Alan R~~~~

Good Camps Guide

BRITAIN and IRELAND
2002

Quality Camping and Caravanning Parks

Compiled by: Deneway Guides & Travel Ltd

Maps created by Customised Mapping (01985 844092) contain background data provided by GisDATA Ltd. Maps are © Customised Mapping and Gis DATA Ltd 2001

Clive Edwards, Lois Edwards & Sue Smart have asserted their rights to be identified as the authors of this work.

First published in this format 2001

© **Haynes Publishing & Deneway Guides & Travel Ltd 2001**

Published by: Haynes Publishing, Sparkford, Nr Yeovil, Somerset BA22 7JJ
in association with
Deneway Guides & Travel Ltd, Burton Bradstock, Bridport, Dorset DT6 4QA

British Library Cataloguing-in-Publication Data:
A catalogue record for this book is available from the British Library.

ISBN: 0 901586 81 1

Printed in Great Britain by J H Haynes & Co Ltd

Contents

Introduction

Welcome to the 35th edition of our Guide, now, for the first time, in full colour throughout!

Alan Rogers himself, now sadly deceased, published the first of the Guides that still bear his name back in 1968, introducing it with the words "I would like to stress that the camps which are included in this book have been chosen entirely on merit, and no payment of any sort is made by them for their inclusion".

As campers and caravanners ourselves it was this objective approach that attracted us to become regular readers of his Guides, and which eventually led to our taking over the editing and publishing of the Guides when Alan retired in 1986.

Whilst the content and scope of the Guides have expanded considerably in the fifteen years since we took over, mainly due to the huge growth in the number of campsites throughout the UK and Europe during those years, our selection of sites to be featured still employs exactly the same philosophy as Alan defined over thirty years ago.

The Alan Rogers' Approach to Selecting Sites

Firstly, and most importantly, our selection is based entirely on our own rigorous inspection. Parks cannot buy their way into our guides - indeed the extensive Site Report which is written by us, not by the site owner, is provided free of charge so we are free to say what we think and to provide an honest description. This is written in plain English and without the use of icons or symbols.

The criteria which we use when selecting sites are numerous, but the most important by far is the question of good quality and standards. Whatever the size of the site, whether it's part of a campsite chain, or even a local authority site, makes no difference in terms of it being required to meet our exacting standards in terms of its quality. In other words, irrespective of the size of the site, or the number of facilities offered, the essentials (the welcome, the pitches, the sanitary facilities, the cleanliness and the general maintenance) must all be of a good standard.

Our selection of sites is designed to cater for a wide variety of preferences, from those seeking a small peaceful campsite in the heart of the countryside, to those looking for an 'all singing, all dancing' site in a popular seaside resort, and for those with more specific needs such as sports facilities, cultural or historical attractions, even sites for naturism.

We rely on our small, dedicated team of Site Assessors, all of whom are experienced campers, caravanners or motorcaravanners, to visit and recommend parks, following which our Sites Director makes the final decision on those to be included in the following year's guide. Once a park is included, it will be regularly inspected to ensure that standards are being maintained. We also appreciate the feedback we receive from many of our readers, and we always make a point of following up complaints, suggestions or recommendations for possible new sites. However, should you have a specific complaint about a park this should be addressed to the Park Operator at the time, preferably in person. Please bear in mind that although we are interested to hear about any complaints, we have no contractual relationship with the sites featured in our guides and are therefore not in a position to intervene in any dispute between a reader and a park.

How to use the Guide

A few words of explanation regarding the layout may be useful:

Regions and counties

For England we have used official Tourist Board Regions and the counties. For Wales and Scotland, where there are many official regions, we have adopted our own regional structure based on the needs of the average holidaymaker. For Ireland (North and South) we use the counties.

Index

Not one, but two - on pages 300/304 you will find each campsite indexed by its number, and on pages 297/299 you will find an index of the villages or towns nearest to where the sites are situated.

Maps

These appear on pages 293/296. The approximate position of each campsite is indicated on the map by the symbols: ● or ■ and the name of the site. The colour of the ite name indicates whether the campsite is open all year or not. The maps are intended to help you find the approximate location of campsites, not to navigate by! Each Site Report includes succinct directions as to how to find the site, based on the assumption that you will be using a proper road map, such as those produced by the Ordnance Survey, the AA or RAC, etc. and for convenience we have also included an Ordnance Survey Grid Reference in our Site Report in respect of sites in mainland Britain.

The Site Reports

These are really self-explanatory, but please remember that all prices shown are per night, and all telephone numbers assume that you are 'phoning from within the country where the site is situated - thus if you want to telephone a site from abroad you will need to prefix the number with the appropriate International Dialling Code.

Example of an entry:

County or area
Park name
Address

number

Main text
A description of the park in which we try to give an idea of the general features of the site - its size, its situation, its strengths and weaknesses. This column should provide a picture of the site itself with reference to the facilities provided if they impact on its appearance or character. We retain reference to pitch numbers, electricity (with amperage), hardstandings etc. in this section as pitch design, planning and terracing affects the site's overall appearence. Similarly we continue to include reference to caravan holiday homes, etc. but no longer indicate if they are available to let (this type of information will appear in our new guide 'Campsite Accommodation to Let'). Importantly at the end of this column we indicate if there are any restrictions, e.g. no tents, adults only etc.

Facilities:
The second column in smaller print contains all the "nitty gritty" information on the site facilities.

Please see the notes below.

Charges

Tel/Fax:
Reservations:
Open
Directions:
Please see the notes below.

Facilities:

Toilet blocks: are now covered in less detail than in previous editions as standards have greatly improved. We assume that toilet blocks will be well equipped with all necessary shelves, hooks, plugs and mirrors; will have free hot water supplied everywhere; have a clearly identified chemical toilet; provide well built water and waste water points and bin areas. If this is not the case we comment. We do, however, continue to mention certain features that some of our readers find very important: washbasins in cubicles, facilities for babies, facilities for those with disabilities and motorcaravan service points. Disabled readers are also advised to telephone the park of their choice before turning up to ensure that facilities are appropriate to their particular needs (see page 286).

Shop: basic or full supplies, and opening dates.

Bars, restaurants, takeaway facilities and entertainment: we try hard to supply opening and closing dates and to identify if there are discos or other noisy entertainment.

Children's play areas: fenced and with safety surface (e.g. sand or bark).

Swimming pools: if particularly special, we cover in detail in the first column but reference is always included in the second column. Opening dates and levels of supervision are provided where we have been notified.

Leisure facilities: e.g. playing fields, bicycle hire, organised activities and entertainment including children's clubs.

Dogs: If dogs are not accepted or restrictions apply, we state it here. Check the quick reference list on page 280.

Miscellaneous: Here we cover such points as whether you need a torch, if the site provides caravan storage, whether American motorhomes are accepted, etc. Note: reference to public telephones has been cut - it is very rare for a site not to have one and also many people have mobile phones.

Off site: This briefly covers leisure facilities, tourist attractions, restaurants etc nearby. Geographical tourist information is more likely to be in the first column.

Charges: are the latest provided by the parks. In those few cases where 2001 or 2002 prices are not given, we try to give a general guide. Prices for sites in the Republic of Ireland are given in Euros (€1 = IR£0.788). The pricing structures vary considerably and we try to be as uniform and succinct as possible in what is included since some parks have a simple tariff, while others have a vast complex of possibilities. The same is true of reservations and what is written cannot wholly replace the official park tariff and reservation form.

Opening dates: are those advised to us during the early autumn of the previous year - park operators can, and sometimes do, alter these dates before the start of the following season - often for good reasons - so if you intend to visit a park shortly after its published opening date, or shortly before its closing date, it really is wise to check that it will actually be open at the time required. Similarly some parks operate a restricted service during the low season, only opening some of their facilities (e.g. swimming pools) during the main season - where we know about this, and have the relevant dates, we indicate it, but if you are at all doubtful again it is wise to check.

Directions: Given last, with a coloured background, in order that they may be read and assimilated more easily by a navigator en route. It is possible that a few may have changed due to road improvement schemes, etc. since we visited the park. If this has happened we trust that any delay caused is or was of only minor proportions. The 6-figure Ordnance Survey Grid Reference (O.S.GR:) point is provided by the park for those wishing to locate a site by this means.

Quick Reference Sections

Our Guide includes several Quick Reference Sections, (see pages 278, 281, 284) which should enable you to quickly identify those parks that are open all year, those which welcome dogs, and those which don't, parks where fishing facilities are available, where there are facilities for launching small boats, and where there are bicycles for hire, those with riding stables or golf courses, and those which are strictly 'adults only'.

Alan Rogers' Discounts

We have been able to negotiate special 'Alan Rogers' discounts with some of the parks featured in this Guide, and with a number of tourist attractions, whereby on presentation of a current edition of the Guide, readers will be able to enjoy a reduction compared with the normal public price. Details are shown in the relevant Site Report or, in the case of attractions, on the relevant advertisement page.

 Where a park offers a discount to our readers this is indicated in the Site Report by a small Alan Rogers' Logo, and a brief description of the discount available.

Our Site Assessors

Finally we'd like to say a special thank you to to our Site Assessors for all their efforts and hard work, and for the many miles they travel, their patience with our detailed site reports and their commitment to the philosophy of the guides. Special thanks are due to Chris and Gerry Bullock for being out and about, continuing their work on facilities provided by parks for disabled visitors. See pages 286/287 for their comments and recommendations. The Disabled Discrimination Act (DDA) 2000 requires parks to make reasonable adjustments for wheelchair users and persons with disabilities.

We are, of course, also out and about ourselves, visiting Parks, talking to owners and readers, and generally checking on standards, new developments, etc. We wish all our readers thoroughly enjoyable Camping and Caravanning in 2002, and let's hope for some good weather, and no Foot and Mouth Disease.

Lois Edwards MAEd, FTS
Clive Edwards BEd, FTS
Sue Smart   Directors

TAKE IT EASY AND SAVE MONEY

THE ALAN ROGERS'
travel service

Get the site you want
Get the dates you want
Get the ferry you want
Get the price you want

To Book
Ferry ✓
Pitch ✓
Accommodation ✗

01892 55 98 98

The all-season "leave it to us solution " We'll book your chosen Alan Rogers' approved campsite(s) - choose from around 200 across Europe, including Ireland and the Channel Islands. We'll organise your low cost ferry and insurance as well as providing a comprehensive Travel Pack with maps and directions too.
We're with you all the way!

Call us now for your FREE colour Readers Travel Guide
01892 55 98 98   www.alanrogers.com

12 nights pitch fees + ferry for car and passengers from £249
Save Money, and Take It Easy!

- *No more trying to contact foreign sites direct*
- *No more doubt as to whether your pitch really is booked*
- *No more ringing round all the ferry companies for the best price*
- *No more foreign currency booking fees*

Camping Cheque

The low season 'go as you please' solution. With over 200 sites across Europe, all committed to fully open facilities in low season, there's no need to commit yourself to a fixed itinerary.
Move freely from site to site as you wish, and enjoy incredibly low ferry prices as well. This discount scheme offers fantastic savings.

Enjoy the freedom   Enjoy the flexibility
Enjoy the ferry prices   Enjoy the savings

Call us now on 01892 559855 for your FREE Camping Cheque brochure
www.campingcheque.co.uk

10 Camping Cheques + ferry for car and passengers from £249
SUPER-LOW FERRY PRICES GUARANTEED

Camping Cheques now operate in Britain and Ireland. The parks involved are clearly identified in this guide - look for the CAMPING CHEQUES logo.

South West Tourism

Isles of Scilly, Cornwall, Devon, Somerset, Bath, Bristol,

South Gloucestershire, Wiltshire and Dorset

Address: Woodwater Park, Exeter, Devon EX2 5WT
Tel: 0870 442 0830 Fax: 0870 442 0840
E-mail: post@swtourism.co.uk

Internet: http://www.westcountrynow.com

If you've only ever thought of the West Country as a heavenly place for summer holidays it's time to think again. More than 400 attractions now stay open all year, so whatever the season, there's always a reason to visit the West Country. In a region where British winters are mildest, you can walk for miles in lovely countryside, along spectacular coastal paths and rolling moorland. If you need reviving drop into a country inn. You'll find the warm climate is mirrored by warm hospitality from people with time to chat.

Good food is an art in the West Country. Rich pastures provide the grazing for quality meats, while fresh fish and seafood is landed at quaysides along 600 miles of coast. Local cheeses and tasty Cornish pasties will tempt the taste buds and who can resist a West Country cream tea?

Spring comes early in the West, where the gentle climate encourages a profusion of flowers to bloom early. Cornwall's Festival of Spring Gardens takes place during early March through April and May, with over 70 gardens open to the public on different days.

Cornwall

While you're in Cornwall, take time out to visit some of area's other attractions like the Pilchard Works at Newlyn in Cornwall or the Wheal Martyn China Clay centre at St Austall and see the stunning scenery of Land's End. Artists have always loved the quality of light in the West and you will be equally inspired by the art exhibitions and the architecture of the Tate Gallery in St Ives.

Devon

Home to the English Riviera with the cosmopolitan atmosphere of Torquay, Paignton and Brixham on the palm fringed south coast. Nearby Salcombe and Dartmouth with the Royal Britannia Naval College, now open to the public, stands proud over the Dart Estuary are popular for watersports. Further west is the dramatic moorland of Dartmoor with wild ponies and granite tors. Clovelly, Ilfracombe and Lynton on the North coast are a stark contrast to the green moorland with long golden beaches and pretty harbours. For shopping and heritage visit the cities of Plymouth for The Hoe, Barbican area and National Marine Aquarium or the cathedral city of Exeter with it's beautiful Tudor buildings.

Somerset

The west is covered by Exmoor where you can travel by steam train from Bishop's Lydeard to the coast at Minehead. Visit lush gardens at Hestercombe and historic Forde Abbey. Glaston-bury Tor and Abbey have links to past dating thousands of years and while the caves and Gorge at Cheddar are spectacular. Weston Super Mare bustles with the noise of families as they enjoy the carnival atmosphere while the city of Taunton has a great range of shops, theatres and cafes.

Dorset

Land of Thomas Hardy and one of the best coastlines in the country for fossils which can be found along the three mile stretch of Chesil Beach or the cliffs of Lyme Regis. The seaside town of Weymouth is popular due to it's bustling nightlife and charming Georgian town houses.

Wiltshire

Where the West Country begins - is less than an hour from London. The cities of Bristol and Bath and beyond them, Exeter, Plymouth and Penzance, are all served by fast, direct rail services from London, the Midlands and the North.

To find out about exhibitions and events currently happening in the West Country, contact the Tourist Information Centre in the town or city you plan to visit. To get the number of the local TIC call 0870 442 0880.

For information on the Dorset and East Devon Heritage Coast bid, see page 63.

Cornwall
Polmanter Tourist Park

005 Halestown, St. Ives, Cornwall TR26 3LX

Polmanter is a good example of a sympathetic conversion of a farm from agricultural to leisure use and the Osborne family have developed the park well. The converted farm buildings provide a cosy bar lounge overlooking the heated swimming pool, toddler's pool and sunbathing area. Good value meals are served in the bar and there is a family area with high chairs. The new conservatory between the bar and the pool provides extra space for families (open all day, with a hot drinks machine). Occasional entertainment is organised in season. The 240 tourist pitches (no statics) are well spaced in several fields with growing shrubs and hedges giving individual pitch areas and connecting tarmac roads. There are 16 hardstandings, 190 electric hook-ups (16A) and 80 deluxe pitches with electricity, water and waste water. It is a busy park with a happy atmosphere within 1½ miles of St Ives - a footpath leads from the park (20 minutes downhill) or there is a bus service from the park in high season (hourly, 10 am. - midnight). The park gates are closed midnight - 6.30 am. with outside parking. A member of the Best of British group.

Facilities: The toilet blocks vary – as the park has grown, so extra blocks have been added. There are now four, the latest being modern and good, the others refurbished and tiled. All can be heated and still incorporate the ideas of the first block, which include a wall cupboard for clothes in each shower to keep them dry. Two fully equipped en-suite family shower rooms, plus a baby changing room. Extra dishwashing sinks in the new block and good laundry provision. Well stocked, self service shop (shop and pool Whit - mid Sept). Bar, with food and family area (Easter, then Whitsun - mid Sept). Takeaway (4.30 - 7 pm). Swimming pool. Tennis courts. Children's play areas. Sports field. Games room with two pool tables, table tennis and games machines. **Off site:** Golf 1 mile, fishing, riding, bicycle hire and boat launching facilities within 2 miles. New indoor pool at St Ives. Note: Dogs are banned from the St Ives beaches in high season.

Charges 2001

Per unit incl. 2 persons, car and awning	£9.00 - £14.00
extra adult	£2.50 - £4.50
child (3-15 yrs)	£2.00 - £3.50
electricity (16A)	£2.00
multi-service pitch	£3.00 - £4.00
dog	£1.00

Tel/Fax: (01736) 795640. E-mail: phillip_osborne @hotmail.com. **Reservations:** Made with £30 deposit. For 15/7-26/8 only: multiples of 7 nights with arrival on Fri, Sat or Sunday for electric pitches, multiples of 7 nights but any day arrival for non-electric pitches. **Open** Easter - 31 October (full facilities to 10 Sept). 'Camping Cheque'

Directions: Take B3074 to St. Ives from the A30 and then first left at a mini-roundabout taking 'Holiday Route' (B3311) to St. Ives (Halestown). At T-junction turn right for Halestown, right again at the Halestown Inn then first left. O.S.GR: SW509392.

Cornwall
Little Trevarrack Tourist Park

047 Laity Lane, Carbis Bay, St Ives, Cornwall TR6 3HW

Little Trevarrack is a traditional Cornish park covering 16 acres with views from the top of the site across St Ives bay towards Hayle and the surrounding countryside. It is now being updated by Neil Osborne, the son of the owners of Polmanter Park. There are 254 pitches, in five open fields (top ones with gentle slopes), 168 with 16A electricity. Bushes have been planted which will in time form hedging to provide individual type pitches. A new toilet block and children's play area have been built. Reception is clearly marked in the 'Kids Play Zone' which is situated at the site entrance. Carbis Bay is less than a mile and in high season a bus runs hourly into St Ives (10.00- 23.30 hrs). This is a developing site which will provide a quiet, peaceful base from which to explore St Ives and the southern tip of Cornwall.

Facilities: The new toilet block is central, modern and well equipped. An older, original block is open for the peak season only. Dishwashing sinks under cover. Laundry behind reception in the Kids Play Zone. Small shop in reception providing basics (but Tesco is nearby, also fish and chips and pasta restaurants). Children's play area and playing field. No kites allowed. Note: Dogs are banned from the St Ives beaches in high season.

Charges 2001

Per unit incl. 2 persons	£8.50 - £13.00
extra adult	£2.00 - £3.00
child (3-15 yrs)	£1.75 - £2.50
dog	£1.00
electricity	£2.00

Tel/Fax: (01736) 797580. **Reservations:** Made with deposit of £25 per week booked. **Open** 1 April - 15 September.

Directions: Follow signs for St Ives and take A3074 at Carbis Bay. Site is signed on left opposite junction to Carbis Bay beach. Follow road for 150 yds, cross small crossroads and site is on right. O.S.GR: SW527378.

Cornwall
Ayr Holiday Park

003 Higher Ayr, St. Ives, Cornwall TR26 1EJ

On first arrival Ayr Park seems to be all caravan holiday homes, but behind them, with marvellous views over St Ives Bay and Porthmeor beach, is a series of naturally sloping fields providing 40 touring pitches. Level, hard-core, terraced areas also provide places for motorcaravans and caravans with 35 electrical connections (16A). With an extra field for tents open in July and August, the facilities could be a little hard-pressed, but were coping well when we visited in August. St Ives centre and supermarkets are within easy walking distance, also the new Tate Gallery. There is direct access to the coastal footpath.

Facilities: Modern, well maintained toilet block, consisting of various parts with controllable showers (some accessed direct from the outside and some with toilet), hairdryer, dishwashing sinks under cover and good laundry facilities. Motorcaravan waste point. Games room with pool table and TV, hot drinks and snack machines. Adventure play area and football field. Spa shop nearby. One dog per pitch, up to medium size, is permitted but dogs are not allowed on St Ives beaches in high season.

Charges guide

Per adult	£2.35 - £3.70
child (5 -16 yrs)	£1.10 - £1.80
pitch	£4.40 - £9.50
car or m/cycle	£1.20
dog	£1.05
electricity	£2.25

Tel: (01736) 795855. Fax: (01736) 798797. E-mail: andy@ayrholidaypark.demon.co.uk. **Reservations**: Made with £35 deposit. **Open** Easter/1 April - 31 Oct.

Directions: 300 yds after leaving the A30 turn left on A3074 at mini-roundabout following signs for St Ives for heavy vehicles and day visitors (not town centre direction). After approx. 2 miles this joins the B3311 and then the B3306 about 1 mile from St Ives (an octagonal building on your left). Still heading for St Ives turn left at a mini-roundabout following camping signs through residential areas. Park entrance is 600 yds at Ayr Terrace. O.S.GR: SW515388.

Cornwall
Trevalgan Holiday Farm

004 Trevalgan Farm, St Ives, Cornwall TR26 3BJ

We already have some very different sites in the St Ives area and Trevalgan is different yet again. Based on a working farm, it is a friendly, no frills site on the cliffs 1½ miles west of St Ives, providing 120 clearly marked pitches (43 with 16A electricity) in a level stone walled field. The pitches vary in size as the park is very popular with walkers. There is direct access to the coastal path and it is a 25 minutes walk to St Ives. With tractor rides (in high season), plus farm and hill trails and a farm pets corner with baby chickens, two donkeys etc. it is in all, quite an original type of park. A member of the Countryside Discovery group.

Facilities: A purpose built toilet block has curtained washbasins, plus baby room, laundry and washing up, and even a hot drinks machine. Small shop (1/6-15/9). 'Farm House Kitchen' with takeaway (July/Aug), popular for breakfast or evening meals. Gas available. Games field, children's play area and crazy golf. Games room in a barn with table tennis, pool, fruit machines and a comfortable upstairs TV room. **Off site**: Fishing 3 miles, bicycle hire, riding, golf, all within 2 miles. In July/Aug. bus service once a day from the park to St Ives (10 am. returning at 5 pm). Dogs are banned from the St Ives beaches in high season.

Charges guide

Per adult	£3.50 - £5.50
child 3-14 yrs	£2.50 - £4.50
under 3 yrs	£1.50
dog	50p
electricity	£2.50

Tel/Fax: (01736) 796433. E-mail: trevalgan@aol.com. **Reservations**: Contact park. Open Easter - 30 September.

Directions: Approach site down a narrow Cornish lane from the B3306 St Ives - Lands End road, following sign. O.S.GR: SW490400.

Cardinney Camping Park

002 Crows an Wra, St Buryan, Cornwall TR19 6HX

A friendly Geordie welcome awaits from the owner, Kevin Lindley, when you visit Cardinney, which is perfectly situated for visiting the famous Lands End beauty spots and tourist attractions and also within easy driving distance of small Cornish beaches and coves. The level field is semi-divided into three camping areas and is neatly kept with some landscaping. Bushes have been planted, along with a central Cornish stone wall, allowing for 105 marked, level pitches, 56 with 10A electricity and some with hardstanding. The combined café and bar acts as reception and a social point providing breakfasts, takeaway food at most times and good cheer in the evenings. Coastal, cliff top walks, surfing beaches and the Minnack Open Air Theatre are nearby.

Facilities: The facilities are simple compared to many of the more sophisticated sites in Devon and Cornwall, the toilet block originally built over 30 years ago but adapted over the years. It includes a baby cubicle, laundry facilities and one outside dishwashing sink with hot water. Games room with TV, pool table and video games. Tourist information chalet. **Off site**: Fishing 3 miles, bicycle hire 5 miles, riding 7 miles.

Charges 2001

Per unit incl. 2 adults	£5.00 - £8.00
extra adult	£2.00
child (2-15 yrs)	£1.00
electricity	£1.75

Pets free. Less for stays over 2 weeks. **Tel**: (01736) 810880. Fax: (01736) 810998. E-mail: cardinney@btinternet.com. **Reservations**: Made with £10 per week deposit. **Open** 1 February - 30 November.

Directions: Park is signed before Crows an Wra on main Penzance - Lands End A30 road, 5 miles west of Penzance. O.S.GR: SW426285.

River Valley Country Park

006 Relubbus, Penzance, Cornwall TR20 9ER

River Valley is a quiet park in the natural environment of a pleasant river valley. Run by Brian and Eileen Milson, it provides 150 large touring pitches well spaced in nooks and bays around the perimeters of small meadows or in natural clearings. All are clearly defined with shrubs or hedges and new trees have been planted to supplement these or in the more open areas to edge the individual pitch spaces, making the park very attractive and the pitches more private. Most pitches have electrical connections (15A), some have hardstanding and there are special sections for families, couples, tents, dogs, etc. There are now 38 caravan holiday homes, some privately owned, in more or less separate areas, beside the river at the far end of the park or on the hillside at the back. There is no children's playground, but lots of very tame ducks on the river. A fence separates the park from the river and there is a pleasant walk for 2½ miles alongside it, popular for dog walks. St Michael's Mount is only 3 miles and can be reached by footpath. Much of the valley is a protected nature reserve and the park encourages wildlife by not using weedkillers and by leaving parts uncut - badgers, foxes, herons, kingfishers and glow-worms are regular visitors. A member of the Best of British group.

Facilities: Three good quality, carefully maintained toilet blocks are well placed for all pitches. Two male and two female family shower rooms have been added in the block at the far end. Some private cabins for ladies and a special make-up room with hair dryers. Separate laundry facilities and baby bath. Covered dishwashing sinks. Motorcaravan service point (fresh water top up and waste water emptying). Shop/reception. **Off site:** Bicycle hire 5 miles, riding or golf 3 miles.

Charges 2000

Per unit incl. 2 adults	£6.00 - £11.00
extra adult	£1.00 - £3.25
child	50p - £1.25
awning/pup tent	£1.00
dog	£1.00
electricity	£1.50

Min. charge 2 adults per vehicle; large motorcaravans add £1.00. **Tel**: 0845 60 12 516. Fax: 01736 763398. E-mail: rivervalley@surfbay.dircon.co.uk. **Reservations**: Any period with deposit (£20) and fee (£1). **Open** all year except Jan. and Feb.

Directions: From A30 at St Michaels Mount roundabout, take A394 towards Helston. At next roundabout take B3280 to Relubbus. In approx. 3 miles in village turn left just over a small bridge. O.S.GR: SW566320.

Calloose Caravan Park

Leedstown, Hayle, Cornwall TR27 5ET

011

This friendly, family touring park is quietly situated in an inland valley covering 8½ acres, about 4 miles from Hayle, with an extra ½ mile to the beaches beyond, 9 to St. Ives on the north coast and 6 to Helston and Praa Sands on the south. Attractively landscaped with almost a tropical feel, units are personally sited. The terrain is mainly flat but is dry, with two slightly raised areas on terraces. There are 120 tourist pitches (96 with 16A electricity, 8 with water and 28 gravel hardstandings) close together with individual markers, and 17 caravan holiday homes. In the main meadow areas, pitches are arranged round the perimeter with some free space in the middle. A heated swimming pool and separate paddling pool are neatly landscaped with a sunbathing terrace and access for disabled people. A large, recreation block with a themed bar and family room serves bar meals. Entertainment is organised most evenings in the main season including weekly barbecues in peak season. Sun lounger and mountain bike hire and extensive local information are available in reception. All public areas have wheel chair access. A popular park, booking is essential.

Facilities: Both toilet blocks are well kept, providing washbasins in cubicles, a family shower room, baby room, en-suite unit for disabled visitors, dishwashing sinks under cover. Laundry room and first aid room. Well stocked shop and off-licence (including gas). Swimming pool (40 x 20 ft. open mid-May to mid-Sept). Bar with bar meals (daily in the main season, slightly restricted in early season). Takeaway (mid-May - late Sept). TV lounge, pool table, games room with skittle alley. All-weather tennis court. Crazy golf (floodlit). Table tennis. Adventure playground. Four acres of recreation fields include dog exercise fields, a full size football pitch and mountain bike scramble track. **Off site:** Village with shops, pubs, etc. is within walking distance. Golf 4 miles, fishing 2 miles, riding 5 miles.

Charges guide

Per unit incl. 2 persons	£7.00 - £13.00
awning	free
extra person (over 3 yrs)	£1.00 - £3.00
pup tent (max. 1.8 x 1.2 m)	£1.00 - £2.00
dog	£1.00 - £2.50
electricity (10A)	£2.00
'super' pitch	plus £2.00

Tel/Fax: (01736) 850431. **Reservations:** Made with £20 deposit per pitch, balance on arrival. **Open** 1 April - 30 September.

Directions: From crossroads of B3280 and B3302 in Leedstown take the B3302 towards Hayle. First right, then left on ½ mile access road to park. O.S.GR: SW599353.

Boscrege Caravan Park

Ashton, Helston, Cornwall TR13 9TQ

048

A pretty little site hidden deep in the countryside, Boscrege will suit those who want a quiet peaceful base for their Cornish holiday. The main large touring field nestles at the foot of Tregonning Hill with its striking hill top cross, and has neatly cut grass with a gentle slope from the top. The pitches are generously spaced around the edge, backing on to hedging and leaving plenty of room in the centre for ball games. Two small, attractive paddock areas, one with caravan holiday homes, the other for tourers, complete the total provision of 46 pitches, 36 with 10A electricity. It is a welcome retreat for couples and families with young children. Little people will love the miniature classic cars with their battery powered engine - 20p a time!

Facilities: The traditional style toilet block is nicely fitted out with two washbasins in cabins and a smaller basin for children (M/F). Dishwashing sinks, laundry sink, washing machine and dryer. Reception keeps emergency supplies (nearest shop at Godolphin). Children's play area for smaller children and central ball area. Amusement machines and pool table.

Charges 2001

Per unit	£6.50 - £13.00
electricity	£2.50
extra small tent	£2.50

No charge for dogs (max. 3). **Tel/Fax:** (01736) 762231. E-mail: enquires@caravanparkcornwall. com. **Reservations:** Made with deposit of £35 per week or part week. **Open** Easter/1 April - 31 October

Directions: From Helston take A394 for Penzance. At top of Sithney Common Hill turn right just before Jet garage onto B3302 (Hayle) road. Pass Sithney General Stores on left and take next left for Carleen and Godolphin. Continue on this road to Godolphin village and turn left at side of Godolphin Arms signed Ashton. Proceed up hill and at top where road turns sharply left go straight over into lane leading to Boscrege. O.S.GR: SW593305.

Mullion Holiday Park
nr Helston, Cornwall TR12 7LJ

For those who enjoy plenty of entertainment, both social and active, in a holiday environment, Mullion would be a good choice. The site is situated on the Lizard peninsula with its sandy beaches and coves. It is a holiday home park with all the trimmings – indoor and outdoor pools, super children's play areas, clubs, bars, and a wide range of nightly entertainment. These facilities form the core of the park and are well organised and managed. The touring area past the holiday homes has a more relaxed atmosphere and is set on natural heathland with clumps of bramble and gorse which provide breaks and recesses making for a more informal layout. Linked by a circular gravel road, all 160 pitches are numbered, 10 with hardstanding and 105 with electricity connections (16A). Land drainage could be a problem if there is heavy continuous rain. A resident warden is now based at the entrance to the touring section. Eurotents for hire. There is much to see in the area including Goonhilly Satellite Station and Flambards Village, the theme park, Lizard Point and Lands End.

Facilities: Central modern toilet block with additional 'portacabin' style facilities for high season. Dishwashing sinks under cover, two laundry sinks and two washing machines. Large launderette in main complex. Freezer pack service. Large supermarket with off licence. Pub with family room, restaurant and takeaway (half board or breakfast options). Moonshine Club with live shows and cabarets, big screen satellite TV. Excellent outdoor children's play areas (fenced). Toddlers' soft play area. Amusement arcade, bowling alley. Heated outdoor swimming pool and paddling pool (26/5-8/9). Heated indoor fun pool with slide, both supervised. Sauna and solarium. Crazy golf, pitch and putt. Mountain bike hire. Barbecue.

Charges 2001

Per pitch (incl. free club membership)	£8.25 - £15.50
electricity	£2.95
awning	£2.50
dog (one only)	£2.50
'super hook-up' incl. TV point, fresh water	£4.50

Half board or breakfast options available. **Tel**: (01326) 240000. Fax: (01326) 241141. **Reservations**: Contact site. High season and Spr. B.H. bookings must be Sat. - Sat. **Open**: 12 May - 15 September.

Directions: From Helston take A3083 for The Lizard and continue for 7 miles. Site on left immediately after the right turning for Mullion. O.S.GR: SW698185.

Award winning Holiday Parks in areas of outstanding natural beauty and close to glorious sandy beaches.

☆ Spacious Level Pitches
☆ Electric & Super Electric Hook-up
☆ **Free** Indoor & Outdoor Heated Pools
☆ **Free** Live Nightly Entertainment
☆ **Free** Children's Clubs
☆ On Park Restaurant, Supermarket, Off Licence, Bars and Take-Away

☎ **MULLION** • 01326 240 000
☎ **SANDFORD** • 01202 631 600

 www.weststarholidays.co.uk   @ touring@weststarholidays.co.uk

Quote R1

There is a sense of timelessness about Trelowarren – perhaps it is the mature parkland or the mellow manor house, home to the Vyvyan family since 1427. Whatever, it is a beautiful, tranquil park set on the eastern side of the Lizard Peninsula, close to the banks of the Helford river. Access from the main road is via a single track road for one mile but it is well worth it. Set in 20 acres, there are three distinctive areas for camping all with neatly cut grass and providing 125 places for caravans and motorcaravans and 75 for tents. First is the walled gardens with some pitches on a slight slope, then the apple orchard edged by the woods with a secluded area known as the quarry at the lower end, with some level but mainly sloping pitches. The third area is more open, with views across the valley and running parallel to the orchard, separated by Cornish stone walling. It has some mature trees and the main toilet block. There are 25 level hardstandings in this area which will fit even the large American motorhomes. Just past the walled garden area through a small door, is the stable courtyard with a delightful 'bistro' and a Countryside Centre that charts the development of the Lizard from pre-history to the present day – a must to try and understand this unique area, which is now home to the Goonhilly Earth Station. Also here is the Trelowarren Pottery and Weaving Centre with various exhibitions organised by the Cornwall Craft Association, not to mention the house and gardens (now being rebuilt to the original design but incorporating 20th century techniques, plants and architectural incident). Combined with the woodland walks (way-marked), Trelowarren becomes a most attractive place to spend some time with something for everyone in a relaxing, yet interesting and peaceful environment.

Facilities: The main sanitary facilities in original stone buildings are modern and attractively equipped with some washbasins in cubicles for ladies, and a bath. Five washing up sinks are under cover. Laundry room, complete with original stone walls and floor, providing three sinks, a washing machine and dryer. En-suite facility for disabled visitors. Baby room with three sinks. Extra small basic sanitary block with toilets, washbasins in walled garden area. Motorcaravan service point. Takeaway (1/7-3/9) and attractive little 'Inn'. Craft and Countryside Centre next door with licensed bistro which is open at lunch-times and some evenings (with jazz and folk music).

Charges 2002

Per person	£3.25 - £4.00
child (3-16 yrs)	£1.50 - £1.95
dog, extra car or boat	£1.00
electricity	£1.80

Pitch and awning incl. No credit cards. **Tel**: (01326) 221637. FAX: (01326) 221427. **Reservations**: Made with £10 deposit. **Open**: 1 April/Easter - 30 September, (as are all other facilities on the park which are open to the public).

Directions: From Helston take A3083 for the Lizard. Just after Culdrose Naval Air Station turn left on B3293, signed St Keverne. Avoid turnings to both Gweek and Mawgan and watch for the Trelowarren signs on the left before reaching Goonhilly Earth Station. O.S.GR: SW719239.

Silver Sands Holiday Park

007 Kennack Sands, Ruan Minor, Helston, Cornwall TR12 7LZ

Silver Sands is a small, peaceful 'away-from-it-all' park in a remote part of the Lizard peninsula, the most southerly part of mainland Britain and an 'area of outstanding natural beauty'. The park is only reached after passing Culdrose Naval Base and the Goonhilly Earth Station down a single track road. Silver Sands is tucked away behind two other parks which provide static holiday homes with very little else. A half mile footpath leads down through a small valley to the twin beaches of Kennack Sands (one is dog-free) divided by a small headland. This is generally an unspoilt walking area with the coastal path passing through and under the care of English Nature. The park itself has 16 caravan holiday homes, along with 14 touring pitches with 5A electrical hook-ups for caravans and motorcaravans. They are large, attractively situated and divided into individual bays by growing flowering shrubs and bushes. An adjoining tent field has similar pitches (4 with electricity) where the shrubs are growing and the pitches in bays are slightly sloping. Reception is housed in an elderly static van, has a good supply of tourist information. A member of the Countryside Discovery group.

Facilities: The sanitary block is old and quaint, but it is well maintained. It includes, a laundry room, baby changing unit, dishwashing sinks and a microwave. Some play equipment and an undeveloped three-acre field can be used for walking, kite flying, etc. **Off site:** Shop 20 yards on the next site and pub within walking distance. Fishing 1 mile, bicycle hire 5 miles, boat launching 2 or 7 miles, riding 5 miles, golf 6 miles.

Charges 2001

Per touring unit incl. 2 persons	£5.50 - £7.50
extra adult	£2.00 - £3.00
child (3-13 yrs)	£1.10 - £1.80
awning or extra pup tent	free - £1.00
dog	£1.30 - £1.60
electricity	£1.60

Less £1.50 for cyclists or hikers with pup tent. Reductions for some bookings. No credit cards. **Tel/Fax:** (01326) 290631. E-mail: enquiries@ silversandsholidaypark.co.uk. **Reservations**: Made with 25% deposit, min. £30; balance on arrival. **Open** 1 May - 15 September.

Directions: From Helston take A3038 Lizard road. After Culdrose turn left on B3293 passing Goonhilly after 4 miles. At the next crossroads turn right (signed Kennack Sands), continue for 1½ miles then left to Gwendreath on single track road - site is 1 mile. O.S.GR: SW732170.

Chacewater Park

001 Cox Hill, Chacewater, Truro, Cornwall TR4 8LY

For those who want to be away from the hectic coastal resorts and to take advantage of the peace and quiet of an 'adults only' park, this will be an excellent value for money choice. Chacewater has a pleasant rural situation and the site is run with care and attention by Richard Peterken and his daughters Debbie and Mandy. It provides 100 level touring pitches, all with electricity and 60 with hardstanding, in two large field areas (with a slight slope) edged with young trees or in smaller bays formed by hedging. There are 29 fully serviced pitches with electricity, water, drainage and sewage connections and one area for dog owners. Reception is not at the entrance but through the park to one side in a pleasant courtyard area and it also provides a small library. Truro is only 5 miles and there is a good choice of beaches north or south within 5-10 miles. This park only accepts adults over 30 yrs.

Facilities: The main toilet block provides well equipped showers and two en-suite units, along with dishwashing sinks under cover and a laundry room. This block has been supplemented by a new one providing similar facilities near reception. Adults only accepted (over 30 yrs).

Charges 2001

Per unit incl. 2 adults	from £9.00
extra person	£4.00
electricity	95p
dog	£1.00

Weekly rates for pre- booked pitches. Discounts for senior citizens excl. August. **Tel:** (01209) 820762. Fax: (01209) 820544. E-mail: chacepark@aol.com. **Reservations**: Made with £20 deposit per week or part week, balance on arrival. **Open** 1 May - 30 September.

Directions: Chacewater can be approached either from the A390 road or from the A30. Park is ½ mile west of the village - follow signs. O.S.GR: SW742439.

Liskey Holiday Park

Greenbottom, Truro, Cornwall TR4 8QN

013

Liskey is a quiet, family run park, pleasantly landscaped with rockery plants and well manicured grass – first impressions of loving care are carried all through the park. The main, slightly sloping camping area is beautifully landscaped with trees, shrubs and heathers and the level, well spaced pitches have good views across the countryside. The 4 seasonal and 81 touring pitches have 10A electricity and 12 are fully serviced with level hardstanding and a gravel area for awnings. There are all weather pea-gravel pitches for tents. Seven holiday homes are in a separate area. There is a great feeling of spaciousness, mainly because the enthusiastic new owners do not try to fit in too many units. Breathable groundsheets are welcome on the grassy pitches. A pub with good food and real ale is only 600 yards and buses to Truro pass the gate. Liskey is a good place for the family that can amuse itself without the need for discos and gaming machines.

Facilities: The central, very clean and well maintained toilet block can be heated. A second block is planned for 2002. Some washbasins are in cubicles. Family bathroom (50p). Well equipped laundry room and dishwashing sinks under cover. Motorcaravan service point. Shop for basics at reception, plus excellent maps. Room with TV and tourist information. Adventure playground. Volleyball and basketball nets. Play barn, table tennis. Winter caravan storage. **Off site**: Coarse fishing ¼ mile, bicycle hire 3 mile, riding 2 miles, golf 1 mile. Within 5 miles are beaches and facilities for tennis and boat launching. Truro supermarkets 3 miles.

Charges 2001

Per unit incl. 2 persons	£8.50 - £11.00
extra person over 3 yrs	£2.00
electricity (10A)	£2.00
serviced pitch	£3.00

Low season discounts for over 50s, fully retired. **Tel**: (01872) 560274. Fax: (01872) 561413. E-mail: enquiries@liskeyholidaypark.co.uk. **Reservations**: Made with £3 deposit per night booked or payment in full if less than 5 days. **Open** 1 March - 31 October.

Directions: From the A30 take A390 to Truro. At the next roundabout turn right (signed Threemilestone) and, immediately at mini-roundabout, right again towards Chacewater. Park is 600 yds on right past small business unit. O.S.GR: SW772452.

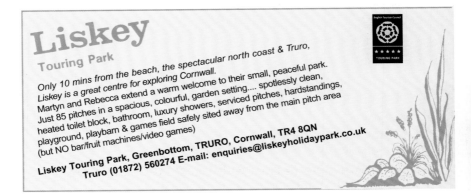

Liskey

Touring Park

Only 10 mins from the beach, the spectacular north coast & Truro, Liskey is a great centre for exploring Cornwall.
Martyn and Rebecca extend a warm welcome to their small, peaceful park.
Just 85 pitches in a spacious, colourful, garden setting.... spotlessly clean, heated toilet block, bathroom, luxury showers, serviced pitches, hardstandings, playground, playbarn & games field safely sited away from the main pitch area
(but NO bar/fruit machines/video games)

Liskey Touring Park, Greenbottom, TRURO, Cornwall, TR4 8QN
Truro (01872) 560274 E-mail: enquiries@liskeyholidaypark.co.uk

Carnon Downs Caravan and Camping Park

018 Carnon Downs, nr Truro, Cornwall TR3 6JJ

Under the new ownership of Simon Vallance, this is a thoughtfully laid out, level park with attractive hedging and flowering shrubs providing some pleasant bays for caravans. Gravel roads connect 110 pitches, 100 with electricity (10/15A) and 20 with hardstanding. Of these 12 are fully serviced. Tent pitches, some with electricity, are well spaced around the outside of two level fields, the centre of one for goal posts and adventure-type play equipment, the other containing the reception unit. Here you will receive a warm welcome, a neatly presented layout plan of the park, and a touring information pack. Some of the park's amenities are to be found in the round-house next to the TV and information room. The round-house used to house the donkeys that turned the mill which once operated on the site! Although one side of the park is next to the A39 road, it is well screened with a band of mature woodland so noise should be minimal. This quiet, quality family park is well situated to explore the tip of Cornwall. A member of the Best of British group.

Facilities: Two well maintained toilet blocks can be heated and provide good facilities including some washbasins in cubicles. Showers are unisex, and once you have got used to the idea, it works well. One block includes three very good family bath/shower rooms, one suitable for use by disabled people or mothers and toddlers. Two good laundries, one in each block. Mother and toddler room (heated), including two baby sinks and a full sized bath. Motorcaravan service point (ask at reception). Gas, newspapers and caravan accessories. Recycling centre. Caravan storage. **Off site:** A 'Brewsters' pub is 100 yds across the road. Fishing 3 miles, riding or bicycle hire 2 miles, golf 1 mile.

Charges 2001

Per unit incl. 2 persons	£7.25 - £12.75
extra adult	£2.00
child (5-14 yrs)	£1.70
electricity (10/15A)	£2.00
all-service hardstanding	£2.00
small 2 man tent plus car	less £1.00
walker or cyclist (single)	less £3.00

Tel: (01872) 862283. E-mail: park@carnon-downs caravanpark.co.uk. **Reservations**: Made with £20 deposit p/week. **Open** all year.

Directions: From Truro take A39 Falmouth road. There is direct access from the Carnon Downs roundabout after 3 miles. O.S.GR: SW805406.

Pennance Mill Farm Chalet and Camping Park

045 Maenporth, Falmouth, Cornwall TR11 5HY

Pennance Mill Farm has been in the hands of the Jewell family for three generations and is listed as a typical Cornish farmstead and you can still watch the cows being milked and enjoy tractor rides. The camping park is friendly and relaxed, situated in three sheltered south-facing and fairly level meadows with views over the fields and providing for 70 pitches, 50 of which have 16A electricity. An old mill wheel reminds one of the site's origins and you book in at the farmhouse. Continuing on past the site for half a mile, you come to the sandy beach at Maenporth and within walking distance are tennis courts, a golf course and pitch and putt. Across the road and up a footpath you can reach Mean Valley Holiday Park where you can use their shop and club bar, enjoy good value food and where there is a nice atmosphere and some entertainment.

Facilities: There are two toilet blocks, the first near the entrance is the original one but it is well kept and provides a washing machine, dryer and laundry sinks. The new block in the top meadow is heated and well equipped and includes covered washing up sinks. Small farm shop including some basic provisions (open 9.00-10.30 and 5.30-6.30). Gas available. Children have a small play meadow with a swing and climbing frame, and table tennis.

Charges guide

Per adult	£2.50 - £3.00
child (over 3 yrs)	£1.00
pitch	£2.50 - £3.00
awning	£1.00
dog	50p
electricity	£2.00

Tel: (01326) 317431 or 312616. Fax: (01326) 317431. **Reservations**: Contact park. **Open** Easter - November.

Directions: Using A39 Truro - Falmouth road, follow brown international camping signs to Hillhead roundabout. Turn right towards Maenporth, then straight on at mini-roundabout. Continue for 2 miles towards Maenporth beach, down to bottom of hill and park is immediately on left. O.S.GR: SW789307.

Trethem Mill Touring Park

St Just-in-Roseland, nr St Mawes, Truro, Cornwall TR2 5JF

009

St Mawes is a very popular, pretty village on the Roseland peninsula, which is itself an 'area of outstanding natural beauty'. Only three miles away, Trethem Mill is well placed for either sailing, walking the coastal path around the peninsula, visiting the gardens of Trelissick or Heligan, or simply lazing on the nearby beaches. The Akeroyd family continue to work hard to turn Trethem Mill into a park of which to be proud. Trethem is a 'strictly touring' park with 84 pitches, of which 50 have 16A electricity and with several now classified as all-weather. The pitches are large, most on slightly sloping ground, and are clearly divided by hedging giving your own area. Generally there is a good spacious feel to the site, with a tarmac circular access road. At the busiest times an extra field, also with tarmac access, is brought into use. The park has been carefully landscaped and is a mass of colour, the area around reception being particularly pretty where a small watermill has been built amongst the flowers – the sound of gently flowing water is very relaxing – and there are pet animals (do not feed). Trethem Mill aims to attract couples and families who seek peace and tranquillity, and can manage without a bar and on site entertainment.

Facilities: The centrally located toilet block has been refurbished to a very high standard and it is kept spotlessly clean. Heated in cooler weather, it is well equipped, complete with baby room. Laundry and dishwashing sinks. Reception/shop, only small but very well stocked and licensed. Freezer for ice packs (free). Motorcaravan services. Children have a games room, TV room and a well equipped, fenced playground (closed at 9 pm). Large field alongside the park is used as a recreation and ball game area. **Off site:** Fishing 1½ miles, boat launching 2 miles, bicycle hire 4 miles, riding 8 miles, golf 6 miles.

Charges 2001

Per unit incl. 2 adults	£7.00 - £11.00
per person, hiker or cyclist	£4.00 - £5.50
extra adult	£2.00 - £2.50
child (4-16 yrs)	£1.50 - £2.00
electricity	£2.00
dog	£1.00
extra car or pup tent	£1.00

Tel: (01872) 580504. Fax: (01872) 580968. E-mail: reception@trethem-mill.co.uk. **Reservations:** Made with £30 deposit. **Open** 27 March - 13 October.

Directions: From Tregony follow A3078 to St Mawes. Approx. 2 miles after passing through Trewithian, watch for caravan and camping sign. O.S.GR: SW862364.

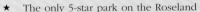

Silverbow Park

012 Goonhavern, nr Truro, Cornwall TR4 9NX

Silverbow has been developed by the Taylor family over many years and they are justifiably proud of their efforts. It is a select, and spacious park seeking to encourage couples and quiet families with young children (no teenagers over 12). The Taylors believe Silverbow is a way of life and staying is an experience – they have certainly created a relaxed and tranquil atmosphere. Hard work, planting and landscaping has provided a beautiful environment set in 21 acres which has, in the past, taken part in the well known 'Gardens Scheme'. There are 90 tourist pitches which are all of good size and include 69 'super' pitches in a newly developed area, with electricity, water and drainaway, which are even larger. Many are on a slight slope with some attractive views. There are also 15 park-owned, high quality leisure homes. Much free space is not used for camping, including an excellent sports area with two all-weather and one grass tennis courts (free coaching in season), two outdoor badminton courts, as well as wild meadow and wooded areas ideal for walks. More recently, a natural area with ponds has been created to encourage wild-life (the park was the first in Cornwall to gain a Bellamy gold award for conservation). The park is 2½ miles from the long sandy beach at Perranporth (30 minutes walk away from traffic) and 6 miles from Newquay.

Facilities: Three toilet blocks, all of excellent quality, have private cabins for each sex, four family shower/toilet rooms, two accessible for wheelchairs, and one bath on payment for each sex. Enclosed washing-up sinks. Laundry room. Recycling bins. Free freezer service. Shop (mid May-mid Sept). Attractive, kidney shaped, heated swimming pool and small paddling pool (open mid-May - mid-Sept) sheltered by high surrounding garden walls. Games room with pool table, table tennis and tourist information. Children's adventure playground and general play field. Tennis and badminton courts. Short mat bowls. Mountain biking from the park (but no bikes on site). **Off site**: Gliding, riding and fishing nearby. Concessionary green fees are available at Perranporth golf club. Pub within walking distance.

Charges 2001

Per unit incl. 2 adults	£6.00 - £14.00
extra adult under 50 yrs	£3.00 - £5.50
extra child 2-12 yrs or adult over 50	£2.00 - £3.60
dog	free - £1.50
fully serviced pitch incl. electricity	£3.00

Children over 12 yrs with or without parents not accepted. Discounts available. **Tel**: (01872) 572347. **Reservations**: Made with £20 p/week deposit (Sat. - Sat. only 17/7-21/8). **Open** 2 May - 10 October.

Directions: Entrance is directly off the main A3075 road ½ mile south of Goonhavern. O.S.GR: SW781531.

Penrose Farm Touring Park

Goonhavern, nr Truro, Cornwall TR4 9QF

014

Penrose Farm is a quality, family park for tourers only, on the edge of the village of Goonhavern. The park is level and sheltered, the 100 pitches spread over five fields with flower beds and bushes set amongst them. These flowers and those at the entrance are very colourful and give the park a neat, orderly and well cared for feel. The present, enthusiastic owners, Alan and Sharman, enjoy getting to know their customers, many of whom come every year, and take pride in the pitches and facilities the e. Children not only have an excellent adventure playground but also an indoor animal centre with guinea pigs, rabbits, chickens, fish, terrapins and birds to admire. There are 52 pitches with 16A electricity and 8 pitches with hardstanding (4 with electricity). Alan always ensures that each unit has plenty of space and does not feel overcrowded. It is only a short walk to the village and its popular pub, and buses to Newquay stop in the village. The superb beach at Perranporth is only 2½ miles. To retain its quiet family image, there are no plans for bars or entertainment and only couples and families are admitted.

Facilities: The fully equipped toilet block also provides four excellent family rooms containing an adjustable shower, washbasin, WC and hairdryer. One of these rooms is also accessible for wheelchairs. The owners have a love of plants and all these amenities are enhanced with beautiful pot plants and flowers. Well equipped laundry. Dishwashing sinks provided. Small shop for gas and basics (Easter, then May - Sept). Adventure playground. Caravan storage. Bicycle hire can be arranged. **Off site**: Fishing or riding ½ mile, golf 1 mile.

Charges 2002

Per unit incl. 2 persons	£8.00 - £12.00
extra person (5 yrs and over)	£3.00
awning, extra car, dog	free
electricity (16A)	£2.00

Families and couples only. Less 50p for over 60s if booked. **Tel**: (01872) 573185. E-mail: penrosefarm2001@hotmail.com. **Reservations**: Made with £30 deposit. **Open** 1 April - 31 October.

Directions: Take A30 from Exeter past Bodmin and Indian Queens. Just after wind farm take B3285 to Perranporth. Park is on the left as you enter Goonhavern village. O.S.GR: SW790535.

Trevornick Holiday Park

Holywell Bay, Newquay, Cornwall TR8 5PW

022

Trevornick, once a working farm, is now a modern, busy and well run family touring park providing a wide range of amenities. It recently won the coveted 'Investors in People' award (one of the first parks to do so) and this is reflected in the standards and management of resources and in the welcoming attitude of the staff. The park has grown to provide caravanners and campers (no holiday caravans) with 450 grass pitches (386 with electricity and 35 fully serviced) on five level fields and two terraced areas. There are few trees, but some good views. Providing 'all singing, all dancing' facilities for fun packed family holidays, the farm buildings now provide the setting for the Farm Club. Recently refurbished, it has licensed facilities and food, children's rooms and a cafeteria 'De caff' with terrace and takeaway, plus much entertainment. The rest of the development has provided an 18 hole golf course, with a small, quiet club house offering bar meals and lovely views out to sea. Next door is the Holywell Bay 'fun' park (site pass gives reduced rates). The sandy beach is 5 minutes by car or 20 minutes walk through the sand dunes past the Holywell. The park offers 60 'Eurotents' to hire.

Facilities: Five toilet blocks of a standard modern design provide coin-operated showers (20p), a family shower room, two bathrooms (50p), baby bath, dishwashing, laundry facilities, and provision for disabled visitors. Well stocked supermarket with fresh bread made on site (both from late May). Bars (with TV), restaurant, cafe and takeaway. Entertainment (every night in season). Good size, outdoor, heated and supervised pool (also late May) with slide. Sauna. Super Fort Knox style adventure playground, crazy golf, Kiddies Club and indoor adventure play area (supervised for 2-8 year olds at a small charge). Games room. Pitch and putt. Golf. Bicycle hire. Coarse fishing with three lakes. Dogs are accepted in one field only. **Off site:** Boat launching 4 miles, riding within 1 mile.

Charges 2001

Per adult	£3.25 - £5.95
child (4-14 yrs)	free - £3.85
car	80p
electricity	£3.00
serviced pitch incl. electricity	£7.50
dog	£1.95

Families and couples only. **Tel** (01637) 830531. Fax: (01637) 831000. E-mail: info@trevornick.co.uk.
Reservations: Made with £20 deposit per week (Sat. to Sat. only July/Aug). **Open** Easter - mid September.

Directions: From A3075 approach to Newquay - Perranporth road, turn towards Cubert and Holywell Bay. Continue through Cubert to park on the right. O.S.GR: SW776586.

Relax ...we've got the holiday for you!

As touring and camping specialists we have everything you need for a brilliant holiday. Superb location overlooking Holywell Bay. First-class facilities and a wonderful friendly atmosphere.

Enjoy...No Tent?

Book a luxury fully equipped, pre-erected Eurotent which sleeps 4/6 – astounding value!

Smile ...for a great fun holiday!

Glorious safe swimming and surfing beach. Amazing full entertainment programme, marvellous children's club, heated pool, coarse fishing and a brilliant 18-hole golf course. You'll have a fantastic time!

'Voted Family Park of the Year by Practical Caravan Readers'

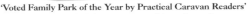

Phone NOW for a copy of our brochure
☎ 01637 830531
www.trevornick.co.uk · email: info@trevornick.co.uk

Caravan TOP 100 FAMILY PARKS

CORNWALL'S FINEST PARCS

trevornick Holiday Park

HOLYWELL BAY · NEWQUAY · CORNWALL TR8 5PW

Trevella Caravan and Camping Park

Crantock, Newquay, Cornwall TR8 5EW

017

One of the best known and most respected of Cornish parks with its colourful flower-beds and driveway (a regular winner of a 'Newquay in Bloom' award), Trevella is also one of the first to fill up and has a longer season than most. Well organised, the pitches are in a number of adjoining meadows, most of which are on a slight slope. Of the 250 pitches for touring units (any type), some 200 can be reserved and these are marked, individual ones. Over 200 pitches have electricity connections (10A), with 33 'premium' serviced pitches (with hardstanding, electricity and TV hook-ups, water, waste water, sewage). Trevella is essentially a quiet family touring park with an accent on orderliness and cleanliness; on-site evening activities are limited. Access is free to three fishing lakes, two on site (permits from reception); with some fishing instruction and wildlife talks for youngsters in season. There is a pleasant walk around the lakes, a protected nature reserve, and it is also possible to walk to Crantock beach but check the tides first. A member of the Best of British group.

Facilities: The sanitary facilities are kept very clean, three blocks providing sufficient coverage with individual washbasins in private cabins for ladies, hair dressing room and a baby room. Launderette. Well stocked supermarket and heated outdoor pool (both Easter - October). Freezer pack service. Nicky's Kitchen offers hot dishes and snacks to take away or eat there, open late. Games room with pool tables and table tennis. Separate TV room. Crazy golf, large adventure playground, separate play and sports area and a pets corner. Fishing on site. **Off site**: Shuttle bus service to Newquay in high season. Nearest beach is ½ mile on foot, 1 mile by car and Newquay is 2 miles. Pubs and restaurants at Crantock, 1 mile. Riding 1 mile, golf 3 miles.

Charges 2001

Per adult	£3.25 - £5.75
child (3-16 yrs)	£1.50 - £2.75
car	70p - 80p
dog	60p - £1.20
electricity	£2.50
full services incl. electricity	£5.75

Families and couples only. **Tel**: (01637) 830308 (24 hr). Fax: (01872) 571254. E-mail: holidays@trevella. co.uk. **Reservations**: Made with £20 deposit and £2 booking fee (16/7-27/8: Fri/Fri or Sat/Sat only). **Open** Easter - 31 October.

Directions: To avoid Newquay leave A30 or A392 at Indian Queens, straight over crossroads with A39 and A3058, left at A3075 junction and first right at camp sign. O.S.GR: SW802598.

Newperran Tourist Park

Rejerrah, Newquay, Cornwall TR8 5QJ

016

This is a large, level park in rural Cornish countryside and on high ground making it quite open but also giving excellent views of the coast and surrounding district. Although it has its own manager, it is under the same family ownership and direction as Trevella Park, with the same sort of standards. Newperran is a little further back from the sea, but only 2½ miles from Perranporth beach, and there is a free heated swimming pool on site. Those who prefer traditional camping to a holiday camp atmosphere should appreciate this park. It certainly has its full share of amenities, but it is a quiet park used mainly by families and with few evening activities. It does now have an attractive 'village inn' with a garden, open every evening, more in high season. The park consists of a number of flat, well drained, hedged meadows divided into 250 individual pitches. Some fields have larger and reservable plots, with more free space in the middle. There are 113 electrical hook-ups (10A) including 13 'all-service' pitches. Goonhavern village is within walking distance with pubs and post office. A member of the Best of British group.

Facilities: Sanitary facilities comprise four clean, permanent blocks. Most washbasins are in cabins, there are two bathrooms, hair dressing room and a unit for disabled visitors. Dishwashing sinks. Launderette. Good self-service licensed shop. Pub. Café with hot snacks to eat there or take away. Outdoor swimming pool. TV room with some children's video shows. Adventure playground and separate play area for under-fives. Crazy golf. Children's room and activity programme in season. Free fishing at Trevella. **Off site**: Riding or golf 2 miles.

Charges 2001

Per adult	£3.25 - £5.75
child (3-16 yrs)	£1.60 - £2.90
car	70p - 80p
dog	60p - £1.00
electricity (10A)	£2.40
full services incl. electricity	£5.75

Tel: (01872) 572407. (1/10-1/5: (01637) 830308). Fax: (01872) 571254. E-mail: holidays@newperran.co.uk. **Reservations**: Advised in high season; made with £20 p/w deposit and £2 fee. **Open** mid-May - mid-September.

Directions: Turn off A3075 to west at camping sign 7 miles south of Newquay and just north of Goonhavern village. O.S.GR: SW794546.

Trevella & Newperran

CARAVAN AND CAMPING PARK

TOURIST PARK

Both parks have spotless facilities including modern toilet and shower blocks with individual wash cubicles, razor points, babies room, hairdressing room, hairdriers, launderette, crazy golf, games room, TV room, cafe, shop and off licence, free heated swimming pools and adventure play areas.

THE FAMILY RUN HOLIDAY PARKS

Our parks are renowned for their cleanliness and hygiene and we spare no effort to maintain this reputation.
- Concessionary green fees at Perranporth's excellent links golf course.
- Nature reserve and well stocked lake at Trevella offers Free Fishing (no closed season).

VOTED TWO OF THE TOP 10 TOURING PARKS IN CORNWALL

TREVELLA PARK
22 CRANTOCK, NEWQUAY, CORNWALL TR8 5EW.   TEL: 01637 830308

www.trevella.co.uk

Trevella just outside Newquay and its seven golden beaches. A breathtakingly beautiful secluded family park. As well as touring pitches there are holiday caravans for hire with toilet, shower and colour Satellite TV.

★★★★★ HOLIDAY PARK

NEWPERRAN TOURIST PARK
22 REJERRAH, NEWQUAY, CORNWALL TR8 5QJ.   TEL: 01872 572407

www.newperran.co.uk

Newperran has been developed from a small Cornish farm in a picturesque, beautifully cared for setting. It is a level park with perimeter pitching ideal for caravans, tents, motor homes and the perfect family holiday.

★★★★ TOURING PARK

TELEPHONE FOR COLOUR BROCHURES OR WRITE FOR BROCHURE TO THE SITE OF YOUR CHOICE.

Newquay Holiday Park

Newquay, Cornwall TR8 4HS

020

This park lies peacefully on a terraced hillside only just outside the town, 2 miles from the beaches and town centre. Its main feature is an attractively laid out group of three heated swimming pools with a giant water slide (lifeguards in attendance) and surrounding 'green' sunbathing areas. Mainly a touring park, it has 356 marked pitches for any type of unit in a series of hedged fields, some sloping. Some fields are just for caravans, others are for tents, plus 138 caravan holiday homes (for hire). Most pitches are individual ones marked out by lines on ground but with nothing between them. Electricity points (16A) are provided for caravans and tents, plus 10 special 'star' pitches with hardstanding, water and drainage. Entertainment is provided each night with live music, discos etc. in the site's Fiesta Club which also has a bar, TV lounge and games room with pool and snooker tables (all open when the site is open). A bus service runs to Newquay from the site.

Facilities: Two good-sized, modern toilet blocks provide fairly basic free hot showers. An extra block is opened for the main season when facilities may be under pressure. Baby bath. Covered external dishwashing sinks. Full launderette with free ironing. Well stocked self-service shop (gas available) and takeaway food bar (both all season and good value). Lounge with Sky TV. New restaurant. Outdoor pool complex. Pitch and putt and crazy golf. Good children's play area, children's club and recreation field for football and volleyball. Amusement arcade. No dogs or pets are accepted. **Off site**: Fishing and bicycle hire 2 miles, golf 200 yds, riding 2½ miles.

Charges 2002

Per unit incl. 2 adults	£7.10 - £13.10
child (3-15 yrs)	free - £4.10
vehicle	85p
electricity (16A)	free - £2.50
star pitch supplement	£3.50

Min. charge per night in high season £13.10. Families and mixed couples only. **Tel**: (01637) 871111. Fax: (01637) 850818. E-mail: bookings@ newquay-holiday-parks.co.uk. **Reservations**: Recommended for peak season; made with £18.50 deposit per week plus £10 cancellation insurance (peak weeks Sat. - Sat. only). **Open** Easter - October.

Directions: Park is east of Newquay on A3059 road 1 mile east of junction with A3058. O.S.GR: SW853626.

Trekenning Tourist Park

Newquay, Cornwall TR8 4JF

031

Trekenning is owned by John Fynn, his daughter Tracey and son-in-law Dave and they have succeeded in developing a popular park with good facilities, a nice change from the 'all singing, all dancing' Newquay sites. Easy access just off the A39 roundabout at St Columb Major leads to a large sloping field with neatly cut grass and all the facilities in the opposite corner. In total there are 75 pitches, 68 with 10A electricity. Some have been levelled, others are tucked away at a lower level shaded by tall trees. A well hidden tent field with just a water point is edged by a wooded small stream. The star of the show is undoubtedly the kidney shaped pool and paddling pool which are in a garden-like setting with gazebos and sun loungers, with a terraced lawn and patio at the top. This leads to the games room and cosy upstairs bar. Entertainment is provided every night in the main season (ie. singers, quiz nights, connect-4 nights, discos on Fridays). The A39 runs parallel to one side of the site, so there is possible road noise.

Facilities: Two sanitary blocks, one providing normal showers and vanity style washbasins, the other with two en-suite bathrooms and six large family showers, well refurbished. Laundry room. Covered dishwashing sinks. Children's play area. Outdoor pool. Games room. Bar with food and takeaway facilities (all July/Aug). Barbecue area. **Off site**: Fishing 1 mile, riding and golf 2 miles, bicycle hire 6 miles.

Charges guide

Per adult	£3.75 - £5.40
child (3-15 yrs)	£2.55 - £3.90
electricity	£2.90
extra vehicle	£1.10
dog	£2.00

Tel: (01637) 880462. Fax: (01637) 880500. E-mail: trekenning@aol.com. **Reservations**: Made with £20 deposit. **Open** Easter/1 April - 30 September

Directions: Take A3059 turning to Newquay from St Columb Major then turn immediately left; park is signed. O.S.GR: SW907625.

A Warm Welcome to

Parkdean *Holidays*

EMAIL: enquiries@parkdean.com
www.parkdeanholidays.com

Newquay
HOLIDAY PARKS

EMAIL: enquiries@newquay-hol-park.demon.co.uk
www.newquay-holiday-parks.co.uk

BROCHURE HOTLINE
HOLIDAY HOMES & TOURING · ALL PARKS
01637 871111

Fantastic Locations & Great Value for Money

Holywell Bay — Holiday Park

Next to glorious sandy beach
- Touring/Camping Facilities • Marked Pitches
- Electric Hook-Ups • Free Showers
- Refurbished Club • Sky TV★ • Entertainment
- Maxi Million Club★ • Themed Play Area★
- Heated Pool • Amusements • Shop
- Take-Away • Launderette • Full Facilities
- Holiday Homes also available

Newquay — Holiday Park

Superb location in south facing parkland
- Touring/Camping Facilities • Marked Pitches
- Electric Hook-Ups • Free Showers • Shop
- Refurbished Club • Sky TV★ • Entertainment
- Maxi Million Club★ • Heated Pool
- Themed Play Area★ • Restaurant★
- Take-Away • Launderette • Amusements
- Pool • Snooker • Crazy Golf • Pitch n' Putt
- Full Facilities • Holiday Homes available

★ NEW IN 2001   ★ NEW FOR 2002

St Minver — Holiday Park

Set in grounds of old manor house
- Touring/Camping Facilities • Electric Hook-Ups
- Club & Bar • Sky TV • Entertainment
- Indoor Pool • Maxi Million Club
- Pool Tables • Play Area for under 5's
- Adventure Playground • Amusements
- Take-Away & Snack Bar
- Crazy Golf • Shop • Launderette
- Full Facilities • Holiday Homes available

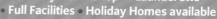

Hendra Holiday Park

Newquay, Cornwall TR8 4NY

021

Hendra is a long-established holiday park for the family that likes to be entertained, as the entertainment programme here is very comprehensive. There are comedians, show bands, cabaret, dancing, bingo, discos, plus entertainment and clubs for children. The 600 pitches are on various well mown, slightly sloping grass fields with country views and mature trees, some more sheltered than others. There are tarmac roads and lighting and 200 pitches have electric hook-ups (16A). Some landscaped hardstanding 'super' pitches have water, electricity, light, sewer drainage and satellite TV connections (dogs not accepted on these pitches). Many pitches also have water, drainage and hardstanding. There are caravan holiday homes for hire but they are separate from the tourers. The entrance and reception are very attractive with a mass of well tended flower beds which, along with the other facilities, form a village-like centre to the park. The 'star of the show' is the Oasis complex consisting of a 30 m. indoor, heated fun pool with three flumes, river rapids, water falls and beach. The complex is open to the public – really a mini water-park. The new outdoor heated pool with grass sunbathing area is free to campers. Activities are well catered for (see opposite). The park is only 1½ miles from Newquay and its fabulous surfing beaches and a bus to the town passes the gate.

Facilities: The three toilet blocks have been refurbished to provide vanity style washbasins, free showers and some facilities for babies and disabled visitors. Large launderette. Motorcaravan services. Gas supplies. Well stocked shop. Various bars and restaurants, open all season (limited hours in early season), breakfast included. Pizzeria (main season only). Takeaway. Swimming pool complex – timed 1/ hour sessions cost £2 per family group (max. 4 persons). Outdoor pool. Children's play areas. Tennis. Minigolf. Large playing fields. Table tennis, pool tables and a large array of slot machines. **Off site:** Fishing or riding 1 mile, bicycle hire or golf 2 miles.

Charges 2001

Per adult	£3.30 - £5.65
child (3-14 yrs)	free - £3.50
vehicle	£1.00
awning	free
'super' pitch (electricity, water, chemical disposal, TV point, hardstanding, no dogs)	£7.50
hardstanding pitch (electricity, water, drainage)	£3.85
electricity only	£2.80
dog	£1.70

Families and mixed couples only. Various special offers. **Tel:** (01637) 875778. Fax: (01637) 879017. E-mail: hendra.cornwall@dial.pipex.com.
Reservations: Made with deposit (£20) and fee (£3).
Open February - end October.

Directions: Park is on left side of A392 Indian Queens - Newquay road at Newquay side of Quintrell Downs. O.S.GR: SW833601.

Southleigh Manor Naturist Holiday Club

St Columb Major, Cornwall TR9 6HY

024N

Southleigh is a welcoming family naturist site in the mature grounds of a large house. For those who have ventured to try the naturist sites in our France guide and who also may appreciate that special ambience at home, we are happy to include Southleigh Manor, now under the new ownership of Kathy and Bob Prescott. The respect that the naturist has for the environment and for fellow beings provides a very special, caring atmosphere and this can be truly experienced on this site. The 50 pitches are in the south facing, sheltered lawned garden and orchard with mature trees. There are 2 hardstandings and 48 electrical connections (5/10A), plus 8 touring vans to let. Barbecues, social evenings and quiz nights are organised, and there is the opportunity to enjoy Cornwall's naturist beaches and many tourist attractions, which combine to provide a relaxed holiday atmosphere.

Facilities: The purpose built toilet block has identical, well equipped, unisex units at each end. Laundry room. Small shop - bread, milk, papers (late May - 31 Aug). Bar area. with bistro planned for 2002). Small open air swimming pool heated (most of the season). Sun room/leisure suite including sauna and spa bath in the house. Boules, volleyball, table tennis and minigolf. Children's play area with tree house and gaily painted train. **Off site:** Fishing 4 miles, bicycle hire 7 miles, riding 2 miles, golf 5 miles.

Charges 2001

Per unit incl. 2 adults	£12.00 - £13.50
child (13 yrs and under)	£1.20 - £1.40
electricity	£1.95
dog	95p

Club membership £2.50 per couple/family for stay. No credit cards. **Tel:** (01637) 880938. Fax: (01637) 881108. E-mail: southleighmanor@success4 business.com. **Reservations:** Made with £50 per week deposit. **Open** April - 31 October.

Directions: From north on A30 Bodmin - Truro road, after village of Victoria pass Roche Cross and go under iron railway bridge and then first right on A3059 towards St Mawgan and St Columb. Site is on left in 3 miles. From A39, take A3059 at Newquay/St Columb roundabout and site is on right, almost immediately. O.S.GR: SW904622.

Cornwall

Sea View International

Boswinger, Gorran, St Austell, Cornwall PL26 6LL

Sea View is one of the best examples of a well cared for, quality park and this is reflected in the number of awards it has won in the last 20 years. Now in the hands of the third generation of the Michell family, the park is constantly being improved with the aim of providing quality camping for the discerning camper. Although somewhat exposed, the park is colourful with flower beds and flowering shrubs and has well manicured grass of exceptional quality. The area around the swimming pool is particularly attractive, with sunbathing areas with free sun-beds on tiled terraces surrounded by flowers creating private little areas, all with magnificent views of the sea and the distant headland. An attractive covered, flowered walkway, created with hanging baskets, connects the two excellent toilet facilities which are topped by a handsome clock tower. There are no bars, restaurant or evening entertainment which seems to be the main reason many return year after year - booking for July/Aug. is advisable. Reception has a free ice machine and coffee – a nice touch. Many of the 163 large, level pitches have views, all have 16A electricity and 47 are fully serviced, including hardstandings suitable for large motorhomes. There are 38 caravan holiday homes for hire in a separate area. Anyone not restricted by school holidays will find May and June a particularly good time to visit, the gardens of Heligan and Trelissick and Lanhydrock House being at their best at that time. The area is full of places to visit from theme parks to the seal sanctuary, not forgetting the safe beaches, one of which is only a ½ mile walk. This park is well worth consideration. A member of the Best of British group.

Facilities: The toilet blocks are excellent – centrally positioned, well maintained, with good quality fittings and central heating. Large showers, baby baths, facilities for disabled visitors (two showers and WCs), and a hairdressing area, plus bathrooms (on payment). An extension provides an enlarged, smart dishwashing area with two small campers' kitchens (one with a microwave, one with a mini-grill and hob) and a well equipped laundry. Motorcaravan service point with car washing facilities. Shop plus gas (June-end Sept). Takeaway (Whitsun-mid Sept). Swimming pool open all season, heated end May-mid Sept. Excellent large playing field allowing plenty of room for leisure activities including tennis, volleyball, badminton, football, putting, table tennis, crazy golf, petanque, a fenced play area for under-sevens, and an adventure playground. Barbecue area with tables and seats at the top of the park has a very descriptive weather map which is updated daily. Bicycle hire. Certain breeds of dog are not accepted. **Off site:** Fishing ½ mile, boat launching 2 miles, riding 1 mile, golf 9 miles.

Charges 2001

Per unit incl. 2 persons and awning	£6.00 - £17.00
extra adult	£1.00 - £4.00
child (5-14 yrs)	£1.00 - £3.00
pup tent (outside 18/7-27/8)	free - £2.00
electricity	£1.90
dog (limited breeds and numbers)	free - £2.00
special facility pitch	£3.00

Tel: (01726) 843425. Fax: (01726) 843358. E-mail: enquiries@seaviewinternational.com. **Reservations**: Min 7 nights, w/e - w/e, 28/7-1/9. other times, any length, with £30 deposit and £2 fee. **Open** 1 April - 3 October.

Directions: From St Austell take B3273 towards Mevagissey; 1 mile before Mevagissey village turn right at Gorran and camp sign and continue towards Gorran for 5 miles. Fork right at camp sign and follow signs to park. O.S.GR: SW991412.

Cornwall
Pentewan Sands Holiday Park

025 Pentewan, nr St. Austell, Cornwall PL26 6BT

Pentewan Sands is a popular, well managed family park with an ideal position right beside a wide sandy private beach. The beach offers safe bathing and is managed by the park. A busy, 32 acre holiday park with lots going on, there are 501 individual touring pitches, 401 with electricity, and 120 caravan holiday homes. The good-sized pitches are on level grass with nothing between them, marked and numbered by frontage stones, mostly in rows adjoining access roads. A good sized free heated swimming pool with a small children's pool is beside the Clubhouse and bowling centre. The Clubhouse contains two licensed bar lounges upstairs and a further one downstairs opening on to the pool area, open all day and serving a variety of good value food in season. A full entertainment programme, beach activities, water sports and a children's club are organised, and a small water sports centre is on the beach. The sailing club adjoining offers membership to campers, scuba diving, windsurfing courses, etc. No jet-skis are permitted and no 4WD vehicles allowed on the beach. There is access to the Pentewan Valley Trail, a six mile route for cycling or walking following the old carriageway to Mevagissey with its throngs of tourists (only two miles by the main road). The park has been owned by the Tremayne family for 60 years, along with the beach, and there are links with the award winning Lost Gardens of Heligan.

Facilities: The four main toilet blocks serve their purpose, receiving heavy use in peak season but now with individual cleaners. They include two bathrooms and a baby room, plus facilities for disabled people, a well equipped laundry room, and washing up sinks. Motorcaravan service point. Large, self-service shop (from Easter but hours may be limited). Bistro and fast food (Whitsun - mid-Sept). Bars, bar meals. Entertainment programme and children's club. Swimming pools (supervised and open Whitsun - mid Sept). Adventure playground. Tennis courts (one full size, one compact). Bicycle hire. Slipway and boat launching service (Whit - mid Sept). Freezer service for ice packs, battery charging service. Gas available. Security barrier at entrance. Caravan and boat storage. Dogs are not accepted. **Off site**: Riding or golf 2 miles.

Charges 2001

Per unit incl. 2 adults	£6.45 - £16.50
extra adult	£1.60 - £3.60
child (3-15 yrs)	£1.00 - £2.70
awning	free
extra small tent, boat or car	£1.30 - £1.80
electricity (10A)	£2.80

Sea front pitch plus 10-20%. **Tel**: (01726) 843485. Fax: (01726) 844142. E-mail: info@pentewan.co.uk. **Reservations**: Made Sat - Sat or Wed - Wed with deposit (£35-£75, acc. to season), £4 booking fee and compulsory cancellation insurance (£3-£6). **Open** Easter/1 April - 31 October. 'Camping Cheque'

Directions: From St Austell ring road take B3273 for Mevagissey. Park is 3½ miles, where the road meets the sea. O.S.GR: SX018468.

Cornwall
Heligan Woods Caravan Park
041 St Ewe, St Austell, Cornwall PL26 6ER

A peaceful park in a mature garden setting, Heligan Woods (formerly Pengrugla) is now under the ownership of Pentewan Sands and the Tremayne family. We are happy to feature the park to complement the Pentewan site with its busy beach life and many activities. Part of the boundary actually edges the Lost Gardens of Heligan although nothing can be seen. At some time the land used to develop the park must have been part of the Gardens and one can enjoy the mature trees and flowering shrubs which have been further landscaped to provide an attractive situation for a number of private holiday homes. Facing out over a part of Heligan's 'Lost Valley' these are interspersed with touring pitches, with some below on sloping grass and others in a more level situation amongst trees and shrubs. In all, there are 100 good sized pitches, 80 with 16A electricity.

Facilities: A modern toilet block is heated, fully equipped and well kept, including a unisex room with bath and small size bath. Dishwashing sinks under cover. Laundry room with two washing machines, two dryers, iron and board, but no hand washing sink. Small shop with good takeaway (fish and chip style; Easter, then Whitsun - 14 Sept). Adventure playground. Access to the Pentewan Trail to ride or cycle into Mevagissey or Pentewan. **Off site**: The facilities of Pentewan Sands are open to Heligan Woods visitors. Riding 4 miles, golf 5 miles.

Charges 2001

Per unit incl. 2 adults	£6.30 - £15.05
extra adult	£2.10 - £3.10
extra child (3-15 yrs)	£1.00 - £2.25
dog	£1.00
electricity	£2.20

Tel: (01726) 842714. Fax: (01726) 844414. E-mail: info@pentewan.co.uk. **Reservations**: Made with deposit (£35-£75, acc. to season); write to Pentewan Sands (no. 025). **Open** 1 April - 31 October.

Directions: From St Austell ring road take B3273 for Mevagissey. After 3½ miles, pass Pentewan Sands, continue up the hill and turn right following site signs. Park is on left just before reaching Heligan Gardens. O.S.GR: SW999464.

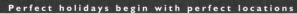

Cornwall

Croft Farm Touring Park

046 Luxulyan, Bodmin, Cornwall, PL30 5EQ

This secluded park is just one mile from the new Eden Project. Croft Farm was once part of a larger site and you pass some of the residential homes on the way in. Mature trees and shrubs edge most of the site, except for an open field. A number of mobile homes are on site, some privately owned and some for hire by the site, along with three holiday cottages. In the top field with good views, there are 30 individual pitches with new hedges planted. The original mature area provides a further 27 pitches (with 10A electricity for the majority), 15 with hardstanding and 5 of these fully serviced. The park has won a Bellamy Gold award and it is the first time we have seen recycling complete with compost unit. The half mile woodland trail is also part of the conservation effort and takes you through the rest of the park's natural areas which are indeed left very natural! The village pub is ¼ mile and the newly opened Eden project on the door step.

Facilities: The heated toilet block (£5 deposit for key) is of older design but has been neatly updated to provide showers with a plastic door instead of a curtain and plenty of room to change with a good seat, a baby room and one en-suite basin and toilet for ladies. Dishwashing under cover, one laundry sink with spin dryer. 'Field kitchen' with sinks in the top field. Reception has a newspaper ordering service and keeps basic necessities. Grass area with adventure play equipment and goal net. Games room with pool table and amusement machines. **Off site**: Fishing 1 mile. Golf or riding 3 miles.

Charges 2001

Per unit incl. 2 adults	£7.70 - £10.50
extra adult	£2.00
child (5-15 yrs)	£1.20
electricity	£2.00
serviced pitch	£1.00
awning	£1.00
dog	50p
small tent per person	£2.80 - £3.25

Tel: (01726) 850228. Fax: (01726) 850492. E-mail: lynpick@globalnet.co.uk. **Reservations**: Made with £20 deposit p/week or £3 p/night for shorter visits. **Open** 21 March - 31 October

Directions: From A391 Bodmin - St Austell road follow directions for the Eden project. When you come to the entrance of the project continue straight on for approx. 1 mile, and site is on the left side of this road in the direction of Luxulyan. O.S.GR: SX045588.

Cornwall
Penhaven Touring Park
Pentewan, St Austell, Cornwall PL26 6DL

026

Family owned, Penhaven is a level 13 acre touring park, with the road on one side (this can be a little noisy on busy Saturdays) and a river on the other. There is a bridge from the site giving access to the Pentewan Valley Trail, a two mile walk or cycle ride to Pentewan village and beach along this quiet, traffic-free track, with links to Mevagissey via Heligan. Owned and developed by the Hackwell family for over 10 years, the park comprises three fields with 105 good sized, grassy pitches which are numbered, 80 with 10A electricity, 5 with hardstanding and 4 fully serviced. The North field is used for rallies and has a refurbished 'portacabin' style toilet unit. The south field is used for ball games, caravan storage and as a tent area for 35 tents on a 28 day licence (no tarmac road and no lighting). The Middle field has all the main facilities which include a heated swimming pool (unsupervised) with a paved sunbathing surround and loungers. Heligan Gardens are nearby, the new Eden Project is 4 miles and the beach is only 1 mile. A busy park, but away from the hectic coastal sites, Penhaven will probably appeal to people who don't want a bar and evening entertainment.

Facilities: Fully equipped heated toilet block and three family shower rooms (key on request with deposit) and one unit for use by disabled visitors. Dishwashing sinks under cover. Well equipped laundry with washing lines provided. Motorcaravan services. Shop. In high season a van on site sells takeaway snacks. Outdoor pool (mid May - early Sept). Small play area. Bicycle hire. **Off site:** Restaurant in the nearby village of London Apprentice. Buses pass the gate for St Austell and Mevagissey. Fishing near, boat launching 1 mile, golf 3 miles, riding 8 miles.

Charges guide

Per unit incl. 2 persons	£8.80 - £18.00
extra adult	£3.35 - £4.45
child (5-15 yrs)	£1.60
extra car, boat or trailer	£1.50
electricity (10A)	£2.10
dog	80p

Tel: (01726) 843687. Fax: (01726) 843870. E-mail: penhaven.cornwall@virgin.net. **Reservations**: Made for min. 3 days with £20 deposit per week. **Open** 1 April - 31 October.

Directions: From St Austell on A390, take B3273 to Mevagissey and park is on left, 1 mile from London Apprentice before the village of Pentewan. O.S.GR: SX008481.

Cornwall
Powderham Castle Tourist Park
Lanlivery, nr Lostwithiel, Cornwall PL30 5BU

028

This is a most pleasant, peaceful touring park with plenty of sheltered green space and a natural, uncommercialised atmosphere. This has been enhanced by careful planting of trees and shrubs to form a series of linked paddocks with a small unfenced stream running through. The nearest beach at Par is some 4 miles. The park has 38 private caravan holiday homes in a separate field and 75 numbered touring pitches spread round the perimeter of the paddocks, each with 10-15 pitches. All have electricity connections (5/10A) and 7 have hardstanding (awning groundsheets must be lifted alternate days). A large, well equipped children's activity play area with a super range of adventure type equipment on grass is in one of the hedged paddocks with a fenced paddling pool. Indoor tennis courts (Bodmin) and a swimming pool are near. The village pub is within walking distance and there are several good local restaurants. The Eden Project is very close.

Facilities: The single central toilet block is good but is quite a walk from some pitches. Hot showers are on payment, with curtained cubicles in the ladies' and a family washroom with shower, basin, WC, etc. Separate dishwashing area with five sinks. Fully equipped laundry room. Motorcaravan service point. Seasonal pitches and caravan storage available. Children's play area. Torch useful. **Off site:** Fresh water fishing 1½ miles or sea fishing 3 miles, bicycle hire 4 miles, riding 2 miles, golf 1½ miles.

Charges 2001

Per unit	£3.50 - £5.00
adult	£1.70 - £2.60
child (3-16 yrs)	60p - £1.30
electricity	£1.75
awning (no groundsheet), extra small tent, car	free

No single sex groups (excl. bona fide organisations). No credit cards. **Tel**: (01208) 872277. **Reservations**: Made with £20 deposit. **Open** Easter/1 April - 31 October.

Directions: Park approach road leads off A390 road 1½ miles southwest of Lostwithiel. Follow white or brown camping signs. No other approach roads are advised. O.S.GR: SX083592.

Carlyon Bay Caravan and Camping Park

Bethesda, Carlyon Bay, St Austell, Cornwall PL25 3RE

Tranquil open meadows edged by mature woodland, well cared for by the Taylor family, provide a beautiful holiday setting with a busy Blue Flag beach five minutes walk from the top gate at this park. The original farm buildings have been converted and added to, providing an attractive centre to the park, also home for the owners, with a certain individuality of design which is very pleasing, particularly in the impressively tiled toilet blocks which are of excellent quality and design. The 180 pitches in five areas are spacious and allow for a family meadow, a dog free meadow, and an area for couples, etc. All are on flat, terraced or gently sloping grass with flowers and shrubs in some areas. The 104 pitches with electricity (5/10A) are marked. There is even a 'discreet' area, well screened and hidden, for naturists. The only official naturist beach in Cornwall, Polgaver Bay, at the far end of Carlyon Bay can be reached by walking over the cliff tops (and is now charged for). The attractive kidney shaped, heated pool (Easter-Sept) with children's paddling pool, is walled and paved for sunbathing. It is part of the central, covered area used for entertainment. Socially the park provides entertainment in high season for families and children but those who wish for more can choose between the Cornish Leisure World complex on the beach, with its pool, bars and discos, or the social club near the entrance to the park which welcomes campers. The coastal footpath passes near. All Cornwall's attractions are within touring distance. Buses to St. Austell and Fowey run from the park entrance.

Facilities: Three modern toilet blocks provide a mix of facilities from vanity style washbasins to en-suite toilets and basins, comfortable, roomy, pre-set showers with divider, shelf, etc, facilities for hair-care and make-up and thoughtful provision for babies - almost 'home from home'! Dishwashing sinks under cover at all blocks. Fully equipped laundry room (hot water metered). TV lounge, crazy golf, table tennis and pool table. Swimming pool. Two children's play areas, one adventure type. Modern reception with a good little shop and takeaway (May-mid Sept). **Off site**: Golf course near the park entrance.

Charges 2001

Per unit incl. 2 persons and car	£8.00 - £17.00
extra adult	£3.00 - £3.50
child (3-17 yrs incl.)	£1.50 - £2.50
awning or small pup tent	free - £1.00
dog	£1.00 - £1.50
electricity	£2.00
serviced pitch	£3.00

Motorcaravan less £1.00, hiker/tent less £2.00 per night. **Tel**: (01726) 812735. Fax: (01726) 815496. E-mail: jeffst@globalnet.co.uk. **Reservations**: Made with £30 deposit and £2 fee (min. 6 nights 19/7-17/8). **Open** April - October.

Directions: From Plymouth direction on A390, pass Lostwithiel and 1 mile after village of St Blazey, turn left at roundabout beside Britannia Inn. After 400 yds turn right on a concrete road and right again at site sign. O.S.GR: SX053526.

Cornwall
Polruan Holidays Camping and Caravanning

019 Polruan-by-Fowey, Cornwall PL23 1QH

Polruan is a rural site in an elevated position not far from Fowey. With 32 touring pitches and 11 holiday homes to let, this is a very pleasant little site. The holiday homes are arranged in a neat circle, with a central area for some tourers, including 7 pitches with gravel hardstanding and electricity. The remaining touring pitches are in an adjacent field with 4 electricity hook-ups, which is part level for motorcaravans and part on a gentle slope for tents. There are marvellous sea views, but it could be a little exposed when the wind blows off the sea. A raised picnic area, with a table provided, gives more views across the estuary to Fowey. This is a nice little park in a popular tourist area, within walking distance (down-hill all the way, and vice-versa!) of the village, where there are various hostelries and a passenger ferry to Fowey. A member of the Countryside Discovery group.

Facilities: The small sanitary block of older design is centrally situated and includes a laundry sink plus a washing machine – in the ladies'. New dishwashing sinks. Motorcaravan service facilities. Recycling bins. Reception (with a small terrace) doubles as a small shop for basics and gas, and provides a freezer for ice packs, tourist information and bus timetables (for Looe, etc). Sloping field for children's play with swings. **Off site**: Riding or bicycle hire 3 miles, fishing ½ mile, golf 10 miles.

Charges 2001

Per unit	£6.75 - £10.25
extra person	£1.75
electricity	£2.00

No credit cards. **Tel/Fax**: (01726) 870263. E-mail: polholiday@aol.com. **Reservations**: Advised for July/Aug. and made with £30 deposit. **Open** Easter - October.

Directions: From main A390 at East Taphouse take B3359 towards Looe. After 5 miles fork right signed Bodinnick and ferry. Watch for signs for Polruan and site to left. Follow these carefully along narrow Cornish lanes to site on right just before village. O.S.GR: SX133509.

Cornwall
Trelay Farmpark

040 Pelynt, by Looe, Cornwall PL13 2JX

Situated a little back from the coast, just over three miles from Looe and Polperro in a rural situation, this is a well cared for park. Neat, tidy and quiet, there is no farm adjacent. On your right as you drive in, and quite attractively arranged amongst herbaceous shrubs, are caravan holiday homes (13 privately owned, some let by the park). The touring area is behind and slightly above, on level to gently sloping, neatly cut grass. An oval hard-core road connects the good sized, numbered pitches that border the site and back onto hedges, the majority with rural views. There are 23 pitches with electricity hook-ups, with a further 30 pitches for tents, etc. Outside the main season the central area is kept free for ball games. You will receive a good welcome from the enthusiastic owners, Heather and Graham Veale and their family, who live in the chalet bungalow near the entrance where the small reception is located.

Facilities: The excellent chalet-type toilet block is purpose built, heated, well equipped and maintained. There are some semi-private washbasins. For disabled visitors an en-suite unit (with ramp) is accessed by key from reception and includes a baby bath. Two dishwashing sinks and a laundry sink. Washing machine and dryer. Gas supplies. Free use of fridge/freezer. Tourist information including map sales and loan. **Off site**: Village with pub and shops within ½ mile. 'Coastal Hoppa' bus from the gate on Thursdays. The Eden Project is 10 miles west.

Charges 2002

Per unit incl. 2 persons	£7.00 - £8.50
extra person under 5 yrs	£1.00
over 5 yrs	£2.00
electricity	£1.60
dog	50p

No credit cards. **Tel/Fax**: (01503) 220900. **Reservations**: Advised for July/Aug. **Open** 1 April - end October.

Directions: From A390 Lostwithiel road take B3359 south at Middle or East Taphouse towards Looe and Polperro. Site is signed ½ mile past Pelynt on the left. From Looe take A387 towards Polperro and after 2 miles turn right onto B3359 towards Pelynt. Site is signed 1 mile on right. O.S.GR: SX210545.

 Alan Rogers' discount
Less 50p per night

Killigarth Manor Holiday Centre

Polperro, Looe, Cornwall PL13 2JQ

A substantial part of Killigarth Estate is occupied by caravan holiday homes but a separate part is allocated to touring units and it is a good choice for those that like a range of facilities and entertainment. It provides 202 marked, level or gently sloping grass pitches, of which 75 are taken by seasonal units, and a tenting paddock. There are 73 electric hook-ups (16A) for tourers. A range of bars (eg. Smugglers' Bar, Sportsman's Lounge and Harbour Lights Club) and a large entertainment area with stage, mini-cinema, family room, amusements and games areas, a new restaurant, takeaway and bar snacks, a heated indoor pool (adult £2, child £1), fitness centre with gym, sauna and sun bed, and a sun terrace with beautiful views. Early evening 'young entertainment' is followed later by live shows, discos or groups and a programme of competitions, quizzes or family films in a big screen cinema. This park is popular with families with children of all ages and there is much to do in the area.

Facilities: One large, spacious and fully equipped toilet block is supplemented by a small 'portacabin' unit with toilet facilities for peak season. Dishwashing facilities under cover. Facilities for disabled visitors are in the main block. Well equipped laundry with sinks. Well stocked mini-market (all season). Bars and restaurant. Indoor pool. Fitness centre. New indoor play area for under-fives and other play areas. Tennis court (£3/hour). Bicycle hire. Skittle alley, croquet, draughts, badminton and crazy golf. Bus service in high season. **Off site:** Fishing and boat launching approx. 1 mile

Charges 2001

Per pitch	£2.50 - £5.50
adult	£3.00 - £3.50
child (3-16 yrs)	£1.50 - £1.80
electricity	£2.00

Pup tents not permitted to share a pitch with another unit. Special offers available.

Tel: (01503) 272216. Fax: (01503) 272065. E-mail: killigarthmanor@breathmail.net. **Reservations**: Made (Sat. - Sat. in main season) with £30 deposit. **Open** 4 April - 25 October.

Directions: From Looe take A387 towards Polperro. After 3½ miles, fork left immediately past a bus shelter and phone box at sign to Killigarth. Site is / mile. O.S.GR: SX213519.

Polborder House Caravan and Camping Park

032 Bucklawren Road, St Martin's-by-Looe, Cornwall PL13 1QR

Polborder House may appeal to those who prefer a quiet, well kept little family site to the larger ones with many on-site activities. With good countryside views, up to 31 touring units can be accommodated on well tended grass. Pitches are marked with some hedging and there are 28 electrical connections (10A). A number of hardstandings and 4 serviced pitches have been added recently. The owners live on the park. The site is well situated with Seaton only 2 miles, Looe 2½ and the nearest beach 20-25 minutes walk from a gate in the corner of the park.

Facilities: The sanitary block (key entry) is well kept, of ample size and provides hot showers on payment, baby room with washing and changing facilities, fully equipped laundry room, and three covered sinks outside for dishwashing. En-suite toilet unit for disabled visitors has a ramped approach. Rubbish recycled. Motorcaravan services. Shop (all season) for gas and basics, including off licence. Toddler's play area. **Off site**: Fishing, golf and boat launching within 2 miles, riding 8 miles. Restaurant 500 m.

Charges 2001

Per unit incl. 2 persons	£6.50 - £9.50
extra person	£1.50 - £2.00
child (4-15 yrs)	75p - £1.00
awning or child's tent	£1.00
dog	75p
electricity	£1.85

Less 10% for senior citizens for booked stays over 5 nights. **Tel**: (01503) 240265. Fax: (01503) 240700. E-mail: rlf.polborder@virgin.net. **Reservations**: Any period, £20 deposit (non-refundable). **Open** 1 April - 31 October.

Directions: Park is about ¼ mile south of B3253; turn off 2 miles east of Looe and follow signs to park and Monkey Sanctuary at junctions; care is needed with narrow road. O.S.GR: SX283555.

Alan Rogers' discount
Less 50p per pitch, per night

Whitsand Bay Holiday Park

035 Millbrook, Torpoint, Cornwall PL10 1JZ

Whitsand Bay is a family holiday park that caters well for children. It must also be one of the most unusual places to stay and is, in fact, a designated ancient monument in an 'area of outstanding natural beauty'. The site has been converted from a Coastal Gun Battery built in 1890 to protect Plymouth and the views are magnificent across to Plymouth and the Tamar Estuary with Dartmoor in the background, over the sea towards the Rame peninsula, Whitsand Bay and west to the Lizard, Looe, and Bodmin Moor. Covering 27 acres, some wild and natural, you can explore the original gun emplacements and enjoy the views or venture into the dark, damp underground tunnels and earthworks. It is obvious that the solidly constructed clubhouse, laundry and chapel are part of the original fortifications. In fact the laundry room was part of the Quartermaster's store. The Battery Club has been developed to provide a cosy bar. The approach along the clifftop road is deceptive as the earthworks completely hide what is, in essence a self contained village including holiday caravans and chalets of older design. The 120 marked grass touring pitches, connected by tarmac roads, vary in size, are terraced and enjoy mainly landward views. Sixty have electricity (16A) and quite a few are taken by seasonal lets.

Facilities: The two toilet blocks are acceptable with metered showers – we understand they are shortly to be upgraded. Each block has a washing up sink. Laundry room. Well stocked shop. Café open all day in season, with takeaway. Barbecue area. Bar with family area alongside a larger bar and dance hall and disco area with entertainment in high season. Indoor, heated pool and paddling pool, sauna and sun bed. Adventure play area, multi-sport court, amusement arcade and table tennis. 'Kids Club'. **Off site**: A steep 200 ft. cliff path provides access to Whitsand Bay (unsuitable for small children or the infirm). Fishing ½ mile, boat slipway 2 miles, golf 2 miles. Riding 5 miles.

Charges guide

Per pitch incl. adults, children (max. 6)	
awning and space for car	£8.00 - £16.00
electricity (16A)	£2.00
dog	£1.00
two-man tent with car	£5.00 - £10.00

Woodland mini-pitches for cyclists or walkers less 50%. Club membership incl. **Tel**: (01752) 822597. Fax: (01752) 823444. E-mail: rob@whitsandbayholidays.co.uk. **Reservations**: Made with £10 deposit p/week. **Open** March - December.

Directions: Take the Torpoint ferry and on disembarking follow A374 Liskeard road for 3 miles. At village of Antony fork left for Millbrook (B3274) and continue for 2 miles to T-junction. Turn left for Whitsand Bay, then almost immediately right following narrow road overlooking the bay for a further 2 miles. Park is hidden on the left - watch for sign. O.S.GR: SX417506.

Alan Rogers' discount
Stay 2 nights, get third free

Colliford Tavern Campsite

030 | Colliford Lake, nr St Neot, Liskeard, Cornwall PL14 6PZ

Colliford Tavern must be unique, quietly situated high on Bodmin Moor near Colliford Lake but hidden and protected by tall pines. The project has been developed over the last ten years by the Edwards family with much care and attention and offers a family run free house with excellent, home cooked food and ale in an old world atmosphere complete with 90 year old well and en-suite accommodation. There is a bar, dining room, a family room with outside terrace, garden, water wheel and a good fenced play area with Wendy House. Open to campers and caravanners, some original suggestions for food which can be quite special or simpler bar-type food are worth trying. The camping area is quiet and simple and has been kept very natural with short grass (helped by the rabbits) and sheltered from the moor by tall pines. The main field provides 40 fairly level pitches with 19 electric hook-ups (16A) and 6 hardstandings backing on to the pine trees. The smaller, lower area is nearer to all the facilities. Reception is in the Tavern building. The site gate is closed at night but there is a 24 hour bell. Ideally situated for Colliford Lake and the Moor with its rich history, flora and fauna, be it for walking, fly fishing (permits available) or birdwatching, the park is also suitable for excursions to the north or south coast.

Facilities: The cheerful, pine-fitted toilet block is well equipped, heated and carefully maintained with a baby room, unit for disabled people (no shower), laundry sink and two washing up sinks. Service wash and tumble dry available Monday to Friday. Restaurant and bar. Some occasional family entertainment. Barbecues permitted with prior permission.

Charges 2001

Per unit incl. 1 adult	£6.00 - £7.25
2 adults	£8.00 - £10.00
extra person (over 4 yrs)	£2.00 - £2.75
electricity	£1.95
dog	50p

Tel/Fax: (01208) 821335. E-mail: info@colliford-tavern.co.uk. **Reservations**: Advised for high season and made with £10 deposit, plus £5 for electric hook-up. **Open** Easter - end September.

Directions: Approaching on the A30 travelling south, pass the Jamaica Inn on the right and site is signed a further 1-1½ miles on the left. Follow for ½ mile and site is signed beside Colliford Lake Park. O.S.GR: SX168730.

Glenmorris Park

023 | Longstone Road, St Mabyn, Cornwall PL30 3BY

The beaches of north Cornwall and the wilds of Bodmin Moor are all an easy drive away from Glenmorris Park A quiet, family run park, there are 75 reasonably level pitches (52 with 16A electricity) on well drained, well mown grass. There is no bar but the local village inn has a good reputation for food. The Camel Trail for either cycling or walking all the way to Bodmin, Wadebridge or Padstow is only 2 miles. Bodmin and Wadebridge are only 5 or 6 miles for supermarket shopping. All in all, this is a pleasant park for relaxing or to use as a base to explore the towns and beaches of Cornwall.

Facilities: Glenmorris has fairly modern toilet facilities that are clean and well maintained. Dishwashing sinks and laundry with washing machine, dryer and iron. Heated, outdoor swimming pool and paddling pool (late May - early Sept), surrounded by sheltered, paved and grass sunbathing areas. Excellent, fenced adventure playground with bark safety base. Games room for teenagers. Caravan storage. **Off site:** Fishing, riding or golf 3 miles, bicycle hire 5 miles.

Charges guide

Per unit incl. 2 adults and awning	£5.00 - £7.50
extra adult	£1.00 - £2.25
child (3-16 yrs)	75p - £1.50
extra vehicle or pup tent	free - £1.00
electricity (16A)	£2.00
hiker or cyclist's tent (2 adults, no car)	£5.00 - £6.50

Weekly rate available. **Tel/Fax**: (01208) 841677. E-mail: glenmorris.cornwall@virgin.net. **Reservations**: Made with £15 deposit. **Open** Easter - 31 October.

Directions: From Bodmin or Wadebridge on A389, take B3266 north signed Camelford. At village of Longstone turn left signed St Mabyn and brown camping sign. Site is 400 yds. on right. Ignore all other signs to St Mabyn. O.S.GR: SX053735.

Cornwall
Trerethern Touring Park
043 Padstow, Cornwall PL28 8LE

Trerethern is a traditional park of wide open fields, although there have been attempts to divide it up with hedging that is gradually developing in places despite the rabbits and the elements. There is room for 300 units but only 100 are taken so there is plenty of open space and the views across Bodmin Moor and the estuary are marvellous. The grass is neatly cut and the pitches mostly level, although there is a gentle slope in parts. Electricity (10A) is available on 67 pitches, there are 10 water points and 9 hardstanding places for motorcaravans, 7 of these with electricity plus an emptying point (the site can accommodate 32-34 ft motorhomes). The 'Kernow' pitches have private facilities. The owners live on site and, along with site wardens, ensure a well run and orderly park. Padstow itself is a mile away either by public footpath through the fields (20-30 minutes) downhill or for bicycles by the road. A bus service passes (the site is a request stop) and reception holds timetables. Rick Stein has now opened a bistro alongside his restaurant so you may just get a reservation!

Facilities: Two sanitary blocks are simple but clean and tidy, with two washbasins in cabins in the smaller block. A toilet with washbasin and ramped access is provided at the back of the main toilet block at the far side of the park. A unique feature is the four individual en-suite washrooms for use with the 'Kernow' pitches (three more planned). These have a key and are for private use, with a pass key for the shower room (see below for cost). The small block which also houses the private units is locked at night so if you need the loo in the night it could be a little walk! Dishwashing sinks. Laundry facilities with two washing machines, spin dryer, tumble dryer and iron. Reception cum shop for gas and basic supplies. Children's play area. **Off site**: Nearest beach is at Padstow, others are within 5 miles. Access to the Camel Trail cycle route. Riding or fishing 2 miles, golf 5 miles.

Charges 2001

Per unit	£3.00 - £4.00
adult	£2.25 - £3.25
child (under 15 yrs)	£1.00 - £1.50
dog	50p
electricity	£2.25
'Kernow' pitch incl. electricity	£4.50 - £5.50

Key deposit £5. No credit cards. **Tel/Fax**: (01841) 532061. E-mail: camping.trerethern@btinternet.com. **Reservations**: Made with deposit (£15 p/week). **Open** Easter/1 April - 2 October.

Directions: Park is signed from the A389, SSW of Padstow. Follow unmade approach road, then turn into park. O.S.GR: SW912739.

Cornwall
Budemeadows Touring Holiday Park
037 Poundstock, Bude, Cornwall EX23 0NA

Budemeadows is an attractive, family run touring park located south of Bude. It is maturing well with growing hedging and trees and, although close to the A39 through road, offers a good, quiet option being only about a mile from the sandy surfing beaches at Widemouth Bay and 3 miles from Bude with all its amenities. It has been thoughtfully planned and provides large, separated (low hedging or fencing) pitches, some slightly sloping but with panoramic rural views, others more sheltered and nearer the facilities. Some 146 units of any type are taken and there is plenty of room for these numbers with 80 electrical connections (10A) and 26 hardstandings. An attractive feature is the centrally situated, fenced pool area with a comfortably heated pool and toddlers pool (also heated), patio and grass sunbathing area, and gazebos. Also thoughtfully provided are picnic tables, brick built barbecues, a large scale outdoor chess set, table tennis and skittles. A mobile 'Catch a Snack' van calls evenings in high season. The owners live on site.

Facilities: The pine clad toilet block can be heated and has good controllable showers, six private cabins for ladies with basin and WC, one for men. A second similar block provides full facilities for disabled visitors. There are also three family shower units, a family bathroom, baby bath and changing room, dishwashing sinks and a laundry room with tourist information. Motorcaravan service point. Shop (Spr. B.H. - mid Sept). Gas supplies. Large adventure playground. TV and games room with pool table and board games. Caravan storage. **Off site**: Boat launching in Bude, lake fishing 5 miles, riding 3 miles, golf 4 miles.

Charges guide

Per adult	£4.45 - £5.99
child (3-14 yrs)	£2.75 - £3.50
dog	£1.00 - £1.50
electricity	£2.99 - £1.99

Pitch and awning included. **Tel/Fax**: (01288) 361646. E-mail: wendyjo@globalnet.co.uk. **Reservations**: Made with deposit (£5 p/night or £35 p/week). **Open** all year.

Directions: Park entrance is from a lay-by to the east off the A39 just north of a turning to Widemouth Bay. O.S.GR: SS216017.

Lakefield Caravan Park and Equestrian Centre

Lower Pendavey Farm, Camelford, Cornwall PL32 9TX

036

Lakefield is a small touring park with a BHS and RDA approved equestrian centre. It was previously a working farm and with only 40 pitches, it is no wonder that the owners, Maureen and Dennis Perring, know all the campers. The well-spaced pitches with 24 electric hook-ups (16A) are on level grass in sight of the small lake (fenced) and its feathered inhabitants. The white-washed shop/reception, converted from one of the old barns and including a fascinating picture gallery, is open all day and all season which impressed us for such a small site. A tea room offers cream teas, cakes and sandwiches. A dozen picnic tables are dotted about the site, with some children's play equipment on grass. In a barn is an animal corner with calves, lambs, chickens, etc. and 'Wabbit World' is fascinating. The BHS approved riding school, very much part of the site, offers lessons and hacks with qualified supervision and instruction and 25 horses, from miniature Shetlands to thoroughbreds. All abilities are catered for (sand menage, show jumping paddock, beginners cross country course and pony rides) and this is the Riding for the Disabled (RDA) Centre for north Cornwall. Pony days and activity days are organised. Tintagel, Boscastle, Bodmin Moor and the many beaches and coves of the north Cornwall coast wait to be explored. Cornwall's first wind farm watches over the site.

Facilities: The toilet block is clean and bright. Washing machine and dryer in the ladies' and a dishwashing sink and a laundry sink outside but under cover. No facilities for disabled visitors. Shop and tea room. Gas supplies. Mountain bike hire. Torches may be useful. **Off site**: Fishing (sea 4 miles, coarse 5 miles), golf 2 miles.

Charges 2001

Per unit incl. 2 adults	£6.00 - £10.00
extra adult or child (5 yrs or over)	60p
electricity	£2.00

No credit cards. **Tel/Fax**: (01840) 213279. E-mail: lakefield@pendavey.fsnet.co.uk. **Reservations**: Made with £20 deposit per week. **Open** 1 April - 31 October.

Directions: Follow B3266 north from Camelford. Park access is directly from this road on the left just before the turning for Tintagel, clearly signed. O.S.GR: SX097852.

Wooda Farm Park

Poughill, Bude, Cornwall EX23 9HJ

Wooda Farm is spacious and well organised, with some nice touches. A quality, family run park, it is part of a working farm, 1¼ miles from the sandy, surfing beaches of Bude. In peaceful farmland with plenty of open spaces (and some up and down walking), there are marvellous views of sea and countryside. The 200 pitches, spread over four meadows, are on level or gently sloping grass, 160 with electricity connections (10A), 21 with hardstanding and 21 grass, hedged 'premium' pitches (electricity, water, waste water) linked by tarmac roads. Situated beside the shop and reception at the entrance are 55 holiday letting units. There is a small farm museum and friendly farm animals - children (and adults) are welcome to assist at feeding time! Tractor and trailer rides, pony riding and trekking, archery and clay pigeon shooting with tuition are provided according to season and demand, likewise barn dances, plus a woodland walk (where the pixies can be found) and an orchard walk. There is much to do in the area – sandy beaches with coastal walks, and Tintagel with King Arthur's Castle and Clovelly nearby. A member of the Best of British group.

Facilities: Three well maintained solid toilet blocks, one heated include a unit suitable for disabled people, a baby room with small bath and two new private family washrooms with shower and bath. Washing up sinks under cover. Two fully equipped laundry rooms. Self-service shop with off-licence (8.30 - 8.30 in main season). Attractive courtyard bar with bar meals and a pleasant restaurant, Linney's Larder, with home cooking (closed Mon. and Sat. outside main season). Children's play area in separate field on grass, with plenty of room for ball games, 9 hole 'fun' golf course (clubs provided). Games room with TV, table tennis and pool. Coarse fishing in 1½ acre lake (permits from reception, £1.50 per half day, £2.50 per day). Certain breeds of dogs are not accepted. Caravan storage. Off Site: Local village inn is five minutes walk. Leisure Centre and Splash Pool in Bude.

Charges guide

Per unit incl. 2 persons	£7.50 - £11.00
extra adult	£1.50 - £2.50
child (3-15 yrs)	£1.00 - £1.50
awning/pup tent	£1.00 - £1.50
dog	£1.00 - £1.50
electricity (10A)	£2.00
fully serviced pitch (incl. electricity)	£3.50 - £4.50
with TV point	£4.50 - £6.00

Tel: (01288) 352069. Fax: (01288) 355258. E-mail: enquiries@wooda.co.uk. **Reservations**: Made with £20 p/week deposit. **Open** Easter/1 April - October (facilities from Spr. B.H - Sept).

Directions: Park is north of Bude at Poughill; turn off A39 on north side of Stratton on minor road for Coombe Valley, following camp signs at junctions. O.S.GR: SS225080.

Dolbeare Caravan and Camping Park

044 St Ive Road, Landrake, Saltash, Cornwall PL12 5AF

Bob and Ruth Mahy will make you very welcome at their small, but well kept park. In a rural setting, but very easily accessible from the main A38, the park consists of a large rectangular field of neatly cut grass edged with trees and sloping slightly at the top, connected by a gravel roadway. Caravans and motorcaravans go around the edge, with some terraced pitches with hardstanding, and tents tend to go in the central area where there is also play equipment and water and refuse points. All 60 pitches are numbered and of comfortable size, 51 with electricity (16A). An extra field doubles as a rally and games field and part is set aside for a dog exercise area. The Mahys have thoughtfully provided leaflets on 'Where to Eat', 'Where to Walk', and 'Suggestions for what to do' with a good supply of tourist information with maps in a caravan near the caravan storage area. Dog kennels nearby can provide day care from £3.50, but the drawback is that there could be some noise depending on season and wind direction. A very usefully situated park said to be 20 minutes from everywhere - e.g. Plymouth, beaches, National Trust properties, Dartmoor and Bodmin Moor.

Facilities: The well kept heated toilet block to one side of the field provides pre-set showers with curtain and seat, plus two outside, but covered washing up sinks. Laundry next to reception at the entrance provides a sink (H&C), washing machine, dryer, iron and board. Reception doubles as a small shop for basics including gas (limited hours out of main season). Boules pitch opposite reception (a set of boules can be hired). Site barrier closed 11 pm. - 7.30 am. **Off site**: Fishing 3 miles, golf 8 miles.

Charges 2001

Per unit incl. 2 adults and car	£7.50 - £8.50
extra adult	£2.00
child (5-16 yrs)	£1.00
electricity	£1.50 - £1.80
awning	£1.00
small tent per person	£2.50 - £3.00

Tel: (01752) 851332. E-mail: dolbeare@compuserve.com. **Reservations**: Contact park. **Open** all year.

Directions: After crossing the Tamar Bridge into Cornwall, continue on A38 for a further 4 miles. In village of Landrake turn right following signs and site is ¾mile on right. O.S.GR: SX366616.

Riverside Caravan Park

081 Longbridge Road, Marshmills, Plymouth, Devon PL6 8LD

Riverside is well placed for those visiting Plymouth, the maritime capital of the southwest, to use the car ferries or en-route to Cornwall. It is also ideally situated for touring Dartmoor and south Devon. Although under 4 miles from the city centre, its location on the banks of the River Plym in a wooded valley is a quiet one – in fact riverside walks can take you up to Dartmoor. Attractive shrubs and trees, flower beds, well kept grass and tarmac roads give a neat, park-like appearance. Over 220 units of any type are taken on flat, numbered pitches, including 170 with 10A electrical connections and 60 'winterised' (ie. with hardstanding). There is a separate area for tents and a large, hard area is retained for late arrivals and large American motorhomes. An added advantage is that the site is security patrolled at night.

Facilities: The two sanitary blocks, one subdivided into two, are of different construction and have been modernised and decorated somewhat haphazardly. Some washbasins in private cabins with toilets for ladies in one block. Indoor dishwashing sinks. Laundry facilities with irons on loan. A shop at the entrance open to all (Spr. B.H. - mid-Sept). Lounge bar (fully open from July with nightly entertainment), coffee bar and restaurant with takeaway meals (6-10 pm), games and TV rooms. Play area. Heated swimming pool (60 x 30 ft), with children's paddling pool, open Spr. B.H. - mid-Sept. Fishing on site. **Off site**: Bicycle hire 3 miles, boat slipway 2 miles, tennis and dry ski slope 1 mile.

Charges 2001

Per adult	£2.50 - £3.50
child (3-10 yrs)	£1.10 - £1.25
pitch	£2.50 - £4.00
electricity	£2.00 - £2.50
hardstanding	free - £1.00
awning	free - £1.00
dog, extra car or boat	£1.00

Special breaks for the over-50s. No single sex groups. **Tel**: (01752) 344122. E-mail: info@riversidecaravanpark.com. **Reservations**: Made with £15 deposit per week or part week. **Open** all year.

Directions: From A38 dual-carriageway from Exeter, take Marsh Mill exit (the first signed to Plymouth city centre). Follow good camp site signs to third exit, turning left after a few yards. O.S.GR: SX518576.

Harford Bridge Park

Peter Tavy, Tavistock, Devon PL19 9LS

Harford Bridge has an interesting history - originally the Wheal Union tin mine until 1850, then used as a farm campsite from 1930 and taken over by the Royal Engineers in 1939. It is now a quiet, rural, mature park inside the Dartmoor National Park. It is bounded by the River Tavy on one side and the lane from the main road to the village of Peter Tavy on the other, with Harford Bridge, a classic granite moorland bridge, at the corner. With 16½ acres, the park provides 120 touring pitches well spaced on a level grassy meadow with some shade from mature trees and others recently planted; 40 pitches have electricity and 8 have 'multi-services'. Out of season or by booking in advance you may get one of the delightful spots bordering the river (these without hook-ups). Some holiday caravans and chalets are neatly landscaped in their own area. At the entrance to the park a central grassy area is left free for games, which is also used by the town band, village fete, etc. It is overlooked by reception which also stocks camping accessories, postcards, stamps. etc. but not groceries. While the river (unfenced) will inevitably mesmerise the youngsters and the ducks and chickens attract their interest, a super central adventure play area on a hilly tree knoll will claim them. With its own and the local history, plus its situation, this is a super place to stay.

Facilities: The single toilet block is older in style but has been refurbished and is well kept, properly maintained, and fully equipped. Facilities include a baby bathroom, good launderette and drying room. Freezer pack facility. Games room with additional campers' information, table tennis and separate TV room. Children's play area – two restored Wickstead stainless steel slides, a 45 year old carnival carousel roundabout and tunnels are just part of a well presented, safe and marvellous provision. Tennis court (free). Two communal barbecue areas. Fly fishing (by licence, £3 p/day, £10 p/week). **Off site**: Bicycle hire, riding and golf, all within 2½ miles.

Charges 2002

Per unit, incl. 2 persons	£6.50 - £10.50
extra adult	£2.20 - £2.70
child	£1.10 - £1.60
electricity	£1.00
awning	£1.00
dog	£1.00

Less 10% for stays over 7 days (not electricity or fishing). **Tel**: (01822) 810349. Fax: (01822) 810028. E-mail: enquiry@harfordbridge.co.uk. **Reservations**: Made for any length with first night's fees. **Open** Late March - early November.

Directions: Two miles north of Tavistock, off A386 Tavistock - Okehampton road, take the road to Peter Tavy. O.S.GR: SX504768.

Alan Rogers' discount
Less £1 per unit

Higher Longford Caravan and Camping Park

Moorshop, Tavistock, Devon PL19 9LQ

Situated within the Dartmoor National Park boundaries, this small park has views up to the higher slopes of the moor. The site has been reorganised and landscaped to provide a neat, sheltered field with 40 level pitches arranged on each side of a circular access road, three smaller touring areas for 12 units in total and a seasonal camping field for a further 40. Facilities include 62 electrical hook-ups, 12 multi-serviced pitches and an area of hardstanding for motorhomes in poor weather. Private residential caravans and two chalets are in a separate area and some attractive converted cottages form a courtyard area with the farmhouse, reception and bar. Within the 14th century farmhouse is a small shop with gas and some fresh farm produce. It adjoins a pleasant, cosy bar and restaurant with open fire and TV, a spacious extension, useful in poor weather. Higher Longford is an ideal centre for touring Dartmoor, either by car, on foot, or astride a local pony.

Facilities: The main toilet block provides roomy showers and smallish washbasins, including one en-suite cabin for ladies. This is supplemented by extra heated facilities in the courtyard, which include showers with a communal dressing area. Full laundry facilities. Covered and indoor dishwashing sinks. Motorcaravan services. Ice block service. Licenced shop, bar and restaurant/takeaway (all 31/3-31/10). Pool/snooker table. Caravan storage. **Off site**: Plymouth and the cross-channel ferries are a 30 minute drive, Tavistock (3 miles) has a good market and the Goose Fair in October. Game or coarse fishing 3 miles, golf 1 mile, bicycle hire or riding 3 miles.

Charges 2001

Per unit incl. 1 person	£7.00 - £7.50
2 persons	£8.00 - £8.50
family (2 adults, 2 children)	£9.50 - £10.00
extra adult	£2.00
extra child (over 3 yrs)	£1.00
electricity	£2.00

Less 50p per night for booked stays over 7 nights. **Tel**: (01822) 613360. Fax: (01822) 618722. E-mail: stay@higherlongford.co.uk. **Reservations**: Made with £10 deposit. **Open** all year.

Directions: Park is clearly signed from B3357 Princetown road, 2 miles from Tavistock. O.S.GR: SX520747.

Old Cotmore Farm

104

Stokenham, nr Kingsbridge, South Devon TQ7 2LR

A charming and secluded park, two miles from Start Point, Old Cotmore Farm – that is the farmhouse, two cottages and a small touring site – is owned by Sue and John Bradney. The only livestock to be seen now are a few chickens and ducks, and maybe some horses. They have worked hard to improve the facilities and now provide 30 pitches, all with electric hook-up, on neatly cut grass. Partly in a garden type situation to one side of the driveway with some pitches sloping, and partly on a level, smallish field with children's play equipment in the centre. Pitches here tend to be used for families with children, with those on the other side of the drive kept for adults only. Helpful wardens will assist you to pitch. A small stream runs along one side with a pretty, fenced pond area and bridge near the entrance. Reception is past the pitches towards the farmhouse and adjoining the toilet block which has been converted from original farm buildings. A separate field with a 28 day licence has water points, two sinks (H&C) and two toilets, but it may put pressure on the main block when in use. Mrs Bradney holds a children's club once a week in high season. The site is in an area of Outstanding Natural Coastal Beauty, with Slapton Sands, Salcombe and Kingsbridge near and Dartmouth just a little further – an ideal area for walking, boating, diving, windsurfing and safe bathing.

Facilities: The ladies' and men's sections of the toilet block provide modern facilities with a degree of individuality. A separate en-suite unit provides for disabled visitors and also includes a baby bath and changing table. A new utility room has dishwashing sinks and a laundry sink, three washing machines and two dryers, plus tourist information. Reception stocks gas and basic necessities - warm baguettes can be ordered. Mountain bike hire. Table tennis. **Off site:** Riding 4 miles, golf 8 miles. Two pubs are within one mile either way.

Charges guide

Per unit incl. 2 persons	£7.00 - £9.00
tent incl. 2 persons	£6.50
extra adult	£2.00
child (3-12 yrs)	£1.00
car, extra car or boat	£1.00
dog	£1.00
electricity	£2.00

Less £1.00 per pitch in low seasons. Tel: (01548) 580240. Fax: (01548) 580875. Reservations: Made with 25% deposit; contact park. **Open** 14 March - 15 November.

Directions: From Kingsbridge on A379 Dartmouth road, go through Frogmore and Chillington to Carehouse Cross mini-roundabout at Stokenham. Turn right towards Beesands and follow camp signs for 1 mile. Site entrance is on right just past the post box - look out for the churns! Roads are a little narrow in places. O.S.GR: SX804417.

Moor View Touring Park

082

California Cross, nr Modbury, Ivybridge, Devon PL21 0SG

Moor View has a gently sloping position with terraced, individual, fairly level grass pitches with marvellous views across to the Dartmoor Tors. It provides 68 pitches of varying size, connected by hardcore roads, all with 10A electricity and 15 with hardstanding. Bushes and shrubs on the lower terraces are growing well, giving the park a more mature feel. A two acre field provides space for children or for the odd rally. There is also a fenced play area on grass near a small river pool. The amenities have been designed in one block near the entrance, not too far from the furthest pitches and include a reception cum shop with basic food and some camping accessories. Burgh Island and Bigbury Bay are nearby, Dartmoor is within striking distance. This is a park in a lovely corner of Devon, with enthusiastic owners, Alan and Julia Marshall. A member of the Countryside Discovery group.

Facilities: Traditional type toilet facilities have access from a courtyard area and are kept clean, providing all necessary facilities including a laundry room and sink, and covered dishwashing sinks. Shop (basics). Takeaway in season (to order, 6.30-7.30 pm). Children's play area. Games room with pool table, table tennis and video machines. TV room. **Off site:** Golf 5 miles, riding and fishing 6 miles. Pub within walking distance, small town of Modbury 3 miles.

Charges 2001

Per pitch incl. 2 adults	£8.00 - £10.00
extra adult	£2.00
child (3-14 yrs)	£1.50
small tent	less £1.00
electricity (10A)	£1.75
water hook-up	50p

Tel: (01548) 821485. E-mail: moorview@tinyworld.co.uk Reservations: Made with £10 deposit. **Open** Mid-April - mid-October.

Directions: On A38 from Exeter, pass exit for A385 (Totnes) and continue for a further 2 miles. Just past Woodpecker Inn leave the A38 at Wrangaton Cross, signed Ermington, Modbury and Yealmpton. Turn left and follow straight on at crossroads (Kitterford Cross) signed Modbury, Loddiswell, Kingsbridge for 3 miles to California Cross. Leave garage on left and follow towards Modbury (B3207). Park is ½ mile on left. O.S.GR: SX705533.

Camping and Caravanning Club Site Slapton Sands

083 Middle Grounds, Slapton, Kingsbridge, Devon TQ7 1QW

Slapton is a charming village with tiny lanes and cottages, a shop and two historic pubs, one dominated by the ruined tower of an old monastery. The village (unsuitable for camping traffic) is about half a mile inland from the shingle beach of Slapton Sands and the fresh water Ley which is administered as a nature reserve by the Field Studies Council. The Camping and Caravanning Club site is situated on the road which leads from the Sands, on a well kept meadow overlooking the bay – the sea views are panoramic from most areas of the site, with shelter provided by some large bushes and the surrounding hedge. There are 126 grass pitches, some with a slight slope, and electricity (16A) is available for 48 (including 11 with hard-standing). Motorcaravans, trailer tents and tents are accepted without problems but planners will only permit 8 caravan pitches which are kept for club members. The Field Studies Centre arranges guided walks and short study courses on a wide variety of interests and can issue fishing permits for the Ley (perch and pike, of legendary size, in the summer months). Beach fishing is also popular. This area was used for rehearsals for the WW2 Normandy landings, when the population was evacuated - there are memorials. Dartmouth is 7 miles, Kingsbridge 8 miles and a variety of beaches and coves around the beautiful South Hams coastline are within easy reach.

Facilities: The modern toilet block is central, can be heated and is kept very clean, with washbasins in private cabins. Useful parent and child room and separate unit for disabled visitors (with key). Dishwashing facilities, laundry sinks, washing machine and dryer (and outside lines). Motorcaravan service point. Reception has a small library, gas and freezer for ice blocks. Small children's play area. Chip van calls weekly. **Off site:** Riding ½ mile.

Charges 2001

Per adult	£3.75 - £5.30
child (6-18 yrs)	£1.65
non-member pitch fee	£4.30
electricity	£1.65 - £2.40

Tel: (01548) 580538 (no calls after 8 pm).
Reservations: Necessary and made with deposit; contact site. **Open** March - October.

Directions: From A38 Exeter - Plymouth road, take A384 to Totnes. Just before town, turn right on A381 to Kingsbridge, then A379 through Stokenham and Torcross to Slapton Sands. Half way along the beach road (partly single track, contolled by lights) turn left to Slapton village and site is 200 yds on right. Note: Avoid the very narrow Five Mile Lane from the A381 which is signed Slapton (just after a filling station) 6 miles from Kingsbridge. O.S.GR: SX825450.

Galmpton Touring Park

085 Greenway Road, Galmpton. Brixham, Devon TQ5 0EP

Within a few miles of the lively amenities of Torbay, Galmpton Park lies peacefully just outside the village of Galmpton, overlooking the beautiful Dart estuary just upstream of Dartmouth and Kingswear. Some 120 pitches, 60 marked for caravans, are arranged on a wide sweep of grassy, terraced meadow, each pitch with its own wonderful view of the river. Situated on the hillside, some parts have quite a slope, but there are flatter areas (the owners will advise and assist). There are 95 electrical connections (10A) and 20 pitches are fully serviced. There is a separate tent field. Galmpton is a quiet and simple park (with the gates closed 11.30 pm - 7.30 am) in a most picturesque setting, within easy reach of all the attractions of South Devon. A member of the Countryside Discovery group.

Facilities: A central, substantial looking toilet block provides clean facilities including three washbasins in private cabins, baby unit and hair care areas. Dishwashing room also with a washing machine, dryer, iron and ironing board. New reception/shop selling a wide range of basics including gas. Good adventure play equipment. Dogs (max. 2 per unit) are accepted at the owner's discretion and only outside the school summer holidays. Caravan storage. American motorhomes are not accepted. **Off site:** Local pub is five minutes walk.

Charges 2001

Per unit incl. 2 persons and awning	£6.50 - £11.00
extra adult	£2.00
extra child	£1.00
electricity	£1.90
dog (off peak only)	50p

Various discounts available. Tel: (01803) 842066. Fax: (01803) 844458. E-mail: galmptontouringpark@ hotmail.com. Reservations: Made with £20 deposit p/week booked. Open Easter - 30 September.

Directions: Take A380 Paignton ring road towards Brixham until junction with the Paignton - Brixham coast road. Turn right towards Brixham, then second right into Manor Vale Road. Continue through the village, past the school and site is 100 yds on the right. O.S.GR: SX885558.

Devon

Woodlands Leisure Park

Blackawton, nr Dartmouth, Devon TQ9 7DQ

084

Woodlands is a surprise, a nice one – from the road you have no idea of just what is hidden away deep in the Devon countryside. To achieve this, there has been sympathetic development of farm and woodland to provide a leisure centre, open to the public and with a range of activities and entertainment appealing to all ages, plus a touring caravan park. Children (and many energetic parents too!) will be kept amused for hours by a variety of imaginative adventure play equipment or amazing water toboggan runs and 'Arctic Coasters' hidden amongst the trees and many farm animals, birds and boats. Those more peacefully inclined can follow woodland walks around the attractive ponds. A Falconry Centre gives opportunities to watch displays (or for the birds to watch you!) There is plenty of play equipment for younger children too, including an indoor play barn with a circus theme. Opened for the millennium, the 'Empire of the Sea Dragon', a new two million pounds indoor play centre, has provided marvellous wet weather facilities – the biggest indoor venture in the UK. With a two night stay, campers on the touring park are admitted free of charge to the leisure park. The camping and caravan site overlooks the woodland and the leisure park, taking 220 units on two sloping, grassy fields, one original, the other newly developed. These have been fully terraced to provide groups of four to eight flat, very spacious pitches, 90% with electrical connections (10A) and a shared water tap, drain and rubbish bin. The level terraces are divided by young hedging and shrubs that are growing nicely in the original field. A popular park, early reservation is advisable.

Facilities: Two modern, heated toilet blocks are well maintained and kept very clean. The newer block includes private bathrooms (coin-operated, 20p) and seven family shower cubicles. Each block has a well equipped laundry room, dishwashing area and a freezer for ice packs. Baby changing facilities. The leisure park café, with terrace, provides good value meals and cream teas with entertainment (music, Morris men, etc.) at busy times and a takeaway service for campers. Opening hours of the café and adjoining gift shop (with gas and a few basic food supplies) vary according to season and demand. TV and games room. Dogs are accepted on the campsite but not in the leisure park (kennels available). Caravan storage. **Off site:** The charming town of Dartmouth and the South Hams beaches are near. Fishing 3 miles, golf ½ mile, riding 5 miles.

Charges 2001

Per unit, incl. 2 persons	£7.50 - £14.50
extra person (over 2 yrs)	£3.75
awning or extra small pup tent	£2.50
large tent or trailer tent (120 sq.ft. plus)	plus £2.00
extra car, boat or trailer	£1.00
dog	£2.50
electricity	£1.95

Free entry to leisure park for stays 2 nights or more. Tel: (01803) 712598. Fax: (01803) 712680. E-mail: bookings@woodlandspark.com. Reservations: Accepted for min. 3 nights with £35 deposit, except July/Aug. when min. 7 days and £50 deposit. Balance in full 21 days before arrival. **Open** 1 April - 4 November.

Directions: From A38 at Buckfastleigh, take A384 to Totnes. Before the town centre turn right on A381 Kingsbridge road. After Halwell turn left at Totnes Cross garage, on A3122 to Dartmouth. Park is on right after 2½ miles. O.S.GR: SX813521.

Beverley Holidays

Goodrington Road, Paignton, Devon TQ4 7JE

087

Beverley Park is a quality holiday centre, attractively landscaped and with views over Torbay. With pools, a large dance hall, bars and entertainment, all is run in an efficient and orderly manner. The holiday caravan park has 197 caravan holiday homes and 23 lodges, mainly around the central complex. The 189 touring pitches are in the lower areas of the park, all reasonably sheltered, some with views across the bay and some on slightly sloping ground. All pitches can take awnings and have 16A electricity (15 m. cable), 38 have hardstanding, 21 are fully serviced. Tents are accepted and a limited number of tent pitches have electrical connections. The park has a long season and reservations are essential for caravans. Entertainment is organised at Easter and from early May in the Starlight Cabaret bar. There are indoor and outdoor pools, each one heated and supervised. The adult pools are generous in size and the Oasis fitness centre provides a steam room, jacuzzi, sun bed, excellent fitness room, swimming lessons, etc. The park is in the heart of residential Torbay, with views across the bay and with sandy beaches less than a mile away. It is a popular park with lots to offer, well maintained and well run. A member of the Best of British group.

Facilities: Toilet blocks are adjacent to the pitches. These are good (particularly the new ones) and, although they can receive heavy use and need regular attention, they are well maintained and heated. Showers and washbasins have free hot water, baths are on payment. Unit for disabled visitors and facilities for babies. Laundry. Gas supplies. Motorcaravan service point. Large general shop, 'express diner', bars and takeaway service (all Easter, then 4 May - 26 Oct). Swimming pools. Tennis court. Crazy golf. Children's playground. Nature trail. Amusement centre with pool, table tennis and amusement machines. American motorhomes are accepted (max. 20 ft). Dogs are not accepted. **Off site**: A regular minibus service runs to Paignton (timetable at reception) or normal services from outside the park. Fishing, bicycle hire, riding and golf all within 2 miles.

Charges 2001

Per serviced pitch incl. 2 persons	£11.00 - £22.00
electric pitch	£9.00 - £20.00
tent	£7.00 - £18.00
with electricity	plus £2.00
extra adult	£4.00
child (4-14 yrs)	£3.00
awning or extra pup tent	£3.00

Max. 6 persons per reservation. Tel: (01803) 843887. Fax: (01803) 845427. E-mail: enquiries@beverley-holidays.co.uk. Reservations: Made with £25 deposit (7, 14 or 21 days 17/7-3/9, min. 2 nights all other times); balance payable more than 28 days before arrival. **Open** 17 February - 30 November; tents 1 April - 31 October.

Directions: Park is south of Paignton in Goodrington Road between A379 coast road and B3203 ring road and is well signed on both. O.S.GR: SX882584.

Widdicombe Farm Tourist Park

The Ring Road, Compton, Paignton, Devon TQ3 1ST

090

Widdicombe Farm, just 3 miles from Torquay and with easy access from the A380, offers 200 numbered pitches (156 for touring units). Electricity connections (10A) are available on 180 pitches and 12 are fully serviced. Surrounded by farmland, the pitches are on gently sloping grass terraces giving a very rural feel. Many trees and shrubs have been planted and there are tarmac access roads. A few pitches are fairly close to the A380 and there may be some traffic noise. Touring areas are separated into sections for families, couples or tents and some hardstandings are available. A large comfortable bar offers family entertainment and opposite the bar is a 'do it yourself' barbecue area with large gas barbecues, patio area and seating (£2 per session). The proprietors live on site.

Facilities: There are three sanitary blocks – the original heated block near reception and two newer blocks, one at the top of the site with provision for disabled visitors and another in the new lower section (with toilets and washbasins only). Baby room. Dishwashing under cover. Small laundry with two machines and dryers. Shop and the 'Poppy' restaurant that provides evening meals, breakfasts, cream teas and takeaway (both Easter - mid Oct). Family bar. Games room with video games and pool tables, children's play area and a recreation field for ball games. Certain breeds of dog are not accepted. Caravan storage. **Off site:** Fishing, bicycle hire, riding and golf, all within 2 miles.

Charges 2001

Per unit incl. 2 persons	£6.00 - £10.50
extra adult	£2.50
child 3-16 yrs £1.50, under 3 yrs	50p
dog	£1.00 - £1.50
electricity (10A)	£1.80

Bargain breaks available. Tel: (01803) 558325. Fax: (01803) 559526. E-mail: enq@torquaytouring.co.uk. Reservations: Advised for July/Aug. (min. 4 days) and made with deposit (£20 per week) and fee (£2). **Open** 16 March - 17 November.

Directions: From Newton Abbot take A380 south for approx. 5 miles; site is well signed off this road. O.S.GR: SX874641.

Dornafield

Two Mile Oak, Newton Abbot, Devon TQ12 6DD

088

The entrance to Dornafield leads into the charming old courtyard of a 14th Century farmhouse giving a mellow feeling that is complemented by the warm welcome from the Dewhirst family. The reception, shop, tourist information/ecology room have been sympathetically converted from the farm outbuildings, with the games room from the old milking parlour, complete with stalls. Once booked in, you may continue down the lane (in spring time overlooked by a tree covered bank and alive with wild flowers) to the Buttermeadow, a tranquil valley providing 75 individual, numbered pitches on flat grass, separated by grassy ridges and in some places, wild rose hedges. You will pass the walled Orchard area, secluded and cosy for tents. Or take the road up the hill and reach Blackrock Copse, the development of large luxury pitches with all facilities including a chemical disposal point for each pitch and TV connections, very cleverly concealed and 38 with hardstanding. All electricity points are 10A. Whilst having been carefully designed, the environment has been kept natural. Both Buttermeadow and Blackrock have super woodland adventure play areas, well maintained and complete with Wendy houses. Dornafield is also a member of the Caravan Club's 'managed under contract' scheme, with both members and non-members made welcome. Dornafield's rural situation is delightful and, being away from the coast and without any evening activities, it is a haven for those seeking a quiet, restful holiday. A member of the Best of British group and a park that is well worth consideration.

Facilities: Perhaps the finest features of the park are the toilet blocks. The original one in Buttermeadow is good, heated, with some washbasins in cubicles and comfortable roomy showers, but the new block up the hill could be said to be 'state of the art' with under-floor heating and a heat recovery system. It is stylish yet warm providing everything for your comfort including a large clock! Both blocks have facilities for disabled visitors and babies, laundry rooms and covered washing up areas. They are bright, cheerful and spotlessly clean. Shop, Gas supplies. All year caravan storage. All-weather hard tennis court. Games room with table tennis. Play areas. **Off site:** The local inn is within half a mile. Fishing 2½ miles, golf 1 mile.

Charges 2001

Per unit incl. 2 adults	£8.50 - £13.00
adult	£3.50 - £4.50
child (5-16 yrs)	£1.10 - £1.20
awning	free - £1.00
pup tent or porch awning	free - 80p
tents over 100 sq.ft.	free - £1.50
full services	£1.00 - £2.00
electricity (10A)	£1.50 (£2.25 outside 19/4-2/10)
dog	£1.00

Tel: (01803) 812732. Fax: (01803) 812032. E-mail: enquiries@dornafield.com. Reservations: Any length, £10 p.w. low season, £25 p/week high season. **Open** 17 March - 3 November.

Directions: Park is northwest of A381 Newton Abbot - Totnes road. Leave A381 at Two Mile Oak Inn, opposite garage, and turn left at crossroads after about ½ mile. Entrance is on the right. O.S.GR: SX848683.

Ross Park

Park Hill Farm, Ipplepen, Newton Abbot, Devon TQ12 5TT

091

Ross Park has to be seen to appreciate the amazing floral displays with their dramatic colours, that are a feature of the park. These are complemented by the use of a wide variety of shrubs which form hedging for most of the 110 pitches providing your own special plot, very much as on the continent. For those who prefer the more open style, one small area has been left unhedged. There are views over the surrounding countryside but as the foliage has developed these are not quite as extensive but there is more protection on a windy day. The owners, Mark and Helen Lowe, continue to strive to provide quality facilities and maintain standards, and this is reflected in the awards they have won. There are nice personal touches, as seen in the utility room with the beautiful photographs of the countryside and suggestions for visits cross-referenced to a map. Also giving an individual touch is the impressive, heated conservatory with yet more named exotic and colourful plants. Seating is provided here as it is directly linked to the New Barn which provides a comfortable lounge, a mezzanine bar with bar snacks and a restaurant. The touring area is divided into bays or groups by the hedging and shrubs and provides 110 pitches all with electricity (10/16A), 82 of which have a hardened surface, some made larger with an increased gravel area. Herbs for your barbecue can be found beside the tourist information chalet. An orchard area alive with daffodils in the spring and a conservation area with information on wild flowers and butterflies, and with extended views, completes these environmentally considered amenities. Barn dances with barbecue are organised on Sundays in high season. A well cared for park worthy of consideration.

Facilities: The main toilet facilities next to the New Barn open from under a veranda style roof, colourful with hanging baskets. They comprise six well equipped, heated en-suite units, one with baby changing facilities, one suitable for disabled people. At the rear are further separate shower, washbasin and toilet facilities. Below the New Barn are more toilets and washbasins in a new well kept, heated 'portacabin' style unit. New fully equipped laundry room and utility room providing dishwashing sinks, freezer and battery charging facilities. Dog shower. Motorcaravan service point. Recycling bins. Comfortable reception cum shop. Gas supplies. Bar, bar snacks and restaurant with a la carte menu (all April - end Oct, plus Christmas and New Year). Games room, table tennis, full sized snooker table and billiards room. 7-acre park area for recreation with bowling and croquet greens and large well equipped adventure playground for older children. Caravan storage. **Off site:** Dainton Park 18 hole golf course is adjacent. Fishing 3 miles, riding 1 mile.

Charges 2001

Per unit incl. 2 persons	£7.70 - £13.00
extra adult	£3.25 - £4.25
child (4-16 yrs)	£1.50
electricity (16A)	£1.70 - £2.20

Christmas packages available. No credit cards. Tel/Fax: (01803) 812983. E-mail: enquiries@ rossparkcaravanpark.co.uk. Reservations: Made with £20 deposit. **Open** all year except Jan. and first two weeks of Feb.

Directions: From A381 Newton Abbot - Totnes road, park is signed towards Woodland at Park Hill crossroads and Jet filling station. O.S.GR: SX845671.

Finlake Holiday Park

Chudleigh, Devon TQ13 0EJ

092

This extensive 130 acre park on the edge of Dartmoor has been purpose built as a modern touring park with a lively entertainment and leisure complex. Approached by a long, sweeping drive, with views up to the moor, the park is on well landscaped, undulating ground surrounded by woodland. There are 318 flat numbered pitches in two main areas, with some terracing on the higher parts. Pitches in the area around the central complex may well be affected by noise from the bars, etc. – for a quieter place, ask for a pitch further away (Lakeside or Deer Park). The pitches are of varying size, all with hardstanding and electric point (10A), 51 also with water. A separate, enclosed field is retained for tents and there is a special area for dog owners. Also open to the public, the park offers extensive leisure activities including a 9-hole pitch and putt course, two fishing lakes, fitness track, tennis courts, quad bikes and track for children and walks in the woodland around the park with pony riding at a centre 100 m. from the entrance. The modern, attractively designed central complex provides three bars around a pool terrace, two with entertainment and one with a restaurant. There is a lively, free organised entertainment programme over a long season (out of season only one bar is open). A fitness suite has been added (small additional charge, open all year) with beauty treatment room and qualified instructors. The indoor and outdoor pools (with slide) are supervised in high season but are also easily observed from the bar areas and terrace. The Lakeside Bar, open in high season and for adults only, overlooks the fishing lake. A torch would be useful.

Facilities: Five modern toilet blocks set around the park are being progressively refurbished and extended. Heated and of good quality, they include family shower rooms, bathrooms for ladies, suitable toilet/washrooms for disabled people and washing-up sinks outside, under cover. The facilities can come under pressure at peak times but are supplemented by 'portacabin' style unit with electricity for the tent field. Fully equipped launderette. Motorcaravan service points. Supermarket (Easter-Oct, limited opening early and late season). Gas supplies. Bars and restaurant. Gym. Swimming pools. Fishing. Two tennis courts. 'Quads for Kids'. Children's play area. Caravan storage all year. **Off site:** Riding centre adjacent. Bicycle hire 6 miles, golf 3 miles.

Charges guide

Per unit incl. 2 persons	£7.50 - £16.50
electricity	£1.80
tent	£5.50 - £12.00
extra person (from 3 yrs)	£1.50 - £2.50
water and drainage	£1.00 - £2.00
awning	free
pup tent	£1.00 - £2.00
dog	£1.00 - £2.00

Special theme weekends - details from park. Bookings from young groups not accepted. Tel: (01626) 853833. Fax: (01626) 854031. Reservations: Made with 25% deposit, balance 28 days before arrival. **Open** all year.

Directions: Park is signed on A38 dual-carriageway; take exit for Chudleigh Knighton, Kingsteignton, Teign Valley. O.S.GR: SX850778.

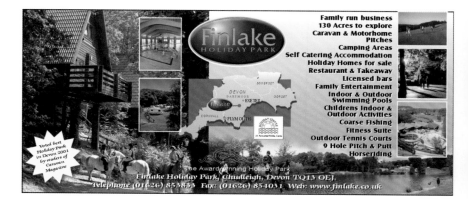

Devon
Ashburton Caravan Park
Waterleat, Ashburton, Devon TQ13 7HU

For tents and motorcaravans only, the four acres of Ashburton Park nestle in a hidden valley below Dartmoor, bordered by mature woodland. The Ashburn, a shallow stream with rocky pools, evenly divides and screens two acres of holiday homes from the two acre camping area. Sheltered and south facing, the park is a tranquil retreat, although for the energetic a half mile steep uphill walk brings you to the moor or by 1½ miles of Devon lanes to Ashburton village. There are 35 level or gently sloping pitches, 8 with electricity (16A), on either side of a tarmac road that culminates in a small field area. Each visitor receives a copy of the 'Dartmoor Visitor', the information paper supplied by the Dartmoor National Park authorities - the campsite is actually within the boundaries of the Park. There are limited bus services to Newton Abbot, Exeter or Plymouth. A well maintained, tranquil small park for nature lovers.

Facilities: First class, purpose built toilet block provides washbasins in cabins for ladies and a toilet and washbasin for disabled visitors (baby bath, etc. available). Washing machine and dryer, plus free spin dryer and iron. Reception/information centre provides gas, a freezer pack service, tourist information, maps and walks and a daily weather report. Dogs (limited breeds only) are welcomed if exercised off the park. Torches useful. **Off site:** Shops, banks, post office, a small heated swimming pool and pubs, etc. are in Ashburton, a pleasant walk away by the river. Bicycle hire 1 mile, riding and golf 3 miles.

Charges 2001

Per unit incl. 1 person	£4.00
2 persons	£7.50 - £10.00
extra person (over 1 yr)	£1.50 - £2.25
dog	70p
electricity	£1.80

No credit cards. Tel/Fax: (01364) 652552. E-mail: info@ashburtondevon.freeserve.co.uk. Reservations: Made for min. 3 nights with £15 deposit. **Open** Easter - mid October.

Directions: In the centre of Ashburton turn northwest into North Street. As built-up area thins out bear right before bridge following signs for 'Waterleat' (tent symbol) for approx. 1½ miles. Park is on the left. O.S.GR: SX752721.

Devon
Lemonford Caravan Park
Bickington, Newton Abbot, Devon TQ12 6JR

Lemonford is a well run, neat and tidy site for all ages and families on the southern edge of the National Park, some 3 miles from both Ashburton and Newton Abbot. It has the look and atmosphere of the 'cultivated' caravan park, in close proximity to the main road, yet set in a sheltered and peaceful dip bordered by the pretty River Lemon. Well mown grass and smart, trimmed hedges create the tranquil, attractive atmosphere the owners work hard to maintain. There are 85 touring pitches (65 with 10A electricity, over 45 with hardstanding) on level grass and grouped in four areas according to whether they are to be used by families, couples or individuals. The park is well located for excursions, two good pubs are within walking distance, one along the banks of the river, and there is a leisure pool in Newton Abbot.

Facilities: Two modern toilet blocks, one new, can be heated and provide some private cabins, a ladies' bathroom (£1 payment) and a family bathroom. Dishwashing area under cover. Laundry facilities. Shop. Gas supplies. Freezer service. Children's play area. Putting green. Fishing in the River Lemon. No commercial vehicles are accepted. **Off site:** Fishing 4 miles, riding and bicycle hire 3 miles, golf 2 miles.

Charges 2001

Per unit incl. 2 persons	£5.50 - £9.00
extra person	£1.50
child (3-15)	£1.10
awning	£1.00
electricity	£1.70
dog	70p

Special low season offers. No credit cards. Tel/Fax: (01626) 821242 or 821263. Fax: (01626) 821242. E-mail: mark@lemonford.co.uk. Reservations: Advised for July/Aug. and made with £15 deposit (min. 3 nights July/Aug). **Open** Mid March - 31 October.

Directions: From Exeter, turn off A38 Plymouth road at A382 (Drumbridges) exit signed Newton Abbot, Bovey Tracey. At roundabout take third exit to Bickington. Continue for 1 mile to Toby Jug Inn in the village and park is on left at the bottom of the hill. From Plymouth, take A383 (Goodstone) exit, cross A38 and take first left to Bickington to site on right. O.S.GR: SX793723.

Devon
Parker's Farm Holiday Park

096 Higher Mead Farm, Ashburton, Newton Abbot, Devon TQ13 7LJ

Well situated with fine views towards
Dartmoor, Parker's Farm is a modern
touring site on a working farm. Close
inspection reveals a unique chance to
experience Devon country life at first hand,
with pigs, sheep, goats, calves and
rabbits, etc. in pens to feed and touch or
the milking to get involved with. In addition
the Parker family have added a family bar
which provides entertainment during the
season (quiz night, bingo, guitar player)
and fills the gap created by the closure of
the local pub. Farm walks are
tremendously popular and take place four
evenings a week in high season, on
request at other times. The 100 touring
pitches, with electricity (12A), are set
directly above the farm buildings on
terraces giving broad, flat groups of
pitches, all with good views across the
valley (to the A38 which may give some
road noise). Hardstandings are available.
Young trees and hedges have been
planted and are maturing nicely on the
lower terraces. Parker's Farm will suit
those who don't seek the sophisticated
amenities of more developed parks and a
warm welcome awaits - in the words of
one camper, 'You come here and feel you
belong'.

Facilities: Two modern and clean shower and toilet
blocks provide good facilities with a family shower
room and baby bathroom, plus an en-suite room for
disabled visitors, dishwashing and laundry. Small
shop (Whitsun-mid Sept). Restaurant, family bar
(Whitsun-mid Sept.) and entertainment. Games room
with table tennis and pool, an indoor play and TV
area, a large outdoor play area, with trampolines
around the park, and made-safe farm implements
and tractors. Caravan storage. Rallies welcome.
American motorhomes accepted by prior
arrangement. **Off site:** Bicycle hire 5 miles, golf 4
miles, riding 5 miles.

Charges 2001

Per unit incl. 2 persons	£5.00 - £9.50
extra adult	£1.30
child (3-15 yrs)	£1.20
awning	£1.30
pup tent	£1.20
electricity	£1.80
dog	60p

Tel: (01364) 652598. Fax: (01364) 654004. E-mail:
parkersfarm@btconnect.com. Reservations: Made
with £10 deposit **Open** Easter - 31 October.

Directions: From Exeter on A38, 26 miles from
Plymouth, turn left at Alston Cross signed
'Woodland Denbury ½ mile'. Site is ¼ mile. O.S.GR:
SX757702.

Devon
Holmans Wood Caravan and Camping Park
Chudleigh, Devon TQ13 0DZ

Close to the main A38 Exeter - Plymouth road, with easy access, this attractive, neat park makes a sheltered base for touring south Devon and Dartmoor. The hedged park is arranged on well kept grass surrounding a shallow depression, the floor of which makes a safe, grassy play area for children. Many attractive trees are growing and the park is decorated with flowers. In two main areas and accessed by tarmac roads, there 115 level pitches (including a number of seasonal pitches) and 14 mobile homes. There are 109 pitches with electrical hook-ups (10A) and 70 with hardstanding, electricity, TV aerial hook up, water and drainage. Grassy areas are provided for tents. Adventure play equipment is provided for children, with badminton and tennis nets and an extra meadow for recreation. There may be some traffic noise on pitches to the west of the park. This is a pleasant, well run park and with no other on-site amenities would suit couples or families who prefer a peaceful stay.

Facilities: The single, good quality toilet block includes facilities for babies and disabled visitors, a dishwashing room and a laundry room. Children's play area. Caravan storage. **Off site**: Pub/restaurant nearby in Chudleigh village. The beach or Dartmoor are 7 miles and Haldon Forest for walks is 2 miles. Sunday market at Exeter Racecourse (2 miles). Fishing 1 mile, golf or riding 4 miles.

Charges 2001

Per unit incl. 2 persons	£6.59 - £8.95
deluxe pitch	£7.95 - £10.65
extra adult	£1.65 - £2.20
child (4-14 yrs)	£1.39 - £1.69
awning or child's tent	£1.69
porch awning	95p
dog	90p
electricity	£2.00

Tel: (01626) 853785. Fax: (01626) 854707.
Reservations: Any length, £30 deposit per week.
Open Mid-March - end October.

Directions: From Exeter on A38 Plymouth road, ½ mile after the racecourse and just after a garage, take Chudleigh exit (signed). Park is immediately on the left. From Plymouth turn off A38 for Chudleigh/Teign Valley, then right for Chudleigh. Continue through the town and park is 1 mile. O.S.GR: SX882811.

Devon
Clifford Bridge Park
Clifford, nr Drewsteignton, Devon, EX6 6QE

This eight acre riverside touring park provides peace and tranquillity within the Dartmoor National Park, three miles from the nearest village with any facilities. In a wooded valley on the banks of the River Teign, it can only be approached on narrow lanes (single track for the last mile), but is a good base with plenty to do for those who like country pursuits 'away from it all'. Fingle Bridge is 3½ miles and Castle Drogo (National Trust) 5 miles. The site is licensed for 24 touring caravans or motorcaravans and 40 tents. Pitches are of a good size on a flat grassy meadow, mainly around the perimeter with some backing onto the river. Plenty of grassy space is left free for recreation and there is a free swimming pool. There are 3 hardstandings and 25 electrical connections (6A). First class walks are possible from the site and game fishing is available on permit.

Facilities: The toilet block, near the entrance to the park, is not large or modern but is satisfactory and kept clean, with free hot water in the smallish washbasins and showers. Hand and hair dryers. An adjacent 'portacabin' style unit provides extra facilities in high season. Dishwashing sinks are outside, under cover. The farm outbuildings house a shop (Spr.B.H - 1/9), gas supplies, games room with pool table, amusement machine and tourist information, and a small laundry room around a courtyard. Swimming pool (54 x 24 ft. open and heated Spr.B.H - 1/9). **Off site**: riding or golf 6 miles, bicycle hire 3 miles.

Charges 2001

Per unit incl. 2 persons	£7.40 - £12.60
small motorcaravan	£6.60 - £10.70
backpacker or cyclist per person	£2.50- £3.50
extra person	£2.50 - £3.50
child 8-16 yrs	free - £2.50
4-7 yrs	free - £1.75
awning	£1.60
extra pup tent	free - £1.00
dog	free - 50p
electricity	£1.80

Discounts available. No credit cards. Tel: (01647) 24226. Fax: (01647) 24116. E-mail: info@clifford-bridge.co.uk. Reservations: Advised for school holidays and made for any length with £30 deposit. **Open** Easter - 30 September

Directions: To avoid much single-track road approach via the A30, turning off 11 miles west of Exeter to Cheriton Bishop. Left there (at Old Thatch Inn), 2 miles to crossroads where right for Clifford Bridge, 1 mile of single track, over crossroads and bridge and left to park. O.S.GR: SX782897.

With its mature park and woodland, once part of a Victorian estate, this interesting and unusual park could appeal to many, particularly those with children. Very close to Dartmoor, in the beautiful Dart valley, the park is open to the general public on payment. It features a variety of unusual adventure play equipment (eg. a giant spider's web) arranged amongst and below the trees, 'Lilliput Land' for toddlers, woodland streams and a lake with raft for swimming and inflatables, fly fishing and marked nature and forest trails - all free to campers except fishing. It can become busy at weekends and school holidays. Supervised courses in caving, canoeing, archery or climbing are arranged in school holiday periods (contact the park for details). The camping and caravanning area is in the more open parkland overlooking the woods and is mainly on a slight slope with some shade from mature trees. There are 170 individual pitches of very reasonable size, marked by lines on the grass with 85 electrical connections (10A). The entire estate is kept very clean and tidy.

Facilities: The original good quality toilet block can be heated, providing a baby room, shower for disabled visitors, dishwashing sinks, launderette and freezer. A second block serves the 50 newer pitches. Fully equipped, it includes a separate unit for disabled visitors (access by key) and washbasins in cubicles for ladies. Motorcaravan service point. Shop (all season). Restaurant and adjoining snack bar with takeaway (July/Aug). Small, heated swimming pool. Tennis courts. Bar (July/Aug, plus Easter and B.Hs) with TV and games room with pool and amusement machines. Max. two dogs per pitch. American motorhomes are only accepted in dry periods (no hardstandings). **Off site**: Bicycle hire or riding 4 miles, golf 6 miles.

Charges 2001

Per adult	£4.75 - £6.50
child (over 3 yrs)	£3.95 - £5.15
dog	£1.00
electricity	£1.85

Tel: (01364) 652511. Fax: (01364) 652020. E-mail: enquiries@riverdart.co.uk. Reservations: Low or mid season, any length with £3 fee; high season (strongly recommended), £20 deposit plus £3 fee for 7 days or less; £40 + £3 for longer. **Open** 1 April - mid September.

Directions: Signed from the A38 at Peartree junction, park is about 2 miles west of Ashburton, on the road to Two Bridges. Disregard advisory signs stating 'no caravans' as access to the park is prior to narrow bridge. O.S.GR: SX734701.

Dartmoor View Holiday Park

Whiddon Down, Okehampton, Devon EX20 2QL

078

With easy access from the A30 road, this peaceful park has been much improved by the friendly new owners. It is bordered by mature trees and hedges and has a well tended look with pretty flower beds around. There are 72 flat, grassy touring pitches (8 hardstandings) of which 50 have electricity (16A) and 14 have water and waste water. Reception is near the entrance, together with a family bar with entertainment some evenings in season. Children have some good quality play equipment and there is a heated outdoor swimming pool (10 x 5 m) with children's pool, fenced with paved surrounds and a small 9 hole putting green. The site is close to the Dartmoor 'letter-boxing' area.

Facilities: The heated sanitary facilities are well maintained and equipped with three unisex cabins. Laundry and campers' kitchen. Licensed shop. Family bar (1/4-1/10). TV and games rooms. Swimming pool (1/6-15/9). Children's play area. Putting green. No kite flying is permitted. First aid caravan. Caravan storage. **Off site:** Fishing or riding 5 miles, golf 3 miles.

Charges 2001

Per unit, incl. 2 persons	£7.50 - £9.75
small one person tent	£5.00 - £6.75
extra person	£2.00
child (3-11 yrs)	£1.50
dog	£1.00
electricity	£2.25
all service pitch	£2.00
hardstanding	£1.00
awning or pup tent	£1.00

Spring or autumn special prices. Tel: (01647) 231545. Fax: (01647) 231654. E-mail: anyone@dartmoorview. co.uk. Reservations: Any length, with deposit of £25 p/week or £4 p/night. **Open** March - November.

Directions: On A30 dual-carriageway at the Merrymeet roundabout, take the Whiddon Down road. Park is ½ mile on the right. O.S.GR: SX685928.

Yeatheridge Farm Caravan Park

East Worlington, Crediton, Devon EX17 4TN

106

Yeatheridge is a friendly, family park with riding, fishing lakes, and indoor pools. Based on a 200-acre farm, 9 acres have been developed over many years into an attractive touring park. With splendid views of the local hills and Dartmoor away to the south, and Exmoor easily accessible to the north, you can explore three woodland walks ranging from 1 to 2½ miles and the banks of the River Dalch. There are two deep coarse fishing lakes (bring your own rod), the top one offering family fishing and the lower one for serious fishing (age 14 or over and free of charge). Horse riding is available on site (best to bring your own hat) with short rides for £1.80 and 50 minute park rides for £7.00. The ponies and goats are also popular with adults and children alike. The touring area was very neat and tidy during our stay in late August and, although the park was almost full, it did not feel crowded, as units are sited around the perimeter or back onto hedges, leaving open central areas. The 104 numbered, grass pitches are flat, gently sloping or on terraces and appeared sufficiently large, 80 with electricity connections (10A). A maximum of 24 pitches are for caravan holiday homes. Other visitors found the relative seclusion of the park gave a good feeling of security to parents. The owners, Geoff and Liz, try very hard to make everyone feel at home.

Facilities: The central sanitary facility, with very hot water and cabins for ladies, showed signs of heavy use (particularly the rather fierce push-button showers). For 2002, this may be alleviated by the addition of a new building by the pools. Dishwashing (hot water 10p). Shop open long hours with local produce. Club bar has good value drinks and a fish and chip van is on site, open Friday, Saturday and Tuesday evenings. Indoor swimming pools and toddlers pool open for long hours, the water slide has shorter hours, as it requires supervision. Fenced play area with a fort for under 10's (with parental supervision) and football field. TV room. Pool table, table tennis and skittles. Fishing and horse riding.

Charges 2001

Per unit incl. 2 persons	£6.50 - £9.00
extra person over 4 yrs	free - £1.80
awning or pup tent	free - £1.80
dog - first two	50p each
extra dog	£2.00
electricity	£2.00

Tel: (01884) 860330. E-mail: info@yeatheridge.co.uk. Reservations: Advised for Bank and school holidays and made with £35 deposit; contact park. **Open** April - September.

Directions: Park is off the B3042 Witheridge - Chawleigh (not in East Worlington). From M5 take exit 27 onto A361 to Tiverton. Turn left onto A396 for ½ mile then right on B3137 almost to Witheridge, then left on B3042 for 3 miles to site, well-signed down concrete roadway on left. O.S.GR: SS771112.

Devon
Springfield Holiday Park
Tedburn Road, Tedburn St Mary, Exeter, Devon EX6 6EW

Quietly situated to explore both Dartmoor and Exmoor, yet easily accessible, Springfield has room for 88 units on its 9 acres, mainly on level, grass terraces with views across the Devon countryside. Over 50 pitches have 10A electricity. There are some seasonal units and 19 caravan holiday homes which are to be found at the lower part of the park. The reception cum shop is on the right as you drop down into the park and gravel access roads radiate out from here along the terraces and link up at the bottom where a new family 'terrace bar' has been built with a grass terrace making the most of the rural views. Good value meals are served to eat in or takeaway, even cream teas and the odd musical evening. Martin and Eileen Johnson, the owners, are keen to help everyone enjoy their stay and can provide plenty of local information on Dartmoor walks and where to find the best fishing lakes, etc. A new bridge on the A30 provides much easier access to the site and to Dartmoor.

Facilities: The two toilet blocks are of older design with pre-set showers (20p external meter), a family bathroom and baby changing facilities. Washing up and laundry sinks (H&C), three washing machines and two dryers. Facilities could be stretched in high season. Well stocked licensed shop featuring local produce. Gas supplies. Terraced bar with bar meals or takeaway (open Easter, then May - Sept evenings and Sunday lunch). Small heated swimming pool, naturally sheltered (unsupervised). Children's play area and games room. **Off site:** Fishing 6 miles, bicycle hire 8 miles, riding 10 miles, golf 2 miles.

Charges 2001

Per caravan or motorcaravan	£8.00 - £10.00
tent	£7.50 - £9.00
walker or cyclist	£5.00 - £6.00
extra person (over 3 yrs)	£1.50
full or half awning, pup tent	£1.00
dog	£1.00
electricity	£1.80

Tel: (01647) 24242. Fax: (01647) 24131.E-mail: springhol@aol.com. Reservations: Made with deposit (£20 per unit per week or £5 per night with electricity). **Open** 15 March - 15 November.

Directions: From M5 junction 31 take A30 towards Okehampton. Take third exit from the A30 (Woodleigh junction) and follow signs over bridge to park. O.S.GR: SX788936.

Devon
Minnows Camping and Caravan Park
Sampford Peverell, nr Tiverton. Devon EX16 7EN

Minnows is an attractive park with views across the Devon countryside, separated from the Grand Western canal by hedging. Easily accessible from the M5, it is suitable as an ideal touring centre for Devon and Somerset, for cycling or walking, or simply for breaking a long journey. A small, neat park, open for nine months of the year, it provides 45 level pitches all with 16A electricity. Of these, 37 are all weather (grass and gravel), including 3 fully serviced for motorcaravans. A further 3½ acres have been added to the park providing space for more and larger pitches, a children's playground and a large field for ball games, etc. The village of Sampford Peverell, with pub and general store, is only a half mile walk via the towpath, with Tiverton 7½ miles. In fact, there are 12 miles of level walking on the towpath or one can take a trip on a horse-drawn barge. The site is also on the Sustran cycle route (route 3). Tiverton Parkway station (BR) is 1 mile and buses run from the village to Tiverton. Coarse fishing permits for the canal are available from reception. Part of the Caravan Club's 'managed under contract' scheme, non-members are also very welcome.

Facilities: The heated toilet block is well maintained with all modern facilities and constant hot water. Facilities for disabled visitors, a baby bath on request. Covered dishwashing sinks and one for laundry, plus a spin dryer and washing machine. Motorcaravan service point. Gas supplies. Newspaper delivery can be arranged. Excellent tourist information. Children's play area. All year caravan storage. Site gates closed 9 pm. and locked 11 pm.- 7.30 am. **Off site:** Bicycle hire 5 minutes walk away. Golf driving range near, full course 4 miles; riding 6 miles.

Charges 2001

Per caravan, motorcaravan or trailer tent	£4.00
small tent and car	£2.00
adult	£2.75 - £3.75
child (5-16 yrs)	£1.10 - £1.20
dog	free
extra tent or car	£1.00
electricity	£1.50 - £2.25
serviced pitch	plus £1.00

Awning free with breathable groundsheets on grass. Credit cards accepted for £10 or over. Tel/Fax: (01884) 821770. Reservations: Made with £10 deposit. **Open** 8 March - 12 November.

Directions: From M5 junction 27 take A361 signed Tiverton. After about 600 yds leave on the first exit signed Sampford Peverell. After about 200 yds turn right at roundabout and cross bridge over A361 to a second roundabout. Go straight ahead and park is immediately ahead. From North Devon on A361 go to M5 junction 27 and return back up the A361 as above. O.S.GR: ST042148.

 Alan Rogers' discount
Apply to park

Hidden Valley Touring and Camping Park

West Down, Ilfracombe, N. Devon EX34 8NU

071

Aptly named, this award-winning, family park has been carefully developed in keeping with its lovely setting between Barnstaple and Ilfracombe. In a valley beside a small stream and lake (with ducks), it is most attractive and is also convenient for several resorts, beaches and the surrounding countryside. The owners, Martin and Dawn Fletcher, run the park to high standards. The original part of the park offers some 74 level pitches of good size on three sheltered terraces. All have hardstanding, electricity hook-ups (16A) and free TV connections (leads for hire), with a water point between each pitch. Kingfisher Meadow, a little way from the main facilities and reached by a tarmac road, provides a further 60 pitches entirely on grass (so suitable for campers with tents), all with electricity, water, waste water and TV hook-ups. A good value, family restaurant serves home cooked meals in attractive surroundings. Essentially this is a park for those seeking good quality facilities in very attractive, natural surroundings, without too many man-made distractions - apart from some slight traffic noise during day time.

Facilities: Two modern toilet blocks (one heated), are tiled and have non-slip floors. One for each area, they provide some washbasins in cubicles, some en-suite with toilets in the Kingfisher Meadow block, baby changing room, laundry facilities including washing machine, dryer and iron, and dishwashing sinks under cover, plus complete facilities for people with disabilities. There are supplementary clean 'portacabin' style facilities in the original area. Motorcaravan service facilities. Gas supplies. Small shop with off licence. Lounge bar. Restaurant. Takeaway. Games room. Two good children's adventure play areas have wooden equipment and safe bark surfaces (one near a fast flowing stream). Up to two dogs are accepted (otherwise by prior arrangement). Caravan storage. **Off site**: Fishing or golf 2 miles, bicycle hire 4 miles, riding 5 miles.

Charges 2001

Per unit incl. 2 persons	£5.00 - £13.00
extra person over 5 yrs	£1.00
extra tent	£1.00
extra car or boat	free - £1.00
dog	free - £1.00
electricity (16A)	£1.75 - £2.00

Tel: (01271) 813837. Fax: (01271) 814041. E-mail: hvp@aol.com. Reservations: Accepted with £25 deposit. **Open** all year.

Directions: Park is on A361 Barnstaple - Ilfracombe road, 3½ miles after Braunton. O.S.GR: SS499408.

Step out of this world...
into Hidden Valley

Nature at its best

to find out more about our award winning park call us on
01271 813837
or visit our website at www.hiddenvalleypark.com

West Down Nr. Ilfracombe
North Devon EX34 8NU

GOLD

TOURING PARK

96-97-98 99-2000

AA PREMIER PARK

Woolacombe Bay Holiday Village

107 Sandy Lane, Woolacombe, Devon EX34 7AH

Woolacombe Bay, and its sister site Golden Coast nearby, are well known holiday parks providing a range of holiday accommodation from caravan holiday homes to chalets and apartments, with many on site amenities including pools, restaurants and bars, and providing a wide range of entertainment. A new camping section has been developed at the Woolacombe Bay park, for tents and trailer tents only, whereby touring visitors can enjoy all the activities and entertainment of both parks. Partly terraced out of the hillside and partly on the hill top with some existing pine trees but with many more trees planted for landscaping, the site has magnificent views out across the bay. Marked and numbered pitches have been provided on grass for 146 tents, 94 with electrical connections (10/16A). All should be level, having been terraced where necessary and they are connected by gravel roads. Some up and down walking is needed for the toilet block. A courtesy bus service runs between the two parks, the third park in the group (Twitchen Parc - see below) and the beach during the high main season, although there is a footpath to the beach from the site. All three parks have varied entertainment programmes and children's clubs.

Facilities: A super new central toilet block has excellent facilities, including en-suite shower and washrooms and separate toilets; also included is a sauna and steam room – unusual but nice. Separate dishwashing and laundry rooms. Unit for disabled visitors. Supermarket. Bars, restaurant and entertainment. Indoor (heated) and outdoor pools with flumes and slides. Sauna and gym. Health spa and beauty suite. Tennis courts. Dogs are welcome at Woolacombe Bay but not at Golden Coast. **Off site:** Fishing or riding 1 mile.

Charges 2001

Per adult	£3.95 - £10.65
child (5-15 yrs)	£2.00 - £5.35
dog per week	£10.00

Tel: (01271) 870343. Fax: (01271) 870089. E-mail: goodtimes@woolacombe.com. Reservations: Advised for peak season. **Open** Easter - end October.

Directions: Take A361 Barnstaple - Ilfracombe road through Braunton. Turn left at Mullacott Cross roundabout towards Woolacombe then right towards Mortehoe. Park is on left before village. O.S.GR: SS463445.

Twitchen Parc

073 Mortehoe, Woolacombe, Devon EX34 7ES

Set in the grounds of an attractive Edwardian country house, Twitchen Parc is under the same ownership as Woolacombe Bay. Its main concern lies in holiday caravans and flats, but it also provides marked pitches for tourers at the top of the park, with some views over the rolling hills to the sea. With a newly developed touring field, they include 155 pitches with 16A electricity, many with tarmac hardstanding, mostly arranged around oval access roads in hedged areas. Further non-electric pitches are behind in two open, unmarked fields which are sloping (blocks are thoughtfully provided). A smart, modern entertainment complex incorporates a licensed club and family lounge with snacks, a restaurant, adults only bar, teenage disco room and a cartoon lounge. Twitchen is very popular for families with children. If they become bored, there are always the excellent beaches nearby with a footpath down to the sea. All the facilities of the Golden Coast and Woolacombe Bay Parcs are free to visitors at Twitchen, with a courtesy bus running regularly between the three parks and to the beach.

Facilities: There are two sanitary blocks, the larger one of an unusual design with different levels and rather narrow corridors. Dishwashing and laundry facilities at each block plus a good modern launderette at the central complex. Shop and takeaway. Club, bars, restaurant and entertainment for adults and children, day and evening. Outdoor pool (heated mid-May - mid-Sept). Indoor pool with sauna, children's paddling pool, fountain and a viewing area. Games rooms for table tennis, pool, snooker and arcade games. Good children's adventure play area. American motorhomes are accepted (up to 30 ft).

Charges 2001

Per caravan or motorcaravan	£11.50 - £25.95

High season per week only: per pitch incl. electricity 27/5-3/6 £125, 15/7-26/8 £225.

Tent pitch:	
per adult	£3.95 - £10.65
child (5-15 yrs)	£2.00 - £5.35
dog per week	£10.00

Special offers available. Tel: (01271) 870343. Fax: (01271) 870089. E-mail: goodtimes@woolacombe.com. Reservations: Made with deposit (£2 per pitch per night). **Open** 1 April/Easter - end October.

Directions: From Barnstaple take A361 towards Ilfracombe and through Braunton. Turn left at Mullacott Cross roundabout towards Woolacombe and then right towards Mortehoe. Park is on the left before village. O.S.GR: SS466456.

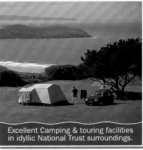

Easewell Farm Holiday Park

072

Mortehoe, Woolacombe, N. Devon EX34 7EH

Near to the sandy beaches of Woolacombe, Easewell Farm is a family run site, run with families in mind. This is a traditional touring park which during the day is a hive of activity, but the nights are quiet and peaceful. The largest of the camping fields is sloping with superb views across the headland to the sea. Two smaller fields are terraced and one area has hardstandings. Together they provide 250 pitches, 90 with electricity connections (15A) and 20 also with TV and water connections. The shop is well stocked (gas available), there is a takeaway and restaurant and an attractive bar with patio overlooking a small duck pond. The park has its own very well maintained 9 hole golf course which is popular and has reduced fees for campers. One of the huge redundant farm buildings has been put to excellent use - divided into three areas, it provides table tennis and pool, a skittle alley and two lanes of flat green bowling with changing rooms. Walks to the local village and along the coastal path are easy from the site and a bus to Ilfracombe and Barnstaple stops 100 yds. from the entrance.

Facilities: The central toilet block is continually upgraded and can be heated. Two washbasins in the ladies have extending hoses for hair washing, controllable showers (no dividers) and there is a small area with baby bathing facilities. Dishwashing sinks under cover. Laundry. All these facilities are arranged around the farmhouse area and include a very well equipped unit for disabled people with everything in one large room including a hairdryer. Motorcaravan service point. Shop. Bar. Golf. A small heated indoor swimming pool is well used, as are games and TV rooms. Fenced play area with bark chipping base. In high season only one dog per pitch is allowed. **Off site:** Fishing or riding 1 mile, bicycle hire 3 miles.

Charges 2001

Per caravan incl. 2 persons	£8.00 - £12.00
tent or motorcaravan incl. 2 persons	£7.00 - £10.00
extra person incl. children	£1.50
electricity	£2.00
'supersite' incl. electricity	plus £4.00
awning or pup tent	free

Tel/Fax: (01271) 870225. Reservations: Made with £20 deposit per week booked. **Open** Easter - 30 September.

Directions: From Barnstaple, take A361 Ilfracombe road through Braunton. Turn left at Mullacott Cross roundabout on B3343 to Woolacombe, turning right after 2-3 miles to Mortehoe. Park is on right before village. O.S.GR: SS465455.

Greenacres Touring Caravan Park

070

Bratton Fleming, Barnstaple, Devon EX31 4SG

A neat, compact, rural park on the edge of Exmoor, Greenacres is managed and run alongside, but separately from, the working farm owned by the family. Drive through the farm access to the park (clearly signed) - you will need to go back and call at the house to book in. No tents are taken. The site has 30 good sized, well drained pitches with connecting gravel paths to the road – in theory you can get to your unit without stepping on the grass; 22 electric hook-ups (16A). The top area is level, the lower part next to the beech woods is semi-terraced to provide six hardstandings and some hedged places. There are marvellous views outside the beech hedge that shelters the site. To the west of Exmoor, the park is very suitable for the coast at Ilfracombe and Combe Martin, or for exploring the moor. The family has opened up a woodland walk across the fields to a secluded valley picnic area beside a stream to take advantage of the marvellous views and surroundings.

Facilities: The toilet block, in the centre of the horseshoe layout has been well designed with showers (1M, 1F) on payment (20p) and an en-suite room for disabled visitors. Laundry room, with spin dryer, iron and board, and dishwashing room. Gas supplies. Tourist information hut. An area for children with net and swings is separated by a Devon bank from the 2 acre dog field. **Off site:** Fishing 3 miles, riding 5 miles, golf 12 miles.

Charges 2001

Per unit incl. 2 persons	£4.00 - £7.50
extra person	75p - £1.25
child (under 7 yrs)	free
awning	free - £1.50
dog	free
electricity	£1.50

Less 10% for stays over 10 days. No credit cards. Tel: (01598) 763334. Reservations: Made with £5 deposit. **Open** Easter/1 April - 31 October.

Directions: From North Devon link road (M5, exit 27) turn north at South Molton onto A399. Continue for 9 miles, past turning for Exmoor Steam Centre and on to Stowford Cross. Turn left towards Exmoor Zoological Park and Greenacres is on the left. O.S.GR: SS663404.

Stowford Farm Meadows

Combe Martin, Ilfracombe, Devon EX34 0PW

069

Dating from the 15th century, Stowford Farm is set in 450 acres of rolling countryside, all of which is available for recreation and walking. With a nice spacious feel and a village-like atmosphere, this large touring park has been developed in the fields and farm buildings surrounding the attractive old farmhouse. There are 570 pitches for all units on four slightly sloping meadows. Unseparated, the numbered and marked pitches are accessed by tarmac or hard-core roadways, most have electricity (10A) and there are well placed water points. If breathable groundsheets are used, awnings are free in low seasons and cheaper in high season. The original stables have become the Old Stable Bars, refurbished to a high standard and entertainment in high season includes barn dances, discos, karaoke and other musical evenings. Children will also be entertained by the under cover mini-zoo (Petorama) where they can handle many sorts of animals (on payment). In low season some facilities may only open for limited hours. Stowford provides plenty to keep families occupied without leaving the park, including a new woodland walk. It is also a friendly, countryside base for exploring the North Devon coast and Exmoor.

Facilities: The four identical toilet blocks have their own personal cleaners and are kept very clean, providing good, functional facilities. Showers are on payment and each block has laundry facilities and under cover dishwashing sinks. Private washrooms and facilities for disabled visitors in reception area. Well stocked shop (with holiday goods, gas and camping accessories) and a good value takeaway service with a restaurant area. Bars and entertainment in season. Swimming pool (22 x 10 m; heated Easter - Oct) at a small charge (90p). Riding stables on site. 18-hole pitch and putt course. Games room (pool tables, table tennis and amusement machines) and snooker room. Crazy golf. Bicycle hire. 'Kiddies kar' track (all charged for). Large children's play area. Games and activities organised in high season. Dogs welcome in one section (max. 2 per pitch). Summer parking and winter caravan storage. New caravan workshop and repair centre. **Off site**: Fishing and boat launching 4 miles.

Charges 2001

Per unit and car incl. 2 persons	£4.60 - £9.70
extra person (over 5 yrs)	free - £2.00
awning with groundsheet	£2.00 - £2.50
extra car or small tent	£2.00
dog	60p - £1.00
electricity	£1.25 - £1.75

Reduced fees for over-50s in low and mid seasons. Tel: (01271) 882476. Fax: (01271) 883053. E-mail: enquiries@stowford.co.uk. Reservations: Any length, deposit £2 per night, £12 per week, £20 per fortnight. Balance due 28 days before arrival. **Open** Easter - end October.

Directions: From Barnstaple take A39 towards Lynton. After 1 mile turn left on B3230. Turn right at garage on A3123 and park is 1½ miles on the right. O.S.GR: SS560427.

Lady's Mile is a popular, large family touring park that caters well for children. It has extensive grassy fields (with some trees for shade), in addition to the main, landscaped camping area which is arranged in broad terraces. There are 486 pitches, mostly marked by lines but with nothing between them, and 450 with electrical connections (10A). It is a 20 minute walk to a good sandy beach at Dawlish Warren but the park also has a good sized, free outdoor swimming pool with 200 ft. plus slide, a children's pool and a paved surround (May-Oct), plus a super heated indoor pool (20 x 10 m.) with 100 ft. flume and separate paddling pool (both with lifeguards). A large and attractive bar complex, with a family area overlooking the indoor pool, provides food and entertainment. Below is a spacious games room including pool tables and video games, and a new separate disco and bar. A sloping recreation field is ideal for kite flying and the large fenced children's adventure playground has a safe, sand surface. A nine hole golf course is on site (free but with small charge for hire of clubs) and a multi-sports pitch. In spite of its size, the park is popular over a long season, with reservation necessary.

Facilities: There are four toilet blocks of various ages and styles, but of a good standard, well spaced around the main areas of the park with an additional shower block. This should be an adequate provision overall. Facilities for disabled people and four family bathrooms (50p). Dishwashing sinks are under cover with free hot water. Two launderettes. Mini-market and fish and chip takeaway (both Easter - mid Sept). Bars. Indoor and outdoor pools. Adventure play area. Games room. Golf (9 hole). Tarmac area at reception for late arrivals. Winter caravan storage. **Off site**: Riding and bicycle hire 1 mile, fishing 3 miles.

Charges 2001

Per unit incl. 2 adults	£7.50 - £12.50
2-man tent (no car)	£6.00 - £10.00
awning or child's tent	£1.20 - £2.50
extra adult	£1.20 - £2.50
child (2-14 yrs)	£1.20 - £2.50
boat or extra car	£1.00 - £2.50
dog	£1.00 - £2.00
electricity	£2.00

Low season special offers. Low season discount for OAPs. Tel: (01626) 863411. Fax: (01626) 888689. E-mail: info@ladysmile.co.uk. Reservations: Made for Sat to Sat only in peak seasons, with £15 deposit. **Open** 13 March - 31 October.

Directions: Park is 1 mile north of Dawlish with access off the A379 (Exeter - Teignmouth) road. O.S.GR: SX969778.

Peppermint Park

Warren Road, Dawlish Warren, Dawlish, Devon EX7 0PQ

First impressions of this extensive family run park are perhaps somewhat formal. However, this is quickly dispelled by the friendly reception staff, abundent flowers and the way the pitches have been laid out on the slightly sloping ground. There are 250 pitches, ranging in size, each with electricity (10A), with at least another 60 hook-ups available for tent campers. Tarmac roads thread through the site giving easy access to all areas, each pitch being marked and numbered. Visitors to Peppermint Park can use the full facilities at the adjacent sister site (Golden Sands), which include a large indoor pool. Peppermint Park's own pool complex includes a water slide in the larger pool. Nightly entertainment is staged in the Peppermint Club in high season and at Golden Sands at other times. This site's 'jewel in the crown' is the walking distance (700 yds) to the large, safe beaches of Dawlish Warren and its associated pleasure complex - ideal for families. For others, there is the adjacent coastal footpath or the city of Exeter (7 miles) with its cathedral and historic Quay complex. A passenger ferry operates from Starcross (2 miles) across the estuary to Exmouth in high season.

Facilities: The two modern sanitary blocks are kept in spotless condition and can be heated. Two units (WC, washbasin and shower) are provided for disabled visitors. Fully equipped mother and baby room. Laundry (washing machines, dryers and free irons) and dishwashing. Shop with gas. Restaurant, bar and takeaway in high season (1/7-30/8). Entertainment. Swimming pool (26/5-30/8). Children's playground on a hill. Field for ball games. Small coarse fishing lake (£2.50 for adult day ticket). **Off site**: Dawlish Warren nature reserve is adjacent and includes an 18 hole links golf course.

Charges 2001

Per unit incl. 2 persons	£5.50 - £11.00
tent incl. 2 persons and car	£5.50 - £9.50
extra adult	£1.20 - £2.50
child (2-13 yrs)	£1.00 - £2.30
electricity	£2.00
dog	£1.00 - £2.30

Tel: (01626) 863436. Fax: (01626) 866482. E-mail: info@peppermintpark.co.uk. Reservations: Made with £15 deposit (Sat. - Sat. only 24 July - 28 Aug). **Open** 15 April - 28 October.

Directions: Leave M5 at junction 30 and take A379 Dawlish road. After passing through Starcross (7 miles) turn left to Dawlish Warren just before Dawlish. Continue for 1½ miles down hill and park is on left in 300 yds. O.S.GR: SX978788.

About 1½ miles from a sandy beach at Dawlish Warren this popular, family site takes over 400 touring units on a variety of fields and meadows with beautiful country views. Although not individually marked, there is never a feeling of overcrowding. The smaller, more mature fields, including a pleasant old orchard for tents only, are well terraced. While there are terraces on most of the slopes of the larger, more open fields, there are still some quite steep gradients to climb. There are some 300 electrical connections (10A). One area has 62 park-owned, holiday homes. A well designed, central complex overlooking the pool and decorated with flowers and hanging baskets, houses reception, a shop and off-licence and a bar lounge, the 'Cofton Swan', where bar meals are usually available (all Easter - 30 Sept). A family room and bar are on the first floor of this building and there is an outdoor terrace and some light entertainment in season. The adjacent supervised kidney-shaped heated pool with paddling pool and slide, has lots of grassy space for sunbathing. Coarse fishing is possible in three lakes on the park and there is a woodland trail towards Dawlish Warren.

Facilities: Toilet facilities comprise three blocks, one on each side of the road dividing the park for the touring pitches and the third near the holiday home area. The newest, at the top of the larger fields is first rate, with laundry and facilities for disabled visitors and babies. Hair dryers. Dishwashing facilities under cover. In addition four 'portacabin' style units with basic toilet facilities are provided for the peak season. Two launderettes. Gas available. Ice pack hire service. Bar lounge. Shop. Fish and chip shop - breakfast possible. Swimming pool (overall length 100 ft. open Spr. B.H - mid Sept). Games room (busy in high season). Adventure playground in the woods overlooking the pools and two other well equipped play areas. Coarse fishing (from £16.50 per rod for 7 days, discount for senior citizens outside July). Winter caravan storage. **Off site:** Golf 3 miles. Beach 1½ miles.

Charges 2001

Per unit incl. 2 persons	£6.50 - £11.50
extra adult	£1.30 - £2.60
child (2-13 yrs)	£1.10 - £2.40
awning or child's tent	£1.30 - £2.60
boat, dog or extra car	£1.10 - £2.40
electricity	£2.00

Small low season discount for Senior Citizens. Tel: (01626) 890111. Fax: (01626) 891572. E-mail: info@coftonholidays.co.uk. Reservations: Made for min. 3 nights, 4 nights in peak season with £20 deposit. **Open** Easter - 27 October.

Directions: Access to the park is off the A379 road 3 miles north of Dawlish, just after Cockwood harbour village. O.S.GR: SX965797.

This is the heart of Cofton Country in South Devon

A family-owned Park in beautiful landscaped surroundings offering some of the best facilities for caravanners and campers in the area. There are also cottages, luxury apartments and holiday homes (new 2002 models) available.

Heated Swimming Pools • 'Swan' Pub and family lounges • Large well-stocked Mini-Market and off-licence • Coarse Fishing Lakes. • Woodland Walks • THREE Children's play areas • Take Away foods • Games Room with pool table & amusements • Facilities for disabled • Electric hook-ups* • Toilet blocks with showers, wash hand basins and hairdryers • Free hot water • Caravan Storage • Senior Citizens' discount in Low and Mid season

***FREE ELECTRIC HOOK-UPS**
LOW & MID SEASON
Advance bookings only, Minimum 3 Nights Stay

Cofton Country
HOLIDAYS

COFTON COUNTRY HOLIDAYS, STARCROSS, NR. DAWLISH, SOUTH DEVON EX6 8RP.
Tel: 01626 890111 Fax: 01626 891572.
email: info@coftonholidays.co.uk
www.coftonholidays.co.uk

AA
DE LUXE PARK   LISTED

TOURING CARAVANS • CAMPING • HOLIDAY HOMES
COTTAGES • LUXURY APARTMENTS

Devon

Coast View Holiday Park

Torquay Road, Shaldon, Teignmouth, Devon TQ14 0BG

108

On the coast road between Teignmouth and Torquay with magnificent views over Lyme Bay, this family run park has a section of caravan holiday homes and chalets. However, the touring area of 100 pitches is quite separate. On terraced grass, some pitches are part sloping. There are 28 electricity connections (16A). At present, due to recent reconstruction of the park, there is little or no shelter but as the site is terraced into the hillside, there is adequate protection from the prevailing southwest winds. To the right of the park entrance is an attractive indoor swimming pool. and an entertainment area comprising a clubroom with bar (bar meals and snacks), takeaway, TV room and games room. All these facilities are open all season. Entertainment is organised each night and also activities in the mornings for children. Good for holidaymakers of all ages, this park offers superb views with excellent facilities.

Facilities: The new toilet block is spacious with free hot showers and open washbasins, and includes a baby room. Separate dishwashing and laundry facilities. Licensed shop for basic provisions. Indoor pool and children's pool. Clubroom with bar, takeaway and games room (arcade games, table tennis and pool). Adventure playground and indoor soft play area. Crazy golf. **Off site:** Fishing or golf 1 mile, riding 3 miles. The park is convenient for the beach (1½ miles) and the coastal footpath is adjacent. Torbay is 5 miles. A bus service stops at the gates.

Charges 2001

Per caravan incl. up to 8 persons	£7.00 - £16.00
motorcaravan or tent (up to 8 persons)	£7.00 - £14.00
tent incl. 2 persons	£6.00 - £8.00
electricity	£1.75
dog	free - £3.00

Tel: (01626) 872392. Fax: (01626) 872719. Reservations: Contact park. **Open** 22 March - 27 October.

Directions: From A380 Exeter - Newton Abbot road, take A381 to Teignmouth. On entering town turn right over Shaldon Bridge on B3199 for Torquay. Park is on right in approx. 1½ miles. O.S.GR: SX932714.

Devon

Webbers Farm Caravan and Camping Park

Castle Lane, Woodbury, nr Exmouth, Devon EX5 1EA

110

Over the past twenty years this park has been gradually enlarged from an initial open field site to one that can boast modern facilities, yet retain its essentially rural character. The 115 marked, grass pitches are large, with the majority level and a few gently sloping. There are 100 electricity connections (10/16A). Although essentially a farm site, there is no problem with animal noise – this is a sheep farm and children are encouraged to participate in a hands-on experience and there is a paddock with a donkey and Shetland pony. A short drive takes you to the two miles of glorious sand at Exmouth, with Woodbury Common (excellent heathland walks) just over a mile away. This is a mature, friendly and modern park in a lovely situation. A member of the Countryside Discovery group.

Facilities: There are three modern sanitary blocks, the newest (built in '99) with full bathroom facilities (£1). Baby room and two units for disabled visitors (WC, shower and washbasin). A new block planned for 2002 will include family rooms. Dishwashing and laundry facilities. Unusual in terms of number, are seven chemical disposal points, located at each water point (and adequately separated). Small shop (limited cold food only). Gas supplies. Children's play area. Games field. All year caravan storage. **Off site:** Woodbury village within walking distance with excellent pub/restaurant, post office, etc. Exeter 6 miles. Fishing or golf 2 miles; riding 5 miles; bicycle hire or boat launching 10 miles.

Charges 2001

Per pitch incl. 2 persons	£7.50 - £11.00
extra person (over 5 yrs)	£2.00
awning or extra tent	£1.50
electricity	£2.00

Tel: (01395) 232276. Fax: (01395) 233389. E-mail: reception@webbersfarm.co.uk. Reservations: Essential for peak periods and made with £20 deposit. **Open** Easter - 29 September.

Directions: Leave M5 at junction 30 and follow A376 Exmouth road. At second roundabout take B3179 (Budleigh Salterton and Woodbury). In village centre follow brown signs to park on right. O.S.GR: SY017874.

East Devon and West Dorset Heritage Coast

The Dorset and East Devon Coast has been proposed as a World Heritage Site - 'a natural or cultural feature or area which has such universal value that it is regarded as the heritage of all mankind' (UNESCO). The coastline has been nominated due to its outstanding geology. The coast contains a fascinating glimpse into the Earth's ancient past, with a complete record through almost 200 million years of earth history during the Triassic, Jurassic and Cretaceous periods of geological time. Also contained within this coast are a number of important fossil localiites and features such as landslides. The final decision will be taken by UNESCO's World Heritage Committee in December 2001.

Forest Glade International Caravan and Camping Park

Cullompton, Devon EX15 2DT

100

Set in the Blackdown Hills (designated an area of outstanding natural beauty), Forest Glade is owned and run by the Wellard family, deep in mid-Devon away from the hectic life on the coast. A sheltered site set amongst woodland with extensive walking without using your car, there are 80 touring pitches, 70 of which have 16A electricity connections and 24 hardstanding. The pitches are all level, mostly backing onto the forest, and there is also a rally field. There is a small heated, covered pool with a paddling pool and a patio area outside. The surrounding forest makes this a dog lover's paradise (dogs are accepted). Touring caravans must book in advance and the easiest route for them will be explained then (phone bookings accepted). Although set in the country, the beaches of East Devon are a fairly easy drive away. A member of the Best of British group.

Facilities: There is one main toilet block, heated in cold weather, with some washbasins in cubicles, and washing up sinks. Separate room with WC, low level washbasin and shower for disabled visitors. Laundry with washing machines and dryers, ironing facilities and a stool to sit on. Extra facilities of 'portacabin' style with toilets, washbasins and showers are at the swimming pool, but these are only available when the pool is open (Easter, then early May - late Sept, plus Oct half term). Motorcaravan service facilities. The shop (all season) is quite well stocked including gas and locally made bread and pastries with a takeaway (open evenings except Sunday). Adventure playground. Games room with table tennis, video games and two pool tables. All weather tennis court. Sauna. Caravan storage. **Off site:** Fishing or riding 1½ miles, golf 6 miles, bicycle hire 5 miles.

Charges 2001

Per unit incl. 2 adults	£6.25 - £11.75
child (5-9 yrs)	£1.00
student (10 yrs - end of study)	£2.00
awning	free
backpacker or cyclist per person	£2.50
dog	50p
electricity	£1.90

Tel: (01404) 841381. Fax: (01404) 841593. E-mail: forestglade@cwcom.net. Reservations: Any length with deposit of £4 p/day or £20 p/wk, (£15 for B.H. w/ends). Essential for B.Hs and school holidays. **Open** 23 March - 28 October.

Directions: Park is 5½ miles from M5 exit 28. Take A373 for 3 miles, turning left at camp sign towards Sheldon. Park is on left after approx. 2½ miles. This access is not suitable for touring caravans owing to a steep hill - phone the park for alternative route details. O.S.GR: ST101073.

MEMBERS WELCOME

Ideal for site seeing.

The Camping and Caravanning Club

Horsley Club Site

FOR YOUR FREE GUIDE TO THE GREAT SITES OF BRITAIN CALL

024 7685 6797

PLEASE QUOTE REF 9638

Experience our Great Sites of Britain

For a fantastic camping or caravanning holiday, why not head for one of our superb sites.

We have over 90 sites covering the length and breadth of the Country in locations that will take your breath away.

Nearly all of our sites are open to non-members and all visitors will receive discount vouchers for local attractions plus with our Camping Miles Passport scheme the more you camp the greater the rewards with free camping nights and prizes to be won.

The Regional Tourist Boards have given our sites excellent gradings so you are guaranteed of quality as well as great value for money.

You can also join our Club and visit our sites for less. Club membership is **only £27.50*** and can be recouped in just 8 nights camping.

SEND FOR YOUR FREE SITES GUIDE TODAY

*plus £4 joining fee waived if paid by direct debit or continuous credit or debit card agreement.

CHOOSE FROM OVER 90 SITES IN THE UK.

FOR FURTHER INFORMATION VISIT OUR WEBSITE:
www.campingandcaravanningclub.co.uk

Oakdown Touring and Holiday Home Park

Weston, Sidmouth, Devon EX10 0PH

Oakdown is an award winning, exceptionally well kept and environmentally conscious park. It is always neat and tidy and we continue to note developments there, under the special care, guidance and attention of Mr and Mrs Franks and their son Alastair, the manager. They now provide one of the most comfortable, well equipped and attractively laid out family parks we know, complete with welcoming staff who help pitch your unit (and live on site). The park has a spacious, uncrowded feel with large pitches semi-screened in small bays or groves and edged with trees. There is a marvellous range of trees (all 70 types are named) providing variety, privacy and home for wildlife. A circular concrete road links the 120 pitches, all of which have electricity (16A), 29 with water, waste water and drainage and 89 with hard-standing. Tourist information is provided on a wall board of the toilet block, together with the history of the park. This is interesting as it was within the boundaries of a secret wartime radar station which accounts for the very solid construction of the block. An interesting footpath edged with wild flowers leads through the fields to the nearby Donkey Sanctuary and one can walk further to the beach and sea (2 miles, steep in parts). There are, in fact, over 113 varieties of wild flower (some named) to be seen and 45 varieties of wild bird. A family of Lesser Spotted wood-peckers have caused interest, skylarks and goldfinches are regular visitors and buzzards wheel overhead. Badgers and foxes visit (after 10.30 pm) and trees and bushes have been planted to encourage butterflies and more birds. It is the care of and attention to all things natural that makes this park rather special. The 'reed bed' development is progressing well, together with a bird-hide and wildlife pond. A member of the Best of British group.

Facilities: The central toilet block with piped music provides good, fully equipped, heated sanitary facilities, all well maintained. One private cabin for ladies. Two unisex family bathrooms (with bath, shower, toilet, washbasin and coin operated entry) also double as useful units for disabled people. Dishwashing sinks. Laundry facilities plus free use of a freezer and a microwave. Motorcaravan service point. Recycling point (glass, paper, cans). Fax service. TV room. Well equipped, grass based children's play area with adventure style equipment and play castle. No cycling, skate-boarding or kite flying is permitted. Certain breeds of dog are not accepted. Site has closed circuit TV. Secure, alarmed caravan storage. **Off site:** Adjoining the touring park is Oak Grove, with 46 holiday homes, some for hire (under the same ownership). Riding 6 miles, golf 2 miles.

Charges 2001

Per standard pitch incl. 2 persons	£7.75 - £11.70
super pitch (water, drainage)	£11.50 - £15.60
extra person (5 yrs and over)	£1.75
dog	£1.00
awning	£1.70
porch awning or child's pup tent	£1.00
electricity	£2.20

Less 70p for senior citizens in low season. Tel: (01297) 680387. Fax: (01297) 680541. E-mail: oakdown@btinternet.com. Reservations: Made with £20 p/w deposit, min. 3 days at B.Hs. and 3/4 Aug. (Sidmouth Folk Festival). **Open** 22 March - 3 November.

Directions: Turn south off the A3052 (Exeter - Lyme Regis) road between Sidford and Colyford, 2½ miles east of the A375 junction and park is on left. O.S.GR: SY167902.

Somerset

Quantock Orchard Caravan Park

Flaxpool, Crowcombe, Taunton, Somerset TA4 4AW

The old adage 'small is beautiful' certainly fits Quantock Orchard, nestling at the foot of the Quantocks in quiet countryside, yet close to many of the attractions of the area. Crowcombe Station on the West Somerset Steam Railway is only a short walk. The park has been most attractively developed by the owners, Mr and Mrs Biggs and is well cared for. Mature apple trees, recently planted trees, shrubs and pretty flower beds with a nice use of heathers, make a very pleasant environment and the clock tower on the sanitary block adds interest. With access from gravel roads, there are 55 touring pitches, part separated by growing shrubs and hedging, and 20 for tents. Of various sizes, 52 have 10A electrical hook ups, 20 with hardstanding, 4 have TV hook-up and 2 are fully serviced (one large with patio and TV). A leisure suite provides a sauna, steam room, jacuzzi, spa, mini-gym and conservatory rest area. It is complemented by the outdoor heated swimming pool, which is walled with paved sunbathing surrounds. Four purpose built barbecues and picnic tables are set in the central grass area and rarer breeds of duck waddle around the park.

Facilities: The central, heated sanitary block has some nice touches and is very well maintained. Some washbasins in cubicles for ladies, excellent family bathroom (recently refurbished) and separate mother and baby room. Good dishwashing provision, microwave, and laundry facilities. Motorcaravan service point. Well stocked licensed shop includes caravan and camping accessories. Mountain bikes for hire (some with buggies for children). Fish and chip van visits (twice weekly in summer). Swimming pool (40 x 20 ft. and open May - Sept). Leisure suite (open to the public; visitor membership optional with a range of tariffs to suit all; children must be accompanied). Games room, Sky TV. Fenced safe-based children's play area. Only 'air-flo' style groundsheets are permitted on grass pitches. Caravan storage Oct. - March. **Off site:** The Carew Arms serving meals is within walking distance in the mellow village of Crowcombe. The Brendon and Exmoor hills, Minehead, Dunster Castle and Taunton are within 10-15 miles.

Charges 2001

Per unit incl. 2 adults	£7.50 - £11.50
extra adult	£3.00
child 3-4 yrs	95p
child 5-15 yrs	£1.95
child's pup tent with caravan	£1.20
electricity	£2.00 - £2.20
backpacker or cyclist per person	£3.75 - £4.95

Winter weekend special rates. Tel/Fax: (01984) 618618. E-mail: qocp@flaxpool.freeserve.co.uk. Reservations: Made with £10 per week deposit, per booking (non-returnable). **Open** all year.

Directions: Park is west off A358 road (Taunton - Minehead), about 1 mile south of Crowcombe village. O.S.GR: ST140363.

Hoburne Blue Anchor Park

138 Blue Anchor Bay, nr Minehead, Somerset TA24 6JT

Although mainly a holiday park, with 300 caravan holiday homes, Blue Anchor nevertheless offers good facilities for 103 touring units. Trailer tents are accepted but not other tents (other than pup tents with a touring booking). Virtually in a separate touring area, the level pitches all have hardstanding and 16A electricity. A feature of the park is a good sized, irregularly shaped indoor swimming pool with an area for small children, complete with a mushroom shaped fountain. With views of the sea from the pool, it is heated and supervised. Although not actually within the park itself, there are both restaurants and takeaway food facilities within easy walking distance. The park's situation, directly across the small road from the beach, is unusual and gives some beautiful views across the Bristol Channel to South Wales. Dunster Castle, Exmoor, the Quantocks and Minehead are close and the West Somerset Steam Railway runs along one side of the park. Part of the Hoburne Group.

Facilities: Toilet facilities provide large, free hot showers (with push-button), dishwashing and laundry sinks under cover, and a fully equipped launderette in a single, modern block serving just the touring area. Excellent, attractive children's play area in the copse. Crazy golf. Small supermarket/shop with coffee shop (open 8 am - 9 pm in high season, less at other times). American motorhomes are accepted (max. 36 ft). Dogs are not accepted. **Off site**: Riding 5 miles, golf 4½ miles.

Charges guide

Per unit, incl. up to 6 persons electricity and awning incl.	£6.50 - £16.00
extra pup tent	£3.00

Weekend breaks available. Tel: (01643) 821360. Fax: (01643) 821572. E-mail: enquiries@hoburne.co.uk. Reservations: For stays of 1-6 days, payment required in full at time of booking; for 7 nights or more £50 deposit. Min. bookings at B.Hs. **Open** 1 March - 31 October.

Directions: From M5 junction 25, take A358 signed Minehead. After approx. 12 miles turn left onto A39 at Williton. After 4 miles turn right onto B3191 at Carhampton signed Blue Anchor. Park is 1½ miles on right. O.S.GR: ST025434.

Halse Farm Touring Caravan and Camping Park

136 Winsford, Minehead, Somerset TA24 7JL

A truly rural park with beautiful, moorland views, you may be lucky here and glimpse red deer across the valley or be able to see Exmoor ponies and foals graze outside the main gate on one of the highest points on Exmoor. Two open, neatly cut fields that are level at the top, back onto traditional hedging and slope gently to the middle and bottom where wild flowers predominate. One field provides electricity points (10A) and is used for motorcaravans and caravans, the other is for tents. There is no reception - you leave your unit by the toilet block and walk down to the farm kitchen to book in. The pretty village of Winsford is 1 mile (footpath from farm) with a post office, shop, pub and restaurant. Mrs Brown has encapsulated maps available (at a small cost) detailing six walks of varying distances, starting and finishing at the farm. Also available is a list of the wild birds, flowers, etc. to be found on the site. A member of the Countryside Discovery group.

Facilities: The central toilet block is of good quality and heated. Well equipped and maintained, it includes a toilet, washbasin and shower for visitors with disabilities, washing machine, dryer and iron, and tourist information. Gas is available at the farm. Play equipment. **Off site**: Fishing 4 miles, bicycle hire 5 miles, riding 2 miles. Tarr Steps and Barle Valley 3 miles. Winsford Village 1 mile.

Charges 2002

Per unit incl. 2 adults	£6.00 - £8.00
1 person tent and car	£3.00 - £4.00
extra adult	£2.00 - £3.00
child 0-5 yrs	50p
5-16 yrs	£1.00 - £1.50
awning	£1.00
electricity	£1.70 - £1.85

Less 10% for 7 days paid in advance 10 days before arrival. No credit cards. Tel: (01643) 851259. Fax: (01643) 851592. E-mail: ar@halsefarm.co.uk. Reservations: Advised for July/Aug. and made with £10 deposit. **Open** 25 March - 29 October.

Directions: Turn off A396 Tiverton - Minehead road for Winsford (site signed). In Winsford village turn left in front of the Royal Oak (not over ford) and keep on uphill for 1 mile (go slowly round the sharp bend at the bottom). Cross cattle grid onto moor and turn immediately left to farm. Caravans should avoid Dulverton - keep to the A396 from Bridgetown (signed). O.S.GR: SS898342.

Burrowhayes Farm Caravan and Camping Site

West Luccombe, Porlock, Minehead, Somerset TA24 8HT

137

This delightful park with riding stables on site, is on the edge of Exmoor. The stone packhorse bridge over Horner Water beside the farm entrance sets the tone of the park, which the Dascombe family have created over the last thirty years having previously farmed the land. The farm buildings have been converted into riding stables with escorted rides available (from 7/4). Mature trees, neat grass, partly sloping with marvellous views, or level nearer the clear, bubbling river, allows for 20 caravan holiday homes in their own area, 66 tents and 54 touring caravans or motorhomes. Electrical hook-ups are available (10A). With walking, birdwatching, plenty of wild life to observe, pretty Exmoor villages and Lorna Doone country nearby there is much to do. Children can ride, play in the stream or explore the woods at the top of the site. Limited trout fishing is available in Horner Water (NT permit) alongside the park.

Facilities: The toilet facilities, in the reception and stable block area, are well maintained and equipped with a laundry room, baby changing unit, and indoor washing up. Well stocked shop doubles with reception (from 22/3; 08.30-18.00 in the main season). **Off site**: Minehead 5 miles. Local pub 20 minutes walk. Bicycle hire or golf 5 miles.

Charges 2001

Per unit incl. 1 or 2 persons	£6.00 - £8.00
extra person	£2.50 - £3.00
child (3-15 yrs)	£1.00 - £1.50
1-man tent	£4.00 - £5.00
awning	£1.00
porch awning or pup tent	75p
electricity	£2.00

Tel: (01643) 862463. E-mail: info@burrowhayes.co.uk. Reservations: Made with £10 deposit per pitch. **Open** 15 March - 31 October.

Directions: From A39, 5 miles west of Minehead, take first left past Allerford to Horner and West Luccombe. Site is on right after ¼ mile. O.S.GR: SS897460.

Waterrow Touring Park

Wiveliscombe, Taunton, Somerset TA4 2AZ

152

Beside the River Tone in a pretty part of South Somerset, Tony and Anne Taylor have enthusiastically developed Waterrow into a charming, landscaped touring park for adults only. Nestling in a little sheltered valley, it is very peaceful and convenient for an overnight stop (just over 30 minutes from M5 jct 25) or as a base for exploring nearby Exmoor and the Brendon Hills. There are 45 touring pitches, 22 of which are on level hardstanding (2 doubles in the centre with flower beds around). The remainder are on flat or gently sloping grass with little shade as yet but with bushes and trees planned. Most have electrical connections (16A), spring and mains water are available and TV aerial points have been installed. Converted barns have been put to good use, providing local tourist information, a small library, nature and conservation notes and diary and a visual record of the park's development. Further down the park, below the touring area, wide steps lead to a private nature reserve where you can find the recently constructed Otter Holt, go fly fishing for wild brown trout, take a riverside walk or just relax and watch the birds. This adults only site is open all year.

Facilities: Well fitted out and clean 'portacabin' style sanitary units, one each for men and ladies, can be heated. Showers are fairly small. Dishwashing and laundry facilities are behind. Basic grocery provisions are available in reception and you may order jacket potatoes before lunchtime for the evening for just 60p. The Taylors will 'dog sit' for you if you are visiting somewhere your pet is not allowed. Caravan storage with 'store and stay' system. **Off site**: Bicycle hire 10 miles. Coarse fishing 5 miles. The Rock Inn is a short walk and provides good value meals and real ales. Wiveliscombe and its shops just three miles away.

Charges 2001

Per unit incl. 2 persons	£8.00 - £9.00
(adults only 18 years and over)	
extra adult	£2.00
electricity	£2.00 - £2.50
TV connection	£1.00
awning	£1.00
dog	50p

Rallies by arrangement. Tel: (01984) 623464. Fax: (01984) 624280. E-mail: taylor@waterrowpark.u-net.com. Reservations: Advised for B.Hs and high season and made with £10 deposit. **Open** all year.

Directions: From M5 exit 25 take A358 (signed Minehead) round Taunton for 4 miles, then at Staplegrove onto the B3227 for 11.5 miles to Wiveliscombe where straight over at lights towards Waterrow (still on B3227). Park is on left shortly after the Rock Inn. O.S.GR: ST053251.

Home Farm Holiday Park and Country Club

148 Edithmead, Burnham-on-Sea, Somerset TA9 4HD

Home Farm is impressive - neatly and attractively laid out covering 44 acres, well organised and professionally run. Over 600 level pitches (including privately owned holiday homes) are regularly laid out on level mown grass. They are all clearly marked, accessed by tarmac roadways and divided into various sections, for example an area for those with pets or a tenting area. Including 183 pitches with hardstanding, there are 20 serviced pitches for motorcaravans with water and grey water drainage. Electrical connections (16A) are available everywhere (fewer in the tenting area) with plenty of water points in all the sections, but one central refuse area. A large, modern pool with paved surrounds and a paddling section is neatly walled and overlooked by a pool-side terraced cafe and takeaway. A sun-bed is also provided. The club house (with free membership) is a feature of the site providing carvery meals, a range of entertainment, a function room, wide screen TV, an attractive conservatory and outside barbecue area. In all, it is an excellent provision and Burnham-on-Sea is only a mile away - there is a footpath from the site crossing the railway line. With Berrow Sands and Brean Down there is over seven miles of beach to choose from!

Facilities: Toilet blocks, five in total, are good, heated and well situated for all parts of the park. Hot showers in the newest block are family size minus dividers, there are also some bathrooms (key with £5 deposit). Baby changing room. Dishwashing facilities under cover and a very well equipped laundry room. Facilities for disabled visitors. Dog shower! Shop with general groceries, camping accessories and camping gaz. Bar. Restaurants, takeaway (open B.Hs., weekends and high season). Swimming pool. Well equipped children's play area and children's club for 4-10 year olds runs in the school holidays. Amusement machines and pool tables. Fishing and boating lakes (paddle and bumper boats to hire). BMX and go-karting tracks. Five-a-side football pitch. Reception holds a good supply of tourist information.

Charges guide

Per pitch incl. 2 persons electricity and awning incl.	£7.50 - £16.50
extra person over 10 yrs	£2.50 - £4.50
child 4-9 yrs	£1.50 - £3.00
extra car or small tent	£2.50 - £4.00
dog	£1.00 - £2.00
hardstanding	£2.00 - £3.00

Club membership free. Security barrier card £2 (£1 refundable). Special breaks available. Tel: (01278) 788888. Fax: (01278) 780113. E-mail: homefarmholidaypark@compuserve.com. Reservations: Contact park for details. **Open** all year.

Directions: Home Farm is / mile from M5 junction 22 and the A38. It is signed from the B3140 into Burnham-on-Sea. O.S.GR: ST327493.

Slimeridge Farm Touring Park

153 Links Road, Uphill, Weston-super-Mare, BS23 4XY

This attractive small touring site is next to the beach in Uphill village at the southern end of Weston Bay. There are 50 pitches (a few taken on seasonal lets), on level grass with electricity (10A) available, separated from the beach by stone walling. The view across the bay is quite something, with Brean Down and Steep Holm Island standing out. However it is worth noting that, because of its situation close to the beach, the site could be affected by the tide in extreme adverse winter weather conditions. You book in at the warden's caravan and a circular tarmac road connects the marked and numbered pitches which are allocated by the wardens. There are five hardstandings for motorhomes. Weston-super-Mare with all its leisure activities and entertainment is 2 miles. The park is under the same ownership as no. 148, Home Farm Holiday Park, a much larger site at Burnham-on-Sea with a wide range of facilities and entertainment. Slimeridge guests are entitled to free membership of Home Farm Country Club and free use of its pool.

Facilities: A modern toilet block with electronic code entry system is well equipped and includes en-suite shower facilities that are also provided for handicapped visitors. Laundry room and washing up sinks. Chemical disposal unit also used for waste water. **Off site**: Post office, general stores and pubs within close walking distance. Golf (note: golfers have right of way to cross the park as the golf course is split by the site). Cheddar Gorge, Wooky Hole and Glastonbury are within easy driving distance.

Charges 2002

Per unit incl. 2 adults electricity and awning incl.	£5.50 - £13.50
extra adult	£1.50 - £3.50
child (4-9 yrs)	£1.00 - £2.00
extra car or small tent	£2.00
dog	50p - £1.50

Min. stay 2 nights at B.Hs. No credit cards. Tel/Fax: (01934) 641641. E-mail: homefarmholidaypark@ compuserve.com. Reservations: Made with deposit of £5 p/night; no refunds given. **Open** 1 March - 30 October

Directions: Site is south of Weston-super-Mare. From A370 follow sign for Uphill village and beach. O.S.GR: ST312585.

Somerset
Greenacres Camping
Barrow Lane, North Wootton, nr Shepton Mallet, Somerset BA4 4HL

Greenacres is a rural site in Somerset countryside for tents, trailer tents and motorcaravans only. Hidden away below the Mendips and almost at the start of the 'Levels', it is a simple green site – a true haven of peace and quiet. The grass is neatly trimmed over the 4.5 acres and hedged with mature trees, though there is a view of Glastonbury Tor in one direction and of Barrow Hill in the other. All of the 39 pitches are around the perimeter of the park, leaving a central area safe for children to play. At the narrower neck end, 5 pitches have electricity hook-ups (16A) and are ideal for those without children or birdwatchers. Wild life abounds. A speciality is the 'Turf Rider' that tows the cart used to give children an evening ride. There are many nearby attractions should you tire of the peace and quiet, such as Wookey Hole, Cheddar Caves and Gorge, Longleat, the beautiful small city of Wells, Clarks Village, etc. You can cycle into Wells or Glastonbury using Sustran Route 3.

Facilities: The central wooden toilet block is simple but perfectly acceptable and kept clean. Hot showers are accessed directly from the outside. Two dishwashing sinks, two laundry sinks (H&C) and a spin dryer, with an iron, board and hairdryer available from the park office. A selection of play equipment, a badminton net and a caravan to use as a play house. The park office is across the lane (gate is usually keep shut), at the owner's bungalow. Here too are fridges and freezers for campers' use (free), a library, tourist information and bicycle hire. Batteries may be charged or borrowed. Dogs are not accepted. **Off site**: In North Wootton itself, ¾mile walk, is a large pub/restaurant and a vineyard. Leisure centre in Wells. Fishing and riding nearby.

Charges 2002

Per adult	£5.00
child (4-16 yrs)	£2.00

No credit cards. Tel/Fax: (01749) 890497. E-mail: harvie.greenacres@talk21.com. Reservations: Made with £2 deposit. **Open** March - October incl. plus Carnival Fortnight in Nov.

Directions: From A39 Glastonbury - Wells road turn east at Brownes Garden Centre and follow camping signs. From A361 Glastonbury - Shepton Mallet road follow camp signs from Pilton or Steanbow. O.S.GR: ST553416.

Somerset
Batcombe Vale Caravan and Camping Park
Batcombe Vale, Shepton Mallet, Somerset BA4 6BW

Set in a secluded valley with fields gently rising around it, contented black and white cows grazing with watchful buzzards cruising the thermals above and views across the distant hills, this is just a very special place. Home to Donald and Mary Sage, Batcombe Vale House is a mellow, attractive building covered with wisteria, to one side of the valley overlooking the lakes and the 'wild' landscape. Different trees and shrubs have been skilfully placed to enhance the natural environment providing a range of colour and shape. It is actually designated an 'area of outstanding natural beauty' and there are 120 acres around the valley where you may wander and picnic in the fields - a haven for wild flowers, birds and butterflies. For those who fish, two lakes have carp and tench. As you descend slowly down the narrow entrance drive you see the 30 pitches, attractively set and terraced where necessary, in an oval with the lakes, one after another, below. The grass is neatly cut, the pitches are level, marked and numbered and 16 have 16A electricity. The grass is left natural around the pitches and paths mown where needed. There is a range of circular walks or you can potter about in a small rowing boat (free gentle exercise provided care is taken). A marvellous site, it is a privilege to be able to share and enjoy it with the Sage family.

Facilities: The small rustic toilet block covered in honeysuckle meets all needs, including a freezer and dishwashing sinks. Groundsheet awnings must be lifted daily. Fishing (current licence required). Caravan storage. One dog per pitch is welcome (no dangerous breeds). **Off site**: Bruton (for shops, etc.) is 2 miles. Launderettes at Shepton or Frome. There are many places to visit nearby, from Glastonbury with the Tor, to Cheddar Gorge and the Caves.

Charges 2002

Per unit incl. 2 adults	£10.00
extra adult	£3.50
child 8-18 yrs	£2.50
child 4-8 yrs	£1.00
full awning	£1.00
electricity	£1.50
dog	£1.00

Coarse fishing (up to 20 lbs) adults £3 p/day (child £1.50) or £2 p/day times length of stay. No commercial vehicles or motorcycle 'packs' - family groups only. Tel: (01749) 830246. E-mail: DonaldSage@compuserve.com. Reservations: Only essential for B.Hs and school holidays; made with £5 deposit and £1 fee (min. 2 nights). **Open** Easter - September.

Directions: Bruton is south of Shepton Mallet and Frome but north of Wincanton where the A359 intersects the B3081. Site is 2 miles north of Bruton and signed in the town. The road is narrow in places but an easier way for caravans is clearly signed. O.S.GR: ST681379.

The Old Oaks Touring Park

139 Wick Farm, Wick, Glastonbury, Somerset BA6 8JS

The Old Oaks, an adults only park from 2002, is tucked below and hidden from the 'Tor' in a lovely secluded setting with views across to the Mendips. Developed over the last ten years on a working farm, there are 40 extra large pitches in a series of paddocks, most with 10A electricity, 18 with hardstanding and 4 fully serviced (including sewage). Mainly backing on to hedges, they are attractively arranged and interspersed with shrubs and flowers in a circular development or terraced with increasing views. A quiet orchard area or a separated hedged paddock for camping and a larger field with chemical disposal facilities complete the provision. Mature trees and hedges combine with the mellow farm buildings to give a sense of timelessness, tranquillity and peace. An interesting development features reed beds to deal with waste water, a traditional method, which is now coming into its own again. The reception/ shop is modern, yet in keeping. Whether you fish or not, the pond which is well stocked with carp, roach and tench is worth a visit not only for its view of the Tor, but also to see the ducks and the chickens on your way. There is parking for disabled visitors within 25 yards of the pond. In an area steeped in history and legend, this very well equipped and maintained park should meet the needs of the discerning camper or caravanner. A member of the Best of British group.

Facilities: The heated toilet block, converted from the old stables, is of excellent quality and well equipped. Neatly paved outside, it has digital security locks (a public footpath from the Tor passes through the farm). Some washbasins are in cubicles. Two en-suite rooms (shower, toilet and basin) and a bathroom (£1). Disabled visitors have two rooms, one with a toilet and basin, the other with a shower, toilet and basin, both with level access. Fully equipped laundry room. Dishwashing under cover. Motorcaravan service facilities. Two recycling points. Freezer for ice packs (free). Useful dog wash. Shop for basics and locally baked bread in the main season and an off licence (limited hours). Bicycle hire (together with helmets and panniers). Fishing (£3 per half day, £5 per day). Adults only accepted (18 yrs and over). **Off site:** Riding 5 miles and golf 6 miles. Market day is Tuesday.

Charges 2002

Per pitch	£3.00 - £4.00
adult	£2.50 - £3.50
awning with breathing groundsheet	75p - £1.00
dog	50p - 75p
electricity (10A)	£1.75
'all service' pitch	£1.00 - £1.50
(free to disabled badge holders).	

Tel: (01458) 831437. Fax: (01458) 833238. E-mail: info@theoldoaks.co.uk. Reservations: Advised for high season and made with £15 deposit. **Open** 1 March - 31 October.

Directions: Park is north off A361 Shepton Mallet - Glastonbury road, 2 miles from Glastonbury. Take unclassified road signed Wick for approx. 1 mile and the park is on the left. O.S.GR: ST521394.

The Isle of Avalon Touring Caravan Park

140 Godney Road, Glastonbury, Somerset BA6 9AF

This pleasant, modern park, owned by Mike and Sharon Webb, has a friendly atmosphere and is only a short walk from the centre of Glastonbury. Developed on flat, grassy ground, the park has been landscaped, part with trees and shrubs, part open, to provide 70 individual pitches. Well spaced and connected by hard roads, they have hardstanding with adjacent grass for awning and electrical points (5/10A). A further 50 tent spaces are on the adjoining, level field. Water and refuse points are well distributed and attractively surrounded by trees and shrubs. All visitors are personally seen to their pitches. A well stocked shop with some camping accessories and reception with gas and tourist information is at the entrance with a cared for, attractive and spacious feel. The top corner of the tenting field is left clear as a play area. Nearby Street, famous for its shoes, now boasts 'Clarks Village', a range of factory outlets including shoes!

Facilities: The single, excellent, tiled toilet block is comfortable and spacious, and can be heated. Some washbasins in cubicles for women and excellent units for disabled visitors (plus ramps to the shop and reception). Large laundry room and dishwashing area. Motorcaravan disposal point. Shop. Bicycle hire. Dogs are accepted but by prior arrangement only on tent pitches. American motorhomes are welcome. Winter caravan storage. **Off site:** Glastonbury centre, with shops, restaurants and cafés, and the Abbey 10 minutes walk. Indoor and outdoor swimming pools at Street. Riding or golf 2 miles, fishing 200 yds.

Charges 2001

Per unit	£5.00 - £6.00
American style motorhomes	+£1.00
adult	£2.00
child (3-14 yrs)	£1.50
awning	£1.50
pup tent	£1.75
electricity	£2.00
dog	£1.00

No credit cards. Tel/Fax: (01458) 833618. Reservations: Any length with £10 deposit. **Open** all year.

Directions: Park is on west side of the town bypass (A39), just off B3151 (Wedmore Road) with good signs from the bypass. O.S.GR: ST495397.

Long Hazel International Caravan and Camping Park

150 Sparkford, Yeovil, Somerset BA22 7JH

Pamela and Alan Walton, who live at this neat, small site, are really enthusiastic about their park in the Somerset village of Sparkford and will make you most welcome. With neat, level grass, attractive beech hedging, silver birches and many newly planted trees, the park has a comfortable feel. It provides 76 touring pitches for all types of units, 25 with hardstanding and 50 with electrical hook-ups (16A). The entrance has been widened for easier access. There is a post office/shop in the village selling bread baked on the premises and the Sparkford Inn provides good food. Sparkford is also home to the famous Haynes Motor Museum (½ mile), a must for those interested in the history of the world's motor industry, and the Fleet Air Arm Museum is near at Yeovilton. You will also find several National Trust properties and gardens in the area and the park is the midway site for the Leland Trail. Details of safe cycle routes and walks are available at reception. The park edges the A303 bypass; although it is well hedged, there could be road noise in some areas.

Facilities: The well equipped heated toilet block is kept immaculate. Well planned en-suite facilities for visitors with disabilities. Motorcaravan discharge point. Gas available from reception. Central recreation area providing play equipment, badminton net, bowls green and a 9-hole putting green. Many pitches are large enough for American style motorhomes. **Off site:** Riding or fishing 8 miles, golf 5 miles.

Charges 2001

Per unit incl. 2 persons	£8.00 - £10.00
extra person (over 5 yrs)	£2.00
awning	£2.00
extra single tent	£5.00
electricity	£2.00

No credit cards. Tel/Fax: (01963) 440002. E-mail: longhazelpark@hotmail.com. Reservations: Contact park. **Open** 1 March - 31 December.

Directions: From Yeovil direction on A303 take road into village of Sparkford and park is signed on the left 100 yds before the Inn. O.S.GR: ST604263.

Mendip Heights Camping and Caravan Park

143 Priddy, nr Wells, Somerset BA5 3BP

Historic Priddy is the highest village in the Mendips and is famed for its annual Sheep Fair in August. Nearby are extensive Roman lead-workings, Bronze Age burial mounds, the Priddy Circle and access to Swildons Hole, one of the popular cave systems in the Mendips. This well kept, family run park is half a mile from the village with tranquil views across the Mendip fields, characterised by dry stone walling. It has a simple charm with field margins left natural to encourage wildlife and nest boxes in the mature trees edging the three fields which comprise the site. These provide space for 90 units on mostly level short grass with 21 electric hook-ups (10/16A) and 8 with hardstanding. The only marked pitches are those with electric hook-up, so visitors can site themselves where they like. Activities can be arranged covering canoeing, abseiling, archery, caving, mountain biking and others, with equipment provided. Free guided walks are also usually provided at 2 pm. on Sundays during B.Hs and the summer holidays. The park is on the Padstow-Bristol Sustran Route 3. Other than all that activity, places like Cheddar Gorge, Wookey Hole, Glastonbury with the Tor, Wells and Bath are within 20 miles. A member of the Countryside Discovery group.

Facilities: The toilet block, although of older design, is bright and cheerful, spotlessly clean and heated, with coin operated showers and a baby changing area. Dishwashing and laundry facilities. The reception/shop doubles as the village shop and is therefore open all season selling groceries, Calor gas, etc. with an off licence and tourist information. Wendy house, swings and table tennis for children. Torches useful. Off site: Two traditional village pubs with very different characters stand by the village green within walking distance (½ mile). Fishing 6 miles, riding 2 miles.

Charges 2002

Per adult	£3.25 - £4.95
child (4-16 yrs)	£1.30
electricity	£1.80
dog	£1.00

No charge for awning or extra car. Pup tent or gazebo £1.00 in peak season. Tel: (01749) 870241. Fax: (01749) 870368. E-mail: camping@ mendipheights.co.uk. Reservations: Made with £10 deposit (min. 3 nights for electricity at B.Hs). Open 1 March - mid November.

Directions: From M5 exit 21 (Weston-super-Mare) take A371 to Banwell. Turn left on A368, right on B3134 and right on B3135. After 2 miles turn left at camp sign. From M4 westbound exit 18, A46 to Bath, then A4 towards Bristol. Take A39 for Wells and right at Green Ore traffic lights on B3135; after 5 miles turn left at camp sign. From Shepton Mallet, follow A37 north to junction of B3135 and turn left. Continue on B3135 to traffic lights at Green Ore. Straight on and after 5 miles turn left at camp sign. O.S.GR: ST522518.

Broadway House Holiday Caravan and Camping Park

Cheddar, Somerset BS27 3DB

141

An interesting and well maintained park offering a range of facilities on continental lines, Broadway has been developed by the Moore family with 'T.L.C.' over a period of 30 years. On a gently sloping area at the foot of the Mendips near Cheddar Gorge, the park takes 250 touring units of all types. From the entrance, after a neat caravan holiday home area, a series of touring areas graduates upwards, culminating in a tent and overflow rally field. The central access avenue is lined by trees with the groups of pitches on either side separated by ranch style fencing or hedging and landscaped with trees and shrubs and interesting 'bygones'. Most pitches have electrical connections (16A) and 30 have water and drainage. This park aims to cater for the normal active family - single sex groups are actively discouraged. There is a secluded, walled, heated pool (60 x 25 ft.) and children's pool (open Easter - Sept; unsupervised) with grass sunbathing area and shade from silver birches, but a sun bed is also provided! The range of activities organised from the park is wide and includes abseiling, canoeing, hill-walking, archery, shooting, caving, mountain biking (bicycle hire on site), windsurfing can also be arranged and there is a dry ski slope nearby. Two animal enclosures house a variety of interesting animals and Sonny the parrot is a character with a history! A nature trail including a 'pixie walk' leads from the park - Cheddar Wood is a site of special scientific interest. The shop has a wide range of goods and there is a bar and café with an extensive, reasonably priced menu available at peak periods. This is really a park to be experienced - there is always something to see and do from the moment you turn in the gates and everything is well signed.

Facilities: The large, purpose built, tiled toilet block at the start of the touring area has a good provision of showers, plus eight private cabins. Behind are 10 family shower units with shower, bidet and washbasin, two of which are 'disabled friendly'. Extra facilities, newly refurbished with bathroom (coin operated) and a unit for disabled visitors are near reception, with a 'portacabin' type unit (no showers) in the top tenting field. Baby room, coin operated hairdryers, washing up sinks and a well equipped launderette. Motorcaravan service point. Shop. Swimming pool. Adventure playground, football field, indoor table tennis, barbecue area, target golf, boules pitch, skateboard ramp, croquet. Games/amusements room, family room and large screen TV and tourist information room. Electronic barrier security. Not all breeds of dog are accepted. **Off site**: Fishing ½ and 5 miles. .

Charges guide

Per adult	£2.00 - £4.00
child (3-14 yrs)	£1.00 - £2.00
caravan or tent and car	£1.00 - £6.00
motorcaravan	£1.00 - £2.50
premier pitch (incl. 3 services)	plus £2.00
electricity (16A)	£1.50
awning, pup tent or extra car	free - £1.00
dog	£1.00
two small dogs	£1.50

Special discounts for longer stays and for O.A.P.s. Min. charge £3.50. Credit cards accepted with 5% surcharge. Tel: (01934) 742610. Fax: (01934) 744950. E-mail: enquiries@broadwayhouse.uk.com. Reservations: Advisable in high season, with £5 deposit per night. **Open** 1 March - 30 November.

Directions: Park entrance is on the A371 towards Axbridge, about 1 mile northwest of Cheddar. O.S.GR: ST449547.

Somerset

Southfork Caravan Park

Parrett Works, Martock, Somerset TA12 6AE

Don't be put off by the address which is historic – it was once a 17th century flax mill, now no more. Mr and Mrs Metcalfe own and run this excellent, modern, well drained site just outside the lovely village of Martock. With 30 touring pitches on grass with a gravel access road (20 with 10A electrical hook-ups), it is an orderly, quiet park on two acres of flat, tree lined meadow near the River Parrett. All the expected facilities are close to the entrance and as the owners live on the premises, the park is open all year. Most things are available, including an NCC approved caravan repair centre. Despite the rural setting, the A303 trunk road is just ten minutes away. Information about access to many cycle routes and numerous walks, including the Parrett Trail, is available from reception.

Facilities: The heated well maintained toilet block is fully equipped. Laundry room and dishwashing sink. Shop and limited off licence with gas supplies and comprehensive camping and caravan spares and accessories (open all year except Christmas and New Year). Children's play area. **Off site:** Fishing available (and licences) on the River Parrett a few yards from the park. Golf 3 miles. This area of South Somerset contains much of interest, including the Fleet Air Arm Museum, Haynes Motor Museum and Cricket St Thomas Wildlife Park.

Charges 2001

Per unit incl. 2 persons	£7.00 - £9.00
extra person	£1.00
child under 5	free
awning	50p - £1.00
dog	50p
electricity	£1.80 - £2.30

Tel: (01935) 825661. Fax: (01935) 825122. E-mail: southfork.caravans@virgin.net. Reservations: Advisable for B.Hs. and peak season and made with £10 deposit. **Open** all year.

Directions: From A303 between Ilchester and Ilminster take signs for South Petherton or Martock; park is mid-way on the road between the two villages (follow signs). O.S.GR: ST447187.

Alan Rogers' discount
Less £1 per night (max. 7)

Somerset

Bath Marina and Caravan Park

Brassmill Lane, Bath BA1 3JT

Bath Caravan Park is a good, purpose-designed touring park for caravans and motorcaravans only, under the same ownership as the next door Marina. A useful, well run park from which to visit historic Bath or Bristol, there is a park-and-ride facility for Bath outside the entrance, and the Bath to Bristol cycle path is nearby. It provides 89 pitches (no tents) with concrete hardstanding and 16A electricity, pleasantly interspersed with grass and flowering trees and bushes. A newer circular area near reception provides landscaped hardstanding for the caravan only with extra, separate hardstanding for the car. One 'super' pitch next to the toilet block has full services (electricity, water, drain and TV aerial). A reader tells us that TV reception is not good. A gate provides access to the 'Boathouse', a bar with a terrace fronting the River Avon and useful for bar snacks.

Facilities: Two heated toilet blocks (with digital security system) provide showers (lacking shelf space but with plenty of hooks and stools outside), vanity style washbasins in semi cubicles and hair dryers. Each block has dishwashing sinks outside, under cover, a unit for disabled people and a fully equipped laundry room. Reception/shop (for essentials and gas) has tourist information as well as necessities for the Marina. Children's play park next door. Fishing. **Off site:** Bicycle hire, riding, golf or boat launching within 2 miles

Charges 2001

Per pitch	£9.00
adult	£2.00
child (5-15 yrs)	£1.00
electricity (16A)	£2.00
dog	free

Winter special (1/11-28/2): £12 per unit inclusive. Tel/Fax: (01225) 424301 or 428778. Reservations: Any length with £10 deposit. **Open** all year.

Directions: From M4 exit 18 take A46 for Bath for approx. 8 miles to A4 T-junction. Turn right following signs for Bath city centre to main traffic lights at A36 intersection. Turn left on A36 signed Bristol. After 2 miles, just after Little Chef on right, turn right at traffic lights crossing over river to Newbridge. Immediately turn right next to Murco petrol station into Brassmill Lane. Park is 100 yds on right. O.S.GR: ST720655.

Bath

Dating back to the 4th century AD, this historic city is poised once more to come alive as the Spa Resort of Britain when visitors to the city will be able to enjoy water treatments and holistic therapy at The Bath Spa Project. Another reason to visit the city is the beautiful Georgian architecture of the Royal Crescent and The Circus.

Bath Chew Valley Caravan Park

151

Ham Lane, Bishop Sutton, North Somerset BS39 5TZ

A small and secluded garden site for adults only, Chew Valley is run with much tender love and care by Ray and Val Belton. The result is that caravans are sited on neat lawns amongst colourful beds of flowers and the car is tucked away on the car park, providing a tranquil and restful atmosphere. Ray will place your caravan for you, levelling it if necessary. Groundsheets are not permitted to protect the grass. Neat hardstandings are on 14 pitches and, again to protect the grass, motorcaravans must always use them. This park will particularly appeal to garden lovers and has actually been featured on BBC TV's Gardeners' World. A very nice touch is the small nursery 'Gone to Pot' where Val (the garden expert) does all her growing and where those staying on site can purchase some of the plants found on the park. A small library with coffee available is next to reception. Chew Valley lake is a walk of about half a mile with trout fishing available and Blagdon lake is popular for birdwatching. There are several circular walks in the area – visitors may borrow the route plans and a walking stick from reception. A Best of British group member. This is an adults only park.

Facilities: The heated toilet block is attractively wallpapered giving a 'home from home' feel, with washbasins in cubicles and all the other fittings which make life comfortable. Two separate en-suite units. Useful utility room for dish or hand washing with a spin dryer, together with a washing machine and tumble dryer for service washes only. Motorcaravan service point. **Off site:** The village is only 100 yds up the road with a useful general store, newsagent, two pubs and a post office. Supermarkets are within 15 minutes drive. Golf 1 mile, riding 8 miles. Bristol and Bath are within an easy distance and Cheddar Gorge or Longleat make excellent days out.

Charges 2001

Per pitch incl. 2 persons, electricity, awning, pets and TV hook-up	£15.00

No credit cards. Tel: (01275) 332127. Fax: (01275) 332664. E-mail: enquiries@chewvalley.co.uk. Reservation: Advisable for B.Hs. **Open** all year.

Directions: From Bath direction on A368 turn right opposite the Red Lion pub in Bishop Sutton. Road appears a little narrow but continue past a small track to the left (50 yds) for a further 50 yds. Park entrance appears on your left with neat, clear entrance. O.S.GR: ST584599.

Baltic Wharf Caravan Club Site

144

Cumberland Road, Bristol BS1 6XG

This excellent, city centre site, open all year, is operated by the Caravan Club. A gem of a little site in Bristol's re-developed dockland, it is well laid out and maintained with access via a lockable gate to the Baltic Wharf dockside. It is screened from the road by a high wall with a boatyard on one side and residential apartments on the other, and is well designed with a good use of trees. The view across the dock towards Clifton village and Bristol is unique and you can even glimpse the suspension bridge (effectively lit up at night). The 58 pitches are accessed by a circular tarmac road - the central nine are on grass (these are not used in the winter), the rest on stone chippings and ideal for all year round use (steel pegs are provided). All are supplied with 16A electricity. It is a 30 minute walk to the city centre, a ferry is available (weekends only in winter) or a regular bus service (every 30 minutes, 7.30 am.- 6 pm). An extra ferry runs from the SS Great Britain. This is a well serviced situation and a popular site so advance booking is necessary. Arrive by 8 pm.

Facilities: The toilet block (coded access) is heated for winter use and provides good clean facilities including controllable showers and, for ladies, washbasins in cubicles. Good new facilities are provided for disabled visitors, plus toilets for the walking disabled and showers in the main block. Dishwashing under cover. Good fully equipped laundry room. Motorcaravan service point. Tourist information room. Dogs are welcome but there is no dog walk. Wardens live on the site. **Off site:** Small general store with off licence and newsagent 200 yds. Pub nearly next door. Golf 2 miles. The Sustran cycle route 3 ends here.

Charges 2001

Per pitch (non-member)	£7.00 - £8.00
adult	£3.75 - £4.75
child (5-16 yrs)	£1.20
electricity	£1.50 - £2.25

TV reception is poor but a booster may be hired for 55p per night. Tel: 0117 926 8030 (8 am. - 8 pm. only). Reservations: Always advised, essential in high seasons, and made with £5 deposit; contact the Wardens with SAE for confirmation. **Open** all year.

Directions: Easiest access is to follow signs for the 'Historic Harbour' and SS Great Britain. The site is just west of the SS Great Britain, on the right behind a high wall - look carefully for the club sign (no brown signs to follow). O.S.GR: ST572718.

Camping and Caravanning Club Site Devizes

Spout Lane, Seend, Melksham, Wiltshire SN12 6RN

First opened in 1998, this newly constructed site occupies a level field with gravel roads and centrally located facilities. It is also adjacent to the Kennet and Avon Canal (opened in 1810, and recently extensively restored), and the towpath now provides a traffic-free route passing the Caen Hill flight of 29 locks into Devizes (4 miles). In the other direction the towpath runs towards Melksham (also 4 miles). In total there are 50 hardstanding and 45 grass pitches, 75 with electricity (16A). The site is central for visiting many places of interest including the stone circles at Stonehenge and Avebury. A more unusual outing is to Sandridge Farm, renowned for its speciality bacons, hams and sausages. The farm shop is open from 9-5 daily, and from May to Sept. visitors can see the pigs and piglets (admission free - wellies advisable). The Vale of Pewsey cycle route can be accessed from the canal towpath to the east of Devizes, and runs for 41 miles between Great Bedwyn and Corsham.

Facilities: The modern, heated toilet block provides spacious hot showers, washbasins in cubicles, laundry, dishwashing room, and a mother and baby room. Facilities for disabled visitors are in a suite (with alarm system) by reception. Motorcaravan services are in the late arrivals parking area. Small playground with rubber safety base. Reception opens 09.00-10.30 and 16.30-17.30, and stocks basic foods and drinks, snacks and gas supplies, fishing licences, cycle passes for the canal towpath and local tourist information.

Charges guide

Per adult:	£4.80 - 5.30
child	£1.65
pitch fee (non-members)	£4.30
electricity	£1.65 - 2.40

Tel: (01380) 828839 (not after 8.00 pm, please). Reservations: Advised for B.Hs and peak season; contact site. **Open** all year.

Directions: From Devizes take A361 westbound, and ½ mile before Seend village, take A365 towards Melksham. Cross the canal bridge, take next left by 'Three Magpies' and the site entrance is on your right. Approaching from the M4 junction 17, use A350 to Melksham and A365 to the site. O.S.GR: ST 951619.

Piccadilly Caravan Park

Folly Lane West, Lacock, Chippenham, Wiltshire SN15 2LP

Piccadilly is set in open countryside close to several attractions in northern Wessex, notably Longleat, Bath, Salisbury Plain, Stourhead, and Lacock itself. It is a small, quiet family owned park that is kept neat and tidy. Landscaped shrubs and trees are maturing, giving the impression of three separate areas. There are 40 well spaced, clearly marked pitches, 11 of which have hardstanding. Electrical connections (10A) are available on 34 pitches. A bus service runs from Lacock village to Chippenham.

Facilities: The one toilet block is well maintained and equipped, should be adequate in size for peak periods and can be heated in cool weather. Dishwashing area. Laundry room with baby changing facilities. Small, bark-based children's playground and a large, grassed ball play area. Limited gas supplies. Papers can be ordered. **Off site**: Fishing 1 mile, bicycle hire 6 miles, riding 4 miles, golf 3 miles.

Charges 2002

Per unit incl. 2 persons	£9.00
extra person over 5 yrs	£1.00
electricity	£1.50

No credit cards. Tel: (01249) 730260. Reservations: Any length; deposit of 1 nights fee. **Open** Easter/1 April - October.

Directions: Park is signed west off A350 Chippenham - Melksham road (turning to Gastard with caravan symbol) by Lacock village. 300 yds. to park. O.S.GR: ST911682.

Bristol

A modem vibrant city which has experienced a dramatic transformation in the past few years. '@Bristol', a brand new attraction for all ages takes you to a world where you can explore science and technology for yourself. The Harbourside now has a row of cafes, theatres and bars overlooking the city and the waterfront. Visit Harvey's Cellars to watch craftsmen fill the famous Bristol Blue bottles with delicious sherry or go aboard the SS Gt Britain at the Docks.

Plough Lane Caravan Site

168 Plough Lane, Kington Langley, nr Chippenham, Wiltshire SN15 5PS

Opening for its first season in '98 and catering for adults only, this is a good example of a well designed, quality, modern touring site. The 35 pitches are half hardstanding, half grass and all have electricity (16A). Access roads are gravel and the borders are stocked with newly planted shrubs and trees. The site gate has an alarm system for security at night. Local facilities include a supermarket, two public houses, and two garages - both stocking Calor and Camping Gaz. This site is an ideal base for visiting Bath, Westonbirt Arboretum and the many attractive villages of north Wiltshire and south Gloucestershire. This is an adults only park.

Facilities: The sanitary building is heated, spacious, light and airy, and has all the usual facilities including some washbasins in cubicles, with a hairdressing area for ladies. Separate en-suite room for disabled visitors with ramp access. Dishwashing sinks under cover. Fully equipped laundry with two further dishwashing sinks. **Off site:** Golf less than 1 mile.

Charges 2001

Per unit incl. 2 adults and electricity	£11.00
extra adult	£3.00

No credit cards. Tel/Fax: (01249) 750795. E-mail: ploughlane@lineone.net. Reservations: Made with £10 deposit. **Open** 1 March - 4 November.

Directions: From M4 junction 17 turn south on A350 for 2 miles, then left at traffic lights where site is signed. From Chippenham head north on A350 (towards M4), approaching traffic lights (signed for site and Kington Langley) you need the right hand lane. O.S.GR: ST915765.

Longleat Caravan Club Site

169 Warminster, Wiltshire BA12 7NL

What a magnificent situation in which to find a caravan park, amidst all the wonders of the Longleat Estate including the Elizabethan House, Safari Park, the collection of mazes (including the world's largest), not to mention Doctor Who and the Daleks and the Adventure castle! These are just some of the attractions to be found here to suit all ages amidst a beautiful rural parkland setting. Visitors can roam the woodlands (leaflets are available on a range of walks) and enjoy the views, watch the wildlife and marvel at the azaleas, bluebells, etc. according to the season or listen to the occupants of the Safari Park. The site itself, well managed by Caravan Club wardens, is situated in 10 acres of lightly wooded, level grassland within walking distance of the house and gardens. Following full refurbishment, there will be 98 hardstanding pitches around the perimeter of the park and 66 central grass pitches, all with 16A electricity connections. Water points and re-cycling bins are neatly walled with low night lighting. A separate wooden chalet houses tourist information but the wardens will help you to get the best out of your stay at Longleat. Tents are not accepted (except trailer tents).

Facilities: Two new heated toilet blocks will provide washbasins in cubicles, controllable showers and a vanity section with shelf, mirrors and hairdryers. There will be a baby/toddler room, facilities for disabled visitors, a laundry and a covered dishwashing area. The former toilet block is to be transformed into a games room. Motorcaravan service point. Children's play area. Office is manned 9 am - 6 pm and stocks basic food items, papers can be ordered and gas is available. Paperback exchange library. Fresh fruit and vegetable van drives around the site and a fish and chip van calls.

Charges 2001

Per pitch (non-member)	£6.00 - £8.00
adult	£2.75 - £4.50
child (5-16 yrs)	£1.10 - £1.20
electricity	£1.50 - £2.25

Open 31 March - 30 October. Tel: (01985) 844663. Fax: (01985) 844964. Reservations: Advisable for B.Hs and school holidays and made with £5 deposit.

Directions: The main entrance to Longleat which caravans must use is signed from the A362 Frome - Warminster road near to where it joins the A36 Warminster bypass. Turn into the estate and follow the Longleat House route through the toll booths for 2 miles then follow caravan club signs for 1 mile. There are shorter ways to leave the site. O.S.GR: ST806434.

Alderbury Caravan and Camping Park

167 Southampton Road, Whaddon, Salisbury, Wiltshire SP5 3HB

Under new ownership, this small village touring park is convenient for visiting Salisbury and the New Forest. At the southern end of Alderbury/Whaddon village, it is on level ground with a gravel access road to the 39 numbered pitches; 26 have access to electricity (16A). The park has some mature trees for shade, as well as younger trees, shrubs and flowers. More recently seven hardstandings, extra chemical disposal and waste water points, site lighting, more shrubs and trees have been added. The village shop and post office, a pub serving meals, public phone and a bus stop are within easy level walking distance of the entrance. There are hourly bus services to Salisbury, Southampton and Romsey. The country lanes around the area are good for cycling and walking. Salisbury Museum, the Cathedral and its Close are all well worth a visit. There is some road noise, most noticeable at the far end of the park.

Facilities: The central toilet block is practical, clean and well maintained. It provides hot showers in cubicles with curtain, a separate unit for disabled visitors, and a dishwashing sink also in a separate room. **Off site:** Fishing 1 mile, bicycle hire 3 miles, riding 2 miles, golf 5 miles.

Charges 2001

Per unit incl. 2 adults	£7.50 - £9.50
extra adult	£2.00 - £2.25
child (under 14 yrs)	£1.00 - £1.25
awning	£1.25 - £1.50
electricity	£2.25

No credit cards. Tel: (01722) 710125. Reservations: Contact park for details. **Open** all year.

Directions: From Salisbury take A36 towards Southampton and, after 3 miles (at far end of the dual carriageway section), turn left at sign to Alderbury and Whaddon, then right, over bridge, and left for park entrance. From Southampton on A36 towards Salisbury, continue past the A27 (Romsey) junction and over Pepperbox Hill. At end of a downhill straight, left onto slip road marked Alderbury, park is signed. O.S.GR: SU198263.

Monkton Wyld Farm Touring Caravan Park

173 Charmouth, Dorset DT6 6DB

Opened in 1991 by Simon and Joanna Kewley, Monkton Wylde is maturing nicely. Planting of flowering shrubs and trees continues (hydrangea and lavender) making an attractive, peaceful park, and a woodland walk has been created in 80 acres of the beautiful countryside surrounding the park. An abundance of mature trees around the perimeter provides shade and plenty of space between the 60 pitches gives a feeling of spaciousness. Most pitches have 16A electricity and around 35 have hardstanding. On site facilities are limited but an area at the top of the park has been turned into a children's play area, with a good area for ball games, a climbing frame, trampoline, etc. There is no reception as such, however a wooden chalet near the entrance provides information regarding pitch vacancies and the owners or the resident wardens (high season) are never far away. The gate is locked at 11 pm. A separate site has been developed next to the existing park for Camping and Caravanning Club members, managed by the Club. Bread, milk, groceries and papers may be obtained from here in the main season (09.00-19.00 hrs).

Facilities: The modern, well maintained toilet block has a fully equipped family room with baby changing facilities that can also be accessed by wheelchairs. Individual showers with folding screen are very spacious. Small laundry with washing machine and tumble dryer. Washing up is under cover. Gas supplies. Children's play area. Caravan storage. **Off site:** Fishing or riding 2 miles, bicycle hire, golf and boat launching 3 miles. Shops and local pubs are within a mile's walking distance and Charmouth and Lyme Regis are only 3 miles (buses leave from just along the road to both towns).

Charges 2001

Per unit incl. 2 adults	£6.50 - £11.50
extra adult	£1.50
child (5-16 yrs)	50p - £1.00
electricity	£2.00
dog	free - 75p
pup tent	free - £1.00

No extra charge for awnings, 2nd car, boats or visitors. No credit cards. Tel: (01297) 34525. Warden (May - Sept) (01297) 631131. Fax: (01297) 33594. E-mail: holidays@monktonwyld.co.uk. Reservations: Made with deposit of £3 per night booked. **Open** 30 March - 28 October.

Directions: Park is signed on A35 between Charmouth and Axminster, approx. 1½ miles west of Charmouth. Turn right at Greenway Head (B3165 signed Marshwood) and park is 600 yds on the left past the Club site. Don't go to Monkton Wylde hamlet - the road is very steep. O.S.GR: SY329966.

This family owned park, run with care, occupies a prominent position beside the road into Charmouth village with marvellous views southwards to the hills across the valley. By the nature of the terrain the pitches are terraced in two fields to provide over 200 well spaced places for touring units, some for seasonal units and over 80 for caravan holiday homes. The tenting field of mainly sloping grass also has super views. Electric hook ups (10A) are provided on 144 pitches and 30 have hardstanding, water and waste water. Five are special 'Millennium' pitches with a washing machine and dryer for individual use. Other accommodation includes smart pine lodges, apartments and motel rooms. All the facilities are located in a modern building to one side of the wide tarmac entrance. A range of family entertainment includes a children's club during school holidays with Dino Dan (the dinosaur). The smaller indoor pool and jacuzzi is open all year, the adjacent outdoor pool is walled, paved and sheltered. Neither pool is supervised, both are heated. A comfortable site for families, the beach and village are within easy walking distance. Charmouth is known for its fossil finds and its connection with Jane Austen.

Facilities: The lower toilet block is modern and light with roomy showers, and has an adjoining washing up area. The other block is traditional in design with rather psychedelic tiles, but it is heated, clean, neat and tidy. Laundry room adjoining, plus dishwashing sinks (under cover). Well stocked shop (March-Nov). Licensed club bar (limited hours Nov - March). Restaurant (open evenings 6-9 pm. March - Nov) including takeaway. Indoor pool (charged for, open all year, limited hours Nov - March). Outdoor pool and paddling pool (key-coded entrance). Nine-pin bowling alley for hire at £5 per half hour. Super large children's play area in the field below the tenting field is open dawn to dusk - be tempted to try the maypole swing and bobsleigh ride! In low seasons opening hours of the various facilities may vary. **Off site:** Fishing 1 mile, riding 3 miles, golf 2 miles.

Charges 2001

Per pitch incl. up to 6 persons	£8.00 - £17.00
serviced pitch	£16.00 - £25.00
extra pup tent	£3.00
dog (max. 2)	£1.00
electricity	£2.00

Club membership included. Only one van or tent per pitch. **Open** all year. Tel: (01297) 560259. Fax: (01297) 560787. E-mail: enq@newlandsholidays.co.uk. Reservations: Made with £30 deposit per week.

Directions: Approaching from Bridport leave the A35 at first sign for Charmouth at start of the bypass and site almost directly on your left. O.S.GR: SY373935.

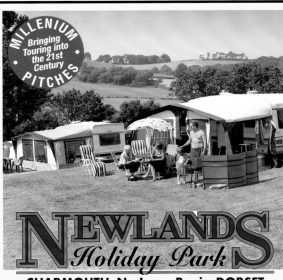

Family park in beautiful Dorset countryside - just a short stroll to Charmouth village and beach.

Terraced Touring and Tenting pitches with electric hook-ups available.

Indoor and Outdoor Swimming Pools.

Full amenities incl. Club, Restaurant and Bowling Alley.

Pine lodges, Holiday Homes & Apartments also available.

Open all year

CHARMOUTH, Nr. Lyme Regis, DORSET

CHEQUES

Camping Cheque
ACCEPTED

Free colour brochure:
Newlands Caravan Park, Charmouth, Dorset DT6 6RB
Tel: **01297 560259** Fax: **01297 560787**
www.newlandsholidays.co.uk
E-mail: enq@newlandsholidays.co.uk

Wood Farm Caravan Park

176 Axminster Road, Charmouth, Dorset DT6 6BT

Wood Farm is an excellent, family run park, maintained to high standards and with an indoor swimming pool. Situated on the western side of Charmouth beside the A35 (some road noise may be expected) and only a mile or two from Lyme Regis and its beaches, it is part of the Caravan Club's 'managed under contract' scheme (non-members are also very welcome). On sloping, well landscaped ground, it has open views across the countryside. There are 200 pitches for touring units of which 180 are neat, level all-weather pitches with hardstanding, electricity (10A) and TV connections, and provision for awnings. These are divided by neat, box-like leylandii hedging which has almost become a feature of the park. Water and waste water hook-ups are also available. One grassy terraced field takes about 25 tents and there are 80 caravan holiday homes in their own areas. A member of the Best of British group.

Facilities: Four good, modern toilet blocks can be heated and include some washbasins in curtained cubicles for ladies. The excellent lower block provides wash cubicles, and en-suite facilities for disabled people. One block has a baby care unit and laundry sinks with a spin dryer. Separate laundry room. Covered dishwashing sinks. Motorcaravan service point. Shop by reception. Fish and chip van opens 2-4 times a week (acc. to season). All visitors are offered temporary membership to the good heated indoor swimming pool (27 x 54 ft.) on payment of £1.50 per session. Recreation hall providing a snooker room and family games area with table tennis. Outdoor tennis court. Children's play field. Small coarse fishing lake (carp, rudd, roach, tench) is adjacent - day and weekly tickets (rod licence required, also available from park). **Off site**: Golf 1 mile, beaches and shops ¾ and 2 miles.

Charges 2001

Per unit incl. side awning	£1.50 - £5.50
adult	£3.50 - £4.75
child (5-16 yrs)	£1.10 - £1.20
electricity (10A)	£2.00 - £2.75
mains water pitch	£1.50
dog, extra car, trailer or pup tent	£1.00

Special senior citizens low season discounts. Tel/Fax: (01297) 560697. E-mail: holidays@woodfarm.co.uk. Reservations: Made with £30 deposit (non-returnable), min. 5 nights in high season, 3 nights other times. **Open** 22 March - 3 November.

Directions: Park is ½ mile west of Charmouth village with access near roundabout at junction of A35 with A3052 (Lyme Regis) road. O.S.GR: SY356940.

Binghams Farm Touring Caravan Park

177 Melplash, nr Bridport, Dorset DT6 3TT

Binghams is a small, purpose built park, for adults only. In a pleasant, rural situation two miles from the market town of Bridport, with views seaward towards West Bay and inland across Beaminster Downs and Pilsdon Hill, it is open all year. The park provides an area of individual pitches with 10A electricity and over 40 hardstandings, nicely landscaped with shrubs and trees growing between the pitches, plus an open sloping field overlooking the valley with 20 electrical hook-ups. The entrance to the park is neatly tarmaced and resident ducks and chickens provide interest. A cottage has been converted into two flats to let. A path is provided to the river which links with the main footpaths for Bridport (20 minutes) or local hostelries. A limited bus service runs on the main road. The Brit Valley is an unspoilt area of West Dorset with an ancient heritage and coastal West Bay is only a couple of miles. This is an adult only park.

Facilities: The original farm buildings have been sympathetically converted to provide reception, a good heated toilet block and the other amenities. The toilet block, with under floor heating for winter use, provides well fitted, tiled, curtained showers, hairdryers, a separate, fully equipped room for the less able with ramped access and a laundry room. Dishwashing under cover. Upstairs lounge bar serving bar food in high season (closed Tues/Wed). Games room with table tennis, books, chess and pool table. Gas available. Winter caravan storage. Gates closed 23.00-08.00 hrs. Adults only. **Off site**: Sea fishing and golf 3 miles.

Charges 2001

Per pitch incl. 2 persons and awning	£8.00 - £12.00
extra adult	£2.00
dog	£1.00
electricity (10A)	£2.00

Tel: (01308) 488234. E-mail: binghamsfarm@hotmail.com. Reservations: Made with £25 non-returnable deposit per week or part. **Open** all year.

Directions: At main roundabout on A35 road, on east side of Bridport, take A3066 towards Beaminster. Watch for site entrance after approx. 2 miles on the left. O.S.GR: SY482963.

On slightly sloping ground with superb open views, both coastal and inland, Highlands End is quietly situated on the Dorset Heritage Coastline. With access to the coastal path, a path in front of the park runs along the cliff top and then leads down to a shingle beach a little further along. It is a good quality park with 180 caravan holiday homes, mostly privately occupied, and 195 touring pitches in two areas nearest to the sea - one has to travel through the holiday homes to reach them. All have electricity (10A) and 45 also offer water, drainage, hardstanding and a gravel awning area. A further area is used for tents in high season. A modern, attractive building houses a lounge bar, good value restaurant, family room and games room, with some musical evenings in high season. The park's amenities also include an excellent, air-conditioned indoor heated swimming pool, a gym room, sun beds, steam room and sauna (all charged). The owners have a long time interest in the fire brigade and an historic fire engine (1936 Leyland Pump Escape) along with memorabilia make an interesting display in the bar. The park was used to film scenes for Nick Berry's TV series based on nearby West Bay harbour. A well run park and a member of the Best of British group.

Facilities: The two toilet blocks near the tourist sections are excellent, well maintained and can be heated. They provide washbasins (some in cubicles with toilets), large, comfortable, showers, covered washing-up sinks and a dishwashing room. En-suite facilities for disabled visitors and a baby care room. Laundry room. Motorcaravan service point. Well stocked shop beside reception (opening times vary with the season), including gas supplies. Bar and restaurant/takeaway (open Spr. B.H.- late Sept). Tennis court. Swimming pool (with attendant; 20 x 9 m. and charged £2 per session, £1 for children) and gym. Pitch and putt. Adventure play area. **Off site:** Golf or fishing 2 miles.

Charges 2001

Per unit incl. 2 persons and awning	£8.00 - £12.50
extra adult	£2.75 - £3.00
child (4-17 yrs)	£1.25 - £1.50
dog	£1.25 - £1.50
electricity	£1.75 - £2.00
all service pitch	plus £1.50
(hardstanding, water and drainage, excl. electricity)	

Tel: (01308) 422139. Fax: (01308) 425672. E-mail: holidays@wdlh.co.uk. Reservations: Essential in high season and made with £20 deposit (min. 4 days in high season). Contact West Dorset Leisure Holidays, Eype, nr Bridport, Dorset DT6 6AR. **Open** 20 March - 1 November.

Directions: Follow Bridport bypass on A35 around the town and park is signed to south (Eype turning), down narrow lane. O.S.GR: SY452914.

Golden Cap Holiday Park

Seatown, Chideock, nr Bridport, Dorset

Golden Cap, named after the adjacent high cliff (the highest in southern England) which overlooks Lyme Bay, is only 150 yards from a shingle beach at Seatown and is surrounded by National Trust countryside and the Heritage Coastline. The park is arranged over several fields on the valley floor, sloping gently down towards the sea. It is in two main areas, having once been two parks, each separated into fields with marvellous views around and providing 108 tourist pitches. All have electricity and 28 also have hardstanding with drainaway and gravel awning area. An extra sloping tent field is used for peak season (torch useful) and there are 211 caravan holiday homes in their own areas. The most attractive indoor swimming pool at Highlands End (under the same ownership) is three miles away and open for campers on payment. Beaches are nearby, sea fishing, boat launching, riding or fossil hunting are possible in the area, plus good walks including access to the coastal path. A well run park and a member of the Best of British group.

Facilities: The main toilet block is modern and of very good quality, with spacious shower cubicles (some with toilet and washbasin), good facilities for visitors with disabilities (Radar key) and a baby care room. Two other smaller blocks around the park. Laundry room. Motorcaravan service point. Useful and well stocked shop (8 am - 6 pm, or 9 pm in high season). Takeaway service each evening in peak season. Gas supplies. Tourist information rooms. American motorhomes not accepted. **Off site:** Pub with food service close.

Charges 2001

Per unit incl. 2 persons and awning	£8.00 - £12.50
extra adult	£2.75 - £3.00
child (4-17 yrs)	£1.25 - £1.50
dog	£1.25 - £1.50
electricity	£1.75 - £2.00
all service pitch	plus £1.50
(hardstanding, water and drainage, excl. electricity)	

Tel: (01308) 422139. Fax: (01308) 425672. E-mail: holidays@wdlh.co.uk. Reservations: Essential in high season and made with £20 deposit (min. 4 days in high season). For information or booking contact: West Dorset Leisure Holidays, Eype, Bridport, Dorset DT6 6AR. **Open** 20 March - 1 November.

Directions: Turn off A35 road at Chideock, (a bigger village with shops and restaurants) 3 miles west of Bridport, at sign to Seatown opposite church. Park is less than 1 mile down narrow lane. O.S.GR: SY423919.

Family run parks for families with direct access to a beach are rare in Britain and this one has the added advantage of being in beautiful coastal countryside in West Dorset. It is an ideal situation to explore the 'Hidden County' and the resort of Weymouth (17 miles) and is next to the sea and a beach of fine pebbles, sheltered from the wind by pebble banks. The River Bride edges the park and joins the sea here. Approached by a fairly steep access road, the park itself is on level, open ground. The 500 plus touring pitches, over 300 with 10A electricity, are on an open, undulating grass field connected by tarmac or hard-core roads. Caravan pitches (10 x 11 m.) are now marked, evenly spaced in lines. Some tent pitches are in the main field, with others well spaced around the edge of a sloping extra field. In separate areas there are 230 caravan holiday homes, with 60 for hire. This lively holiday park has an extensive range of facilities that includes a swimming pool, and three bars with an evening entertainment programme in season. Daytime entertainment caters for all ages - don't miss the donkey derby! The overall impression is of a large, busy holiday park with a friendly reception and happy atmosphere.

Facilities: Toilet facilities are in two refurbished blocks, plus another with washbasins and toilets only, all with free hot water. A 'portacabin' stle unit serves the tent field. In all, it is a good provision for a busy beach park. The main blocks have facilities for disabled people (Radar key), and a baby care room (key system). Laundry and washing up sinks cope well at peak times. Launderette. Bars with entertainment. and licensed restaurant (weekends only in late season; closed Mondays all season). Good value supermarket and takeaway. Heated and supervised outdoor swimming pool and children's pool (15/5-30/10) with swimming and diving lessons available. Adventure play area, pets corner and pony trekking (own stables on site). Bicycle hire. **Off site:** Golf course adjacent. Fishing possible from Chesil Bank. Good connection to footpaths to the attractive, thatched village of Burton Bradstock or West Bay.

Charges 2001

Per unit incl. up to 6 persons	£9.00 - £20.00
extra person	£2.00
electricity	£2.00
small tent incl. 2 walkers or cyclists	£6.50 - £11.50
dog	£2.50.

Single sex groups not admitted. Tel: (01308) 897317. Fax: (01308) 897336. E-mail: enquiries@fbhp.co.uk. Reservations: Made for min. 1 week with £20 deposit p/week, plus £1 fee. Short break reservations available - ring for details. **Open** 16 March - 10 November.

Directions: Park is immediately west of the village of Burton Bradstock, on the Weymouth - Bridport coast road (B3157). O.S.GR: SY980898.

Fun filled days on privately-owned family park next to our own private beach. Large Camping & Touring fields and Self Catering Holiday Caravans.

- Heated outdoor swimming pools
- Club Complex with licensed restaurant and bars
- Nightly Entertainment (*Whitsun-Mid Sept.)
- Children's activities and amusements
- Beach fishing and wind-surfing
- Horse/Pony Rides
- Supermarket and take-away foods
- Fine country and cliff walks
- Golf course adjoining park
- Caravan sales
- High level of facilities and amenities

FRESHWATER BEACH HOLIDAY PARK
Burton Bradstock, Near Bridport, Dorset DT6 4PT
Tel: 01308 897317 • Fax: 01308 897336

Email: info@freshwaterbeach.co.uk • www.freshwaterbeach.co.uk

East Fleet Farm Touring Park

Chickerell, Weymouth, Dorset DT3 4DW

East Fleet Farm has a marvellous situation on part level, part gently sloping meadows leading to the shores of the Fleet, with views across to the famous Chesil Bank with the sea beyond. The Fleet is a lagoon renowned for its wildlife and popular with bird watchers. The park itself has been developed within the confines of a 300-acre working dairy and arable farm and is maturing nicely as bushes and trees grow. The 270 pitches are a comfortable size so there is no feeling of crowding. Of these, 97 are level and marked with 10A electric hook-ups, 25 also having hardstanding. The bar is in a newly converted barn and has a terrace complete with views over the Fleet (open high season and B.Hs) and provides bar meals. The busy resort of Weymouth with its safe bathing beaches and many watersports facilities is only 3 miles away (bicycle hire and boat launching possible). There is a bus service from the top of the lane (approx. ½ mile) and Abbotsbury Swannery and Gardens are nearby.

Facilities: The central toilet block is built in natural stone and provides adequate rather than luxurious facilities with coin-operated showers (one heated). Dishwashing under cover (H&C). Fully equipped laundry room with a self-contained unit for disabled people off it. Extra new toilets and a family bathroom are beside the bar. Reception plus shop with basic groceries, bread, papers and gas, etc. opens longer in high season. Games room with pool table. Children's play area but, remember, elsewhere this is a working farm. **Off site**: Riding or golf 2 miles.

Charges 2001

Per unit incl. 2 persons	£5.00 - £10.00
extra adult	50p - £2.50
child (5-16 yrs)	25p - 50p
awning	free - £1.75
dog	25p - £1.00
electricity (10A)	£1.75 - £2.25

Senior citizen discount in June (10%). Tel: (01305) 785768. E-mail:enquiries@eastfleet.co.uk. Reservations: Write with £20 deposit. **Open** 15 March - 31 October.

Directions: Park is signed from B3157 Weymouth - Bridport road, approx. 3 miles west of Weymouth. The narrow, uneven approach road is by the army camp on the southern side of the B3157. O.S.GR: SY639798.

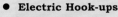

Sandyholme Holiday Park

Moreton Road, Owermoigne, Dorchester, Dorset DT2 8HZ

A peaceful haven in Thomas Hardy country, Sandyholme provides 44 holiday homes (privately owned or to hire) and 40 numbered pitches for touring units on level, short grass fields with one corner lightly wooded. The next door field is operated by the local farmer on a 28 day licence with use of the park's facilities (extra facilities opened in high season ensure no problems). The Holme Club (free membership) is a pleasant provision, open every evening at B.Hs during April and May, then mid-July to mid Sept. It has a cosy bar and patio, and a good bar meal menu. An unusual feature is a rather special duck pond with an amazing variety of ducks from all over the world with a pleasant walk and seats around the edge (an electric fence keeps the foxes at bay!) There are walks and cycling direct from the site or in Puddletown and Wareham Forests, or along the coastal path. Lulworth Cove, Durdle Door and Weymouth, with its sandy beach, are all near at hand.

Facilities: Two identical toilet blocks, although of older design, are bright and well maintained, with pre-set showers (20p). Laundry facilities in both blocks, and dishwashing sinks (10p). The shop/reception stocks all basic necessities including papers and gas. Bar and bar meals. Good, fenced, safe-based children's adventure play area. Games room with pool table and amusement machines. **Off site**: Fishing is available on an adjacent farm, bicycle hire or golf 5 miles, riding 6 miles.

Charges guide

Per pitch incl. all persons	£6.50 - £12.00
awning or pup tent	£1.00
dog	£1.00 p/n or £5 p/w
electricity	£2.00

Tel: (01305) 852677. Fax: (01305) 854677. Reservations: Made with £20 deposit (non-refundable); include SAE for receipt. **Open** Easter/ 1April - 31 October.

Directions: On A352 Dorchester - Wareham road going west, watch for short dual carriageway section before Weymouth - Osmington roundabout. Turn north through Owermoigne village and park is on the left (clearly signed) after approx./ mile. O.S.GR: SY768863.

Photo: Purbeck, Dorset, South West Tourism

Southern Tourist Board

East Dorset, Hampshire, Isle of Wight, South Wiltshire, Oxfordshire, Berkshire and Buckinghamshire

Southern Tourist Board
40 Chamberlayne Road, Eastleigh, Hampshire SO50 5JH
Tel: 023 8062 5505 Fax: 023 8062 0010
E-mail: info@southerntb.co.uk
Internet: http://www.visitsouthernengland.com

The Southern Tourist Board covers three distinctive areas:

The South Coast comprises Weymouth and Portland with its safe sandy beach and the Isle of Portland joined to the mainland by the unique Chesil beach, and Swanage with the famous Studland beach and Purbeck hills. The cosmopolitan resort of Bournemouth, with its seven miles of golden sand, and the New Forest renowned for its trees and ponies, with its famous yachting havens of Lymington and Buckler's Hard. The Isle of Wight is just a short ferry trip across the Solent and offers a wealth of activities for all ages with a mild and sunny climate. Portsmouth, the flagship of Maritime England, is now the home of the 'Mary Rose' and several other historic ships, also Southampton, with its maritime connections including the 'Titanic' and the International Boat Show.

Rural Southern England comprises green rolling hills and scenic wooded valleys covering North and West Wiltshire, parts of Dorset, Hampshire, Kennet and Avon Canal country and the New Forest and the Test Valley. Worthy of mention is the beautiful medieval city of Salisbury with its inspirational Cathedral and Close, and Winchester, ancient capital of the Kingdom of Wessex.

Thames and Chilterns, dominated by the River Thames, its tributaries and the Chiltern Hills offers a mix of internationally famous cities and sporting events, royal pomp and traditional English village life. Buckinghamshire inspired John Betjeman and John Milton finished 'Paradise Lost' in his cottage at Chalfont St Giles. Benjamin Disraeli, the 19th Century Prime Minister came from near High Wycombe and the scenic village of Great Missenden was home to the great children's story teller Roald Dahl. Oxford is the city of dreaming spires. The golden stone university buildings have shaped a graceful and timeless city which no visitor forgets. The Oxfordshire Cotswolds has picturesque villages, the regal splendour of Blenheim Palace and market towns such as Chipping Norton. Berkshire is within 50 miles of London and is well known for its racing connections, and Royal connections at Windsor and Eton.

Photo: Peter Tirmuss, Southern Tourist Board

Wareham Forest Tourist Park

North Trigon, Wareham, Dorset BH20 7NZ

A peacefully located, spacious park in an unspoilt corner of Dorset, this site becomes very busy in high season. Developed to high standards by the present owners, it provides formal pitching, with or without hardstanding, for caravans or natural pitches for tents in pine wood or open field. Drainage appears satisfactory (although there is an unfenced dyke in the pinewood). The setting in Wareham Forest is attractive offering space for 200 units, 102 with hardstanding and all with electrical connections. There are also 8 luxury pitches on hardstanding with water, drainage, TV aerial, dustbin and light (available 1/3-31/10 only). There are forest walks and the park is well situated to explore the Dorset coast and Thomas Hardy country.

Facilities: Two well maintained, spacious toilet blocks are of a good standard with some washbasins in cubicles for ladies, plus adjustable showers on payment. The block used in the winter months is centrally heated. Facilities for disabled people. Well equipped laundry rooms and deep sinks for washing up. Motorcaravan service point. Café for breakfasts, etc. (main season). Small licensed shop with gas (part of the café, limited hours). Games room with video amusement machines next door. Open-air, heated swimming pool (60 x 20 ft). Large adventure play area. Entrance closed 11 pm. - 7 am. Resident wardens on site. Torches necessary. Caravan storage facilities. **Off site:** Fishing 5 miles, bicycle hire or golf 3 miles, riding 8 miles. In high season a bus service to and from Wareham leaves the site six times daily (mornings and teatime).

Charges 2001

Per pitch: standard	£4.00 - £6.00
serviced	£6.00 - £8.00
adult	£1.50 - £3.00
child (2-14 yrs)	£1.00 - £2.00
awning, boat, trailer, extra car	60p - £1.20
extra tent	60p - £2.20
dog	50p - £1.50
electricity	£2.00 - £2.25.

Couples and families only. Discount for OAPs in low season. Tel/Fax: (01929) 551393. E-mail: holiday@wareham-forest.co.uk. Reservations: Made with £25 non-returnable deposit and £2 admin. fee, balance 28 days before arrival. **Open** all year.

Directions: Park is north of Wareham between Wareham and Bere Regis, located off the A35 road. O.S.GR: SY899903.

Wareham Forest Tourist Park

OPEN ALL YEAR For further details and free coloured brochure write or phone: Tel/Fax: (01929) 551393. Peter & Pam Savage, Wareham Forest Tourist Park, North Trigon, Wareham, Dorset BH20 7NZ. www.wareham-forest.co.uk email holiday@wareham-forest.co.uk. Credit cards accepted

Rowlands-Wait Touring Park

Rye Hill, Bere Regis, Dorset BH20 7LP

205

Bernard and Linda Hammick have worked hard to make Rowlands-Wait into a most attractive park catering for all types of humans and units! The top of the park, edged by mature woods (full of bluebells in spring) is a haven for tents (and squirrels) with marvellous views and providing 30 places in three descending fields. The rest of the park is a little more formal, and nearer to the central toilet block, but most pitches back on to hedging or trees and they are generally level. Many walks are possible from the park with information provided on wildlife. A warm welcome awaits, particularly for those new to camping and caravanning, and a reader reports the park as "very friendly and relaxed, with few rules". The park takes bookings for groups or rallies all year. A member of the Countryside Discovery group.

Facilities: The purpose built toilet block is well equipped, with free hot water except for the showers (10p, 3-4 minutes). Laundry room. Covered dishwashing area. Recycling bins. Shop (high season) providing milk, papers and basic essentials and a freezer for ice packs. Play area for little ones with miniature assault course and castle is well placed near reception. Games room with pool table, table tennis and table football behind the sanitary block. Crazy golf. Bicycle hire. Torch useful. **Off site:** The village, a 10 minute walk, has shops, two pubs, etc. plus a bus service for Dorchester and Poole. Fishing 5 miles, golf 3 miles, riding 9 miles.

Charges 2001

Per unit incl. 2 persons	£6.30 - £9.30
extra adult	£1.60 - £2.10
child (under 16 yrs)	90p
awning, pup tent	free - £1.00
extra car, boat or trailer	free - £1.00
electricity (10A)	£2.00
dog	free - 60p

Tel/Fax: (01929) 472727. E-mail: ar@rowlandswait. co.uk. Reservations: Made with £15 deposit per week. **Open** 16 March - 31 October, and winter by arrangement.

Directions: Park is south of Bere Regis, just off the road to Wool, well signed from A35/A31 roundabout. O.S.GR: SY842933.

Alan Rogers' discount
Less 50p per night

Manor Farm Caravan Park

1 Manor Farm Cottage, East Stoke, Wareham, Dorset BH20 6AW

204

Near to the Purbeck hills, this is a small, rural park beside, but not part of, a working farm. David and Gillian Topp own and carefully run this simple park which is set in a hedged, level field, semi-broken up by evergreens. It provides 50 level, well spaced pitches, 30 for touring units, with 43 electrical connections (16A), on neatly cut grass. An ice pack service and gas exchange are provided and there is a sturdy children's play unit. East Stoke village has a pub, Wool is 2 miles with a pub and shops. Wareham and Swanage are near.

Facilities: The timber-clad toilet block (key system) is at the top of the field and is adequate inside providing all necessary facilities and kept very clean. Showers are metered (20p). A toilet for disabled people is in the men's room. Sink for washing up and one for laundry with a spin dryer (all 20p). Caravan storage. Dogs are accepted at the discretion of the owner. **Off site:** Fishing, bicycle hire, boat launching, riding all 3 miles, golf 4 miles.

Charges 2001

Per unit incl. 2 persons	£7.80 - £9.80
extra adult	£2.00
child (3-13 yrs)	£1.20
dog	£1.25
electricity (16A)	£2.20

No groups, singles, motorcycles or rallies. No credit cards. Tel/Fax: (01929) 462870. E-mail: info@ manorfarmcp.co.uk. Reservations: Made with £20 deposit. **Open** April - 30 September.

Directions: Off A352 Wareham - Wool road, turn into lane by church, over manned level crossing and park is ½ mile on right. Or from B3070 turn right signed East Stoke, then next right signed Manor Farm and site is on left. O.S.GR: SY872867.

Ulwell Cottage Caravan Park

Ulwell, Swanage, Dorset BH19 3DG

Nestling under the Purbeck Hills in this unique corner of Dorset on the edge of Swanage, Ulwell Cottage is a family run holiday park with indoor pool and wide range of facilities. A good proportion of the park is taken by caravan holiday homes (140), but an attractive, undulating area accessed by tarmac roads is given over to 77 numbered touring pitches. There are 68 electricity hook-ups (16A) and 18 hardstandings, 8 of which are serviced. The mixture of level and sloping pitches, interspersed with trees and shrubs, is quite pretty. The colourful entrance area is home to the Village Inn with a courtyard adjoining the heated, supervised indoor pool complex (both open all year and open to the public) and modern reception. The hill above the touring area, Nine Barrow Down, is a Site of Special Scientific Interest for butterflies overlooking Round Down. It is possible to walk to Corfe Castle this way. With Brownsea Island, Studland Bay, Corfe village and the Swanage Railway, Ulwell Cottage makes a marvellous centre for holidays.

Facilities: The sanitary block serving the touring section is modern and cheerful with bright yellow doors, and can be heated. It is supplemented by an older block in the holiday home section. Both well equipped, a laundry room and baby washing sinks are in the lower block. Dishwashing under cover. Well stocked shop with gas available (Easter - mid Sept). Bar snacks and restaurant meals with a family room. Takeaway (June-Sept). Indoor pool. Amusement arcade with video games. Playing field and play areas with a long slide and boat. **Off site:** Bicycle hire or riding 2 miles, fishing 1 mile, golf 1 mile.

Charges 2001

Per unit incl. up to 6 persons	£12.00 - £24.00
with electricity	£12.00 - £26.00
fully serviced with hardstanding	£13.50 - £27.50
extra tent, car or boat	£1.50

Less £2 for two persons only, less £1 for three persons. Tel: (01929) 422823. Fax: (01929) 421500. E-mail: enq@ulwellcottagepark.co.uk. Reservations: Made with 25% deposit; Sat.- Sat. only in high season. **Open** all year except 8 Jan - 28 Feb.

Directions: From A351 Wareham - Swanage road, turn on B3351 Studland road just before Corfe Castle, follow signs to right for Swanage and drop down to Ulwell. O.S.GR: SZ019809.

Merley Court Touring Park

208 Merley, Wimborne, nr Poole, Dorset BH21 3AA

Merley Court must be one of the best examples today of a family touring park and is a credit to the Wright family. It is a well planned, attractively landscaped park, run with consistent care and attention to high standards. The latest addition is the Leisure Garden, an historic walled garden (the Grade II listed walls date back to the 18th century) formerly part of the Merley House estate, the design and construction of which was overseen by John Nash. With flower collections, rock garden and sunken garden lovingly tended by Mrs Wright, it offers space for picnics and recreation facilities including croquet, crazy golf, petanque, badminton, volleyball and basketball or perhaps just an evening stroll. The touring area has 160 pitches for all types of unit, all with 16A electricity, on clearly marked neat lawns interspersed with a variety of shrubs, palms and plants and the odd ornamental urn. This provision includes 11 neat all-service pitches with water, waste water and satellite TV connection. Some attractive tent pitches nestle in a small wooded valley with woodland walks and a dog walk, complete with the graves of past doggie friends. The park's club complex is well furnished, providing a lounge bar where meals are available, a large indoor games room with pool tables and a family room that opens out onto a spacious and attractive sheltered patio. This in turn leads through to the paved, walled swimming pool area. A member of the Best of British group.

Facilities: Three heated, well designed toilet blocks are of good quality, two with pre-set well equipped showers. Separate facilities for disabled visitors and for babies. Excellent dishwashing and laundry facilities. Motorcaravan service point. Shop in the Leisure Gardens carries gas and caravan accessories. Café and takeaway. Bar with food (limited hours in low and mid season). Outdoor pool (30 x 20 ft) with children's section open mid May - Sept. Tennis and short tennis. Table tennis. Two children's play areas. Games room with pool tables. Conference/meeting venue available in the Orangery within the Leisure Garden. Dogs are not accepted in high season (14/7-31/8). Secure caravan storage (all year). Barrier card £5 deposit. **Off site:** Fishing, bicycle hire, riding and golf all within 5 miles. The park is only 6 miles from Poole, 8 from Bournemouth. Tower Park leisure and entertainment centre is nearby, Kingston Lacy House, Knoll Gardens and Brownsea Island are also near.

Charges 2001

Per standard pitch incl. 2 persons	£7.50 - £12.50
all service pitch (excl. electricity)	£10.00 - £15.00
extra adult	£3.00
child (3-13 yrs)	£2.00
awning (no tent as well as awning)	£1.00
dog (outside 14/7-31/8)	£1.00
electricity (16A)	£2.00

Min. 5 nights Easter, 7 nights Spr B.H. and high season. Less 10% for senior citizens in low season (excl. B.Hs). Tel: (01202) 881488. Fax: (01202) 881484. E-mail: holidays@merley-court.co.uk. Reservations: Made with deposit (£35 p/w), balance due 28 days before arrival. **Open** all year except 8 Jan - 28 Feb.

Directions: Park is signed at an exit from the A31/A349 roundabout on the Wimborne bypass. O.S.GR: ST008984.

Whitemead Caravan Park

209 East Burton Road, Wool, Dorset BH20 6HG

The Church family continue to make improvements to this attractive little park which is within walking distance of the village of Wool, between Dorchester and Wareham. Very natural and with open views over the Frome Valley water meadows, it provides 95 numbered pitches on flat grass sloping gently north and is orchard-like in parts. The pitches are well spaced and mostly back onto hedges or fences. There are 65 electrical connections for tourers (10A) and no caravan holiday homes. The park is 4½ miles from the nearest beach at Lulworth and is handily placed for many attractions in this part of Dorset (train services and limited bus service close). Possibly some rail noise.

Facilities: The single, comfortably sized toilet block includes a baby room which doubles as a facility for disabled visitors. Dishwashing and laundry sinks, washing machine, spin and tumble dryer. Takeaway (breakfasts at weekends). Shop (limited hours) with off licence and gas. Games room with pool table and darts. Children's playground. Caravan storage. **Off site**: Ship Inn 300 m. Riding or golf 3 miles.

Charges 2001

Per caravan, tent or motorcaravan	£4.25 - £8.25
person over 5 yrs	£1.00
awning or tent (over 15 x 15)	£1.00 - £1.50
dog	75p
electricity	£2.00

No credit cards. Tel/Fax: (01929) 462241. E-mail: nadinechurch@aol.com. Reservations: Made with £15 deposit, min. 3 nights at B.Hs. **Open** 20 March - 31 October.

Directions: Turn off main A352 on eastern edge of Wool, just north of level crossing, onto East Burton road. Site is 300 m. on right. O.S.GR: SY841871.

 Alan Rogers' discount
Less 50p in mid and low seasons

Wilksworth Farm Caravan Park

206 Cranborne Road, Wimborne, Dorset BH21 4HW

Wilksworth Farm is a spacious, quiet park with a heated outdoor pool, and is well suited for families. It has a lovely rural situation just outside Wimborne and around 10 miles from the beaches between Poole and Bournemouth. With its duck pond at the entrance, it is well designed on good quality ground with fairly level grass and some views. It takes 65 caravans (awning groundsheets up in daytime) and 25 tents mainly on grass but with some hardstandings. All pitches have electrical connections, 10 also with water and drainage. There are some 77 privately owned and self contained caravan holiday homes. Facilities are in converted farm barns or designed to be in keeping with the listed buildings.

Facilities: The good quality, central toilet block is well maintained. The ladies' part has been completely refurbished with under-floor heating throughout (the men's due for 2002). Family bathroom and facilities for disabled visitors, a shower/bath for children and baby changing point. Covered dishwashing sinks outside. Laundry room. Reception and shop (basics only, limited hours, Easter - 30 Sept). Gas supplies. Freezer for ice packs. Attractive coffee shop with full menu and takeaway service (weekends and B.Hs only outside the main season). Heated 40 x 20 ft. swimming pool (unsupervised, but fenced and gated, open May - Sept) with small children's pool. Football ground. Excellent adventure play area. BMX track, golf practice net and two tennis courts, one full and one short size. Games room with table tennis, pool, some games machines. Winter caravan storage. **Off site**: Golf, fishing and riding 3 miles. Tower Park entertainment centre 6 miles, Kingston Lacy (NT) 3 miles and Wimborne town centre (with its Minster) 1 mile.

Charges 2001

Per pitch incl. 2 adults	£6.00 - £14.00
child (3-16 yrs) July, Aug. & Spr. B.H	£1.00
other times one free with each adult	
extra adult	£2.00
dog	£1.00
boat, extra car or pup tent	£1.00
electricity	£2.00
full services	£1.00

No credit cards. Tel/Fax: (01202) 885467. Reservations: Advised for July/Aug. and B.Hs. Made with payment in full at booking or £20 per week deposit; balance more than 28 days beforehand (min. 5 days at B.Hs). **Open** 1 March - 30 October.

Directions: Park is 1 mile north of Wimborne, west off the B3078 road to Cranborne. O.S.GR: SU010019.

Pear Tree Touring Park

211 Organford Road, Holton Heath, Poole, Dorset BH16 6LA

Pear Tree is obviously the pride and joy of its owners, Mr and Mrs Broome, and this clearly shows. It is a neat, well cared for park catering for families and couples only. Set in 7½ acres, with mature trees and views across to Wareham Forest, the 125 good sized, grassy pitches are separated into areas by high hedges and shrubs. There are 120 pitches with 10A electricity, 50 with full services (water, waste water and electricity) of which 26 have hardstanding. Only breathable groundsheets are permitted for awnings. The tent area is a lovely secluded spot with many mature trees. Reception and a small shop supplying milk, bread, gas and other basics is at the park entrance where the gates (with key) are closed at 9 pm. (no late arrivals area, so book in before 9 pm) and tourist information. A large, hedged, separate children's play field is at the top of the park with swings, climbing frame, trampolines and ball games area. A bus service stops outside for Wareham (2½ miles) or Poole (8 miles).

Facilities: The main heated toilet block (opened by key) provides coin-operated hot water throughout (20p), with a baby changing unit and two WCs for disabled visitors. A separate small block is near the tent area. All is kept spotlessly clean. Motorcaravan service point. Shop (basics only). Fish and chip van calls three times weekly in high season. Children's play area. Dogs are only accepted outside July/Aug. All year caravan storage. **Off site**: The Clay Pipe Inn is just 500 m. Fishing lake 500 m. (day tickets from reception). Bicycle hire. Riding 5 miles, golf 2 miles.

Charges 2001

Per unit incl. 2 persons	£8.00 - £11.00
extra adult	£3.00
child (3-14 yrs)	£1.50
dog (not July/Aug)	£2.00
electricity (10A)	£2.20 - £2.50

Security key deposit £10 (refundable). Tel: (01202) 622434. Fax: (01202) 631985. E-mail: info@ visitpeartree.co.uk. Reservations: Made with £25 deposit (min. 4 nights in high season). **Open** Easter - mid October.

Directions: Park is just west off A351 (Wareham - Poole) road at Holton Heath near Sandford Park. O.S.GR: SY940915.

The Inside Park Touring Caravan & Camping Park

Blandford Forum, Dorset DT11 9AD

The Inside Park is set in the grounds of an 18th century country house that burned down in 1941. Family owned and carefully managed alongside a dairy and arable farm, it is a must for those interested in local history or arboriculture and is a haven for wildlife and birds. The reception/toilet block and games room block are respectively the coach house and stables of the old house. The 9-acre camping field, a little distant, lies in a sheltered, gently sloping dry valley containing superb tree specimens - notably cedars, with walnuts in one part - and a dog graveyard dating back to the early 1700s under a large Cedar of Lebanon. In total there are 125 spacious pitches, 90 with electricity (10A) and some in wooded glades. The six acres adjoining are the old pleasure gardens of the house where campers can walk and exercise dogs in the former garden, now mostly overgrown and providing what must be one of the largest children's campsite adventure-lands in the UK. No vehicle access to the park is allowed after 10.30 pm. (separate late arrivals area and car park). The market town of Blandford with its leisure and swimming centre (temporary membership for Inside Park guests) is 2 miles and the area is excellent for walking and cycling (test your fitness on a 5 mile mountain bike course). Extensive walking routes are marked through the farm and woodland, with a guide showing points of interest available in the shop and farm tours are organised.

Facilities: The toilet block provides some washbasins in cubicles, comfortably sized showers with non-slip floors and a room for disabled visitors or mothers and babies. Dishwashing sinks. Laundry room in the same block. Recycling bins. Shop with basics, gas and camping provisions (limited opening out of main season). Mobile fish and chips twice weekly. Spacious games room with pool tables, table tennis, etc. and a tourist information section. Safe based children's adventure play area. Day kennelling facilities for dogs. Winter caravan storage. **Off site:** Fishing and riding 2 miles, golf 3 miles.

Charges 2001

Per pitch	£3.00 - £4.80
adult	£2.50 - £3.00
child (5-16 yrs)	free - £1.10
dog	60p - 90p
electricity	£2.25

Tel: (01258) 453719. Fax: (01258) 459921. E-mail: inspark@aol.com. Reservations: Essential for B.Hs and high season; made with £10 deposit (min. 4 nights 14/7-2/9). **Open** Easter - 31 October.

Directions: Park is about 2 miles southwest of Blandford and is signed from roundabout junction of A354 and A350 roads. If approaching from the Shaftesbury direction, do not go into Blandford but follow the bypass to the last roundabout and follow camp signs. O.S.GR: ST864045.

Sandford Holiday Park

210 Holton Heath, nr Poole, Dorset BH16 6JZ

Sandford Park is a pleasant, well run park with many first-class amenities near the popular coastal areas of Dorset. It has a large permanent section with 248 static holiday homes and lodges. However, the touring sections can accommodate around 500 units of any type, mainly on individual pitches, on level grass with mature hedging in the main area, all with 10A electrical connections. Early booking is advisable. Sandford is a large, very busy holiday park with a wide range of entertainment. The clubhouse (free membership) is spacious with a dance floor, bar and seating area, and caters for different tastes and age groups. There is also a large air-conditioned ballroom for entertainment and dancing. Both are open over a long season, also a variety of bars, restaurants (book in busy periods) and simple hot meals, breakfasts and takeaway in peak season. The heated outdoor swimming pool and a very large play pool with a sandy beach, ideal for children, are attractively situated with a snack bar, terraced area and go-kart track. There is also an impressive, heated and supervised indoor pool which is a nice addition.

Facilities: The main toilet block in the touring area provides facilities for disabled visitors and a baby room. It is supplemented by the former main block and subsidiary 'portacabin' style units in the touring and static areas (one a bath block). Could be under pressure at peak times. Large launderette. Ladies' hairdresser. Bars, restaurants. TV lounges. Outdoor swimming pool (25 m. long, open May-Sept. and supervised) and indoor pool. Large supermarket and other shops, including well stocked camping accessory shop (all open peak season only). Soft indoor play area for children (April - Oct and Christmas, supervised). Children's playground, two tennis courts, mountain bike hire, table tennis, two short mat bowling greens (outdoor) and a large crazy golf course. Riding lessons available at stables on site. Dogs or pets are only permitted in the touring section from 2 Sept.

Charges 2001

Per pitch	free - £6.25
adult	£4.45
child (3-13 yrs)	£1.50 - £2.65
electricity	£2.75
'super hook-up' (16A electricity, TV, water)	£4.50
dog (1 only, after 2 Sept)	£2.50
boat and trailer	£1.50 - £2.00

Special offers and special interest weeks. Tel: (01202) 631600. E-mail: bookings@ weststarholidays.co.uk. Reservations: Early booking advisable (min. 3 days). **Open** February - January.

Directions: Park is just west off A351 (Wareham - Poole) road at Holton Heath. O.S.GR: SY940913.

See advertisement on page 13

Mount Pleasant Touring Park

214 Matchams Lane, Hurn, Christchurch, Dorset BH23 6AW

Mount Pleasant is a surprisingly pretty, rural park for its situation near Bournemouth, however it is on the edge of the New Forest. Under new ownership, it is a neat tidy park with 170 numbered pitches on mostly level, sandy grass with circular connecting tarmac roads. Neatly fenced and interspersed with pine trees, rhododendron bushes and newly planted evergreens, there are 95 pitches for touring units, 86 of them marked and with 10A electricity, with a separate, more open and sloping area for tents. A card operated security barrier is at the entrance. Bournemouth is around 10 minutes by car (depending on the traffic). The nearest bus service is 2 miles. Due to its situation between Bournemouth airport and the A338 dual-carriageway there may be road or aircraft noise. Despite this, it is a very popular, well run park.

Facilities: Two good, purpose built modern toilet blocks can be heated and provide some washbasins in cubicles, a toddler room and a separate, en-suite unit for disabled visitors. Laundry room. Good basic shop with information area. Mobile takeaway including breakfast (open all season, closed afternoons). Adventure play area. **Off site:** Fishing or golf 2 miles. Riding or boat launching facilities 4 miles. Dry ski centre within ½ mile with bars and restaurants.

Charges 2001

Per unit incl. up to 2 persons	£7.00 - £12.00
small tent	£5.50 - £9.50
extra person (over 4 yrs)	£1.00 - £2.00
dog	£1.00 - £1.50
electricity (10A)	£2.00

Tel: (01202) 475474. Fax: (01202) 475428. E-mail: enq@mount-pleasant-cc.co.uk. Reservations: Made with £30 deposit (non-refundable). **Open** 1 March - 31 October (try phoning for winter stays).

Directions: From A338 Ringwood-Bournemouth road, take B3073 in direction of Hurn airport. Follow camp signs at first mini roundabout onto Matchams Lane. O.S.GR: SZ129987.

Grove Farm Meadow Holiday Park

Stour Way, Christchurch, Dorset BH23 2PQ

This is a quiet, traditional park with caravan holiday homes and a small provision for touring caravans. The grassed flood bank which separates the River Stour from this park provides an attractive walkway. The river bank has been kept natural and is well populated by a range of ducks and a resident swan family and early in the season they parade their young through the park. There are just under 200 caravan holiday homes (118 privately owned, 77 for hire), regularly sited in rows. For touring units 44 level grass pitches, all with 15A electricity, are clearly numbered, backing on to fencing or hedging and accessed by tarmac roads. Some are fully serviced (with hardstanding, shingle base for awnings and chemical disposal point), the other grass pitches sharing service points. The impressive modern reception has a good collection of tourist information. The Littledown Centre, said to be the south coast's premier leisure facility is nearby. Bournemouth is 10 minutes by car, Christchurch 5.

Facilities: The toilet block is nicely tiled with a bathroom for each sex (50p), a separate toilet and washbasin with ramp access for disabled visitors. Baby room. Dishwashing sinks. Spin dryer, iron and board and a washing line, with a launderette near reception. Games room with pool table and video games. Play area beside the river bank. Good, well stocked shop (8-8 in high season but limited hours in early March and late Oct). Fishing. Bicycle hire can be arranged. No dogs or other pets are accepted.
Off site: Boat launching 4 miles, public 9 hole golf course (pay as you go) nearby.

Charges guide

Per 'luxury' pitch incl. 2 persons, 10A electricity and awning	£9.00 - £18.00
large pitch	£8.00 - £16.00
standard pitch (no awnings)	£6.00 - £14.00
extra person over 5 yrs	£1.00 - £2.00

Tel: (01202) 483597. Fax: (01202) 483878. E-mail: enquiries@meadowbank-hols.demon.co.uk. Reservations: Made for Sat-Sat or Sun-Sun in high season, min. 3 nights at other times, with £30 deposit. Contact Meadowbank Holidays at above address. **Open** 1 March - 31 October.

Directions: From A388 Ringwood - Bournemouth road take B3073 for Christchurch. Turn right at the first roundabout and Stour Way is the third road on the right. O.S.GR: SZ136946.

234 Shamba Touring Park

234

Ringwood Road, St Leonards, Ringwood, Hampshire BH24 2SB

The Gray family have been gradually upgrading Shamba over the last few years and it is developing into a comfortable, friendly park with good sized, well drained pitches (150 in total, all with 10A electricity). Most of the amenities are good and as the owners have a young family themselves, they seem to be aware of the needs of little people and cater well for them. The Grays live on site as well and have managed to create a relaxed, pleasant atmosphere. Bournemouth with its beaches is 8 miles, Ringwood 2½ miles and the Moors Valley Country Park 1 mile. The site is near the A31 so there could be some road noise. The access road is rather uneven, but persevere and you will find a pleasant site.

Facilities: The showers are in a separate heated block. The rest of the provision is adequate if a little dated, although it is kept clean and includes facilities for children. Covered dishwashing sinks. Laundry sink, two washing machines and two dryers. Improvements are planned. Well stocked shop. Cosy bar with snacks, takeaway and a small family room. Large play area and a games room with video games and table football. Small heated outdoor fenced pool. **Off site:** Riding and a fishing lake 500 yds.

Charges 2001

Per pitch incl. 2 persons	£8.50 - £13.00
extra person	£2.00 - £2.50
electricity	£2.00
dog	£1.00 - £2.00

Tel/Fax: (01202) 873302. E-mail: holidays@ shamba.co.uk. Reservations: Made with £25 non-returnable deposit. **Open** 1 March - 31 October

Directions: Site is signed directly off the A31 Ringwood - Wimborne Road, 400 yds. down a small lane. Approaching from the east, after passing Little Chef, you will need to go round the next roundabout back on yourself, then immediately left down lane. O.S.GR: SU104026.

Red Shoot Camping Park

235

Linwood, nr Ringwood, Hampshire BH24 3QT

Red Shoot is set on three acres of open, slightly sloping, level grassland, in the heart of the New Forest. A rural retreat with panoramic views of the surrounding countryside and forest, it is very popular in high season. There are around 130 good sized pitches, 45 with electricity (16A), served by a circular gravel road. There is no site lighting so a torch would be useful. The adjacent Red Shoot Inn (under separate ownership) serves hot or cold meals and brews its own real ales - Forest Gold and Tom's Tipple. There are ample opportunities for walking, cycling and naturalist pursuits. Local attractions include watersports at the New Forest Water Park near Ringwood, a Doll Museum in Fordingbridge, cider making in Burley, and Breamore House just north of Fordingbridge.

Facilities: Toilet facilities are fairly modern, well maintained and practical, but not luxurious. Dishwashing sinks under cover. Laundry plus baby bath. Good unit for disabled visitors. Well stocked shop including camping equipment and gas. Fenced playground. Mountain bike and tandem hire.

Charges 2001

Per adult	£3.90
child (0-14 yrs)	£1.00 - £2.30
car or m/cycle	£1.10
electricity	£2.30
awning	£1.50
dog	70p

VAT not included. Min. stays at B.Hs (plus £4 surcharge per weekend). Less 20% in low seasons (min. 3 nights). Tel: (01425) 473789 or 478940. Fax: (01425) 471558. E-mail: enquiries@redshoot-campingpark.com Reservations: Advised for w/ends and peak season made with £15 deposit per week or part week. **Open** 1 March - 31 October.

Directions: From A338 about 1.75 miles north of Ringwood, turn east (signed Linwood and Moyles Court). Follow signs, over a staggered cross-roads, and continue straight on for another 1.75 miles to Red Shoot Inn. O.S.GR: SU188095.

Ashurst Caravan and Camping Site

Forestry Commission, Ashurst, nr Lyndhurst, Hampshire

230

An attractive Forestry Commission site on the fringe of the New Forest, Ashurst is set in a mixture of oak woodland and grass heathland which is open to the grazing animals of the Forest. Smaller than the Hollands Wood site (23 acres), it provides 280 pitches, 180 of which have been gravelled to provide semi-hardstanding; otherwise you pitch where you like, applying the 20 ft. rule on ground that can be uneven. There are no electricity connections. Some noise must be expected from the adjacent railway line - the station is just five minutes walk away. Reception is run by the very helpful site managers. There is a late arrivals area and separate car-parking area for those arriving or returning after the gate has closed (11.30 pm).

Facilities: The single central toilet block has been refurbished and provides everything necessary, including hairdryers, a well equipped unit for visitors with disabilities (key required) and a good laundry room. It could be under pressure when the site is full in the main season. No barbecues in dry weather. Dogs are not accepted. A torch is useful. **Off site:** A local garage sells gas. Nearby pub accessible by footpath across an adjacent field. Shops and local buses within a five minute walk. Guided forest walks are organised during the main season.

Charges 2001

Per unit incl. up to 4 persons	£6.40 - £12.50
extra person (over 5 yrs)	£1.00
extra car, gazebo or pup tent	£3.60

Less 20% all year for disabled guests and outside 7/7-28/8 for senior citizens. Reservations: Necessary for B.Hs and peak times (min. 3 nights with £30 deposit). Contact (at all times): Forest Holidays, Forestry Commission, 231 Corstorphine Road, Edinburgh EH12 7AT. Tel: (0131) 314 6505. E-mail: fe.holidays@forestry.gsi.gov.uk. **Open** 24 March - 29 September.

Directions: Site is 2 miles east of Lyndhurst, set back from the A35 Southampton - Bournemouth road, 5 miles southwest of Southampton. O.S.GR: SU332102.

Hollands Wood Caravan and Camping Site

Forestry Commission, Lyndhurst Road, Brockenhurst, Hampshire SO43 7QH

231

Hollands Wood is a large, spacious 168-acre secluded site in a natural woodland setting (mainly oak), in the heart of the New Forest, with an abundance of wildlife, including the famous New Forest ponies. The site is arranged informally with 600 level unmarked pitches but it is stipulated that there must be at least 20 feet between each unit. There are no electrical connections and possible traffic noise from the A337 which runs alongside one boundary. One area of the site is designated a dog free zone. The site has no shop, but it is only about ½ mile from Brockenhurst village where there are shops for supplies and gas, etc, plus trains and buses. Barbecues are not permitted in dry weather. The site can get very busy and we include the smaller Ashurst site as an alternative.

Facilities: Two large utilitarian toilet blocks (and a third smaller, older one) are fully equipped, if somewhat basic. Facilities for disabled people and baby changing surfaces. Two laundry rooms with washing machines and dryers. These facilities are under pressure at peak times. Motorcaravan service point. Night security with the barrier closed 23.30 - 07.30 hrs (overnight area). Torches essential.

Charges 2001

Per unit incl. up to 4 persons	£7.20 - £13.80
extra person (over 5 yrs)	£1.00
extra car, gazebo or pup tent	£3.90

Less 20% all year for disabled guests and outside 7/7-28/8 for senior citizens. Reservations: Necessary for B.Hs and peak times (min. 3 nights with £30 deposit). Contact (at all times): Forest Holidays, Forestry Commission, 231 Corstorphine Road, Edinburgh EH12 7AT. Tel: (0131) 314 6505. E-mail: fe.holidays@forestry.gov.uk. **Open** 22 March - 25 September.

Directions: Site entrance is on east side of A337 Lyndhurst - Lymington road, half a mile north of Brockenhurst. O.S.GR: SU303038.

Sandy Balls Holiday Centre

Godshill, Fordingbridge, Hampshire SP6 2JY

Sandy Balls must be one of the oldest 'camp sites' in the UK, celebrating its 75th anniversary in 1995. Ernest Westlake, grandfather of the present owners and an educationalist and idealist, bought the ancient woodland overlooking the Avon Valley in 1919 to save it from the axe and today, while the majestic oaks, beeches, Scots pine and larch have matured, new facilities have been designed to be in sympathy with the setting. Sandy Balls is now an award winning, well run park and is protected as a nature reserve.

Set within 120 acres, with a wide range of leisure facilities developed around a 'village' centre, it is open all year. Its extensive area comprises a series of fields that include terrain of different types: light woodland with 206 caravan and chalet holiday homes, and some tent areas with unmarked pitches, touring units for the most part on open meadows, and some general parts including woodland not used for camping. They include 256 all service pitches for touring units with electrical connections (10-16A), water, drainaway and TV connection (site satellite dish), on concrete or gravel with gravel hardstanding for awnings (steel pegs can be provided if required). In winter only 50 pitches are available. The central area with the park's facilities (see below) is pleasantly laid out and designed to blend with the forest surroundings. It includes a large indoor heated swimming pool and a solar heated outdoor pool. A nice addition is Valencio's pizzeria for eating in or takeaway. The park recently won a 'Good Lighting Award' from the British Astronomical Association for the design of its lighting that enables visitors to better appreciate the night sky; a new and unusual award for a park to win. Sandy Balls provides a range of all-round family entertainment, including a woodland leisure trail where wild animals and birds can be observed in their natural surroundings, as well as the New Forest on your doorstep. An ideal park for families and couples.

Facilities: There are three modern toilet blocks with under-floor heating and one of `portacabin' type that remains as overflow in the tent field (28 day). One block has a bath in each section (M&F) and all have washbasins in cubicles. The blocks are spacious and airy and should be adequate for peak season, with 'Northfield' having been added to provide extra, good quality facilities. Toilets for disabled visitors and baby changing facilities are provided in at least two blocks. Excellent launderette plus washing machines in all the toilet blocks. Motorcaravan service point and recycling stations - look for the green coloured sheds. Supermarket with own bakery. Takeaway. Restaurants, bars and family room. Wide screen TV and entertainment (every evening in high season). Indoor pool (66 x 30 ft) and outdoor pool (25/5-30/8). both with lifeguards and free at all times (in high season, sessions are timed according to demand). Well equipped fitness gym, jacuzzi spa bath, steam room, toning tables, sauna and solarium and dance studios. Games room with pool and table tennis. Adventure playground and children's play areas including soft ball area. River fishing on permit. Riding stables. Bicycle hire. Petanque, archery, orienteering and hot air balloon rides. Tourist information. Dogs are only allowed on certain fields.

Charges 2001

Serviced pitch weekends and high season	£17.00
mid-week	£12.75
non-serviced pitch weekends/high season	£15.00
mid-week	£11.25
Mid and high seasons only: adult	£1.50 - £3.50
young adult (12-17 yrs)	£1.25 - £2.00
child (3-11 yrs)	75p - £1.50
additional car or m/cycle	50p
dog	50p - £1.25

Tel: (01425) 653042. Fax: (01425) 653067. E-mail: post@sandy-balls.co.uk. Reservations: Made with deposit and compulsory cancellation insurance. **Open** all year.

Directions: Park is northwest off B3078 (Fordingbridge - Cadnam) just west of Godshill village, and about 1½ miles east of Fordingbridge. O.S.GR: SU168147.

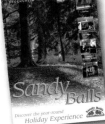

Hampshire

Hill Cottage Farm Caravan Park

236 Sandleheath Road, Alderholt, Fordingbridge, Hampshire SP6 3EG

First opened in 2000, this is a newly constructed, modern site set in 47 acres of beautiful countryside on the Dorset and Hampshire border. The 32 pitches, all on hardstandings with electric hook-ups (16A) are arranged around a circular gravel roadway. Secluded and sheltered, they have views across the surrounding countryside. A field alongside the camping area is used for tents and rallies, and has space for ball games and a small children's playground. Also on site are a tennis court and a lake for coarse fishing, and there are many woodland walks in the area. Overall this site is more suitable for adults and small children – it is not really designed for active teenagers. A 20 minute woodland walk will take you to the village centre with a pub, church, Post Office and store. Local attractions include Rockbourne Roman Villa, Cranborne Chase, The Dolls Museum at Fordingbridge, Salisbury, and Ringwood with its Wednesday market.

Facilities: A large modern barn-style building provides excellent heated facilities, including covered dishwashing sinks, a laundry room with washing machines and dryers, plus facilities for disabled people and babies – in all, a very generous provision. The first floor of this building has a games room with a full size snooker table, two pool tables and a darts board, plus a separate function room. Drive over motorhome services by reception. Children's playground.

Charges 2001

Per unit incl. 2 adults and electricity	£10.00-12.00
extra adult	£1.40
child	95p
awning	£1.00
dog	50p

Tel: (01425) 650513. Fax: (01425) 652339.
Reservations: Made with minimum £10 deposit. Advised for B.Hs and peak season. **Open** all year.

Directions: From Fordingbridge take B3078 westwards for 2 miles to Alderholt. On entering the village, at a left hand bend, turn right towards Sandleheath (site is signed), and the site entrance is approximately 300 yards on your left. O.S.GR: SU 120130.

Lytton Lawn Touring Park

Lymore Lane, Milford-on-Sea, Hampshire SO41 0TX

228

Lytton Lawn is the touring arm of Shorefield Country Park, a holiday home park and leisure centre. Situated 2½ miles from Shorefield itself, campers and caravanners staying at Lytton Lawn are entitled to free membership of the Leisure Club there. The comprehensive amenities at Shorefield are of a very good standard and are mostly free (extra charges are made for certain activities). They comprise a very attractive, heated indoor pool (20 m), a solarium, sauna, spa bath and steam room and two all weather tennis courts, open all year with trained attendants. There are outdoor pools, crazy golf, restaurant facilities including a bistro and a range of entertainment and activity programmes, fitness classes and treatments, all well managed and organised. Lytton Lawn provides 135 marked pitches, including 53 'premier' pitches (hardstanding, 16A electricity, pitch light, water and waste water outlet) in a hedged area of natural grass. This section, with its heated toilet block, is open for a longer season. The rest of the pitches, all with electricity (tenters note), are in the adjoining, but separate, gently sloping field, edged with mature trees and hedges and with a further toilet block. Access roads are tarmac or gravel. The New Forest, Isle of Wight, Bournemouth, Southampton and the beach at Milford on Sea are near.

Facilities: Two purpose built, modern toilet blocks are tiled and well fitted. Dishwashing, washing machine and dryer in each block. Baby changing facilities in one block and facilities for disabled visitors (Radar key). Simple shop (Easter - end Oct), with a supermarket, bistro (Easter - Oct) and takeaway (main season) at Shorefield. Small fenced children's play area and hedged field with goal posts. Only one dog per pitch is accepted. Off site: Village pub 10 minutes walk. Golf, riding, coarse fishing (all within 3 miles), sailing, windsurfing and boat launching facilities (1½ miles).

Charges 2001

Per 'premier' pitch incl. all persons, electricity, water, drainage and TV connection	£11.00 - £26.00
Basic pitch incl. electricity	£9.50 - £24.00
pup tent or awning free, together	£2.50
dog (1 only)	£3.00

Tel: (01590) 648331. Fax: (01590) 645610. E-mail: holidays@ shorefield.co.uk. Reservations: Made with deposit and cancellation insurance - contact Shorefield Holidays Ltd, Shorefield Road, Milford on Sea, nr Lymington, Hampshire SO41 0LH. **Open** all year except 4 Jan - 9 Feb.

Directions: From M27 follow signs for Lyndhurst and Lymington on A337. Continue towards New Milton and Lytton Lawn is signed at Everton; Shorefield is signed at Downton. O.S.GR: SZ293937.

Oakdene Forest Park

St Leonards, Ringwood, Hampshire BH24 2RZ

227

Set in 55 acres of park and woodland, with direct access to the Avon Forest and near the New Forest, Oakdene provides caravan holiday homes to let or 135 pitches for all types of touring unit. These pitches are numbered, many with electricity connections (10A) and including 43 'Premier' pitches. Free membership is provided for the Leisure and Country Club offering a bar, buffet and a range of entertainment. A super new indoor swimming pool with a flume and an outdoor pool have been built. Oakdene is part of the Shorefield group at Milford on Sea and massive investment is being carried out (as can be seen by the pools) and future plans aim to provide the quality and standard of facilities and entertainment found at Shorefield and Lytton Lawn (no. 228).

Facilities: Sanitary facilities include free hot showers, a purpose built launderette and dishwashing sinks. Shop (Easter - Oct). Café/bistro and bar (13 March - 28 Oct). Outdoor pools (26 May - 10 Sept). Crazy golf. Children's adventure play area and Cyril the Squirrel's Kids Club. Bicycle hire.

Charges 2001

Per pitch incl. electricity and water	£5.70 - £26.00
dog	£3.00

Lower prices for mid-week. Min. stays at B.Hs. Tel: (01590) 648331. Reservations: All bookings are handled by   Shorefield Holidays, Shorefield Road, Milford on Sea, nr. Lymington, Hampshire SO41 0LH. Tel: (01590) 648331. Fax: (01590) 645610. E-mail: holidays@shorefield.co.uk. **Open** all year except January.

Directions: Park access leads off the main A31 westbound carriageway about 2½ miles west of Ringwood. O.S.GR: SU101016.

South Coast
and New Forest

With two high quality destinations to choose from, Shorefield Holidays offers you the best of both worlds in touring locations

LYTTON LAWN
TOURING PARK

Set in beautiful natural parkland close to Milford beach and the historic New Forest with views to the Isle of Wight. Peaceful, unspoilt and relaxing. Electricity hook-up, showers, laundrette, shop, 'Premier Pitches' and a children's area. Optional Leisure Club facilities 2$^1/_2$ miles away, at Shorefield.

OAKDENE
FOREST PARK

Over 55 acres of beautiful parkland giving direct access to the Avon Forest, and only 9 miles from Bournemouth's sandy beaches. New 'Premier Pitches', indoor and outdoor pools, sauna, steam room, spa bath, flume, gym, adventure playground, club with entertainment, cafeteria, takeaway, general store and launderette.

SHOREFIELD
HOLIDAYS LIMITED

RALLIES WELCOME AT BOTH SITES

2000
DAVID BELLAMY
CONSERVATION AWARD
GOLD

For further details telephone
01590 648331 Ref. A.R.

Oakdene Forest Park, St. Leonards, Ringwood, Hants BH24 2RZ
Lytton Lawn, Lymore Lane, Milford on Sea, Hants SO41 0TX
e-mail: holidays@shorefield.co.uk   www.shorefield.co.uk

ENGLAND FOR EXCELLENCE
THE ENGLISH TOURIST BOARD
AWARDS FOR TOURISM

Hoburne Bashley Park

225 Sway Road, New Milton, Hampshire BH25 5QR

A pleasant, well run park with many holiday homes (380, including some for hire), Bashley Park also has a very sizeable tourist section and can take 420 touring units. However, tents, trailer tents and pup tents are not accepted. Spread over three flat meadows and a woodland area, complete with visiting squirrels, individual pitches with electricity are marked out. Many are now separated by fences and growing hedges, and have hardstanding - a useful development. Groundsheets must be lifted daily. Set in pleasant park-like surroundings not far from beaches, Bournemouth and the New Forest, the site has a good clubhouse with excellent facilities. This overlooks an 18 m. circular outdoor swimming pool (heated mid-May - mid-Sept) and 18 m. children's paddling pool, a sensible size and fun with its geysers and beach effect. An impressive indoor pool complex houses a water flume, sauna, spa bath and steam room. Evening entertainment is provided (also for children) in the club with live or taped music (Spring B.H. to mid-Sept) and it has a ballroom, large lounges and bars, a restaurant, and simple hot food takeaway all day. A popular park with lots going on, Bashley is part of the Hoburne group.

Facilities: Four well constructed toilet blocks, one central to each area, are fully tiled with modern fittings. Two have been refurbished in cheerful yellow and blue with washbasins in cabins. They have push-button, pre-set showers (no dividers, but shower heads are set fairly low). Launderette. Clubhouse with bars, restaurant and takeaway. TV room. Video arcade and games room with two full-size snooker tables, plus three pool tables spread among other rooms. Children's club. Shop (mid-May - end Sept). Indoor and outdoor swimming pools. Crazy golf. Golf course (9 hole, par 3). Tennis courts (3). Bicycle hire. Children's play area. Only one dog or pet permitted per unit. Up to 6 American motorhomes are accepted (40 ft. max). **Off site:** Fishing or riding 1 mile.

Charges guide

Per unit incl. all persons	£10.00 - £25.00
multi service pitch	£10.50 - £30.00
pet (1 only)	£2.00

Weekend breaks available. Tel: (01425) 612340. Fax: (01425) 632732. E-mail: enquiries@hoburne.co.uk. Reservations: Necessary for peak season and made for any length: 1-6 nights with payment in full at booking; 7+ nights, £50 p/w. deposit, balance 3 weeks before arrival. **Open** 28 February - 31 October.

Directions: Park is on the B3055 about / mile east of the crossroads with the B3058 in Bashley village. O.S.GR: SZ246969.

Camping and Caravanning Club Site Chichester

232 Main Road, Southbourne, Hampshire PO10 8JH

This is a small, neat park, just to the west of Chichester and north of Bosham harbour. Formerly an orchard, it is rectangular in shape with 60 pitches on flat, well mown lawns on either side of gravel roads. All pitches have 16A electricity, 32 with level hardstanding. Although the new A27 bypass takes most of the through traffic, the site is by the main A259 road so there may be some traffic noise in some parts (not busy at night). Opposite the park are orchards through which paths lead to the seashore and the location is ideal for touring this part of the south coast or inland. There are shops, restaurants and pubs within easy walking distance in the nearby village and the park is on a main bus route. Unfortunately there is no overnight area for late arrivals; the gates are shut between 11 pm. and 7 am. with no parking outside. An excellent caravan shop is near. Chichester has a leisure centre and market day is Wednesday. Also nearby are Bignor Roman villa, Apuldram Roses and the Weald and Downland open-air museum.

Facilities: The well designed, brick built toilet block is of first class quality. Fully tiled and heated in cool weather, with facilities for people with disabilities (access by key). Washing machines and dryers. Gas supplies. No ball games permitted on the park. Dogs can be walked in the lane opposite the entrance. Security barrier. **Off site:** Fishing or golf 5 miles, riding 6 miles.

Charges 2001

Per adult	£4.80 - £5.30
child (6-18 yrs)	£1.65
non-member pitch fee	£4.30
electricity	£1.65 - £2.40

Tel: (01243) 373202 (no calls after 8 pm). Reservations: Necessary and made with deposit (min. 2 nights); contact site. **Open** 7 February - 26 November.

Directions: Park is on main A259 Chichester - Havant road at Southbourne, 750 yards west of Chichester Caravans. O.S.GR: SU774056.

Isle of Wight

Isle of Wight Tourism, Westridge Centre, Blading Road, Ryde, Isle of Wight PO33 1QS
Tel: 01983 813818 Fax: 01983 823031

Internet: www.island_breaks.co.uk

The island is a popular destination with a certain old world charm, combining coast and countryside activities and scenery with a mild, sunny climate and a network of footpaths and bridleways. It has a wide range of tourist attractions and sports facilities. Ferry companies offer mid-week discount packages for touring caravan owners. We found that most of the park owners are knowledgeable about deals and we suggest you contact the parks and let them arrange the most economical crossing.

A new museum has opened in Sandown - Dinosaur Isle. The first purpose built museum for dinosaurs in Britain, it is located on the east coast at Sandown. The striking exterior of the building has been modelled on a pterodactyl. An introductory exhibition deals with the geology and fossils of the island, which is one of the most fruitful regions for dinosaur excavation in Europe, running back 120 million years.

Red Funnel Ferries

As the original cross-Solent operator, Red Funnel celebrated 135 years of running a ferry service between Southampton and Cowes with the introduction of three super modern car ferries. The new ships have been fitted out to a very high standard and we were very impressed with the on-board facilities which include a shop, bar, restaurant, seating areas and sun deck. Each vessel is able to carry up to 140 cars and there are 19 sailings a day in high season. The crossing time is 55 minutes.

The Orchards Holiday Caravan Park

Newbridge, Yarmouth, Isle of Wight PO41 0TS

In a village situation in the quieter western part of the island, The Orchards is a busy and lively family holiday park combining 63 holiday caravans (in a separate area) with a neat touring area. Run personally by the proprietor, it provides a pleasant, comfortable base from which to explore, situated about four miles from the beaches and from Yarmouth. A pool complex provides a medium size, heated swimming pool and children's pool (late May - early Sept) with a grass sunbathing area, supplemented by an irregularly shaped indoor pool with spa pool (on payment, open all year and supervised), attractively glass walled with terrace and café bar for relaxing – a nice addition. About 175 marked pitches are arranged on gently sloping meadow, broken up by apple trees, mature hedges and fences. All have electricity and 84 have hardstanding, including 12 with water hook up and drain. The large reception provides useful tourist information. A meeting room (up to 50 persons) is suitable for small rallies. Golfing and walking holidays are arranged. Part of the Caravan Club's 'managed under contract' scheme, non-members are also very welcome, the park is also a member of the Best of British group.

Facilities: Sanitary facilities are provided by three blocks of varying age and size which together should be an ample provision. A few washbasins are in private cabins. Baths on payment. The latest block, a smart mobile unit, provides en-suite facilities (shower, WC and basin). Facilities for disabled visitors (a hardstanding pitch close by can be reserved). Full laundry facilities. Motorcaravan service point. Ice pack and battery charging services. Gas supplies. Well stocked shop and takeaway service (mid-March - Oct, limited opening at quiet times). Indoor and outdoor pools. Football pitch. Muilti-court. Exercise stations. Pool, table tennis, TV and amusements rooms (no evening entertainment on site). Coarse fishing on site (no closed season).
Off site: Bicycle hire, boat launching 4 miles, riding 1 mile. Membership is available for the village social club and a small discount at Freshwater golf course (4 miles) - ask at reception.

Charges 2001

Per unit incl. 2 adults	£7.95 - £11.55
extra adult	£3.35 - £5.15
child	£1.50 - £3.25
electricity (16A)	£2.20 - £3.05
all-service pitch	plus £3.15
dog	75p - £1.35

No pitch fee for hikers or cyclists. Packages incl. ferry travel available - ring park for best deal. Tel: (01983) 531331 or 531350. Fax: (01983) 531666. E-mail: info@orchards-holiday-park.co.uk. Reservations: Made for min. 5 days with £30 p/wk deposit. **Open** all year excl. 3 Jan - 15 Feb.

Directions: Park is in Newbridge village, signed north from B3401 (Yarmouth - Newport) road. O.S.GR: SZ412878.

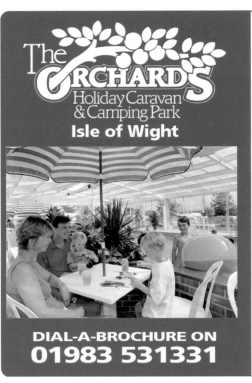

- Special ferry inclusive package holidays for caravanners and campers

- Holiday caravans to let, some with double glazing and central heating

- **Indoor pool** (open all year) **Outdoor pool** (open late May-early Sept)

- Superb self service shop / takeaway food bar (open late March-October)

- Coarse fishing (all year)

- Small rallies welcome

The Orchards, Newbridge, Yarmouth, Isle of Wight, PO41 0TS
info@orchards-holiday-park.co.uk
www.orchards-holiday-park.co.uk

Southland Camping Park

Newchurch, Sandown, Isle of Wight PO36 0LZ

247

Southland was opened in 1981 in the grounds of a former nursery and it has matured nicely with many attractive shrubs and trees. In the peaceful country setting of the Arreton valley, it is a sheltered and well run park with 120 large, level pitches backing on to and separated by hedging. Comfortable and spacious, all have electricity (10/16A) and some water points. Nearby Arreton and Newchurch have craft shops and in August there is the National Garlic Festival. Sandown and Shanklin are 3 miles, the beach at Lake, 2½ miles. A member of the Countryside Discovery group.

Facilities: The excellent toilet block is well maintained – the ladies' is modern, with washbasins in spacious cubicles, low level washbasins for children, three en-suite basin and shower cubicles, and a hairdressing area. Bathroom (on payment), baby room, a good unit for disabled people, and two new family shower rooms also suitable for disabled visitors. Laundry and dishwashing sinks. Motorcaravan service point. Shop. Fenced children's play area. Only raised barbecues are permitted. More than one dog per pitch by prior arrangement only. **Off site**: Fishing ½ mile, riding 2 miles, bicycle hire or golf 3 miles. Main bus route stops at the top of the road, two pubs are within walking distance and there is direct access to walks and bridleways. Concessions at Heights Sports Centre for visitors.

Charges 2002

Per adult	£3.60 - £5.65
child (3-15 yrs)	£1.65 - £3.10
electricity	£2.00
dog	£1.10

Packages incl. ferry travel available. Special low season offers. Tel: (01983) 865385. Fax: (01983) 867663. E-mail: info@southland.co.uk. Reservations: Made for any length with £30 deposit per pitch, per week (or part week). **Open** Easter - end September.

Directions: Park is signed from A3055/6 Newport-Sandown road, southeast of Arreton. O.S.GR: SZ557847.

Appuldurcombe Gardens Caravan and Camping Park

Wroxall, nr Ventnor, Isle of Wight PO38 3EP

248

This well kept little park would be a pleasant spot for a stay on the Isle of Wight. Quietly situated in a village and once part of the grounds of Appuldurcombe House, it is a little back from the sea - Ventnor beach 2½ miles and Shanklin 3 - with distant views and good walks nearby. It has a good, sheltered, heated swimming pool (60 x 25 ft.), with underwater floodlighting (Spr. BH.- end Aug) and an attractive bar and lounge, with dance floor, beside the pool, where there is limited entertainment at Spr. B.H. and school holidays. It is therefore quite a lively park - there are also 40 holiday caravans for hire in the attractive, old walled garden and two 8-bed flats. The 100 marked touring pitches, 48 with electricity (10A), are arranged on either side of gravel access roads on a slightly sloping grassy meadow. A further field with a pond is available for recreation, with goal posts, and a little stream flows past the reception block. The park can be peaceful and quiet in early and late season, whilst being busily active in high season.

Facilities: Two small toilet units serve the site. The older one, now very dated, is behind reception and to one side of the touring field. The other unit, more recently refurbished, is close to the pool in the old walled garden with facilities for disabled visitors. Small shop in school holiday periods, otherwise limited. Swimming pool, and bar. **Off site:** Fishing, bicycle hire, riding, golf and boat launching facilities within 3 miles.

Charges 2002

Per adult	£3.50 - £5.50
child (3-13 yrs)	£2.50
pitch	£1.00 - £2.25
dog	50p or £3.00 per week
electricity	£2.50

Tel: (01983) 852597. Fax: (01983) 856225. E-mail: appuldurcombe@freeuk.com. Reservations: Made with £10 non-refundable deposit per week booked. **Open** 1 April - 31 October.

Directions: From Newport take A3020 Sandown road, turning right to Shanklin. Follow through Godshill to Whiteley Bank roundabout and turn right for Wroxall. Continue for 1 mile past Donkey Sanctuary and site is to right in village - watch for sign. The entrance to the site access lane is off a narrow road on a blind bend and the access lane itself is too narrow for two units to pass (unguarded stream on one side and corners with jutting out walls). O.S.GR: SZ548803.

Kite Hill Farm Caravan and Camping Park

Firestone Copse Road, Wootton Bridge, Ryde, Isle of Wight PO33 4LE

249

Kite Hill Farm is a traditional touring site on the northern side of the island, near Fishbourne. It is set in a designated area of outstanding natural beauty, in an elevated position above the old mill pond of Wootton Creek, where you may find kingfishers and herons. In the woods below the site you might catch a glimpse of the island's other famous inhabitant - the red squirrel. The site's 50 unmarked pitches are on a large gently sloping field, with 48 electric hook-ups (10A). There is a small children's playground plus a very large area for ball games, etc. (kite flying is not allowed due to light overhead power cables). Torches would be useful. Wootton Bridge village has a fish and chip shop, plus a mini-market that is open long hours, and several supermarkets are only ten minutes away by car. The Firestone Copse, managed by the Forestry Commission, is nearby with walking trails and wildlife. Local attractions include the Steam Railway, Butterfly World, Brickfields Horse Country, Robin Hill Theme Park, and Haseley Manor - the island's oldest manor.

Facilities: The tiled modern sanitary unit, has controllable, high pressure showers. Dishwashing and laundry sinks, washing machines, dryer and ironing. Full facilities for disabled persons. Gas available from reception. Children's play area. **Off site**: Fishing, riding and golf, all within 3 miles. Bus stop close (every 15 minutes to most parts of the island).

Charges 2002

Per unit incl. 2 adults	£7.00 - £8.00
extra adult	£3.00 - £3.50
child (5-15 yrs)	£1.50 - £2.10
electricity	£2.00
dog	free

Tel: (01983) 882543. Fax: (01983) 883261. Reservations: Advisable for B.Hs and peak season, made with £15 p/week deposit. **Open** all year.

Directions: From A3054 (Newport - Ryde road), just east of Wootton Bridge, half way up hill (where site is signed) turn right into lane, site entrance is 250 yds. on right. O.S.GR: SZ550918.

Heathfield Farm Camping

Heathfield Road, Freshwater, Isle of Wight PO40 9SH

250

Heathfield is a pleasant contrast to many of the other sites on the Isle of Wight, in that it is a 'no frills' sort of place, very popular with tenters, cyclists and small motorcaravans. Despite its name, it is no longer a working farm. A large, open meadow provides 60 large, level pitches, 30 with electricity (10A), and a very large open area for non-electric pitches. A play field for ball games also has two picnic tables and two barbecues provided. There is no shop as you are only eight minutes walk from the centre of Freshwater. The site overlooks Colwell Bay and across the Solent towards Milford-on-Sea and Hurst Castle. It is ideal for visiting attractions on the western side of the island including Totland and Freshwater Bays, The Needles and Old Battery, Compton Down, and Mottistone Manor Garden. The Military road which runs from Freshwater Bay to St Catherine's Point gives spectacular coastal views.

Facilities: The main sanitary unit is housed in a modern, ingeniously customised, 'portacabin' type unit including one washbasin cubicle for ladies and a baby room. Showers are slightly different in that they have two pushbutton controls, one for pre-mixed hot water, the other for cold only (provided at the special request of some of the regular customers). A second similar unit has WCs and washbasins in cubicles, plus facilities for disabled visitors. Laundry and dishwashing sinks. Recycling bins. Motorcaravan service point. Gaz and ice pack service. Children's play field. No commercial vehicles are accepted. Gate locked 22.30-07.00 hrs.

Charges 2002

Per adult	£3.50 - £4.00
child (3-15 yrs)	£1.50 - £2.00
dog	£1.00
electricity	£1.75

Min. pitch fee July/Aug. £7.50. One night booking supplement £2.00 - £4.00. No credit cards. Tel: (01983) 756756. Fax: (01983) 756756. Reservations: Advisable for B.Hs and peak season; made with £15 deposit. **Open** 1 May - 30 September.

Directions: From A3054 north of Totland and Colwell turn into Heathfield Road where site is signed. Site entrance is on right after a short distance. O.S.GR: SZ334878.

Lincoln Farm Park

257 High Street, Standlake, nr Witney, Oxfordshire OX8 7RH

From its immaculately tended grounds and quality facilities, to the efficient and friendly staff, this park is a credit to its owner. Situated in a small, quiet village, it is well set back and screened by mature trees, with wide gravel roads, hedged enclosures, attractive brick pathways and good lighting. All 90 numbered, level touring pitches are generously sized and have electrical connections (10/16A), 75 with gravel hardstanding and adjacent grass for awnings, and 22 are fully serviced (fresh and waste water, electricity and satellite TV). Although only a relatively small site its leisure facilities are quite outstanding. One indoor swimming pool is always appreciated, but two (30' x 15' and 40' x 20') plus a toddlers' pool, spa pools, saunas, steam room, sun bed and a fitness suite really offer something rather special. Charges for all of these are modest, and outside of the open sessions everything can be hired privately by the hour. Oxford and the Cotswolds are conveniently close. A member of the Best of British group.

Facilities: The two heated toilet blocks are of notable design and quality, well maintained and exceptionally clean, with showers (sensibly sized and designed), and washbasins in cubicles. A well equipped, separate unit for disabled people is adjacent to a specially reserved pitch with direct access. Two family bathrooms (incorporating baby bath and changing facilities). Each block also contains a laundry room, dishwashing sinks under cover (more throughout the site), freezers, fridges and microwaves. Motorcaravan service point. Shop (basic supplies). Information kiosk. Outdoor chess/draughts, putting green and sizeable adventure play area (bark chipping and rubber base). Indoor swimming pools. Up to two dogs are welcome with allocated walks. **Off site:** Fishing (lake and river) 300 yds - 5 miles, riding centre and water sports nearby.

Charges 2001

Per unit incl. 2 persons	£10.95 - £13.95
extra adult	£2.25
child (5-14 yrs)	£1.50
full awning (no groundsheets)	£1.25
porch awning	75p
electricity	£2.25 - £2.50
'super' pitch (excl. electricity)	£4.00
dog	75p

Low season offers. Tel: (01865) 300239. Fax: (01865) 300127. Reservations: Made with £15 non-returnable deposit. **Open** 1 February - 18 November.

Directions: Take A415 Witney - Abingdon road and turn into Standlake High Street by garage; park is 300 yds on the right. O.S.GR: SP396029.

Barnstones Caravan and Camping Park

260 Great Bourton, nr Banbury, Oxfordshire OX17 1QU

Three miles from Banbury and open all year round, this small, neat park provides an excellent point from which to explore the Cotswolds, Oxford and Stratford-upon-Avon. The 49 level pitches all have gravel hardstanding with a grass area for awnings (no groundsheets are allowed) and 10A electricity; 20 of these are fully serviced. Shrubs, flowers and an oval tarmac road convey a tidy impression throughout and the low level lighting is subtle but effective. A rally field is near the main road, so some traffic noise is to be expected. New arrivals should report to the warden's caravan at the park entrance. The church in Great Bourton (250 m) has a most unusual lych gate and there is a canal-side walk to Banbury (3 miles).

Facilities: The newly upgraded toilet block is small, but it can be heated and is quite adequate for the number of people it serves. It has adjustable, unisex showers and a separate dishwashing and laundry room. Small, fenced play area for children (grass and bark chipping base) adjacent to the entrance road. Gas is available. **Off site:** Nearest shop 1 mile. supermarket 3 miles, pub 150 yds. Fishing, bicycle hire, golf and riding, all within 3 miles.

Charges 2001

Per unit incl. 2 persons	£5.50
extra person 5-12 yrs	50p
over 12 yrs	£1.00
1-man tent	£3.50
awning	50p - £1.00
electricity	£1.50
fully serviced pitch incl. electricity	£8.50

OAPs less 50p per night. No credit cards. Tel: (01295) 750289. Reservations: Contact park. **Open** all year.

Directions: From M40 take exit 11 for Banbury. Turn off following signs for Chipping Norton, straight on at two small roundabouts. At third roundabout turn right on A423 signed Southam and in 2½ miles turn right signed Great Bourton, Site entrance is 100 yds on right. O.S.GR: SP455454.

 Alan Rogers' discount
Less 50p per unit, per night

Cotswold View Caravan and Camping Site

258 Enstone Road, Charlbury, Oxfordshire OX7 3JH

On the edge of the Cotswolds and surrounded by fine views, this well-run family site offers a warm welcome. It successfully combines a working farm, touring site and self catering country cottages. Wide gravel or tarmac roads ensure easy access to the 125 pitches (all with 10A electricity) in the 10-acre touring area. Part of this are has been carefully developed more recently to a high standard and will naturally take some time to mature. The small reception also serves as a licensed shop selling freshly baked bread, home-made cakes and eggs from their own hens. Farmhouse breakfasts (ordered the night before) are served in the farmhouse itself where B&B is also offered. The farm's animals (sheep, hens, pigs, rabbits, ducks, goats, ponies and a donkey) add great interest to one's stay. Well defined and maintained trails around the enclosures enable the animals to be safely observed, whilst additional trails and woodland plantations provide more walking opportunities, particularly for dogs which can be allowed off the lead. Convenient for touring the Cotswolds, there is also a good train service for day trips to London.

Facilities: Two well maintained toilet blocks provide excellent facilities including washbasins in cubicles, showers with ample changing space, two family rooms, baths (50p), hairdryers, central heating and even soft piped music! Both blocks have good units for disabled people. Baby changing facilities, laundry room, freezers for ice packs and dishwashing sinks under cover. Motorcaravan service point. Shop. Children have two sheltered grass areas in which to play and a games room with table tennis, pool table and football table. Hard tennis court. Outdoor chess. Bicycle hire. Skittle alley for hire. American motorhomes accepted. New barrier system (£5 deposit). **Off site**: Fishing 1 mile, riding 10 miles, golf 7 miles.

Charges 2002

Per unit incl. 2 persons	£8.00 - £11.00
extra adult	£1.75
child (5-16 yrs)	£1.00
electricity	£2.00
dog	free

Tel: Freephone 0800 085 3474. Fax: (01608) 811891. E-mail: bookings@cotswoldview.f9.co.uk. Reservations: Advisable for B.H.s and peak season. **Open** Easter - 31 October.

Directions: From A44 Oxford - Stratford-on-Avon road, take B4022 to Charlbury, just south of Enstone. Park is 2 miles on left. O.S.GR: SP365210.

Wysdom Touring Park Caravan Site

262 The Bungalow, Burford School, Burford, Oxfordshire OX18 4JG

You'll have to go a long way before you find anything else remotely like this site! The land is owned by Burford School and the enterprising caretaker and his wife, caravanners themselves, suggested that they create this wonderful place to raise money for the school (hence cheques payable to Burford School). It is really like putting your caravan or motorcaravan (no tents accepted) into their own private garden. The 19 pitches are separated by hedges, all have electricity hook-ups (16A) and a picnic table and some have their own tap. When we visited, the site was a true riot of colour. This is a lovely location for exploring the Cotswolds, Burford calls itself the 'Gateway to the Cotswolds'. Note: there is a narrow turn into the site off the school drive and this site is not therefore considered suitable for large motorhomes. It is best to avoid school pick-up and drop-off when the drive can be congested.

Facilities: The small sanitary building offers all you need although with only one shower per sex, whilst it meets statistical requirements there may be a queue at times. **Off site**: Burford is yards away with its famous shop lined hill full of antique shops, old coaching inns and all those 'interesting' shops it is so much fun rooting about in. Burford Golf Club next door – you can walk from your caravan to the first tee.

Charges 2001

Per unit incl. 2 persons and electricity	£7.00 - £8.00
extra person	£1.50
dog in excess of one	50p

No credit cards. Tel: (01993) 823207. Reservations: Contact park. **Open** all year.

Directions: From roundabout on A40 at Burford, take A361 and site is a few yards on the right signed Burford School. Once in school drive watch for narrow entrance to site on right in about 100 yards. O.S.GR: SP249117.

Bo Peep Farm Caravan Park

Aynho Road, Adderbury, Banbury, Oxfordshire OX17 3NP

261

Set amongst 85 acres of farmland and woodland, there is an air of spacious informality about this peaceful, friendly park and it blends perfectly with the views surrounding it. Part of the Caravan Club's 'managed under contact' scheme, non-members are also very welcome. All of the 114 numbered, pitches are large, have 16A electricity and, with the exception of eight that slope gently, are otherwise quite level. Gravel roads connect the various areas, such as Poppy Field, The Paddocks and The Warren, with reasonable shelter provided by hedges and trees. Pitches are mostly grassy and set around the perimeters, leaving central areas free for a liberal sprinkling of picnic tables. A separate 4 acre field is reserved for tents and 18 seasonal units occupy the hardstandings and some other pitches. Children are welcome but there is no play area. A network of circular walks around the site, including the pleasant river walk, has wide, well-kept paths; even bench seats and waste bins are provided. A 15 acre field has been acquired which can be used for recreation and, in the longer term, a lake is planned, plus the reclaiming of farmland to redevelop as woodland and more walks, a clear indication that owners Andrew and Margaret Hodge seek to improve an unusual site even further.

Facilities: The original toilet block has been supplemented by a larger, purpose-built unit, all clean and heated. Ample showers with changing space, hairdryers. Dishwashing sinks under cover. Laundry rooms. Motorcaravan service point. Low level lighting. Small shop with off licence, gas and basic supplies. Information centre (with maps, leaflets, sample menus from local pubs, etc). Fishing (apply to office). Caravan storage. Caravan cleaning area. **Off site:** Golf course next door. Banbury is just 3 miles, the famous Blenheim Palace 6 miles. Great day trips to Stratford upon Avon, Warwick and its castle and even Silverstone can be entertained from this base.

Charges 2001

Per adult	£4.00
child (over 5 yrs)	£2.00
pitch (non-member)	£5.00
electricity	£1.50
Tent campers:	per adult £4.00; child £1.20

No credit cards. Tel/Fax: (01295) 810605. E-mail: warden@bo-peep.co.uk. Reservations: Advised and made with £10 deposit. **Open** 16 March - 1 November.

Directions: Adderbury village is on the A4260 Banbury - Oxford road. At traffic lights in Adderbury turn on B4100 signed Aynho; park is clearly signed, ½ mile on the right (½ mile drive). O.S.GR: SP482353.

Wellington Country Park

Riseley, nr Reading, Berkshire RG7 1SP

269

The Wellington Country Park is open to all on payment of an entry fee (entry for campers included in pitch fee) and many visit it for a day out. It contains a boating and fishing lake, a large adventure playground and other activities for children, nature trails, deer park, fitness course, crazy golf, narrow-gauge railway, animal farm and a dairy museum. The camping site is in a wood within the 350 acre park. It has 70 pitches, 18 with hardstanding and 42 with electricity hook-ups (10A). There are several individual pitches and some small groups all within woodland clearings which gives a very rustic and casual feel to this site. It is a very pleasant setting and we found it quite nostalgic, the site being of the older and more traditional style of camping found some 20 years ago. Once the Country Park closes at 5.30 pm. all is very quiet. Access is through a locked gate and you must make advance arrangements if you plan to arrive after 5.30 pm when the main park shop closes (a late arrivals field at the entrance has no sanitation).

Facilities: The ladies' toilet facilities were completely refitted in 2000 and we understand that the men's will have similar treatment. This work will bring the standards up greatly, with comfortable facilities including washbasins in cubicles and well equipped showers with good dry areas. Dishwashing sinks, and ample laundry. Small shop stocks basics (from 1/5; no gas) with very limited hours. Fishing. Family events. Torch useful. **Off site:** Riding nearby. Legoland and Windsor are 30 minutes drive.

Charges 2001

Per unit incl. up to 2 adults and 2 children	£13.00
Mon - Thursday off-peak	£7.50
extra adult	£1.50
child	£1.00
dog	free
electricity	£1.75

Fee includes fishing permit for ONE person. Tel: (0118) 932 6444. Fax: (0118) 932 6445. Reservations: Made with £13 non-returnable deposit (min 2 nights July/Aug. or 3 nights at B.Hs). **Open** 1 March - 31 October.

Directions: Park is signed at Riseley, off A32/A33 road between Reading and Basingstoke, and from M4. It is 4 miles south of M4 exit 11 and 7 miles north of M3 exit 5. O.S.GR: SU727628.

Highclere Farm Country Touring Park

275 Newbarn Lane, Seer Green, Beaconsfield, Buckinghamshire HP9 2QZ

Only 25 miles from London and 10 miles from Legoland and Windsor, this is a peaceful park that backs onto fields and woodland. Developed around a working chicken farm, there are also sheep, horses and a pot-bellied pig to provide that country feel. There are 60 level grass pitches, most with 10A electricity and gravel hardstanding, the rest being reserved for tents. Converted chicken houses also form the basis for the excellent en-suite bed and breakfast facilities. The atmosphere is friendly, but informal, with reception doubling as a small shop that can supply all types and sizes of fresh laid eggs. A fenced children's play area plus a footpath are at the top of the park. A bus service to Uxbridge passes the site, London is 35 minutes by train, whilst Windsor Castle and Thorpe Park are also within easy reach. A member of the Countryside Discovery group.

Facilities: The heated sanitary facilities, fully equipped, have been converted from a chicken house with large showers (20p), all is very clean and cosy. A unit with toilet and washbasin is provided for disabled people. Laundry room including washing up and laundry sinks. Shop. Children's play area. **Off site:** Fishing 8 miles, bicycle hire 3 miles, riding or golf within 1 mile.

Charges 2002

Per unit	£10.00 - £13.00
tent	£8.00 - £10.50
extra pup tent	£1.00
electricity	£2.00

Awning, dog or extra car incl. Tel: (01494) 874505. Fax: (01494) 875238. E-mail: highclerefarm@ netscapeonline.co.uk. Reservations: Contact park. **Open** all year except February.

Directions: From M40 take exit 2, then follow A40 towards London. Take first left for Seer Green, then follow site signs. O.S.GR: SU977927.

South East England Tourist Board

East Sussex, West Sussex, Surrey and Kent

'Traditional Kentish Oast Houses'
South East England Tourist Board

South East England Tourist Board

East Sussex, West Sussex, Surrey and Kent

South East England Tourist Board
The Old Brew House, Warwick Park,
Tunbridge Wells, Kent TN2 5TU
Tel: (01892) 540766 Fax: (01892) 511008
E-mail: enquiries@seetb.org.uk
Internet: http://www.southeastengland.uk.com

Picture yourself soaking up the sun on a secluded beach, strolling through golden downland or enjoying a lively city break in the distinctive and beautiful counties of Kent, East and West Sussex and Surrey.

For visitors enjoying history and heritage, there's a feast of interesting places to see. Step back in time to the ages of Chaucer, Kipling and Churchill; discover 1066 Country where the Normans invaded and changed the history of England; or track down the secret coastal history of smugglers and pirates.

The South East has long been a favourite with great garden makers. The temperate climate and ideal growing conditions have produced world-famous gardens to delight every taste from the romantic gardens built around the ruins at Scotney Castle to the modern sculpture Gardens of Gaia.

Many of the rich and famous have also chosen to make their home in South East England. Sir Winston Churchill and his family lived at Chartwell in Kent from 1922 until his death and Dickens readers will enjoy visits to Broadstairs where 'Bleak House' (now a museum) was his holiday home and Rochester, the scene of many of his novels.

The region boasts over 500 miles of long distance footpaths and cycle routes through some of the best landscapes in England, through chalk downland, wooded valleys and dramatic cliff top walks, and over 250 miles of coastline offers everything from traditional bucket-and-spade family seaside holidays to romantic breaks.

If cosmopolitan, lively cities are more to your taste, look no further than the City by the Sea, Brighton, with the exotic Royal Pavilion and famous piers, whilst historic Canterbury and Arundel offer beautiful cathedrals and are full of character and culture.

When looking for the perfect gift to take home, antiques hunters will enjoy Petworth, Tenterden or Westerham. For a more modern shopping experience try Bluewater near Dartford, the largest retail park in Europe, or hunt for bargains at the McArthur Glen Designer Outlet in Ashford or De Bradelei Wharf in Dover.

Families will never be short of things to do either. Choose from the award winner Drusillas Park at Alfriston which has a reputation as being the best small zoo in England or The Historic Dockyard at Chatham which charts 400 years of naval history for a great family day out.

The South East offers endless holiday ideas to suit every budget with the chance to sample excellent cuisine from fresh local seafood to village pubs serving traditional ale made from local hops. There is a wealth of theatres and outdoor venues providing live music, festivals and full dramatic productions, and London's West End is just a stone's throw away.

Photo: South East England Tourist Board

Camping and Caravanning Club Site Chertsey

281

Bridge Road, Chertsey, Surrey KT16 8JX

This is an old-established site (1926), a flagship for the Club, which is splendidly located on the banks of the River Thames, only a few minutes walk from the shops and amenities of Chertsey. In the summer, lovely flower displays greet you as you drive in. There are 200 numbered pitches in total (for all types of unit), 100 with 16A electricity and 33 with hardstanding. They are either in open, field-like areas, beside the river creek or in little nooks and corners, which avoids the regularity of some sites. Squirrels, rabbits and ducks abound and mature trees and plants create a pretty site with views across the water and towards Chertsey bridge, although unfortunately there is some road noise and, depending on flight paths, aircraft noise. A good, under cover tourist information area is next to reception, suitable for disabled people. The rail station for London is at Chertsey or Weybridge. Fishing is possible (£1 per day, NRA licence needed). Canoeing can be arranged (Chertsey is the main base of the Club's canoe section). The river can flood but the site has a well established warning system and will not allow camping near the river when floods are expected.

Facilities: The main toilet block is centrally situated next to the recreation hall (with table tennis). The other is at the site entrance in the same building as reception and the shop. Well equipped, there are washbasins in cabins, hairdryers, laundry and dishwashing rooms. Separate facilities for wheelchair users are approached via a ramp. There is an area for hanging clothes out. Motorcaravan service point. Well stocked shop for essentials and gas (8-11 am. and 4-6 pm). Children's play area on bark. Short dog walk areas. Torches are necessary. Caravan storage.

Charges 2001

Per adult	£4.80 - £5.30
child (6-18 yrs)	£1.65
non-member pitch fee	£4.30
electricity	£1.65 - £2.40

Tel: (01932) 562405 (no calls after 8 pm).
Reservations: Necessary and made with deposit; contact site. **Open** all year.

Directions: Suggested: from M25 use junction 11. Turn left at roundabout on A317 towards Shepperton and continue to second set of traffic lights. Turn right then almost immediately left watching for green Club camp sign just before Chertsey bridge; the opening is narrow. O.S.GR: TQ052667.

Camping and Caravanning Club Site Horsley

282

Ockham Road North, East Horsley, Surrey KT24 6PE

London and all the sights are only 40 minutes away by train, yet Horsley is a delightful, quiet unspoilt site with a good duck and goose population on its part lily covered lake (unfenced). It provides 135 pitches, of which 70 have 16A electrical connections and 29 are all weather pitches (most with electricity). Seventeen pitches are around the bank of the lake, the rest further back in three hedged, grass fields with mostly level ground but with some slope in places. There is a range of mature trees and a woodland dog walk area (may be muddy). The soil is clay based so rain tends to settle - sluice gates remove extra water from the lake area when the rain is heavy. A recreation hall with TV and table tennis (bring your own bats) is sometimes used for bingo. Basic provisions, gas and books are kept in reception and resident wardens will make you comfortable. Guildford and the R.H.S. gardens at Wisley are close by.

Facilities: Two purpose built, heated toilet blocks with good design and fittings, with some washbasins in cabins, a Belfast sink and parent and child room with vanity style basin, toilet and wide surface area. Also well designed facilities for disabled people, and new drying areas. Children's play area. Fishing is possible from May (£3 per day, NRA licence required). **Off site**: Shops and the station are 1 mile, pubs 1½-2 miles. Golf 1½ miles, riding 2 miles.

Charges 2001

Per adult	£3.75 - £5.30
child (6-18 yrs)	£1.65
non-member pitch fee	£4.30
electricity	£1.65 - £2.40

Tel: (01483) 283273 (no calls after 8 pm.)
Reservations: Necessary and made with deposit; contact site. **Open** March - October.

Directions: From M25 junction 10, travel 2½-3 miles towards Guildford and take first left on B2039 to Ockham and East Horsley, continuing through Ockham towards East Horsley. Site is on right - watch carefully for small club sign. O.S.GR: TQ083552.

White Rose Touring Park

Mill Lane, Wick, nr Littlehampton, West Sussex BN17 7PH

289

Situated about midway between the imposing castle at Arundel and the beaches of Littlehampton, White Rose makes an excellent base from which to enjoy the many attractions of this popular district. Watersports centres, race courses, beaches, historical and cultural interests, downland walks and the resorts of Bognor and Brighton are within easy reach. There are 140 pitches for tourists, 88 with electricity (10/16A). The flat grassy meadow is surrounded by trees and divided into two areas. The first part has individually hedged pitches, as on the continent, on either side of concrete access roads, with electricity hook-ups and shared water/waste water connections. The second area includes 14 'super' pitches (each having electricity, fresh and waste water and sewage connections, TV aerial socket and night light), further full sized pitches with no electricity, plus special pitches for small tents and small motorcaravans. A busy road runs along one side of the park and road noise could be disturbing in the early mornings during the week to a few pitches.

Facilities: The central toilet block is heated and fully equipped, with two washrooms provided for disabled people (key from reception). Reception has a few basic supplies and gas. Central play area for children. Trailed boats by prior arrangement only. **Off site:** Supermarket / mile. Fishing, boat launching, bicycle hire, riding and golf within 2 miles.

Charges 2001

Per pitch incl. unit, car and up to 3 people	£12.00
super pitch	£16.00
fully serviced pitch (electric, water, drain)	£14.00
extra person	£1.00

Reductions for 1 week or 1 month outside 10 July - 31 Aug. Tel: (01903) 716176. Fax: (01903) 732671. E-mail: snowdondavid@hotmail.com. Reservations: Made with deposit of 1 nights fee p/week reserved. **Open** all year except 14 Jan - 15 March.

Directions: Take A284 Littlehampton road from A27 just to the east of Arundel station, pass the campsite behind the pub at this junction and park is signed along on the left. O.S.GR: TQ026041.

Raylands Caravan Park

Jackrells Lane, Southwater, nr Horsham, West Sussex RH13 7DH

288

A pleasant, reasonably priced park (owned by Roundstone Caravans at Southwater), deep in the heart of the Sussex countryside, Raylands is well maintained and thoughtfully landscaped. The 65 caravan holiday homes occupy an area of their own and touring units use marked, numbered pitches on gently sloping grass meadows separated into smaller areas by trees and hard access roads. Electricity (15A) is available to 50 of the 65 pitches. The park manager seems to have engendered a friendly atmosphere and is willing to advise on the very numerous attractions the locality has to offer. London and Brighton are easily reached by rail from nearby Horsham and the region abounds with places of historical, cultural and sporting interests. The clubhouse (weekends only in low season) has snacks and good value full meals at weekends (to early Sept) with a special bar/dining room for non-smokers. There is some road noise from the A24.

Facilities: The single toilet block is centrally situated with hot showers on payment. Separate en-suite facilities for disabled visitors. Laundry room. Bar, restaurant. Large field for children's ball games. Children's games room with pool, table tennis, video games and TV. Adult's games room has pool, darts and a small library. Tennis court. **Off site:** Supermarket and other shops are under 2 miles. Swimming pool 3 miles. Fishing, bicycle hire riding and golf, all 2 miles.

Charges 2001

Per unit incl. 2 persons	£10.00
extra person	50p
hiker or cyclist tent, 1 person	£7.00
2 persons	£8.50
electricity	£1.50

Tel: (01403) 731822. Fax: (01403) 732828. Reservations: Essential for BHs, advisable for peak season, with £10 deposit. **Open** 1 March - 31 October.

Directions: Leave A24 Worthing - London road for Southwater and follow signs for approx. 2 miles on narrow lanes to park. O.S.GR: TQ170265.

Honeybridge Park

Honeybridge Lane, Dial Post, West Sussex RH13 8NX

294

Honeybridge's owners, Jeff and Val Burrows, continue to develop this 15 acre park which now has around 140 pitches, including 40 with gravel hardstanding and 118 with electric hook-ups (16A) and also a large number of seasonal caravans. Recent developments include an increase in the number of individually hedged places. The other pitches are on slightly sloping grass with little to separate them. The reception building houses a small shop, and the park provides a discount voucher pack for local attractions. A large wooden, adventure-style playground is provided for the children on an area of grass well away from the pitches, and simple family entertainment is organised on special occasions. A recent addition is a games room with darts, table tennis and free use of many board games. A TV is to be installed. This site is ideally situated for visiting the South Downs with its many attractive villages.

Facilities: The toilet unit can be heated in cool weather and provides all modern facilities including some washbasins in cubicles. It could be under pressure in peak season. Unit for disabled persons. Dishwashing and laundry sinks, a washing machine and dryer. Motorcaravan service point. Children's play area. Games room. Security barrier (card access, £10 deposit) is locked 11 pm - 7 am. **Off site:** Pub and tea shop in Dial Post. Billingshurst and Horsham are both 8 miles. Fishing 1 mile, golf or riding 10 miles.

Charges 2002

Per adult	£2.50 - £3.50
child (5-14 yrs)	£1.00
pitch	£4.00
2-man small tent (backpackers)	£8.50
electricity	£2.00
dog	free

Senior citizen discounts. Tel/Fax: (01403) 710923. E-mail: enquiries@honeybridgepark.co.uk.
Reservations: Made with £10 p/night deposit (June-Aug); contact park. **Open** all year.

Directions: Two miles south of the junction of A24 and A272 at Dial Post, turn east by Old Barn Nurseries. Follow signs to site (½ mile approx). O.S.GR: TQ150190.

Sheepcote Valley Caravan Club Site

East Brighton Park, Brighton, East Sussex BN2 5TS

293

Brighton is without doubt the South of England's most popular seaside resort and now that the Caravan Club has taken over and modernised the Sheepcote Valley Site, there is a first class base from which to enjoy the many and diverse attractions both in the town and this area of the south coast. The site occupies a quiet situation in an almost fully enclosed valley in the South Downs, a mile north of the town's interesting Marina which has a superstore and good variety of shops and restaurants. A wide tarmac road winds its way through the site from reception, with pitches on either side, leading to terraces with grass pitches on the lower slopes of the valley. With a total of 249 pitches, 169 have electricity connections (16A), 82 have hardstanding and 13 have water, drainage and TV sockets. Two grass terraces are for tents and these have hard parking near as a low fence prevents cars being taken onto the camping areas. Although there are a number of trees, many are young so do not yet provide shade. Flower beds add to the attractiveness of the site. The site fully lives up to the very high standards expected from the Caravan Club and provides a first class venue both for a quiet holiday and as a base from which to explore this interesting and historic town and delightful Sussex downland countryside either by car or on foot.

Facilities: Two well built, brick, heated sanitary blocks have excellent facilities including all washbasins in private cabins. In the main season a 'portacabin' type building provides additional services near the tent places. Well equipped room for wheel chair users, another one for walking disabled and two baby and toddler wash rooms. Laundry facilities. Motorcaravan service point. Gas available. Children's play area with safety base. **Off site:** Brighton is only two miles away with a bus service from the entry road. Extensive recreation grounds adjacent.

Charges 2001

Per pitch (non member)	£7.00 - £8.00
person	£3.75 - £4.75
child (5-16 yrs)	£1.10 - £1.20
electricity	£1.50 - £2.25

Tel: (01273) 626546. Fax: (01273) 682600.
Reservations: Advised for high season with £5 deposit. **Open** all year.

Directions: Site is in eastern part of Brighton and well signed from A259 coast road opposite the Marina through to site entrance. O.S.GR: TQ341043.

Washington Caravan and Camping Park

London Road, Washington, nr Worthing, West Sussex RH20 4AJ

295

Washington is an unusual campsite with superb equestrian facilities and a bias towards tenting families. It provides only 21 hardstanding pitches for caravans or motorcaravans, and a large gently sloping grassy field with enough space for 80 tents. The 23 electric hook-ups (16A) are on slot meters (50p). Security is good, but unobtrusive. There is some road noise from the A24. The latest development is a new equestrian centre adjacent to the campsite, including an Olympic standard floodlit arena, a small children's pony arena, stabling and paddock facilities. There are excellent riding opportunities on the bridle paths of the South Downs Way.

Facilities: A heated chalet style building houses sanitary facilities of an excellent standard, including spacious shower rooms (on payment) and indoor dishwashing and laundry facilities. No on-site shop but eggs, bread, butter and milk can be obtained from reception. Drinks machine and freezer. **Off site:** Local pub and a nearby restaurant. Local attractions include Highdown Chalk Gardens at Worthing, Nutbourne Vineyard and Steyning Museum.

Charges 2001

Per caravan or motorcaravan incl. 2 persons	£9.50
extra person	£3.00
electricity (metered)	50p
Per tent	£2.00
person	£3.00
car or m/cycle	£1.00

Weekly terms acc. to time of year. Tel: (01903) 892869. Fax: (01903) 893252. E-mail: washcamp@ tinyworld.co.uk. Reservations: Contact site for details. **Open** all year.

Directions: Site entrance is just east of the junction of A24 and A283 at Washington, 6 miles north of Worthing. O.S.GR: TQ125130.

Horam Manor Touring Park

Horam, nr Heathfield, East Sussex TN21 0YD

290

In the heart of the Sussex countryside, this rural touring park is part of (but under separate management from) Horam Manor which has a farm museum, nature trail and the well known Merrydown Winery. The 90 pitches, 54 with electricity are on two open meadows joined by a tarmac/gravel road. The field nearer reception is undulating, the second field is flatter but slopes - levelling blocks are needed for motorcaravans. Pitches are of generous size, those with electricity being numbered and marked. Both areas are ringed with a variety of mainly tall trees. The park, back from the main Eastbourne to Tunbridge Wells road, is a haven of peace and tranquillity. The Craft Centre to the side of the site has some interesting exhibits, farm machinery and riding stables. The nature trail (free access for campers) has walks ranging from ½ -1½ hours in length. A member of the Countryside Discovery group.

Facilities: The modern, well built toilet block (unheated) is fully equipped and is said to be cleaned four times daily. Family room (access by key from reception) with shower, washbasin and toilet, suitable also for disabled visitors. Laundry and washing up sinks. Washing machine. Gas available. Up to two dogs per unit are accepted. Fishing is possible in 10 lakes on the estate (adults £3). **Off site:** Tennis (small fee) 200 yds. Bicycle hire and golf within 1 mile. Village shop. Two inns are within walking distance and the Barn cafe at the Farm Centre serves drinks and snacks (10 am. - 5 pm).

Charges 2002

Per unit incl. 2 adults and 2 children (under 18 yrs) £12.50; extra adult £3.50; extra child £1.15; electricity £2.45 (10/9-10/5) - £1.95; extended awning £2.50; dogs (max 2) free.

No credit cards. Tel: (01435) 813662. E-mail: horam. manor@virgin.net. Reservations: Contact park. **Open** 1 March - 31 October.

Directions: Entry to the park is signed at the recreation ground at southern edge of Horam village. O.S.GR: TQ577169.

Crazy Lane Tourist Park

296 Crazy Lane, Sedlescombe, nr Battle, East Sussex TN33 0QT

Formerly known as Whydown Farm, this peaceful, traditional style, two acre park has just 36 pitches arranged on grassy terraces, all with electric hook-ups (5/10A). It may be best to phone to make sure space is available before travelling long distances. Set in the heart of '1066 country' with its historical links, other local attractions include the very pretty village of Sedlescombe, two steam railways, an organic vineyard, Rye with its quaint cobbled streets and of course Battle itself. This is an ideal park for couples.

Facilities: The tiny but well maintained sanitary unit includes controllable hot showers (on payment), laundry facilities with washing machine and dryer, dishwashing sinks and a suite for disabled visitors. New reception/shop added recently.

Charges 2001

Per unit incl. 2 adults	£8.00 - £9.00
extra person over 12 yrs	£1.25
awning or extra car	£1.00
electricity	£2.00

Open March - October. Tel: (01424) 870147. E-mail: info@crazylane.co.uk. Reservations: Contact site for details.

Directions: From A21, 100 yards south of junction with B2244 (to Sedlescombe) turn into Crazy Lane, where site is signed. O.S.GR: TQ782170.

Bay View Caravan and Camping Park

292 Old Martello Road, Pevensey Bay, East Sussex BN24 6DX

The Adams family have developed this friendly beach-side park with care over the last few years, a fact which is obvious as soon as you arrive and see the tidy state of everything. There are 3½ acres of mainly flat grass with gravel access roads and a low bank on three sides giving some shelter if it is windy. Careful use of fencing adds to the attractiveness, whilst also keeping the rabbits off the flowers. The 49 pitches (80 sq.m, all with 10/16A electricity and 10 with hardstanding) are neatly marked out by numbered posts, while five caravan holiday homes are at the back of the park. A large overflow field opposite the entrance with small 'portacabin' style sanitary facilities is used in the peak season. At other times this space may be used for games. Apart from all the attractions of Sussex, you may swim, fish, windsurf, sail or just enjoy the view from this very pleasant park. A newly developed cycle/walking path leads into Pevensey Bay and Eastbourne. A marina complex is under construction nearby.

Facilities: The central toilet facilities are housed in a very well maintained 'portacabin' style building which is heated when necessary. Showers on payment (20p). Laundry room with washing machine, dryer, spin dryer, iron and board, plus tourist information. Motorcaravan service point. Well stocked, good value shop (open long hours as the owners live next to it). Gas available. Popular, well made and fenced children's play area with bark surface and adventure equipment (10 years and under). Winter caravan storage. **Off site**: Golf 2 miles.

Charges 2002

Per unit	£4.95 - £5.60
2 person tent	£4.35 - £4.70
adult	£2.30 - £2.60
child (2-16 yrs)	£1.60 - £1.80
awning	£1.60 - £1.75
dog	60p - £1.00
electricity	£2.10

Couples and families only. No commercial vehicles, large vans or pick-ups. No credit cards. Tel: (01323) 768688. Fax: (01323) 769637. E-mail: holidays@bay-view.co.uk. Reservations: Made with deposit (£25). **Open** Easter/1 April - October.

Directions: Park is about 1 mile west of Pevensey Bay and 2 miles east of Eastbourne, off the A259 Pevensey Bay road. O.S.GR: TQ648028.

Black Horse Farm Caravan Club Site

309 385 Canterbury Road, Densole, Folkestone, Kent CT18 7BG

This neat, tidy and attractive six-acre park, owned by the Caravan Club, is situated amidst farming country in the village of Densole on the Downs just 4 miles north of Folkestone, 8 northeast of Dover and 11 south of Canterbury. This makes it ideal for a night stop travelling to or from the continent via the Channel Ports or the Tunnel, or as a base for visiting the many attractions of this part of southeast England. Accessed directly from the A260, the tarmac entrance road leads past reception towards the top field which has gravel hardstanding pitches with a grass area for awnings (possibly some road noise), past hedging to the smaller middle area with 8 hardstandings, then to the large bottom field which has been redeveloped to give 104 large pitches, all with electricity (16A). A late arrivals area and pitches for 'one-nighters' are now located in the top field. A new area for tents and summer use should be complete.

Facilities: The carefully thought out and well constructed toilet blocks, one below reception and the other at the far end of the site, have washbasins in private cabins with curtains, good sized shower compartments, a baby room and facilities for disabled visitors, laundry and washing-up facilities, all well heated in cool weather. Motorcaravan service point. Gas supplies. Caravan storage. **Off site**: Riding 1 mile, golf or fishing 5 miles. Opposite the entrance is a general store and newsagent and within 100 m, a pub and filling station.

Charges 2001

Per pitch (non-member)	£6.00 - £8.00
adult	£3.50 - £4.50
child (5-17 yrs)	£1.10 - £1.20
electricity	£1.50 - £2.25

Tel: (01303) 892665 (not after 8 pm.) Reservations: Advised at all times - contact the Warden. **Open** all year.

Directions: Directly by the A260 Folkestone - Canterbury road, 2 miles north of junction with A20. Follow signs for Canterbury. O.S.GR: TR211418.

Hawthorn Farm Caravan and Camping Site

310 Martin Mill, Dover, Kent CT15 5LA

Hawthorn Farm is a large, relaxed park close to Dover. Set in 27 acres, it is an extensive park taking 224 touring units of any type on several large meadows which could accommodate far more, plus 157 privately owned caravan holiday homes in their own areas. Campers not requiring electricity choose their own spot, most staying near the two toilet blocks leaving the farthest fields to those liking solitude. There are 120 pitches with electricity (10/16A), 46 of which are large pitches separated by hedges, the remainder in glades either side of tarmac roads. A well run, relaxed park with plenty of room, mature hedging and trees make an attractive environment. Being only 4 miles from Dover docks, it is a very useful park for those using the ferries and is popular with continental visitors. Close to the sea at St Margaret's Bay, it is a fairly quiet situation apart from some rail noise (no trains 23.30 - 05.30). Member of the Best of British group.

Facilities: The toilet blocks (now heated) are well equipped and of good quality including dishwashing and laundry sinks. Launderette. Motorcaravan services. Breakfast and other snacks are served at the shop (closed 31/10) and a pub is nearby. Gates close at 8 pm. - cards are available. A torch would be useful. Caravan storage. **Off site**: Riding ½ mile, golf 3 miles, bicycle hire, fishing and boat launching 4 miles.

Charges 2001

Per car, caravan/tent incl. 2 persons	£9.00 - £12.00
extra adult	£2.00 - £2.50
child (7-16 yrs)	£1.50 - £2.00
hikers and bikers (2 man tent)	less £2.00
dog	£1.00
electricity	£2.00

Less 10% for 4 nights booked (and paid for on arrival). Tel: (01304) 852658. Fax: (01304) 853417. E-mail: info@keatfarm.co.uk. Reservations: Contact park for details. **Open** 1 March - 31 October.

Directions: Park is north of the A258 road (Dover - Deal), with signs to park and Martin Mill where you turn off about 4 miles from Dover. O.S.GR: TR341464.

Yew Tree Park

306 Stone Street, Petham, nr Canterbury, Kent CT4 5PL

Yew Tree Park is a small, quiet site located in the heart of the Kent countryside overlooking the Chartham Downs. Just 5 miles south of Canterbury and 8 miles north of the M20, it is ideally placed either to explore the delights of the ancient city or the many attractions of eastern and coastal Kent. Its nearness to the Channel ports also makes it useful for a night stop on the way to, or on return from, the continent. If catching a late evening ferry you may remain on site after 12 noon for a small payment. With some caravan holiday homes, the site also has 45 pitches for tourers and tents. The 20 with electricity (10A) are marked on mainly level grass either side of the entrance road, the remainder unmarked on a rather attractive, sloping area which is left natural with trees and bushes creating cosy little recesses in which to pitch. This neat, tidy, well cared for park that resident proprietors, Derek and Dee Zanders, have created makes an excellent base away from the hurly-burly of life where you can enjoy the rural scenery and also have the opportunity for walking, riding, visiting local places of interest or for cross-Channel excursions.

Facilities: Two brick-built sanitary blocks (one for each sex) can be heated. Washbasins with warm water from a single tap, and four showers (on payment). Extra toilets on the edge of the camping area. Recently added is a toilet/shower room for families or disabled visitors. Laundry and dishwashing sinks, plus a washing machine, dryer and iron. Shop (from April). Gas supplies. Swimming pool (60 x 30 ft. open June-Sept). Torches may be useful. Dogs are not accepted. **Off site:** Riding 4 miles, golf 6 miles. The County cricket ground is 4 miles.

Charges 2001

First two adults, per person	£3.00 - £4.00
extra adult	£2.00 - £3.00
child 2-11 yrs	75p - £1.10
child 12-16 yrs	£1.00 - £1.60
caravan or trailer tent	£2.50 - £4.00
motorcaravan or tent	£1.50 - £3.50
small tent	£1.20 - £3.00
electricity (deposit required)	£2.00 - £2.20

Tel/Fax: (01227) 700306. E-mail: info@yewtreepark. com. Reservations: Made with deposit of £5 per night. **Open** March - October.

Directions: Park is on B2068 Canterbury-Folkestone road. From south, take exit 11 from the M20. From Canterbury, ignore signs to Petham and Waltham on B2068 and continue towards Folkestone. From either direction, turn into road beside the Chequers Inn, turn left into park and follow road to owners' house/reception. O.S.GR: TR138507.

Alan Rogers' discount
Less 10% in low season

Camping and Caravanning Club Site Canterbury

307 Bekesbourne Lane, Canterbury, Kent CT3 4AB

Situated just off the A257 Sandwich road, about 1½ miles from the centre of Canterbury, this site is an ideal base for exploring Canterbury and the north Kent coast, as well as being a good stop-over to and from the Dover ferries, and the Folkestone Channel Tunnel terminal. There are 200 pitches, 86 with electric hook-ups (10/16A) and, except at the very height of the season, you are likely to find a pitch, although not necessarily with electricity. Most of the pitches are on well kept grass with hundreds of saplings planted, but there are also 24 pitches with hardstanding. Some pitches do slope so blocks are advised. A good sized overnight area for late arrivals can be reached even when the barriers are down. The site is adjacent to Bekepond nature reserve and within walking distance of Howletts Zoo. Although the busy A257 is close, there is minimal noise from the traffic. Note: power lines cross the site.

Facilities: Two modern toilet blocks, the main one with a laundry room, a room for dishwashing, an outside vegetable preparation area, and recycling bins. Motorcaravan service point. Reception stocks a small range of essential foods, milk and gas. Excellent tourist information room. Children's play area with equipment on bark chippings. **Off site:** Golf adjacent, bicycle hire 2 miles.

Charges 2001

Per adult	£3.75 - £5.30
child (6-18 yrs)	£1.65
non-member pitch fee	£4.30
electricity	£1.65 - £2.40

Tel: (01227) 463216 (no calls after 8 pm). Reservations: Necessary and made with deposit; contact site. **Open** all year.

Directions: From A2 take Canterbury exit and follow signs for Sandwich - A257. After passing Howe military barracks turn right into Bekesbourne Lane opposite golf course. O.S.GR: TR172577.

Pine Lodge Touring Park

A20 Ashford Road, Hollingbourne, nr Maidstone, Kent ME17 1XH

305

Set in the heart of Kent, near Leeds Castle and central for the historical and scenic attractions of this county, this park is on a slight slope, the rectangular field surrounded by rolling hills, farmland and trees. A gravel, one-way road circles the site with pitches set against hedges around the perimeter and around a figure of eight in the centre with picnic areas. Trees have been planted for decoration and shade. Of the 100 pitches, 85 have electricity (16A), several have hardstanding and 3 are serviced. It is a useful park near the main London - Folkstone - Dover M20 and access from the A20 road is wide, but there may be background traffic noise. The park is very convenient for events staged at Leeds Castle and is a useful overnight stop between London and the Channel ports.

Facilities: Good sanitary facilities at the entrance to the park include metered showers (token), laundry and washing up facilities, plus a shower and toilet room for disabled visitors. Motorcaravan services. Basic supplies and gas are available from reception plus tourist information. Small children's play area. Dogs are not accepted. **Off site**: Local shops 1 mile (Bearsted) or 3½ miles (Maidstone). Fishing 3 miles, riding 2 miles, golf 1 mile.

Charges 2001

Per unit incl. 2 adults	£10.00 - £12.00
extra adult	£2.00
child (3-14 yrs)	£1.00
electricity	£1.50 - £2.25
awning or extra tent	£1.00

Hikers or cyclists please enquire. Tel: (01622) 730018. Fax: (01622) 734498. Reservations: Contact park. **Open** all year.

Directions: From M20 junction 8, at A20 roundabout, turn towards Bearsted and Maidstone and park is about ½ mile on the left. O.S.GR: TQ808548.

Broadhembury Caravan and Camping Park

Steeds Lane, Kingsnorth, Ashford, Kent TN26 1NQ

304

In quiet countryside just outside Ashford, near to Folkestone and the ferries, this well landscaped, sheltered park takes 65 touring units of any type, plus 25 caravan holiday homes (5 for hire). All pitches are on level, neatly cut grass backing onto hedges, 50 have electrical connections (10A), 4 are fully serviced and have 16A electricity, 8 have double hardstanding plus a grass area for an awning. The park is friendly and popular and often becomes full in the main season, with a good proportion of continental visitors, so reservation is advisable. Security arrangements are excellent - the gates are closed at 11 pm. in high season with coded entry. For those who would like a trip to France, the new International Railway Terminal is at Ashford (Paris in 2 hours) - take your passport. A member of the Best of British group.

Facilities: The single small well equipped toilet block is kept very clean, and can be heated in cool weather. Alongside is a new campers' kitchen, fully enclosed with dishwashing sinks, plus a microwave, fridge and freezer, all free of charge. Small laundry room. Motorcaravan service point. Well stocked shop and comprehensive tourist information. TV and pool room, games room with table tennis. Two children's playgrounds (grass or wood-chip bases) and a play field away from the touring area. Dog exercise field - up to two dogs per pitch are accepted. **Off site**: Fishing 500 m, bicycle hire or riding 2 miles and golf 1 mile

Charges 2002

Per unit incl. 2 persons	£10.00 - £15.00
extra adult	£2.20
child (5-16 yrs)	£1.80
electricity (10A)	£2.20
one awning or pup tent included	
'super' pitch	plus £6.00

Less 10% outside July/Aug. for bookings of 7 nights or more.Tel/Fax: (01233) 620859. E-mail: holidays@ broadhembury.co.uk. Reservations: Essential for B.Hs and peak season and made with £5 per night deposit (min. 3 nights at Easter or Spr. B.H). Balance 21 days before arrival for B.Hs, on arrival at other times. **Open** all year.

Directions: From M20 junction 10 take A2070. After 2 miles follow sign for Kingsnorth. Turn left at second crossroads in Kingsnorth village. O.S.GR: TR010382.

Tanner Farm Touring Caravan and Camping Park

303

Goudhurst Road, Marden, Kent TN12 9ND

Developed as part of a family working farm, Tanner Farm is recognised as a top class quality park. This is the heart of the Weald of Kent with orchards, hop gardens, lovely countryside and delightful small villages. The owners are much concerned with conserving the natural beauty of the environment and visitors are welcome to walk around the farm and see the Shire horses at work. The park extends over 15 acres, most of which is level and part a gentle slope. The grass meadowland has been semi-landscaped by planting saplings, etc. which units back onto (the owners don't wish to regiment pitches into rows). Places are numbered but not marked, allowing plenty of space between units which, with large open areas, gives a pleasant, comfortable atmosphere. There are 100 pitches, all with 16A electricity, 13 with hardstanding, 4 with water tap and 1 with waste water point also. The farm drive links the park with the B2079 and a group of refurbished oast houses (listed heritage buildings) with a duck pond in front, along with rare pigs, pygmy goats, lambs, etc. make a focal point. The friendly managers will advise on local attractions, shops and pubs. There are many National Trust attractions in the area (Sissinghurst, Scotney Castle, Bodiam Castle) The park is a member of the Caravan Club's 'managed under contract' scheme although non-members are also welcome.

Facilities: Two heated, well cared for sanitary units include some washbasins in private cubicles in both units. Purpose built facilities for disabled visitors. A bathroom (£1 token) and baby facilities have been added in the newer block (this block is not opened Nov - Easter). Small launderette. Dishwashing sinks. Motorcaravan service point. Small shop in reception (opening hours and stock limited in winter). Gas supplies. Small children's play area. Fishing on site (on payment). Torch may be useful. Caravan storage all year. **Off site**: Riding and golf within 6 miles, leisure centres and sailing facilities near and good shopping facilities at Maidstone and Tunbridge Wells.

Charges 2001

Per adult	£2.75 - £3.75
child	£1.10 - £1.20
pitch	£3.00 - £4.00
2-man tent plus car (all incl.)	£9.00 - £9.50
plus bicycles	£6.50 - £7.00
electricity	£1.50 - £2.25
all service pitch	plus £2.00

Only one car per pitch permitted. Tel: (01622) 832399. Fax: (01622) 832472. E-mail: tannerfarmpark @cs.com. Reservations: Essential for high season and B.Hs, recommended for other times. Made with deposit (£5 for 1-3 nights; £10 over 3 nights and B.Hs). A popular park, early reservation is advised. **Open** all year.

Directions: Park is 2½ miles south of Marden on B2079 towards Goudhurst. O.S.GR: TQ732417.

Quex Caravan Park

311

Park Road, Birchington, nr Margate, Kent CT7 0BL

This park does not accept tents. Although there are a fair number of privately owned holiday homes, they do not intrude on the touring area which is in a sheltered glade under tall trees. There are 60 touring pitches with 48 electric hook-ups (16A). Local attractions include Quex House and gardens, the model village and motor museum at Ramsgate, whilst in the seaside resort of Margate you can walk through 1,000 years of history at the Caves, or visit the Hollywood Bowl. Reception can provide you with a map of the local area. A member of the Best of British group.

Facilities: The well equipped central sanitary unit is in a heated chalet style building with all the usual facilities. Dishwashing sinks under cover. Laundry room with sink, washing machine and dryer. Well stocked shop. More than one dog per pitch is accepted by prior arrangement only. **Off site**: Supermarkets close by. Fishing, golf or riding 3 miles.

Charges 2001

Per unit incl. 2 adults	£9.00 - £12.00
extra adult	£2.00 - £2.50
child (5-16 yrs)	£1.50 - £2.00
dog	£1.00
electricity	£2.00

Less 10% for 4 nights booked (and paid for on arrival). Tel/Fax: (01843) 841273. E-mail: info@ keatfarm.co.uk. Reservations: Contact site for details. **Open** 7 March - 7 November.

Directions: From roundabout at junction of A28 and A299, take A28 east towards Birchington and Margate. At Birchington carry straight on at roundabout by church, then take next right, then right again, and left at mini roundabout. Site is on right in ½ mile (well signed). O.S.GR: TR320685.

Kent

Gate House Wood Touring Park

Ford Lane, Wrotham Heath, Sevenoaks, Kent TN15 7SD

312

This sheltered park, which opened for its first season in '98, has been created in a former quarry where all the pitches are on well drained grass. A spacious paved entrance with a new reception building and well stocked shop, leads on to the park itself. The 60 pitches are level and open with a few small trees, two brick built barbecue units, and 40 electric hook-ups (10A). A children's playground has swings, seesaw and a slide, all set on a safety base, and the entire site is enclosed by grassy banks on three sides, with a wild flower walk around the top. Local attractions include Brands Hatch Circuit, the International Karting Circuit at Buckmore Park, and the nearby Country Park at West Malling.

Facilities: Comprehensive toilet facilities are smart and well maintained, including a well equipped family room, which is also designed for disabled people. The laundry and dishwashing room is at one end of the modern heated building. Children's playground. No dogs or other pets, commercial vehicles or caravans/motorcaravans greater than 25' overall are admitted. **Off site:** Within walking distance are three pubs and a Cantonese restaurant. Trains run to London Victoria from Borough Green (2½ miles).

Charges 2001

Per unit incl. 2 adults	£8.00 - £9.50
hiker's tent (incl. 2 adults)	£6.00 - £7.00
extra adult	£1.50
child (3-12 yrs)	£1.00
awning or extra car	£1.00
electricity	£1.70 - £2.20

No credit cards. Tel: (01732) 843062. Reservations: Made with deposit (£5 for 3 days, £10 over 3 days or £10 p/week for longer stays). **Open** 1 April - end October.

Directions: From M26 junction 2a, take A20 eastwards towards Wrotham Heath and Maidstone. Just past junction with A25, and opposite the Royal Oak pub, turn left into Ford Lane, and park is immediately on left. O.S.GR: TQ630580.

London Tourist Board

London Tourist Board

Glen House, Stag Place,
Victoria, London SW1E 5LT
Tel: 0207 932 2000 Fax: 0207 932 0222
Internet: www.londontown.com

London is the largest city in Europe, covering some 610 square miles with a population of nearly seven million. However, the centre is fairly compact and covers the financial district called 'The City', the entertainment and shopping area known as 'The West End' and Westminster, seat of Parliament and home of royalty. London's wealthiest neighbourhoods, such as Knightsbridge, Kensington and Chelsea, lie to the west.

East of the city is the culturally intriguing East End and the ambitious Docklands development and further down-river, historical Greenwich.

For information on West End shows, visit the web site:
www.officiallondontheatre.co.uk

For more details about London's restaurants visit the web site:
www.eatlondon.net

For information on shopping visit:
www.shop-london.net.

Experience the London Eye, phone 0870 5000600 or:
www.ba.londoneye.com.

The world's highest observation wheel sweeps the London skyline at an incredible 450 feet. Thirty-two high tech capsules carrying up to 25 passengers each, offer unique and breathtaking views of London, day and night.

Photo: BA London Eye, London Tourist Board

Crystal Palace Caravan Club Site

Crystal Palace Parade, London SE19 1UF

327

The Caravan Club's site at Crystal Palace in south London provides easy access to the city centre and all its many attractions. A pleasant and efficiently run site, it is arranged in terraces overlooking the ruins of the old Crystal Palace, its park and National Sports Centre. It is surprisingly quiet given its location (with the possible exception of regular police sirens and over-flying aircraft). In peak season it is even busier than Abbey Wood with many overseas visitors and advance booking is always necessary. However, as most of the pitches are on gravel hardstanding, it is particularly useful for out of season stays. There are places for 84 caravans or motorcaravans, all with electricity connections (16A). Tents are placed on the site's well mown lawns at the top near reception. In summer an overflow area across the approach road (with portacabin style sanitary facilities) takes further tents or small motorcaravans. Reception has tourist information and many buses stop outside the site, including services to central London. The Crystal Palace park is extensive and provides open spaces for strolls or picnics and plenty of activities for children. The Sports Centre has two swimming pools, tennis and squash courts and gym facilities, with national events in a variety of sports to watch at certain times. The park and the Sports Centre are due for substantial redevelopment and when this begins access will obviously be restricted. An area at the site entrance should be used for arrivals after 10.30 pm.- the pitch areas have a coded security barrier.

Facilities: The single toilet block can be heated in cool weather with curtained washbasins for ladies, washbasin for disabled visitors and a laundry room. The block is kept locked and new arrivals are given a key (without deposit). Washing up sinks and neat rubbish bins are outside, under cover. Motorcaravan service facilities. Gas available. **Off site:** Shops, pubs, etc. / mile.

Charges 2001

Per pitch (non-member)	£7.00 - £8.00
adult	£3.75 - £4.75
child (5-16 yrs)	£1.20
electricity	£2.25 - £1.50

Tent campers - apply to site. Tel: (020) 8778 7155 (08.00-20.00 hrs). Fax: (020) 8676 0980.
Reservations: Essential at all times and made with £5 deposit - contact site. **Open** all year.

Directions: On A205 South Circular road travelling east, pass Dulwich College and golf course on right (avoid College Road - width restriction), turn right at traffic lights (Harvester pub on left). Within / mile at traffic lights turn right into Sydenham Hill; in 350 yds at roundabout turn left (still Sydenham Hill). Site entrance is 1 mile opposite mini-roundabouts (take care on these). Travelling west on A205 South Circular, immediately after passing under Catford railway bridge, keep left onto A212 signed Crystal Palace. After 2¼ miles site entrance is on left at top of Westwood Hill before two mini-roundabouts. O.S.GR: TQ341724.

Photo: BA London Eye, London Tourist Board

Hertfordshire
Lee Valley Caravan Park

321 Charlton Meadows, Essex Road, Dobbs Weir, Hoddeson, Hertfordshire EN11 0AS

Stretching for 26 miles along the Lee Valley and covering 10,000 acres from Ware to the east end of London, Lee Valley Park is administered by the Lee Valley Regional Park Authority. Extensive development of the park into a leisure area now means it offers a wide variety of outdoor and sporting pursuits, including riding, water sports, golf, cycle tracks and places of interest. Set between Hoddesdon, Broxbourne and Nazeing, and under the same management as Lee Valley Campsite, the caravan park is situated in the far north of the complex. The touring section consists of a large, open, well mown meadow with space for 100 units (36 with 10A electricity) and is quite separate from 100 caravan holiday homes. There is no shade in the touring area, but tall trees surrounding the site offer adequate shelter, and it has a neat, tidy and well cared for appearance. Trains run from Broxbourne (about 2 miles) to London, with the journey taking about 30 minutes. Dobbs Weir industrial estate and garden centres are near, although surrounding trees screen out noise and create some privacy.

Facilities: The single, heated toilet block (access by key) has been recently refurbished and is of good quality. Facilities include a baby room, laundry, rotary clothes dryers and good en-suite facilities for disabled visitors. **Off site:** No shop on site, but a free bus service to a nearby superstore is provided three times a week, and a bar/restaurant is just 100 yards from the entrance. Some fishing is possible from the canal towpath that runs past the site, with further opportunities nearby and a swimming pool is just 2 miles.

Charges 2002

Per adult	£5.44
child (3-16 yrs)	£2.20
electricity	£2.25

Min charge £7.64 (but not backpackers). Checking out time 5 pm. Tel/Fax: (01992) 462090. E-mail: info@leevalleypark.com. Reservations: Made with £5 deposit - write to park for reservation form. (For information contact PO Box 88, Enfield, Middlesex: tel: 01992 700766). **Open** March - 31 October.

Directions: Take exit 25 from M25 and then north on A10 for 4 miles; take the Hoddesdon exit, turn left at second roundabout following signs for Dobbs Weir and park is on the right within 1 mile. O.S.GR: TL383082.

London
Lee Valley Campsite

325 Sewardstone Road, Chingford, North London E4 7RA

This site provides an excellent base from which to visit London, having both easy access to the M25 and excellent public transport links into the centre of London. Close to Epping Forest and in the heart of the Lee Valley there is much to enjoy in the surrounding area; from walking and cycling, to golf, fishing and riding. With capacity for 200 units of all types the site is mostly level, with several bush sheltered avenues and plenty of trees throughout. There are 20 pitches with tarmac hardstanding and 100 with electricity (10A). Two local buses stop by the site at fairly frequent intervals in season, with another alternative, and equally good service, every 20 minutes to Walthamstow underground station just 500 yards away. Alternatively you can park at South Woodford or Chingford stations and use the train for London visits.

Facilities: The three toilet blocks (one heated) have been refurbished and are kept clean. Well equipped room for disabled visitors. Clothes and dishwashing facilities. Washing machines, dryers, rotary clothes lines and irons. Well stocked shop, gas available. Children's playground.

Charges 2002

Per adult	£5.60
child (under 16 yrs)	£2.45
electricity	£2.25

Min charge £8.05 per unit/night. Tel: 020 8529 5689. Fax: 020 8559 4070. E-mail: scs@leevalleypark.com. Reservations: Any length up to 14 days with £5 deposit. **Open** Easter - 27 October.

Directions: From M25 exit 26 (Waltham Abbey) from where site is signed take A112 towards Chingford and site is about 3 miles on right. It can also be approached on A112 from the North Circular Road. O.S. GR: TQ378970.

Perfectly Placed for the
City of London
and the countryside of Hertfordshire and Essex

Lee Valley Regional Park is a perfect place to stay. All sites have modern facilities, offer value for money and are located in pleasant surroundings with their own leisure attractions.

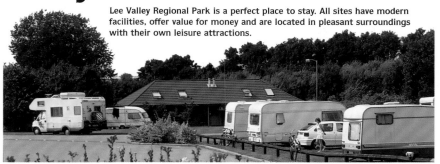

Lee Valley Caravan Park, Dobbs Weir, Hoddesdon, Herts
Enjoy the peace and tranquillity of this riverside site with good fishing, walking and boating nearby. Get to the West End by train and tube in under an hour.
Tel/Fax: 01992 462090

Lee Valley Campsite, Chingford, London
Situated on the edge of Epping Forest and close to the historic town of Waltham Abbey, this site is easily accessible from the M25 and just 42 minutes from the West End by public transport.
Tel: 020 8529 5689
Fax: 020 8559 4070

Lee Valley Cycle Circuit Campsite, Leyton, East London
Set in 40 acres of open parkland, this site is only four miles from the Tower of London. Stay here and you'll reach London's major attractions in less than 30 minutes
Tel: 020 8534 6085

For more information, call the Lee Valley Park Information Centre on 01992 702200 or find us on the web at: www.leevalleypark.com

London
Lee Valley Cycle Circuit Campsite
Quartermile Lane, Stratford, London E15 2EN

This site is set in 40 acres of parkland, only 4 miles from the Tower of London. It is a short bus ride to the nearest Underground station for easy access to Central London. The adjacent Cycle Circuit offers bicycle hire on an off-road, 1.6 km. circuit and id opposite a nature reserve.

Tel: 020 8534 6085. Fax: 020 8536 0959.

Directions: Site is a short distance from Eastway/Ruckholt Road, linked directly to the A102M. Follow signs for Spittalfields Market or camping signs.

Abbey Wood Caravan and Camping Site

326 Federation Road, Abbey Wood, London SE2 0LS

This quietly situated Caravan Club site in southeast London is one of the nearest sites to central London and it becomes very full and crowded in the summer months with campers of many nationalities. Run by the Caravan Club, there are reductions for their members. Reservations are made for all units except tents and are very advisable for July/Aug. and B.Hs. Tent campers, for whom there is a special railed area with cars parked separately, must take their chance. Stays are limited to a maximum of 14 days. Although within a built-up area, this grassy site is in a quiet and pleasant setting with many mature trees. Most parts, especially those for caravans, are sloping but many of the 360 pitches are levelled. A curving line of gravel hardstandings is provided for 14 motorcaravans. There is not much on-site activity but nearly all those staying here want to visit London. A train service runs every 15 minutes from Abbey Wood station (5 mins walk) to either Charing Cross or Cannon Street. The Royal Observatory and the Thames Barrier are nearby. A car park at the entrance has electrical connections for late arrivals (after 10.30 pm). Security could be a problem - be aware.

Facilities: Three traditional type toilet blocks, all heated in cool weather, have washbasins (with shelf and mirror, curtained for ladies), mostly controllable showers, dishwashing sinks and laundry room. Motorcaravan service facilities. Bread, milk and cold drinks available from the office in high season. Gas available. Good travel and information centre (open 8.30- 11 am) can provide tickets for travel and attractions. Children's playground with sand base. **Off site:** Golf 4 miles. Sports centre at Crook Log, 1 mile.

Charges 2001

Per pitch (non-member)	£6.00 - £7.00
adult	£2.75 - £4.50
child (5-16 yrs)	£1.10 - £1.20
electricity	£2.25 - £1.50

Tent campers - apply to site. Tel: 010 8311 1465 (08.00-20.00 hrs). Fax: 010 8311 7708. Reservations: Essential for Easter, Spring B.H. July/Aug with £5 deposit. **Open** all year.

Directions: From east on M2/A2 or from central London: on A2 turn off at A221 junction (third exit off the A2) into Danson Road (signed Bexleyheath, Welling and Sidcup). Follow sign Bexleyheath to Crook Log (A207 junction); at traffic lights turn right and immediately left into Brampton Road. In 1½ miles at traffic lights turn left into Bostal Road (A206); in ¼ mile at traffic lights turn right into Basildon Road (B213). In 300 yds turn right into McLeod Road, in about ½ mile at roundabout turn right into Knee Hill; in 100 yds turn right (second right) into Federation Road. Site on left in 50 yds. From M25, north, west or south approach: leave at junction 2 onto A2 (signed London), then as above. Note: route is well signed with International caravan and camping signs. O.S.GR: TQ472785.

The Grange Country Park

330 East Bergholt, Colchester, Essex CO7 6UX

Set in the heart of Constable country, this neat 11 acre park has a heated pool and high season entertainment. It offers 120 pitches, many with electrical connections (16A). All are on flat grass with well lit, tarmac roads throughout the site. There are 41 fully serviced 'executive' pitches, a separate area for tents and 52 privately owned caravan holiday homes. In addition to a communal barbecue point, many pitches also have their own facilities (equipment can be hired from reception). The range of amenities includes a 60 x 30 ft. outdoor, heated swimming pool plus a children's paddling pool, with snack bar, grass seating area, sauna and solarium. Single groups, motorbikes and commercial vehicles are not accepted. Facilities available may be limited during winter (Nov. - March).

Facilities: Three modern heated toilet blocks have good, clean facilities. En-suite unit for disabled visitors. Two laundry rooms. Shop (April - Sept, limited hours out of peak season). Swimming pool (Whitsun - 7 Sept and supervised during high season). Bar and restaurant, offering reasonably priced meals and entertainment in high season. Games and TV rooms. Small children's play area on grass and matting. Dogs are accepted but max. 2, and no dangerous breeds. Nature trail.

Charges 2001

Per unit incl. 2 adults	£9.00 - £13.00
premier pitch incl. electricity	£14.00 - £18.00
extra adult	£1.50 - £2.50
child (3-14 yrs)	£1.00 - £2.00
electricity	£2.25 - £2.50
dog (max. 2)	£0.50 - £1.00

Less 10% for stays over 10 nights. Tel: (01206) 298567/298912. Fax: (01206) 298770. E-mail: enquiries@grangecountrypark.co.uk. Reservations: Made with £10 deposit and £2 fee. **Open** all year except 4 Jan. - 1 Feb.

Directions: Park is between Ipswich (8 miles) and Colchester (10 miles). Follow signs for East Bergholt from the A12 (4 miles). O.S.GR: TL097352.

Discover Britain with us...

East of England Tourist Board

Essex, Suffolk, Norfolk, Cambridgeshire, Hertfordshire and Bedfordshire

Toppesfield Hall, Hadleigh, Suffolk IP7 5DN

Tel: (01473) 822922 FAX (01473) 823063

E-mail: eastofenglandtouristboard@compuserve.com

Internet: http://www.eastofenglandtouristboard.com

Step into the East of England and you step into a subtly different world. It is England as you like it - the perfect mix of soft and gentle countryside, ancient cities, charming towns, storybook villages, bird-reserved beaches and old-fashioned seaside fun. Somehow this welcoming region has missed the relentless march of time - so take your time and let the pleasures quietly unfold for you.

The East of England is ideal for short breaks, and especially for cycling and walking holidays - it is here that you can truly 'get away from it all'.

In **Bedfordshire** and **Hertfordshire** you can visit the peaceful canals, go antique hunting, or see Old Warden Park - where you can find the Shuttleworth Collection of historic aircraft, a Swiss Garden and a Falconry Centre. Or visit some of the country's greatest stately homes - Knebworth House, Woburn Abbey, and Hatfield House.

In **Cambridgeshire** there is, of course, the fascinating university city of Cambridge, with King's College Chapel, the Botanical Garden and the varied museums. Not far from Cambridge is Oliver Cromwell Country, the ancient cathedral cities of Ely and Peterborough, or the Georgian town of Wisbech where you can visit the 'hidden' garden of Peckover House. The flat Fenland is a network of canals and rivers, ideal for narrowboat trips, and for something completely different there is the Imperial War Museum at Duxford, Europe's premier aviation museum.

Essex is the home of charming villages, unspoilt coastline and a rich maritime history - so close to London. The landscape has been immortalised by the artist John Constable, while towns such as Saffron Walden, Finchingfield and Coggeshall are 'pretty as a picture'. There are fabulous gardens, such as the Gardens of Easton Lodge, Beth Chatto's Garden and the gardens of stately homes such as Hyde Hall, Audley End and Marks Hall.

Photo: Sandringham, East of England Tourist Board

Norfolk has miles of beautiful coastline where you can enjoy seaside fun or nature trails, or visit the ancient ports such as Kings Lynn. The man-made waterways of The Broads, are ideal for exploring by boat. Or take a stately tour of Holkham Hall, Houghton Hall, Blickling Hall, Oxburgh Hall, and of course, the Queen's country retreat, Sandringham - with special exhibitions to celebrate the Queen's Golden Jubilee.

Suffolk is where you'll find space, peace and picturesque villages set in gently rolling countryside. Lavenham, Long Melford and Kersey are medieval remnants of a more wealthy time, while the larger towns of Bury St Edmunds and Ipswich have a rich heritage with lots to explore. And if you fancy a flutter, head for Newmarket, the horse racing capital since the 17th century.

Suffolk
Moat Barn Touring Caravan Park
Dallinghoo Road, Bredfield, Woodbridge, Suffolk IP13 6BD

333

Mike Allen opened this small, new touring park in April 2000. Family run, it provides just 25 level pitches, all with electricity hook-ups (10A). As yet, the hedges have not matured, but the pitches are spacious and the park provides a tranquil environment making it a very pleasant place to use as a base. Walkers and cyclists will enjoy this location – the park is on the Suffolk Heritage Cycle Route, and also the Hull - Harwich National Cycle Route. Moat Barn also offers bed and breakfast.

Facilities: The well equipped sanitary block can be heated. A separate unit houses a dishwashing sink. Laundry and shop planned. Motorcaravan service point.

Charges 2002

Per unit incl. 2 adults	£9.00
extra person or car	£1.00
electricity	£2.00

Tel: (01473) 737520. Reservations: Advised, especially for B.Hs and made with £10 deposit. **Open** April - October.

Directions: From Ipswich on A12 to Lowestoft, after Hasketon roundabout take first left signed Bredfield. At village pump turn right and follow road past public house and church. Continue through S-bends and, after 200 yards, site entrance is on left, just after farm buildings. From Lowestoft, take right turn to Bredfield just before Hasketon roundabout, then as above. O.S.GR: TM 270537.

Suffolk
Low House Touring Caravan Centre
Bucklesham Road, Foxhall, nr Ipswich, Suffolk IP10 0AU

331

Set in 3½ acres, this beautiful garden site has 30 pitches and an abundance of trees, shrubs and flowers. In two sections, you drive through one field (the rally field) to reach the more secluded, sheltered garden area. We understand from the owner that there are 90 different varieties of trees on site, and an ornamental tree walk can be followed around the edge of the park. All the pitches have electrical connections (most 16A, but some 10A) and they back onto trees that provide plenty of shade and the opportunity to observe a range of wildlife. The rally field has a more open aspect, but is still well sheltered and tranquil. Reception and the office are in the cottage of the enthusiastic and helpful owner, John Booth. A good bus service to Ipswich stops just outside the site. Low House lies between Felixstowe (8 miles) and Ipswich (5 miles) and would be a useful stopover for the Felixstowe port or Harwich. Note: Tents are only accepted subject to space.

Facilities: The modern, heated sanitary block is spotlessly clean with hot showers (50p). There are chemical disposal facilities, but no dishwashing sinks. No on-site provisions but a supermarket is 2 miles (towards Ipswich). Frozen goods can be stored. Calor gas is available. Small children's adventure play area. Pets area with rabbits and ornamental fowl. A torch would be useful. **Off site**: Pub in Bucklesham village (1½ miles) and other good pubs nearby. Golf 2 miles.

Charges guide

Per unit incl. 2 adults and children	£7.50
extra adult	£2.00
child (5-15 yrs)	£1.00
awning (please lift groundsheets)	free
electricity (16A)	£1.50 - £2.20

No commercial vehicles. No credit cards. Tel: (01473) 659437. Fax: (01473) 659880. E-mail: john.e.booth@ talk21.com. Reservations: Advanced booking advised - phone any time. **Open** all year.

Directions: Turn off A14 (was A45) Ipswich ring road (south) via slip road onto A1156 (signed Ipswich East). Follow road over bridge which crosses over the A45 and almost immediately turn right (no sign). After ½ mile turn right again (signed Bucklesham) and site is on left after / mile. O.S.GR: TM225423.

Little Lakeland Caravan Park

348 Wortwell, Harleston, Norfolk IP20 0EL

This peaceful hideaway with its own fishing lake, is tucked behind the houses and gardens that border the village main street. It is a traditional, mature little site with 58 pitches and a number of caravan holiday homes and long stay units, but there should always be around 22 places for tourers. The pitches are mostly individual with mature hedges and trees separating them. Fishing in the lake is free for campers. Places to visit nearby include The Cider Place at Ilketshall St Lawrence, The Otter Trust at Earsham, and there are numerous local way-marked walks around Wortwell and nearby Harleston which also has a market every Wednesday. A member of the Countryside Discovery group.

Facilities: A modern, heated toilet block provides washbasins all in cubicles for ladies, and one for men. Fully equipped laundry. Separate en-suite room for disabled visitors also has facilities for baby changing. A further unit (also heated) by reception provides a shower, WC and basin per sex and is used mostly in the colder months. Recycling bins. Reception stocks gas and some basic essentials. Small children's play area, and library of paperback books in the summer house. Fishing (max. 4 rods per unit). **Off site**: Riding 6 miles, golf 4 miles.

Charges 2002

Per unit incl. 2 adults	£8.20 - £10.30
extra adult	£2.20
child (4-16 yrs.)	£1.00
electricity (10A max)	£1.80

No credit cards. Tel/Fax: (01986) 788646. E-mail: information@littlelakeland.co.uk. Reservations: Advisable for B.Hs and peak season; made with £20 deposit or full fee if less. **Open** 15 March - 31 October.

Directions: Approaching from Diss, leave A143 at roundabout signed Wortwell. Continue to village, pass 'The Bell' public house then a garage on the right, after which turn right at first bungalow (Little Lakeland Lodge) watching carefully for signs. Site is down lane, 250 yards on right. O.S.GR: TM270850.

The Grange Touring Park

349 Yarmouth Road, Ormesby St Margaret, Great Yarmouth, Norfolk NR29 3QG

The appealing overall appearance of this family touring site is that of a garden, with many hanging baskets, flower beds, bluebells and daffodils under the trees in spring, and all carefully tended by the resident wardens. The 70 level grassy pitches are arranged around tarmac access roads, 62 with electricity (5A). Next to the campsite is The Grange itself - a free house offering a wide range of meals, beers and real ale, plus children's play equipment (open all year). The site owner also has a holiday campsite at Hemsby (4 miles) with its own wide sandy beach, which guests at The Grange are welcome to use. Local attractions include Caister Castle and Motor Museum, Norfolk Rare Breed Centre, Yarmouth greyhound stadium and ten pin bowling.

Facilities: A modern stylish toilet building is exceptionally well appointed, and spotlessly clean, housing all the usual facilities including a baby changing room in the ladies'. Laundry room with washing machine and dryer. Washing lines are provided at the rear of the building. Children's swings. Mobile shop calls daily in high season. Gas available from reception. **Off site**: Fishing 4 miles, golf 3 miles.

Charges 2001

Per unit incl. 4 persons	£7.00 - £11.50
extra adult	£2.00
awning	£2.00
electricity	£1.70
extra car or boat	£2.00
first dog free, extra dog by arrangement	£2.00

Tel: (01493) 730306. Fax: (01493) 730188. E-mail: john.groat@virgin.net. Reservations: Advisable for B.Hs (min. 3 nights), school holidays and peak season and made with deposit (£10 for under 7 days or £20 per week). **Open** 20 March - 26 September.

Directions: Site is north of Great Yarmouth and east of Ormesby St Margaret, just south of the roundabout where the B1159 road joins the A149. O.S.GR: TG515140.

This popular well established family holiday park is in a semi-rural location, but within easy reach of Great Yarmouth. On site is an area with 109 privately owned caravan holiday homes, plus 35 site owned units for rent. A separate open, grassy area provides around 150 touring pitches, some slightly sloping, with only 100 having electrical hook-ups (16A), plus 2 fully serviced pitches. A large restaurant/bar providing club style entertainment in season and a takeaway service (noon-7 pm) overlooks a heated outdoor swimming pool. Campers can also use the indoor pool and other facilities at Liffens Welcome Holiday Centre close by. The excellent children's playground and a fenced, hard-surfaced multi-court for ball games are far enough from the pitches to preserve peace and quiet. The site also operates a post office/shop which is adjacent to the site, and a regular bus service runs from here to Great Yarmouth. The remains of a Roman fortress border the site.

Facilities: Two sanitary units of differing ages provide clean but fairly standard facilities with a unit for disabled persons, a baby room, and dishwashing sinks. The laundry is located in a separate older unit. Restaurant, bar and takeaway. Swimming pool (60 x 30 ft; open 29/5-10/9) with new water slide. Children's playground. Crazy golf. Bicycle hire planned. Multi-court. Torches advised. **Off site**: Golf 2 miles, fishing/mile.

Charges 2001

Per unit incl. 4 persons	£8.00 - £15.00
extra person	free - £2.00
fully serviced pitch	plus £4.00
awning	£1.50 - £2.00
extra pup tent	£5.00
electricity	£3.00
dog (one only)	£2.00

Special offer breaks available. Tel: (01493) 780357. Fax: (01493) 782383. Reservations: Essential for high season and made with £20 p/week deposit. **Open** 2 April - 30 October.

Directions: From junction of A12 and A143 at roundabout south of Great Yarmouth take Burgh Road westwards, straight over at next roundabout, then second left into Butt lane. Site is on right. Avoid width restricted road closer to Great Yarmouth. O.S.GR: TM490050.

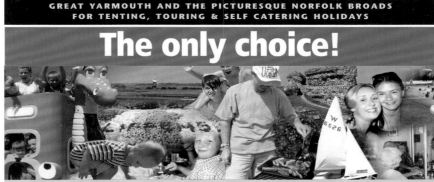

Kelling Heath Holiday Park

343 Weybourne, Sheringham, Norfolk NR25 7HW

Kelling Heath is a holiday park set in a 250-acre estate in a designated area of outstanding natural beauty overlooking the north Norfolk coast. A spacious park, the 384 caravan holiday homes (36 to let, the rest privately owned) and the 300 touring pitches blend easily into the part-wooded, part-open heathland. A wide range of on-site facilities, including a club complex, fitness centre and nature trail, provide activities for all ages. The touring area is quiet and peaceful, away from the facilities, on fairly level grass amid pine trees and open heath with gorse and heather. It has 246 marked pitches with electrical hook-ups (16A) and a further 54 unmarked pitches. The central reception area, between the statics and the tourers, has been attractively paved and pedestrianised with village stores, bar and bandstand. 'The Forge', a complex comprising an entertainment bar, adults only bar and family room, provides a comprehensive range of entertainment and amusements all season. Opened in 2001, the Health and Fitness club includes an indoor pool (19 x 9 m). Other facilities include two hard tennis courts, a small outdoor, heated fun pool, sports field, play areas and a small lake for free fishing (permit holders only). The North Norfolk steam railway has a halt within walking distance, giving access to Cromer.

Facilities: Three toilet blocks serve the site, the most modern of which is heated with a glazed conservatory that provides covered access all year to disabled people. Baby changing. Dishwashing and laundry sinks. All blocks have a few washbasins in private cubicles, baby baths and, in season, a nappy disposal service. Washing machines (3) and tumble dryers (2), with irons from reception (£20 deposit). Village stores. Gas available. Bar, restaurant and takeaway. Indoor and outdoor pools. Fitness centre with spa pool, sauna, steam rooms and gym with fully trained staff (membership on either daily or weekly basis). Nature trail. Adventure play area with assault course. Tennis. Fishing. Entertainment programme. Torch useful.

Charges 2001

Per unit	£10.85 - £15.95
pitch with electricity	£12.85 - £17.95
extra person (under 16 yrs)	free - £1.95
extra car or pup tent	£2.00
dog (max. 2)	£1.50

Min 7 day stay in high season. No single sex groups. Tel: (01263) 708181. Fax: (01263) 588599. E-mail: info@kellingheath.co.uk. Reservations: Necessary for July/Aug. on a weekly basis with £30 booking remittance. **Open** 19 March - 16 December.

Directions: Park is signed on A148 Holt - Cromer road, between High Kelling and Bodham. On A149 Sheringham road turn right at the church in Weybourne. O.S.GR: TG117418.

The Old Brick Kilns Caravan & Camping Park

340 Little Barney Lane, Barney, Fakenham, Norfolk NR21 0NL

This tranquil, family run park, owned by Alan and Pam Greenhalgh, has been developed on the site of an old brick kiln resulting in land on varying levels. It provides areas of pitches (eg. the Dell, the Orchard) which have been well drained and grassed over. Banks around the park and trees provide shelter, home for a variety of wildlife with a wide range of trees and shrubs. Garden areas include a butterfly garden, of which a central conservation pond is the main feature. There are 60 pitches, all with electricity (10/16A) and semi hardstanding. Drinking water is supplied by a 285 ft. bore and excellent, roofed service areas provide water and waste disposal. Amenities include a large, comfortable bar area and restaurant, open selected evenings and weekends. A friendly, helpful atmosphere prevails and as the park is 8 miles from the coast, it is ideally situated to explore North Norfolk. A member of the Best of British group.

Facilities: Toilet facilities are very good with under-floor heating, washbasins in curtained cubicles, and hand and hair dryers. Facilities for babies and disabled people (unisex), a laundry room and dishwashing. A small toilet block is at the furthest end. Motorcaravan service point. Shop with gas. Bar and restaurant. Patio area outside with barbecue. Gas barbecues for hire. TV room, information centre, table tennis, giant chess and a mini library. Bicycle hire. Fenced children's play area with bark surface. Fishing. Winter caravan storage. B&B available. **Off site**: Riding 6 miles, golf 5 or 8 miles

Charges 2001

Per pitch	£5.25 - £7.75
adult	£2.00
child 0-15 yrs	50p - £1.50
dog (max. 2)	free
electricity	£2.00

Tel: (01328) 878305. Fax: (01328) 878948. E-mail: enquire@old-brick-kilns.co.uk. Reservations: Advised and made with £15 deposit (non-refundable). **Open** all year excl. 7 Jan - 20 Feb.

Directions: From Fakenham take A148 Cromer road. After 6 miles, fork right on B1354 Aylsham road and in 300 yds, turn right, signed Barney, and then first left along a narrow country lane with passing places, for ¼ mile. O.S.GR: TG004332.

Norfolk

Woodhill Park

350

Cromer Road, East Runton, Cromer, Norfolk NR27 9PX

Woodhill is a seaside site with good views and a traditional atmosphere. It is situated on the cliff top, in a large gently sloping open grassy field, with 300 marked touring pitches. Of these, 175 have electricity (16A) and many have wonderful views over the surrounding countryside. A small number of holiday homes which are located nearer to the cliff edge have the best sea views. Although the site is fenced there is access to the cliff top path. Nearby attractions include 'Karttrax' at Cromer (go-karting), boat trips to see the seals off Blakeney Point, the Shire Horse Centre at West Runton, the North Norfolk Steam Railway, and at Sheringham you can find 'The Splash' fun pool complex with wave machine.

Facilities: The three sanitary units (the newest is part of the heated reception building) are fully equipped. Laundry with washing machines and dryer (iron available from reception). Fully equipped unit for disabled persons. Well stocked mini-market plus gas exchange. Adventure playground and plenty of space for ball games. Crazy golf. 9 hole golf course adjacent to the site. **Off site**: Bicycle hire nearby.

Charges 2001

Per unit	£8.00 - £9.20
small pitch (non-electric)	£4.50 - £5.95
multi-service pitch	£10.60 - £11.95
adult	£1.45
child	80p
dog	85p

Tel: (01263) 512242. Fax: (01263) 515326. E-mail: info@woodhill-park.com. Reservations: Accepted for min. 3 nights with £15 p/week non returnable booking fee. **Open** 20 March - 31 October.

Directions: Site is beside the A149 coast road between East and West Runton. O.S.GR: TG190420.

Two Mills Touring Park

342 Yarmouth Road, North Walsham, Norfolk NR28 9NA

Two Mills is a quiet site for adults only. Situated in the bowl of a former quarry, it is therefore a real sun trap, both secluded and sheltered. The park is neatly maintained with natural areas, varied trees, wild flowers and birds. It is a good centre from which to explore the north Norfolk coast, the Broads or for visiting Norwich and a footpath from the park joins the Weavers Way. There are 54 level, marked pitches for tourers, 33 all weather gravel, including five 'panorama' pitches (hardstanding, patio area, water and waste water drainage) and 21 on grass. All are generously sized and have electricity (10/16A). A small, secluded area is reserved for tents (no plastic groundsheets). A member of the Best of British group. This is an adult only park.

Facilities: The central, very well maintained, heated toilet block has some washbasins in cabins, en-suite facilities for disabled people, laundry and dishwashing rooms. Small shop. Community room with TV and tea and coffee facilities. Ice service. Fish and chip van calls Thursday evenings. Dogs accepted by arrangement only with kennels provided. **Off site:** Hotel/pub across the road. Town 20 minutes walk. Fishing, golf or riding 5 miles, bicycle hire 1½ miles and the coast is 5 miles.

Charges 2002

Per unit incl. 2 adults	£8.00 - £11.00
panorama pitch per week	£91.00 - £115.50
extra person	£2.50
awning	£1.00 - £1.50
dog	50p
electricity	£2.00

Senior citizen discounts. Tel/Fax: (01692) 405829. E-mail: enquiries@twomills.co.uk. Reservations: Made with £10 deposit; balance payable on arrival. **Open** all year except 4 Jan - 28 Feb.

Directions: Approach from southeast on A149 and watch for caravan sign approx. 1½ miles before North Walsham (also signed White Horse Common). The road runs parallel to the A149 and site is on right after 1/ miles. O.S.GR: TG292287.

Little Haven Caravan and Camping Park

345 The Street, Erpingham, Norwich, Norfolk NR11 7QD

Within easy reach of the coast and the Broads, this is an attractive and peaceful little site under new ownership and it has excellent facilities. Only adults and accompanied children over 14 years are accepted. The 24 grassy pitches, all with electricity (16A), are arranged around the outside of a gravel access road, with a central lawn and decorative pergola, a neat little garden and a seating area. There is no shop, but two pubs serving food and traditional ales are within walking distance. An ideal base for cycling, walking, horse riding, or just relaxing, the Weavers Way footpath is within half a mile of the site, whilst riding stables and a craft centre are at nearby Alby. Also close by is magnificent Blickling Hall with its superb state rooms, gardens and park, or a short drive takes you to the historic market town of Aylsham. This is an adult only park.

Facilities: The well maintained toilet unit is heated and provides modern facilities including spacious hot showers and two covered dishwashing and laundry sinks. Gas available. Site is unsuitable for American motorhomes.

Charges 2001

Per unit incl. 2 adults	£8.00 - £10.00
extra adult	£3.00
extra car	£2.00
extra small tent	50p
dog	free
electricity	£2.00

Single person discount £1.50. Less 10% in low season for Senior Citizens Mon - Thurs. No credit cards. Tel/Fax: (01263) 768959. E-mail: pat@haven30.fsnet.co.uk. Reservations: Advisable for B.Hs and peak season and made without deposit. **Open** 1 March - 31 October.

Directions: From A140 Cromer - Norwich road, going south towards Aylsham and 3 miles south of Roughton, past the Horseshoes pub and Alby crafts, take first turning right signed Erpingham 2 miles. Site is 175 yards on right. O.S.GR: TG190320.

Norfolk

The Garden Caravan Site

346 Barmer Hall, Syderstone, Kings Lynn, Norfolk PE31 8SR

An imaginative touring site in an enclosed, south facing, walled garden, this newly developed site has 30 spacious marked pitches, all on gently sloping grass in the most attractive setting behind the Hall itself. There are 30 electrical connections (16A), each with a TV hook-up as reception is variable, possibly due to the high wall and woodland surrounding the site. However, this does mean that the site is peaceful and a little sun-trap, a haven from the busy world outside. Attractive mature trees, shrubs and climbers provide shade at various times of the day. Reception is housed in a small kiosk (not always manned, so pitch yourself and pay later). Barmer Hall is not far from Sandringham, and there are plenty of peaceful lanes to explore on your bicycle or take a woodland walk from the little door in the wall at the rear of the site. Maybe visit Norfolk Lavender, Langham Glass or the Thursford Collection of steam engines, mechanical organs and Wurlitzer fame. The North Norfolk coast and beaches, numerous golf courses and bird sanctuaries are all within easy reach.

Facilities: Toilet facilities are in a new building (heated when necessary) including extremely spacious hot showers and free hot water throughout. Dishwashing sinks are under cover at one end of the building. There is no shop, but gas, ices, soft drinks and free range fresh eggs are usually available. **Off site:** Bicycle hire 4 miles, riding 6 miles, golf 10 miles.

Charges 2001

Per adult	£3.00 - £4.00
child	£2.00
electricity	£2.00
TV aerial hook-up	£1.00

No credit cards. Tel: (01485) 578220 (house) or 578178 (site). Fax: (01485) 578178. E-mail: nigel@mason96.fsnet.co.uk. Reservations: Advised for B.Hs and peak season. **Open** 1 March - 1 November.

Directions: Approx. 4 miles west of Fakenham turn off A148, taking B1454 northwards and turning to Barmer Hall after a further 4 miles, where site is signed - the road is marked 'unsuitable for motor vehicles' but ignore this and follow past and behind the Hall and farm buildings. O.S.GR: TF810330.

Alan Rogers' discount
Less 10% for adults in June

Norfolk

Gatton Waters Lakeside Touring Site

344 Hillington, St Sandringham, Kings Lynn, Norfolk PE31 6BJ

Developed around two fishing lakes (formerly stone quarries), Gatton Waters has a pleasant open aspect. The 60 caravan (all with electric hook ups) and 30 tent pitches are set further away, around the lakes and quite a number are occupied by seasonal caravans. However, there is room for those seeking either to fish (day tickets available) or for a quiet base to visit Sandringham (2.2 miles) or the north Norfolk coast (8 miles). Everything is kept as natural as possible and skylarks, pheasants, ospreys and leverets are frequently to be seen, in addition to the many types of ducks, etc. on the lakes. In keeping with the natural, relaxed atmosphere of the site the owners made the decision to go 'adult only' in '98, and have been encouraged by the positive response they have received. Only adults over 18 years are accepted.

Facilities: Two new toilet blocks can be heated and also provide dishwashing facilities. Extra facilities are near reception. Motorcaravan services. The reception/bar, housed in an old Norfolk barn, provides a friendly welcome, an open fire and serves real ale (closed Tuesdays). Evening meals and Sunday lunches are served (weekends only out of main season and not October). Caravan storage. **Off site:** Riding or golf 8 miles

Charges 2001

Per unit incl. 2 persons	
caravan or trailer tent	£5.00 - £9.00
tent incl. 2 persons	£4.00 - £9.00
extra person	£1.00
electricity	£1.75 - £2.00

No credit cards. Tel: (01485) 600643. E-mail: gatton.waters@virgin.net. Reservations: Advisable during peak periods and made for min. 3 days at B.Hs. **Open** April - 1 October.

Directions: From Kings Lynn follow A148 Cromer road. Site is signed after sign to West Newton, but before sign to Sandringham and village of Hillington (all to the left). O.S.GR: TF705255.

The Dower House Touring Park

339 Thetford Forest, East Harling, Norfolk NR16 2SE

Set in 20 acres of Britain's largest woodland forest on the Suffolk and Norfolk borders, the Dower House provides quiet woodland walks and cycle ways, with an abundance of wildlife. It is also an ideal centre from which to explore Breckland. The present owners acquired the park some years ago and have worked hard to upgrade the facilities, yet without compromising its natural features. There is provision for 60 tents and 100 vans on unmarked, fairly level, open grass with some mature oaks, in four field areas surrounded by forest, with the Dower House at the centre. Electrical hook-ups (10-16A) are available on three fields with wheel hardstandings on one. Six pitches for visitors with mobility problems are linked by a path to the main facilities. The Dower House, as well as being the home of the owners, houses a pleasant bar and a patio area used for special feature weekends (e.g. Morris dancing, Star Gazers and Swinging 60s).

Facilities: Two toilet blocks - a small, refurbished one near the entrance, and a larger one with a baby room. A separate building houses the showers (5 for each sex and 20p) and a unit for disabled people. Dishwashing room, including a lower sink for children or disabled people. Laundry room with washing machine and dryer. Bar serving food (weekends only in low season) and a takeaway. Licensed shop daily in season, on request at other times. Gas supplies. TV and quiet rooms. Small swimming pool (late May - early Sept), with paddling pool. Caravan storage. Torches necessary. **Off site:** Fishing 1½ miles.

Charges 2001

Per unit incl. 2 persons	£8.90 - £11.50
extra adult	75p - £2.00
extra child	50p - £1.00
hikers or cyclists (2 persons) incl. tent	£6.50 - £8.80
electricity	£2.25 - £2.50

Tel: (01953) 717314. Fax: (01953) 717843. E-mail: info@dowerhouse.co.uk. Reservations: Accepted by phone. **Open** 15 March - 29 September.

Directions: From A11 (Thetford - Norwich) road follow signs to East Harling and park is signed. Turn right at church and right at T junction; park is on right. From A1066 Thetford-Garboldisham road follow signs for East Harling and park is on left after Forestry Commission site. Follow unmade road for approx. 1 mile driving slowly past the Gamekeepers cottage. O.S GR: TL969853.

in the heart of Thetford Forest...

the Dower house

BH&HPA

DAVID BELLAMY CONSERVATION AWARD GOLD

English Tourism Council TOURING AND CAMPING PARK ★★★★ Excellent

Enquiries to David or Karin, The Dower House, Touring Park Thetford Forest, East Harling, Norfolk, NR16 2SE (01953) 717314 www.dowerhouse.co.uk

Breckland Meadows Touring Park

347 Lynn Road, Swaffham, Norfolk PE37 7PT

Within walking distance of the historic market town of Swaffham, this is a pleasant little park with enthusiastic owners that would make a good base to explore Norfolk and the local area. The 45 pitches are on fairly level, neat grass, all with electricity (16A), some with hardstanding. There may be some road noise at times but newly planted trees should reduce this as they mature. Adjacent to the site is the Swaefas Way, a seven mile circular walk which links to the better known Peddars Way. Local attractions include the Thursford Collection of steam engines, mechanical organs and Wurlitzer fame. Swaffham (½ mile) has a popular Saturday market.

Facilities: The toilet block has been refurbished and is neat, clean and heated when necessary. It provides all the usual facilities, a separate toilet and washbasin unit for disabled visitors, and outside covered washing-up facilities. Gas available. **Off site:** Fishing 5 miles, riding 4 miles, golf 2 miles.

Charges 2001

Per unit incl. 2 adults	£6.00 - £8.00
extra adult	£2.00
child (5-15 yrs)	50p
tents	from £6.00
awning	£1.00
electricity	£2.00

Tel: (01760) 721246. Fax: (01760) 725994. E-mail: info@brecklandmeadows.co.uk. Reservations: Essential for B.Hs and advised for peak season; made with non-refundable £10 deposit. **Open:** All year, but reservation essential Nov - Feb.

Directions: Park is just west of Swaffham on the old A47, approx. 1 mile from town centre. O.S.GR: TF809094.

Highfield Farm Touring Park

Long Road, Comberton, Cambridge, CB3 7DG

356

Situated five miles from Cambridge, this eight acre park is set in a delightfully quiet touring location. Family run and very well kept, the welcome is always warm and the facilities of superior quality. Divided into five enclosures by hedges and conifers, there are also shady glades for those who wish to retreat even further; plus one enclosure is reserved for those without children. Offering 60 numbered pitches for caravans or motorcaravans, and 60 for tents, personal space is further enhanced by the fact that the centre of each enclosure is left free. All pitches have 10A electricity, 50 have gravel hardstanding, and most are level. Basic provisions are available from reception and there are nearby shops and pubs. Two play areas (swings and tree house) plus two sizeable areas for football, kite flying or merely running. A good dog walk is provided, which can be extended to a pleasant 1½ mile walk, with seats, around the farm perimeter. A member of the Best of British group.

Facilities: Three heated toilet blocks provide more than adequate coverage. The original block offers controllable showers on payment, and an additional set of unisex showers. The other two blocks (fully tiled) also provide showers on payment (10p), some washbasins in cubicles, all outstandingly clean and well maintained. Baby changing room but no dedicated provision for disabled visitors, although one block has extra wide doors and easy access. Hot water is free to 10 covered dishwashing sinks spaced throughout the site. Fully equipped laundry. Motorcaravan service point. Children's play areas. Bicycle hire from site. Gates closed midnight to 7.30 am. **Off site:** Fishing 3½ miles, golf 2 miles.

Charges 2002

Per unit incl. 2 persons	£7.75 - £9.25
m/cyclist tent	£6.75 - £7.50
hiker/cyclist tent	£6.50 - £7.25
extra adult	£2.00
child (5-16 yrs)	£1.50
awning/pup tent	£1.00
electricity	£1.75

No credit cards. Tel/Fax: 01223 262308. Reservations: Made for any length with £10 deposit and 50p fee. **Open** 23 March - 31 October.

Directions: Park is 5 miles southwest of Cambridge city centre near eastern edge of Comberton village. From M11 take exit 12, the A603 towards Sandy and right after ½ mile on B1046 to Comberton. From A428 turn south at Hardwick roundabout and follow international camping signs to Comberton. O.S GR: TL391571.

Ferry Meadows Caravan Club Site

358 Ham Lane, Peterborough, Cambridgeshire PE2 5UU

Only 3 miles from Peterborough and closer still to the East of England Showground, Ferry Meadows occupies 30 acres of the much larger Nene Country Park. The meadows, lakes and woodlands provide ample opportunities to sample the numerous facilities on offer. Open all year, this Caravan Club site (open to non-members) provides 254 pitches – 160 grass pitches on one side of the park and 94 gravel hardstandings on the newer side, just across the road. Privacy, shade and character are assured by the abundance of trees, bushes and shrubs that are part of the park as a whole. All pitches have electricity (16A) and tents are accepted on the grass section of the site. Families with children may prefer the grass section, from where they can keep a watchful eye on the well-equipped play area. The Country Park covers over 500 acres within which are miles of walks and cycle ways, horse routes, lakes for coarse fishing, sailing and windsurfing, a wetland nature reserve, archery field, two golf courses and a miniature railway. Well laid out for the disabled visitor, free wheelchair hire is available on request. Also passing within nostalgic earshot and yielding the occasional aroma of bygone eras is the Nene Valley Steam Railway, complete with Thomas the Tank Engine.

Facilities: Two modern, heated toilet blocks are of the usual good standard, with curtained washbasins and en-suite facilities for disabled visitors. Each section has dishwashing sinks under cover, as well as a laundry room. Motorcaravan service point. The office stocks basic provisions (nearest shops 1½ miles). Children's play area. Tourist information room with ideas on where to go. Peterborough offers ice and roller skating, whilst other attractions include Spalding Flower Festival and Burghley Park.

Charges 2001

Per pitch (non-member)	£6.00 - £8.00
adult	£3.50 - £4.50
child	£1.10 - £1.20
electricity	£1.50 - £2.25

Tel: (01733) 233526. Reservations: Essential for B.Hs, July/Aug and all w/ends. **Open** all year.

Directions: From A1 south, do not turn onto A1139, but turn left at next junction (signed Showground, Chesterton, Alwalton). At T-junction turn left on A605, continue straight at three roundabouts, following signs for Nene Park to site in Ham Lane. O.S.GR: TL151975.

Old Manor Caravan Park

355 Church Road, Grafham, Huntingdon, Cambridgeshire PE28 0BB

This small, attractive park has connections that reach back to the days of Oliver Cromwell, who occupied the old white cottage which is now reception. The grounds formed part of his garden and even today the horse pond and part of the moat remain. A tarmac road leads to the 80 numbered and generously sized grass pitches, most with 10A electrical connections. Some all-weather pitches are planned. A variety of trees and hedges provide shade throughout the six acre, level grounds. Well drained, neat and carefully maintained, the park has ample water and refuse points. Cambridge, the Imperial War Museum at Duxford, Woburn Abbey and the Shuttleworth Collection at Old Warden are nearby.

Facilities: The single, toilet block is well maintained and exceptionally clean. Parent and baby room. Dishwashing and laundry rooms, plus a free freezer for ice blocks and food storage. Basic provisions are available from reception (1/3-31/10), with the nearest shops being at West Perry or Buckden (5 and 3 miles respectively). Small playground. Large, heated outdoor pool (small extra charge; unsupervised). New security barrier.

Charges 2002

Per unit incl. 2 adults	£11.00 - £13.00
extra person	£3.00 - £3.50
child (5-15 yrs)	£1.50 - £1.75
awning	£1.00
dog (max. 2)	£1.00
electricity	£2.00 - £3.00

Tel: (01480) 810264. Fax: (01480) 819099. E-mail: camping@old-manor.co.uk. Reservations: Made with £10 non-returnable deposit (min 3 nights at B.Hs). **Open** all year (reduced facilities Nov-Feb incl).

Directions: Leave the A1 at Buckden roundabout and follow B661 towards Grafham Water for approx. half a mile. O.S.GR: TL160 680.

Alan Rogers' discount
One night free for one week booked

**COUNTRYSIDE
DISCOVERY**

is a group of quality,
rural caravan and
camping parks all
situated in
country locations

COUNTRYSIDE
DISCOVERY

For a **FREE** brochure with full details of all our parks and types
of accommodation, please telephone our brochure line on –
01986 788646 – 8 am to 8 pm

Britain's best rural caravan and camping parks

Heart of England Tourist Board

Lincolnshire, Derbyshire, Nottinghamshire, Staffordshire, Leicestershire, Northamptonshire, West Midlands, Warwickshire, Gloucestershire, Worcestershire, Shropshire and Herefordshire

Heart of England Tourist Board
Larkhill Road, Worcester WR5 2EZ
Tel: (01905) 761100 Fax: (01905) 763450
or Premier House, 15 Wheeler Gate, Nottingham NG1 2NA
Tel: (0115) 959 8383 Fax: (0115) 959 8686
Internet: www.visitbritain.com/heart-of-england

This central area of England, bordering Wales on the west, Lincolnshire on the east and with Birmingham, at its heart covers:

Derbyshire

The Peak District is ideal for leisure and activity holidays, with spectacular crags, dales and moorland. There are ample opportunities for walking, cycling or the more daring challenges of rock climbing, gliding or hang-gliding.

Staffordshire

Stunning countryside and moor-lands, combine with Britain's number one theme park, Alton Towers. Stoke on Trent, the birthplace of British ceramics, is where Josiah Wedgwood, Sir Henry Doulton and Josiah Spode worked their magic transforming base clay to objects of beauty. Visitor centres and factory shops tell their story.

Nottinghamshire

Nottingham Castle above the city presides over a modern vibrant city and nearby Sherwood Forest is still alive with tales of Robin Hood and his merry men.

Leicestershire

Home to the pork pie of Melton Mowbury fame and Stilton cheese.

Rutland

England's smallest county, just 20 miles across. Rutland Water is a Mecca for watersports.

Northamptonshire

Known as the county of 'spires and squires', Kings and Queens of England used to hunt in Rockingham Forest but today its royal connection is centred on Althorp the resting place of Diana, Princess of Wales. It is also home to Silverstone, Britain's Formula 1 Grand Prix circuit.

Lincolnshire

From the gently rolling landscape of the Lincolnshire Wolds and dramatic open landscape of the Fens, to the cathedral and antique shops in Lincoln, traditional seaside resorts and the network of tranquil waterways. There is a huge variety in the setting of vast skies and unforgettable sunsets.

Warwickshire

Shakespeare Country, birthplace of the world's greatest playwright and home of the Earls of Warwick. Warwick castle must be the finest mediaeval castle in England.

Birmingham

One of the UK's most important cities and a leading international centre.

Worcestershire

Ranks as one of England's most attractive counties. Home to Malvern Water, Worcestershire Sauce and the Morgan sports car.

Shropshire and Herefordshire

Where England meets Wales and a mix of heritage and history brought to life in Ellis Peters' Brother Cadfeal series, the medieval whodunits based on Shrews-bury. Herefordshire is the home of cider and timber framed buildings are a feature.

Gloucestershire

From the Cotswold hills and villages, the Forest of Dean, the Wye valley to Regency Cheltenham with its world standard festivals of literature, jazz and famous for its horse racing not to mention the art of chasing a Double Gloucestershire cheese down a hill!

Tallington Lakes Caravan and Camping

376 Barholm Road, Tallington, Stamford, Lincolnshire PE9 4RJ

This large, 160-acre site spreads around a series of lakes that provides for many watersport activities including water-ski (slalom and jump courses), jet-ski, sailing (sailboards and dinghies), and angling. The touring campsite has recently been brought up to date and now has around 120 pitches, of which 66 have electric hook-ups (10A), and 11 are on hardstandings. Major roads are tarmac, with gravel roads around the pitches, but the small hedges and shrubs separating the pitches are new and will need time to mature. The complex also has a good number of permanent holiday homes. Local places of interest are Stamford Museum, Burghley House, Sacrewell Farm and Country Centre and the Nene Valley Railway.

Facilities: The newly built, heated sanitary unit, opened in early 2000. includes facilities for babies, small children and disabled visitors, plus a room with dishwashing sinks. Additional WCs and showers (also used by the water skiers). Laundry. Excellent motorcaravan service point has facilities for chemical disposal, fresh and waste water, and a drive-over drain. Bar and restaurant. Watersports. Dry-ski slope, snowboard centre and tennis. Small, well fenced, children's adventure style playground (age 5-12 yrs). Key-card for the sanitary unit and barrier (£10 refundable deposit).

Charges 2001

Per adult	£1.50
motorcaravan	£6.00
caravan	£6.00
awning or pup tent	£1.50
tent	£4.50
dog (max. 2 per unit)	£1.00
electricity	£1.50

Tel: (01778) 347000. Fax: (01778) 346213. E-mail: info@tallington.com. Reservations: Accepted with full payment. **Open** all year excl. February.

Directions: From A16, midway between Stamford and Market Deeping, just east of the railway crossing at Tallington, turn north into Barholm Road and site entrance is on the right. (site is signed). O.S.GR: TF085090.

Walesby Woodlands Caravan Park

366 Walesby, Market Rasen, Lincolnshire LN8 3UN

Surrounded by mature Forestry Commission woodland, this family owned, small touring park is therefore mainly very peaceful (if the wind is in a certain direction trains may be heard in the distance). The new owners, Paul and Christine Burrows will make you welcome. About 1½ miles away is the small town of Market Rasen, but further afield and within easy driving distance, are Lincoln, the east coast including Skegness and, of course, the Lincolnshire Wolds. There are 64 well spaced pitches, 60 with 10A electricity, marked out on a single, mainly flat, grassy field divided by a central gravel road and with a double row of trees providing useful visual screening. The Viking Way passes through Walesby and there are many other shorter walks in the forest and surrounding area.

Facilities: The single toilet block (with a deposit charged for the key) is spacious and ample for the site. It has toilet facilities for disabled people and outside, covered, dishwashing sinks. Laundry room. Small shop with information section (all season). Battery charging. Gas supplies. Children's play area. No kite flying - overhead wires. Winter caravan storage. **Off site:** Market Rasen racecourse is 2 miles. Fishing 3 miles, riding 2 miles, golf 1½ miles.

Charges 2001

Per unit incl. 2 persons	£8.00
extra person	£1.25
child (2-12 yrs)	£1.00
awning or child's pup tent	£1.25
electricity	£2.00

Tel: (01673) 843285.Reservations: Any length, with deposit. **Open** 1 March - 31 October.

Directions: Park is northeast of and signed from the main approach roads to Market Rasen. O.S.GR: TF117907.

Bainland Country Park

Horncastle Road, Woodhall Spa, Lincolnshire LN10 6UX

A family park with many amenities, Bainland has 170 spacious, level pitches in hedged bays, linked by roads forming circles and islands. Of these, 51 are 'super' pitches with hardstanding for car and caravan, honeycombed for awning, individual water, drainage and chemical disposal, electricity and TV aerial hook-ups. The remaining pitches are either on gravel hardstanding or level grass, all with 16A electricity. The friendly reception is housed in a pleasant Swiss-style building containing the shop and the heated indoor pool, overlooked by the bistro and spacious bar area, which in turn overlook the golf course and outdoor bowls area. A children's adventure play area has been created in a large hollow with a sand base. For adults there is the 18 hole, par 3 golf course, and a tennis club with a year round floodlit tennis dome with 3-4 courts including badminton (the dome comes off in the summer). Barbecues, jazz, country and western evenings are organised. Bainland is 1½ miles from Woodhall Spa, with its old fashioned charm and Dambusters associations, yet deep in the heart of the Lincolnshire Wolds, surrounded by mature trees and with direct access to woods for walking. A member of the Best of British group.

Facilities: Two solid toilet blocks are to be supplemented by two new ones. Heated and equipped for all basic necessities (except, perhaps, for showers in peak times), they include a baby care centre, unisex shower room for families, hair care room, family bathroom, fully equipped unit for disabled people. Maintenance can be variable. Laundry room. Enclosed dishwashing and separate hand washing sinks. Motorcaravan service points. Licensed shop (March - Oct). Bistro (all year) and bar, both also open to the public. Indoor pool and jacuzzi (under 16s must be accompanied by an adult). Golf. Tennis and badminton. Play areas, trampoline, crazy golf, croquet, TV and games room and soft play area. The great range of leisure activities, including the pool, are individually booked and paid for at reception (open 08.00-22.00 hrs). Winter caravan storage. **Off site**: Fishing 3 miles, riding 6 miles.

Charges 2001

Per unit incl. electricity and awning	£9.00 - £14.00
serviced pitch	£11.00 - £17.00
pup tent	free - £3.00.

Firework display (min. 2 nights, 5/6 Nov) £25.00; serviced pitch £30.00. Discounts for senior citizens. Tel: (01526) 352903. Fax: (01526) 353730. E-mail: bookings@bainland.com. Reservations: Advised and made for any length. Deposit at B.Hs. only (one night's fee). **Open** all year (in winter, super pitches only).

Directions: Entrance to park is off B1191 Horncastle road just outside Woodhall Spa by derestriction sign. O.S.GR: TF214637.

Classified as one of the top parks in Lincolnshire, Bainland is situated on the edge of the Wolds, surrounded by woodland, 1½ miles from the centre of Woodhall Spa.

The Park of over 40 acres, caters for caravans, motorhomes and campers alike with Super and Standard pitches, electric hook - ups and satellite T.V. points.

OPEN ALL YEAR

TOP AWARD WINNING PARK

Bainland Country Park

18 hole Par 3 Golf Course

Practice Putting Green

All weather Bowling Green

Indoor/Outdoor Tennis

Crazy Golf

Trampoline

Table Tennis

Indoor Swimming Pool

Childrens Adventure Playground

Sauna

Jacuzzi

Sunbed

Childrens 'Poachers Den' soft playroom

Bar

Restaurant

Rallies Welcome

Horncastle Road, Woodhall Spa, Lincolnshire, LN10 6UX Tel: Woodhall Spa (01526) 352903

Lakeside Park

North Somercotes, nr Louth, Lincolnshire LN11 7RB

367

With a splendid water feature at the entrance, good tarmac access roads and well tended grounds throughout, first impressions here are most rewarding. Set in 47 acres of pine forest, this park is continually seeking to improve and develop the service it offers. The majority is occupied by 300 privately owned holiday homes, all proudly maintained, with the touring section in a separate 15 acre field, but furthest from the leisure areas and activities. Although rather open, a programme of long term landscaping has commenced, intended to impart more character to this area. The number of grass based touring pitches, all level and with 16A electricity has been reduced to 150, whilst hardstanding 'super' pitches have been increased to 50. The outdoor pool remains popular (from July), although the heated indoor 'Tropicana' complex, with jacuzzi and sauna, is an outstanding facility and well worth the small charge (adult £2.20, child £1.50). Both pools are well maintained and supervised at all times. An impressive, new development, with family, cabaret room and stylish bar is the Waterfront Club, providing a varied entertainment programme all season. Staff are friendly and helpful. The nearest beach, at Mablethorpe, is 15 minutes by car, and Grimsby, Alford and Louth are also accessible. No tents are accepted.

Facilities: The original heated toilet facilities have been augmented by another newer block so the provision should be adequate (although showers are rather slow to drain and cleaning can be variable). Indoor dishwashing facilities. Launderettes. Motorcaravan service facilities. Licensed shop (from April). Bar, restaurant and takeaway (daily 12-2 and 6-11 except Sunday). Indoor and outdoor pools. Children's play areas. Amusement arcade. Games room. 7 acre fishing lake. Tennis. Nine hole golf course (£5 per day). Gas available. Caravan storage. Security barrier (£10 deposit for card) and night patrols. **Off site:** Riding 4 miles.

Charges 2001

Per unit incl. up to 5 persons

awning and electricity	£7.00 - £22.00
'super' pitch	plus £3.00
extra person	£5.00
dog (max. 2)	£1.00

Min. 3 night stays at B.Hs. Tel: (01507) 358315 or 358428. Fax: (01507) 358135. E-mail: lakeside@donamott.com. Reservations: Advised for B.Hs and main summer season with deposit (£5 per night booked). Open March - end November.

Directions: Park is on A1031 road, 7 miles north of Mablethorpe towards Cleethorpes. O.S.GR: TF430960.

Cherry Tree Site

Huttoft Road, Sutton-on-Sea, Lincolnshire LN12 2RU

365

Cherry Tree is a good example of a small, good value touring park. The grass is neatly trimmed and well drained, and is divided by evergreen hedging to site your unit against. Some hedges are well grown, the rest recently planted. Connected by a one-way circular gravel road, there are 60 good sized pitches all with 10A electricity. Buses stop outside hourly, and a shop and pub are within 10 minutes walk. It is also possible to walk to the sea via the road. Mablethorpe beach is known for its sand yacht racing and Skegness, with all its popular attractions is just down the road. A very warm welcome awaits from Geoff and Margaret Murray.

Facilities: The brick built toilet block can be heated and is immaculately kept, providing controllable hot showers (20p) and a new en-suite unit for disabled visitors. Combined dishwashing and laundry room with washing machine, spin dryer and tumble dryer. Neat reception. Well fenced children's play area on grass. Gas available. Off site: Tennis and bowls nearby, fishing 1½ miles, golf 1 mile, riding 4 miles.

Charges 2001

Per pitch	£1.50 - £3.50
adult	£2.25
child (3-16 yrs)	£1.00
awning or extra pup tent	75p
electricity	£1.75

Min. stay 3 nights at B.Hs. No credit cards. Tel: (01507) 441626. E-mail: murray.cherrytree@virgin.net. Reservations: Made with £20 deposit (non-returnable). Open 2 March - 28 October.

Directions: Park is 1½ miles south of Sutton-on-Sea on A52 coast road to Skegness, with the entrance leading off a lay-by on the left. O.S.GR: TF518828.

Skegness Sands Touring Site

373 Winthorpe Avenue, Skegness, Lincolnshire PE25 1QZ

This very well organised touring site is actually part of a much larger caravan holiday home park, but it has its own entrance and, indeed, its own, more intimate character. It is a modern, well appointed site adjacent to the promenade and beach. There are 85 pitches, all level and with electricity (16A). Most are grass but there are now 40 gravel hardstandings, 4 of which are fully serviced. Site lighting is good throughout, there are regular security patrols and the vehicle entry gates are locked 11 pm - 6 am. The gate to the promenade is kept locked at all times, campers getting a key. Local attractions include Funcoast World, Fantasy Island, Hardys Animal Farm, a seal sanctuary. The site is a member of the Caravan Club's 'managed under contract' scheme, but non-members are made very welcome.

Facilities: The good quality, heated sanitary unit includes washbasins in curtained cubicles plus three family bathrooms comprising WC, washbasin and shower and a well equipped room for disabled people. Two dishwashing sinks are outside under cover. Laundry room. Gas supplies on site. Hairdressing salon. Indoor heated swimming pool (open end May - 30 Sept; adult £2, child £1.50) located in the 'static' area of the site. Small children's playground. **Off site**: Well stocked shop/post office 200 m. Pubs, fast food outlets and a supermarket are all within easy walking distance. 'Hail and ride' bus service to Skegness and Ingoldmells at 200 m. Stock car racing, ten pin bowling and golf near.

Charges 2001

Per adult	£2.85 - £4.75
child (5-16 yrs)	£1.20
non-member pitch fee	£6.00 - £8.00
electricity	£1.50 (summer) - £2.25 (winter)
fully serviced pitch	plus £3.00

Tel: (01754) 761484. Reservations: Advised for B.Hs, school holidays and peak season. **Open** all year.

Directions: Site is north of Skegness. Turn from the A52 opposite 'Garden City' public house into Winthorpe Avenue and site entrance is on the left at far end of road. O.S.GR: TF570640.

Foreman's Bridge Caravan Park

375 Sutton St James, Spalding, Lincolnshire PE21 0HU

Foreman's Bridge is an extremely pleasant and compact park that continues to win awards. It also makes an excellent base from which to explore the Fens, including Spalding, famous for its annual flower festival. Fishing and cycling are popular pastimes in the area, indeed bicycle hire and fishing licences are both available from the site, with fishing possible in the river that runs just past the entrance. Arranged around a large, level and grassy meadow are 40 pitches, 32 with electricity (10A) and 20 with gravel hardstanding. Fruit trees, flower beds, hanging baskets and planted troughs provide bursts of vibrant colour.

Facilities: The modern, brick built toilet unit is spacious and kept very clean, providing really large individual shower rooms with seats and washbasins (showers on payment). Dishwashing room. Laundry room with washing machine, dryer and ironing. Recycling of glass, aluminium and paper. Motorcaravan service points. Basic provisions and gas are kept. Fishing. Bicycle hire. Site barrier (£5 deposit for card). Winter caravan storage. **Off site**: Nearest shop 2 miles. Riding 8 miles, golf 5 miles.

Charges 2002

Per unit incl. 2 adults	£6.00
small 1 person tent	£4.50
extra adult	£2.00
child	£1.00
awning	£1.00
dog	50p
electricity	£2.00

No credit cards. Tel/Fax: (01945) 440346. E-mail: foremansbridge@btinternet.com. Reservations: Advisable for Flower Festival, B.Hs (min. 3 nights), and peak season; made with £10 deposit. **Open** 1 March - 30 November.

Directions: From A17 Spalding - Kings Lynn road turn south on B1390 at Long Sutton towards Sutton St James for approx. 2 miles. Site entrance is on the left immediately after the bridge. O.S.GR: TF410198.

Pilgrims Way Caravan and Camping Park

370 Church Green Road, Fishtoft, Boston, Lincolnshire PE21 0QY

In a rural setting, this delightful, family run park is two miles from Boston and its famous church tower. There are 20 individual pitches all with access to electricity (10A) and including 5 with hardstanding. The park's facilities are housed in a good quality conversion at one end of what was once a workshop. Local attractions include the 'Boston stump', the Pilgrim Fathers Memorial and Maud Foster Windmill, all in and around the town. Further afield is Heckington village and its unique eight sailed windmill (6 miles) and the Aviation Heritage Centre (12 miles). Boston market days are on Wednesdays and Saturdays and the town also has a fine marina, two sport and leisure centres (one with swimming pools), a ten-pin bowling alley and a tennis centre.

Facilities: Heated in low season, the sanitary facilities are thoughtfully planned and exceptionally clean and well maintained. Entry is by keypad and all of the usual facilities are provided, including , dishwashing and laundry sinks, plus an excellent fully equipped unit for disabled persons. Laundry with washing machine and dryer. Gas available. Groundsheets, kite flying and ball games are not allowed. Site is not really suitable for American motorhomes. Dogs are accepted only by prior arrangement. **Off site**: mini-market, baker and fuel station within 1 mile, supermarket just 2 miles. Golf, fishing, bicycle hire and riding within 2 miles.

Charges 2002

Per unit incl. 2 persons	£8.00
electricity	£2.00
extra person or car	£1.00

No credit cards. Tel/Fax: (01205) 366646.
Reservations: Advised for B.Hs and peak season.
Open 1 April/Easter - 30 September.

Directions: From A52, 1 mile east of junction with A16, turn south by the 'Ball House' public house, continuing past the Boston Bowl towards Fishtoft, where the site is on your left. O.S.GR: TF360420.

Low Farm Touring Park

377 Spring Lane, Folkingham, Sleaford, Lincolnshire NG34 0SJ

This quiet secluded park is a lovely spot to either just relax or to tour the Lincolnshire countryside. Jane and Nigel Stevens are working hard to make this site a pleasant place to stay and have a really well laid out park offering good quality facilities which are very clean and tidy. The site is in countryside and offers some good views of Lincolnshire, and about 200 yards from the site is the village of Folkingham with good eating and drinking houses and shops. There are some pleasant walks around the village. The site offers 36 touring pitches, 24 of which have electric hook-ups.

Facilities: Controllable free showers. Washing up and laundry. Bar at weekends in high season. **Off site:** For larger shops and other interesting places, Sleaford, Bourne and Lincoln are within easy reach.

Charges 2001

Per unit	£6.50 - £7.50
electricity	£1.50 - £2.00
awning	50p
dog	free

Tel: (01529) 497322. **Open** Easter - October.

Directions: Site is on the main A15 Lincoln - Peterborough road, 2 miles from the roundabout junction with the A52. From this roundabout follow the A15 towards Peterborough and Folkingham is about 1.5 miles. Go through the village and down the hill. At the bottom, at campsite sign, take the road opposite to your right and site is at end of lane. O.S.GR: TF070333.

Rivendale Caravan and Leisure Park

Buxton Road, Alsop-en-le-Dale, Ashbourne, Derbyshire DE6 1QU

When we first visited this new park we were struck by the size of the project the owners had taken on. Now three years later, they are very near to achieving their goal of being one of the premier sites in the Peaks National Park. The reception, shop, bar and restaurant are up and running (including an excellent breakfast). Located in an old quarry, the park provides 100 pitches with hardstanding, 80 of which have 16A electrical hook ups. Set out in small groups with names such as 'Little Delving' or 'Crickhollow', each pitch is separated from its neighbour and some have a grass area. Up to 40 tents can be taken on a separate grassy area (metal tent pegs advised but drainage good). The touring park will eventually take up about 11 acres of the total land space of 37. An environmental pond has been completed (fenced for safety) and trees and plants around the site are maturing to add character. With the National Park on hand and towns such Ashbourne and Bakewell nearby, there is lots to do and see.

Facilities: The sanitary facilities are first rate with under-floor heating, some washbasins in cubicles for ladies, and an excellent en-suite room for disabled visitors. Laundry room. Glass and paper recycling bins. Bar (evenings) and café (mornings, lunch times and evenings, both with limited opening in low season). Special events and games in main season. Shop (all essentials). **Off site**: The park is almost on The Tissington Trail offering walking and off road cycling. Riding 3 miles, fishing 5 miles, bicycle hire 2½ miles.

Charges 2001

Per pitch incl. 2 adults	£7.20 - £9.50
pitch with water connection	plus £2.70
tent pitch on field	£6.80
extra person (over 3 yrs)	£1.00
awning	£1.50
dog	75p
electricity	£2.20

Tel: (01332) 843000. Fax: (01332) 842311. E-mail: rivendale@fsmail.net. Reservations: Made with £10 deposit. **Open** all year excl. February.

Directions: Park is about 7 miles north of Ashbourne. After Tissington, on A515 from Asbourne, look for turning on right for Alsop village. Site is 100 yds on the right. Care should be taken when leaving as there is a very fast section of the A515 here. O.S.GR: SK161566.

A peaceful 37 acre park with a superb, south-facing, sheltered pitching area in a natural sun-trap. Ideal for cycling and rambling in the surrounding Peak District with lots to see and do close by - from sailing at Carsington Water - to a day out at Chatsworth and Alton Towers.

Tel: 01332 843000 or 01335 310311
Fax: 01332 842311

www.rivendalecaravanpark.co.uk

Convenient for Chatsworth, Alton Towers, Dovedale, Hartington, Bakewell, Ashbourne.

The low season 'go as you please' solution. With over 200 sites across Europe, all committed to fully open facilities in low season, there's no need to commit yourself to a fixed itinerary. Move freely from site to site as you wish - this discount scheme offers fantastic savings.

Enjoy the freedom   Enjoy the flexibility
Enjoy the ferry prices   Enjoy the savings

Call us now on 01892 559855 for your FREE Camping Cheque brochure
www.campingcheque.co.uk

Camping Cheques now operate in Britain and Ireland. The parks involved are clearly identified in this guide - look for the CAMPING CHEQUES logo.

Highfields Camping and Caravan Park

380

Fenny Bentley, nr Ashbourne, Derbyshire DE6 1LE

Run by the Redfern family, Highfields is set on high, flat ground in the Peak District National Park with marvellous views. It takes 50 touring units and 50 seasonal vans in open, hedged fields accessed by tarmac roads, with an area for tents, another for vans with concrete slabs for jockey wheels and an area for adults only. There are 8 hardstandings and 89 electrical connections (16A), with 55 privately owned caravan holiday homes in separate fields. A site shop stocks basics and gas, and a room, complete with in-built barbecue, table and chairs, is available for hire. An indoor, heated swimming pool is open all season (restricted times if the park is not very full), with a small charge. Although not supervised at all times, the pool is monitored from reception by closed circuit TV. People frequently venture off the site to enjoy the Peak District - Dovedale and Ilam are only a mile or two's distance by footpath and the Tissington Trail with access to the High Peak Trail passes by the park.

Facilities: The main toilet block is kept locked (deposit for key) and is well maintained. Hot water is metered to laundry and dishwashing sinks, and to the showers. Baby bath provided. A smaller block is in the far static field and further sanitary facilities are provided adjacent to the new rally room. All blocks are heated when necessary. Shop. Children's playground. Bicycle hire. Swimming pool (90p per session). American motorhomes accepted. Winter caravan storage. **Off site**: Pub and restaurant close. Fishing 3 miles, golf 5 miles, riding 2 miles, boat launching 5 miles.

Charges 2001

Per unit incl. 2 persons	£10.00
extra adult	£2.00
child (under 16 yrs)	75p
electricity (16A)	£2.50
dog	75p

Tel: 0870 741 8000. Fax: 0870 741 2000. Reservations: Made with payment of one night's fee; min. stay at B.Hs - 3 nights. **Open** 1 March - 31 October.

Directions: Park is west off A515 Buxton - Ashbourne road, just north of Fenny Bentley village (take care at sharp turn to site road when approaching from Ashbourne). O.S.GR: SK170510.

Lime Tree Park

384

Dukes Drive, Buxton, Derbyshire SK17 9RP

A select park with high quality, modern facilities, Lime Tree is in a convenient, edge of town location that makes a very good base for touring the Peak District. The 99 touring pitches, 64 with access to electricity (10A), are on the two upper terraces which have the best views but are slightly more exposed until the new plantings mature. Below are areas set aside for late arrivals and the caravan holiday homes (most privately owned, some for rent). On site is a small shop for gas and basics, and a new, extended children's playground with a grass and rubber safety base. The nearest pub serving food is just around the corner and Buxton town centre is a comfortable stroll away. A member of the Best of British group.

Facilities: A new toilet building serves the caravan and motorcaravan area, complete with patio and pergola frontage, together with the refitted original unit which serves the tent area. Both units are heated with top quality fittings, including washbasins (some in cubicles), a baby room with the very latest design of baby bath, and a family room with facilities for disabled people. Dishwashing sinks are outside under cover. Laundry room with washing machine and dryer. Motorcaravan service area. Shop. Children's play area. Games/TV room. **Off site**: Fishing, bicycle hire, riding and golf, all within 5 miles. Alton Towers is 22 miles.

Charges 2001

Per unit incl. 2 adults	£8.25 - £10.50
extra adult	£1.50
extra child (5-15 yrs)	75p
hiker, cyclist or m/cyclist	£3.50 - £4.00
awning	£1.50
dog	50p
electricity	£2.00

Open 1 March - 31 October. Tel: (01298) 22988. Reservations: Made with £10 deposit.

Directions: From Buxton take A515 (Ashbourne) road south, turning sharp left into Dukes Drive after the hospital on the outskirts of the town, under the railway viaduct, and site is on right. O.S.GR: SK069725.

Darwin Forest Country Park

382 Darley Moor, Two Dales, Matlock, Derbyshire DE4 5LN

Between Matlock and Bakewell, this park, as its name implies, is set amongst 44 acres of mixed woodland close to the Peak District National Park. A large proportion of the park is given over to pine lodges for holiday letting but it also provides 50 touring pitches. All with hardstanding and electric hook-up (10A), they are clearly defined with hedging or open fencing in level grass bays amongst the pines – the unspoilt woodland is home to a variety of birds and wildlife. The pleasant Forester's Inn provides meals and a beer garden. The indoor swimming pool has a railed off section for children, spectator area and terrace, with good changing and shower facilities (see charges below). This is a useful park from which to explore the picturesque towns and villages of the Peak District. The Peak District Steam Railway currently operates a two mile section from Darley Dale to Matlock Riverside.

Facilities: The modern toilet block is tiled and well equipped, with washbasins in cabins, free hairdryers, a full unit for disabled people, laundry room and covered washing up area. Small shop for basics and Calor gas. Inn. Heated indoor pool (40 x 20 ft) – charges: adult £1.00 - £2.50, child (4-14 yrs) 50p - £1.50. Children's adventure play area on bark. Games room with pool tables. Tennis court, short-tennis. Minigolf. **Off site:** Fishing 2 miles, bicycle hire 8 miles, riding 2 miles, golf 4 miles. Chatsworth House 4 miles, Alton Towers 40 minutes.

Charges 2001

Per unit incl. all persons:	
Fri. and Sat. nights	£12.00
other nights	£10.00 - £12.00
awning	£2.00
electricity	£2.00 - £2.50

Tel: (01629) 732428. Fax: (01629) 735015. E-mail: admin@darwinforest.co.uk. Reservations: Advised and made with deposit. **Open** March - October.

Directions: Park is best approached via the A632 Chesterfield - Matlock road. North of Matlock take B5057 signed Darley Dale and park is on the right before descending into the village of Two Dales. O.S.GR: SK287633.

The Perfect Setting For Your Caravan Holiday in the heart of the Derbyshire Peak District

FOR A FREE BROCHURE CALL 01629 732428

Orchard Park Touring Caravan and Camping Park

395 Marnham Road, Tuxford, nr Newark, Nottinghamshire NG22 0PY

This well established family run site has been created in an old fruit orchard in a quiet location. It has 65 pitches, including 28 with hardstanding, 20 of which were occupied by seasonal units at the time of our visit. All pitches have access to electricity (10A). Reception is at the owner's house and at the far end of the park is a children's play area with swings and slide, a grassy area for ball games and a nature walk with wild flowers, birds and butterflies. Local attractions include Tuxford Windmill, Sundown Adventureland children's theme park, Laxton Medieval village and Victorian Times, with its working horse-drawn carriage driving centre, at nearby Kirton.

Facilities: The specially designed toilet unit (with piped music) has the usual facilities including a well equipped room for disabled persons. Two dishwashing sinks outside. Laundry with washing machines, dryer and sinks. Small shop with basic essentials and gas; more services (some open to 10 pm) are in the village (½ mile). Children's play area. New entrance barrier (£5 deposit for key).

Charges 2001

Per unit incl. 2 adults	£7.50 - £8.00
extra adult	£1.00
child (4-15 yrs)	50p
awning or child's pup tent	£1.00
electricity	£1.50

Tel: (01777) 870228. Fax: (01777) 870320. Reservations: Advised for B.Hs (min. 3 nights) and peak season with £10 deposit. **Open** March - Oct.

Directions: From the A1 turn onto A6075 towards Lincoln, continue through village to the eastern outskirts, turning right towards High Marnham. Site is on right ½ mile after railway bridge (well signed in village). O.S.GR: SK750710.

Smeaton's Lakes Touring Caravan Park

394 Great North Road, South Muskham, Newark-on-Trent, Nottinghamshire NG23 6ED

This 82-acre site is really ideal for fishermen, with three fishing lakes (coarse, carp and pike) and river fishing on the Trent. Smeaton's Lakes is a new site with tarmac access roads and a modern building near the entrance housing reception and the sanitary facilities (quite a walk from some of the pitches). Ground maintenance is good and there are now 130 pitches on grass, 48 with hardstanding (more to come) and 76 with electricity connections (16A). This site is probably the best choice for visiting events at nearby Newark Showground, or Newark town (1 mile) with its castle, the Millgate Folk Museum, the Air Museum and various weekly markets. The park is also well placed for visiting Southwell Cathedral, Lincoln with its castle and cathedral or Nottingham with its Lace Hall, Castle or Caves and, for people who like to look at motorhomes, Brownhills is close by.

Facilities: Toilet facilities (with keypad access) are heated and include a good unit for disabled people, but no laundry room. Laundry and dishwashing sinks are outside. At busy times these facilities could be stretched. Reception keeps gas, soft drinks, dairy produce, etc. and newspapers can be ordered. On site concessions for lake and river fishing. Security cameras and night-time height barrier (about 6 ft). **Off site:** Bus stop is at the end of the entry lane and buses run into Newark every hour until 10 pm.

Charges 2001

Per unit incl. 2 adults	£7.50 - £8.50
extra adult	£1.00 - £1.50
children (over 5 yrs)	75p - £1.00
electricity	£2.00 - £2.50

No credit cards. Tel: (01636) 605088 or 673250. E-mail: lesley@smeatonslakes.co.uk. Reservations: Essential for electric hook-ups. **Open** all year.

Directions: Site lies on A6065 west of the town, south of junction of A616 towards Ollerton (well signed). O.S.GR: SK792558.

Riverside Caravan Park

392 Central Avenue, Worksop, Nottinghamshire S80 1ER

A town centre touring park, this excellent site is attractive and surprisingly peaceful. Riverside is within easy walking distance of the town centre pedestrian precinct and shops, and the Chesterfield Canal runs close to its northern side offering delightful tow-path walks or fishing (children would need to be watched). Adjacent to the County cricket ground, this site is ideal for those who cannot resist the thwack of leather on willow. Of the 60 marked level pitches, 50 are on gravel hardstanding, some separated by trees and low rails, and all have electric hook-ups (10A). There is excellent site lighting. This is also a good base for exploring Creswell Craggs, Clumber Park, the Dukeries Cycle Trail, and Rufford Mill Craft Centre and Country Park.

Facilities: The modern sanitary unit near reception can be heated and has all the usual facilities, although showers are on payment (20p). There is no laundry, but a launderette is close by in the town. **Off site:** Activities available locally include squash, flat or crown green bowling, bicycle hire and campers are also very welcome at the cricket ground clubhouse. Worksop provides well for golfers with three courses in the area. One of the town's most interesting buildings, the medieval Priory Gatehouse, is open free of charge. Market days are Wednesday, Friday and Saturday.

Charges 2002

Per adult	£3.75 - £4.00
child (5-16 yrs)	£1.50
electricity	£2.00

No credit cards. Tel: (01909) 474118. Reservations: Advised for B.Hs, peak season and weekends, with £5 deposit. **Open** all year.

Directions: Easiest approach is from roundabout west of the town (A57) - third roundabout from the A1, junction of A57/A60. Turn into Newcastle Avenue, then left into Stubbing Lane, right into Central Avenue, left into Cricket Ground, follow through to camping site (well signed). O.S.GR: SK580790.

Silvertrees Caravan Park

396

Stafford Brook Road, Penkridge Bank, Rugeley, Staffordshire WS15 2TX

Silvertrees, as its name suggests, is in a beautiful wooded setting with many silver birches on the edge of Cannock Chase, but it only takes caravans and motorhomes. In the evenings the deer roam down the little valley in which the site is situated and there is evidence of much more animal and bird life – the park is actually designated a Site of Special Scientific Interest (SSSI). Of the older style, it comprises three paddock areas with 50 mobile homes (most privately owned), plus 50 touring pitches on gently sloping grass. Double paving stones for the main wheels mark each pitch – chocks would be useful. All pitches have 16A electrical hook-ups. The park is set in 20 acres of woodland adjoining the natural heathland of the chase so there is plenty to do. Helpful wardens and the owners live on site. There is a little library in reception and much useful tourist information in the games room. A member of the Countryside Discovery group. Tents are not accepted.

Facilities: The small, heated toilet block provides two showers each for men and women (20p) with shared changing area, laundry and dishwashing sink, and a washing machine and dryer. It could be under pressure at B.Hs. Small, unheated fun pool (3 ft deep, open May - Sept) in the valley bottom. Good tennis court, adventure play area, ball field. Comfortable games room with table tennis, video games, TV and an unusual ceiling. Gas supplies. Barbecues must be raised off the ground. Only certain breeds of dog are accepted. **Off site:** Fishing 1 mile, riding 6 miles, golf 3 miles. Supermarket 2 miles. Bus service outside park. Pub with food within walking distance. Alton Towers is nearby.

Charges 2001

Per pitch incl. 2 persons, electricity	£8.00 - £10.00
extra person	£1.00
awning	£2.00

Credit cards accepted (+3%). Tel/Fax: (01889) 582185. Reservations: Made with £20 deposit and essential at B.Hs. (when min. 3 nights). **Open** April - October.

Directions: Park is 2 miles from Rugeley just off the Penkridge - Rugeley road. It is signed from Rugeley off the A51. O.S.GR: SK014173.

Glencote Caravan Park

397

Station Road, Cheddleton, nr Leek, Staffs ST13 7EE

At the entrance to the Churnet Valley, three miles south of the market town, Glencote is a pleasant, family run park of six acres. It has 60 numbered pitches set on flat grass, 50 with patio style hardstandings, with tarmac access roads. All pitches have electrical connections (10A) and a dedicated water supply. Pretty flower-beds and trees make a very pleasant environment. An attractive, sunken children's play area, on grass and bark with an abundance of shrubs and flowers, sits alongside the small (fenced) coarse fishing pool, together with a barbecue area with a tented cover. Attractions nearby include a renovated Flint Mill powered by two giant water wheels and Cheddleton railway centre. The Churnet Valley, an Area of Outstanding Natural Beauty is good for walking, the Staffordshire Way is also near. For the more energetic, canoeing and hang gliding opportunities are close. Alton Towers is 10 miles (you may leave your unit on site after 3 pm. for an additional £2 charge).

Facilities: The good, modern toilet block is centrally situated and can be heated. Facilities include one private cabin for ladies, a small laundry room, and two dishwashing sinks under cover. Gas supplies. Max. 2 dogs per unit. **Off site:** In the village of Cheddleton, ½ mile away, is a small supermarket and a post office. A variety of inns are within easy walking distance - the Boat Inn beside the canal is very good value. Riding 10 miles, bicycle hire 5 miles, golf 4 miles.

Charges 2001

Per unit incl. 2 persons	£9.00
child (under 16 yrs)	£1.50
extra adult	£2.00
pup tent or extra car	£1.00
electricity (10A)	£1.80

For each 7 nights booked, one night free (except electricity). Min. stay of 3 nights at B.Hs. Tel: (01538) 360745. Fax: (01538) 361788. Reservations: Advised for peak season and made with deposit of £18 (2 nights) or £25 (over 2 nights). **Open** Easter - end October.

Directions: Park is signed off A520 Leek - Stone road, 3½ miles south of Leek on northern edge of Cheddleton Village. O.S.GR: SJ982524.

Hoburne Cotswold

Broadway Lane, South Cerney, Cirencester GL7 5UQ

Since this park is adjacent to the Cotswold Water Park, those staying will have easy access to the varied watersports there which include sailboarding and water ski-ing. On the park itself there is a lake with pedaloes and canoes for hire. Its wide range of other amenities include an outdoor heated swimming pool and an impressive, large indoor leisure complex. There are 340 well marked touring pitches for any type of unit, all with hardstanding (only fairly level) and a grass surround for awning or tent; 40 are serviced 'super' pitches. Of good size but with nothing between them, all have electricity (some need long leads). There are also 150 holiday units, mainly for letting. The large clubhouse has a big general lounge with giant TV screen, entertainment at times, food service (or food bar in lounge), big games room and a lounge bar which overlooks the outdoor pool and lake with a patio. Part of the Hoburne group.

Facilities: Six toilet blocks, all quite small, but clean and well maintained with pre-set showers. Baby changing facilities. Basic facilities for disabled visitors are in toilet block 4 and at the clubhouse. The site has heavy weekend trade. Launderette. Supermarket. Indoor leisure complex including pool with flume, spa bath, sauna, steam room (all free) and sun bed (charged). Outdoor pool (open Whitsun - early September; 44 x 22 ft). Clubhouse with bar, food and entertainment. Football field. Tennis courts. Good quality adventure playground with bark base. Crazy golf. Fishing lake (permits from reception). No dogs or pets are accepted.

Charges 2001

Touring pitch incl. electricity	£10.50 - £24.50
pup tent	£3.00

Weekly rates and weekend breaks available. Tel: (01285) 860216. Fax: (01285) 862106. E-mail: enquiries@hoburne.co.uk. Reservations: Bookings of 1-6 nights payable in full at time of reservation; caravans with £50 deposit for 1 week. Min. 4 nights booking at B.Hs. **Open** March - 31 October.

Directions: Three miles from Cirencester on A419, turn westtowards Cotswold Water Park at new roundabout on bypass onto B4696. Take second right and follow signs. O.S.GR: SU055957.

Tewkesbury Abbey Caravan Club Site

Gander Lane, Tewkesbury, Gloucestershire GL20 5PG

There are two important reasons why the Caravan Club site at Tewkesbury is so popular: firstly, it is within five minutes walk of the town centre and is overlooked by the Norman Abbey, the focal point of the town and secondly, it is a good base for exploring the eastern end of the Cotswolds as well as some of the country's most delightful towns. Gloucester, Cheltenham, Stow-on-the-Wold, Bourton-on-the-Water, Chipping Norton and Broadway are just a few that immediately spring to mind. The Malvern hills are also within driving distance. Covering nine acres, the site has 170 pitches reached by tarmac roads. All are on grass, but some slope so blocks are essential, and all have electric hook-ups (16A). The entrance to the site is locked at night but there is a late arrivals area just outside. A popular site and one of the largest sites operated by the Caravan Club with friendly and helpful wardens.

Facilities: There are three toilet blocks, all built and maintained to the Club's high standards and they can be heated. The one in the reception building is without showers. One block has facilities for disabled visitors and two have laundry rooms. Motorcaravan service facilities. Reception sells basic supplies and gas. Food shops, restaurants, pubs, etc. are all within easy walking distance. **Off site**: Fishing 400 yds, riding 5 miles, golf 1 mile.

Charges 2001

Per pitch (non-member)	£6.00 - £8.00
adult	£3.50 - £4.50
child (5-17 yrs)	£1.10 - £1.20
awning	free
electricity	£2.25 - £1.50

Tel: (01684) 294035 (8 am. - 8 pm. except emergencies). Reservations: Are accepted and are essential all B.Hs. and June-Aug. **Open** April - October.

Directions: From all directions follow signs for town centre and head for the Abbey which is easily distinguished. Turn by the Abbey into Gander Lane, follow down passing two car parks to site at end of the lane. O.S.GR: SO894324.

Moreton-in-Marsh Caravan Club Site

413

Bourton Road, Moreton-in-Marsh, Gloucestershire GL56 0BT

This excellent, busy, but rural, tree-surrounded site in the heart of the Cotswolds offers everything one would hope for from a camping holiday. Only 250 yards from the town, there is plenty of choice for food and pubs. The site has 180 pitches, all with electricity, 120 with hardstanding and most offering TV sockets. Milk, bread, papers and ice-cream are available from reception. A large play field provides a climbing frame with bark base and space for football, volleyball, boules and crazy golf. Kite flying is not allowed because of low power cables. Moreton-in-Marsh is famous for its Tuesday street market and is always a busy town, being only a few miles from the pretty villages of Bourton-on-the-Water and Stow-on-the-Wold, just two of the many interesting Cotswold villages worthy of a visit in this lovely area of England.

Facilities: The two toilet blocks offer very good facilities with spacious showers, washbasins in cabins, with facilities in each block for the walking disabled (4 inch step). Excellent en-suite room for disabled visitors in another building and a large laundry. Play field.

Charges 2001

Per pitch (non-member)	£6.00 - £8.00
adult	£3.50 - £4.50
child (5-16 yrs)	£1.10 - £1.20
extra car, boat or trailer	£1.00
electricity	£1.50 (31/3-2/10) or £2.25

Tel: (01608) 650519. Reservations: Contact site. **Open** all year.

Directions: From Evesham on A44, site on left after Bourton-on-the-Hill village, 150 yards before town sign. From Moreton-in-Marsh take A44 towards Evesham and site is on right, 150 yards past the Wellington museum. O.S.GR: SP200323.

Camping and Caravanning Club Site Winchcombe

414

Brooklands Farm, Alderton, nr Tewkesbury, Gloucestershire GL20 8NX

This is a popular, quiet site in a rural location, close to the Cotswold attractions. Some pitches surround a small coarse fishing lake, with others in a more recently developed area with open views over the surrounding countryside. In total there are 80 pitches, 53 with electric hook-ups (10A) and 42 with gravel hardstandings. The reception building flanks a small gravel courtyard car park and late arrivals area approached from a tarmac drive. Places to visit include Gloucester Docks and the National Waterways Museum, whilst south of Gloucester are Owlpen Manor near Uley, and the Painswick Rococo Garden. The Wildfowl and Wetlands Trust at Slimbridge, first opened in 1946 by Sir Peter Scott is also well worth a visit. Much closer to the site is the GWR (Gloucester Warwickshire Railway) at Toddington or Winchcombe.

Facilities: The main, heated sanitary unit, kept very clean and tidy by the wardens, is well equipped. Dishwashing sinks are under cover. To the rear of the site is a small, 'portacabin' style sanitary unit (also heated). Well equipped unit for disabled people. Laundry with washing machine and dryer. Gas supplies. On Saturdays between 5-6 pm. a fish and chip van calls. Large games room with a bowling alley, table tennis and a pool table. Small outdoor children's play area. **Off site:** Several pubs and restaurants in the area.

Charges 2001

Per adult	£3.75 - £5.30
child	£1.65
non-member pitch fee	£4.30
electricity	£1.65 - £2.40

Tel: (01242) 620259 (not after 8.00 pm, please). Reservations: Contact site. **Open** 16 March - 15 January.

Directions: From M5 exit 9, take A46 Evesham road for 3 miles to Toddington roundabout, then take B4077 towards Stow-on-the-Wold, for a further 3 miles to the site entrance. Ignore signs for Alderton village. O.S.GR: SP 007324.

Somers Wood Caravan and Camping Park

407 Somers Road, Meriden, Warwickshire CV7 7PL

Somers Wood is a useful site near the NEC, open all year but for adults only. Although near Birmingham, it is attractively situated and edged by pine woods, with views of the adjacent 16 hole golf course (including driving range) and coarse fishing lake; both being available for visitor's use. Log buildings blend comfortably into their surroundings providing reception, with the owners' home at the entrance and separate sanitary facilities. An oval, gravel road provides access to the 48 large pitches, all on hardstanding with 10A electricity connections. This is a very useful park for those visiting the NEC and for certain shows, such as the National Boat, Caravan and Leisure Show in February, it can be busy, although at other times it is quiet and peaceful. This is an adult only park.

Facilities: The central, heated sanitary block is fully equipped. Two dishwashing sinks are on the veranda area. Laundry service at reception. Rally field available. **Off site:** Local shops and restaurant less than 1 mile and visitors also welcome to use the bar and restaurant at the golf club.

Charges 2001

Per pitch incl. 2 persons	£14.00
extra adult	£2.00
extra car or trailer	£3.00
electricity	£2.50

No credit cards. Tel/Fax: (01676) 522978. E-mail: enquiries@somerswood.co.uk. Reservations: Advised for B.Hs and certain NEC exhibitions; made with deposit of £3 per night booked. **Open** all year.

Directions: From M42 junction 6 (NEC) take A45 towards Coventry. Almost immediately, on left-hand side, take A452 signed Leamington. Turn right at roundabout on A452 then turn left into Hampton Lane at the next roundabout, signed Stonebridge Golf Centre and site is signed with golf and fishing centres on the left. O.S.GR: SP228819.

Bosworth Water Trust

390 Market Bosworth, Nuneaton, Warwickshire CV13 6PD

Essentially designed for the water sports enthusiast, the camping area at Bosworth has 80 pitches on mostly level grass with electricity (5A) available to 31. This RYA recognised centre offers a range of watersports - dinghy and board sailing, canoeing, rowing and fishing (swimming is not advised in the lake). Tuition is available for all watersports activities - lifejackets and wet suits can be hired - and there is a 'Kids Club' every Saturday (call site for brochure). On arrival you will need £2 to operate the Centre's entrance barrier. Local attractions include Snibston Discovery Park, Twycross Zoo, Mallory Park motor racing circuit, steam trains and the battlefields.

Facilities: The good quality, heated toilet facilities in the main building are designed more for the watersports users, with communal showers and changing area, however the adjacent small 'portacabin' style unit does have conventional separate shower cubicles. This unit may be replaced in the future, as the current facilities could be slightly over-stretched during peak times. Reception serves a good range of snacks, soft drinks, ices, etc. Gas available. **Off site:** Riding 1 mile, golf ½ mile.

Charges guide

Per unit incl. all persons	£8.00
pup tent	£2.00
awning	£1.00
extra car	£1.00
electricity	£2.00

Fishing and lake fees: 50% discount for campers. No credit cards. Tel/Fax: (01455) 291876. Reservations: Recommended at B.Hs, school holidays and peak season. **Open** all year.

Directions: Site is off B585 about 1 mile west of Market Bosworth. O.S.GR: SK370020.

Camping and Caravanning Club Site Clent Hills

404

Fieldhouse Lane, Romsley, Halesowen, West Midlands B62 0NH

Conveniently close to Birmingham and only a couple of miles or so off the M5/M42 intersection, this site is a real surprise in terms of being quiet and peaceful and very pretty with good views. Its only disadvantage is that it is on sloping ground, but the present, helpful wardens are happy to assist in pitching anyone who has a problem (mainly motorcaravanners); in fact, there are some level pitches and these are all earmarked for motorcaravans. The 115 pitches are of a good size, 47 with electricity (10A) and 14 with hardstanding (more to be added). The modern reception building, arrivals area and larger car parking area are at the entrance. Generally this is a well run and attractive site, very usefully situated.

Facilities: The central sanitary toilet block can be heated and provides the latest facilities, including washbasins in cabins, hairdryers, baby room and a toilet and shower for disabled people. It was spotless when seen in high season. Washing machine, dryer and ironing facilities. Small children's play area with rubber safety surface. Gas supplies. Caravan storage. **Off site:** Fishing 3 miles, riding 1 mile.

Charges 2001

Per adult	£3.75 - £5.30
child (6-18 yrs)	£1.65
non-member pitch fee	£4.30
electricity	£1.65 - £2.40

Tel: (01562) 710015 (no calls after 8 pm). Reservations: Necessary and made with deposit; contact site. **Open** March - October.

Directions: From M5 junction 4 take A491, branch right to Romsley on B4551 and watch for site signs in Romsley village by shops. Site is on left. O.S.GR: SO955795.

Ranch Caravan Park

418

Honeybourne, nr Evesham, Worcestershire WR11 5QG

The Vale of Evesham is noted for being a sheltered area growing fruit and other produce from early spring through to late autumn. Ranch lies not far from both Evesham and Broadway in quiet country surroundings of 50 acres and is also only half an hour's drive from Stratford-on-Avon. A free swimming pool (55 x 30 ft.) with a slide is open and heated June - Sept. The park takes 120 touring units – caravans, motorcaravans or trailer tents but not other tents – on flat, partly undulating, hedged meadows with well mown grass and a spacious feel. Pitches are not marked but the staff site units. There are around 100 electrical connections (10A) and 8 fully serviced pitches (electricity, TV, water and sewer connections), with 20 new hardstandings added for 2001. There are 169 caravan holiday homes in their own section.

Facilities: Two very well appointed, modern sanitary blocks, with hot showers on payment, make a good provision. Comfortable clubhouse (weekends only in early and late season) with value for money meals and entertainment at B.H. weekends and Saturdays in school holidays. Small games room with TV (incl. Sky), video machines and pool table. Children's playground. Tents are not accepted. **Off site:** Fishing 2 miles, bicycle hire 4 miles, riding stables close.

Charges 2001

Per unit incl. 2 adults	£10.50 - £15.50
extra person (over 5)	free - £1.75
awning	free - £1.75
electricity	£2.50
full services	£2.50
dog	free - £1.75

Tel: (01386) 830744. Fax: (01386) 833503. E-mail: enquiries@ranch.co.uk. Reservations: Advised for peak weeks and B.Hs. Made with £5 per night deposit and essential for B.Hs. (when min. 3 days). **Open** 1 March - 30 November.

Directions: From A46 Evesham take B4035 towards Chipping Campden. After Badsey and Bretforton follow signs for Honeybourne down unclassified road (Ryknild Street, Roman road). Park is through village on left by station. O.S.GR: SP112444.

CARAVAN PARK · RANCH · HOLIDAY CENTRE
- ESTABLISHED FAMILY-RUN PARK
- LOCATED IN THE VALE OF EVESHAM
- TOURERS WELCOME
- ELECTRIC AND MULTISERVICE HOOK-UPS AVAILABLE
- LICENSED CLUB SERVING MEALS
- HEATED OUTDOOR SWIMMING POOL
- SHOP
- LAUNDRY

HONEYBOURNE, EVESHAM, WORCS. WR11 5QG

Tel: EVESHAM (01386) 830744

Kingsgreen Caravan Park

419 Kingsgreen, Berrow, Malvern, Worcestershire WR13 6AQ

A friendly, comfortable, farm site with views of the Malvern Hills, Kingsgreen is situated in an attractive rural location. An ideal site for adults who like the quiet life, there are no amusements for children. The surrounding countryside is ideal for walking or cycling, and the small, fenced fishing lake on the site is well stocked (£3 per day). There are 45 level, grass and gravel pitches, all with electricity (16A), plus an additional area for tents. Some old orchard trees provide a little shade in parts. The site is 7 miles from the market town of Ledbury with its half timbered buildings and within easy driving distance of Malvern, the Three Counties showground, Cotswolds, Forest of Dean or Tewkesbury with its 12th century Abbey.

Facilities: Modern toilet facilities (key on deposit) provide hot showers (25p token from reception) and a separate unit for disabled people (WC and washbasin). Dishwashing sinks under cover. Laundry room with washing machine, dryer, sink and iron and board (all metered). Gas and barbecue fuels are stocked and a milkman calls daily with milk, eggs, bread, soft drinks, etc. **Off site:** Nearest shop and pub 1½ miles. Bicycle hire 2 miles, riding 3 miles, golf 5 miles.

Charges 2001

Per unit incl. 2 adults	£6.00
tent incl. 2 adults	£5.00 - £6.00
extra person over 2 yrs	£1.00
dog	50p
awning	£1.00
electricity	£1.50

No credit cards. VAT not included. Tel/Fax: (01531) 650272. Reservations: Essential for peak season and B.Hs. **Open** 1 March - 31 October.

Directions: From M50 junction 2, take A417 towards Gloucester, then first left, where site is signed, also signed the Malverns, back over the motorway. Site is 2 miles from the M50. O.S.GR: SO767338.

Lickhill Manor Caravan Park

421 Stourport-on-Severn, Worcestershire DY13 8RL

A well managed touring or holiday site within easy walking distance (15 minutes) of the town centre via a footpath along the River Severn which lies a short distance below the site. There are opportunities for fishing and boating. The touring field has 90 marked, level, grassy pitches accessed via gravel roadways, all with electricity (10/16A). The 124 holiday homes, well screened from the touring area amongst tree lined avenues, are not visually intrusive, and there is a separate rally field (with 50 hook-ups). There is an extended children's playground and the site has recently created wildlife ponds and planted over 1,000 native trees and shrubs. With its new sanitary block, roads and landscaping and friendly welcoming staff, this park promises to mature into one of the best in the area. Stourport is a lively bustling town with some splendid public parks, amusements and sports facilities. Kidderminster, the Forestry Commission Visitor Centre at Bewdley, the Severn Valley Railway and West Midland Safari Park are a short drive from the site.

Facilities: A second sanitary building was added in '98 to serve the touring pitches and complement the older unit at the other end of the park. This heated building provides sparkling modern facilities including a comprehensively equipped suite for disabled guests which also double as a family washroom with facilities for baby changing. Excellent drive over motorcaravan service point. Recycling bins. Gas supplies. Children's playground. **Off site:** Riding 1 mile, bicycle hire 3 miles. Six golf courses within 5 miles. A small parade of shops and the nearest pub are 10 minutes walk.

Charges 2001

Per unit incl. 4 persons	£7.00 - £10.00
small tent	£7.00
large tent	£9.00
awning	£1.50
extra person, car, trailer or boat	£1.00
dog	50p
electricity	£2.00

Weekly rates available. Senior citizen discounts. Tel: (01299) 871041. Fax: (01299) 824998. E-mail: enquiries@lickhillmanor.co.uk. Reservations: Advised for B.Hs. and peak season. **Open** all year.

Directions: From centre of Stourport take B4195 northwest towards Bewdley. After 1 mile turn left at crossroads (traffic lights), into Lickhill Road North where site is signed. O.S.GR: SO790730

The Boyce Caravan Park

Stanford Bishop, Bringsty, nr Worcester WR6 5UB

420

The Boyce is a very peaceful park on rolling downland, with distant views of the Malvern Hills. Within its 17 acres are 20 touring pitches and 140 permanent caravan holiday homes. The relatively new landscaping and screening is maturing and electrical connections (10A) are available throughout. There is a fenced and gated playground for smaller children, plus plenty of open space for ball games (no cycling on the park). The adjacent disused railway line is now the dog walk (dogs accepted by arrangement, no dangerous breeds). Coarse fishing is available across a meadow, and the area is rich in wildlife. Nearby Shortwood Farm has Jacob sheep, cider making, sheep shearing and a farm trail, and at the Pig Pen you can handle the piglets (wellingtons recommended). The new reception building offers good tourist information including maps of local walks. Bromyard with its shops and restaurants is 4 miles, and the cathedral cities of Hereford and Worcester are within easy driving distance.

Facilities: The modern toilet unit, built to serve the touring section, can be heated and provides controllable hot showers (10p for 4 mins), and a hairdressing area. Utility room housing dishwashing and laundry sinks, a washing machine, dryer, iron, and a freezer for campers' use. Gas available. **Off site:** Local pub 500 yards serving meals including breakfast. Riding 5 miles and several golf courses in the area.

Charges guide

Per unit incl. 2 adults	£7.50
extra person over 5 yrs	£1.00
extra car	£1.00
1-man tent	£4.00
awning/pup tent	£1.50
electricity	£1.50

No tent pitches at B.H. weekends. No credit cards. Tel: (01886) 884248. Fax: (01886) 884187. Reservations: Made with deposit of one night's fee; contact park for details. **Open** 1 March - 31 October.

Directions: From A44 (Worcester - Leominster), turn on B4220 1 mile east of Bromyard. After 1½ miles, turn opposite 'Herefordshire House' inn (signed Linley Green), site is 500 m. and signed. O.S.GR: SO698527.

Broadmeadow Caravan and Camping Park

Broadmeadow, Ross-on-Wye, Herefordshire HR9 7BH

432

This modern, spacious park, with open views and its own fishing lake, is convenient for the town of Ross-on-Wye. The approach to the site is unusual, but persevere and you will find one of the best laid out, immaculately maintained sites with the very highest quality facilities. Recently constructed, level and with good lighting, it offers 150 large pitches on open grass, and is especially good for tents. Each set of four pitches has a service post with water, drain, electricity points (16A) and lighting, and is within view of the clock-tower on one of the sanitary buildings. The town centre is within easy walking distance. Although the A40 relief road is at the eastern end of the site, the traffic noise should not be too intrusive (but tenters be aware). This is a good base for touring Herefordshire, the Wye Valley or the Forest of Dean.

Facilities: Two superb modern sanitary buildings are fully equipped, including hairdryers, baby rooms, family bathrooms each with WC, basin and bath, and a comprehensive unit for disabled visitors with alarm and handrails. A dishwashing room and a laundry with sinks, washing machine, dryer, iron (tokens from reception), are at each building. New entrance barrier and keypad entry system on this and all external doors. Small fenced playground. Well fenced fishing lake (coarse fishing £5.50 per day). **Off site:** Bicycle hire in town, riding 8 miles, golf 3 miles. Supermarket 200 m.

Charges 2001

Per pitch	£6.00 - £7.00
adult	£2.50
child (4-14 yrs)	£2.00
awning or pup tent	£1.75
dog	£1.00
electricity	£2.50

Tel: (01989) 768076. Fax (01989) 566030. Reservations: Made with £10 deposit. **Open** Easter/1 April - 30 September.

Directions: From A40 relief road turn into Ross at roundabout, take first right into industrial estate, then right in ½ mile, before Safeway supermarket, where site is signed. O.S.GR: SO610240.

Poston Mill Park

430 Peterchurch, Golden Valley, Herefordshire HR2 0SF

Poston Mill Park is a pleasant, neat park in farmland a mile from Peterchurch in the heart of the Golden Valley. It offers 82 touring pitches set on level grass, including some very pleasant pitches near the River Dore, with mature trees and conifers around the perimeter. All pitches have electricity, water and TV connections (leads to hire), and 35 have waste water and sewage outlets. The park covers 33 acres and also has 80 caravan holiday homes. An attractive walk along one side of the park, edging the River Dore (fishing available), follows the line of the old Golden Valley railway and there is a footpath from the site over the fields. Next to the park is 'The Mill' restaurant for lunches, evening meals and takeaway. The restaurant also has a TV room and sells bread and milk. Peterchurch village is only 1 mile. A member of the Best of British group.

Facilities: There is one central sanitary block with a smaller block near the holiday home area. Of reasonably modern construction and fully equipped, they include a unit for disabled people (toilet and basin only) and a baby changing room. Motorcaravan service point. Small, well equipped laundry room housing a campers' fridge and a freezer for ice packs. Gas supplies. Large children's play area. Pitch and putt. Tennis court. Petanque and croquet. Bicycle hire. Golf driving range. Football pitch. Games room with snooker and darts. Winter caravan storage. **Off site:** Riding 3 miles.

Charges 2001

Per unit incl. 2 adults	£8.00 - £11.00
1 man tent	£4.75 - £7.75
extra person	£1.00
child (3-10 yrs)	50p
awning or extra pup tent (incl. 1 person)	£1.50
dog	50p
electricity	£2.00
TV hook-up	£1.00, own lead 50p

Min. charge at B.Hs. 5 nights. Tel: (01981) 550225. Fax: (01981) 550885. E-mail: enquiries@poston-mill.co.uk. Reservations: Made with £10 deposit. **Open** all year.

Directions: Park is 1 mile southeast of Peterchurch on the B4348 road. O.S.GR: SO356371.

Luck's All Caravan and Camping Park

431 Luck's All, Mordiford, Hereford HR1 4LP

Set in around 9½ acres on the bank of the river Wye, Luck's All has 80 large, well spaced and level touring pitches, of which 55 have electricity (10/16A). The river is open to the site but lifebelts and safety messages are in evidence. Canoes are available for hire – or bring your own – and fishing permits may be obtained from the local tackle shop. A small, unfenced playground and a large grassy area for games are provided for children. The site shop has basic supplies and gas, plus home-made cakes - a mini-market is within 1½ miles. Amongst the local places worthy of a visit are the Cider Museum and King Offa Distillery in Hereford, Belmont Abbey and Queenswood Country Park. The park is also a good base for touring the Wye Valley. A member of the Countryside Discovery group.

Facilities: The main sanitary facilities, housed in a new building, provide showers (20p) and a separate unit for disabled visitors with ramped entrance, WC, washbasin, shower and hand-dryer. Dishwashing sinks. A smaller, older unit near the entrance to the park provides extra facilities for peak periods and a fully equipped laundry room. Shop (basics only). Fishing. Canoeing. Winter caravan storage. **Off site:** Golf 5 miles, bicycle hire 9 miles.

Charges 2001

Per unit incl. 2 adults	£7.50 - £8.00
small 2-man tent	£6.50 - £7.00
extra person over 5 yrs	£1.50
dog	75p
awning	£1.00 - £1.25
pup tent on same pitch	£3.00
electricity	£1.75

Tel: (01432) 870213. Reservations: Essential for B.Hs. and peak season and made with £15 deposit. **Open** Easter/1 April - 31 October.

Directions: Between Mordiford and Fownhope, 5 miles southeast of Hereford on B4224, the park is well signed. O.S.GR: SO571355.

 Alan Rogers' discount
Less £1 in June, Sept and Oct.

The Millpond Touring Caravans and Camping

433 Little Tarrington, nr Hereford, Herefordshire HR1 4JA

This peaceful little site with its own fishing lake is set in 30 acres of countryside. Opened in '97, it only has 30 large pitches on open grassland, all with electricity (8A). The large fishing lake (unfenced) is well stocked with a good mix of coarse fish, has facilities for disabled fishermen and offers reduced rates for campers. The large acreage surrounding the site has a mix of well-established trees that have been supplemented with many new plantings, and well-mowed paths encourage you to wander and enjoy the great variety of trees, wild flowers, birds and the peaceful surroundings. Site lighting is minimal (local authority regulations) so a torch might be useful, but it is an ideal site for amateur astronomers. A railway track is at the rear of the site, so there may be a little noise.

Facilities: A new building houses heated sanitary facilities, laundry and dishwashing sinks, a unit for disabled persons and a "common room" with a good supply of tourist information. Note: The site is not really suitable for American motorhomes. **Off site:** The local pub is only a 10 minute walk, but there is no shop in the village. Hereford 7 miles.

Charges 2001

Per unit incl. 2 adults and awning	£8.00 - £9.00
small tent incl. 2 persons	£7.00 - £9.00
large tent	plus £2.00
extra person	50p
electricity	£2.00

Tel/Fax: (01432) 890243. E-mail: enquiries@millpond.co.uk. Reservations: Made with £10 deposit (1-6 nights), £20 per week. 50% of total for B.Hs. Advised for B.Hs and peak season. **Open** 1 March - 31 October.

Directions: Little Tarrington is midway between Hereford and Ledbury. The site is just north of A438 on eastern edge of Tarrington village (signed). O.S.GR: SO627409.

Fernwood Caravan Park

438 Lyneal, nr Ellesmere, Shropshire SY12 0QF

Fernwood is set in a lovely area known as the Shropshire 'Lake District' - the mere at Ellesmere is the largest of nine meres - and the picturesque Shropshire Union Canal is only a few minutes walk. The park itself is a real oasis of calm and rural tranquillity with its floral landscaping, the setting and the attention to detail, all of a very high standard with planted and natural vegetation blending harmoniously. In addition to 165 caravan holiday homes, used normally only by their owners, the park takes 60 caravans, motorcaravans or trailer tents (but not other tents) in several well cut, grassy enclosures (plus 25 seasonal long stay). Some are in light woodland, others in more open, but still relatively sheltered situations. All pitches have electricity (10A). One area is set aside for adults only. There is always generous spacing, even when the site is full.

Facilities: The refurbished toilet block for tourers can be heated and includes a unit for disabled people, but no dishwashing sinks. Motorcaravan service points. Well tiled laundry room near the shop and adjacent are WCs for ladies and men. Small shop doubling as reception (open from 1 April, sometimes limited hours). Coarse fishing lake. Forty acres of woodland for walking. Children's play area on grass.

Charges 2001

Per unit incl. electricity	£10.50 - £14.50
awning	free - £1.75
extra car	free - £1.00

One night free for every 7 booked in advance. Tel: (01948) 710221. Fax: (01948) 710324. E-mail: fernwood@caravanpark37.fsnet.co.uk. Reservations: Necessary for peak season and B.Hs (min. 3 nights) with deposit of £5 per night. **Open** 1 March - 30 November.

Directions: Park is just northeast of Lyneal village, signed southwest off the B5063 Ellesmere - Wem road, about 1½ miles from junction of the B5063 with the A495. O.S.GR: SJ453338.

FERNWOOD CARAVAN PARK

- ESTABLISHED FAMILY-RUN PARK
- PEACEFUL WOODLAND SETTING
- TOURERS WELCOME
- ALL PITCHES HAVE ELECTRICAL HOOK-UPS
- PICTURESQUE LAKE
- CHILDRENS PLAY AREA
- SHOP
- LAUNDRY

LYNEAL NR. ELLESMERE SHROPSHIRE SY12 0QF

TEL: (01948) 710221

Severn Gorge Park

442 Bridgnorth Road, Tweedale, Telford, Shropshire TF7 4JB

This six acre touring park, in a woodland setting, has 51 pitches, all with electricity hook ups (10/16A), and 40 with hardstanding (including a few seasonal tourers). A development of park homes has been constructed on one side of the park. There could be some road noise from the A442 which runs down one boundary. A barrier is locked at 11.45 pm, but parking and a late arrivals area is outside. The main local attraction has to be the Ironbridge Museums, featuring the Blists Mill Victorian Town, where you can discover and enjoy a working Victorian town. Hawkstone Park, with its walks and follies, is very popular and the Cosford Aerospace Museum is essential visiting for those interested in aviation.

Facilities: The sanitary buildings can be heated and have been upgraded to provide comprehensive facilities including facilities for disabled visitors and a baby room, plus a dishwashing conservatory leading to an ample laundry (8 am.- 9 pm). Motorcaravan service points. Small, limited shop (8.30 am - 5.30 pm daily). Gas supplies. Small play area. Large field nearby with a three hole pitch and putt and a small lake (unfenced) stocked for fishing. Kite flying is discouraged because of nearby overhead cables. Maximum of two dogs per pitch. Winter caravan storage. **Off site:** Pub 10 minutes away with a tempting 'Ale and Hearty' menu served until 9 pm. Golf 1 mile, riding 3 miles.

Charges 2001

Per unit	£3.60 - £4.20
adult	£2.60 - £3.15
child (5-15 yrs)	£1.05 - £1.30
awning	£1.05
dog (max 2)	£1.05
electricity	£2.35 - £2.60

Tel/Fax: (01952) 684789. Reservations: Contact park for details. **Open** all year.

Directions: From M54 junction 4 follow signs (A442) onto the A442 signed Kidderminster. Take slip road signed Bridgnorth to next roundabout, turn right and pick up park signs. O.S.GR: SJ704052.

Westbrook Park

439 Little Hereford, Ludlow, Shropshire SY8 4AU

Bordering the River Teme, this 45 pitch, all-touring park is of the older style, but it does retain the simplicity and tranquillity lost on so many other developed parks. In a peaceful orchard setting, the pitches are well spaced and level, and there are several with hardstanding. All have electricity connections (but only 6A) and TV aerial hook-ups. This is a simple, unpretentious park near the lovely market towns of Tenbury Wells, Leominster and Ludlow.

Facilities: The timber-clad sanitary block houses roomy, curtained showers (20p for 5 mins) which are showing their vintage – but they are clean and they do work. Simple laundry room with washing machine, dryer and sinks (hot water 10p). Simple play equipment but Gert and Daisy, the Shetland ponies, are the favourites. Bicycles not permitted. Fishing (£3 per day). Riverside walks. Caravan 'storage and use'.

Charges 2001

Per unit incl. 2 adults	£8.00 - £11.00
one man tent	£4.75 - £7.75
extra person over 10 yrs	£1.00
3-10 yrs	50p
awning	£1.50
dog	50p
electricity	£1.75

Min. B.H. stay 3 nights.Tel: (01584) 711280. Fax: (01584) 711460. Reservations: Advised for B.Hs (min. 3 nights) and made with £10 deposit. **Open** all year.

Directions: From A49 Ludlow - Leominster road turn east at Woofferton onto the A456 signed Tenbury Wells, Kidderminster. After 2 miles turn right just before the bridge over river and the Temeside Inn. Park is down the lane on the left. O.S.GR: SO547679.

Stanmore Hall Touring Park, Bridgnorth

440   Stourbridge Road, Bridgnorth, Shropshire WV15 6DT

This good quality park is situated in the former grounds of Stanmore Hall, where the site's huge lily pond, fine mature trees and beautifully manicured lawns give a mark of quality. Open views take precedence over maximising the number of units, with the result that all pitches are generously sized. In addition, caravans can be orientated in any direction, thus breaking the feeling of regimentation. There are 131 pitches, all with 16A electricity, 30 of which are hardstanding 'super pitches' with TV connections. A limited number of 'standard' hardstanding pitches are available, but the majority are on grass. Some pitches are reserved for adult only use (over 21 years). Access and internal roads are tarmac; site lighting is adequate. Reception is located within the shop. The adjacent conservatory and patio overlook the lake, accommodating everything from humbler ducks to the resident peacocks who strut proudly around their domain. But there's something else too; this is a peaceful site with personality. Little wonder it needs advance booking and people keep returning to enjoy its atmosphere. Open all year round, there are even groups who spend Christmas and New Year here. The site is a member of the Caravan Club's managed under contract scheme but non-members are also very welcome.

Facilities: Access to the centrally heated sanitary block is by key. The facilities are excellent and cleanliness outstanding. Washbasins in private cubicles, and a room for disabled people (which includes equipment for baby care), demonstrate thoughtful design. Full laundry facilities. Motorcaravan service points. Licensed shop (open all year) is well stocked, including caravan accessories and repair items. Limited, bark based children's play area. Dogs are limited to two per unit. **Off site:** Fishing 1½ miles, golf 2 miles. The Severn Valley is full of interest – Bridgnorth nearby, the Clee Hills and Ironbridge Gorge Museum are just a few suggestions.

Charges guide

Per pitch	£3.80 - £4.20
adult	£3.40 - £4.20
child	£1.45 - £1.60
awning or pup tent	£1.00
dog (max. 2)	75p
extra car or trailer	£1.20
electricity	£2.00 - £2.75
full services	£2.50 - £3.00

Tel: (01746) 761761. Fax: (01746) 768069. E-mail: stanmore@morris-leisure.co.uk. Reservations: Advisable and made with £10 deposit. **Open** all year.

Directions: Site is 1½ miles from Bridgnorth on the A458 (signed Stourbridge). O.S.GR: SO742923.

Oxon Hall Touring Park

443   Welshpool Road, Shrewsbury, Shropshire SY3 5FB

Oxon Hall is a purpose-built park, well situated for visiting Shrewsbury. It is under the same ownership as Stanmore Hall (no. 440) and has been developed from a green field site by an experienced park operator to a very high standard. When we first made contact a couple of years ago, the place felt a little bleak, but nature has done its bit and on our latest visit, a much greater feeling of maturity existed. Of the 130 pitches, half are all-weather, full service pitches (fresh and waste water facilities, TV hook-up), the others being either grass or with hardstanding. An area is set aside as an 'adults only' section. All pitches have 16A electricity. Some extra long hardstandings are provided for American motorhomes. Virtually adjacent to the park is the Oxon 'park and ride' which makes a trip into Shrewsbury some 2 miles away very simple. The famous Ironbridge Gorge Museum and the mysteries of the Welsh Borders are all easy day trips from this excellent base.

Facilities: Toilet facilities here are first rate with washbasins in cubicles, ample showers, baby room, facilities for disabled visitors, dishwashing room and laundry, all situated at the entrance in a centrally heated building which also houses reception and the shop - perhaps a hike from some of the pitches. Motorcaravan service point. Entry controlled by electronic barriers. Up to two dogs are welcome per pitch. **Off site:** Golf, riding and fishing nearby.

Charges guide

Per unit	£3.80 - £4.20
adult	£3.40 - £4.20
child (5-15 yrs)	£1.45 - £1.60
awning or pup tent	£1.00
extra car or trailer	£1.20
dog (max. 2)	75p
'super' pitch	plus £2.50 - £3.00

Tel: (01743) 340868. Fax: (01743) 340869. E-mail: oxon@morris-leisure.co.uk. Reservations: Made with £10 deposit. **Open** all year.

Directions: From junction of A5 and A458, west of Shrewsbury, follow signs for Oxon 'park and ride'. Park is signed just ½ mile from junction. O.S.GR: SJ455138.

Beaconsfield Farm Touring Caravan Park

441 Battlefield, Shrewsbury, Shropshire SY4 4AA

Just north of the historic market town, a neat stone entrance and a tarmac drive of half a mile through open fields lead to this purpose-designed park for adults only. Neatly laid out in a rural situation, with a well stocked trout fishing lake and a small coarse pool forming the main feature, the ground has been levelled and grassed to provide 60 well spaced pitches, 25 'de-luxe' hardstanding pitches with 16A electricity connections (with 10A hook-ups to the other pitches). The park is well lit with a circular tarmac access road. A large timber chalet-style building with a tiled Canadian maple roof provides reception and a coffee shop that is open during reception hours. New for 2000 was a snooker room in a purpose built log building that will eventually incorporate a bistro. Added for 2001 was a bowling green – use is free, but woods may be hired by those without such essential caravanning kit. Limousins and pedigree Suffolk sheep graze in neighbouring fields and a 'park and ride' scheme operates nearby for those interested in Shrewsbury and its medieval past, bought to life by the Brother Cadfael novels. This is a top class park, maturing by the year. A member of the Best of British and the Countryside Discovery groups. This park is now 'adults only' (25 yrs) all year round.

Facilities: Heated toilet facilities (£2 key deposit) are of excellent quality, with curtained, roomy, pre-set showers and free hairdryers. Dishwashing room, plus washing machine, dryer, free irons and boards. Motorcaravan service point. Indoor heated swimming pool, available all year, with two daily open sessions (adult £2.50, child £1) and to hire privately at other times (£3 and £1, min. £10 per hour). New bowling green. Security barrier in operation. Only two dogs per unit are accepted. Adults only park. **Off site:** Golf 2 miles. Riding 7 miles.

Charges 2001

Per grass pitch incl. 2 persons	£8.50 - £10.50
de-luxe pitch	£10.50 - £12.50
extra adult	£3.00
awning or child's tent	£1.50
dog (max. 2)	75p
electricity	£2.00

No credit cards. Last arrivals 7 pm. (8 pm. Fridays). Tel: (01939) 210370 or 210399. Fax: (01939) 210349. E-mail: mail@beaconsfield-farm.co.uk. Reservations: Advised for B.Hs and July/Aug. and made with £20 deposit. **Open** all year.

Directions: Site is north of Shrewsbury and off the A49 Whitchurch road just before the village of Hadnall. Turn opposite the New Inn at brown camping sign towards Astley and park entrance is 400 m. on right. O.S.GR: SJ523196.

 Alan Rogers' discount
Less 50p per night

Yorkshire Tourist Board

North, South, East and West Yorkshire

Yorkshire Tourist Board
312 Tadcaster Road, York YO24 1GS
Tel: (01904) 707961 Fax: (01904) 701414
24 hour brochure hotline: (01904) 707070
E-mail: info@ytb.org.uk
Internet: http://www.yorkshirevisitor.com

Variety is the spice of life in Yorkshire, a region of scenic contrasts with an historic past and a wealth of new attractions, which makes an ideal destination for visitors at any time of the year. Rural charm and scenic softness, rugged castles, stately homes and ancient churches are packed into a compact area with excellent transport communications, making the region a favourite spot for short breaks.

For many people, the scenic grandeur of the Yorkshire Dales National Park - 680 square miles of unspoilt countryside, rivers, caves, castles and unforgettable views - is a major attraction. This is the landscape made famous world-wide in the books and TV programmes featuring Dales Vet, James Herriot.

The great city of York, with its unparalleled wealth of ancient sites, continues to be a powerful magnet for visitors: more than 2 million visit the Minster each year. Other top attractions are the National Railway Museum and the Jorvik Viking Centre, and the fascinating Castle Museum.

Kingston Upon Hull is a maritime city with powerful links to Britain's proud seafaring tradition, and north of here is the lovely market town of Beverley, with its Georgian Houses in the shadow of the Minster.

The North York Moors National Park has miles of open moorland with picturesque villages nestling in hollows. The North Yorkshire Moors Railway, starting at Pickering, is one of many steam railways in the region.

On the coast, traditional family resorts like Scarborough, Bridlington and Cleethorpes have added many new attractions in recent times, and offer the holidaymaker a wide range of activities, from the relaxed to the energetic. And of course, don't forget the fascinating fishing port of Whitby, once home to Captain James Cook, and the charming smaller resorts including Filey and the "smuggler's village" of Robin Hood's Bay. For anyone interested in experiencing the coastal wildlife, a visit to the RSPB nature reserve at Bempton Cliffs is a must.

The towns and cities of West Yorkshire make interesting destinations, with their powerful blend of heritage combined with the spirit of renovation and renewal. Leeds shows the way with the recent opening of the Royal Armouries and the only branch of Harvey Nichols outside of London. Salts Mill, Saltaire is home to the largest collection of work by Bradford born artist David Hockney, as well as floors of excitingly eclectic shopping opportunities. Nearby is the Bronte village of Haworth, high on the Pennine moors.

South Yorkshire was made famous on the big screen, with hits such as The Full Monty and Brassed Off, so why not pay it a visit? As well as the busy market town of Doncaster and the vibrant city of Sheffield, the area has country parks, nature reserves and woodlands, and fascinating places of historical interest including Conisborough Castle and Brodsworth Hall. One of the region's most highly praised new attractions, the science adventure centre Magna is also here.

Calderdale district offers an intriguing cocktail of bustling towns and vast swathes of open moorland. In nearby Kirklees is Holmfirth, the setting for TV's "Last of the Summer Wine", one of many film and television locations in Yorkshire.

A memento of your time in Yorkshire is a must and there are many locally made craft products for you to choose from. Whitby Jet became fashionable after Queen Victoria was so taken by it and still remains a popular semi-precious stone to this day. Sheffield was once provider of most of the country's cutlery and is still regarded as home to some of the best crafted in the country. For those with a sweet tooth, try Harrogate toffee or Pontefract Cakes or, for something a little more permanent, Yorkshire is home to an array of craft shops. One thing is for sure, whatever you are looking for, there will be something to suit every taste.

Yorkshire

Thorpe Hall Caravan and Camping Site

451 Rudston, Driffield, East Yorkshire YO25 4JE

This pleasant small touring park is in the grounds of Thorpe Hall, just outside the village of Rudston and 4½ miles from the sea at Bridlington. Enthusiastically managed by Jayne Chatterton, it is set on flat grass, largely enclosed by the old kitchen garden wall. The 90 pitches are numbered and well spaced with 78 electrical hook-ups (16A) and TV connections. A separate area takes tents and there are no caravan holiday homes. There is always a chance of finding space, though it is best to book for B.H.s and peak weeks. Information sheets on a range of local walks are provided and Thorpe Hall Gardens are open to park visitors between 1-4 pm. A member of the Countryside Discovery group.

Facilities: The solid, central toilet block can be heated. Ladies have three washbasins in private cabins and a bath. Well equipped unit for disabled visitors with a bath. Launderette. Covered dishwashing sinks. Small shop with gas, essentials and local produce. Games room with two pool tables, table football and table tennis. Satellite TV room. The site's own coarse fishing lake is now open nearby. **Off site**: Bicycle hire, golf and boat launching at Bridlington (4½ miles), riding 2 miles. Footpath to the village with a shop, post office, garage, a pub serving bar meals and a new restaurant, plus a twice weekly bus service to Bridlington

Charges 2001

Per unit incl. all persons	£6.00 - £11.50
tent field	£5.00 - £10.30
electricity (16A)	£2.10

Less 10% on booked stays of 7 days or over. No credit cards. Tel: (01262) 420393. Fax: (01262) 420588. E-mail: caravansite@thorpehall.co.uk. Reservations: Made with advance payment (min. 4 nights at Spr. B.H). **Open** 1 March - 31 October.

Directions: Site is by the B1253 road, 4½ miles from Bridlington, on east side of Rudston . O.S.GR: TA105676.

Yorkshire

St Helens in the Park

454 Wykeham, Scarborough, North Yorkshire YO13 9QD

St Helens is a high quality touring park with pleasant views, set within 30 acres of parkland. The 250 mainly level pitches have a spacious feel and the 52 pitches with hardstanding are used by seasonal lets in the summer months but are available for tourers in winter. Electrical hook-ups (10A) are available on 240 pitches, also in the late arrivals area. Set on a hillside (hence the views), the park's buildings are built in local stone and all is maintained to a high standard. The Downe Arms, a short stroll away, is known for its good food and it occasionally runs family discos in high season. Scarborough is only 5 miles with its beaches and summer shows.

Facilities: The four heated toilet blocks are well equipped and maintained, two having been extended and refurbished recently. Some washbasins in cabins and baby baths. The new unit for disabled visitors is of a very high standard. All four blocks have dishwashing sinks under cover. Good laundry room is next to the well stocked shop (Mar-Oct). Takeaway cabin providing simple meals on certain evenings each week during busy periods. The adventure playground set on bark is part of a three acre area set aside for children with goal posts and a mountain bike track. Small games room with pool table and amusement machines. **Off site**: Nearby Wykeham Lakes offer fishing (trout and coarse), scuba diving, windsurfing and sailing (in your own boat).

Charges guide

Per unit incl. 2 persons	£7.40 - £9.40
extra person (over 3 yrs)	£1.00
awning	£1.80
porch awning	£1.30
pup tent	£6.00
dog	50p
electricity	£2.10

Tel/Fax: (01723) 862771. E-mail: caravans@ wykeham.co.uk. Reservations: Made with £10 deposit (min. 4 nights for Spr. and Aug. B.Hs). **Open** all year excl. 15 Jan. - 13 Feb. (reduced facilities Nov-Feb).

Directions: Park access road leads off the A170 (Pickering - Scarborough) road in Wykeham village 2 miles west of junction with B1262. O.S.GR: SE963835.

Far Grange Park

473 Skipsea, Driffield, East Yorkshire YO25 8SY

Far Grange is a very well maintained holiday park that will especially appeal to families. A comprehensive leisure centre is located at the park entrance, well away from the touring pitches. The indoor pool, fitness suite, sauna and solarium (with charges) are excellent facilities with lifeguards who are happy to give assistance to swimmers with disabilities if needed. This area also includes bars with shows, cabaret acts and dancing (adults only). A family room provides games and shows for children and discos for teenagers. These rooms are very tastefully decorated and furnished, making a pleasant, relaxing environment. There are also facilities for pool, snooker, darts and a TV room (all requiring children to be accompanied by parents). Outside is an attractive patio area. The 130 touring pitches all have electrical hook-ups (10A) and include 66 'super' pitches (these available for long weekends all winter). The cliffs here are high and in summer a steel stairway is put in place to give access to the long beach. This is a large, popular site with many caravan holiday homes and seasonal tourers, but with lots of space and plenty to do whatever the weather.

Facilities: Tiled toilet blocks are heated in low season and provide some washbasins in cabins, baths and mother and baby rooms, also a bathroom for wheelchair users. These facilities are clean and well maintained. In the central reception area is a well stocked supermarket (with gas), takeaway, amusement arcade and a well appointed laundry. Indoor leisure complex. Bar with bar meals served in the evenings and Sunday lunches. Restaurant. The park grounds are extensive with plenty of room for team games, tennis, a fitness trail for young and old, an excellent adventure playground with a skateboard ramp, and a play area for younger children (both with rubber safety bases). Fishing. **Off site:** Adjacent is golf, pitch and putt and bowls and, across the road from the entrance, is a country park with fishing and wildfowl lake, visitor centre and a dipping pond for youngsters – an idyllic place to get away for a walk and a picnic.

Charges 2001

Per unit incl. 2 persons	£11.00 - £14.00
3 persons	£11.00 - £15.00
4 persons	£11.00 - £16.00
'super' pitch	£16.00 - £19.00
extra person (3 yrs and over)	£1.00
dog, car or small tent	all £1.00

Min. charge for Easter £55. Less 10% for booked stays over 7 days excl. March and Oct. Tel: (01262) 468293 or 468248. Fax: (01262) 468648. E-mail: enquiries@fargrangepark.co.uk. Reservations: Made with £20 per week deposit (min. 7 days B.Hs and high season). **Open** 1 March – 31 October.

Directions: From A165 (Bridlington - Beverley) take B1242 Skipsea road. Park is on the seaward side of this road, about 1½ miles south of Skipsea. O.S.GR: TA186530.

Northcliffe Holiday Park

453 High Hawsker, nr Whitby, North Yorkshire YO22 4LL

Northcliffe is a high quality, family park with splendid sea views, set within the North Yorkshire Moors National Park. As well as touring units, it caters for 170 caravan holiday homes, although they are entirely separate. The modern park is well planned and attractive, the very friendly owners keeping everything neat and tidy. The toilet facilities are especially good. The 30 touring pitches are of a good size, all with electrical hook-up, and 16 fully serviced. These 16 have 16A electricity, the rest have 10A. Many trees and flowering bushes have been planted to provide wind breaks. The park is situated on the Heritage Coast and one can walk the Cleveland Way into Whitby or to Robin Hood's Bay. Available at reception are leaflets on walks and countryside notes (75p) produced by the park. Whitby and Scarborough with their sandy beaches are within easy reach as are the moors. York is about an hour away. A member of the Best of British group.

Facilities: The toilet block (refurbished and extended in '99) is heated in early and late seasons and uses a coded number pad entry system. Some washbasins in cabins. Good facilities for babies and for disabled visitors. Dishwashing room. Well equipped laundry. Well stocked shop (with gas) incorporating an attractive tea-room with range of reasonably priced food to eat in or takeaway (8 am - 8 pm in high season, mornings and evenings in low season, from 1 April). Two fenced play areas with good quality fittings and safety bases. Grass area for games. Indoor room with pool table and amusement machines. Dogs are not accepted. **Off site:** Fishing 4 miles, riding 5 miles, golf 4 or 6 miles.

Charges 2001

Per unit incl. up to 4 persons	£7.00 - £11.00
pitch incl. 10A electricity	£9.00 - £13.00
'super' pitch with 16A electricity	£11.00 - £15.00
extra adult	£2.00 - £3.00
child (under 16 yrs)	£1.00 - £1.50

Less 10% if 7 nights booked. Tel: (01947) 880477. Fax: (01947) 880972. E-mail: enquiries@northcliffe-seaview.com. Reservations: Made with deposit and fee, min. 2-6 nights acc. to pitch type and season. **Open** 14 March - 31 October.

Directions: Three miles south of Whitby on A171 (Scarborough) road turn left onto the B1447 signed High Hawsker and Robin Hood's Bay. Go through Hawsker village and continue on Robin Hood's Bay road. At top of hill turn left onto private road - go on ½ mile towards sea. O.S.GR: NZ936080.

Cayton Village Caravan Park

455 D23 Mill Lane, Cayton Bay, Scarborough, North Yorkshire YO11 3NN

Cayton Village Caravan Park is just three miles from the hustle and bustle of Scarborough. Originally just a flat field with caravans around the perimeter, four years of hard work, a lot of time and even more expense has produced a park which is very pleasing to the eye and of which the owner, Carol, can be proud. The entrance is a mass of flowers. The late arrivals area here has electrical hook-ups, very handy as the gates are locked at night and anyone leaving early is also expected to use it so as not to disturb others. The 200 pitches, of which 160 are for touring units, are numbered and everyone is taken to their pitch. There are 170 with electricity and 18 'super' pitches. A short walk across a field takes you to Cayton Village which has a popular pub providing excellent meals, a shop/post office and a church, and Cayton Bay is half a mile. The North York Moors are a short distance away, as is the Forestry Commission's Dalby Forest Drive with its scenic drive, mountain bike trails and way-marked walks. The steam railway at Pickering is a big attraction.

Facilities: Three toilet blocks (key code locks) can be heated. Some showers are pre-set, others controllable. Two family shower rooms, family bathroom and baby changing facilities. These facilities are under pressure at busy times when cleaning can be variable. Reception and shop (8.30 am. to 8 pm). The shop's comprehensive stock includes gas and caravan spares. Adventure playground with safety surface. Superb dog walk (an enormous well mown field, floodlit at night). Caravan storage. Off site: Fishing and bicycle hire ½ mile, riding 4 miles, golf 3 miles. Regular bus service from the village to Scarborough or Filey.

Charges 2001

Per unit incl. 4 persons	£7.10 - £10.00
extra person (over 3 yrs)	£1.00
awning	£2.00
dog	£1.00
electricity	£2.00
'super' pitch	£13.50 - £16.50
with hardstanding	£14.50 - £17.50

Special offers available. Tel: (01723) 583171 (winter (01904) 624630). E-mail: info@caytontouring.co.uk. Reservations: Are advised and made for min. 3 nights (4 at B.Hs) with £20 deposit. **Open** Easter - 1 October.

Directions: From A64 Malton - Scarborough road turn right at roundabout (with MacDonalds and pub) signed B1261 Filey. Follow signs for Cayton, in Cayton Village take second left after Blacksmiths Arms down Mill Lane (at brown caravan site sign) and park is 200 yds. From roundabout to park is 2¼ miles. From A165 turn inland at Cayton Bay traffic lights and park is ½ mile on right. O.S.GR: TA057837.

Jasmine Park

474 Cross Lane, Snainton, Scarborough, North Yorkshire YO13 9BE

This is an area of North Yorkshire that is very popular so although we have other parks nearby, we feel there is room for another. Jasmine is a very attractive, quiet, well manicured park with owners who go to much trouble to produce masses of plants to give a very colourful entrance. Set in the Vale of Pickering, the park is level, well drained and protected by a coniferous hedge. The 106 pitches (54 for touring units) are on grass, with electricity connections (10A) for all caravans and some tents. There is no play equipment for children, although a field is provided for football, etc. Masses of tourist information is provided in a log cabin and the owners are only too happy to advise. The market town of Pickering and the seaside town of Scarborough are both 8 miles. Many local attractions are within easy reach, including Castle Howard, Dalby Forest, Sledmere House, Nunington Hall, Goathland (the setting for ITV's 'Heartbeat') and the North York Moors Railway. Some privately owned log cabins and seasonal tourers are also on the site. This is a quiet, peaceful park for a restful holiday. A member of the Countryside Discovery group.

Facilities: The toilet block is kept very clean and includes a large room for families or disabled visitors containing a bath, shower, WC and washbasin (access by key). Laundry room with dishwashing sinks, washing machine, dryer and iron (hot water metered). Motorcaravan service point. Licensed shop selling essentials and gas. Dogs are welcome but there is no dog walk. **Off site:** Riding 2 miles. Golf driving range 2 miles. Fishing 5 miles.

Charges 2001

Per unit incl. 2 persons	£7.00 - £10.00
extra adult	£1.00
child (5-14 yrs)	75p
awning or tent over 150 sq.ft.	£1.50
extra car	£1.00
electricity	£2.00

Min. stay at Easter 4 nights, other B.Hs 3 nights. Tel/Fax: (01723) 859240. E-mail: info@ jasminepark.co.uk. Reservations: Made with £10 deposit and S.A.E. **Open** 1 March - 31 December.

Directions: Snainton is on the A170 Pickering - Scarborough road and park is signed at eastern end of the village. Follow Brakers Lane to park on left in 1 mile. O.S.GR: SE928813.

Flower of May Holiday Park

452 Lebberston Cliff, Scarborough, North Yorkshire YO11 3NU

Flower of May is a large, family owned park for both touring caravans and caravan holiday homes situated on the cliff tops, 4½ miles from Scarborough and 2½ miles from Filey. There is a cliff walk to the beach but it is only suitable for the reasonably active - there is an easier walk down from a car park one mile away. The entrance to the park is very colourful and the reception office is light and airy. The range of leisure facilities grouped around reception, includes an indoor pool with areas for both adults and children, a water flume and a jacuzzi. In the same building are two squash courts, 10 pin bowling, table tennis and amusement machines. The leisure centre is also open to the public (concessionary rates for campers) but during high season is only available to local regulars and the campers on the park. The park is licensed for 300 touring units and 184 caravan holiday homes (45 to hire, the remainder privately owned). The touring pitches are pretty level, arranged in wide avenues mainly on grass and divided by shrubs. There are 210 with electricity (5A), including 45 'star pitches' with water and drainage also. Riverside Meadows at Ripon and Rosedale Country Caravan Park near Pickering are under the same ownership as Flower of May.

Facilities: The three toilet blocks, all refurbished in a light and colourful style, are fully tiled with washbasins in both cabins and vanity style, plus baby rooms and facilities for disabled visitors. Well stocked and licensed shop (closes end Sept) near the leisure centre, as is the laundry room. Two modern bar lounges, one for families and one for adults only, with discos in season, a games room with TV, large adventure playground with safety base, and a café plus takeaway fish and chips. The Plough Inn near the park entrance offers a good bar meal. Pay and play golf course (£5 a round). Indoor swimming pool. Dog exercise area, but numbers and breeds are limited (one per pitch) and not allowed at all at B.Hs and the six week summer holiday. **Off site:** Fishing, boat slipway or riding 2 miles, bicycle hire 4 miles.

Charges 2001

Per unit incl. up to 4 persons	£8.00 - £12.50
awning	£2.00
extra person (over 3 yrs)	£2.00 (£5 at B.Hs)
extra car (on car park only)	£2.00
dog (see above)	£1.00
electricity	£2.00
'star' pitch	plus £4.00

10% discount on pitch fee for weekly bookings. No credit cards. Tel: (01723) 584311. Reservations: Made with £20 deposit per week and £1 booking fee (Sat.-Sat. only for Spr. B.H. and 13/7-31/8). **Open** Easter - 31 October.

Directions: Park is signed from roundabout at junction of A165 and B1261 from where it is 600 yds. O.S.GR: TA088836.

Rosedale Caravan and Camping Park

477 Rosedale Abbey, Pickering, North Yorkshire YO18 8SA

In a beautiful location below Rosedale Moor and on the edge of a popular village, this is a campsite that is highly suitable for walkers. The surrounding hillsides are a maze of public footpaths and these and nearby Cropton Forest can all be reached without using your car. The site itself has a wide entrance on the edge of the village and as it is within the National Park, the buildings are in the local stone and in keeping with the area. The site is reasonably level, with 200 pitches, a few with hardstanding and with 28 electricity connections (10A). One field is for tents only, there are some caravan holiday homes (private) and seasonal touring pitches in their own areas, with the remainder for touring caravans and motorcaravans. The majority have superb views of the surrounding hills. In summer the Dales bus runs through the village, connecting several of the popular villages. The 13 mile Rosedale circuit follows the route of the old iron-ore railway, giving magnificent views and reminders of bygone industries.

Facilities: The toilet blocks are due to be refurbished, together with laundry and dishwashing sinks. Reception provides maps and a small selection of camping accessories, plus gas supplies. Games room with pool and video games. Large play area with space for ball games. Entrance barrier controlled by card (£5 deposit). **Off site:** The village has a general store with daily papers, a post office, bakery, pubs and a restaurant. There is a glass blower at the village blacksmith. A 9 hole golf course, set on a picturesque hillside is 500 yards. The Ryedale Folk Museum at Hutton-le-Hole is 3½ miles.

Charges 2001

Per unit incl. up to 4 persons	£8.00 - £12.50
2-man tent	£4.00 - £6.00
awning	£2.00
extra person (over 3 yrs)	£2.00 (£5 at B.Hs)
dog	£1.00
electricity	£2.00

10% discount on pitch fee for weekly bookings. No credit cards. Tel: (01751) 417272. E-mail: rosedale@flowerofmay.com. Reservations: Contact site. **Open** 31 March - 31 October.

Directions: Rosedale is signed from the A170, 2 miles west of Pickering. Site is in the village of Rosedale Abbey, 8 miles north of the A170. O.S.GR: SE725958.

See also Riverside Meadows on page 172

Yorkshire
Lebberston Touring Park
Home Farm, Filey Road, Lebberston, Scarborough YO11 3PE

Lebberston Park is a quiet, spacious touring site, but it takes no tents. It is highly suitable for anyone seeking a quiet relaxing break, such as mature couples or young families. There is no play area and no games room so teenagers may get bored. The only concession to children is a large central area with goal posts. The site itself has a very spacious feel. It is gently sloping and south facing and the views are superb. There are 125 numbered pitches, all with 10A electricity and 6 with hardstanding. The circular access road is tarmac, the grass is well manicured and the entrance a mass of flowers. Reception is part of an attractive log cabin, which is also the home of the owners and their young family. The resorts of Filey, Bridlington, Scarborough and Hornsea provide something for everyone, the moors and the Dalby forest are also within a short distance. Because there is such a popular and busy area we feel justified in adding another site to the guide, especially one of such quality.

Facilities: Recently upgraded toilet blocks are of high quality, with large shower cubicles and washbasins in cubicles with curtains. Both blocks have dishwashing sinks and one has a family bathroom (20p). The room for disabled visitors is very good. Laundry with washing machine, dryer, spin dryer, iron and board. A key is supplied for the laundry, bathroom, telephone booth and the disabled room. Reception sells a few supplies plus papers, ice cream and gas. **Off site**: Local pub within walking distance. Each new arrival is given details of parking in Scarborough including a parking disc.

Charges 2001

Per unit incl. 2 persons	£6.50 - £8.00
B.Hs (min 3 or 4 nights)	£11.00
extra adult	£1.00
child (5-14 yrs)	75p
awning	£1.50
trailer tent over 8 sq.m.	£1.50
electricity	£2.00

Tel: (01723) 585723. Reservations: Made with £10 non-returnable deposit. **Open** 1 March - 31 October.

Directions: From A64 Malton - Scarborough road turn right at roundabout (MacDonalds, pub and superstore) signed B1261 Filey. Go through Cayton, Killerby and in 4½ miles site is signed on right. O.S.GR: TA082823.

Yorkshire
Golden Square Caravan and Camping Park
Oswaldkirk, Helmsley, York YO62 5YQ

Golden Square is a popular, high quality, family owned touring park. Mr and Mrs Armstrong are local farmers who have worked hard to turn an old quarry into a very attractive caravan park with a number of levelled bays that have superb views over the Vale of Pickering. The 130 pitches are not separated but they do have markers set into the ground and mainly back onto grass banks. In very dry weather the ground can be hard, steel pegs would be needed (even in wet weather the park is well drained). All pitches have electrical connections (10A), 24 have drainage and 6 are 'deluxe' pitches (with waste water, sewage, electricity, water and TV aerial connection). The licensed shop is very well stocked, selling home-made fresh bread and cakes, dairy produce, fresh vegetables and groceries, newspapers, gas and gifts. Visitors may have membership of the Ampleforth College sports centre, with its indoor pool, tennis and gym, etc. The area abounds with footpaths and three well known long distance footpaths are near. Dog owners are well catered for with two or three enormous fields for exercising alongside the park.

Facilities: Two heated well cared for toilet blocks are of excellent quality, with some washbasins in private cabins. Showers are pre-set and metered (token) and a bathroom (token) also houses baby changing facilities. Both ladies' and men's blocks have full facilities for disabled visitors. Dishwashing sinks are under cover. Laundry with washing machines, dryers, a spin dryer and iron and board. Motorcaravan service point. The tourist information room also houses a microwave and an extra iron and board. Shop. Two excellent play areas allow tiny tots to be kept separate from older children. Games field and a barn with table tennis and pool table. Bicycle hire. All year caravan storage. **Off site**: Riding 2 miles, golf 3 miles, fishing 5 miles. Nearby Helmsley and Ampleforth have shops and pubs with food.

Charges 2001

Per unit incl. 2 persons and all children up to 10 yrs		
		£6.50 - £10.50
extra person (10 yrs or over)		£1.50
awning		£1.20 - £1.40
electricity		£2.00
'de-luxe' pitch all incl.		£15.00 - £20.00

No credit cards. Tel: (01439) 788269. Fax: (01439) 788236. E-mail: barbara@goldensquarecaravanpark. com. Reservations: Essential for B.Hs and made with £10 deposit (£20 for B.Hs). **Open** 1 March - 31 October.

Directions: From York take B1363 to Helmsley . At Oswaldkirk Bank Top turn left on B1257 to Helmsley. Take second left turn signed Ampleforth to site. O.S.GR: SE605797.

Foxholme Touring Caravan and Camping Park

458 Harome, Helmsley, North Yorkshire YO62 5JG

Foxholme is an unusual park with only 60 pitches for caravans and a small field for a few tents. Nearly all the pitches are individual ones in clearings in the quite dense coniferous plantation. The trees give a lot of shade and quite a lot of privacy (manoeuvring may be difficult on some of the pitches). All pitches have electricity (6A, a few need long leads) and six places have hardstanding. Some picnic tables are provided. The site is managed by wardens with reception usually open 9 am. - 9 pm. with an hour for lunch. Very basic provisions are kept. The park is set in quiet countryside and would be a good base for touring, being within striking distance of the moors, the coast and York. There are no on site activities but the indoor pool at the Pheasant Hotel in Harome may be used by campers (£3 per session).

Facilities: The toilet block is of good quality, built in local stone, with all washbasins in cubicles. Laundry room with washing machine and sinks and a washing up room. Two further small blocks provide WCs only in other parts of the park. Motorcaravan service point. Torches useful. Caravan storage. **Off site**: Nearest shops at Helmsley and Kirkbymoorside, both 4 miles. Bicycle hire, riding and golf 4 miles.

Charges 2002

Per unit	£7.50 - £8.00
awning	£1.50
electricity	£2.50

No credit cards. Tel: (01439) 770416, 771241 or 771696. Fax: (01439) 771744. Reservations: Made for any dates with £10 deposit. **Open** Easter - 31 October.

Directions: Turn south off the A170 between adjoining villages of Beadlam (to west) and Nawton (to east) at sign to Ryedale School, then 1 mile to park on left (passing another park on right). From east ignore first camp sign at turning before Nawton. From west turn right / mile east of Helmsley, signed Harome, turn left at church, go through village and follow camp signs. O.S.GR: SE661831.

FOXHOLME TOURING CARAVAN PARK

HAROME, HELMSLEY, NORTH YORKSHIRE YO62 5JG
Telephone: (01439) 771241, 770416 or 771696   Fax: (01439) 771744
AA 3 PENNANT - CARAVAN CLUB APPROVED - CAMPING CLUB APPROVED

A quiet, rural site for touring vans, motor caravans and some tents. All pitches in well sheltered clearings in the 6 acres of 39 year old woodland. All weather roads; Some hardstandings; Luxury toilet block graded excellent by the A.A. Washbasins in cubicles; H&C showers; Laundry room; Small shop; Gas exchange; Mains electric hook-ups available.

BEAUTIFUL COUNTRYSIDE,

CLOSE TO THE NORTH YORK MOORS NATIONAL PARK
Please send stamp for brochure to G.C. Binks

Vale of Pickering Caravan Park

460 Carr House Farm, Allerston, nr Pickering, North Yorkshire YO18 7PQ

Vale of Pickering is a level park edged by grassy banks and, although over the years that the site has been developing these have been partly hidden by foliage, trees and attractive flower beds, they do give shelter from the wind. It is a well designed, neat and tidy park. The family owners, who are local farmers, have put a lot of thought into planning the site. There are 120 pitches, 75 of which are for touring units, all with electrical connections (10A), plus further pitches for tents. The well stocked, licensed shop also stocks a few caravan accessories and gas (open according to demand in low season). There is a local pub at Yedingham (1½ miles).

Facilities: The refurbished toilet block is tiled, heated and well maintained, providing some washbasins in cabins, showers (20p) and a bath. Separate toilet and washbasin for disabled visitors. Dishwashing sinks (2p for hot water). Launderette. Microwave. Motorcaravan service point. Shop. Good play area and play field. **Off site**: Fishing 1 mile, bicycle hire and riding 3 miles, golf 5 miles.

Charges 2001

Per unit incl. 2 adults and 2 children (under 12 yrs)	
	£6.50 - £9.50
extra adult	£2.00
child	£1.00
awning	£1.50
electricity	£2.00
2 dogs free, extra dog	£1.00

No credit cards. Tel: (01723) 859280. Fax: (01723) 850060. E-mail: tony@valeofpickering.co.uk. Reservations: Made with £10 deposit (min. 3 nights at B.Hs with £20 deposit). **Open** 14 March - 31 Oct.

Directions: Park is 1 mile off the main A170 (Scarborough - Helmsley) road at the village of Allerston. O.S.GR: SE879808.

Brompton on Swale Caravan and Camping Park

480 Brompton on Swale, Richmond, North Yorkshire DL10 7EZ

Brompton is a quiet family site in a delightful setting on the banks of the river Swale, only two miles from the ancient market town of Richmond (the Lass of Richmond Hill fame). This caravan park is on level meadows of well cut grass with pitches marked by a slab for the jockey wheel. Of the 214 pitches 100 are allocated to seasonal lets and the remainder to tourers. There are some fully serviced pitches and 177 with electricity (10/16A). The ones alongside the river are ideal for families with older children as they can easily be supervised in their unending efforts to catch tiddlers and crayfish. Fishing permits are available from reception for both fly and coarse fishing on the river. There is a security barrier (key for toilets and barrier £5 deposit) and a late arrivals area with hook-up. The town of Richmond can be reached by a riverside walk. Its cobbled market square is dominated by the 100 feet high keep of the Norman castle and is home to the Green Howards museum and a Georgian theatre. The site is on the route of the long distance Coast-to-Coast trail.

Facilities: Both shower blocks can be heated and have facilities for disabled visitors and baby changing. Showers have a curtain divider, and washbasins are open plan, vanity style. One block has two rooms for families or disabled people. Each block has dishwashing sinks. Laundry with washing machines, dryers and an iron. Motorcaravan service point. Licensed shop at the entrance with wide range of produce and gas. Fenced play area. **Off site:** Swimming pool and leisure centre in Richmond.

Charges 2001

Per unit incl. 2 persons	£8.50
awning/gazebo	£2.00
electricity	£2.50
backpacker, cyclist or m/cyclist	£3.80
extra person (12 yrs or over)	£2.00
fully serviced pitch	£16.00
dog (max 2)	50p

Tel: (01748) 824629. Fax: (01748) 826383. E-mail: brompton.caravanpark@btinternet.com. Reservations: Made with £10 deposit (min 3 nights at B.Hs). **Open** 15 March - 31 October.

Directions: Park is by the B6271 road, 1.5 miles southeast of Richmond. O.S.GR: NZ197004.

Constable Burton Hall Caravan Park

469 Constable Burton Hall, nr Leyburn, North Yorkshire DL8 5LJ

This tranquil park is in beautiful Wensleydale and the emphasis is on peace and quiet, the wardens working to provide a relaxing environment. Being in the grounds of the Hall, it has a spacious, park-like feel to it. On part level, part sloping, well trimmed grass, the 120 pitches (40 for touring units) are of a good size and all have electrical connections (10A). There are 5 pitches for tents. Ideally placed for visiting the Northern Dales, the gardens of the Hall are open to the public, with a collection of maples and terraced gardens developed by Mrs Vida Burton. There is no shop on site but nearby Leyburn will provide all your needs. Opposite the park entrance is the Wyvill Arms for bar meals. Ball games are not permitted on site.

Facilities: Two toilet blocks built of local stone, blending in with the local surroundings, have been refurbished recently, are well tiled and kept immaculately clean, and can be heated. The former deer barn has been adapted for use as a laundry room and extra washrooms with basins for both men and women. Gas supplies. Gates closed 10 pm - 8 am. **Off site:** Fishing, riding or golf within 4 miles.

Charges 2001

Per unit incl. 2 persons	£7.50 - £10.00
extra adult	£2.00
child (5-16 yrs)	75p
awning	£1.80
electricity	£2.00

No commercial vehicles. No credit cards. Tel: (01677) 450428. Reservations: Made with deposit (£20 for B.Hs. £5 other times). **Open** Late March - 31 October.

Directions: Park is by the A684 between Bedale and Leyburn, ½ mile from the village of Constable Burton on the Leyburn side. O.S.GR: SE152907.

Street Head Caravan Park

468 Newbiggin, Bishopdale, Leyburn, North Yorkshire DL8 3TE

Street Head is a no frills, simple site next door to the local hostelry and with marvellous views. There are 50 privately owned holiday homes arranged over two areas, while a separate, fairly level, hedged field with a circular gravel road provides 25 pitches for touring units. Each has hardstanding and 10A electricity. A further separate sloping field is for tents. Thoralby village (⅟ mile) has a post office/general store and West Burton (1½ miles) is very pretty with a pub and shops. Bar snacks are served next door at the Street Head Inn. Aysgarth Falls are only 1½ miles and there are local markets at Hawes and Leyburn.

Facilities: Sanitary facilities provide metered hot showers (20p), free hot water to washbasins, but metered for washing up sinks. Washing machine and dryer. Basic essentials and gas are available from reception (only open for two hours morning and afternoon in the main season, less in low season). Caravan storage. Off Site: Bicycle hire ½ mile, fishing 4 miles.

Charges 2001

Per unit	£9.00
hikers' tent	£8.00
awning	£2.00
electricity	£2.00

No credit cards. Tel: (01969) 663472 or 663571. Reservations: Advised at B.Hs; contact site. **Open** 1 March - end October.

Directions: From A684 travelling west (just after Swinithwaite) take B6160 signed Kettlewell, continue to Newbiggin past turning to West Burton and park is on right. O.S.GR: SD998862.

Woodhouse Farm Caravan and Camping Park

466 Winksley, nr Ripon, North Yorkshire HG4 3PG

This secluded family park on a former working farm, is only 6 miles from Ripon and about 4 miles from the World Heritage site of Fountains Abbey. It is a very rural park with a spacious feel and various pitching areas tucked away in woodland areas or around the edges of hedged fields with the centres left clear for children. There are hard roads and most of the 160 pitches have 16A electricity. There are 56 acres in total, 17½ devoted to the site and 20 acres of woodland for walks. The 2½ acre fishing lake is a big attraction and provides a pleasant area for picnics or walks. The Yorkshire Dales of Nidderdale, Wharfedale, Wensleydale and Swaledale are within easy reach and there are many villages with attractive country inns. Woodhouse Farm has a quiet, secluded location from which many excursions can be made. As in most parts of the Dales, the peace is occasionally disturbed by passing jets, but happily not very often.

Facilities: The clean, functional toilet block nearer the pitches includes heating and roomy showers (20p) and some washbasins in cabins. Covered dish-washing sinks. Two bathrooms and facilities for disabled visitors should now be ready. Extra facilities are in the farm buildings along with a well equipped laundry, reception and shop. Motorcaravan services. New restaurant. Games room, table tennis, pool table and TV. Play equipment. Fishing. Mountain bike hire. Caravan storage. **Off site:** Riding 3 miles, golf 6 miles.

Charges 2001

Per unit incl. 2 persons	£8.00
tent	£7.50
cyclist or hiker with tent	£4.50
extra person (over 5 yrs)	75p

Plus £1 on hook-up pitches at B.Hs. Tel: (01765) 658309. Fax: (01765) 658882. E-mail: woodhouse.farm@talk21.com. Reservations: Contact park. **Open** 1 March - 31 October.

Directions: From Ripon take Fountains Abbey - Pateley Bridge road (B6265). After approx. 3½ miles turn right to Grantley and then follow campsite signs for further 1-2 miles. O.S.GR: SE241715.

Riverside Meadows Country Caravan Park

476

Ure Bank Top, Ripon, North Yorkshire HG4 1JD

Riverside Meadows has a new name and owners who have lots of experience in the caravan park world. All the facilities are being upgraded and brought up to their demanding standards. This is a rural park, although the approach to it belies that fact. The short approach from the main road passes a row of houses and a factory, but once they are passed, the park opens up before you and you are once again back in the countryside. There are plenty of caravan holiday homes but they are, on the whole, quite separate from the touring units. The pitches, practically all with electrical hook-ups, are mainly on gently sloping grass with just a few hardstandings. A meadow separates the park from the River Ure, a favourite place for strolling and fishing (licences available). Close to Ripon is the Lightwater Valley theme park, and a little further are Fountains Abbey, Harrogate, Knaresborough, the Yorkshire Dales and Thirsk with its market and the new James Herriot centre. There is lots to see and do on and off the park for both families and couples.

Facilities: The new, tiled toilet block includes a baby room, dishwashing room, a fully fitted shower room for disabled visitors and laundry facilities. New shop, reception, bar with snacks and games room. Well euipped new children's play area. **Off site:** Golf course within a mile. The delightful market town (city) of Ripon with its ancient cathedral is only 15 minutes walk.

Charges 2001

Per unit incl. 4 persons	£7.00 - £11.00
extra person	£2.00
awning or extra car	£2.00
dog (max. 2)	£1.00
electricity	£2.00

10% discount on pitch fee for weekly bookings. No credit cards. Tel: (01765) 602964. Reservations: Made for min. 3 nights with £20 per week deposit. **Open** Easter - 31 October.

Directions: At the most northern roundabout on the Ripon bypass (A61), turn onto the A6108 signed Ripon, Masham and Leyburn. Go straight on at mini-roundabout and park is signed on right. O.S.GR: SE317727.

See advertisement on page 167

Ripley Caravan Park

463

Ripley, Harrogate, Yorkshire HG3 3AU

Peter and Valerie House are the resident owners of Ripley Park, an 18-acre grass park accommodating 130 units, each with 10A electricity. On fairly level grass (with 20 hardstandings) and connected by a circular gravel road, the pitches are carefully spaced and monitored to ensure that the grass is always in good condition. The trees are growing nicely now to give character and to separate the pitching areas. Recent developments include more trees, new hook-ups, water points and recycling bins. The park has a spacious feel with a small, nicely landscaped lake with resident ducks (pitches here are very popular). Ripley and its castle are a short walk and shows and exhibitions are staged in its grounds during the summer months. This park is very central for the many attractions that Yorkshire has to offer and is mid-way between the spa town of Harrogate and historic Knaresborough.

Facilities: The well designed, central toilet block can be heated in cooler weather and is kept clean and well maintained. It provides washbasins in cubicles, a baby bath, a separate unit for disabled people. Dishwashing sinks under cover. Small laundry. Motorcaravan service point. Shop (with gas). Leisure block beside reception offers a games room with TV, nursery playroom and a heated indoor pool (very reasonably priced at 50p per person). Adventure playground and football area. Two dogs per unit are accepted unless by prior arrangement. Winter caravan storage. **Off site:** Fishing, riding or golf 3 miles. Bus service 150 yds.

Charges 2001

Per unit incl. 2 adults	£6.95 - £8.50
extra adult	£2.00
child (5-18 yrs)	£1.00
small tent incl. 2 persons, no vehicle	£5.00
awning	£1.50
electricity	£1.95
water and drainage	£2.00

Max. per family unit £11.50 (2 adults, 2 children). Tel/Fax: (01423) 770050. Reservations: Made with £10 deposit, min. 3 nights at B.Hs. **Open** Easter - 31 October.

Directions: About 4 miles north of Harrogate, site access is 150 yds. down the B6165 Knaresborough road from its roundabout junction with the A61. O.S.GR: SE291601.

Yorkshire
Moorside Caravan Park
461 Lords Moor Lane, Strensall, York YO32 5XJ

Strensall is only a few miles from York, one of England's most attractive cities and Moorside will provide a peaceful haven after a day's sightseeing. It will impress you with its pretty fishing lake, masses of flowers and the quietness (except for the odd passing daytime train). There are 57 marked pitches on neat well trimmed grass, most with electricity (5/10A) and 18 with paved hardstanding. The whole park is very well maintained making it a very pleasant environment. The small lake is well stocked for coarse fishing (£2 charge) and the pitches bordering the lake are the most popular. York golf course is almost opposite the site entrance. This is an adult only park (no children under 16 yrs).

Facilities: The purpose built toilet block can be heated and houses immaculately kept facilities with washbasins in cubicles for ladies. One WC is suitable for use by disabled visitors. Fully equipped laundry room. Dishwashing area. Tourist information and books to borrow. Caravan storage. **Off site:** Strensall village with shops and places to eat is less than a mile.

Charges guide

Per unit incl. 2 persons	£6.50 - £9.00
extra person	£2.00
awning	£1.00
hardstanding	50p
electricity	£1.50

No credit cards. Tel: (01904) 491208 or 491865. Reservations: Contact park. **Open** March - end October.

Directions: From A1237 York outer ring road, follow Flaxton road. The park entrance is on the left past signs to Strensall village and York Golf Club. O.S.GR: SE647614.

Yorkshire
Fangfoss Old Station Caravan Park
465 Fangfoss, York YO41 5QB

The Station House and its platform give this small site character, its rural situation amongst rolling farmland gives it peace and quietness and its owners, a friendly welcome and clean and comfortable facilities. The grassed over track and sidings provide hardstanding and with the adjacent fairly level grass field, give a total of 75 marked pitches, all with 10A electricity and 18 with hardstanding. York is 10 miles (with 'park and ride'), Hull 28 miles and the Yorkshire Wolds 5 miles. There are nearby market towns and a variety of pubs and restaurants within a 6 mile radius. Fangfoss is 1 mile, Pocklington 4 miles, with sports facilities, etc. This area will encourage walkers and cyclists.

Facilities: A modern central toilet block provides vanity style washbasins (two in cubicles for ladies). A separate wooden utility block, 'The Wendy House', provides washing up sinks, a laundry sink and a food preparation bar (useful for tenters). No washing machine but a laundry service is offered. Reception carries essentials with an off-licence and gas. Some play equipment. Winter caravan storage. **Off site:** Fishing, bicycle hire, riding and golf within 4 miles.

Charges 2001

Per unit incl. up to 4 persons	£7.70 - £12.50
2-man tent	£6.00
awning	£1.00 - £3.00
extra person	£1.00
electricity	£2.00

Tel: (01759) 380491. E-mail: fangfoss@pi2000.co.uk. Reservations: Made with £20 deposit. **Open** 1 March - 31 October.

Directions: On A166 York - Bridlington road, park is clearly signed at Stamford Bridge, on right just after crossing the river. Using A1079 York - Hull road, follow signs at Wilberfoss for 1½ miles (in a northerly direction). O.S.GR: SE748527.

Yorkshire
Rudding Holiday Park

471

Follifoot, Harrogate, North Yorkshire HG3 1JH

The extensive part wooded, part open grounds of Rudding Park are very attractive, peaceful and well laid out. One camping area is sloping but terraces provide level pitches and further pitches are in the very sheltered old walled garden. All 91 touring pitches have electricity (10/16A) and 17 'super pitches' are fully serviced. Some pitches are let on a seasonal basis and a separate area contains 90 owner occupied caravan holiday homes and pine chalets. On the outer edge of the park is an 18 hole golf course and driving range, together with the 'The Deer House', a bar and restaurant open twice daily during B.Hs and school holidays, otherwise only at weekends. Tennis, markets, pubs and restaurants are within a few miles, and the majestic City of York is less than an hour away. This is an attractive park with something for all the family.

Facilities: Two tiled toilet blocks are of a good standard, centrally heated and well maintained. Some washbasins in cabins, a baby room and bathroom. Fully equipped laundry room at each block. Disabled people have well appointed facilities. Motorcaravan service point. Large, well stocked shop (all season, sometimes limited hours). Gas supplies. Restaurant and bar. Heated outdoor swimming and paddling pools with sunbathing areas (Spr.B.H.- early Sept), supervised at all times (extra charge). Adventure playground. Football pitch, games room and minigolf. Golf. Bicycle hire. **Off site:** Buses pass the gate hourly to Harrogate and Knaresborough. Fishing 2 miles, riding 1 mile.

Charges 2001

Per pitch	£9.50 - £13.50
awning	£1.00 - £2.00
electricity	£2.50
'supersite' incl. awning, electricity	£16.50 - £22.50
dog (on lead)	free
Tent: per adult	£3.50 - £4.00
child (under 16 yrs)	£1.25 - £2.50

Special offers - contact park. Tel: (01423) 870439. Fax: (01423) 870859. E-mail: hpreception@rudding-park.com. Reservations: Made with full advance payment (essential for B.H. w/ends). **Open** 16 March - 4 November.

Directions: Park is 3 miles south of Harrogate clearly signed between the A658 and A661 roads. O.S.GR: SE333528.

Yorkshire
Goose Wood Caravan Park

464

Sutton-on-the-Forest, York YO61 1ET

A family owned park in a natural woodland setting, Goose Wood provides a quiet, relaxed atmosphere from which to explore York itself or the surrounding Yorkshire Dales, Wolds or Moors. The park has a well kept air and a rural atmosphere, with 75 well spaced and marked pitches on level grass, all with electricity (16A) and 75 with paved hardstanding and patio pitch. For children, there is a 'super plus' adventure playground in the trees at one side of the park and, for adults, a small coarse fishing lake and attractive, natural woodland for walking, plus a large scale chess set. The park is popular with families in high season when it can be busy at weekends. A 'park and ride' scheme for York operates from nearby all year, six days a week or there is a local bus every two hours, six days a week. The park is 1/ miles from Sutton village and only 7 miles from 'Water World' a new water leisure centre with pool, slides, wave machines, etc. Tents are not accepted at this park. A member of the Best of British group.

Facilities: The excellent toilet block, modern and well maintained, provides good facilities including free showers (four minute push-button which also operates the light and is located outside cubicle), and bathroom (£1). A separate, refurbished unit provides four extra toilets and washbasins, and coin-operated washing up sinks. Motorcaravan service point. Laundry room. Small shop (with gas supplies). Fishing lake. Children's play area. Dogs (max. two per pitch), to be exercised in nearby woodland. No tents are accepted. **Off site:** Riding or golf 1 mile

Charges 2002

Per unit incl. 1 or 2 persons and car	£5.00 - £11.50
extra person	£1.50
awning (no groundsheet), pup tent (1 only) £1.50	
electricity (16A)	£2.50

Tel: (01347) 810829. Fax: (01347) 811498. Reservations: Made with £20 deposit (min. 3 nights at B.Hs). **Open** all year.

Directions: Park is 6 miles north of York; from the A1237 York outer ring-road take the B1363 for Sutton-on-the-Forest and Stillington, taking the first right after the Haxby and Wigginton junction and follow park signs. O.S.GR: SE595636.

Yorkshire
Bronte Caravan Park
479 Halifax Road, Keighley, West Yorkshire BD21 5QF

Bronte Caravan Park is a peaceful haven set in a 50-acre park with wonderful views. It is hard to believe that you are only 1½ miles from the busy town of Keighley, as only the rolling hillsides with a village on the opposite side are visible. Ten acres of the land are devoted to the owners' own deer herd. A two acre lake is in a lovely setting with its island, weeping willows and several varieties of waterfowl, not to mention the local heron or kingfisher. It is well stocked to provide sport for both coarse and fly fishermen. The hillside has been terraced and a stream tumbles down into the lake. The River Worth runs alongside the site (well fenced). The level pitches have gravel surfaces and 10A electricity (some are a little small). There are also 25 pitches for tents. Three pitching areas cater for all needs – two areas are for adults only, the third for families quite separate with an adjacent play area on bark chippings. The Worth Valley railway of 'The Railway Children' fame running alongside the site is a big attraction and one of its smaller stations is only a short walk. Ingrow station with a railway museum and free parking is ½ mile. Haworth and its Bronte heritage (2 miles) is a must with the museum, the parsonage where the sisters lived and the moorland walks. Further away at Bradford is the cinema and photography museum and Cliffe castle museum in Keighley is well worth a visit.

Facilities: The well appointed, central toilet block of local stone includes a very large room for families or disabled visitors. Laundry with washing machine, dryer and iron. Dishwashing sinks under cover. This block is quite a walk from the family pitches but two 'portacabin' style blocks nearer to the pitches are well equipped with toilets, washbasins and an outside dishwashing sink. Children's play area. Fishing (1 rod/1 line, adult or child £2.50). Barrier access (key £10 deposit). **Off site**: Supermarkets 1½ miles.

Charges 2001

Per unit incl. 2 persons	£9.00
tent	£6.00
electricity	£2.00
extra person over 5 yrs	£2.00

Tel: 01535 691746 (office hours). Reservations: Made with £5 deposit (non-returnable). **Open** 1 April - 31 October.

Directions: Park is south of Keighley off the A629 Keighley - Halifax road, on the right approx. 1¼ miles from Keighley.

Yorkshire
Wood Nook Caravan Park
467 Skirethorns, Threshfield, Skipton, North Yorkshire BD23 5NU

Wood Nook is a family run park in the heart of Wharfedale, part of the Yorkshire Dales National Park. The access road is narrow for a short distance, but you will find it is well worth this slight rural inconvenience as the site includes six acres of woodland with quite rare flora and wildlife. Reception is in the farmhouse, as is the small licensed shop (from Easter, gas and basics only). The gently sloping fields have gravel roads and provide 25 pitches with gravel hardstanding. All have electricity (10A, long leads may be required) and there are water points. There is also room for 24 tents and the park has some caravan holiday homes to let. The Thompson family are very friendly, trying always to have time for a chat, although Wood Nook is still a working farm producing beef cattle. The park itself adjoins the fells, with direct access from the top of the site. A visit to the nearby village of Grassington is a must, with its cobbled main street and quaint gift shops. All in all, this is a peaceful park from which to explore the Yorkshire Dales.

Facilities: Farm buildings have been converted to provide modern, neat sanitary facilities which can be heated, are well maintained and kept very clean (opened by key). Washbasins in cubicles for ladies. Roomy showers (in another building) are coin operated. Fully equipped laundry with clothes lines. Dishwashing sinks under cover. Motorcaravan service points. Small, attractive children's play area on top of a small hill. American motorhomes are taken by prior arrangement. **Off site**: Fishing or bicycle hire 2 miles, riding 3 miles, golf 9 miles. The Old Hall Inn at Threshfield offers bar food. Leisure centre with swimming pool nearby.

Charges 2001

Per adult	£2.30
child 3-15 yrs	95p
16-17 yrs as part of a family unit	£1.50
pitch incl. car	£5.00
awning	£1.00
hiker/cyclist	£4.00
electricity	£2.00

Tel/Fax: (01756) 752412. E-mail: enquiries@ wood-nook.demon.co.uk. Reservations: Necessary for high season and B.H.s with £10 deposit. **Open** 1 March - 31 October.

Directions: From Skipton take B6265 to Threshfield, then B6160. After 50 yds turn left into Skirethorns Lane and follow signs for 600 yds, up narrow lane then 300 yds. O.S.GR: SD974641.

Yorkshire
Howgill Lodge Caravan and Camping Park
475 Barden, Skipton, North Yorkshire BD23 6DJ

Howgill Lodge is a traditional family site, set in the heart of the Dales. Arranged on a sloping hillside, the terraced pitches have fantastic views. It is a small park catering for the needs of walkers, tourers and the people who like to just relax. The whole area is a haven for both experienced walkers or the casual rambler, without having to move your car. All the pitches at the upper part of the park are on hardstanding and have electricity connections (10A), the lower ones are mainly on grass (30 in total). Picnic tables and chairs are provided. Reception also houses a small shop which sells most of the basics including fresh foods. Part of the farmhouse has been tastefully converted into a licensed restaurant, open six days a week (noon - 6 pm) in season, weekends only in winter. Pretty villages abound in the area, all with attractive inns and nearby Embsay has the Dales Railway with steam trains. This very pleasant park, with clean facilities, has a very relaxing feel to it. A member of the Countryside Discovery group.

Facilities: Heated toilet facilities are at the entrance, close to reception, with dishwashing sinks outside, under cover. Showers are large and adjustable (on payment). Fully equipped laundry room with washing machine, dryer and iron and four unisex showers also here. Outdoor washing lines are provided. Two small blocks housing WCs are lower down the site for the convenience of tent campers. Shop. Licensed restaurant. No children's play area. Fishing licences are available from reception. B&B is offered. **Off site**: Skipton, an agricultural market town, is only 8 miles and the well known Bolton Abbey, with its beautiful riverside walks is only 3 miles.

Charges 2001

Per unit incl. 2 persons	£9.50
incl. family	£12.00
tent or motorcaravan	£9.00 or £11.00
awning or extra car	£2.00
hiker	£3.30

Tel: (01756) 720655. E-mail: info@howgill-lodge.co.uk. Reservations: Made with £10 deposit. **Open** 1 April - 31 October.

Directions: Turn off A59 Skipton - Harrogate road at roundabout onto B6160 Bolton Abbey, Burnsall road. Three miles past Bolton Abbey at Barden Towers, bear right signed Appletreewick and Pateley Bridge. This road is fairly narrow for 1¼ miles (with passing places). Park is signed on right at phone box. O.S.GR: SE065593.

Yorkshire

Knight Stainforth Hall Caravan and Camping Park

Little Stainforth, Settle, North Yorkshire BD24 0DP

472

This traditional park is located in the heart of the Yorkshire Dales, the whole area a paradise for hill-walking, fishing and pot-holing and with outstanding scenery. The camping area is on slightly sloping grass, sheltered by mature woodland in a very attractive setting. There are 100 touring pitches, 50 with electricity (10A) and 10 with hardstanding. A separate area houses 60 privately owned caravan holiday homes. Buildings near the farmhouse provide reception, a games/TV room and a shop (for basics). A gate leads from the bottom of the camping field giving access to the river bank where the Ribble bubbles over small waterfalls and rocks and whirls around deep pools where, we are told, campers do swim in warm weather. This is not fenced and children should be supervised, although it is a super location for a family picnic. Fishing permits and licences are available from reception and one can fish for trout (or salmon when available). Settle is only 2 miles away, as is Giggleswick and its well known school. Train buffs will want to travel on the Settle – Carlisle railway over the famous Ribblehead Viaduct. The magic of the Dales National Park is on the doorstep and just off the A65 to the west of Settle at Felzor is the Dales Falconry and Conservation Centre.

Facilities: Toilet facilities, in a converted stone barn, are very basic but there is heating and a good supply of hot water, plus three curtained cubicles with washbasins for ladies. A new block is planned. Dishwashing sinks. Laundry room with washing machine and dryers. Shop. Games/TV room. Children's playground. Fishing. Bicycle hire. Security barrier at entrance (£10 deposit). **Off site:** Riding or golf 3 miles.

Charges 2001

Per unit incl. 2 adults	£8.75
extra adult	£2.50
extra child (5-16 yrs)	£1.50
backpacker	£3.90
electricity	£1.75

Weekly rate: 7 nights for the price of 6. Deposit for amenity block key £2. Tel: (01729) 822200. Fax: (01729) 823387. E-mail: info@knightstainforth.co.uk. Reservations: Write or phone for details. **Open** 1 March - 31 October.

Directions: From Settle town centre, drive west towards Giggleswick. Ignore turning marked Stainforth and Horton, and after 200 yards turn right into Stackhouse Lane (signed Knight Stainforth). After 2 miles turn right at crossroads. O.S.GR: SD815671.

Yorkshire

Nostell Priory Holiday Park

Nostell, nr Wakefield, West Yorkshire WF4 1QD

470

A tranquil, secluded woodland park within the estate of Nostell Priory, this site provides 60 touring pitches, all with electrical connections (5A), in a grassy, flat and sheltered area edged with mature trees. There is a hardstanding area suitable for motorcaravans, plus 80 caravan holiday homes in a separate area (5 for hire). Amenities are designed to blend into the environment in rustic wood, including the sanitary block. Nostell Priory itself with its collection of Chippendale furniture and attractive gardens is well worth a visit. The Dales, York and the Peak District are all an easy drive away. A fishing lake is within the grounds, with golf and watersports locally (details in reception). The park is very well cared for and the natural environment is encouraged so there is an abundance of birds and wildlife. A rally field is adjacent to the site. Buses pass the end of the drive (½ mile long).

Facilities: The toilet block although older in style, is very clean and well maintained. The ladies' has been totally refurbished to provide some washbasins in cubicles. Accessed by key, it also includes a separate room for dishwashing. Laundry with two washing machines and a dryer (opening times on the door). Motorcaravan services. Milk and papers can be ordered at reception, the nearest shops are 2 miles Children's play area (no ball games on site). Up to two dogs accepted. **Off site:** Golf 5 miles, boat launching 8 miles.

Charges 2001

Per unit incl. 2 persons	£8.25 - £8.75
extra person (over 7 yrs)	£1.00
awning (no pup tents)	£1.00 - £1.25
electricity (5A)	£1.25
dog (max. 2)	£1.00

Less 10% for 7 night bookings. Less 10% for senior citizens. No single sex groups or units over 21'6" overall length. Tel: (01924) 863938. Fax: (01924) 862226. Reservations: Advised and made with £5 deposit and 50p booking fee (min. 2 nights). **Open** 1 April - 30 September.

Directions: Park entrance is off A638 Wakefield - Doncaster road, 5 miles southeast of Wakefield. Follow drive for ½ mile keeping the rose nursery on your left. O.S.GR: SE394181.

North West Tourist Board

Cheshire, Lancashire, Merseyside, Greater Manchester and the High Peaks of Derbyshire

North West Tourist Board
Swan House, Swan Meadow Road,
Wigan Pier, Wigan WN3 5BB
Tel: (01942) 821222 Fax: (01942) 820002
Internet: http://www.visitnorthwest.com

The North West Tourist Board includes the counties of Cheshire, Greater Manchester, Lanc-ashire and Merseyside, and the High Peak District of Derbyshire.

The north of England expresses itself in a scale and sternness not found in the south of the country, with some magnificent scenery. However, the area suffers from the legacy of the cotton industry and the effects of the Industrial Revolution.

Merseyside with Manchester and Liverpool was at the heart of the cotton business, expanded rapidly and then experienced economic decline. Now Greater Manchester is England's second largest urban area, boasting a very vibrant night life and, with Liverpool, brings together one of the most innovative music and arts scenes in Britain. Liverpool's once thriving docks are now clustered with museums and each pub, restaurant and corner claim a Beatles connection.

Cheshire has distinctive timber framed houses best seen in Chester, which is also a Roman city well worth visiting. Again much of the region was, and is still, industrial; cotton mills can be visited at Style.

The most well known resorts are Lancashire's Blackpool and Morecambe, still with a fairly strong working class flavour developed from the past. Brash and cheerful Blackpool with its three piers and dominated by the Tower, still attracts many visitors who go, not only to visit the Pleasure Beach with its 140 rides, but to see the famous 'illuminations' in September and October. Morecambe is more family orientated

The Peak District National Park wedged between industrial giants like Manchester, Sheffield, Nottingham and Stoke on Trent, serves as a play-ground to 17 million urban neighbours and receives over 26 million visitors a year.

Photo: Blackpool; North West Tourist Board

Abbey Farm Caravan Park

528 Dark Lane, Ormskirk, Lancashire L40 5TX

This quiet, well equipped, family park beside the Abbey ruins has views over open farmland. It is an ideal base for a longer stay with plenty of interest in the local area, including Ormskirk parish church, unusual for having both a tower and a spire. Market days are on Thursday and Saturday. The park is divided into small paddocks, one of which is for 44 privately owned seasonal units, one for tents, the others for touring units, plus a rally field for special events. The 60 touring pitches, all with electricity (10 or 16A), are on neatly mown level grass, separated by small shrubs and colourful flower borders. Some mature trees provide shade in parts. Amenities include a farm walk and a small, free lending library with a good stock of tourist information. The site organises two events annually - a barbecue in early June and a Bonfire Night in November. Wigan Pier, the British Commercial Vehicle Museum, Aintree for the Grand National, the annual Beatles Festival or Southport Flower Show and Martin Mere Nature reserve are some of the attractions within easy reach. A member of the Countryside Discovery group.

Facilities: The main toilet block is modern, heated and spotless, providing controllable hot showers, hand and hair dryers, plus a dual purpose family bathroom, that includes facilities for disabled people. A second smaller unit with individual shower, WC and washbasin cubicles should now be open. Dishwashing sinks are under cover at both units and a laundry room has washing machine, dryer, spinner, ironing board and airing cupboard. A little well stocked shop shares space with reception, with a butcher calling twice weekly. Children have a whole field to themselves, with a small adventure playground and space for ball games. Fishing lake on site for exclusive use of customers (£2 per rod, per day).

Charges guide

Per unit incl. 2 adults standard pitch	£7.75 - £10.75,
serviced pitch	£10.75 - £12.00
extra adult	£1.75
child (5-15 yrs)	£1.00
awning	50p - £1.50
electricity	£1.50 - £2.00

Less 10% for 7 nights booked on or before arrival. Credit cards accepted. Tel/Fax: (01695) 572686. Reservations: Essential for high season or B.Hs. Min charge 3 nights for B.Hs. + £10 deposit. **Open** all year.

Directions: From M6 junction 27 take A5209 (Parbold) road. After 5 miles turn left (just before garage) onto B5240, and then first right into Hob Cross Lane, following signs to site. O.S.GR: SD433099.

Royal Umpire Caravan Park

529 Southport Road, Croston, nr Preston, Lancashire PR5 7JB

Royal Umpire is a spacious park near the coast and the M6 for overnight or longer stays. The entrance to the park is past a large grass area leading to the security barrier with the shop and reception immediately to the left, and slightly ahead, an unusual sunken garden area that is a pleasing feature. Comprising 58 acres, the park has 200 pitches, almost all with 10A electricity, but a few with 16A. About 75% of the pitches now have gravel hardstanding, some with TV and water connections. Tarmac and gravel roads connect the various pitch areas. A good choice of pubs serving bar or restaurant meals is nearby. Gates closed 11 pm. - 7 am. A member of the Best of British group.

Facilities: The two tiled toilet blocks, one beside reception, are an excellent feature. Fully equipped laundry. Dishwashing sinks. Very good facilities for disabled visitors that are shared with baby facilities (entrance with key, £5 deposit). Motorcaravan services. Licensed shop. Large indoor recreation area, somewhat rugged, but effective, with table tennis, pool and various games. Adventure playground. Field area for ball games. Leisure area with outdoor draughts and other games. Rally field. **Off site:** A short walk takes you to the nearby river for fishing. Riding 2 miles.

Charges guide

Per grass pitch incl. 2 persons,	
electricity and awning	£8.20 - £12.70
hardstanding pitch	£9.20 - £13.70
'Royal' pitch	£11.20 - £15.90
'Super Royal'	£12.20 - £17.00
extra adult	£2.50
extra child (5-16 yrs)	£1.70

Less 10% for 7 nights pre-booked. Mid-week stays less. Tel: (01772) 600257. Fax: (01772) 600662. Reservations: Made with £5 per night deposit and £1 fee. **Open** all year.

Directions: From north use M6 exit 28 joining A49 going south (parallel to M6) for 2 miles. Then right across M6 on A581 to Croston (approx. 4 miles). From the south use M6 exit 27 onto A5209 but immediately right on B5250 and follow towards Eccleston, joining A581 at Newtown (approx. 5 miles). Site is clearly signed with wide entrance east of Croston. O.S.GR: SD505189.

Pipers Height Caravan and Camping Park

Peel Road, Peel, Blackpool, Lancashire FY4 5JT

531

Only 4 miles south of Blackpool, this well-run, value-for-money, family park is a useful alternative to the larger holiday sites nearer to town, and is also convenient for visiting Lytham St Anne's with its attractive gardens. There are 140 pitches with electricity (10A) on concrete hardstandings and a further grassy area for tents which also has a small adventure type playground in one corner. Unlike many sites in this area, there are only 28 holiday homes at Pipers Height. Due to its rather flat and exposed location it can be windy at times, even with two grassy dividing banks topped with small trees and shrubs, and there are no dividing hedges between the pitches. The large club room/lounge with bar and restaurant is open evenings in peak season and weekends at other times, providing disco or cabaret entertainment during peak season. Family groups are encouraged at this well-run park.

Facilities: The modern sanitary unit, which can be heated, provides a separate unit for disabled visitors. A refundable deposit (£4) is payable for the amenity building key which includes a barrier card for entry. Dishwashing sinks. Laundry with washing machine and dryer. Club room, bar and restaurant. Small shop stocking basic supplies and gas (open mid-peak season). Games room with pool table and TV. Commercial vehicles are not accepted. **Off site:** Hourly bus service to Blackpool. Riding 1 mile, golf 3 miles.

Charges 2001

Per unit incl. up to 4 adults	£12.00
extra adult	£2.00
child (3-12 yrs)	£1.00
awning	£1.50
electricity	£1.50

Reduced rates for low season. No credit cards. Tel: (01253) 763767. Reservations: Essential for B.Hs, peak season and the illuminations (Sept/Oct) and made with £10 deposit. **Open** 1 March - 30 November.

Directions: From M6 junction 32 take M55 towards Blackpool. Leave at junction 4, taking first left off roundabout, straight on at second roundabout, then right at traffic lights into Peel Road, where site is signed. O.S.GR: SD355327.

Kneps Farm Holiday Park

River Road, Stanah, Thornton-Cleveleys, Lancashire FY5 5LR

530

A well established park with top class modern facilities, Kneps Farm is still operated by the family who opened it in 1967. It is adjacent to Wyre Country Park and makes an excellent base from which to explore the area. A card operated barrier system flanks the reception building which also houses a well stocked shop. The 70 marked and numbered touring pitches are generally on hardstandings with electricity (10A) available to most, and all are accessed from tarmac roads. There are also some grassy pitches and a separate area with 80 caravan holiday homes (most privately owned). A path leads through a gate at the back of the site into the country park. Just down the lane is a public slip-way and the Wyreside Ecology Centre. A list and map are provided of local services and amenities, including pubs, restaurants, takeaway, etc. Other local attractions include Marsh Mill Village with a restored windmill, the Freeport Shopping and Leisure village at nearby Fleetwood (discount shopping), and several bird-watching sites around the estuary and country park.

Facilities: The excellent, large, centrally heated sanitary building is warm and inviting with ten individual family bathrooms, each providing a WC, basin and bath/shower. Separate toilet facilities with electric hand-wash units for men and women. Well equipped room for disabled visitors. Dishwashing sinks. Combined baby care/first aid room. Laundry room with washing machines, dryers, spinner and ironing facility. Shop. Small, fenced children's playground. Up to two dogs are accepted per unit. **Off site:** Fishing ½ mile, golf 2½ miles.

Charges 2001

Per unit incl. 2 adults and 2 children	£12.50 - £16.00
adult couple	£10.00 - £12.50
single adult	£7.50 - £9.25
extra adult	£2.00 - £3.00
extra child	£1.25 - £1.75
electricity	£1.75 - £2.25

Special Senior Citizen rates. Deposit for barrier card and amenity unit key £10. Tel: (01253) 823632. Fax (01253) 863967. Reservations: Essential for B.Hs. and peak season and illuminations, and made with £10 deposit. **Open** 1 March - 15 November.

Directions: From M55 junction 3, take A585 towards Fleetwood. Turn right at traffic lights by Shell station (for Thornton-Cleveleys), straight across next traffic lights, then right at the next roundabout by River Wyre Hotel. After one mile (past school) turn right at mini-roundabout into Stanah Road, continue across second mini-roundabout and eventually into River Road with site entrance ahead of you. O.S.GR: SD350430.

Willowbank Touring Park

536 Coastal Road, Ainsdale, Southport, Lancashire PR8 3ST

Well situated for the Sefton coast and Southport, Willowbank is a new park still under development. It was only in its fourth season when we visited, and things take time and money. The touring park is on the edge of sand dunes amongst mature, wind swept trees. Entrance is controlled by a barrier, with a pass-key issued at the excellent reception building which doubles as a sales office for the substantial static development that is underway at the same site. The owner/operators, Mike and Janet, are very well supported on the touring side by Norman and Christine Roberts who have considerable experience in managing touring parks and have encouraged the development of the touring pitches. Already there are 18 gravel hardstanding pitches, with more planned. Eventually the park will have 99 pitches, but presently only 54 are developed, all with 16A electricity. The park does not accept motorhomes longer than 27 feet. There could be a little noise at times from the nearby main road. This is a young park, being enthusiastically developed.

Facilities: A purpose built, heated toilet block has been developed to a high standard including an excellent bathroom for disabled visitors, although the showers are rather compact. Baby room. Small dishwashing room. Laundry with washing machine and dryer. **Off site:** Beaches and sand dunes are everywhere. Martin Mere, the town of Southport and the hallowed Royal Birkdale are just down the road.

Charges 2001

Per unit incl. 2 adults: standard pitch	£8.00 - £11.00
serviced pitch	£9.50 - £12.50
extra adult	£2.10
child (5-16 yrs)	£1.60
hardstanding	£1.00
dog	50p
backpacker/cyclist	£3.50

Less 5% for stays over 7 days or more. Tel/Fax: (01704) 571566. E-mail: mail@willowbankcp.co.uk. Reservations: Made with £5 deposit and £1 fee. **Open** all year excl. 11 Jan - 28 Feb.

Directions: Park is 4 miles south of Southport. From A565 in Ainsdale turn into Coastal road by traffic lights 1½ miles south of the town centre. O.S.GR: SD308108.

Holgates Caravan Park

535 Middlebarrow Plain, Cove Road, Silverdale, Carnforth, Lancashire LA5 0SH

This attractive, very high quality park is in an outstanding craggy, part-wooded, hillside location with fine views over Morecambe Bay. It takes 70 touring units, with 339 privately owned caravan holiday homes and 11 to rent located in woodland away from the tourist pitches. With just 5 grassy pitches for tents, the remaining 65 large touring pitches, all with electricity (16A), free TV connection, individual drainage and water points are on gravel hardstandings. The main complex, with reception and the entrance barrier, has recently been redeveloped. It provides a well stocked supermarket, boutique, lounge bar, restaurant with good value meals and a terrace with views over the bay. There is also a new heated indoor swimming pool (17 x 17 m; with lifeguard) with a spa pool, steam room and sauna (all free to campers, no unaccompanied under 10s). Children have a choice of two adventure playgrounds and plenty of space for ball games. Also on site is a small but challenging golf course (75p per person). Everything is completed to the highest standards.

Facilities: Two modern, heated toilet buildings, built from local stone, are fully equipped with top quality fittings and including some private cubicles with WC and washbasin. Dishwashing sinks are at each block. Excellent separate provision for disabled visitors with a reserved pitch and parking bay adjacent. Launderette. Shop. Bar and restaurant. Swimming pool. Children's playgrounds. Games room with pool table and video games. Gas is available. Facilities are limited mid-week in January and early February. Admission restrictions include no unaccompanied under 18's or single sex groups, no dangerous breeds of dog or commercial vehicles. **Off site:** Riding, cycling, walking and fishing all within 7 miles. Morecambe or Lancaster are just 12 miles and Kendal 15 miles.

Charges 2001

Per unit incl. 2 adults and 2 children	£10.00 - £20.50
extra adult	£4.50
extra child (5-17 yrs)	£2.50
awning/pup tent	£2.00
electricity (16A)	£2.50

Minimum stays apply for all B.H. weekends. Tel: (01524) 701508. Fax: (01524) 701580. E-mail: caravan@holgates.co.uk. Reservations: Essential for B.Hs and peak season; made with £10 deposit for 1 or 2 nights, £20 for longer. **Open** all year except 3 Nov. - 21 Dec. incl.

Directions: From traffic lights in centre of Carnforth take road to Silverdale under low bridge (12' 9"). After 1 mile turn left signed Silverdale and after 2½ miles over a level crossing carry on and then turn right at T junction. Follow the Holgates signs from here watching for left fork followed by right fork (narrow roads). O.S.GR: SD460755.

Cumbria Tourist Board

Cumbria Tourist Board
Ashleigh, Holly Road, Windermere LA23 2AQ
Main brochure line: 08075 133059 Fax: (015394) 44041
E-mail: mail@cumbria-tourist-board.co.uk

Internet: http://www.gocumbria.co.uk

From the tallest mountain in England to the deepest lake, from the country's steepest roads to the world's biggest liar – Cumbria has a lot to offer and it is no surprise so many visitors return year after year. The heart of the county is the Lake District National Park, well known for the dramatic scenery of mountains and lakes which inspired the lake poets including William Wordsworth and formed the setting for Beatrix Potter's many characters.

Each valley and lake has its own character and charm from powerboats on Windermere to sailing boats on Derwentwater, from the rolling hills east of Coniston Water to the rugged drama of Ulls-water's surrounding mountains. While the Lake District is well known, there are also many quiet, undiscovered areas including the wild moors of the north Pennines and the peaceful green Eden Valley.

In the north, the city of Carlisle still bears of the marks of a turbulent history. Tullie House Museum & Art Gallery, highlights that violent past from the Romans and the Border Reivers to the present day.

The contrasts of Cumbria are best seen in the west where the Lakeland fells drop down to a long and varied coastline. There are many undiscovered and quiet corners from Ennerdale and Eskdale to the sandstone cliffs of St Bees Head, part of a designated Heritage Coast. The Georgian town of Whitehaven was once Britain's third largest port and is now undergoing its renaissance and developing as a major new tourism centre.

The southern coast of Cumbria – the Lake District Peninsulas – were recent winners of the English Holiday Destination of the Year largely due to its spectacular scenery and the mildest climate in the North. This corner of the county has its fun side too with Ulverston not only being home to the world's only Laurel and Hardy Museum but also the birthplace of Quakerism and pole vaulting.

Compact and accessible, Cumbria is a region which can offer something for every taste with many undiscovered and quiet corners waiting to be explored. It is no surprise that National Geographic Traveller Magazine listed the county as one of 50 places in the world which had to be seen in a lifetime.

Newlands Valley - Cumbria TB

Walls Caravan and Camping Park

553 Ravenglass, Cumbria CA18 1SR

Once part of the large Pennington Estate in western Cumbria, Walls is a small, neat park set in five acres of existing woodland amongst a variety of mature trees. It has space for 25 touring units on hardstanding pitches with a grass verge for awnings (plus 25 seasonal units). A circular gravel road provides access and all pitches have electrical hook-ups (10A). A small grass area at the top and back of the park provides a pleasant spot for 10 tents overlooking fields. An attractively designed central courtyard complex includes the owner's home, reception and facilities. All is excellently maintained by Keith and Stephanie Bridges, who provide a very warm welcome and have used the site since it was first developed and now own it. It is a useful site for all sorts of walking – estuary, river or fell – or to explore the Cumbria coast with its Roman connections, the western Lake District or to enjoy the Ravenglass and Eskdale Miniature Railway.

Facilities: The good modern toilet block with all the usual amenities, is well kept with a comfortable feeling often missing in British campsite toilet blocks. Fully equipped laundry room and dishwashing facilities. Motorcaravan service point. Shop (only a few basic necessities, plus gas). **Off site:** Fishing and bicycle hire 3 miles, boat launching 1½ miles, golf 6 miles. The small village of Ravenglass, a single, cottage lined street, is within walking distance, has a pub and holds a Charter Fair in June. Daily bus service runs from Whitehaven to Barrow calling at Ravenglass, or trains from the local station to Carlisle and Barrow.

Charges 2002

Per caravan, frame or trailer tent incl. 2 adults	£9.00
motorcaravan	£8.50
medium tent (2 persons)	£8.00
small tent (1 person)	£4.00
extra person	£1.00
child under 16 yrs	free
awning	£1.00
dog	50p
electricity	£1.75

No credit cards. Tel: (01229) 717250. E-mail: wallscaravanpark@ravenglass98.freeserve.co.uk. Reservations: Contact park. **Open** 1 March - 31 October.

Directions: Park is just off A595 (between Egremont and Millom) on road into village of Ravenglass. O.S.GR: SD096965.

Skelwith Fold Caravan Park

552 Ambleside, Cumbria LA22 0HX

Skelwith Fold has been developed in the extensive grounds of a country estate taking advantage of the wealth of mature trees and shrubs. The 300 privately owned caravan holiday homes and 150 touring pitches are absorbed into this unspoilt natural environment, sharing it with red squirrels and other wildlife in several discrete areas branching off the central, mile long main driveway. Touring pitches (no tents) are on gravel hardstanding and metal pegs will be necessary for awnings. Electricity hook-ups (10A) and basic amenities are available in all areas. Youngsters and indeed their parents will find endless pleasure exploring over 90 acres of wild woodland and, if early risers, it is possible to see deer, foxes, etc. taking their breakfast in the almost hidden tarn deep in the woods. This is a fascinating site where you feel at home with nature at any time of the year, but it is particularly beautiful in the spring with wild daffodils, bluebells and later rhododendrons and azaleas. Only caravans, motorcaravans and trailer tents are accepted.

Facilities: Eight toilet blocks, well situated to serve all areas, have the usual facilities including laundry, drying and ironing rooms. Well stocked, licensed self-service shop, together with a store for gas, battery charging and caravan spares and accessories. Adventure play area. Family recreation area with picnic tables and goal posts in the Lower Glade. **Off site:** Ambleside village 1½ miles. Pubs within walking distance.

Charges guide

Per caravan or trailer tent	£11.00
motorcaravan	£10.50
awning	£2.50
electricity	£1.75

Discounts for weekly or monthly stays. Tel: (015394) 32277. Fax: (015394) 34344. Reservations: Essential for July/Aug and B.Hs. and made for min. 3 days with £10 deposit. **Open** 1 March - 15 November.

Directions: From Ambleside take the A593 in the direction of Coniston. Pass through Clappergate and on the far outskirts watch for the B5286 to Hawkshead on the left. Park is clearly signed approx. 1 mile down this road on the right. O.S.GR: NY358028.

Limefitt Park

Windermere, Cumbria LA23 1PA

Limefitt Park is owned and run by the Whiteley family, who also own Fallbarrow Park, and is centrally situated for the southern Lakes. It is a well managed and popular park with fine views and walks, alongside the beck. With various active pursuits nearby and some evening entertainment, it is designed for families or couples (no organised groups of young people). There are 85 pitches with hardstanding for touring caravans or motorcaravans (20 seasonal). Each has electricity (10A), fresh water tap and waste water point. Cars are parked at an angle on hardstanding in front of each pitch. There are 38 fully serviced pitches for tents or tourers and further pitches for tents, or more caravans and motorcaravans on flat or slightly sloping grass with some terracing and shade provided by trees. The ground by the beck has been developed for log cabins and caravan holiday homes. Activities include walking and fishing, and many local facilities, including bicycle hire, can be booked from the park. American motorhomes, dogs, boats, single persons, groups and rallies are not accepted; to quote, "in order to preserve Limefitt's unique atmosphere and provide restful nights ... we accept families and couples only." The park is popular all season so reservation is recommended.

Facilities: Sanitary facilities consist of one large, central block for the tenting area and a smaller block for the caravan area, accessed by combination locks. Both are of excellent quality, well equipped with modern fittings. Part of one building is dedicated to three toddlers' rooms with half-size bath and changing facilities. Covered washing up and vegetable preparation areas. Camper's kitchen. Launderette. Motorcaravan service point. Supermarket. Bar (real ales), bar meals and takeaway, all open all season. Weekly entertainment. Gas available. Games room with many machines. Away from the camping area is a play field and adventure playground on grass by the river and a small beach area with picnic tables. Dogs are not accepted. **Off site:** Riding 3 miles, golf 5 miles.

Charges 2001

Per unit incl. 2 persons,	
electricity and TV hook-up	£9.50 - £13.00
tent	£9.50 - £13.00
extra adult	£2.00 - £2.50
child (2-14 yrs)	£1.00 - £1.25
awning, pup tent, trailer or 2nd car	£2.00 - £2.50

Max. charge 1 family per pitch £11.50 - £15.50 (excl. supplements). Prices are higher for stays not booked in advance. Tel: (015394) 32300 ext. 49. Fax: (015394) 32848. Reservations: Made with full payment at time of booking; cancellation insurance available. **Open** 22 March - 3 November.

Directions: Limefitt Park lies 2½ miles north up the A592 from its junction with the A591 north of Windermere. O.S.GR: NY416030.

The Larches Caravan Park

Mealsgate, Wigton, Cumbria CA7 1LQ

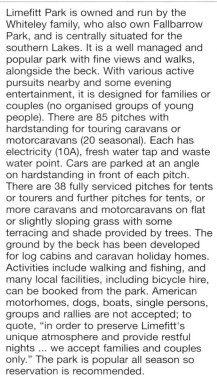

Mealsgate and The Larches lie on the Carlisle – Cockermouth road, a little removed from the hectic centre of the Lake District, yet with easy access to it (and good views towards it) and to other nearby attractions – the Western Borders, Northumberland, etc. It is a quality, family run park which takes 73 touring units of any type and 100 privately owned holiday homes. Touring pitches are in different grassy areas with tall, mature trees, shrubs and accompanying wildlife. Some are sloping and irregular, others on marked hardstandings, with electricity (10A), water and waste water. A well stocked shop, includes gas, camping accessories and off-licence, with events in the surrounding district each day displayed prominently in the window. On arrival everyone is loaned very comprehensive tourist information brochures. The Elliott family provide a warm welcome at this peaceful, well organised park, which is an ideal haven for couples - only adult visitors are accepted.

Facilities: Toilet facilities, in two purpose designed blocks, are of good quality providing en-suite facilities for both sexes. Washbasins for ladies are in cubicles, those for men are set in flat surfaces. A separate unit for disabled visitors can be heated. Laundry room. Camping kitchen with breakfast bar and metered power to a cooker and microwave. Shop. Small indoor heated pool. Table tennis. TV room. Caravan storage. **Off site:** Bus routes to Carlisle and Keswick, walks from the park and good restaurants nearby. Fishing 8 miles, bicycle hire 7 miles, riding 10 miles, golf 3½ miles.

Charges 2002

Per unit incl. 2 adults	£8.00 - £10.00
backpacker	£4.00 - £5.00
extra person, awning or car	£1.00
electricity	£2.00

Discounts for senior citizens and bookings over 7 nights. No credit cards. Tel: (016973) 71379. Fax: (016973) 71782. E-mail: melarches@btinternet.co.uk. Reservations: Made with £1 per night deposit, balance on arrival. **Open** 1 March - 31 October.

Directions: Park entrance is south off A595 (Carlisle - Cockermouth) road just southwest of Mealsgate. O.S.GR: NY206415.

Fallbarrow Park

554

Rayrigg Road, Bowness, Windermere, Cumbria LA23 3DL

Fallbarrow Park is most attractively situated alongside Lake Windermere with a lake frontage of about 600 m; one can stroll among the lawns and gardens near the lake. The park is owned and managed by its founders, the Whiteley family, who are committed to caring for the country-side and raise funds for the District Tourism and Conservation Partnership. The major part of the park is occupied by 260 seasonal holiday homes, but in the 'Lake' area (not actually by the lake, but some pitches have lake views), there are 38 fenced or hedged touring pitches, all with hardstanding, fresh and waste water points, electric hook-up (10/16A) and TV aerial connection. Reception is smart and comfortable, with much tourist information. The Boathouse pub has a spacious and comfortable lounge with bar meals and snacks, a separate restaurant section with varied menu and table service, and an attractive outdoor terrace. TV lounge with occasional entertainment and a large games room with pool table and games machines. The site has a boat park with winter storage and two launching ramps and three jetties can cater for craft up to 18 ft in length.

Facilities: Two excellent toilet blocks serve the touring sections (combination locks) with top quality fittings and heating when required, controllable showers, make up and hairdressing areas and a baby washroom. Dishwashing sinks. Very well equipped laundry which also houses a freezer. Motorcaravan service point. Gas is available at the well stocked supermarket. Restaurant. Bar. American motorhomes are accepted by prior arrangement. Pet area. Fishing on site. Dogs are accepted, but only one per booking (exercise area provided). **Off site**: The centre of Bowness is only a short walk and facilities for pony trekking and numerous visitor attractions are close. Bicycle hire 1 mile, golf 3 miles.

Charges 2001

Per unit inclusive	£14.50 - £20.50
awning	£2.95 - £4.00
boat (max 18 ft.)	£10.00
sailboard or canoe	£2.00

Tel: (015394) 44422, ext. 49. Fax: (015394) 88736. Reservations: Made for 3 nights min. (7 at Spring BH). Payment in full at time of booking. Fallbarrow Park is very popular and reservations are essential for June - Sept. and B.Hs. **Open** 8 March - 9 November.

Directions: Park is beside the A592 road just north of Bowness town centre. O.S.GR: SD401971.

Sykeside Camping Park

Brotherswater, Patterdale, Penrith, Cumbria CA11 0NZ

This small, family owned touring site, set in the northern lakes area (just / mile from Brotherswater Lake) and surrounded by fells, is ideal for active holidays with walking or climbing on high hills. It would also be useful for a touring holiday being a little away from the busiest areas. The park is licensed to take 80 tents which could include 6-8 small motorcaravans, but definitely no caravans, on flat grass in the valley floor. Pitches are not marked and campers arrange themselves. There are 16 electrical connections (5/10A). The stone-built building, an original barn, near the entrance just 200 yards from the field, houses all the facilities. The family also own the Brotherswater Inn, 200 yards from the site and overlooking the fells, which is open all day including meals and has rooms to let.

Facilities: The toilet block includes hot showers (20p); a little basic but clean and functional. No chemical disposal point although one is planned for near the toilet block. Small launderette and dishwashing room. Self-service shop with camping equipment, gas and an ice-pack service, doubles as reception. Cosy, licensed bar and restaurant serving breakfast (8.15-10 am) and evening meals during peak periods (6-9 pm, bar open 5-11 pm). Bunkhouse accommodation provided for 30 persons in various groupings. Fishing available nearby. **Off site:** Bicycle hire 3 miles, riding 8 miles, golf 10 miles.

Charges 2002

Per adult	£2.20 - £2.75
child (4-14 yrs)	£1.50
car or m/cycle	£2.20 - £2.75
motorcaravan, tent or awning	£2.20 - £2.75
dog	£1.00
electricity	£1.60

Min. charge for motorcaravan £5 per night. Tel: (017684) 82239. Fax: (017684) 82558. Reservations: Made with £15 per pitch deposit (not possible to book electric hook-up) with balance on arrival. Easter or Spr. B.H. - min. booking, 3 and 4 days respectively. Reservation is essential in peak seasons. **Open** all year.

Directions: On west side of A592 road about 2 miles south of Patterdale, which lies at the southwestern end of Ullswater - entrance is just behind the Brotherswater Inn. (Note: the road is narrow and hilly, and not suitable for touring caravans and large motorhomes). O.S.GR: NY396005.

Waterfoot Caravan Park

561 Pooley Bridge, Penrith, Cumbria CA11 0JF

Waterfoot is a quiet family park for caravans and motorcaravans only. It is set in 22 acres of partially wooded land, developed in the fifties from a private estate. The 126 private caravan holiday homes are quite separate from 57 touring pitches. Lake Ullswater is only about 400 yards away and a half mile stroll through bluebell woods brings you to the village of Pooley Bridge. Waterfoot's touring pitches are arranged very informally in a large clearing. Most are level, there are some hardstandings and all have 10A electricity. Several pitches are long enough for American RVs, although there is quite a tight corner leading into the main touring area. There is a bar in a large, imposing mansion, in the past a family home then a golf hotel. Public footpaths lead straight from the park. The regular lake steamer service calls at Pooley Bridge, Ullswater yacht club is only 10 minutes drive and the market town of Penrith is 5 miles.

Facilities: The heated toilet block includes some washbasins and showers in cubicles which are activated by a button on the wall outside the cubicle giving five minutes showering time. Large, light and airy dishwashing room and fully equipped laundry. Small shop selling basics, gas and newspapers. Bar with strictly enforced, separate family room open weekend evenings in low season and every evening in high season. Large fenced field with play equipment to suit all ages and goal posts for football. **Off site:** Fishing close, boat slipway or riding 1½ miles, golf 5 miles. Pooley Bridge has a post office/general store, hotels and restaurants. The historic house and gardens of Dalemain are a short walk.

Charges guide

Per unit	£12.00
with electricity	£14.00

No credit cards. Tel: (017684) 86302. Fax: (017684) 86728. Reservations: Essential for B.Hs and summer holidays; contact the Warden. **Open** 1 March - 31 October.

Directions: From M6 junction 40, take A66 signed Keswick. After ½ mile at roundabout take A592 signed Ullswater and site is on right after 4 miles. O.S.GR: NY460245.

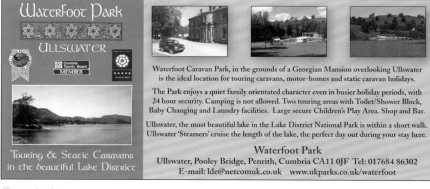

Waterfoot Caravan Park, in the grounds of a Georgian Mansion overlooking Ullswater is the ideal location for touring caravans, motor-homes and static caravan holidays.

The Park enjoys a quiet family orientated character even in busier holiday periods, with 24 hour security. Camping is not allowed. Two touring areas with Toilet/Shower Block, Baby Changing and Laundry facilities. Large secure Children's Play Area. Shop and Bar.

Ullswater, the most beautiful lake in the Lake District National Park is within a short walk. Ullswater 'Steamers' cruise the length of the lake, the perfect day out during your stay here.

Waterfoot Park
Ullswater, Pooley Bridge, Penrith, Cumbria CA11 0JF Tel: 017684 86302
E-mail: lde@netcomuk.co.uk   www.ukparks.co.uk/waterfoot

Pennine View Caravan and Camping Park

560 Station Road, Kirkby Stephen, Cumbria CA17 4SZ

Pennine View was opened in 1990 and is built on reclaimed land from a former railway goods yard. Suitable for night halts or longer breaks, it is a super small park, well managed and well maintained. With a very attractive rockery at the entrance, the whole site is very neat and tidy. Level, numbered pitches with gravel hardstandings are arranged around the perimeter with grass pitches in the centre. The pitches are of a good size (some being especially large) and are all are supplied with electricity hook-ups (16A). One end of the park adjoins the River Eden with steps leading down from the site to huge projecting stone slabs on the river bank (good for sunbathing). There are trout but a licence is needed for fishing.

Facilities: Built of local stone, the modern toilet block is accessed by a digital keypad and includes individual wash cubicles and deep sink for a baby bath. Both ladies and men have a large en-suite unit for disabled visitors. Well equipped laundry room. Dishwashing sinks under cover. Gas available. **Off site:** A nearby hotel offers bar and takeaway pizzas. Kirkby Stephen 1 mile and, although only a small town, its shops should fill most needs.

Charges guide

Per adult	£3.60 - £3.80
child (4-15 yrs)	£1.40
pitch	£1.00 - £2.00
electricity	£1.50 - £2.00
cyclist or backpacker per person	£3.60 - £4.00

Tel: (017683) 71717. Reservations: Made with £5 deposit; min. 3 days Easter and B.Hs. **Open** 1 March - 31 October.

Directions: Park is on the A685 on the southerly outskirts of Kirkby Stephen (just under a mile from the town centre). Turn left at small site sign opposite the Croglin Castle hotel. Site is 50 yds on right. O.S.GR: NY772075.

Cove Camping Park

562 Ullswater, Watermillock, nr Penrith, Cumbria CA11 0LS

Cove Camping is a delightful small site, some of the 50 pitches having great views over Lake Ullswater. A separate area behind the camping field holds 38 privately owned caravan holiday homes. The grass is well trimmed, there are ramps to keep speeds down to 5 mph and the site is well lit. At the top of the park are 17 level pitches with electric hook-ups and one hardstanding suitable for touring caravans and motorcaravans. The rest of the site is quite sloping. Rubbish bins are hidden behind larch lap fencing, as are recycling bins. The park is well situated for walking, boating, fishing and pony trekking activities. The road up from the A592 is narrow, but a self imposed one way system is generally adhered to and the warden will advise on a different way to leave the site.

Facilities: The tiled toilet block is immaculate and heated in cooler months, providing adjustable showers, some washbasins in cabins and, for ladies, a hairdressing area with stool and a baby changing unit. Dividing the ladies' and men's facilities is a foyer containing a freezer (free), coffee machine and tourist information. Laundry with washing machine, dryer and an iron. Washing up sinks are in a separate area. Gas supplies. Small, grass based play area. **Off site:** Shop nearby. Fishing 1½ miles, riding 3 miles, golf 6 mile, bicycle hire 7 miles (will deliver).

Charges guide

Per person (over 3 yrs)	£1.80 - £1.90
caravan, motorcaravan or larger tent	£3.60 - £3.80
pup tent or awning	£1.80 - £1.90
car, boat or m/cycle	£1.80 - £1.90
dog	50p

No credit cards. Tel/Fax: (017684) 86549. Reservations: Made with deposit (caravans or motorcaravans £10, tents £5); contact park. **Open** Easter - 31 October.

Directions: From A66 Penrith - Keswick road, take A592 south, signed Ullswater. Turn right at Brackenrigg Inn (site signed) and follow road uphill for about 1½ miles to park on left. This road is narrow so if you have a larger unit, telephone the park for advice about an alternative route. O.S.GR: NY431236.

The Ashes Caravan Park

565 New Hutton, nr Kendal, Cumbria, LA8 0AS

The Ashes is a friendly, small, adult only park in an extremely peaceful setting in the rolling Cumbrian countryside, yet less than three miles from the M6, and only slightly further from Kendal. Thus it is not only a convenient night stop, but also a useful base from which to explore the Lake District and the Yorkshire Dales. A very tidy park, the central grass area is attractively planted with shrubs and bushes, and there is an open vista with little shade. There are 24 hardstanding gravel pitches, all with electrical connections (10A), with grass for awnings. They are neatly placed around the perimeter, with an oval access road. The whole area slopes gently down from the entrance, with some pitches fairly level and others with a little more slope. No tents are accepted except trailer tents. This is an adult only park.

Facilities: A small, modernised stone building with a slate roof houses the single unisex shower and the washing and toilet facilities (no cabins) It can be heated. **Off site:** Mr and Mrs Mason have prepared a full information sheet with details of laundry, shopping, eating and many other local venues.

Charges 2001

Per unit incl. 2 adults and electricity	£8.50 - £10.50
extra person (over 18's only)	£2.50
awning	£1.50
extra car/trailer	£1.00

No credit cards. Tel/Fax: (01539) 731833. E-mail: ashes-new-hutton@cwcom.net. Reservations: Advisable in July and August. **Open** 1 March - 15 November.

Directions: From M6 junction 37 follow the A684 towards Kendal for 2 miles. Just past a farm B&B and a white cottage turn sharp left at crossroads signed New Hutton. Site is on right in ¾ mile at a left bend. O.S.GR: SD560908.

Wild Rose Park

557 Ormside, Appleby-in-Westmorland, Cumbria CA16 6EJ

Set in the Eden Valley within easy reach of the Lake District and the Yorkshire Dales, Wild Rose is a well known park with an excellent reputation. The entrance is very inviting with its well mown grass, trim borders and colourful flower displays and impressive 'state of the art' entrance barrier and intercom system. It is immediately apparent that this is a much loved park, and this is reflected throughout the site in the care and attention to detail. There are three touring areas, two with their own warden to ensure that everything is always spick and span. The top areas have been upgraded to provide neat, level, fully serviced pitches These are separated by hedges (plus a small fence until the hedge grows) and many have views. The lower touring area on a slightly sloping field caters for both tents and caravans. Next to this are six individual 'super' pitches, fenced or hedged with full services, some including patio, barbecue, picnic table, grass area and satellite TV connections. Privately owned caravan holiday homes occupy their own areas and do not intrude. The final touring field is for 60 tents, gently sloping with an oval roadway linked to the large field or ball game area with its special viewpoint. Wild Rose deserves its excellent reputation, which the owners strive to maintain and improve. Nothing is overlooked from recycling bins, electric dust carts to keep the noise down, 'sac-o-matic' special bags in the dog walk and cycle racks placed around the park. A member of the Best of British group.

Facilities: The three toilet blocks (two heated) are of excellent quality and kept spotlessly clean. Most washbasins are in cubicles, and there are hair-washing basins, baby baths and bottle warmers, full facilities for disabled visitors, and a fully equipped laundry with washing lines and drying rooms. Motorcaravan service point. Exceptionally well stocked shop (with gas). Licensed restaurant with takeaway and conservatory/coffee lounge (all 1/4-5/11), good for Sunday lunches. Outdoor pool kidney shaped pool with sunbathing area (heated mid-May - mid-Sept and open 10 am.- 10 pm). Well kept, fenced play area. Indoor playroom for under fives. Games room with table tennis and video games for older children and two TV rooms, one with a cinema style screen. Bicycle hire. BMX track. Half court tennis. Field for ball games. Certain breeds of dog are not accepted. Caravan storage. **Off site**: Fishing, golf or riding within 4 miles.

Charges 2001

Per unit incl. 2 persons: standard	£7.80 - £13.30
super pitch	£13.50 - £25.00
walker or cyclist	£3.50
extra person (over 4 yrs)	£1.60
awning, toilet or pup tent	£1.90
electricity	summer £2.00, winter £2.50
dog	50p

Less 10% for 7 nights or more. Special winter or long-stay rates. Tel: (017683) 51077. Fax: (017683) 52551. E-mail: mail@wildrose.co.uk. Reservations: Essential for B.Hs and July/Aug; made with deposit of £5 per night + £2 fee, remainder on arrival. Min. 3 nights at B.Hs. **Open** all year.

Directions: Park is signed south off B6260 road 1½ miles southwest of Appleby. Follow signs to park, in the direction of Ormside. O.S.GR: NY697165.

Westmorland Caravan Site

559 Tebay, Orton, nr Penrith, Cumbria CA10 3SB

For caravans and motorcaravans only, this is the ideal stopover for anyone heading either north or south, near the M6 motorway, but far enough away for the traffic noise not to be too disturbing. There are 77 level pitches on gravel, divided into bays of about six or seven units (41 for touring units, 34 seasonal and 7 for caravan holiday homes). All touring pitches have electricity (10/16A). The bays are backed by grassy banks alive with rabbits and birds – a long list in the office describes the large variety of birds to be seen on the site. There is good site lighting and a late arrivals area.

Facilities: The heated toilet block is kept very clean. Showers are pre-set and coin operated (10p) with all other hot water free. Sinks for laundry and dishwashing. Laundry. Reception sells gas. **Off site**: Shops, restaurants and a bar five minutes walk away at the motorway service area (awarded 'Best Motorway Service Station in England 2000').

Charges guide

Per unit	£8.50 - £9.50
awning	£1.00 - £1.50
electricity	£1.85

OAPs less £1. Special rates for 3, 5 or 7 days. Discount on hotel and café meals. No credit cards. Tel/Fax: (015396) 24511. Reservations: Advised for B.Hs and July/Aug. **Open** mid-March - end October.

Directions: From the M6, just north of junction 38, exit for Tebay Services (site signed). Site is accessible from the services travelling north or south. O.S.GR: NY607060.

Northumbria Tourist Board

Northumberland, Durham, Tyne and Wear and Teeside

Northumbria Tourist Board
Aykley Heads, Durham DH1 5UX
Tel: (0191) 375 3000 Fax: (0191) 386 0899
E-mail: enquiries@ntb.org.uk

Internet: http://www.visitnorthumbria.com

Northumbria covers the counties of Northumberland, Durham, Tyne and Wear and the Teeside area. Even before the Victorians invented tourism travellers were drawn to this vast empty area between England's industrial belt and the rugged wilderness of Scotland, bisected by the Pennine Mountains and the start of the Pennine Way. Proud castles, glorious coastline and unspoilt countryside, with a spirit of history and a buzzing modern life - that's Northumbria today.

The Pennine Way was the country's first official long-distance path and still the longest (268 miles), stretching from the Peak National Park to the border. Northumberland borders Scotland and is an ancient rugged area dotted with forts from its passionate past when the Scottish raiding parties ventured south.

The 400 square mile Northumberland National Park stretches south from the now peaceful Cheviot Hills near the border, through the Simonside Hills, to the crags of Whin Sill, where it engulfs part of Hadrian's Wall. When the Romans ruled, this line marked the northern limit of their Empire. The surviving sections of this 73 mile long fortification must be the most impressive legacy of Roman rule. The best part,

popular for walking, is along the crest of Whin Sill crags around Housesteads fort, the most complete fort on the wall.

The coastline is not to be forgotten, deserted white sandy beaches, majestic castles, including Bamburgh and islands. Lindisfarne known for its links with St Cuthbert and early Christianity and the Farnes, remembered locally through the daring of Grace Darling, now a bird sanctuary.

The small city of Durham has a more historical feel, dominated by England's greatest Norman Cathedral. Surrounded on three side by the river Wear, with cobbled medieval streets and restricted car access it is a popular with tourists.For hundreds of years Durham was a quasi-regal state called a 'palatinate' with its own currency, arms and courts with the governors and prince bishops living in the castle, divided from the cathedral by Palace Green. Today it is all part of the university, the third oldest after Oxford and Cambridge in England.

The North East was a coal-producing and ship-building area and proud of its heritage but the high-tech industries have moved in, watched over by the 'Angel of the North'.

Photo: Northumbria Tourist Board

Teeside
White Water Caravan Club Park

574 Tees Barrage A66, Thornaby, Stockton-on-Tees TS18 2QW

Being part of the multi-million pound development at the Tees Barrage, this pleasantly landscaped club site caters for all tastes, especially water sports enthusiasts. The recently opened Tees Barrage has transformed eleven miles of the Tees, providing clean, non-tidal water for many activities. The adjoining White Water Course (Britain's largest purpose-built canoe course) provides facilities for both advanced and beginner canoeists, and hosts major national and international events. Close to the site are wetlands that provide a home for a variety of birds. The site itself provides 117 pitches set in bays and hedged with bushes, all with electricity connections, plus 21 fully serviced pitches (fresh water and waste disposal) on hardstandings. The site is well lit, with a security barrier.

Facilities: The central, heated toilet block of high quality includes washbasins in cubicles, baby changing facilities and a well appointed unit for disabled visitors. Washing up sinks. Laundry room Motorcaravan service point. Play area on fine gravel. Club room with a pool table for wet weather. **Off site:** Supermarket six minutes. Hotel near the entrance. Retail and leisure park, just across barrage bridge, with 14-screen cinema, 10-pin bowling, shops and fast food outlets. North Yorkshire Moors and the Hartlepool Historic Quay within 40 minutes drive.

Charges 2001

Per pitch	£6.00
adult	£2.50 - £3.50
child (5-16 yrs)	£1.10
extra car, boat or trailer	£1.00
electricity	£1.50 (31/3-2/10) or £2.25

Tent campers apply to site. Tel: (01642) 634880. Reservations: Contact site by phone or in writing. Made with £5 deposit. **Open** all year.

Directions: From A1(M) take A66 for Darlington and follow until you pick up signs for Teeside Retail Park and the Tees Barrage. Cross railway bridge and the Barrage bridge, then first right to site on left in ¼ mile. O.S.GR: NZ463194.

Co. Durham
Doe Park Touring Caravan Park

571 Cotherstone, Barnard Castle, Co. Durham DL12 9UQ

This is Hannah Hauxwell country and the Dales, less frequented than other upland areas, provide wonderful walking country; indeed part of the Pennine Way runs near this peaceful site. The farm and park are close to where the River Balder joins the Tees at Cotherstone and the ancient oak wood beside the river is an SSSI (Site of Special Scientific Interest) for its insects and flowers, but is also a haven for bird-watchers. The park's reception is in a new log cabin at the entrance to the pitch area, although at quiet times you may be directed to the farmhouse, formerly Leadgard Hall. This is a mellow three storey, Grade II listed building with a history of its own. Mr and Mrs Lamb or son Stephen will make you very welcome and personally take you to your pitch. The camping fields have a lovely open aspect with wonderful views and the 70 pitches are spacious with well mown grass, all with 10A electricity, over 20 with hardstanding (no tents are taken). A bus service passes the park from Barnard Castle to Middleton and there is a local leisure centre with swimming pool (4 miles). The village of Cotherstone is ½ mile with post office and a restaurant with bar meals, a pleasant walk by road or river bank. Tents other than trailer tents are not accepted.

Facilities: Toilet facilities are at the farmhouse, but the two newer blocks are closer to the pitches. Built in local stone, these are good quality, fully tiled facilities, with the newest one heated. Washbasins in cabins, metered, adjustable showers (20p) and a really well appointed unisex unit for disabled visitors. Dishwashing sinks and small laundry. Eggs and milk are available from the farmhouse, plus gas supplies and battery charging. Although there is no play area, a large grass area in front of some of the pitches can be used for ball games. River fishing on site. Dogs and pets are accepted by arrangement only. **Off site:** reservoirs 3 miles, bicycle hire or golf 4 miles, riding 2 miles.

Charges guide

Per car and caravan or trailer tent	
incl. 2 persons	£6.50 - £7.50
motorcaravan	£6.00 - £7.00
extra person (over 6 yrs)	80p
full awning or extra car	£1.00
electricity	£1.80 - £1.90

Tel/Fax: (01833) 650302. Reservations: Advised for high season and made with £10 deposit (send SAE); min. 4 days at B.Hs. **Open** 1 March - 31 October.

Directions: Follow B6277 from Barnard Castle in direction of Middleton in Teesdale. The farm is signed on the left just after Cotherstone village (there is no need to go into Barnard Castle). O.S.GR: NZ005204.

Camping and Caravanning Club Site Barnard Castle

572 Dockenflatts Lane, Lartington, Barnard Castle, Co. Durham DL12 9DG

For those readers with tents who wish to visit this area, we include this Club site as unfortunately nearby Doe Park does not take tents. Also accepting non-members, the Camping and Caravanning Club site at Barnard Castle was only opened in '96. Originally level farm fields, one side of the site is bordered by mature trees and 11,000 young trees and bushes have been planted so eventually it will become an even more attractive location. Most of the 90 pitches are on grass, with 56 electrical hook-ups (16A) plus 12 hardstanding pitches which have a gravel base with room for both car and caravan and space for an awning on grass. Barnard Castle, an old town with its market cross still standing, is well worth a visit. The Bowes museum in the town is a French style chateau housing one of Britain's finest art collections. Raby Castle, near Staindrop, is an impressive mediaeval castle, formerly the seat of the powerful Neville family. Durham has a castle and cathedral (both World Heritage Sites). High Force, England's highest waterfall is about 12 miles away, and the forest of Hamsterly about 16 miles.

Facilities: The centrally located toilet facilities are of good quality and kept spotlessly clean. Washbasins are in cubicles and free, controllable showers are roomy. Dishwashing sinks, a baby room and a large, fully equipped unisex unit for visitors with disabilities. Large laundry with washing machine, dryer, iron and sink, with outside lines provided. Gas is available. Central children's play area with rubber safety base. **Off site:** Riding centre next to site. Fishing 4 miles, golf 2½ miles. A public footpath leads from the site to Barnard Castle, with a network of public footpaths in the area.

Charges 2001

Per adult	£3.75 - £5.30
child (6-18 yrs)	£1.65
non-member pitch fee	£4.30
electricity	£1.65 - £2.40

Tel: (01833) 630228, (no calls after 8 pm). Reservations: Necessary and made with deposit; contact site. **Open** March - October.

Directions: Follow B6277 from Barnard Castle (towards Middleton in Teesdale) for 1 mile to Lartington. Turn left at club sign into narrow lane with passing places to site entrance on left (there is no need to go into Barnard Castle). O.S.GR: NZ025168.

Fallowfield Dene Caravan and Camping Park

581 Acomb, Hexham, Northumberland NE46 4RP

Although only 2½ miles from Hexham, Fallowfield Dene Caravan Park is very secluded, situated in mature woodland at the end of a no-through road. Set in woodland glades, each with a Roman name (Hadrian's Wall is close), are 113 seasonal pitches and 37 touring pitches, mostly with 10A electricity. The park entrance, with reception and a small shop, is neat, tidy and very colourful. There is no play area or games field, but the surrounding woods are a children's paradise. Fallowfield Dene itself is a network of tracks and there are footpaths from the site entrance. The site is a haven for wildlife with red squirrels, foxes and badgers to be seen. Hadrian's Wall is only a mile away, with Roman forts such as Housesteads Fort and Chesters, being great attractions. In fact the whole area abounds with well preserved Roman remains. Hexham has its Border History museum, housed in the oldest purpose-built gaol in England, where one can learn about the Border Reivers. Bicycle hire can be arranged with advice on routes for exploring the area. This site has a very friendly atmosphere.

Facilities: Brick built toilet blocks (one for each sex) are central and heated in cool weather. Well tiled and kept very clean, there are washbasins in cabins and free hairdryers. A separate, fully equipped room is provided for disabled people and a laundry room with dishwashing sinks. Motorcaravan service point. Small shop for necessities, including gas. Barrier card £5 deposit. **Off site:** Supermarkets and other shops at Hexham or Corbridge. Good restaurant five minutes walk.

Charges 2001

Per adult	£3.00
child (5-17 yrs)	£1.25
car & caravan/trailer tent or motorhome	£3.00 - £4.00
tent	£2.50 - £3.00
car	£1.25
m/cycle	£1.00
awning or dog	50p
electricity	£2.00

Tel: (01434) 603553. Fax: (01434) 601252. Reservations: Made with deposit (£5 for one night, £10 for two or more); min. 3 nights at B.Hs. **Open** 1 April - 31 October.

Directions: From A69 Newcastle - Carlisle road, take A6079 north signed Bellingham and Rothbury. At village of Acomb, site is signed to right. Follow site signs for approx. 1½ miles. The last ½ mile is single track with passing places. O.S.GR: NY938676.

 Alan Rogers' discount
Stay 7 nights, pay for 6

Northumberland
Percy Wood Caravan Park
576 Swarland, Morpeth, Northumberland NE65 9JW

Percy Wood provides excellent, modern facilities whilst still maintaining the feel of camping in woodland. A lot of thought and effort has gone into developing a park which blends with its natural surroundings. Open for 11 months of the year, there are 60 level touring pitches. All have electrical connections (10A) and 20 also have hardstanding and full services. A grass tent field with 5A electricity has a more open aspect with views, and there are also 60 privately owned holiday homes. On the boundary of the park is an 18 hole golf course, with a bar and restaurant, and membership can be arranged. This is an excellent area for rambling and for nature lovers generally. The park is only 4 miles from Throughton Wood and on the bus route for Alnwick and Rothbury. Druridge Bay Country Park is near (lake visitor centre, good for watersports).

Facilities: The central sanitary block is of wooden construction (heated) and in consequence blends naturally with the woodland surroundings. Very well equipped, it includes dishwashing under cover, a laundry room and a baby room. Motorcaravan service facilities. Basic necessities and gas. Children's play area. Outdoor table tennis. Games room with two pool tables and video games. Dogs are accepted on leads (but not certain breeds) **Off site:** Village store and post office ½ mile away and local pubs and a restaurant are within a mile. Fishing 1½ miles.

Charges 2001

Per unit incl. 2 persons,	
awning and 10A electricity	£8.50 - £10.00
fully serviced pitch in July/Aug	plus £1.50
camping field incl. 2 persons, 5A electricity	£8.00
extra person (over 5 yrs)	£1.00
dog	50p

Tel: (01670) 787649. Fax: (01670) 787034. E-mail: enquiries@percywood.freeserve.co.uk. Reservations: Made with 10% non-refundable deposit (min. £10). **Open** all year except February.

Directions: Park is about 2 miles west of the A1 (only signed northbound), 3 miles from the A697. It is 12 miles north of Morpeth and 7 miles south of Alnwick. Site is signed at the northern end of Longframlington on the A697. O.S.GR: NU160042.

Northumberland
Dunstan Hill Camping and Caravanning Club Site
577 Dunstan Hill, Dunstan, Alnwick, Northumberland NE66 3TQ

Northumberland is not very well blessed with good campsites, so we are pleased to feature Dunstan Hill. Off a quiet lane between Embleton and Craster this is a rural site with a tree belt to shelter it from the north wind and access to the beach by a level footpath through the fields, across the golf course and past the ruins of Dunstanburgh Castle. This is 1-1½ miles by car. With gravel access roads, this peaceful site has 150 level, well spaced pitches, 83 with 16A electricity and 10 with hardstanding (more planned). Reception is located in a new building and is manned by very helpful wardens and there is a large area for outside parking and late arrivals at the entrance. This is a wonderful area to visit, with its unspoilt beaches and the whole area is steeped in history with Holy Island, the Farne Islands, Bamburgh, Dunstanburgh, Walkworth and Alnwick castles. Buses pass the site entrance and there are good eating places near.

Facilities: Very clean and well maintained, the two toilet blocks have some washbasins in cubicles, hairdryers and a washroom for children with deep sinks. Fully equipped suite for disabled visitors in one block, a laundry in the other. Motorcaravan service point. Small shop for gas and basic provisions. Bread and milk can be ordered and a mobile shop and the paper man visit. Small children's play area. Torches are useful. **Off site:** Fishing 1½ miles, riding 8 miles.

Charges 2001

Per adult	£3.75 - £5.30
child (6-18 yrs)	£1.65
non-member pitch fee	£4.30
electricity	£1.65 - £2.40

Tel: (01665) 576310 (no calls after 8 pm). Reservations: Necessary and made with deposit; contact site. **Open** March - October.

Directions: From A1 just north of Alnwick take B1340 signed Denwick. Go through village and on to Embleton. Site is signed in Embleton village - avoid signs to Dunstanburgh Castle and follow those for Craster. Site is (south) on the left after approx. ¾ mile, 100 yds past farm site. O.S.GR: NU236214.

Northumberland
Ord House Country Park

East Ord, Berwick-upon-Tweed, Northumberland TD15 2NS

580

Ord House is 40-acre park for 200 privately owned holiday homes and 75 touring caravan and tent pitches. The whole park has a very well cared for appearance, with well mown grass and colourful arrays of flowering bushes. The touring pitches, all with electricity (10A), are in small sections, from the secluded, walled orchard to the more open areas nearer the toilet blocks. There are 39 hardstanding pitches, each with electricity, water and drainage, 19 in the walled garden separated by flowering shrubs and camomile lawns. At the entrance to the park is an area with a few pitches suitable for wheelchair users and close by is a small sanitary unit with WCs and showers plus a large, unisex, well appointed unit (Radar key). The whole site is 'wheelchair friendly' with good access to the airy reception and the well stocked accessory shop. Ord House itself, an 18th century mansion, has been tastefully converted to provide a bar, lounge bar and family room with reasonably priced meals in each. Although there are many caravan holiday homes on the park, they are not overwhelming and their presence does mean that other amenities can remain open all season. A member of the Best of British group.

Facilities: The main, modern toilet building is of excellent quality and cleanliness, very well maintained and can be heated. It has two good large family bathrooms (with two showers, a bath, WC and washbasin). Two rooms for disabled visitors. Dishwashing sinks. Large well equipped laundry. Motorcaravan service point. Gas supplies. Bar (closed two days each week Nov - March) with bar food and family room. Six-hole golf practise area. Bicycle hire. Crazy golf. Table tennis. Draughts. Children's play area. No commercial vehicles are accepted. Dogs only accepted by prior arrangement. **Off site:** Post office stores 50 m. from the entrance. Leisure centre with a pool is 15 minutes walk. Fishing 1½ miles, riding 8 miles, golf 2 miles. Sea fishing can be booked in Berwick.

Charges 2002

Per unit incl. up to 4 people	£9.00 - £13.95
extra person over 6 yrs	£2.50
awning	£2.50
electricity	£2.50
dog	free - £1.50

Extra car, boat and trailer by prior arrangement. 1-man tent less £3.00, 2-man less £2.00. Discounts for longer stays. Tel: (01289) 305288. Fax: (01289) 330832. E-mail: enquiries@ordhouse.co.uk. Reservations: Advisable at all times, essential in high seasons (min. 3 nights at B.Hs). **Open** all year.

Directions: From the A1 Berwick bypass take East Ord exit and follow signs. O.S.GR: NT982515.

Northumberland
Brown Rigg Caravan and Camping Park

Bellingham, nr Hexham, Northumberland NE48 2JY

578

Bellingham is tucked away amidst heather clad moors in the North Tyne valley, just below the Scottish Borders on the edge of the Northumberland National Park - 'full of history, myth and legend', to quote from the Bellingham town guide. John Mowatt went to school here and has returned with his wife and family to establish Brown Rigg in part of the grounds of his old school. This interesting, developing park provides 70 pitches, 26 with electricity (10/16A), for all types of unit on a level grass field between the moor and the road. Reception, a games room and the sanitary facilities have all been converted from the former wooden school dormitory buildings with a central courtyard area and are rather distinctive. A tea shop and plant sales area have been added. Bellingham is half a mile away and an 18 hole golf course has been opened recently. The Pennine Way passes the entrance and Kielder Water is 9 miles to the west, as is Hadrian's Wall to the south.

Facilities: Ladies' toilet facilities, finished in pine, provide washbasins in cubicles, controllable showers on payment (10p) and a free hairdryer. Baby bath available. The unit for men has been tiled. In total, it is a good provision, cleverly adapted and well maintained and is operated on a key system. Washing machine and dryer, free iron and board. Laundry and dishwashing sinks. Motorcaravan service point. Reception provides basic food supplies, gas and battery charging. Games room with pool and table tennis. TV room. Children's play area. **Off site:** Fishing or golf within 1 mile.

Charges 2001

Per unit incl. 2 adults	£8.00 - £9.50
2-man tent	£7.00 - £8.50
1-man tent	£4.00 - £4.50
child's pup tent	£2.00
extra adult	£1.50 - £2.00
child (6-14 yrs)	£1.00
awning	£1.00
one dog free, others	50p
electricity	£1.50 - £2.00

No credit cards. Tel/Fax: (01434) 220175. E-mail: enquiries@northumberlandcaravanparks.com. Reservations: Made with £10 deposit for bookings. **Open** Easter - 31 October.

Directions: Park is on the B6320, south of Bellingham. O.S.GR: NY835826.

Waren Caravan and Camping Park

Waren Mill, Bamburgh, Northumberland NE70 7EE

575

Developed from 100 acres of undulating private heath and woodland, Waren Park is a large, spacious family site with marvellous sea views. A large section of caravan holiday homes (for hire), is separate from a self contained four acre touring area. Enclosed by sheltering banks, this provides 170 reasonably level pitches, 100 with electrical connections (10A). As well as the spacious grounds to wander in, there is much to see nearby from historic castles, the Farne Islands to the Cheviot Hills and miles and miles of sandy beaches.

Facilities: One old toilet block with basic facilities is due for refurbishment. A new block has excellent provision for disabled visitors, baby mats, bathroom and four self-contained rooms with shower, WC and washbasin. Laundry room. Dishwashing sinks. Motorcaravan service point. Licensed shop. Games room. Children's play park and playing fields. Bar serving bar meals with a terrace overlooking outdoor heated swimming pools (June - Sept). **Off site:** Golf, birdwatching and riding nearby.

Charges 2001

Per unit incl. 2 persons	£8.00 - £13.50
extra person (over 5 yrs)	£1.00
1-man tent	£5.00 - £10.00
boat or awning	£1.50
dog (by prior arrangement)	£1.00
electricity	£2.00

Less 10% for bookings of 7 days or over. Tel: (01668) 214366. Fax: (01668) 214224. E-mail: waren@ meadowhead.co.uk. Reservations: Early reservation advisable for high season. Deposit of one night's charge plus £1 fee. **Open** 20 March - 31 October.

Directions: Follow B1342 from the A1 to Waren Mill towards Bamburgh. After Budle Bay turn right and follow signs. O.S.GR: NU154342.

WALES

Wales Tourist Board

Brunel House, 2 Fitzalan Road, Cardiff CF24 0UY

Tel: 029 2049 9909

E-mail: info@tourism.wales.gov.uk

Internet: http://www.visitwales.com

Invigorating. Natural. Rejuvenating. Relaxing. Wales can be all of these things. And much more…

Wales is a compact country with an endless variety of landscape and terrain. Its mountains and lakes, rivers and valleys, coast and country can offer you a break from the pressures of everyday living; Wales has all the benefits of a relaxing escape without any of the disadvantages attributed to travelling long distances.

With a population of just under three million, Wales is a small country with plenty of spirit. It is currently experiencing the most exciting period in its recent history, having in the last few years seen the opening of the National Assembly and hosted the European Summit and Rugby World Cup.

Few parts of the world can claim such a varied landscape in such a small land area; only in Wales can you go from mountains as dramatic as those in Snowdonia to beautiful golden beaches in no time at all. Only in Wales is it but a short journey from city centre to undulating countryside, from inland waterfalls and lakes to coastal cliffs and islands.

Add to this one of Europe's richest cultures, a thriving arts scene, the unique lyrical Welsh language and a wealth of history spanning many centuries and an image emerges of a nation which has much to offer.

Wales' capital, Cardiff, is Europe's youngest, and one of its fastest growing, cities. Many exciting projects are giving the city an air of dynamism and newfound confidence. The barrage in Cardiff Bay is complete and projects such as the new building for the National Assembly and the Wales Millennium Centre are under way. Pride of place goes to Wales' new national stadium – the Millennium Stadium – which has a retractable roof and a 72,500 capacity. Located in the heart of the city, it creates a unique atmosphere during sporting and non-sporting events.

Wales' biggest asset is undoubtedly its country-side. Wales has three National Parks, making up almost a quarter of the country's total area. The dramatic towering mountain scenery of Snowdonia National Park in the north contrasts with the boulder-shaped bare hilltops of the Brecon Beacons in the south and the marine-based coastal beauty of the Pembrokeshire Coast in the west.

Wales also has five designated Areas of Outstanding Natural Beauty, namely the Gower Peninsula, the Wye Valley, the Lln Peninsula, the Anglesey Coast and the Clwydian Range.

An outdoor enthusiast's dream as it evidently is, Wales offers much more. There are many tourist attractions, such as the Great Little Trains, museums, theme and wildlife parks, country houses and estates and of courser more castles per square mile than any other country in Europe.

South Wales

Tourism information for South and West Wales may also be obtained from:

Tourism South and West Wales, Charter Court, Enterprise Park, Swansea SA7 9DB

Tel: (01792) 781212 Fax: (01792) 781300 E-mail: marketing@tsww.com

The Bridge Caravan Park and Camping Site

592 Dingestow, Monmouth, Gwent NP25 4DY

This quiet, family run park is located in a village four miles from Monmouth. The Bridge Caravan Park was established in 1979, being a working farm until a few years ago. Still in the hands of the Holmes family, it provides a peaceful haven bordered by the River Trothy and woodland on one side, and by the farm buildings and church on the other. Over half the park is taken up by seasonal long stay pitches. The touring area is to one side, edged by the river at a lower level. Neat, level grass accessed by a circular tarmac roadway provides 33 pitches for caravans and motorcaravans with electricity (10A) and 16 hardstandings. A further 20 places for tents are available, all with electricity (5A). A pleasant, friendly atmosphere prevails.

Facilities: The purpose built, central toilet block is well maintained and now has a separate shower section, with metered showers in excellent cubicles with dry area. Bathroom for disabled visitors. Washbasins in cubicles and hairdryers. Fully equipped laundry and dishwashing room. Gas available. **Off site:** Village shop, post office and a children's play area. A local pub offers good food a short walk away. River fishing. Bicycle hire 6 miles, boat slipway 4 miles, golf 3 miles.

Charges 2002

Per unit incl. 2 adults	£8.00
extra adult	£1.50
child (5-14 yrs)	£1.00
awning	£1.00
electricity	10A £2.00, 5A £1.50

No credit cards. Tel/Fax: (01600) 740241. Reservations: Contact park. **Open** Easter - 30 October.

Directions: Park is signed off A40 road by junction with A449 (about 4½ miles from junction). O.S.GR: SO458099.

Tredegar House Country Park Caravan Club Site

606 Newport, Gwent NP10 8TW

This immaculate Caravan Club site is ideally situated for breaking a journey or for longer stays. It can accommodates 82 caravans, all with 16A electricity hook-up and 40 with gravel hardstanding. A further grass area is allocated for 30 tents, with its use limited to families and couples – no single sex groups are accepted. Entry and exit from the park are controlled by a barrier (card required). The site itself is set within the gardens and park of Tredegar House, a 17th century house and country park which is open to the public to discover what life was like 'above and below stairs'. Some road noise may be expected at times, but otherwise this is an excellent site.

Facilities: The sanitary block is of an excellent standard with a digital lock system. It includes washbasins in cubicles, a bathroom for visitors with disabilities and a baby and toddler bathroom complete with small bath, toilet, washbasin and changing unit. Dishwashing sinks and laundry. Good motorcaravan service point. Calor gas available. **Off site:** Large supermarket 3 minutes away. Newport is some 3 miles and is a good shopping centre and Cardiff with its castle, shops and much more is only 9 miles.

Charges 2001

Per pitch (non-member)	£6.00 - £8.00
adult	£2.75 - £4.50
child (5-16 yrs)	£1.10 - £1.20
electricity	£1.50 - £2.25

Tel: (01633) 815600. Fax: (01633) 816372. E-mail: cc92@gofornet.co.uk. Reservations: Advisable for peak season - contact the warden. **Open** all year.

Directions: From M4 take exit 28 or from A48 junction with the M4 follow brown signs for Tredegar House. The caravan park is indicated to the left at the house entrance. O.S.GR: ST299855.

Cwmcarn Forest Drive Campsite

593

Cwmcarn, Crosskeys, nr Newport, Gwent NP1 7FA

Set in a narrow, sheltered valley with magnificent wooded slopes (it's hard to believe it was once the site of the Cwmcarn Colliery), this park is not only central for the many attractions of this part of Wales, but there is now also much of the natural environment to enjoy including a small fishing lake. The seven mile forest drive (open daily in season) shares its Visitor Centre with the camp reception and has much to offer - bird watching, badger seeking, the Twmbarlwm ancient hill fort to visit with its magnificent views across the Severn to Somerset, Gloucestershire and Devon. The site has a slightly wild feel, but is stunningly located and has 40 well spaced, flat pitches (30 with 15A hook-ups, 3 with concrete hardstanding and with tarmac for the car) spread over three small fields between the Visitor Centre and the small lake (fishing permits available). Wardens are on hand daily and from Easter to September the Visitor Centre and reception are manned 9 am - 5 pm (6 pm. at weekends), so arrive before then.

Facilities: The single well equipped, heated toilet block (£5 deposit for key) including toilet facilities for the disabled, laundry with washing machine, dryer, iron and board, and a kitchen with two washing up sinks, small cooker and fridge (hot water free). Visitor Centre has a coffee shop open 1-5.30 pm. at weekends from Easter. Guided walks and a new mountain bike route are available. Numeracy trail and environmenteering routes for children. Rallies accommodated. Dogs accepted by prior arrangement. **Off site:** Shops, a leisure centre, pubs and takeaway food are available in the village ¾mile away. Riding 2 miles, golf 6 miles.

Charges 2002

Per unit	£7.20 - £8.20
large tent	£6.20 - £7.20
small ridge tent	£4.80 - £5.80
electricity	£2.00

Tel: (01495) 272001. E-mail: tic@caerphilly.gov.uk. Reservations: No stated policy. 14 day max. stay. Contact the Warden. **Open** January - December.

Directions: Cwmcarn Forest Drive is well signed from junction 28 on M4. From the Midlands and the 'Heads of the Valleys' road (A465), take A467 south to Cwmcarn. O.S.GR: ST230935.

Pembrey Country Park Caravan Club Site

594

Pembrey, Llanelli, Carmarthenshire SA16 0EJ

Sheltered, quiet and peaceful, this Caravan Club site has access to Pembrey Country Park and beach. It provides 115 level grass pitches, accessed by a semi-circular tarmac, one-way road and pleasantly interspersed with clumps of bushes and trees. All but four of the pitches have electricity hook-ups (16A). Tents are taken providing there is room (steel pegs may be needed). However, the real plus for this site is its proximity to the Country Park – access to this is free on foot direct from the site, or the Club has organised a special weekly car pass for £6.50. The Park covers 520 acres of grass and woodland with 7 miles of soft sandy beaches, about a mile of which has a 'Blue Flag' rating (dogs are limited to one area). There are some 64 miles of walks and cycle ways, picnic and conservation areas, a wealth of birds and butterflies, pitch and putt, narrow gauge railway, a dry ski slope (excellent value) and toboggan run, plus an orienteering course, nature trails, and equestrian centre – all part of a really wonderful provision which is both quiet and safe for families. A small drawback could be some noise during the day from aircraft or from occasional meetings at the nearby Pembrey motor racing circuit (on the other hand, enthusiasts can watch the racing from the bicycle trail!)

Facilities: The heated toilet block, well situated for all the pitches, is of the usual good Club standard with curtained washbasins and en-suite facilities for disabled visitors (with key). Fully equipped laundry room. Dishwashing sinks under cover. Motorcaravan service point. Gas available. Small children's play area, giant draughts set and boules pitch. **Off site:** Dogs are restricted on the beach May - Sept. Gower Peninsula 20 miles.

Charges 2001

Per pitch (non-member)	£6.00 - £8.00
adult	£3.50 - £4.50
child (5-16 yrs)	£1.10 - £1.20
electricity	£1.50 - £2.25

Tel: (01554) 834369 (not after 8 pm). Reservations: Essential for July/Aug. and B.Hs; contact the Warden. **Open** 1 April - 5 January.

Directions: Leave M4 at junction 48 onto A4138. After 4 miles turn right onto A484 at roundabout signed Carmarthen. Continue for 7 miles to Pembrey. The Country Park is signed off the A484 in Pembrey village; site entrance is on right 100 yds before park gates. O.S.GR: SN415005.

Abermarlais Caravan Park

596 Llangadog, nr Llandeilo, Carmarthenshire SA19 9NG

Apart from the attractions of south or mid Wales for a stay, this sheltered, family run park could also double as a useful transit stop close to the main holiday route for those travelling to Pembrokeshire. In a natural setting, up to 88 touring units are accommodated in one fairly flat, tapering five-acre grass field edged by mature trees and a stream. Pitches are numbered, and generously spaced around the perimeter or on either side of a central, hedged spine at the wider end, with 42 electrical hook-ups (10A) and some hardstanding. Backpackers have a small, separate area. The park is set in a sheltered valley with a range of wildlife and nine acres of woodland walks. There is also an old walled garden, with some pitches and lawns for softball games, that screens the park, both audibly and visibly, from the A40 road. However, the most sought after pitches are beside the stream, loved by children and a haven for wildlife.

Facilities: The one small toilet block is older in style, but can be heated, is clean, bright, cheerful and adequate with controllable showers. Two external, covered washing-up sinks but no laundry facilities - nearest about 5 miles. Motorcaravan service point. Shop doubling as reception. Gas supplies. Play area with tennis and volleyball nets and play equipment. A torch would be useful. Winter caravan storage. **Off site:** Little Chef restaurant near. Pubs, etc. at Llangadog. Fishing 2 miles.

Charges 2001

Per pitch	£4.50
adult	£1.50
child (over 5 yrs)	£1.00
awning	75p
electricity	£1.75

No credit cards. Tel: (01550) 777868 or 777797. Reservations: Any length, with £5 deposit. **Open** 14 March - 14 November.

Directions: Park is on the A40, between the junctions with the A4069 and A482, between Llandovery and Llandeilo. O.S.GR: SN685295.

Afon Lodge Caravan Park

595 Parciau Bach, St Clears, Carmarthenshire SA33 4LG

Formerly known as Parciau Bach Caravan Park, this small park is personally run by new owners. There are some narrow lanes to be negotiated to get here, but it is well worth it to enjoy its quality and peaceful, rural setting. The 26 privately owned caravan holiday homes are hidden in the wooded slopes at the back of the park - a haven for wild flowers and squirrels. The open field for tents is sloping, but now has individual terraced places with dividing shrub hedges (10 pitches) and a lower level, part terraced for 25 caravan pitches, all with electrical hook-ups (16A), 9 with hardstanding, water and TV connections. All are on neatly cut grass with views across the valley. The owner's pine chalet home, sited on the slope between the touring field and the wooded area houses reception, a tourist information room and the sanitary facilities. A wooded stream area unfortunately does not belong to the park but further up on the site is a small wildlife pond. The park is a haven of tranquillity, even when we visited in peak season. If you tire of the rural atmosphere, Tenby is only 18 miles, with the 7 mile long Pendine Sands 6 miles away or to the north, the Preseli Mountains. Birdwatching opportunities abound. A member of the Countryside Discovery group.

Facilities: Recently extended toilet facilities also include a laundry room and facilities for dishwashing. Children have an adventure play unit and a pets corner. New shop at reception (limited hours, Easter - end Oct). Bar snacks and evening meals are available at the Parciau Bach Inn (weekends only in low seasons; separate ownership) situated above the site. **Off site:** Riding ½ mile, fishing 2 miles, golf 5 miles.

Charges 2002

Per unit incl. 4 persons	£7.80 - £10.50
2 person tent	£5.00 - £7.50
awning	£1.00
electricity	£2.00
TV connection	50p
dog	50p

No credit cards. Tel: (01994) 230647. E-mail: yvonne@afonlodge.f9.co.uk. Reservations: May be advisable for B.Hs. **Open** all year except 9 Jan. - 1 March.

Directions: From St Clears traffic lights, take road to Llanboidy forking right after 100 yds. Follow this road for almost 2 miles and turn right. After less than a mile turn right at small crossroads and park is on left. O.S.GR: SN298184.

Noble Court Holiday Caravan and Camping Park

Redstone Road, Narberth, Pembrokeshire SA67 7ES

597

Centrally situated for southwest Wales, Noble Court is a family owned park with good facilities. The neat entrance sets the standards for the park which is part caravan holiday homes (60) and part touring. Arranged over four hedged fields, each one at a slightly lower level, with an additional tenting field, the last has lovely views over the rural Welsh countryside. All 92 touring pitches have electricity, 25 on grass terraces with waste water connection, fresh water supply and 16A electricity, and the others mainly on gravel based hardstanding. An area is available for rallies. A new half-acre coarse fishing lake is excellent and free for campers. There is good access to a further 20 acres of rural land for walking. The market town of Narberth is half a mile. Noble Court is well placed for all Pembrokeshire has to offer and is easily accessed from the A40.

Facilities: Toilet facilities are in two similar, well equipped blocks. Laundry. Covered dishwashing sinks. Facilities for disabled people with ramped access are in the lower block (access by key). Excellent bar/restaurant, takeaway and a bistro. TV and games rooms. Outdoor heated pool (35 x 20 ft) with beach effect and children's splash pool, nicely paved (from Spr. B.H). Gas supplies. Adventure play area. Fishing. Only one dog per pitch is accepted. **Off site**: Bicycle hire 5 miles, riding 4 miles, golf 3 miles, boat launching 8 miles.

Charges 2001

Per unit incl. up to 4 persons	£10.00 - £16.00
tent pitch incl. 2 persons	£10.00
extra person	£1.50
child (under 12 yrs)	£1.00
dog	free

Tel: (01834) 861191. Fax: (01834) 861484. Reservations: Advised for electricity and made for 1-5 nights payable in full at time of booking, more than 6 nights with £30 deposit. No telephone bookings. **Open** 1 March - 30 November.

Directions: Going west on A40 ignore roundabout with sign to Narberth (on A478) and continue to next junction signed Narberth (B4313) with camping sign. Site is ½ mile on the left and you come on it quite suddenly. O.S.GR: SN111158.

Moreton Farm Leisure Park

Moreton, Saundersfoot, Pembrokeshire SA69 9EA

598

Moreton Farm has been developed in a secluded valley, a 10-20 minute walk from Saundersfoot and 4 miles from Tenby. It provides 20 caravan pitches (all with 16A electricity, and including 16 with hard-standing) and 40 for tents on two sloping, neatly cut grass fields, with 12 pine holiday lodges and 4 cottages occupying another field. The site is approached under a railway bridge (height 10'9", width across the top 6'6", but with alternative access over the railway line for larger vehicles just possible). There are a few trains during the day, none at night. An attractive lake at the bottom of the valley is home to ducks, geese and chickens (fishing is no longer available) – pride of place must go to 'Missy and her girls'! Pembroke and Carew castles and a variety of visitor attractions are close. This is a quiet family site.

Facilities: The toilet blocks (heated) are light and airy, providing excellent facilities with pre-set hot showers (metered), and a ramp to a unit for disabled visitors with toilet and washbasin, a baby bath, dishwashing sinks and laundry facilities. Fenced, outside clothes drying area. Small shop for basics and gas. Children's playground. No dogs or pets are accepted. **Off site**: Fishing or riding 1 mile, bicycle hire 2 miles, golf 4 miles.

Charges 2001

Per caravan incl. 2 persons	£8.00 - £10.00
trailer tent or motorcaravan	£7.00 - £9.00
tent	£5.00 - £7.00
extra adult	£1.00
child (2-17 yrs)	50p
awning	£1.50
electricity	£2.00

No credit cards. Tel: (01834) 812016. Fax: (01834) 811890. E-mail: moretonfarm@btconnect.com. Reservations: Made with deposit (£20 p/wk caravans, £15 p/wk tents), balance 28 days before arrival. **Open** 1 March - 31 October.

Directions: From A477 Carmarthen - Pembroke road take A478 for Tenby at Kilgetty. Park is signed on left after 1½ miles. Watch carefully for sign and park is ½ mile up poorly made-up road and under bridge. O.S.GR: SN122047.

Freshwater East Caravan Club Site

599 | Freshwater East, Lamphey, Pembrokeshire SA71 5NL

This Caravan Club site in the Pembrokeshire Coast National Park is open to non-members (for all units). At the bottom of a hill, it has 126 mainly level pitches bounded by trees and with 16A electrical hook-ups available. Around half of the pitches are on hardstanding. The beach and the Pembroke Coastal Path are about a five minute walk. This is an excellent area for walking with magnificent cliff views and birdwatching. You will find St David's, the smallest cathedral city, well worth a visit. Note:TV aerial connections are available, but you will need your own extension cable.

Facilities: The two heated toilet blocks are modern and clean with washbasins in cubicles, and free hairdryers or sockets for your own. Facilities for disabled visitors. Fully equipped laundry rooms. Waste point for motorcaravans. Small play area. Gas supplies. **Off site:** Shop ½ mile. Fishing within 5 miles.

Charges 2001

Per pitch (non-member)	£6.00 - £8.00
adult	£2.75 - £4.50
child (5-16 yrs)	£1.10 - £1.20
electricity	£1.50 - £2.25

Tel: (01646) 672341 (not after 8 pm). Reservations: Contact the Warden. **Open** 26 March - 1 November.

Directions: From the east on A477, fork left 1¼ miles past Milton onto A4075 Pembroke road. After 2 miles in Pembroke immediately (after railway bridge) turn sharp left at roundabout on A4139 Tenby road. In 1¾miles in Lamphey turn right onto B4584 signed Freshwater East. In 1¾miles turn right signed Stackpole and Trewent and after 400 yds at foot of hill, right into lane at Club sign. Do not tow to the beach area. O.S.GR: SS015979.

Gwaun Vale Holiday Touring Park

600 | Llanychaer, Fishguard, Pembrokeshire SA65 9TA

In a superb rural setting, with wonderful views across the countryside towards the sea, Gwaun Vale provides 30 pitches. On mainly level grass, with one terrace above another, connected by an oval, gravel and tarmac road, 10 pitches have hardstanding and 21 have electricity connections (10A). There are plenty of water points and several picnic tables. A useful little shop doubles as reception with a well presented display of tourist information and variety of books on local walks to buy or borrow. One can also borrow a barbecue, iron and board, a boules set, baby bath or videos! Very convenient for Fishguard and the ferries, day trips to Ireland are possible, as well as windsurfing, boating and fishing trips, and the Pembroke coastal footpath is nearby. A 'must' to see is Wales' answer to the Bayeux Tapestry, a 100 ft. long tapestry on view in Fishguard (the French invaded Britain in 1797 and the tapestry, embroidered by 70 local women, gives a carefully researched account of this invasion and its defeat - full of life and humour).

Facilities: The toilet block, beside reception and to one side of the site is a little old fashioned, but it is neat, clean and heated. Showers 20p (could do with some improvement). Cheerful laundry room with laundry sink, washing machine and dryer and two dishwashing sinks. New shop. Children's play area in a small sloping fenced field with adventure type equipment and a field for dogs adjoining. **Off site:** A family pub serving bar meals is within easy walking distance. Fishing, bicycle hire and riding 2 miles. Golf 7 miles.

Charges 2001

Per unit incl. 1 or 2 persons	£7.00 - £8.00
3 or 4 persons	£8.00 - £9.00
5+ persons	£9.00 - £10.00
electricity (10A)	£1.50

Awning, dog, extra car no charge. No credit cards. Tel: (01348) 874698. E-mail: margaret.harries@ talk21.com. Reservations: Advised for high season and B.Hs. and made with £10 deposit and 50p fee. **Open** 1 April - 31 October.

Directions: Park is on the right, 1½ miles from Fishguard on the B4313; follow brown camping signs from centre. O.S.GR: SM977356.

Cenarth Falls Holiday Park

601 Cenarth, Newcastle Emlyn, Ceredigion SA38 9JS

The Davies family have developed an attractively landscaped, part wooded holiday home park with 80 privately owned units and 7 for hire. However, a neat well cared for, sheltered grassy area at the top of the park provides 30 touring pitches, 29 with sunken grass grid hardstanding and all with electricity (16A). Accessed via a semi-circular tarmac road, they enjoy views across the Teifi valley. An excellent, heated toilet block complements this provision. There is easy ramped access, even to the chemical disposal unit. etc. while the 'Fisherman's Cove', a friendly little private bar (free membership for all guests, weekends only March - May and Sept. onwards), serves good value, home cooked meals, together with some entertainment, especially at weekends. A sunken, kidney shaped heated swimming pool with landscaped surrounds and sun-beds is very pleasant. A footpath leads to the village and the famous Cenarth Falls (with leaping salmon). The National Coracle Centre is well worth a visit. A member of the Best of British group.

Facilities: The toilet block (accessed by key) uses a 'P.I.R.' system that controls heating, lighting, water and air-freshener on entry - very efficient. Tiled with non-slip floors, both men and ladies have an en-suite family room (doubling as provision for disabled visitors), an additional well equipped shower and also one washbasin in a roomy private cabin. Laundry room with two washing machines, two dryers and ironing facilities (used by the whole park). No laundry sinks, but two dishwashing sinks are under cover. Motorcaravan service point. Shop for essential groceries, newspapers, gas. Swimming pool (Whitsun - mid-Sept). Bar. Children's play area. Games room with pool table and video game machine. **Off site:** Fishing ¼mile, bicycle hire 8 miles, riding 7 miles, golf 10 miles.

Charges 2002

Per unit incl. up to 4 people and car	£8.00 - £15.00
extra person	£2.00
awning	£2.00
extra pup tent (space permitting)	£2.50
dog	£1.00
electricity (16A)	£2.00

Tel: (01239) 710345. Fax: (01239) 710344. E-mail: enquiries@cenarth-holipark.co.uk. Reservations: Made with 33% deposit; contact park. **Open** all year excl. 1 Dec. - 10 Jan.

Directions: Follow A484 Cardigan - Newcastle Emlyn road and park is signed before Cenarth village. O.S.GR: SN265421.

Pencelli Castle Caravan and Camping Park

604 Pencelli, Brecon, Powys LD3 7LX

Open all year round, this is a quality park with atmosphere and character. Set amidst the Brecon scenery, it offers excellent facilities in peaceful, rural tranquillity. The owners, Liz and Gerwyn Rees, have retained the country charm but have added a new, all embracing range of spacious, heated, luxury facilities, attractively enhanced by potted plants. A new field, the 'Orchard', incorporates 15 pitches with hardstanding, some fully serviced. Together with the shrubs, fruit trees and stone cider mill, this is a wonderful facility. The 'Oaks' (20 caravans and tents) and the 'Meadow' (40 tents) with its boot and bike wash, are bordered by majestic trees and the Monmouthshire and Brecon Canal, where gaily painted barges slip past. All the fields are level with neatly mown grass and tarmac access roads. Further new attractions are the rabbits, ducks and the red deer which enjoy being hand-fed by visitors. The historic manor house, that dates from 1583, is adjacent to arched barns that house a collection of vintage farm machinery including carts and rare tractors. For mountain bikers and walkers, a path leaves the village to reach the top of the Brecon Beacons or there is an easy towpath ramble to Tal-y-Bont.

Facilities: The new toilet block is exceptionally well designed and includes some private cubicles, two large fully equipped rooms for families or disabled visitors incorporating double showers, baby changing and bath facilities, all humorously decorated for the young at heart. Laundry. Drying room with lockers (a must as this is walking country). Information and planning room. Indoor dishwashing and food preparation room. Motorcaravan service point (with washbasin, soap and hand dryer). Bicycle hire. Dogs are not accepted. **Off site:** The Royal Oak inn with meals is 100 m. Pubs, tea rooms and a post office in Tal-y-bont. Buses pass regularly for Brecon, Abergavenny. Golf or bicycle hire 5 miles. Riding 2 miles.

Charges 2001

Per caravan or motorcaravan incl. 2 persons	£9.50
extra adult	£2.50
child (5-13 yrs)	£2.00
awning	£1.50
electricity	£2.25
Tents: per adult	£4.50.

No credit cards. Tel: (01874) 665451. Fax: (01874) 665452. E-mail: pencelli.castle@virgin.net. Reservations: Advised for peak season and B.Hs. **Open** all year.

Directions: From A40 south after Brecon bypass take B4558 at signs for Llanfrynach and later Pencelli; or if travelling north on A40, approach via Tal-y-Bont. Site at south end of Pencelli. O.S.GR: SO096248.

Brynich Caravan Park

603 Brecon, Powys LD3 7SH

Brynich is a well kept, family run park with a picturesque setting and super views towards the Brecon Beacons, developed over the years by Colin and Maureen Jones to a very high standard. Originally farmland near the Brecon bypass, there are now three level, hedged and neatly mown camping fields with tarmac roads and a mixture of hardwood trees and shrubs maturing nicely. These fields provide for 130 touring units of all types with 108 electric points (10/16A) and hardstanding on many pitches. A nice addition, in a sloping field leading down to a stream, is an extensive dog walk on one side of the Brynich Brook and an adventure play area, reached by stepping stones, on the opposite side. The stream is shallow and an added attraction. Being within the Brecon Beacons National Park, this is a good area for hill walking and climbing. Access to the towpath of the Brecon and Monmouthshire Canal is 200 yds. A member of the Best of British group.

Facilities: Two modern toilet blocks, which can be heated, have well equipped showers, washbasins in cubicles, washing up sinks, and a laundry room. Two fully equipped units for disabled visitors are in one block, one providing left handed toilet facilities, the other right handed (key system) and a baby unit. Fridge, freezer and microwave. Motorcaravan service point. Reception and well stocked shop (with gas). Children's play areas. Large recreation field for ball games. **Off site**: Fishing or bicycle hire 1½ miles, riding 2 miles, golf 3 miles. Watersports near. Local pub serving 'pub grub' within walking distance. Market days in Brecon on Tuesday and Friday.

Charges 2002

Per unit incl. 2 persons	£8.50 - £10.00
extra adult	£2.25 - £3.00
child (4-16 yrs)	£1.25 - £1.75
backpacker	£4.00 - £4.50
awning	£1.50 - £1.75
electricity	£2.00 - £2.25
dog	50p

Tel/Fax: (01874) 623325. E-mail: brynich@aol.com. Reservations: Advisable for hook-ups at B.Hs. and made with £10 deposit. **Open** 28 March - 27 October.

Directions: Park entrance is off the A470 (Builth Wells) road, 250 yds. from the junction with the A40 (Abergavenny) road, 1 mile east of Brecon. O.S.GR: SO069278.

Brynich Caravan Park

Brecon, Powys LD3 7SH
Tel/Fax: 01874 623325
Email: brynich@aol.com
Web address: www.brynich.co.uk

DE LUXE

Family run park with panoramic views of the Brecon Beacons. Well maintained, flat site with closely mown grass and large pitch sizes. Modern shower facilities with free hot water, including disabled and baby rooms - cleanliness a priority. Well-equipped licensed shop, telephone, adventure playground, recreation field and dog exercise field.

Calor Award - Most Improved Park in Wales 1998
AA - Best Campsite in Wales • Practical Caravan Top 100 Parks 2000

Talywerydd Touring Caravan and Camping Park

609 Penbryn Sands, Sarnau, Llandysul, Dyfed SA44 6QY

This family run park is close to a sandy beach on the Ceredigion Heritage Coast. A pleasant little site, it has 40 pitches, most on slightly sloping grass, but with 11 hardstandings and 37 electricity hook-ups (10/16A). Unusually for such a small site there is a nice little restaurant and bar, which is open daily during July and August, and Friday/Saturday evenings at other times. Local attractions are the National Trust owned Penbryn beach, the Coastal Path, a narrow gauge railway at Henllan, several craft and pottery workshops, and woollen mills. Cardigan has a market on Mondays.

Facilities: The main sanitary unit is a modern 'portacabin' type. It is supplemented by two new external access showers at the rear of the bar/restarant building, plus the WCs and washbasins inside. Dishwashing and laundry facilities are in a further 'portacabin' unit. Reception has basic supplies. Small fenced playground and adventure style playground. Games room. Boules. Pitch and putt. Small heated covered pool (May-Sept).

Charges 2001

Per unit incl. 4 persons	£7.00 - £11.50
extra person	£2.00
awning	£1.50
dog	£1.00
electricity	£2.00

Tel: (01239) 810322. Reservations: Made with £20 deposit per week. **Open** 1 March - 31 October.

Directions: Sarnau is 9 mile northeast of Cardigan on A487. From south take second turning signed Penbryn. If approaching from the north also take second turn signed Penbryn. Site entrance is 500 yds on left. O.S.GR: SN300505.

Camping and Caravan Club Site Rhandirmwyn

607 Rhandirmwyn, Llandovery, Carmarthenshire SA20 0NT

This is a popular site with those who like a peaceful life with no on-site entertainment, just fresh air and beautiful countryside. The site is only a short drive from the magnificent Llyn Brianne reservoir and close to the Dinas RSPB nature reserve, where a two mile trail runs through oak and alder woodland alongside the River Tywi and the wildlife includes many species of birds including red kites. The site is in a sheltered valley with 95 pitches on level grass, 55 electric hook-ups (16A), and 12 hardstandings. The village is within walking distance although there is a fairly steep hill to negotiate (but the return is much easier), and you can take a short cut through the woodland grove dedicated to John Lloyd, a former Club Chairman.

Facilities: The single heated sanitary block is kept very clean and tidy. Some washbasins in cubicles, dishwashing sinks and fully equipped laundry. Drive-over motorcaravan service point. Small children's playground with rubber base. **Off site**: The village has a Post Office and general store, and the Royal Oak Inn serves good value meals.

Charges 2001

Per adult	£3.75 - £5.30
child (6-18 yrs)	£1.65
non-member pitch fee	£4.30
electricity	£1.65 - £2.40

Tel: (01550) 760257 (not after 8 pm). Reservations: Advised for high season and made with deposit; contact the wardens. **Open** March - October.

Directions: From centre of Llandovery take A485 towards Builth Wells, after a short distance turn left, signed Rhandirmwyn, continue for approx. 7 miles along country lanes. O.S.GR: SN779435.

Mid Wales

Tourism information for Mid Wales may also be obtained from:
Mid Wales Tourism, Marketing Dept, The Station, Machynlleth SY20 8TG
Tel: 0800 273747 Fax: 01654 703855 E-mail: info@brilliantbreaks.demon.co.uk

Aeron Coast Caravan Park

628 North Road, Aberaeron, Ceredigion SA46 0JF

Aeron Coast is a family park with a wide range of recreational facilities, on the west coast of Wales. Although it has a high proportion of caravan holiday homes (150 privately owned), touring units of all types are provided for in two fields separated from the beach and sea by a high bank (although the best beach is on the south side of this traditional fishing village). Pitches are on level grass with all units regularly and well spaced in lines in traditional style. The main attraction of the park is its excellent recreational provision, both in and out of doors. This includes a heated kidney shaped pool plus a toddlers' pool (unsupervised) and a paved, walled area good for sunbathing, tennis court and small half-court for youngsters, football and a sand pit. The indoor leisure area provides an under-5's room with slide, etc, teenagers-only room with juke box, table tennis, pool and games machines, a large entertainment room and TV room. In high season these are looked after by two students who also arrange other activities such as tennis tournaments, rounders, 5-a-side football, treasure hunts, teenage discos or free films if the weather is poor.

Facilities: Two modern toilet blocks offer excellent facilities (card operated entry system with £10 deposit) including large family showers. Facilities for disabled people and babies are in one block. Basic motorcaravan service point. Swimming pool (1/6-30/9). Club house and bar (from Easter, 12-2 and from 7 pm) with family room serving bar meals and takeaway in school holiday periods. Reception keeps a wide range of tourist information. Shop at the petrol station at the entrance. Only one dog per unit is accepted. **Off site:** Fishing and boat launching ½ mile. A steam railway, craft centre, woollen mills and potteries can be visited locally.

Charges 2002

Per unit incl. 2 persons	£8.00 - £11.00
extra person over 12 yrs	£1.00
child 2-12 yrs	50p
electricity	£1.50

Tel: (01545) 570349. E-mail: aeroncoastcaravanpark @aberaeron.freeserve.co.uk. Reservations: Made with £10 deposit. **Open** 1 March - 31 October.

Directions: Park is on northern outskirts of Aberaeron village with entrance on the right beside a Texaco petrol station - not too easily seen. O.S.GR: SN461633.

Alan Rogers' discount
Less £1 per night
(excl. Bank and school holidays)

Mid Wales
Fforest Fields Caravan and Camping Park
Hundred House, Builth Wells, Powys LD1 5RT

632

This secluded 'different' park is set on a family hill farm in the heart of Radnorshire. Truly rural, there are glorious views of the surrounding hills and a distinctly family atmosphere. This is simple country camping and caravanning at its best, without man-made distractions or intrusions – a place to unwind and watch the stars. The facilities include 50 large pitches on level grass on a spacious and peaceful, carefully landscaped field by a stream. Electrical connections (mostly 16A) are available and there are 10 hardstandings. George and Kate, the enthusiastic owners, have opened up much of the farm for moderate or ample woodland and moorland trails which can be enjoyed with much wildlife to see. Indeed wildlife is actively encouraged with nesting boxes for owls, song-birds and bats, by leaving field margins un-mown to encourage small mammals and by yearly tree planting. George and Kate also run a para-gliding school where beginners are welcome.

Facilities: The toilet facilities are acceptable, if fairly basic, with baby bath, dish and clothes washing facilities including washing machines and a dryer, and heating in cool weather. Milk, eggs and orange juice are sold in reception and gas, otherwise there are few other on-site facilities, but the village of Hundred House, one mile away, has a pub, village stores and post office. A torch is useful. Reception is not manned on a regular basis. **Off site:** Fishing 3 miles, bicycle hire or golf 5 miles, riding 10 miles.

Charges 2002

Per unit incl. 2 persons	£7.50
extra adult	£2.50
child (4-16 yrs)	£1.50
awning	£1.00
electricity	£1.50

Special low season rates for senior citizens. No credit cards. Tel: (01982) 570406. Fax: (01982) 570444. E-mail: office@fforestfields.co.uk. Reservations: Contact park. **Open** Easter - 17 November.

Directions: Park is signed off A481 between Hundred House and Builth Wells. O.S.GR: SO098535.

Mid Wales
Glan-y-Mor Leisure Park
Clarach Bay, Aberystwyth, Ceredigion SY23 3DT

629

Glan-y-Mor, a busy, sea front, holiday-style park, has an enviable situation on this part of the Cambrian coast, on an attractive bay beside the beach, yet within easy reach of Aberystwyth. On a wet day you may not wish to go far with the comprehensive leisure centre on site - it is open eight months of the year with reduced entry fee for campers. Although the balance of pitches is very much in favour of caravan holiday homes (3:1) which dominate the open park and bay, there are 60 touring pitches, 45 with electricity (10A) and 4 new 'super' pitches. They are rather pressed together in two small sections on the lower part of the park. In high season, tents, tourers or motorcaravans can opt for space and fine views (but beware of winds) on a ridge of higher ground above the park. The well equipped leisure centre offers a heated, irregularly shaped pool, jacuzzi, solarium, sauna, steam room and gymnasium. The complex also includes reception, a video and amusement room, 10-pin bowling, bar, buffet bar and dance room (free entertainment nightly, Easter and May-Oct). This is an ideal site for those seeking 'all the bells and whistles'!

Facilities: The heated toilet block is on the lower touring area with dishwashing facilities and laundry room, plus a toilet for disabled people. A 'portacabin' type block (high season only) is on the ridge ground. A suite including shower for disabled people is in a block in the the upper site, with further facilities at the leisure centre (RADAR key). Motorcaravan service point. Supermarket. Play area designed with younger children in mind, and a large sports field. Swimming pool. Licensed restaurant and takeaway (from Easter). Freezer pack service and gas supplies. No dogs are accepted on touring pitches during B.H. and school summer holiday periods. **Off site:** reduced rates are available at local golf courses.

Charges 2002

Per unit incl. 2 persons	£6.00 - £12.00
'super' pitch	£20.00
child	free
extra person over 18 yrs	£2.00
awning	£3.00
electricity	£2.00
dog (not 13/7-2/9)	£2.00

Top camping area max. charge £10 plus £2 electricity. Club membership (but not Leisure complex) included. Tel: (01970) 828900. Fax: (01970) 828890. E-mail: glanymor@sunbourne.co.uk. Reservations: Any length, with £20 deposit; balance 28 days before arrival. **Open** 1 March - 31 October.

Directions: Clarach is signed west from the A487 (Aberystwyth - Machynlleth) in village of Bow Street. Follow signs over crossroads to beach and park. Access for caravans from Aberystwyth on B4572 is difficult. O.S.GR: SN580850.

Penybont Touring and Camping Park

Llangynog Road, Bala, Gwynedd LL23 7PH

634

This is a pretty little park with 92 pitches on level grass for caravans, on either flat or sloping grass for tents. Connected by circular gravel roadways, they are intermingled with trees and tall trees edge the site. Gravel strips are provided for cars and there are 40 electric hook-ups (16A). The park entrance and a stone building housing reception and the shop provide quite a smart image. Penybont has a useful location being the closest park to Bala town, 100 yds from Bala Lake and 3 miles from the Welsh National White Water Centre, with Snowdonia on hand.

Facilities: The sanitary block includes washbasins in cubicles. En-suite unit for disabled visitors doubling as a baby room, operated by key (£4 deposit). Separate laundry room. Outside is a large covered area for dishwashing and bins. Motorcaravan service point. Shop. Barbecues for hire. Caravan storage. **Off site**: Fishing 200 yds, boat launching, bicycle hire and golf ½ mile, riding 3 miles.

Charges 2001

Per caravan or trailer/frame tent	
incl. 2 persons	£10.75
motorcaravan	£9.95
ridge tent	£9.75
extra person (over 5 yrs)	£2.45
awning	£1.95 - £2.25
electricity	£1.95

Tel: (01678) 520549. Fax: (01678) 520006. E-mail: penybont@tinyonline.co.uk. Reservations: Made for exact dates for particular pitches, with deposit of £10 per pitch. **Open** 1 April - 31 October.

Directions: Park is ½ mile southeast of Bala village on the B4391. Bala is between Dolgellau and Corwen on the A494. O.S.GR: SH931349.

Pen-y-Garth Caravan and Camping Park

Bala, Gwynedd LL23 7ES

636

An attractively located touring park in a high valley, Pen-y-Garth has 63 pitches (35 with 10A electrical hook-ups) and two rally fields. Adjacent to the touring area are 54 caravan holiday homes, mainly privately owned. At reception, the well stocked shop has gas and comprehensive tourist information. A good six acre recreation field is opposite the park. Watersports are plentiful in this area with the National White Water Centre 5 miles away and Lake Bala and Lake Vyrnwy close. Portmeirion, Snowdonia, Bodnant Gardens and many of those little railways are easy day trips.

Facilities: The main sanitary block offers free controllable showers. In addition to this block, there are two further men's and ladies' toilets and showers on payment (10p or 20p). All these facilities have been refurbished. Dishwashing and food preparation room with further facilities for dishwashing, a free freezer for ice blocks, and a laundry. Shop (Easter - end Sept). Small games room. Recreation field. Dogs are accepted by prior arrangement. **Off site:** Fishing, bicycle hire, riding and golf, all within 3 miles.

Charges 2001

Per unit incl. 2 persons	£7.95 - £9.50
extra person (over 5 yrs)	£1.75
awning	£1.80
electricity	£1.85

Less 25% for one person with small tent. Min. 3 night stay at B.Hs. Tel: (01678) 520485 (mobile: 0780 8198717). Fax: (01678) 520401. E-mail: stay@ penygarth.co.uk. Reservations: Made with 25% deposit (min. 3 nights at B.Hs). **Open** 1 March - 31 October.

Directions: Take B4391 from Bala and in 1 mile turn right uphill at sign. Park is 600 yds on right before road narrows. O.S.GR: SH940349.

Barcdy Caravan and Camping Park

Talsarnau, nr Harlech, Gwynedd LL47 6YG

Barcdy is partly in a sheltered vale, partly on a plateau top and partly in open fields edged by woods, with fells to the rear and marvellous views across the Lleyn peninsula in one direction and towards the Snowdon range in another. The Roberts family opened to their first visitors sixty years ago, and they still welcome them today. The park provides for all tastes with level or sloping grass pitches, either secluded in the valley or enjoying the view from the plateau or the lower field. There are 108 pitches, including 38 for touring caravans and 40 for tents, with or without 10A electricity (50 electricity points), plus 30 caravan holiday homes. The grounds of the farm include 28 acres of open fields and natural oak woods (a haven for children) and further up the hills are the two Tecwyn lakes for fishing or just to relax by and enjoy the views. Harlech beach and the castle are only 4 miles, the Italianate village of Portmeirion is nearby and Snowdonia is on your doorstep. A member of the Countryside Discovery group.

Facilities: Two toilet blocks, the one at the top of the valley opened in high season only, include large, comfortable showers, that open direct to the outside except for one in each male and female sections. Hot water is free to the washbasins and dishwashing sinks, metered to the showers (25p). Shop for essentials including gas (open 8.30-11 am. and 4-7 pm. Spr. B.H, then mid July-end Aug). Dogs are not accepted. **Off site:** Riding 4 miles, golf 4 or 6 miles.

Charges 2001

Per unit incl. 2 persons	£8.50 - £10.50
plus 2 children	£10.50 - £13.00
extra adult	£3.00
child (up to 16 yrs)	£1.00
electricity (10A)	£2.00

Tel/Fax: (01766) 770736. E-mail: anwen@ barcdy.idps.co.uk. Reservations: Contact park. **Open** Easter - 31 October.

Directions: Park is just off the A496 between villages of Llandecwyn and Talsarnau, 4 miles north of Harlech. O.S.GR: SH622371.

Alan Rogers' discount
Less 10% in low and mid seasons

Hendre Mynach Touring Caravan and Camping Park

Llanaber, Barmouth, Gwynedd LL42 1YR

A neat and tidy family park, colourful flowers and top rate facilities make an instant impression on arrival down the steep entrance to this park (help is available to get out if you are worried). The 220 pitches are allocated in various areas, with substantial tenting areas identified. Thirty gravel hardstandings are available and around the park there are 120 electricity hook-ups (10A) and ample water taps. The quaint old seaside and fishing town of Barmouth is just ¼ mile away, a 15-20 minute walk along the prom. Here you will find 'everything'. The beach is only 100 yards away but a railway line runs between this and the park. It can be crossed at any of three points by pedestrian operated gates which could be a worry for those with young children. Snowdonia National Park and mountain railway, the famous Ffestiniog railway, castles and lakes everywhere provide plenty to see and do – a classic park in a classic area.

Facilities: Two toilet blocks, one modern and one traditional, both offer excellent facilities including spacious showers (20p) and washbasins in cubicles in the new block. Extra showers are provided in mobile units used in peak times. Motorcaravan service point. Well stocked on-site shop incorporating a snack bar and takeaway (Easter - 1 Nov; 08.30-21.00 hrs. in peak times, less at quieter times).

Charges 2002

Per caravan or large motorcaravan	
incl. 2 persons	£8.00 - £14.00
3 or 4 persons	£10.00 - £15.00
electricity (10A)	£2.00
tent or caravanette incl. 2 persons	£8.00 - £12.00
3 or 4 persons	£9.50 - £14.00
extra adult	£3.00
child (2-15 yrs)	£1.00
first dog free, extra dog	50p

Plus £1 for weekends between 24/5-7/9. Special spring and autumn offers. Low season offers for over 60s. Tel: (01341) 280262. Fax: (01341) 280586. E-mail: mynach@lineone.net. Reservations: Made with £20 deposit and £1.50 booking fee. **Open** all year excl. 10 Jan - 28 Feb.

Directions: Park is off the A496 road north of Barmouth in village of Llanaber with entrance down a steep drive. O.S.GR: SH608168.

Daisy Bank Touring Caravan Park

633 Snead, Montgomery, Powys SY15 6EB

For adults only, this pretty, tranquil park in the Camlad Valley has panoramic views, and is an ideal base for walkers. Attractively landscaped with 'old English' flower beds and many different trees and shrubs, this small park has been carefully developed. The Welsh hills to the north and the Shropshire hills to the south overlook the two fields of 20 pitches each. The field nearer to the road (perhaps a little noisy) is slightly sloping but there are hardstandings for motorcaravans, while the second field is more level. All pitches have 16A electricity, water and waste water drainage and TV hook up. With many walks in the area, including Offa's Dyke, a series of walk leaflets is available centred on Bishop's Castle three miles away. The owners will site your van for you and there is a late arrivals area with hook-up. A security bar at the entrance has to be lifted for motorcaravans. Although technically in Wales, the park is 500 yards from the Shropshire border, an area rich in history. This is an adult only park.

Facilities: The cheerful, well equipped toilet block can be heated. Dishwashing sinks at the rear of the block are covered. No laundry facilities (launderette at Churchstoke, 2 miles). Brick built barbecues. Small putting green (free loan of clubs and balls). Gas is stocked. **Off site**: Supermarket 2 miles. Many eating places near. Bicycle hire, riding or fishing 3 miles.

Charges guide

Per unit incl. 2 adults and all services	£11.00
extra person	£2.00
dog	50p

Tel: (01588) 620471. Reservations: Contact park. **Open** all year.

> **Directions**: Site is by the A489 road 2 miles east of Churchstoke in the direction of Craven Arms. O.S.GR: SO303929.

North Wales

Tourism information for North Wales may also be obtained from:
North Wales Tourism, 77 Conwy Road, Colwyn Bay LL29 7LN
Tel: 01492 531731 Fax: 01492 530059 E-mail: croeso@nwt.co.uk www.nwt.co.uk

Camping and Caravanning Club Site Llanystumdwy

658 Tyddyn Sianel, Llanystumdwy, Criccieth, Gwynedd LL52 0LS

Overlooking mountains and sea, Llanystumdwy is one of the earliest Camping and Caravanning Club sites. Well maintained with good facilities, it is on sloping grass. However, the managers are very helpful and know their site and can advise on the most suitable pitch and even have a supply of chocks. There are 60 pitches in total (20 ft. spacing), 45 with 10A electricity connections, spaced over two hedged fields with mainly caravans in the top field with four hardstandings for motor-caravans, and tents lower down. A little library with a supply of tourist information is next to the small reception. A shop and pub are in the village and a bus leaves each hour from outside the site to Pwllheli or Porthmadog. This is a good base from which to explore the Lleyn peninsula or Snowdonia National Park. Portmeirion with its Italianate village is near.

Facilities: A purpose-built toilet block to one side provides excellent, full facilities for disabled visitors including access ramp, one washbasin each in a cubicle for male and female and extra large sinks. Facilities for babies. Laundry (taps with fitting for disabled people). Gas supplies. **Off site**: Riding or fishing ½ mile, golf 2½ miles.

Charges 2001

Per adult	£3.75 - £5.30
child (6-18 yrs)	£1.65
non-member pitch fee	£4.30
electricity	£1.65 - £2.40

Tel: (01766) 522855 (no calls after 8 pm). Reservations: Necessary and made with deposit - contact site. **Open** April - October.

> **Directions**: Follow A497 from Criccieth west and take second right to Llanystumdwy. Site is on the right. O.S.GR: SH469384.

Forestry Commission Beddgelert Campsite

659 Beddgelert, Gwynedd LL55 4UU

This well equipped Forestry Commission site is in the heart of Snowdonia. Set in a marvellous, natural, wooded environment on the slopes of Snowdon there is abundant fauna and flora, tumbling streams and always something to watch from the cheeky squirrels to the smallest bird in Britain. Well equipped and well managed, the site provides 280 pitches - tents in a semi-wooded field area and caravans amongst the trees with numbered hardstandings, and 105 places with 10A electricity. Tents may pitch where they like in their areas leaving 6 m. between units. Metal tent pegs may be best (available from the shop). Free maps of the forest walks are provided in reception and orienteering and fishing are possible. A bus service stops at the top of the entrance lane (two hourly for Caernarfon and Porthmadog).

Facilities: Two fully equipped modern sanitary toilet blocks clad in natural wood provide large, free hot showers (with good dry areas). Laundry equipment is in one block. A small unit provides extra washbasins and toilets in peak season and there is a toilet and washbasin for disabled visitors. Recycling bins. Reception is central, as is a well provisioned shop. Well equipped children's adventure playground. **Off site:** Pub within walking distance (¾ mile) and other eating places nearby. Bicycle hire within 500 m. in forest.

Charges 2001

Per adult	£3.40 - £4.70
child (5-14 yrs)	£1.50 - £2.20
extra car, trailer or pup tent	£2.50
electricity	£2.10 - £2.40

Less 20% all year for disabled guests and outside 7/7-28/8 for the over 60s. Tel: (01766) 890288. Reservations: Necessary for B.Hs and peak times (min. 3 nights with £30 deposit). Contact (at all times): Forest Holidays, Forestry Commission, 231 Corstorphine Road, Edinburgh EH12 7AT. Tel: (0131) 314 6505. E-mail: fe.holidays@forestry.gov.uk. **Open** all year excl. 20/11-20/12.

Directions: Site is clearly signed to the left 1 mile north of Beddgelert on A4085 Caernarfon road. O.S.GR: SH578490.

Bryn Gloch Caravan and Camping Park

660 Betws Garmon, nr Caernarfon, Gwynedd LL54 7YY

Bryn Gloch is a well kept and family owned touring park in the impressive Snowdonia area. Neat and quiet, it takes some 160 units on five flat, wide meadows, with 12 caravan holiday homes. There are tarmac roads and free areas are allowed in the centre for play. There are 150 electrical connections (10A), 6 all weather pitches, 18 'super' pitches and 6 serviced pitches (shared) All these have hardstanding. Fishing is possible on the river bordering the park with a barbecue and picnic area, adventure play area and field for ball games. Tourist information is provided in the complex by reception. Caernarfon with its famous castle 5 miles.

Facilities: The well equipped main toilet blocks include a family bathroom (hot water £1), baby changing room and complete facilities for visitors with disabilities (coded access). The far field has a 'portacabin' style unit containing all facilities, for use in peak season. Well equipped laundry and separate drying room. Motorcaravan service point and car wash. Shop (1/3-30/10). TV and games rooms with pool tables and amusement machines. Minigolf. Entrance barrier with coded access. **Off site:** Riding 2½ miles, bicycle hire or golf 5 miles.

Charges 2001

Per unit incl. 2 persons	£10.00
caravans over 18 ft.	plus £1.00
extra adult	£2.00
child (3-16 yrs)	£1.50
awning or pup tent	£1.50
dog	50p
electricity	£2.50
'super' pitch incl. electricity, etc.	plus £5.50
serviced pitch	plus £4.50

Tel: (01286) 650216. Fax: (01286) 650591. E-mail: eurig@easynet.co.uk. Reservations: Necessary for B.Hs. (min. 3 nights) with payment in full; other times with deposit of first night's fee. **Open** all year, limited facilities 1 Nov - 1 March.

Directions: Park is just beyond Waunfawr, 4½ miles southeast of Caernarfon on A4085 towards Beddgelert. Watch for signs and park entrance is opposite St Garmon church. O.S.GR: SH538578.

Home Farm Caravan Park

664 Marianglas, Isle of Anglesey LL73 8PH

A tarmac drive through an open field leads to this neatly laid out quality park, with caravan holiday homes to one side. Nestling below what was once a Celtic hill fort, later decimated as a quarry, the park is edged with mature trees and farmland. A circular, tarmac access road leads to the 61 well spaced and numbered pitches, which include 9 fully serviced with electricity, water and waste water and a further 19 with electricity and water. All these have hardstanding with 16A electricity; other pitches all have 10A supply. On neatly cut grass, some areas are slightly sloping, and there is a separate area for tents. The 'piece de resistance' of this park must be the children's indoor play area, large super adventure play equipment, complete with tunnels, bridges on safe rubber matting, not to mention an outside fenced play area and fields available for sports, football, etc. and walking. Various beaches, sandy or rocky, are within a mile. A member of the Best of British group.

Facilities: Two purpose built toilet blocks, one part of the reception building, are of the same design and can be heated. They include en-suite provision for people with disabilities (with key) and an excellent small bathroom for children with baby bath and curtain for privacy, a laundry room and good washing up facilities. Motorcaravan service point. Reception provides basic essentials, gas and some caravan accessories. Indoor and outdoor children's play areas. TV and a pool table. **Off site:** Fishing or golf 2 miles, riding 8 miles.

Charges 2001

Per unit incl. 2 persons	£8.00 - £10.75
large or trailer tent	£8.00 - £11.75
extra adult	£1.50 - £2.25
child (5-17 yrs)	£1.00 - £1.50
extra car or boat	£1.50 - £2.00
awning or extra pup tent	£1.50
electricity	£2.00
fully serviced pitch	plus £2.50 - £3.50
dog (max. 2)	50p

Tel: (01248) 410614. Fax: (01248) 410900. E-mail: enq@homefarm-anglesey.co.uk. Reservations: Essential for peak season (min. 3 days at B.Hs) and made with £20 deposit. **Open** April - October.

Directions: From the Britannia Bridge take second exit left signed Benllech and Amlwch on the A5025. Two miles after Benllech keep left at roundabout and park entrance is approx. 300 yards on the left beyond the church. O.S.GR: SH498850.

Bron-Y-Wendon Touring Caravan Park

669 Wern Road, Llanddulas, Colwyn Bay, Clwyd LL22 8HG

Bron-Y-Wendon is right by the sea between Abergele and Colwyn Bay on the beautiful North Wales coast road. This is a quiet park which, by its own admission, is not really geared up for the family unit - there is no children's playground here, although there is a games room with table tennis and a separate TV room. The park is manicured to the highest standards and caters for a large number of seasonal caravans on pitches with gravel bases which are kept very tidy. There are a further 65 grass based, and 20 hardstanding touring pitches, all with electrical hook ups (16A) and tarmac access roads. All pitches have coastal views and the sea and beach are just a short walk away. Colwyn Bay, Conwy, Anglesey, Llandudno, Snowdonia and Chester are all within easy reach, so there is lots to do. Having said how peaceful and quiet everything is (particularly for a seaside park in this area), there is some road noise from the adjacent A55 and during our visit a small train passed on the tracks between the park and the sea (just a few yards away) and at night with little else going on it could be just noticeable.

Facilities: Two toilet blocks, both with heating, provide excellent facilities including men's and women's shower rooms separate from the toilets and washbasins. Good facilities for disabled visitors. Laundry with washing machines and dryers. Mobile shop visits daily. Gas supplies on site. **Off site:** Llanddulas village with shops and several good pubs is very near.

Charges 2001

Per pitch	£5.00 - £7.00
person	£2.00
child (2-12 yrs)	£1.00
awning	£2.00
electricity (16A)	£2.00

Tel/Fax: (01492) 512903. E-mail: bron-y-wendon@ northwales-holidays.co.uk. Reservations: Made with £5 deposit; contact park. **Open** 21 March - 30 October.

Directions: From A55 Chester - Conwy road turn at Llanddulas junction (A547). Turn right opposite Shell garage and park is approx.¼mile, signed on coast side of the road. O.S.GR: SH903785.

 Alan Rogers' discount
Less £1 per unit, per night on stays of 3 nights or more (excl. B.Hs.)

Hunter's Hamlet Touring Caravan Park

665 Sirior Goch Farm, Betws-yn-Rhos, Abergele, Clwyd LL22 8PL

This small, family owned park is licensed for all units except tents (trailer tents allowed). On a gently sloping hillside providing beautiful panoramic views, one area provides 15 well spaced pitches with hardstanding and 10A electricity hook-ups, with access from a circular, hard-core road. A more recent area has been developed next to this of a similar design but with 8 fully serviced 'super pitches' (water, waste water, sewage, TV and electricity connections). Shrubs and bushes at various stages of growth enhance both areas. A natural play area incorporating rustic adventure equipment set amongst mature beech trees with a small bubbling stream is a children's paradise. Milk and papers can be ordered and the Hunters will do their best to meet your needs, even to survival rations! The park is well situated to tour Snowdonia and Anglesey and is within easy reach of Llandudno and Rhyl. Tents (other than trailer tents) are not accepted.

Facilities: The tiny heated toilet block has fully tiled facilities including showers en-suite with toilets for both sexes. A covered area to the rear houses laundry and dishwashing (H&C), washing machine and dryer, iron and board, freezer and fridge. Family bathroom (metered) and basic toilet and shower facilities for disabled visitors. Children's play area. All year caravan storage. Max. 2 dogs per pitch. **Off site:** Fishing or golf 2 miles, riding 10 miles.

Charges 2001

Per unit incl. 2 adults: basic pitch	£9.00 - £11.00
'super pitch' (fully incl.)	£16.00 - £19.00
extra person	£2.00
school age child	£1.00
awning	£2.00
electricity (10A)	£2.00

Less £5 on weekly bookings. Aug. B.H, plus £1.00. Tel/Fax: (01745) 832237. E-mail: huntershamlet@aol.com. Reservations: Made with £20 deposit; B.H. bookings min. 4 nights. **Open** 21 March - 31 October.

Directions: From Abergele take A548 south for 2¾ miles; turn onto B5381 in direction of Betws-yn-Rhos and park is on left after ½ mile. To date there are no local authority caravan signs so watch carefully for the farm after turning - it can be identified by a artistically painted sign with the house and farm name: 'Sirior Goch Farm' and Hunter's Hamlet. O.S.GR: SH929736.

Ty Ucha Caravan Park

670 Maesmawr Road, Llangollen, Clwyd LL20 7PP

Only a mile from Llangollen, world famous for the Eisteddfod, Ty Ucha has a rather dramatic setting, nestling under its own mountain and with views across the valley to craggy Dinas Bran castle. It is a neat, ordered park, carefully managed by the owners and providing 40 pitches (30 with 10A electrical hook-up) for caravans and motorcaravans only. They are well spaced round a large, grassy field with an open centre for play and a small paddock area. One side slopes gently and is bounded by a stream and wood. A path leads from here for various mountain walks, depending on your energy and ability. Because of overhead cables, kite flying is forbidden; no bike riding either. The paddock area provides for those who prefer to be without the company of children or dogs. Eisteddfod is an international festival of music and dance held for six days starting on the first Tuesday of the first full week in July every year – it is a very busy time for the area. No tents are accepted.

Facilities: The single toilet block, although of 'portacabin' style, is clean and well maintained and can be heated. It includes two metered showers for each sex (a little cramped). Dishwashing sink with cold water outside. No laundry facilities but there is a launderette in Llangollen. Gas supplies. Games room with table tennis. Late arrivals area. **Off site:** Hotel ½ mile away with reasonably priced meals. Fishing 1 mile, golf ½ mile.

Charges 2001

Per caravan incl. 2 persons	£7.00
motorcaravan	£6.50
extra person	£1.00
awning (environmental groundsheets)	50p - £1.00
electricity	£2.00

Reductions for OAPs for weekly stays. No credit cards. Tel: (01978) 860677. Reservations: Necessary for B.Hs. and Eisteddfod and made with £10 deposit; 3 days min. at B.H.s. **Open** Easter - October.

Directions: Park is signed off A5 road, 1 mile east of Llangollen (250 yds). O.S.GR: SJ228411.

Alan Rogers' discount
Less 50p per unit, per night

The Plassey Touring and Leisure Park

Eyton, nr Wrexham, Clwyd LL13 0SP

667

Set in 247 acres of the Dee Valley, The Plassey offers many activities. It is not just a touring park but is also a leisure and craft centre with a friendly, busy atmosphere and pleasant environment. The Edwardian farm buildings have been tastefully converted to provide a restaurant, coffee shop, health, beauty and hair studio, a small garden centre and 16 different craft and retail units, open all year to the public. Unusually there is also a small brewery on site, producing its own unique Plassey Bitter! The park itself is spacious with pitches around the outer edges of a series of fields forming circles. There are 110 touring pitches with electrical connections (16A), including 30 new serviced pitches (with hardstanding, water, waste water, electricity, lighting), and five areas taking 120 seasonal caravans which will put pressure on the facilities. There is much to do and to look at in a rural setting at the Plassey but it is probably best enjoyed mid-week and avoiding the busy Bank Holidays. Certainly for peace and quiet, you should try and pitch away from reception, the clubhouse and arcade games.

Facilities: The original toilet facilities beside the entrance and under the clubhouse have been refurbished to a good standard. These are supplemented by a good, new heated block in the top field area with individual washbasin cubicles, a room for disabled visitors or families, dishwashing sinks and laundry. Motorcaravan service point. Shop (all season) and gas. Club house with children's room (open March-Oct.). Indoor, heated swimming pool with sun-bed and sauna (May - Sept, limited hours mid-week, 80p per hour). Badminton courts including indoor one which can be booked. Adventure playground with equipment for smaller children (note: bicycles, skateboards or footballs are not allowed). Nine hole golf course, fishing pools and countryside footpaths. Winter caravan storage. **Off site:** Riding or bicycle hire 5 miles.

Charges 2002

Per unit incl. 2 adults, 2 children, electricity and club membership	£12.00 - £14.50
serviced pitch	£3.00
extra person, dog or extra car	£1.50
awning or pup tent	£2.00

Includes club membership, coarse fishing, badminton and table tennis (own racquets and bats required). B.H. supplement £4 per weekend. Discount for weekly booking. Tel: (01978) 780277. Fax: (01978) 780019. E-mail: enquiries@ theplassey.co.uk. Reservations: Necessary for weekends, B.Hs and July/Aug. and made with £20 deposit. **Open** 5 March - 7 November.

Directions: Follow brown and cream signs (for The Plassey) from the A483 Chester - Oswestry bypass onto the B5426 and park is 2½ miles. Also signed from the A528 Marchwiel - Overton road. O.S.GR: SJ349452.

Alan Rogers' discount
Less 50p per unit, per night

James' Caravan Park

Ruabon, Wrexham, Clwyd LL14 6DW

668

Open all year, this park has a heated toilet block and attractive, park-like surroundings with mature trees and neat, short grass. However, edged by two main roads it is subject to some road noise. The old farm buildings and owner's collection of original farm machinery, carefully restored and maintained, add interest. The park has over 40 pitches, some level and some on a slope, with informal siting giving either a view or shade. Electricity (6/10A) is available all over, although a long lead may be useful. Tourist information and a free freezer for ice packs are in the foyer of the toilet block. This is a useful park with easy access from the A483 Wrexham - Oswestry road.

Facilities: The heated toilet block offers roomy showers (20p) with a useful rail to help those of advancing age with feet washing. En-suite facilities for visitors with disabilities complete with special 'clos o mat' toilet! Motorcaravan service point. Gas available. **Off site:** The village is a 10 minute walk with a Spar shop, fish and chips, a restaurant, launderette and four pubs. Golf 3 miles.

Charges 2001

Per unit incl. 2 persons	£8.00
extra person	£1.00
awning	£2.00
dog	50p
electricity	£2.00

No credit cards. Tel/Fax: (01978) 820148. E-mail: ray@carastay.demon.co.uk. Reservations: Contact park for details. **Open** all year.

Directions: Park is at junction of A483/A539 Llangollen road and is accessible from the west-bound A539. O.S.GR: SJ302434.

SCOTLAND

Scottish Tourist Board
23 Ravelston Terrace, Edinburgh EH4 3TP
Tel: (0131) 332 2433 Fax: (0131) 315 4545

E-mail: inf@stb.gov.uk
Internet: http://www.visitscotland.com

We have used the following Regional Tourist Areas to list our parks:

1. **Scottish Lowlands**
2. **Heart of Scotland**
3. **Grampian**
4. **Highlands and Islands**

Scotland provides superb opportunities to enjoy wild and grand scenery. It also offers towns and cities with a rich cultural life and over the centuries has had a disproportionately large impact on the world with many of its philosophers, scientists and inventors being responsible for the ideas on which we base our understanding of the world.

Lowlands

The area we identify as the Scottish Lowlands or Southern Scotland, covers Dumfries and Galloway, the Scottish Borders, Edinburgh and Lothians, Greater Glasgow and the Clyde valley. In Dumfries and Galloway lonely hills roll down to pastures and dark woods which give way to rich farmlands and a sunny south facing coast. The Borders is an area of tranquil villages, bustling textile towns and a wild coastline running north from Berwick-upon-Tweed. There are magnificent historic houses, great Border abbeys, working woollen mills and craft workshops. Sir Walter Scott, the famous Scottish writer, lived at Abbotsford near Melrose and is buried at Dryburgh Abbey. The Lothians, bordered by the sea waters of the Firth of Forth to the unspoiled Pentland Hills, has a beautiful coastline and rich countryside. Edinburgh is dealt with elsewhere as is Glasgow. Paisley is known for the Paisley shawl and Lanark for the enlightened industrialist Robert Owen whose Utopian ideas on workers welfare in his textile mills

Heart of Scotland

Heart of Scotland covering Loch Lomond, Stirling and the Trossachs, Perthshire, Angus, Dundee and the Kingdom of Fife. Here the Lowlands meet the mountains of the north and west and in old days all routes led to Stirling. Because of its strategic position whoever held Stirling Castle controlled the Scottish nation. The Trossachs with their heather-clad hills are the home of Rob Roy the folk hero. Fife boasts two ancient 'capitals'. Dunfermline, the seat of early Celtic kings and the final resting place of Robert the Bruce and St Andrews, the ecclesiastical capital, now a university town and the 'Home of Golf'.

Grampian

Grampian includes the Grampian Highlands, Aberdeen and the North East Coast and is probably best known for Royal Deeside where Prince Albert built Balmoral Castle as a summer home for Queen Victoria and the Malt Whisky Trail. This is a signed route featuring seven whisky distilleries, each with excellent interpretation facilities for visitors.

Highlands and Islands

The Highlands and Islands is one of the last wildernesses in Europe, from the soaring beauty of Glencoe to the to the idyllic charm of the Isles, and from the crashing waves of the northern coastline to the silence of the windswept moors. Home to the Loch Ness Monster and the famous Fort William to Mallaig railway, one of the greatest railway journeys in the world.

Camping and Caravanning Club Site Culzean Castle

Maybole, nr Ayr, Strathclyde KA19 8JK

This quiet Camping and Caravanning Club site is next door to Culzean Castle (pronounced Kullayne) with its grounds and 17 miles of footpaths and visitors are given a pass to walk in the grounds (when open) as many times as they wish. The 18th century, cliff top castle is built on the site of a former ancient castle and its armoury exhibition is superb. Besides the woodland walks, deer park and aviary, there are three miles of rocky shore, small sandy beaches and stunning views of the Firth of Clyde. A full programme of events is staged at the castle over the season, including special children's weeks, sheep-dog trials, bands, battle re-enactments, ranger walks and craft fairs. The campsite has 90 pitches, some level others slightly sloping, and 60 have electrical hook-ups (10A). A few level pitches are suitable for motorcaravans and 20 pitches have hardstanding. American style motorhomes (less than 27 ft only) are advised to make prior arrangements, as large pitches are limited. Should you have your fill of the castle and its grounds, Maybole with shops, etc. is only 4 miles and the area has a wealth of places to visit. Buses pass the gate.

Facilities: The toilet blocks, kept very clean, can be heated and include some washbasins in cubicles, dishwashing sinks and a well equipped laundry with clothes lines. A unit for disabled visitors has a WC, washbasin and shower - an excellent facility. A small shop with very basic provisions opens for short periods morning and evening. Adventure playground. Units over 27 ft long only accepted by prior arrangement. **Off site:** Golf or bicycle hire 4 miles, fishing 8 miles.

Charges 2001

Per adult	£3.75 - £5.30
child (6-18 yrs)	£1.65
non-member pitch fee	£4.30
electricity	£1.65 - £2.40

Tel: (01655) 760627, no calls after 8 pm. Reservations: Advised for high season and made with deposit; contact site. **Open** March - October.

Directions: From Maybole follow signs for Culzean Castle and Country Park, turning in the town on B7023 which runs into the A719. Country Park entrance is clearly signed on right after 3¾miles; entrance to caravan park is on the right in Country Park drive. O.S.GR: NS247103.

Aird Donald Caravan Park

London Road, Stranraer, Wigtownshire, DG9 8RN

Aird Donald makes a good stopping off place when travelling to and from the Irish ferries, but it is also useful for seeing the sights around Stranraer. The tidy park comprises 12 acres surrounded by conifers, flowering trees and shrubs and the 300 yard drive is lit and lined with well trimmed conifers. There are grass areas for caravans or tents and hardstandings with electricity hook-up (these very handy for hardy winter tourers). A small play area provides for young children, but the local leisure centre is a walk away and caters for swimming, table tennis, gym, etc, and a theatre that hosts everything from country and western to opera. It also has bar facilities. The area has three world famous gardens to visit, numerous golf courses, fishing, riding and watersports.

Facilities: Two toilet blocks, the old original one very basic with free showers, and open all the time, the other new, modern and heated. Kept very clean with excellent, tiled facilities, this one is kept locked with a key deposit of £5 - we recommend you use this facility. It has two types of shower, an electric one which is metered (20p) and two others which are free (strange, because they are all excellent). Washbasins are in vanity units, ladies having one in a cubicle. A unit for visitors with disabilities has a washbasin and WC. Dishwashing sinks and a small laundry with sinks, dryer, twin-tub washing machine, an old fashioned mangle and clothes lines. Motorcaravan service facilities.

Charges guide

Per unit incl. 2 adults, 1 child and electricity	£10.40

No credit cards. Tel: (01776) 702025. E-mail: aird@mimman.u-net.com. Reservations: Contact park. **Open** all year.

Directions: Enter Stranraer on A75 road. Watch for narrow site entrance on left entering town, opposite school. O.S.GR: NX075605.

Brighouse Bay Holiday Park

695 Brighouse Bay, Borgue, Kirkcudbright, Dumfries and Galloway DG6 4TS

Hidden away within 1,200 exclusive acres, on a quiet, unspoilt peninsula, this spacious family park is only some 200 yards through bluebell woods from a lovely sheltered bay. It has exceptional all weather facilities, as well as golf and pony trekking. Over 90% of the 120 touring caravan pitches have electricity (16A), some with hardstanding and some with water, drainage and TV aerial. The three tenting areas are on fairly flat, undulating ground and some pitches have electricity. There are 120 self-contained holiday caravans. On site leisure facilities include a golf and leisure club with 16.5 m. pool, water features, jacuzzi, steam room, fitness room, sun-bed, games room (all on payment), golf driving range and clubhouse bar and bistro. The 18 hole golf course extends onto the headland with superb views over the Irish Sea to the Isle of Man and Cumbria. Like the park, these facilities are open all year. The BHS approved pony trekking centre on the farm offers treks for complete beginners, slow hacks for the nervous or inexperienced or gallops on the beach for the more experienced. A well run park of high standards and a member of the Best of British group.

Facilities: The well maintained main toilet block is large, with 10 unisex cabins with shower, basin and WC, and 12 with washbasin and WC. Covered dishwashing sinks. Launderette. A second, excellent block next to the tent areas has en-suite shower rooms (one for disabled people) and bathroom, separate washing cubicles, showers, baby room, laundry sinks, and covered dishwashing. One section is heated in winter. Motorcaravan service point. Licensed supermarket. Takeaway. Gas supplies. Leisure club with pool. Golf. Mountain bike hire, quad bikes, boating pond, 10 pin bowling, playgrounds, putting, nature trails. Riding (April - Oct). Coarse fishing ponds. Sea angling and all-tide slipway for boating. Caravan storage.

Charges 2001

Per unit incl. 2 persons	£9.50 - £12.75
extra adult	£2.00 - £2.20
child (4-15)	£1.25 - £1.50
awning	£1.80 - £2.00
porch awning or small pup tent	£1.00
electricity	£2.75 - £2.25
fully serviced pitch	£4.20 - £3.95
trailed craft	£3.00 - £3.20
other craft	£1.50 - £1.60
dog	£1.00

Winter rate: from £12.50 incl. all pitch fees. Up to 10% reduction for weekly bookings. Tel: (01557) 870267. Fax: (01557) 870319. E-mail: arogers@ brighouse-bay.co.uk. Reservations: Advance booking is advised and made with £25 deposit. **Open** all year.

Directions: From Kirkcudbright turn south off A755 onto B727 (to Borgue); after 4 miles Brighouse Bay is signed to south. From west take B727 to Borgue and beyond, turning south as above. Or follow Brighouse Bay signs off A75 just east of Gatehouse of Fleet. O.S.GR: NX630455.

Seaward Caravan Park

690 Dhoon Bay, Kirkcudbright DG6 4TJ

Seaward Caravan Park is little sister to the much larger Brighouse Bay Holiday Park, 3½ miles away. Set in an idyllic location overlooking the bay, this park is suitable for all units. The terrain is slightly undulating, but most of the numbered pitches are flat and a good size. There are 35 pitches (18 hardstandings) designated for caravans and motorcaravans, a further 14 for tents, and 43 caravan holiday homes for hire. Electric hook-ups (16A) are on 32 of the touring pitches, 12 also serviced with water tap, waste water disposal, and TV socket. Visitors can play golf on the park's nine-hole course (£3 per round) or watch others play while walking the dog around its perimeter. Facilities at the larger Brighouse Bay Holiday Park are available to all campers at discounted rates. This is a quiet park with excellent views ideally suited for that relaxing holiday or for touring the region.

Facilities: The principal, fully equipped toilet block is to the rear of the park. Two rooms with en-suite facilities suitable for campers with disabilities. Baby room and two more en-suite cubicles being built. Laundry and dishwashing room. No motorcaravan service point but the manager can lift a manhole cover to empty waste water tanks. The reception/shop stocks a variety of provisions, books, gifts, gas, and tourist information. TV/family room. Unsupervised heated outdoor swimming pool with sunbathing area (15/5-15/9). Central play area with bark surface, outdoor chess, rocking horse, table tennis and picnic tables. Excellent games room. Golf. **Off site:** Beach and sea angling nearby, riding or bicycle hire 3½ miles. Kirkcudbright is 2½ miles.

Charges 2001

Per unit incl. 2 adults	£8.25 - £11.25
extra adult	£1.60 - £1.70
child (4-15 yrs)	£1.20 - £1.30
awning	£1.70 - £1.80
porch awning or small tent	£1.00
electricity	£2.25 - £2.75
electric/TV aerial	£2.85 - £3.20
dog	£1.00

Less 5-10% for bookings (not valid with some other discount schemes). Tel: (01557) 331079. E-mail: info@seaward-park.co.uk Reservations: Made with deposit of £25 per week booked, balance on arrival. **Open** 1 March - 31 October.

Directions: Follow international camping signs from Kirkcudbright on A711. O.S.GR: NX680510.

Park of Brandedleys

693 Crocketford, Dumfries, Dumfries and Galloway DG2 8RG

Brandedleys is a first class park providing pitches for some 80 caravans and a limited number of tents, plus 27 self-contained holiday homes (12 of which, with two cottages and three chalets, are let) in three or four flat and variably sloping fields with tarmac access roads. It has excellent installations and amenities. Caravan pitches are on lawns or terraced hardstandings, many with a pleasant outlook across a loch. There are 80 electrical connections (10A), 21 pitches with water and drainage, plus some 'premier' pitches with TV connections and a picnic bench. A small, heated outdoor swimming pool is open when the weather is suitable and the heated indoor pool adjacent to the bar/restaurant is open all season with changing room (both pools free) and a sauna. The bar and licensed restaurant with full menu at reasonable prices, are open for lunch and dinner, with a patio area overlooking Auchenreoch Loch. Walks on the open moors or forest and beautiful sandy beaches 12 miles away. A popular, quality park and a member of the Best of British group.

Facilities: The main centrally heated toilet block has been extensively modernised with clean, well appointed shower cubicles with toilet and washbasin (just one for men), in addition to the normal provision. Hairdryers. Bathroom for disabled visitors. Laundry room, baby and hair care room. Covered dishwashing sinks. A second block of equal size and standard is in the lower field, also with laundry and dishwashing facilities. Shop with good stocks. Bar and restaurant. Takeaway food to order (18.00-21.30 hrs). Swimming pools. All-weather tennis courts, outdoor badminton court and draught board. Games room with TV. Table tennis, pool table and air-hockey table. Football pitch. Putting course and golf driving net. Small playground with grass base and adventure play area for older children by the pool. **Off site:** Fishing (½ mile), golf, riding and pony trekking nearby.

Charges 2001

Per unit incl. 2 persons	£10.00 - £15.00
per family unit	£13.00 - £18.00
awning	£2.00
extra small tent	£3.00
electricity	£2.00
individual water/drainage	£2.00
premier pitch	£5.00
dog (max. 2)	£1.00

No single sex groups. Tel: (01556) 690250. Fax: (01556) 690681. Reservations: Advised for peak dates and made with £20 deposit per pitch. **Open** all year.

Directions: Park is 9 miles from Dumfries on the south side of the A75 Dumfries - Stranraer road, just west of the village of Crocketford. O.S.GR: NX830725.

Lowlands
Hoddom Castle Caravan Park

Hoddom, Lockerbie, Dumfriesshire DG11 1AS

The oldest part of Hoddom Castle itself is a 16th century Borders Pele Tower, or fortified Keep. This was extended to form a residence for a Lancashire cotton magnate, became a youth hostel and was then taken over by the army during WW2. Since then parts have been demolished but the original 'Border Keep' still survives, unfortunately in a semi-derelict state. The site's bar and restaurant have been developed in the courtyard area from the coach houses, and the main ladies' toilet block was the stables. The park is landscaped and spacious, well laid out on mainly sloping ground with many mature and beautiful trees, originally part of an arboretum. The drive to the site is ¼ mile long with a one way system. Many of the 120 numbered pitches have good views of the castle and have gravel hardstandings with grass for awnings, most with electrical connections (10A). In front of the castle are flat fields for tents and caravans not needing electricity. Amenities include a comfortable bar lounge with family room and TV. The park's 9 hole golf course is in an attractive setting alongside the Annan river, where fishing is possible for salmon and trout (tickets available). Coarse fishing is also possible elsewhere on the estate. This is a peaceful place from which to explore historic southwest Scotland.

Facilities: The main toilet block can be heated and is very well appointed, with washbasins in cubicles, refitted showers and en-suite unit for visitors with disabilities. The other two blocks are tiled and kept very clean, with only washbasins and WCs. Each block has dishwashing sinks. Well equipped laundry room at the castle. Motorcaravan service point. Shop (gas available). Bar, restaurant and takeaway (restricted opening outside high season). Games room with pool tables, table tennis and video games. Large, grass play area. Crazy golf. Bicycle hire and mountain bike trail. Fishing. Golf. Guided walks are organised in high season. Caravan storage. **Off site:** Tennis nearby.

Charges 2001

Per unit incl. up to 4 persons	£6.00 - £11.50
small tent incl. 1 or 2 persons	£5.00 - £8.50
extra person	£2.00
awning	£2.00
electricity (10A)	£2.00

Tel: (01576) 300251. Fax: (01576) 300757. Reservations: Necessary for July/Aug and B.Hs. Any length with deductible £5 deposit. **Open** 1 April - 25 October.

Directions: Leave A74M at junction 19 to Ecclefechan. Go into village and take first right (camping sign) and follow signs to T-junction. Turn left over narrow bridge to park entrance immediately on right. Leave A75 at Annan junction (west end of Annan by-pass) and follow signs. O.S.GR: NY155725.

Lowlands
Cressfield Caravan Park

Ecclefechan, nr Lockerbie, Dumfries and Galloway DG11 3DR

Cressfield is just north of the border, close to main routes (A74M/M6) and is an ideal transit park, or for longer stays with the Solway Firth, Dumfries and Galloway tourist features nearby. A purpose designed, modern park, it has been developed to a very high standard in pleasant undulating countryside next to the village of Ecclefechan, and is personally managed by the owner. Open all year, the park provides 153 pitches of which many are taken by holiday homes and seasonal units, leaving around 35 for tourers. The park is landscaped (trees are growing well) and the level pitches, mostly with hardstanding, are connected by tarmac or gravel roads and provided with electric hook-ups (16A). A good rally field is also fully equipped with electrical hook-ups. There is no shop but it is only / mile from the village. For the more active seven golf courses are near, opportunities for coarse or game fishing, cycling, walking, birdwatching and historical Solway to explore. Some road noise is possible.

Facilities: The modern, heated toilet block is central (key system) and provides excellent facilities - well equipped showers and washbasins in cubicles. Bath in the ladies' (20p). Toilet and washbasin, plus a separate shower area for disabled visitors, with shower seats, in both male and female sections. Excellent laundry room. Washing up area under cover. Motorcaravan service point. Gas supplies. Well equipped, fenced children's play area. Putting green. Sports field with goal posts (not wet weather or Nov-March), tennis and badminton nets, netball posts. Giant chess and draughts. Boules. **Off site:** Hotel for meals adjacent. Boat launching 8 miles.

Charges 2001

Per unit incl. 2 adults	£6.50 - £8.50
extra adult	£2.00
child (under 16 yrs)	£1.00
walkers or cyclists with 2-man tent	£5.00
electricity	£2.00 - £2.50

B.H.s - £2 extra per night, per unit. No credit cards
Tel/Fax: (01576) 300702. Reservations: Phone bookings accepted. **Open** all year.

Directions: Approaching from north or south on A74(M) take exit 19 for Ecclefechan (10 miles north of Gretna, 5 miles south of Lockerbie) and follow B7076 for ½ mile to south side of village; park is signed. O.S.GR: NY196744.

 Alan Rogers' discount
Less 50p per unit, per night

Gibson Park Caravan Club Site

High Street, Melrose TD6 9RY

703

This is an ideal transit park, being so close to the A68, but is also a perfect base for exploring this Southern Scotland area or indeed a trip to Edinburgh, as this is only 35 miles away by car or one of the regular buses which run from the park entrance. This small, three acre park has only 60 touring pitches plus, unusually, an extra 12 tent pitches (summer only) next to the adjacent rugby pitch. All touring pitches have electricity (16A) and TV connections (it is a bad signal here), 57 have hardstanding and 10 are serviced with water and drainage. A one way system on the tarmac roads is in operation. This is Sir Walter Scott country - visit Abbotsford House, his romantic mansion on the banks of the River Tweed. Melrose's Abbey ruins are believed to be the final resting place of Robert The Bruce.

Facilities: First rate sanitary facilities are in a new building with spacious showers, washbasins in cabins, centrally heated and all fitted out with purpose made faced boarding giving a very pleasing finish. Laundry facilities. Separate room with shower and WC for disabled visitors. Motorcaravan service point. Gas is available. **Off site**: Situated on the edge of the little town of Melrose, a five minute walk, shops, pubs and restaurants are all in easy reach.

Charges 2001

Per pitch (non-member)	£6.00 - £8.00
adult	£3.50 - £4.50
child (5-16 yrs)	£1.10 - £1.20
electricity	£1.50 - £2.25

Tent pitches apply to site. Tel: (01896) 822969. Fax: (01896) 823641. Reservations: Made with £5 per night deposit. **Open** all year.

Directions: Turn left off A68 Jedburgh - Lauder road at roundabout about 2½ miles past Newton St Boswell onto A6091 Galashiels road. In about 3¼ miles at roundabout turn right onto B6374 to Melrose. Site is on right at filling station opposite Melrose Rugby Club, just before entering town centre. O.S.GR: NT545340.

Crossburn Caravan Park

Edinburgh Road, Peebles EH45 8ED

696

A peaceful, friendly small park, suitable as a night stop, Crossburn is on the south side of the A703 road, half a mile north of the town centre. The entrance has a fairly steep slope down to reception. Passing the caravans for sale and the holiday homes you might think that this is not the site for you, but persevere as the touring area is very pleasant, with attractive trees and bushes. Of the 50 pitches, 46 have electricity (16A), 20 have hardstanding and 8 are fully serviced. There is also a sheltered area for tents. If you decide to stay longer, the area has many things to do. From historic homes, abbeys, woodland walks and sports - it's all there. Edinburgh is 40 minutes drive. Perhaps the night halt may turn into a longer visit.

Facilities: Two toilet blocks, the smaller one (which can be heated) with fairly basic facilities, the other more modern with washbasins in cubicles, free hairdryers and spacious showers. Campers' kitchen (key at reception) with free electric hot plate, kettle and fridge. Shop selling basic food items and large selection of caravan and camping accessories. Large games room with table tennis and games machines. Good play area. Mountain bike hire.

Charges 2001

Per unit incl. 2 persons	£8.50 - £10.00
serviced pitch	plus £2.00
extra person (5 yrs and over)	£1.00
awning	£2.00
hiker or cyclist plus tent	£5.00
electricity	£2.00

Tel/Fax: (01721) 720501. E-mail: enquiries@ crossburncaravans.co.uk. Reservations: Advised for July/Aug. and made with £14 deposit including £2 fee. **Open** Easter/1 April - end October.

Directions: Park is by the A703 road, about ½ mile north of Peebles. O.S.GR: NT248417.

The Monks' Muir

Haddington, nr Edinburgh, East Lothian EH41 3SB

697

The Monks' Muir is set just back from the A1 (the site layout makes traffic noise minimal), a few minutes from Haddington, East Lothian's county town. Edinburgh is about 15 minutes by car, 20 minutes by rail (P&D) or 50 minutes by bus from just outside the site. This is a base from which to explore the city, to enjoy the golden beaches of East Lothian or discover the Border country. Currently there is only space for about 12 units (no marked pitches) taken on fairly level grass beyond a long line of caravan holiday homes.

Facilities: The main toilet block is a fair walk from the touring pitches. A second smaller toilet block nearer the touring units ensures an adequate provision. One block is closed in low season. Motorcaravan services. Shop/café. Boules pitch. Bicycle hire. **Off site**: Fishing and golf within 2 miles.

Charges 2001

Per unit	£5.60 - £12.00
each person (14 yrs or over)	£1.85 - £1.95
electricity	£1.80 - £2.20

Tel: (01620) 860340. Fax: (01620) 861770. E-mail: d@monksmuir.com. Reservations: Made with £7 deposit and £3 booking fee. **Open** all year.

Directions: Park is on the north side of the A1, halfway between East Linton and Haddington. O.S.GR: NT 559762.

Lowlands

Tantallon Caravan Park

706 Dunbar Road, North Berwick EH39 5NJ

Tantallon is a large park with views over the Firth of Forth and the Bass Rock, which is popular with bird-watchers for its world famous gannet colony. Tantallon and Dirleton Castles are also nearby. Access to the beach is through the golf course and then down the road or via cliff paths. The park has 140 quite large, grass touring pitches in two lower, more sheltered areas (Law Park), with the rest having good views at the top (Bass Park). Many have some degree of slope. There are 75 electrical connections (15A) and 10 pitches also with water and waste water. Each area has its own sanitary facilities. Caravan holiday homes for sale or hire are in their own areas. This is a mature, well managed park with good facilities.

Facilities: Bass Park has 8 unisex units with shower, washbasin and toilet. The other areas have open washbasins. Two heated units for disabled visitors. Dishwashing sinks. Good launderette with spin dryer and free iron. Motorcaravan service point. Reception combines with a small shop. Games room with pool table and TV. Good children's playground and better than average putting green. **Off site**: Golf next door, sea fishing, safe sandy beaches in walking distance.

Charges 2001

Per unit	£8.00 - £12.00
electricity	£2.00
awning	£1.00 - £2.00
dog (by prior arrangement)	£1.00

Tel: (01620) 893348. Fax: (01620) 895623. E-mail: tantallon@meadowhead.co.uk. Reservations: Advisable in July and August. **Open** 20 March - 31 October.

Directions: Park is beside the A198 just to the east of North Berwick, which lies between Edinburgh and Dunbar. O.S.GR: NT567850.

Lowlands

Mortonhall Caravan Park

699 38 Mortonhall Gate, Frogston Road East, Edinburgh, East Lothian EH16 6TJ

The Mortonhall park makes a good base to see the historic city of Edinburgh and buses to the City leave from the park entrance every ten minutes (parking in Edinburgh is not easy). Although only 4 miles from the city centre, Mortonhall is in quiet mature parkland, in the grounds of Mortonhall mansion, and easy to find with access off the ring road. There is room for 250 units mostly on numbered pitches on a slight slope with nothing to separate them, but marked by jockey wheel points. Over 170 places have electricity (10A), 16 with hardstanding, water and drainage as well, and there are many places for tents. The park is very popular but only part is reserved and tourists arriving early may find space. An attractive courtyard development houses a lounge bar and restaurant, open to all, with good value meals in pleasant surroundings. Late arrivals area with hook-ups.

Facilities: Two modern toilet blocks with outside, uncovered dishwashing sinks. The only cabins are in the third excellent block at the top of the park, which has eight unisex units incorporating shower, washbasin and WC, and covered dishwashing sinks. The courtyard provides further standard facilities and 'portacabin' type units are added for high season to serve the many tents. Facilities for disabled visitors. Laundry room. Bar/restaurant. Shop. Games and TV rooms. Table tennis. Children's play area. Torches useful in early and late season. **Off site**: Golf near.

Charges 2001

Per unit incl. 2 persons	£9.00 - £13.25
extra person (5 yrs and over)	£1.00
serviced pitch	plus £4.00
electricity	£2.00
awning	£2.50 - £5.00
dog (by prior arrangement)	£1.00

Tel: 0131 664 1533. Fax: 0131 664 5387. E-mail: mortonhall@meadowhead.co.uk. Reservations: Made with 1 night's charge plus £1.50 fee. **Open** 15 March - 31 October.

Directions: Park is well signed south of the city, 5 minutes from A720 city by-pass. Take the Mortonhall exit from the Straiton junction and follow camping signs. Entrance road is alongside the Klondyke Garden Centre. O.S.GR: NT262686.

Lowlands

Drum Mohr Caravan Park

698 Levenhall, Musselburgh, East Lothian EH21 8JS

This family owned, attractively laid out touring park is on the east side of Edinburgh. It is a secluded, well kept modern park, conveniently situated for visits to Edinburgh, the Lothian and Borders regions. It has been carefully landscaped and there are many attractive plants, flowers and hedging. There are 120 individual pitches, 40 with hardstanding, for touring units of any type, well spaced out on gently sloping grass in groups of 12 or more, marked with white posts. There are electric hook-ups on 110 and 8 are fully serviced with water and waste water connections. Free space is left for play and recreation. A brand new, long dog walk through the woods around the park is a useful addition. Musselburgh centre is 1½ miles, Edinburgh 7, with a frequent bus service to the latter. A well run park, managed personally by the owner, Mr Melville. A member of the Best of British group.

Facilities: The two toilet blocks are clean, attractive, of ample size and can be heated. Free hot water to washbasins (one cabin for men, two for ladies in each block) and to four external washing-up sinks, but hot water is on payment for the showers (outside the cubicle) and laundry sinks. Laundry facilities in each block. Motorcaravan service point. Well stocked, licensed shop (gas available, bread and papers to order). Children's playground on sand. **Off site:** Golf course adjacent.

Charges 2002

Per unit incl. 2 persons	£9.00 - £11.00
extra person (over 3 yrs)	£1.50 - £2.00
extra pup tent	£2.00
awning	£1.00
electricity	£2.00
fully serviced pitch incl. electricity	plus £6.00
extra car	£1.00

Tel: 0131 665 6867. Fax: 0131 653 6859. E-mail: bookings@drummohr.org. Reservations: Made for any length with deposit of one night's charge plus £1 fee. **Open** 1 March - 31 October.

Directions: From Edinburgh follow A1 signs for Berwick on Tweed for 6-7 miles. Turn off for Wallyford and follow camp and Mining Museum signs. From south follow A1 taking junction after Tranent village (A199 Musselburgh) and follow signs. O.S.GR: NT371732.

Edinburgh

The capital, a World Heritage Centre and now the home of the Scottish Parliament, is one of the most beautiful cities in the world dominated by its castle. At the very heart is the Royal Mile where you can stroll through the centuries from Parliament Square, the magnificent 15th century St Giles' Cathedral and down to the Palace of Holyrood-house, the Queens's official Edinburgh residence. At the new Museum of Scotland you can absorb the essence of Scottish architecture and material culture from beam engines to Bonnie Prince Charlie.

Edinburgh Caravan Club Site

705

Marine Drive, Edinburgh EH4 5EN

Situated as it is on the northern outskirts and within easy reach of the city of Edinburgh, this large Caravan Club site (open to non-members) provides an ideal base for touring. A bus (numbers 8A and 28A stop just outside the gates) takes you right into the centre of the city and within walking distance of many of its attractions. Enter the site through rather grand gates to find the visitors' car park and reception to the left. There are 150 large flat pitches (103 hardstandings, 12 with water tap and waste water disposal) with electric hook-ups (16A) and TV aerial, and provision for 50 tents in a separate field (hook-ups available) with a covered cooking shelter, and bicycle stands close by. As the bushes planted around the site mature, there will be shade. The nearest hotel/restaurant is about ½ mile, Royal Yacht Britannia and many other attractions in the city, Firth of Forth bridge about 2 miles.

Facilities: Two heated, well kept toilet blocks provide washbasins in cubicles, hair and hand dryers, an en-suite room for campers with disabilities, plus a baby and toddler room with child-size facilities. Each block houses a dishwashing/vegetable preparation area, and a laundry. Drying room. There is no shop, but milk, bread, and newspapers can be ordered, or purchase ice cream and exchange gas cylinders at reception. Fenced play area for youngsters, and a dog walk in the only natural wood in Edinburgh (part of the site).

Charges 2001

Per pitch (non-member)	£7.00 - £8.00
adult	£3.75 - £4.75
child (5-16 yrs)	£1.20
electricity	£1.50 - £2.25

Tent campers apply to site. Tel: 0131 312 6874. Reservations: Made with £5 deposit, balance on arrival. **Open** all year.

Directions: From A720 (signed City Bypass North), turn right at Gogar roundabout onto A8 and follow international camping signs. O.S.GR: NT212768.

Slatebarns Caravan Park

704

Slatebarns, Roslin, Mid Lothian EH25 9PU

Slatebarns is a recently developed, well groomed park, perfectly located for that trip to Edinburgh, a nightstop on the way north or for local walks, including the nearby Pentland Hills. It has only 30 pitches, all with electricity hook-ups (10A), some with hardstanding (with grass for awnings) and some on grass (steel awning pegs useful). Buses run from the village (five minutes' walk) regularly into Edinburgh (30 minute journey, 6 miles), although they are less frequent in the evening. Slatebarns is a small park with little on site for children or teenagers. Managed under contract for the Caravan Club, non-members are also very welcome. An ideal base to get away from the bustle after a full day in Edinburgh, or equally attractive as a touring base or country hideaway.

Facilities: Small purpose built toilet block with washbasins in cubicles for ladies and excellent separate provision for those with disabilities. Good launderette. Very practical motorcaravan service point. Gas supplies. Dogs are not accepted. **Off site**: Village shops, pubs and hotels.

Charges 2001

Per pitch	£2.00
adult	£3.25 - £3.75
child	£1.10
electricity	£1.50 - £2.00 (Oct)

Tel: 0131 440 2192 (up to 8 pm). Reservations: Contact park for details. **Open** Easter - 31 October.

Directions: From Straiton junction on A720 (Edinburgh bypass) go south on A701 signed Bilston, Penicuik. At roundabout in Bilston turn left on B7006 signed Roslin. After 1 mile, in Roslin continue over crossroads signed Rosslyn Chapel. Site entrance is immediately past Chapel. O.S.GR: NT275632.

Strathclyde Country Park Caravan Site

700 Strathclyde Country Park, 366 Hamilton Road, Motherwell ML1 3ED.

The 1,200 acre Country Park is a large green area less than 15 miles from the centre of Glasgow. Well kept and open to all, it provides nature trails, children's adventure play area, sandy beaches and coarse fishing, with an 18 hole golf course 2 km. away. In addition there is a large water sports centre offering sailing, water skiing, windsurfing, canoeing, rowing (all with craft for hire), a water bus, a selection of family `fun boats' and bicycle hire, plus Scotland's own theme park nearby. The touring site, part of the park, is suitable for both overnight or period stays (max. 14 days) and has 100 numbered pitches for caravans, all with electrical connections (10A). Arranged in semicircular groups on flat grass they are served by made-up access roads and the site is well lit. There is also a camping field which holds 150 units or more for special events. It is close to the motorway so there may be some traffic noise.

Facilities: Four solidly built toilet blocks make a good provision. Enclosed sinks for dishwashing or food preparation, Launderette (irons from reception). Block 4 has facilities for visitors with disabilities. Motorcaravan services. Shop with gas available. Bar and restaurant facilities (100 yds) in the Country Park. Children's play equipment. American motorhomes accepted up to 22 ft. 24 hour security.

Charges 2002

Per caravan pitch incl. 2 persons	£8.50
awning	£2.10
tent pitch (3 or 4 persons)	£7.30
small ridge tent	£3.80
extra adult	£1.10
child	90p
electricity	£2.40

No credit cards. Tel: (01698) 266155. Fax: (01698) 252925. E-mail: strathclydepark@northlan.gov.uk. Reservations: Made for any period with deposit of one night's fee. **Open** Easter - 18 October.

Directions: Take exit 5 from M74 and follow sign for Strathclyde Country Park. Turn first left for site. O.S.GR: NS720584.

Glasgow

One of the most magnificent 19th century cities in Europe and now known as Scotland's style capital with its art deco brasseries, stylish shops and cultural centres boasting more than 30 art galleries and museums. Worth visiting is the new elegant Gallery of Modern Art in Queen Street and Charles Rennie Mackintosh's finest building - The Glasgow School of Art. Also interesting along the banks of the River Clyde is the restored Carlton Terrace and Glasgow's newest landmark, the Clyde Auditorium, popularly known The 'Armadillo', due to its distinctive shape.

Trossachs Holiday Park

723 Aberfoyle, Stirling FK8 3SA

Nestling on the side of a hill, three miles south of Aberfoyle, this is an excellent base for touring this famously beautiful area. Lochs Lomond, Ard, Venachar and others are within easy reach, as are the Queen Elizabeth Forest Park and, of course, the Trossachs. This park specialises in the sale and hire of top class mountain bikes. Very neat and tidy, there are 45 well laid out and marked pitches arranged on terraces with hardstanding. All have electricity and TV connections and most also have water and drainage. There is also a large area for tents. There are trees between the terraces and lovely views across the valley. The adjoining oak and bluebell woods are a haven for wildlife, with wonderful walks. You will receive a warm welcome from Joe and Hazel Norman at this well run, family park. A member of the Best of British group.

Facilities: A modern wooden building houses sanitary facilities providing a satisfactory supply of toilets, showers and washbasins, the ladies' area being rather larger, with two private cabins. Laundry room. Well stocked shop (all season) and bike shop. Games room with TV. Play equipment (on gravel). **Off site:** Nearby are opportunities for golf, boat launching and fishing (3 miles). A passport scheme arranged with a local leisure centre (10 miles, 8 passes) provides facilities for swimming, sauna, solarium, badminton, tennis, windsurfing, etc.

Charges 2001

Per unit incl. 2 persons	£9.00 - £12.00
extra adult	£2.00
child (2-14 yrs)	£1.25
porch awning	£1.50
full awning	£2.00
small pup tent	£3.00
electricity and TV connection, hardstanding pitch	£2.00
all services	£3.00

Tel: (01877) 382614 (24 hrs). Fax: (01877) 382732. E-mail: info@trossachsholidays.co.uk. Reservations: Advisable and made for min. 3 days with £15 deposit. **Open** 1 March - 31 October.

Directions: Park is 3 miles south of Aberfoyle on the A81 road, well signed. O.S.GR: NS544976.

Forestry Commission Ardgartan Caravan & Camping Site

726 Ardgartan, Arrochar, Argyll G83 7AR

Ardgartan is a rugged Forestry Commission site in the Argyll Forest Park. Splendidly situated with mountains all around and lovely views of Loch Long, there are lots of sightseeing and activity opportunities. At the northern end of the Cowal Peninsula, the site is on a promontory on the shores of Loch Long, with good sea fishing and facilities for launching small boats. The 160 touring pitches are in sections which are well divided by grass giving an uncrowded air. Most with hardstanding and marked by numbered posts, they are accessed from hard surfaced roads and 46 have electrical hook-ups. There are additional grass areas for tents. Walking and climbing, as well as sea and river fishing (permits obtainable locally), are all possible nearby. The site gate is locked 10.30 pm. - 7.30 am.

Facilities: The main toilet block is opposite the reception and shop with two small others (one for each sex) close by for the busiest periods. It is a basic, but clean provision with facilities for disabled visitors and a launderette. These facilities may be quite stretched when the park is busy. Play equipment is provided (bark surfaces). Raised barbecues are allowed. **Off site:** Arrochar village (2 miles) has fuel, general stores and a restaurant.

Charges 2001

Per adult	£2.90 - £4.30
child (5-14 yrs)	£1.20 - £1.90
electricity	£2.20
select pitch incl. electricity	+£3.40
boat, extra car, trailer or pup tent	£2.80

Less 20% all year for disabled guests and outside 7/7-28/8 for senior citizens. Tel: (01301) 702293. Reservations: Necessary for B.Hs and peak times (min. 3 nights with £30 deposit); contact site. Brochure requests: Forest Holidays, Forestry Commission, 231 Corstorphine Road, Edinburgh EH12 7AT. Tel: (0131) 314 6505. E-mail: fe.holidays@forestry.gsi.gov.uk. **Open** 21 March - 24 October.

Directions: From A82 Glasgow - Crianlarich road take A83 at Tarbet signed Arrochar and Cambletown. Site is 2 miles past Arrochar, the entrance on a bend. O.S.GR: NN275030.

Lomond Woods Holiday Park

724 Tullichewan, Old Luss Road, Balloch, Loch Lomond G83 8QP

A series of improvements over the last few years has made this one of the top parks in Scotland. Almost, but not quite, on the banks of Loch Lomond (¼ mile), this landscaped, well planned park is suitable for both transit or longer stays. Formerly known as Tullichewan Holiday Park, it takes 120 touring units, including 30 tents, on well spaced, numbered pitches on flat or gently sloping grass. Most have hardstanding, 106 have electrical connections (10A) and 8 have water and waste water too. Watersport activities and boat trips are possible on Loch Lomond, with a new visitor attraction, 'Lomond Shores' opened nearby. This is a well run park, open all year, with very helpful management and reception staff. A member of the Best of British group.

Facilities: The single large, heated, well kept toilet block has been totally refitted. It includes some showers with WCs, baths for ladies, a shower room for disabled visitors and two baby baths. Covered dishwashing sinks. Launderette. Motorcaravan service points. Well stocked shop at reception. Games room with TV. Children's playground. Leisure suite providing a sauna, sun-bed and spa-bath (on payment). Bicycle hire. Caravan storage. American motorhomes accepted with prior notice. **Off site:** Fishing and boat launching ¼ mile, riding 4 miles, golf 5 miles. Rail and road connections to Glasgow. Restaurants and bar meals in Balloch (5 mins).

Charges 2001

Per unit incl. up to 2 persons	£10.50 - £13.00
all persons in winter season	£8.50
extra adult	£2.00
child (3-12 yrs)	£1.00
awning or extra small tent	£1.50 - £2.50
electricity	£2.00, £2.50 in winter
fully serviced pitch with electricity	£4.00
dog	50p
hikers (2 persons, no car)	£6.50 - £9.00

Tel: (01389) 755000. Fax: (01389) 755563. E-mail: lomondwoods@holiday-parks.co.uk. Reservations: Made for any length with deposit of first night's charge and £2 fee. **Open** all year except November (reduced facilities Dec-March).

Directions: Turn off A82 road 17 miles northwest of Glasgow on A811 Stirling road. Site is in Balloch at southern end of Loch Lomond and is well signed. O.S.GR: NS389816.

Heart of Scotland
Blair Castle Caravan Park
Blair Atholl, Pitlochry, Perthshire PH18 5SR

730

This attractive, well kept park is set in the grounds of Blair Castle, the traditional home of the Dukes of Atholl. The castle is open to the public, its 32 fully furnished rooms showing a picture of Scottish life from the 16th century to the present day, while the beautiful grounds and gardens are free to those staying on site. The caravan park has a wonderful feeling of spaciousness with a large central area left free for children's play or for general use. There is space for 283 touring units with 196 electricity connections (10/16A), 144 hardstandings and 42 fully serviced pitches with water and waste water facilities also. Caravan holiday homes, 85 privately owned and 28 for hire, are in separate areas. The castle grounds provide many walking trails and the village is within walking distance with hotels, shops, a water mill craft centre and folk museum. A quality park, quiet at night and well managed. For 2002, a new central development will incorporate reception, a shop, games room, laundry and internet gallery. A member of the Best of British group.

Facilities: The four toilet blocks can be heated and are of excellent quality with very high standards of cleanliness. Large hot showers are free, some also incorporating WC and washbasin, and further cubicles with WC and washbasin. Three blocks have facilities for disabled visitors, one with WC and washbasin, the others with a bath also. Baby changing mats. Dishwashing. Good launderette with washing machines, dryers, spin dryer and irons plus a separate drying room and outside lines. Motorcaravan service point. Shop (1/4-28/10). Near reception is a games room with pool, table tennis and table football. Gas supplies. American motorhomes are accepted (max. 30 ft or 5 tons). **Off site**: Mountain bike hire, riding, golf and fishing within 1 mile.

Charges 2001

Per unit with all persons	£8.50 - £10.50
tent (no car) incl. 2 persons	£6.50 - £9.00
extra person	£1.00
child (5-12 yrs)	50p
awning or pup tent	£2.00 - £2.50
dog (max. 2)	50p
electricity	£1.50 - £2.00

Tel: (01796) 481263. Fax: (01796) 481587. E-mail: mail@blaircastlecaravanpark.co.uk. Reservations: Made for any length with deposit of 1 night's charge + £2 booking fee except 15/7-15/8 when min. 3 nights and payment in full. **Open** 1 April - 30 October.

Directions: From A9 just north of Pitlochry take B8079 into Blair Atholl. Park is in grounds of Blair Castle, well signed. O.S.GR: NN868659.

Nether Craig Caravan Park

728 By Alyth, Blairgowrie, Perthshire PH11 8HN

Nether Craig is a family run touring park, attractively designed and beautifully landscaped, with views across the Strathmore valley to the long range of the Sidlaw hills. The 40 large pitches are accessed from a circular, gravel road; 26 have hardstanding (for awnings too) and 10A electrical connections. The majority are level and there are 9 large tent pitches on flat grass. There is a personal welcome for all visitors at the attractive wooden chalet beside the entrance (with a slope for wheelchairs) which doubles as reception and shop providing the necessary essentials, gas and tourist information. A one mile circular woodland walk from the park has picnic benches and a leaflet guide is provided. Otherwise you can just enjoy the peace of the Angus Glens by hill walking, birdwatching, fishing or pony trekking. Alyth with its Arthurian connections is only 4 miles away and Glamis Castle, the childhood home of the Queen Mother, is nearby, as is the beautiful Glenshee and Braemar with its castle.

Facilities: The central, purpose built toilet block is modern, well equipped and maintained, and can be heated. Unit for disabled visitors (entry by key). Separate sinks for dishwashing and clothes are in the laundry room (metered hot water), plus a washing machine, dryer and iron, and a rotary clothes line outside. Shop. Children's play area. Small football field. Caravan storage. **Off site:** Three golf courses are within 4 miles.

Charges 2001

Per unit incl. 2 persons	£10.00 - £12.00
tent incl. 2 persons	£6.00
extra person	£1.00
electricity	£1.80

Tel: (01575) 560204. Fax: (01575) 560315. E-mail: nethercraig@lineone.net. Reservations: Advisable for main season. **Open** 15 March - 31 October.

Directions: From A926 Blairgowrie - Kirriemuir road, at roundabout south of Alyth join B954 signed Glenisla. Follow caravan signs for 4 miles and turn right onto unclassified road signed Nether Craig. Park is on left after ½ mile. O.S.GR: NO265528.

Auchterarder Caravan Park

727 Nether Coul, Auchterarder, Perthshire PH3 1ET

This is a charming small park, purpose designed and landscaped by the owners Stuart and Susie Robertson. In a sheltered position, it is conveniently situated for exploring central Scotland and the Highlands with many leisure activities close at hand (particularly golf) and within walking distance of the village (1 mile). The 21 original pitches, all with electricity (6A) and hardstanding, 12 with drainage, are well spaced around the edge of the elongated, level grass park. Marked pitches with grass frontage back on to raised banks which have been planted with trees. Further pitches have been developed to one side of the site, along with a trout fishing pond (exclusively for campers) and a woodland walk. A tarmac area at the entrance for late arrivals (with electricity) ensures that no one is disturbed. Also at the entrance, a modern pine chalet blending with the environment houses reception and a small library. There is easy access from the nearby A9 road which does create some background road noise, although it is peaceful at night.

Facilities: Excellent toilet facilities with key system and piped music include controllable, well equipped hot showers. Laundry room with sink and washing machine; an iron can be provided. Dishwashing is under cover. Caravan storage. **Off site:** Golf 1 mile, bicycle hire or riding 6 miles. The historic cities of Perth and Stirling are less than half an hour's drive away.

Charges 2001

Per unit incl. up to 4 persons	£6.00 - £8.00
extra person (over 5 yrs)	£1.00
awning	£1.00
electricity and drainage	£1.50 - £2.50

No credit cards. Tel/Fax: (01764) 663119. E-mail: nethercoul@talk21.com. Reservations: Advisable July/Aug. and made with deposit of one night's charge and booking fee (£1). Bookings held until 5 pm. on day reserved. **Open** all year.

Directions: Park is between the A9 and A824 roads east of Auchterarder village, only ½ mile from the main road. It is reached by turning on to the B8062 (Dunning) road from the A824. O.S.GR: NN964138.

Craigtoun Meadows Holiday Park

729 Mount Melville, St Andrews, Fife KY16 8PQ

This attractively laid out, quality park has individual pitches and good facilities, and although outnumbered by caravan holiday homes, the touring section is an important subsidiary. The facilities offered are both well designed and comprehensive with 70 units taken on gently sloping land. Caravans go on individual hardstandings with grass alongside for awnings on most pitches. All caravan pitches are equipped with electricity (16A), water and drainage and have been redesigned to increase size (130 sq.m). There are 24 larger 'patio pitches' with summer house, barbecue patio, picnic table and chairs, partially screened. Tents are taken on a grassy meadow at one end, also with electricity available. Only 'breathable' type groundsheets may be used in awnings. The 157 caravan holiday homes stand round the outer parts of the site. Buses pass the entrance and Craigtoun park with boating pond and miniature railway, etc. is within walking distance. This is a well run park, 2 miles from St Andrews with its golf courses and long, sandy beaches, from where there is a picturesque view of St Andrews and its ruined Abbey and Castle

Facilities: An excellent, de-luxe, centrally heated sanitary building serves the touring area. All washbasins are in cabins and each toilet has its own basin. Showers are unisex, as are two bathrooms, with hand and hair dryers, facilities for disabled people and babies. Dishwashing room. Launderette. Shop. Attractive little licensed restaurant (both restricted hours in low seasons), also providing takeaway. Games room. Mini-gym. Well equipped children's playground, play field and 8 acres of woodland. Barbecue area. All weather tennis court. Small information room. **Off site:** Fishing 5 miles. Golf 1½ miles. Riding 6 miles.

Charges 2001

Per unit incl. 2 persons & electricity	£14.00 - £20.50
3-6 persons	£15.00 - £21.50
backpacker's tent (1 person)	£12.00

Tel: (01334) 475959. Fax: (01334) 476424. E-mail: craigtoun@aol.com. Reservations: Advised for main season; any length with full payment at time of booking. **Open** 1 March - 31 October.

Directions: From M90 junction 8 take A91 to St Andrews. Just after sign for Guardbridge (to left, A919), turn right at site sign and sign for 'Strathkinness, 1¾miles'. Go through village, over crossroads at end of village, left at next crossroads, then ¾mile to park. O.S.GR: NO482151.

Twenty Shilling Wood Caravan Park

731 Comrie, Perthshire PH6 2JY

Everyone gets a warm welcome from the Lowe family when they arrive at Twenty Shilling Wood. Set amongst 10.5 acres of wooded hillside, this unusual park has a few touring pitches for caravans and motorcaravans (no tents), plus a number of owner occupied caravan holiday homes. However, with terracing and landscaping not many of these are visible and flowering trees and shrubs help to hide them. The lowest level is the entrance (controlled by an automatic barrier; £10 deposit for card) where there is a late arrivals area and visitor car park. Just 16 level touring pitches are on gravel with grass bays between them. All have electricity hook-ups (10A) and, because of poor TV reception, a free TV aerial hook up with lead provided. You will be escorted to your pitch. There are many walks in the area from strenuous Munros to a gentle stroll to the Devil's Cauldron waterfall. Glen Turret, Scotland's oldest distillery is at Crieff, 7 miles away, Auchingarrich Wildlife centre is 2½ miles, there are watersports at Loch Earn, 11 miles.

Facilities: The toilet blocks are of an older design but well kept, and have been refurbished to give some washbasins in cubicles for ladies. Dishwashing area and laundry. No shop but rolls, milk and papers can be ordered at reception. Games room with pool table, table tennis (both free) and lounge area with comfortable seating and well stocked library. Fenced adventure playground for all ages. Only two dogs per pitch are accepted. **Off site:** Buses pass the gate. Comrie is 1 mile where most things can be purchased. Golf or fishing within 1 mile, riding or bicycle hire 6 miles.

Charges 2001

Per unit incl. 2 adults	£8.00 - £10.50
extra person (over 5 yrs)	£1.00
awning (rock pegs required)	£1.00
electricity and TV hook-up	£2.00

Tel/Fax: (01764) 670411. E-mail: alowe20@aol.com. Reservations: Advised for B.Hs and July/Aug; made with £10 deposit. **Open** 23 March - 23 October.

Directions: Park is on north side of A85 Crieff - Lochearnhead road, about ¾mile west of B827 junction, ½ mile west of Comrie. O.S.GR: NN762222.

Witches Craig Caravan Park

Blairlogie, nr Stirling FK9 5PX

732

Witches Craig is a neat and tidy park, nestling under the Ochil Hills and the friendly Stephen family take each visitor to their pitch to make sure that they are happy. All 60 pitches have electrical hook-ups (10A) and 14 have hardstanding, 7 of these being large (taking American style motorhomes easily). Reasonably level, the park covers five well maintained acres with the grass beautifully manicured. Seven residential park homes are well kept and surrounded by flowering shrubs. The area has a wealth of historic attractions, starting with the Wallace Monument which practically overlooks the park. Its 220 ft. tower dominates the surrounding area and the climb up its 246 steps gives spectacular views. Being by the A91, there is some day-time road noise. Trees have been planted to try to minimise this but the further back onto the park you go, the less the traffic is heard, although the main touring section with the sanitary facilities is at the front.

Facilities: The modern, heated toilet block is well maintained, and includes one cubicle with washbasin and WC each for ladies and men. Showers are on payment. Baby bath and mat. Good unit for disabled campers. Dishwashing sinks. Laundry. Bread, milk, drinks and papers are available daily (supermarket 2½ miles). Large fenced play area. Field for team games. **Off site:** Riding or bicycle hire 2 miles, fishing 3 miles, golf 1 mile. Buses stop at the park entrance. Within 10 miles there are castles, museums, cathedrals and parks. Many walks from the site into the Ochil Hills. Stirling is known as the 'Gateway to the Highlands' and its magnificent castle is world renowned.

Charges 2001

Per unit incl. 2 adults	£9.75 - £10.75
extra adult	£2.00
child (2-13 yrs)	£1.00
awning (no groundsheets)	£2.00
electricity	£2.00
walker with tent, per person	£4.25 - £5.25

No credit cards. Tel: (01786) 474947. Reservations: made without deposit. **Open** 1 April - 31 October.

Directions: Park is on the A91, 2 miles northeast of Stirling. O.S.GR: NS822968.

Huntly Castle Caravan Park

The Meadow, Huntly, Aberdeenshire AB54 4UJ

755

Huntly Caravan Park was opened in '95 and its hard-working owners, Hugh and Debbie Ballantyne, are justly proud of their neat, well landscaped 15 acre site that is managed under contract for the Caravan Club (non-members welcome). The 76 level grass and 41 hardstanding touring pitches are separated and numbered, with everyone shown to their pitch. Arranged in three bays with banks of heathers and flowering shrubs separating them, 66 of the pitches have electric hook-ups (16A) and 15 are fully serviced with water and waste water also. Two bays have central play areas and all three have easy access to a toilet block, as has the camping area. The park also has 33 privately owned caravan holiday homes. An Activity Centre near the entrance contains two indoor safe play areas (one for up to 2 yrs old, the other up to 9 yrs). In addition there are snooker and pool tables, table tennis, badminton and short tennis. There is a charge for these facilities which are also open to the public, with tea, coffee and ices sold (open weekends and all local school holidays). The area abounds with things to do, from forest trails to walk or cycle, a falconry centre, malt whisky distilleries and an all year Nordic ski track. A member of the Best of British group.

Facilities: The three heated toilet blocks are well designed and maintained, with washbasins (in cubicles for ladies) and large, free showers with lots of changing space. Each block also has a family shower room (even larger), dishwashing sinks with free hot water and a good room for disabled visitors. Well equipped laundry room. Covered cooking shelter (with work tops) for campers should the weather turn inclement. No shop but milk and papers may be ordered at reception. Activity centre. **Off site:** The town of Huntly is only 10 minutes walk with shops and pubs and castle. Fishing, golf or bicycle hire within ½ mile, riding 5 miles

Charges 2001

Per standard pitch incl. 2 persons	£8.95 - £11.00
electricity	£2.10
awning	£1.00 - £1.75
pup tent	£2.00
extra adult	£2.25
child (5-16 yrs)	£1.10
fully serviced pitch	plus £1.50
tent incl. 2 persons	£6.50 - 11.00

Tel: (01466) 794999. E-mail: enquiries@ huntlycastle.co.uk. Reservations: Contact park. **Open** 24 March - 29 October.

Directions: Site is well signed from A96 Keith - Aberdeen road. O.S.GR: NJ526402.

Aden Country Park Caravan Park

753 Old Deer, Mintlaw, Aberdeenshire AB42 8FQ

Aden Country Park is owned by the local authority and is open to the public offering several attractions for visitors including an Agricultural Heritage Centre, Wildlife Centre, Nature Trail and restaurant, as well as open and woodland areas with a lake, for walking and recreation. The caravan and camping site is on one side of the park. Beautifully landscaped and well laid out with trees, bushes and hedges, it is kept very neat and tidy. It provides 48 numbered pitches for touring units, with varying degrees of slope (some level) and all with electrical hook-ups (16A), plus an area for tents. There are also 12 caravan holiday homes in a row on the left as you enter. The park is in a most attractive area and one could spend plenty of time enjoying all it has to offer.

Facilities: The modern, fully tiled sanitary toilet block, with good facilities for disabled visitors, was very clean when we visited. It can be heated and provides free, pre-set hot showers, with dressing area, hairdryer for ladies, and a baby bath, but no private cabins. Dishwashing and laundry facilities are together, with washing machines, tumble and spin dryers and an iron - all metered. Small shop (sweets and ice-creams) in the reception area. Restaurant in the Heritage Centre for meals. For children, two games areas and various items of play equipment (with safety surfaces). **Off site:** Mintlaw ½ mile for shopping. Fishing 1 mile, riding 2 miles.

Charges 2001

Per unit	£9.30 - £10.70
small tent per person	£3.60 - £4.10
awning	£1.00 - £1.15
electricity	£1.80
OAPs out of season, per unit	£4.65

Tel: (01771) 623460. Reservations: Advisable for weekends; write for details. **Open** Easter - 25 October.

Directions: Approaching Mintlaw from the west on A950 road, park is shortly after sign for Mintlaw station. From the east, go to the western outskirts of the village and entrance is on left - 'Aden Country Park and Farm Heritage Centre'. O.S.GR: NJ985484.

Grampian

Aberlour Gardens Caravan and Camping Park

754 Aberlour-on-Spey, Banffshire AB38 9LD

This pleasant park is within the large walled garden of the Aberlour Estate on Speyside. Mr and Mrs Moss, the owners, have made many improvements to the sheltered, five acre, family run park which provides a very natural setting amidst spruce and Scots pine. Of the 64 level pitches, 35 are for touring units leaving the remainder for holiday homes (1 for rent) and seasonal units. All pitches have electrical connections (10A) and 9 are 'all-weather' pitches. This is an ideal area for walking, birdwatching, salmon fishing and pony trekking or for following the only 'Malt Whisky Trail' in the world, while Aberlour has a fascinating old village shop – a 'time capsule'.

Facilities: The toilet block can be heated and has four unisex showers on payment and facilities for visitors with disabilities (can be used as family or baby changing room) . Laundry facilities. Motorcaravan service point. Small licensed shop stocking basics and with an information area. Children's play area. Caravan storage. **Off site:** Fishing 1 or 5 miles, golf 4 miles, riding ½ mile, swimming or bicycle hire 1 mile, bowls 2 miles.

Charges 2001

Per caravan, motorcaravan or trailer tent	
incl. 2 persons	£7.00 - £9.50
tent	£6.75 - £8.00
backpacker and tent per person	£3.75 - £4.50
extra person	£2.00
child (5-16 yrs)	£1.00
electricity	£1.60 - £1.80

Tel/Fax: (01340) 871586. E-mail: abergard@compuserve.com. Reservations: Advised for July/Aug; made with deposit (1 nights fee). **Open** 1 April - 31 October.

Directions: Turn off A95 midway between Aberlour and Craigellachie onto unclassified road and site is signed in 500 yds. Vehicles over 10' 6" high should use A941 Dufftown Road (site is signed). O.S.GR: NJ282432.

 Alan Rogers' discount
Less 50p per unit, per night

Spindrift Caravan and Camping Park

766 Little Kildrummie, Nairn, Highlands IV12 5QU

Mr and Mrs Guillot have put a lot of thought into the landscaping of their park, making it into an absolute gem. It is situated in an elevated position overlooking the distant Monadlaith mountains and a short walk from the River Nairn. The popular seaside resort of Nairn with its shops, restaurants, beach and harbour is some 2 miles away and it is said to take 30 minutes to walk via the riverside path. The park is surrounded by trees and is arranged on three terraces (roads down to the lower pitches have been re-laid and give easy access). The lowest level is used primarily for tents. With 40 pitches altogether, there are 28 electrical connections (16A), all on the highest terrace, although if you have a long cable, reached from the second level too. A part of the top level is set aside for motorcaravans, however there is no dedicated service point. The front porch of the owners house is used as reception and also provides tourist information. It is left open at all times. The river footpath is easily accessible.

Facilities: Two modern well equipped sanitary blocks. Large laundry room with separate dishwashing and laundry sinks. Large table and chairs for campers use in inclement weather. Salmon fishing permits available. **Off site**: Bicycle hire, riding, golf and boat launching within 2 miles. Bus passes the lane end (400 yds). Shops at Nairn.

Charges 2001

Per unit incl. 2 adults and 2 children	£7.50 - £9.50
small tent (2 adults)	£6.50 - £9.00
extra adult	free - £1.00
child	free - 50p
awning	free - £1.00
electricity (15A)	£2.00

No credit cards. Tel: (01667) 453992. E-mail: camping@spindriftcaravanpark.freeserve.co.uk. Reservations: Advised for July/Aug. with £5 deposit. **Open** 1 April - 31 October.

Directions: Follow the signs for Spindrift along the A976 which runs through Nairn. O.S.GR: NH863537.

Torvean Caravan Park

769 Glenurquhart Road, Inverness IV3 6JL

Torvean is a small and neat, select touring park for caravans and motorhomes only. It is situated on the outskirts of Inverness beside the Caledonian Canal and is within easy reach of the town's amenities which include an ice rink, theatre and leisure sports centre. Excursions to the coast and Highlands, including Loch Ness, are possible in several directions. The pitches on level grass are well spaced and clearly marked with a tarmac access road and street lighting giving a very neat appearance. There are 47 touring pitches (27 with 10A electricity connections, 18 fully serviced with fresh water tap, waste water disposal and electricity).

Facilities: Two toilet blocks are of good quality – ladies have two cubicles with washbasin and toilet and a hair washing cubicle. Controllable hot showers on payment. Suite for disabled people with toilet and shower. Launderette. Motorcaravan service point. Children's play area. Only one dog per unit is accepted. **Off site**: Golf adjacent, bicycle hire or fishing 3 miles.

Charges guide

Per unit incl. 2 adults	£9.00 - £9.50
electricity	£2.00
de-luxe pitch incl. electricity	£11.50 - £12.00
extra adult	£1.50
extra child (under 16 yrs)	75p
awning	£2.00 - £3.00
small dog (one only)	£1.00

No credit cards. Tel: (01463) 220582. Fax: (01463) 233051. Reservations: Necessary for July/Aug. and made with first night's charge and £1 fee. **Open** Easter - end-October.

Directions: Park is off the main A82 road on the southwest outskirts of the town by the Tomnahurich Canal Bridge. O.S.GR: NH638438.

Grantown-on-Spey Caravan Park

767 Seafield Avenue, Grantown on Spey, Moray PH26 3JQ

Gerald and Brenda Naylor take care of this excellent park which is owned by Sandra McKelvie and her son John Fleming, and managed under contract for the Caravan Club (non-members are welcome). Peacefully situated on the outskirts of the town, with views of the mountains in the distance, the park consists of well-tended gravel (raked so that it is perfect for each occupant) and grass pitches. Trees and flowers are a feature of this landscaped location. There are 100 pitches for caravans or motorcaravans, of which 5 offer fresh and waste water facilities and 16 have individual fresh water taps. A further 20 pitches are used for seasonal occupation, and there is space for 50 or more tents. More than 80 pitches have 10A electrical hook-ups. Gerald Naylor escorts visitors to their pitch and will help to site caravans if necessary. Caravan holiday homes are located in a separate area of the park. Grantown is a pleasant touring base for the Cairngorms and for the Malt Whisky Trail. A peaceful park with a warden on site at all times.

Facilities: Two modern blocks provide good, clean toilet facilities, with new private wash-cabins for ladies. Dishwashing sinks are covered behind each block. Laundry room with washing machines, and spin dryers and irons. Motorcaravan service point with drive-over emptying facility and a fresh water tap. No on-site shop because the town is just a short distance, however gas cylinders, ice creams, cold drinks and various camping accessories can be purchased at reception. Football field. Games room with table tennis and pool table. Winter caravan storage. **Off site**: Fishing, golf and mountain bike hire within 1 mile, riding 3 miles.

Charges 2001

Per pitch incl. 2 persons	£7.00 - £11.00
2 man tent and vehicle	£6.00 - £8.00
hiker's 2 man tent	£5.00 - £6.00
awning or extra pup tent	£1.50
extra person	£1.00 - £2.00
electricity	£2.00 - £2.50

Tel: (01479) 872474. Fax: (01479) 873696. E-mail: team@caravanscotland.com. Reservations: Advised for peak periods and made with £10 deposit. **Open** 29 March - 31 October.

Directions: Park is signed from the town centre. O.S.GR: NJ028283.

Forestry Commission - Glenmore Caravan & Camping Site

768 Glenmore, Aviemore, Inverness-shire PH22 1QU

Since July 2000 there have been resident wardens here and they have made tremendous improvements to this park, which had been neglected for a while. It would be nice if Forest Enterprises were to invest in new shower/washing and laundry facilities, as although the current facilities are kept very clean, they are out of date and badly positioned. The Glenmore Forest site lies close to the sandy shore of Loch Morlich amidst conifer woods and surrounded on three sides by the impressive Cairngorm mountains. It is conveniently situated for a range of activities, including skiing (extensive lift system), orienteering, hill and mountain walking (way-marked walks), fishing (trout and pike) and non-motorized watersports on the Loch. The campsite itself is attractively laid out in a fairly informal style in several adjoining areas connected by narrow part gravel, part tarmac roads, with access to the lochside. One of these areas, the Pinewood Area, is very popular and has 32 hardstandings (some distance from the toilet block). Of the 220 marked pitches on fairly level, firm grass, 137 have electricity (10A).

Facilities: There are two very basic toilet blocks with heating, but only one shower/laundry block some distance from the majority of the pitches and reached by an underpass. Opened by key pad (you are given a number), the heated block has small, basic, free hot showers. Separate unit for visitors with disabilities. Next to the site is a range of amenities including a well stocked shop, a café serving a variety of meals and snacks, and a Forestry Commission visitor centre and souvenir shop. Barbecues are not permitted in dry weather. **Off site**: The Aviemore centre providing a wide range of indoor and outdoor recreations is only 7 miles and there are several golf courses within a range of 15 miles, as well as fishing and boat trips.

Charges 2001

Per unit incl. up to 4 persons	£7.70 - £10.00
'select' pitch	plus £3.30
electricity	£2.20
backpacker	£3.80 - £4.50

Less 20% all year for disabled guests and outside 7/7-28/8 for senior citizens. Tel: (01479) 861271. Reservations: Necessary for B.Hs and peak times; made for min. 3 nights with £30 deposit. Contact site when open, otherwise Forest Holidays, Forestry Commission, 231 Corstorphine Road, Edinburgh EH12 7AT. Tel: (0131) 314 6505. E-mail: fe.holidays@ forestry.gse.gov.uk. **Open** all year except 1 Nov - 15 Dec.

Directions: Immediately south of Aviemore on B9152 (not A9 bypass) take B970 then follow sign for Cairngorm and Loch Morlich. Site entrance is on right past the loch. O.S.GR: NH976097.

Pitgrudy Caravan Park

770

Poles Road, Dornoch, Highlands IV25 3HY

In a rural situation, Pitgrudy has superb views over the Dornoch Firth and the surrounding Ross-shire hills. There are 40 touring pitches for caravans, motorcaravans or tents, mostly on slightly sloping grass and with electrical connections (10A). A few have hardstanding (unfortunately still on a slope) and six are fully serviced (drinking water, waste water disposal point and electricity). Located at the top of the park are 35 caravan holiday homes, of which 25 are privately owned. The whole park is on immaculately tended grass with tarmac roads. The pleasant little town of Dornoch is less than a mile away with shops, restaurants, plus the cathedral. A member of the Best of British group.

Facilities: Sanitary facilities are provided in a modern, superior 'portacabin' style unit which is very clean and well equipped. Laundry with washing machine, dryer and iron. Dishwashing sinks. Gas supplies. **Off site**: A safe sandy beach is 1 mile and the area is good for walking and golf (there are 7 courses within 15 miles of the park). Fishing 1 mile, bicycle hire or boat launching 3 miles, riding 5 miles.

Charges guide

Per unit incl. 2 persons	£7.50 - £11.00
tent and car	£7.00 - £8.00
small tent	£5.50 - £6.00
extra adult	£1.00
child (under 16 yrs)	50p
awning	£1.50
dog (max. 2)	free
electricity	£2.00

No credit cards. Tel: (01862) 821253 (9 am. - 5.30 pm). Fax: (01862) 821382. Reservations: Made with deposit (1st night's rent) and £1 fee. Bookings and enquiries to: GNR Sutherland, Caravan Sales, Edderton, Tain, Ross-shire IV19 1JY. **Open** 25 April - 30 September.

Directions: At the war memorial in Dornoch, turn north (park signed) on the B9168. Park is ½ mile on the right (45 miles north of Inverness). O.S.GR: NH795911.

Woodend Camping and Caravan Park

772

Achnairn, Lairg, Sutherland IV27 4DN

Woodend is a delightful, small park overlooking Loch Shin and perfect for hill walkers and backpackers. Peaceful and simple, it is owned and run single-handedly by Mrs Cathie Ross, who provides a wonderfully warm Scottish welcome to visitors. On a hill with open, panoramic views across the Loch to the hills beyond and all around, the large camping field is undulating and gently sloping with some reasonably flat areas. The park is licensed to take 55 units, although few pitches would be suitable for caravans or motorcaravans. Most of the 22 electrical hook-ups (16A) are in a line near the top of the field, close to the large, fenced children's play area which has several items of equipment on grass. There are opportunities for fishing and hill walking. The famous Falls of Shin with a Visitor Centre is an ideal place to see the salmon leap (about 10 miles).

Facilities: The modernised sanitary facilities are kept very clean and are quite satisfactory, with dishwashing on small payment. There are books and magazines to borrow in the dishwashing room. Laundry with two machines and a dryer. Kitchen and eating room for tent campers. Reception and a shop at the house, Sunday papers can be ordered, strawberries are on sale in season and daily milk and bread may be ordered. Fishing licences for the Loch (your catch will be frozen for you). **Off site**: Mountain bikes can be hired in Lairg (5 miles). Several scenic golf courses within 20-30 miles.

Charges guide

Per unit incl. electricity	£7.00
tent	£6.00

No credit cards. Tel/Fax: (01549) 402248. Reservations: Not considered necessary. **Open** 1 April - 30 September.

Directions: Achnairn is near the southern end of Loch Shin. Turn off the A838 single track road at signs for Woodend. From the A9 coming north take the A836 at Bonar Bridge, 11 miles northwest of Tain. O.S.GR: NC558127.

Scourie Caravan and Camping Park

773 Harbour Road, Scourie, Sutherland IV27 4TG

Mr Mackenzie has carefully nurtured this park over many years, developing a number of firm terraces with 60 pitches which gives it an attractive layout - there is nothing regimented here. Perched on the edge of the bay in an elevated position, practically everyone has a view of the sea and a short walk along the shore footpath leads to a small sandy beach. The park has tarmac and gravel access roads, with well drained grass pitches and some hard-core hardstandings with 10A electric hook-ups. A few are on an area which is unfenced from the rocks (young children would need to be supervised here). Reception, alongside the modern toilet block, contains a wealth of tourist information and maps. There are very good facilities for disabled visitors on the park and at the restaurant, although the ramps leading to them are a little steep. Mr Mackenzie claims that this is the only caravan park in the world from where, depending on the season, you can see palm trees, Highland cattle and Great Northern divers from your pitch. Red throated divers have also been seen. Trips to Handa Island (a special protection area for seabird colonies) are available from here and Tarbet. The clear water makes this area ideal for diving.

Facilities: The toilet facilities can be heated. Showers have no divider or seat. Fully equipped laundry and dishwashing sinks. Motorcaravan service point. The 'Anchorage' restaurant at the entrance to the park (used as reception at quiet times) is large and well appointed with meals at reasonable prices cooked to order (l/5-15/9). Boat launching facilities. Fishing permits (brown trout) can be arranged. **Off site:** The village has a well stocked shop with post office, gas is available from the local petrol station and mobile banks visit regularly.

Charges guide

Per unit incl. 2 adults	£8.00
1 adult	£7.00
extra adult	£1.00
child (3-16 yrs)	50p
hiker and tent	£5.00
extra tent, vehicle or awning	£1.00
electricity	£2.00

No credit cards. Tel: (01971) 502060. Reservations: Not made. **Open** 1 April - 30 September, but phone first to check.

Directions: Park is by Scourie village on A894 road in northwest Sutherland. O.S.GR: NC153446.

Dunroamin Caravan Park

764 Main Street, Lairg, Sutherland IV27 4AR

Lewis and Margaret Hudson run this small park, close to the centre of Lairg and ideally suited for touring Sutherland and Caithness. Fifty level pitches are reserved for touring caravans, motorcaravans and tents on well-tended grass, and there are ten caravan holiday homes for hire. None of the pitches are marked so the owner directs caravans and motorhomes to the camping area and positions them correctly. Tent campers are able to select their own spot in a field behind the row of holiday homes. There are 15 electrical hook-ups (10/16A) and 8 hardstandings, which are concrete below an inch of grass. A licensed restaurant next to the reception serves breakfasts, snacks and evening meals. Local activities include a weekly ceilidh at the village hall, a multi-sports area, walking, fishing (permits are arranged at park) and watersports on nearby Loch Shin. Three buses run daily to Inverness, and three trains daily further afield (timetable in reception). This is a superb location for exploring the Shin Triangle.

Facilities: Fully equipped central toilet block is clean and tidy with showers (20p for 6 mins). Covered dishwashing sink. No motorcaravan service point although tanks can be drained in a manhole near the entrance. Well equipped laundry. Restaurant (8 am-8 pm). Basic camping requisites and gas exchange at reception; the nearest shop is 300 yds. Bicycles and barbecues can be hired. Max. two dogs per unit. **Off site:** Ferrycroft Country Centre is a 20-minute walk.

Charges guide

Per unit incl. 2 adults	£5.50 - £9.00
backpacker	£4.50 - £7.00
extra person	£1.00
electricity	£2.00
awning	£2.00
dog	£1.00

Less 10% for 7 or more nights. Tel: (01549) 402447. Fax: (01549) 402784. E-mail: dunroamin@hudson38. freeserve.co.uk. Reservations: Made with £20 per week deposit, balance 4 weeks prior to arrival. **Open** 1 April - 1 November.

Directions: On A836 (Lairg - Roagart road), park is on the south side of Lairg. Follow international camping signs. O.S.GR: NC586062.

Reraig Caravan Site

Balmacara, Kyle of Lochalsh, Ross-shire IV40 8DH

776

This is a small, level park close to Loch Alsh with views over to Skye and a wooded hillside behind (criss-crossed with woodland walks). Set mainly on well cut grass, it is sheltered from the prevailing winds by the hill and provides just 40 numbered pitches, 36 with electrical connections (10A) and some hardstandings. Large tents and trailer tents are not accepted at all. Small tents are permitted at the discretion of the owner, so it would be advisable to telephone first if this affects you. Awnings are not permitted during July and August in order to protect the grass. The ground can be stony so there could be a problem with tent pegs. Reraig makes a good base from which to explore the Isle of Skye and the pretty village of Plockton with its palm trees (remember Hamish Macbeth on TV?) Reservations are not necessary but it may be best to arrive before late afternoon in July and August.

Facilities: The single sanitary block has been extensively refurbished and is kept immaculately clean. Children have their own low basins, controllable hot showers are on payment (10p for 2 minutes). Sinks for clothes and dishwashing. Use of a spin dryer is free. Motorcaravan drainage point. **Off site:** Adjacent to the park is the Balmacara Hotel (with bar), shop (selling gas), sub-post office, off licence and petrol station.

Charges 2001

Per unit incl. 2 persons	£8.30
extra adult	£1.50
electricity (10A)	£1.50
awning (May, June, Sept only)	£1.50
backpackers/cyclists, per tent	£6.50

Tel: (01599) 566215. Reservations: Not necessary so not accepted by phone; if considered essential, by letter enclosing cheque/PO for first night's fee (non-returnable). **Open** mid-April - 30 September.

Directions: Take A87 towards Kyle of Lochalsh. Park is signed very soon after sign for Balmacara, on the right just before hotel and petrol station. O.S.GR: NG815272.

Ardmair Point Caravan Park

Ardmair Point, Ullapool, Ross-shire IV26 2TN

771

This spectacularly situated park, overlooking the little Loch Kanaird, just round the corner from Loch Broom, has splendid views all round. The 68 touring pitches are arranged mainly on grass around the edge of the bay, in front of the shingle beach. Electrical hook-ups (10A) are available and some gravel hardstandings are on the other side of the access road, just past the second sanitary block. Motorcaravans are not permitted on the grass pitches and must use the hardstandings. Tent pitches, together with cheaper pitches for some tourers are in a large field behind the other sanitary facilities. The park provides rowing and motorboats for hire and arranges fishing trips. Scuba diving is popular at Loch Kanaird because the water is so clear. Seals are regularly seen in the bay and the whole area is full of interest, including visits to Inverewe Gardens and the Isle Martin bird and seal colonies.

Facilities: Two toilet blocks, both with good facilities. One block has wonderful views from the large windows in the launderette and dishwashing rooms, plus large en-suite rooms for disabled people. Motorcaravan service point. Reception, a restaurant and shop are housed in the same building. Children's play area. **Off site:** Golf or bicycle hire 3 miles.

Charges guide

Per unit incl. two persons	£7.50 - £10.00
awning	£2.00
extra adult	£2.00 - £3.00
child (over 5 yrs)	£1.00
extra tent	£1.50 - £2.50
electricity (10A)	£2.00

Less for 7 or more nights pre-paid. Tel: (01854) 612054. Fax: (01854) 612757. E-mail: p.fraser@btinternet.com. Reservations: Advised for July/Aug. (min. 2 nights). **Open** 1 May - late September, depending on the weather, if in doubt phone.

Directions: Park is off the A835 road, 3 miles north of Ullapool. O.S.GR: NH109983.

Loch Greshornish Camping Site

Arnisort, Edinbane, Isle of Skye IV51 9PS

774

Mr and Mrs Palmer took over this simple, spacious site with simple facilities in 1999. In a beautiful, peaceful setting with views over the loch to the low hills to the northwest of Skye, it is suitable for long or short stays. There are 30 level grass pitches for motorcaravans and caravans, 28 with 10A electric hook-ups. There are also places for up to 100 tents (but numbers never reach that level). A new building houses reception and a small shop selling basic essentials and now including an off-licence. The owners offer bicycle hire (with safety helmets) and canoe hire, with future plans including a children's play area.

Facilities: The refurbished toilet facilities are light, airy and spotlessly clean. The showers are a little cramped. Dishwashing sink in the ladies' and another in the men's. The only acknowledgement of any clothes washing needs is a tumble dryer in a little cabin outside. Camper's shelter with seating, cooking and eating area. Small shop. Bicycle hire. Canoe hire. **Off site:** The local village has two hotels for drinks and meals; Portree, the nearest town, is 15 miles.

Charges 2001

Per caravan or motorcaravan	£1.50
tent	75p
adult	£3.25
child 5-10 yrs	£1.00
11-16 yrs	£2.00
electricity	£1.60

Tel/Fax: (01470) 582230. E-mail: info@greshcamp. freeserve.co.uk. Reservations: Advised for high season. **Open** Easter - 15 October.

Directions: Site is 15 miles west of Portree on the A850 Dunvegan road by Edinbane. O.S.GR: NG343524.

Staffin Caravan and Camping Site

Staffin, Isle of Skye IV51 9JX

775

This simple camping site is on the side of a hill just outside Staffin, where the broad sweep of the bay is dotted with working crofts running down to the sea; it is perhaps more suited to backpackers and small tents. A marked walk from the site leads to the seashore and slipway (good for walking dogs but too far to be taking a boat). With 50 pitches, the site is quite sloping but there are 18 reasonably level pitches with irregular hardstanding for caravans and motorcaravans, all with electrical hook-ups (16A). Skye has many activities to offer and for the truly dedicated walker the Cuillins are the big attraction but the hills above Staffin look demanding!

Facilities: The sanitary block includes large, controllable showers. Washing up sinks are unfortunately not under cover and have only cold water. An older block is only opened at very busy times. Large hardstanding area has a motorcaravan service point. Gas available. **Off site:** Fishing or boat launching 1 mile, bicycle hire 5 miles, riding 9 miles. Staffin village is 400 yards and has a large shop (open six days a week), a restaurant, launderette (useful as the site has no laundry).

Charges guide

Per caravan or motorcaravan incl. 2 persons	£8.00
tent incl. 2 persons	£7.00 - £7.50
tent incl. 1 person	£4.00
extra adult	£3.00
child 5-12 yrs	£1.00
13-18 yrs	£1.50
electricity	£1.50

No credit cards. Tel: (01470) 562213. Reservations: Maybe necessary for peak periods (made with £10 deposit), but will always try to fit you in. **Open** 1 April - 30 September (maybe into October if weather fine).

Directions: Site is 15 miles north of Portree on A855 (2 miles of single track at the start), just before Staffin on the right and up a slope. O.S.GR: NG496668.

Faichem Park

778 Ardgarry Farm, Faichem, Invergarry, Inverness-shire PH35 4HG

Small and unsophisticated, Faichem Park is situated on a hillside in a beautiful setting with glorious views over Ben Tee (2,955 ft) near Loch Ness. The road up to the site has been tarmaced so it is now accessible to all except American motorhomes. For children there is the attraction of helping to feed the animals – sheep and lambs, chickens, many types of ducks and strange marvellous looking types of pheasants (Mr Wilson's hobby), and the pony and the white 'runner' ducks which march like soldiers around the park and farm. There are 30 pitches with plenty of space, including 14 with electrical connections and 10 with level concrete hardstanding. Four barbecues are strategically positioned around the camping area for visitors to use. Dogs are accepted (but care is needed with the livestock) and there is an excellent area above the site for walks. TV reception is good. A flexible system for night-time road illumination allows campers to turn off lights close to their pitch if necessary. There are numerous places to fish in the area, golf in Fort Augustus and Fort William, pony trekking, a pleasure cruiser on Loch Ness (you might see Nessie) and the Great Glen water park (2 miles).

Facilities: A log type cabin houses the toilet facilities which are older in style but very clean (key, £1 deposit). Hot water to the showers is metered but is free to washbasins and dishwashing sinks. Hair and hand dryers. Gas is available and free range eggs are sold at the farm but there is no shop (closest 2 miles towards Fort William). **Off site**: Bicycle hire or boat slipway 2 miles, golf 7 miles. The village is ½ mile with a hotel.

Charges 2001

Per unit incl. 2 persons	£7.00 - £7.50
extra adult	50p
extra child	25p
electricity	£1.50 - £2.00

No credit cards. Tel: (01809) 501226. Fax: (01809) 501307. E-mail: ardgarry.farm@lineone.net. Reservations: Advisable in main season and made with small deposit. **Open** 15 March - 15 October.

Directions: From A82 at Invergarry take A87 (in direction of Kyle of Lochalsh) and continue for 1 mile. Turn right at Faichem sign and bear left up hill, farmhouse and reception is the first entrance on the right, the site is second. From opposite direction on A87, turn left at Faichem sign, take third entrance on left for reception, second left for park. O.S.GR: NH285023.

Alan Rogers' discount
Less 10% in low season

Resipole Farm Caravan and Camping Park

780 Loch Sunart, Acharacle, Argyll PH36 4HX

This quiet, open park is marvellously set on the banks of Loch Sunart, 8 miles from Strontian, on the Ardnamurchan peninsula. With views across the water and regularly visited by wild deer, it offers a good base for exploring the whole of this scenic area or, more locally, for fishing, boating (launching from the site's own slipway) and walking in the unspoilt countryside. There are 60 touring pitches here, more than half with hardstanding and electric hook-ups (10/16A), and 4 with all services. Tents are sited by the hedges. Adjoining the farmhouse is a well equipped bar and restaurant offering reasonably priced home made food in the evenings (vegetarians catered for). Resipole Farm is well located for day trips to Mull via the Lochaline ferry.

Facilities: The central, modern sanitary block can be heated and is kept very clean. Good dishwashing facilities. Excellent provision for diasbled visitors. Laundry facilities. Bar/restaurant. Nine-hole golf course. Caravan storage. **Off site**: Riding 5 miles.

Charges 2001

Per caravan incl. 2 persons	£9.50 - £10.00
motorcaravan or tent	£9.00 - £9.50
cyclists (2 persons)	£7.50
extra adult	£3.00
child up to 5 yrs	50p
6-12 yrs	£1.00
13 yrs upwards	£1.50
electricity	£2.00

Tel: (01967) 431235. Fax: (01967) 431777. E-mail: info@resipole.co.uk. Reservations: Advisable for hook-ups and made for any period with one night's fee. **Open** 1 April - 31 October.

Directions: From A82 Fort William road, take the Corran ferry located 5 miles north of Ballachulish and 8 miles south of Fort William. On leaving ferry, turn south along the A861. Park is on the north bank of Loch Sunart, 8 miles west of Strontian. The road is single track for 8 miles approaching Resipole and care is needed, but it is well worth it. O.S.GR: NM676740.

Invercoe Caravan and Camping Park

779 | Invercoe, Glencoe, Argyll PH49 4HP

On the edge of Loch Leven, surrounded by mountains and forest, Iain and Lynn Brown are continually developing this attractively located park in its magnificent historical setting. It provides 60 pitches for caravans, motorcaravans or tents on level grass with gravel access roads (some hardstandings). You choose your own numbered pitch, those at the loch side being very popular, although the majority of the electrical hook-ups (10A) are to the back of the park. The only rules imposed are necessary for safety because the owners prefer their guests to feel free and enjoy themselves. There is much to do for the active visitor with hill walking, climbing, boating, pony riding and sea loch or fresh water fishing in this area of outstanding natural beauty.

Facilities: The well refurbished toilet block can be heated (shower/wash room locked 10 pm. - 7 am). Dishwashing under cover, excellent laundry facilities with a drying room. Motorcaravan service point with multi-drainage point, fresh water, dustbins, and chemical disposal point. Shop (May-end Sept). Play area with swings. Fishing. **Off site**: Village with pub and restaurant within walking distance. Golf 3 miles. Bicycle hire 2 miles.

Charges 2001

Per unit incl. 2 persons	£10.00
extra adult	£1.00
child (over 2 yrs)	50p
awning	£1.50
electricity (10A)	£1.50
tent incl. 2 persons, no car	£8.00
single person unit	£6.00

Senior citizens less £1 per person outside July/Aug. Tel/Fax: (01855) 811210. E-mail: invercoe@sol.co.uk. Reservations: Advised for electricity for peak season; made with £17 deposit and £3 fee. **Open** Easter/1 April - end October.

Directions: Follow A82 Crianlarich - Fort William road to Glencoe village and turn onto the B863; park is ½ mile along, well signed. O.S.GR: NN098594.

Small family owned park with all round picturesque views of loch, mountain & forest

INVERCOE
Caravan & Camping Park
Glencoe

Shop - Launderette - Showers - Drying Room - Play Area - Telephone
Caravans, Tents and Motorhomes Most Welcome.
Mobile Holiday Homes for Hire (seasonal)   Cottages and Lodges All Year
For Brochure: Tel/Fax 01855 811210   e-mail: invercoe@sol.co.uk www.invercoe.co.uk
Address: Glencoe, Argyll PH49 4HP   Open 1 April - end October

Camping and Caravanning Club Site Oban

781 | Barcaldine by Connel, Argyll PA37 1SG

This Club site at Barcaldine, 12 miles north of Oban, takes 86 units. Arranged within the old walled garden of Barcaldine House, the walls give some protection from the wind and make it quite a sun trap. There are 24 level hardstanding pitches and 52 electrical hook-ups (16A). Being a small site, it has a very cosy feel to it, due no doubt to the friendly welcome new arrivals receive. Through the garden gate, one is immediately in the Barcaldine forest with its miles of forest tracks, absolutely perfect for walking or mountain biking. Unusually for a club site, there is a lounge bar selling very reasonably priced meals most evenings. The loch across the road is handy for sea fishing and a 20 minute walk takes you to a freshwater lake.

Facilities: The central toilet block can be heated and is kept very clean with free hot showers, hair dryers and plenty of washbasins and WCs. Excellent unit for disabled visitors (small ramp). Laundry. Motorcaravan service point. Small shop open a few hours each day for basic provisions and gas. Bar (open til 10.30 pm; no children after 8 pm) with bar meals served 6-8 pm. Small play area with safety base. **Off site**: A not too frequent bus passes the gate. Sea Life Centre 2 miles.

Charges 2001

Per adult	£3.15 - £4.80
child (6-18 yrs)	£1.55
non-member pitch fee	£4.30
electricity	£1.65 - £2.40

Tel: (01631) 720348 (no calls after 8 pm). Reservations: Necessary for high season and made with deposit; contact site. **Open** April - end October.

Directions: From the A85 take A828 over Connel Bridge. After about 5 miles pass Sea Life Centre on left. Park entrance is 1 mile (on right, opposite loch) through archway. O.S.GR: NM966420.

Oban Divers Caravan Park

782 Glenshellach Road, Oban, Argyll PA34 4QJ

Set most attractively in a four-acre valley, yet close to Oban with all its facilities and local attractions, this park has been thoughtfully developed as an extension to the garden of the owner's family home and his diving business which is run alongside the caravan park. A small stream runs through the park, with several types of young eucalyptus and bamboo growing and fuchsias planted along one side at the entrance. Some 60 tons of stone have been sympathetically used to enhance its general appearance. There are only 45 pitches with 12 hardstandings, 34 electrical connections (10A) and plenty of space. Tents are placed mainly on a higher back terrace. An open fronted room is provided for tenters to rest and eat. The single track road leading to the park has few passing places, so it is only suitable for smaller units. There are three bunk houses for groups to rent, two sleeping up to six people, one up to twelve. Local attractions include the Oban distillery, the island of Kerrera for walking, cruises to lochs and islands, plus many more.

Facilities: Toilet facilities are provided in two chalets, the smaller one near the tent pitches. The main chalet provides comfortable facilities with two of the three ladies' washbasins in cabins. Dishwashing and laundry (with a very popular mangle!) with drying rooms (may be closed in very early or late season). Motorcaravan service point. Small shop at reception with gas. Divers' shop with hot drinks machine. Covered barbecue with seating. Children's play items on gravel (those with children can pitch close by). Definitely no dogs accepted. **Off site:** Fishing 1 mile, bicycle hire 2 miles, riding or golf 3 miles.

Charges 2001

Per unit	£7.00
person	50p
electricity	£1.50
awning or extra car	£1.00

Less £1.00 for senior citizens excl. B.Hs and July/Aug. No credit cards. Tel/Fax: (01631) 562755. E-mail: info@obandivers.co.uk. Reservations: Made with £10 deposit. **Open** mid March - end October.

Directions: From north follow A85 one way system through town to traffic island then take ferry terminal exit (Albany St). By Job Centre turn left and then follow signs to Camping Glenshellach. From south go into town to traffic island, then as above. Site is 2 miles from Oban on single track road with passing places. O.S.GR: NM841277.

North Ledaig Caravan Park

784 Connel, by Oban, Argyll PA37 1RT

The views over the Sound of Mull here are magnificent and Mr and Mrs Weir have tried to ensure good views by staggering the pitches and not planting many trees. The park provides 240 pitches for caravans, motorcaravans and trailer tents only. Of these, 230 pitches have electricity (10A) and 228 have hardstanding. A dog walk follows the disused railway track that runs through the park. An award winning 30 acre nature reserve with ponds and walks (strictly no dogs) to attract wildlife has been developed on land across the road. Being well organised and run, this is a quiet park which makes a good base for exploring the area, visiting the islands from Oban or simply relaxing on the shores of the loch. Fishing and sailing are possible from the site (there is a slipway for small boats), hill walking or pony trekking are close. Buses pass the gate five or six times a day. A member of the Caravan Club's 'managed under contract' scheme, non-members are also very welcome.

Facilities: The main sanitary block is centrally located - you may have a bit of a walk depending on your pitch but a new, semi-underground block should be built soon. The current amenities are excellent and include full facilities for disabled visitors and for babies (access by key). Washbasins in cabins for ladies (one for men). Well equipped laundry with irons for hire, and dishwashing. Motorcaravan service area. Further, well renovated sanitary facilities are behind the reception block. Well stocked, licensed shop. Play area. Caravan storage. **Off site:** Bicycle hire and golf 6 km.

Charges guide

Per pitch	£2.00 - £4.00
adult	£2.60 - £4.00
child (5-17 yrs)	£1.10 - £1.20
electricity	£1.50 - £2.25
extra car, trailer or m/cycle	£1.00

Debit cards accepted (not credit cards). Tel/Fax: (01631) 710291. Reservations: Any length, with £10 deposit incl. £1 non-returnable fee. **Open** 27 March - 31 October.

Directions: Park is about 1 mile north of Connel Bridge, on the A828 Oban - Fort William road, 7 miles from Oban. O.S.GR: NM913456.

Glen Nevis Caravan and Camping Park

Glen Nevis, Fort William, Inverness-shire PH33 6SX

783

Just outside Fort William in a most attractive and quiet situation with views of Ben Nevis, this spacious park is used by those on active pursuits as well as sightseeing tourists. It comprises eight quite spacious fields, divided between caravans, motorcaravans and tents (steel pegs required). It is licensed for 250 touring caravans but with no special tent limits. The large touring pitches, many with hardstanding, are marked with wooden fence dividers, 200 with electricity (13A) and 100 also have water and drainage. The park becomes full in the peak months but there are vacancies each day. If reception is closed (possible in low season) you site yourself. There are regular security patrols at night in busy periods. The park's own modern restaurant and bar with good value bar meals is a short stroll from the park, open to all. A well managed park with bustling, but pleasing ambience, watched over by Ben Nevis. Around 1,000 acres of the Glen Nevis estate are open to campers to see the wildlife and explore this lovely area.

Facilities: The four modern toilet blocks make a good provision with hot showers on payment (20p), (extra showers in two blocks); and units for visitors with disabilities. An excellent block in Nevis Park (one of the eight camping fields) has some washbasins in cubicles, showers, further facilities for disabled visitors, a second large laundry room and dishwashing sinks. Motorcaravan service point. Self-service shop (Easter - mid Oct), barbecue area and snack bar (May - mid-Sept). Children's play area on bark. **Off site:** Pony trekking, golf and fishing near.

Charges 2001

Per person	£1.10 - £1.60
caravan	£5.60 - £8.30
motorcaravan or tent	£5.40 - £8.00
small tent	£4.90 - £7.30
backpacker's tent: 1 person	£3.20 - £4.70
2 persons	£3.90 - £5.70
awning	70p - £1.10
fully serviced pitch extra	£1.30 - £2.00

Tel: (01397) 702191. Fax: (01397) 703904. E-mail: camping@glen-nevis.co.uk. Reservations: Advised for July/Aug. **Open** 15 March - 31 October.

Directions: Turn off A82 to east at roundabout just north of Fort William following camp sign. O.S.GR: NN124723.

Linnhe Lochside Holidays

785 Corpach, Fort William, Inverness-shire PH33 7NL

This quiet well run park has a very peaceful situation overlooking Loch Eil, and is beautifully landscaped with wonderful views. There are individual pitches with hardstanding for 65 touring units (12 seasonal) on terraces leading down to the water's edge. They include 32 special ones with electricity connection (16A), water and drainaway, plus 30 with electricity only (10A). A separate area on the lochside takes 15 small tents (no reservation). There are also 64 caravan holiday homes and 11 centrally heated pine chalets for hire. Fishing is free on Loch Eil and you are welcome to fish from the park's private beach or bring your own boat and use the slipway and dinghy park. About 5 miles from Fort William on 'The Road to the Isles', the park is conveniently placed for touring the Western Highlands. Easily accessible are Ben Nevis and the Nevis range (cable car to 2,000 ft.), geological, Jacobite and Commando museums, distillery visits, seal island trips, the Mallaig steam railway and the Caledonian Canal.

Facilities: The toilet facilities are of an excellent standard, are heated in the cooler months and include baths (£1). Dishwashing room. First class laundry and separate outdoor clothing drying room (charged per night). Self-service, licensed shop (end May - end Sept). Gas supplies. Barbecue area. Toddlers' play room and two well equipped children's play areas on safe standing. Up to two dogs per pitch are accepted. Large motorhomes are accepted but it is best to book first. Caravan storage. **Off site**: Bicycle hire 2½ miles, riding or golf 5 miles.

Charges 2001

Per unit incl. 2 persons, electricity	£11.50 - £13.50
special pitch	£12.00 - £14.50
small tent pitch	£8.50 - £10.50
awning, extra tent or car	£1.50
extra person	£1.00
dog (max. 2, not on tent pitches)	50p

Seasonal rates available. Tel: (01397) 772376. Fax: (01397) 772007. E-mail: holidays@linnhe. demon.co.uk. Reservations: Made with £30 deposit for min. 3 nights. **Open** all year except 1 Nov - 19 Dec.

Directions: Park entrance is off A830 Fort William - Mallaig road, 1 mile west of Corpach. O.S.GR: NN072772.

Glendaruel Caravan Park

786 Glendaruel, Kyles of Bute, Argyll PA22 3AB

Glendaruel is in South Argyll, in the area of Scotland bounded by the Kyles of Bute and Loch Fyne, yet is less than two hours by road from Glasgow and serviced by ferries from Gourock and the Isle of Bute. There is also a service between Tarbert and Portavadie. Set in the peaceful wooded gardens of the former Glendaruel House in a secluded glen surrounded by the Cowal hills, it makes an ideal centre for touring this beautiful area. The park takes 35 units on numbered hardstandings with electricity connections (10A), plus 15 tents, on flat oval meadows bordered by over 50 different varieties of mature trees. In a separate area are 28 holiday homes. The converted stables of the original house provide an attractive little shop selling basics, local produce, venison, salmon, wines (some Scottish!) and tourist gifts. Glendaruel is a park for families with young children or for older couples to relax and to enjoy the beautiful views across the Sound of Bute from Tighnabruaich or the botanical gardens which flourish in the climate. The owners, Quin and Anne Craig, provide a warm welcome – they are justifiably proud of their park and its beautiful environment. A member of the Best of British group.

Facilities: The toilet block is ageing but is kept very neat and tidy and can be heated. Washing machine and dryer. A covered area has picnic tables for use in bad weather and dishwashing sinks. Shop (hours may be limited in low season). Gas available. Games room with pool table, table tennis and video games. Behind the laundry is a children's play centre for under 12s and additional play field. Bicycle hire (adults only). Fishing on site. Discount vouchers for local attractions. **Off site:** Sea fishing and boat slipway 5 miles, adventure centre (assault courses, abseiling and rafting) and sailing school close. Golf 12 miles.

Charges 2002

Per unit incl. 2 persons	£8.50 - £10.50
tent per person, no car	£4.00 - £5.00
extra adult	£1.50 - £2.00
child (4-15 yrs)	£1.00 - £1.50
awning, extra tent, extra car, trailer or boat	£1.50
electricity (10A)	£2.00

Special weekly rates and senior citizen discount outside July/Aug. Tel: (01369) 820267. Fax: (01359) 820367. E-mail: mail@glendaruelcaravanpark.co.uk. Reservations: Any length, with £10 deposit and £2 fee. **Open** 29 March - 27 October.

Directions: Entrance is off A886 road 13 miles south of Strachur. Alternatively there are two ferry services from Gourock to Dunoon, then on B836 which joins the A886 about 4 miles south of the park - this route not recommended for touring caravans. Note: the park has discount arrangements with Western Ferries so contact the park before making arrangements (allow 7 days for postage of tickets). O.S.GR: NS001865.

NORTHERN IRELAND

For information on all parts of Northern Ireland contact:

Belfast Welcome Centre
Tel: 028 9024 6609 Fax: 028 9031 2424
E-mail: info@nitb.com

Internet: http://www.discovernorthernireland.com

The natural beauty and variety of the countryside, the historic landscape and the friendly people are what holidaymakers remember best about Northern Ireland. In addition, a wide selection of good quality campsites, uncluttered roads, an abundance of pubs and restaurants and plenty to see and do wherever they go keeps visitors coming back for more.

As Northern Ireland is barely 85 miles from north to south and about 110 miles wide driving is something to be enjoyed. A matter of hours can transport you from the dramatic coastline and the nine Glens of Antrim to the rugged heart of the wild Sperrin Mountains, from the timeless landscape and glittering lakes of Fermanagh to the foothills of the Mourne Mountains sweeping down to Carlingford Lough.

Irish miles: the old granite milestones that still peep out from behind the cow parsley on road verges, especially in County Down, are marked in Irish miles. An Irish mile at 2,240 yards is 480 yards longer than a standard English mile. Distances on road signs, however, are marked in standard miles!

For youngsters and the young-at-heart, action and adventure are never far away. Pan for gold, take a subterranean journey through underground caves, enjoy a literary break or leap from pre-history to the future, then have a go at kayaking, abseiling, archery, horse-riding or any one of the numerous sports and activities on offer throughout Northern Ireland. No matter where you pitch your tent, or park your caravan, you will find good company and great 'craic' just around the corner.

Ferry Services

The following ferry services are expected to operate between the UK mainland and Ireland in 2002:

Irish Ferries
For bookings/enquiries: 08705 171717
or e-mail: info@irishferries.co.uk
www.irishferries.ie/index
Holyhead - Dublin
(ferry 3 hrs 15 mins, fastcraft 109 mins)
Pembroke - Rosslare (ferry 3 hrs 45 mins)

P&O Irish Sea
0870 24 24 777 www.poirishsea.com
Cairnryan - Larne (Super ferry 1 hr 45 mins, Superstar Express 1 hr - no caravans)
Fleetwood - Larne (ferry 8 hrs)
Liverpool - Dublin (ferry 8 hrs, Super ferry 6 hrs)

Sea Cat Scotland
08705 523 523 www.seacat.co.uk
Troon - Belfast (2 hrs 30 mins)
Heysham - Belfast (4 hrs)
Liverpool - Dublin (4 hrs)

Swansea Cork Ferries
01792 45 61 16 www.swansea-cork.ie
Swansea - Cork (10 hrs)

Stena Line
08705 70 70 70 www.stenaline.co.uk
Fishguard - Rosslare
(Super ferry 3 hrs 30 mins, Lynx 99 mins)
Holyhead - Dun Laoghaire (HSS 99 mins)
Holyhead - Dublin Port
(Super ferry 3 hrs 45 mins)
Stranraer - Belfast
(Super ferry 3 hrs 15 mins, HSS 105 mins)

Norse Merchant Ferries
0870 600 4321
www.norse-irish-ferries.co.uk
Liverpool - Belfast (8 hrs 30 mins)
Liverpool - Dublin (8 hrs)

Co. Fermanagh
Share Holiday Village

Smith's Strand, Lisnaskea, Co. Fermanagh BT92 0EQ

This 30 acre park enjoys a quiet and beautiful location on the shores of Upper Lough Erne. The 5 acre touring park, a separate part of this complex, offers all the benefits and self contained aspects of caravanning, plus the opportunity to enjoy all the sports facilities of the village. The 15 pitches have hardstanding, electricity and space for awnings. An important factor here is that Share is committed to the provision of facilities and opportunities for both able bodied and disabled visitors. Caravanners can take temporary Leisure Suite membership for the duration of their stay (£2.50 per day, child under 5 free, and best booked and paid for in advance to ensure availability). If wanting to participate in the outdoor activities, the purchase of an Activity Pass covers sailing, canoeing, windsurfing, banana-ski, archery, mountain bikes, or you may prefer a Viking long-ship cruise. Package deals are available. A 2½ hour session costs £6 per person and includes all equipment and instruction. This centre is an approved British Canoe Union and Royal Yachting Association teaching school and has a 30 berth marina. A multi-purpose Arts Area has been added providing a comprehensive range of art facilities.

Facilities: The sanitary blocks, which can be heated and are kept very clean, are fully equipped including washing up, laundry facilities and a drying room with tumble dryers. Fishing, bicycle hire and boat launching all on site.

Charges 2001

Per caravan or tent	£10.00
2 man tent	£7.00

Touring caravan and campsite packages available. Tel: 028 6772 2122. Fax: 028 6772 1893. E-mail: share@dnet.co.uk. Reservations: Advisable in peak season and for B.H.s and with deposit (weekend or midweek £20, 7 days £50; activity passes 50% of total cost per person). **Open** Easter - 31 October.

Directions: From Lisnaskea village, take B127 sign to Derrylin and Smith's Strand and proceed for 3 miles. Site is clearly signed on the right.

Co. Fermanagh
LoanEden Caravan Park

Muckross Bay, Kesh, Co. Fermanagh BT93 1TX

The owners of LoanEden have built up a reputation for their park, based on a friendly, caring attitude. It is particularly suitable for those who enjoy fishing or riding. First impressions are of an overall neat and tidy appearance, with well tended shrubs, flower beds and wide tarmac driveways. There are many privately owned holiday homes on the site, but these are kept separate from the touring area. The 24 touring and 12 long-stay pitches are level with hardstanding, water, electricity, drainage, rubbish bin and a grass area for an awning. For children there are two outdoor play areas and a new indoor room for football, netball, etc. The 'LoanEden Ramblers' club for 4-11 year olds provides activities in season (£1.50 per child). Young and old can enjoy pony and horse riding tuition under the supervision of the owners' daughter Victoria, an A.I. instructor and son Andrew who is an international rider. The owners organise barbecues and barn dances in aid of charity. There are ongoing plans to further extend this site.

Facilities: The fully tiled central sanitary block is well equipped and includes facilities for disabled people. Laundry area with washing machines, dryers and sinks. Motorcaravan service point. Children's play areas. Riding. **Off site:** Fishing and bicycle hire nearby, golf 5 miles.

Charges guide

Per caravan or motorcaravan	
incl. awning and electricity	£12.00
tent	£8.00
electricity	£1.00

Tel: 028 6863 1603. Fax: 028 6863 2300. Reservations: Advisable for high season and B.Hs. **Open** all year.

Directions: From Enniskillen take A32 Omagh road for 3½ miles and branch left on B82 Kesh road. Continue for 11 miles to village of Kesh. Cross over bridge at north end of village and turn immediately left to park in ½ mile on right.

Bush Caravan Park

835 95 Priestland Road, Bushmills, Co. Antrim BT57 8UJ

An ideal base for touring the North Antrim Coast, this family run, recently extended park is only minutes away from two renowned attractions, the Giant's Causeway and the Old Bushmills Distillery. This fact alone makes Bush a popular location, but its fast growing reputation for friendliness and top class facilities makes it equally appealing. Conveniently located just off the main Ballymoney-Portrush Road (B62), it is approached by a short drive. The site itself is partly surrounded by mature trees and hedging, but views across the countryside can still be appreciated. Tarmac roads lead to 43 well laid out, spacious pitches, with hard-standing and electricity (16A), or to a grass area for tents. Features on site are murals depicting the famed scenery, sights and legends of the Causeway Coast. A further novelty is Bushmills barrels used as picnic tables. The enthusiastic owners organise tours to the Distillery and coastal trips – a musical evening cannot be ruled out.

Facilities: The toilet block (opened by key) is modern, clean and equipped to a high standard. Facilities include controllable showers (token) with excellent provision for people with disabilities. Washing machine, dryer and dishwashing sinks. Central children's play area. Recreation room for all ages.

Charges guide

Per unit incl. all persons	£10.00
frame tent	£8.00
small tent	£6.00
awning	£1.00
electricity	£1.00

Tel: 028 2073 1678 or 028 7035 4240. Fax: 028 7035 1998. Reservations: Advised for high season or weekends. **Open** Easter - 31 October.

Directions: From Ballymoney A26/B62 roundabout proceed north on B62 towards Portrush for 6½ miles. Turn right onto B17 and site is 350 yds on the left.

Curran Court Caravan Park

832 Curran Road, Larne, Co. Antrim BT40 1XB

Formerly run by the local borough council, this park is now managed by the Curran Court Hotel (opposite the park). Attractive garden areas add to the charm of this small, neat site which is very conveniently situated for the ferry terminal and only a few minutes walk from the sea. The 29 pitches, all with hardstanding and electricity (12A), give reasonable space off the tarmac road and there is a separate tent area of 1½ acres. Plans are in hand for another 31 pitches. You may consider using this site as a short term base for discovering the area as well as an ideal overnight stop. The warden can usually find room for tourists so reservations are not normally necessary.

Facilities: The toilet block is clean and adequate without being luxurious – plans are in hand for a new block. Laundry room with dishwashing facilities. Children's play area with good equipment and safety surfaces. Bowls and putting on site. **Off site:** Bicycle hire 1 km. Golf 3 km. Boat launching 500 yds. Many amenities are close including a shop (100 yds), the hotel for food and drink, tennis and a leisure centre with pool (300 yds). Larne market is on Wednesdays.

Charges 2001

Per caravan or motorcaravan	£8.50
tent	£5.00
electricity	£1.50

Tel: 028 2827 3797. Fax: 028 2826 0096. Reservations: Not normally considered necessary. **Open** Easter - 30 September.

Directions: Immediately after leaving the ferry terminal, turn right and follow camp signs. Site is just / mile on the left.

Carnfunnock Country Park Caravan Site

Coast Road, Drain's Bay, Larne, Co. Antrim BT40 2QG

831

In a magnificent parkland setting overlooking the sea, what makes this touring site popular is its scenic surroundings and convenient location. It is 3½ miles north of the market town of Larne on the famed Antrim Coast Road and offers 28 level 'super' pitches, all with hardstanding, water, electricity (15A), drainage, individual pitch lighting and ample space for an awning. The site has a neat appearance with a tarmac road following through to the rear where a number of pitches are placed in a circular position with allocated space for tents. Run by the Borough Council and supervised by a manager, the surrounding Country Park is immaculately kept. The Visitor Centre includes a gift shop and information about local attractions and the restaurant/coffee shop is pleasant and looks towards the sea. Spending time around the parkland, you find a walled time garden with historic sundials, a maze, forest walk, children's adventure playground, putting green, 9 hole golf course, wildlife garden and miniature railway. There is also a summer events programme.

Facilities: A small building beside the entrance gates houses sanitary toilet facilities (entry by key) which are kept clean, but now starting to show signs of wear. There are shower units, facilities for disabled people and dishwashing. Motorcaravan service point. **Off site:** Fishing and boat launching 400 m.

Charges guide

Per caravan or motorcaravan	£13.00
5 nights	£59.00
7 nights	£80.00
tent	£7.00

Tel: 028 2827 0541 or 028 2826 0088. Fax: 028 2827 0852. Reservations: Advisable for week-ends; peak periods and B.Hs. **Open** Easter - 30 September.

Directions: From ferry terminal in Larne, follow signs for Coast Road and Carnfunnock Country Park; well signed 3½ miles on A2 coast road.

Drumaheglis Marina and Caravan Park

36 Glenstall Road, Ballymoney, Co. Antrim BT53 7QN

834

A caravan park which continually maintains high standards, Drumaheglis is popular throughout the season. Situated on the banks of the lower River Bann, approximately 4 miles from the town of Ballymoney, it appeals to watersports enthusiasts or makes an ideal base for exploring this scenic corner of Northern Ireland. The marina offers superb facilities for boat launching, water-skiing, cruising, canoeing or fishing, whilst getting out and about can take you to the Giant's Causeway, seaside resorts such as Portrush or Portstewart, the sands of Whitepark Bay, the Glens of Antrim or the picturesque villages of the Antrim coast road. For tourers only, this site instantly appeals, for it is well laid out with trees, shrubs, flower beds and tarmac roads. There are now 53 serviced pitches with hardstanding, electricity (5/10A) and water points. Ballymoney is a popular shopping town and the Joey Dunlop Leisure Centre provides a high-tech fitness studio, sports hall, etc. There is much to see and do within this Borough and of interest is the Heritage Centre in Charlotte Street.

Facilities: Modern toilet blocks, spotlessly clean when we visited, include individual wash cubicles, and facilities for disabled visitors, plus four family shower rooms. Dishwashing sinks. Washing machine and dryer. Children's play area. Barbecue and picnic areas. **Off site:** Bicycle hire and golf 4 miles, riding ½ mile.

Charges 2001

Per unit incl. electricity	£12.50
per 7 days	£75.00
unserviced	£10.00
per 7 days	£60.00

Tel: 028 2766 6466. E-mail: info@drumaheglismarina.co.uk. Ballymoney Borough Council: Tel: 028 2766 2280; Fax: 028 2766 7659. Reservations: Essential for peak periods and weekends. **Open** Easter - 1 October.

Directions: From A26/B62 Portrush - Ballymoney roundabout continue for approx. 1 mile on the A26 towards Coleraine. Site is clearly signed - follow International camping signs.

Tullans Farm Caravan Park

859 46 Newmills Road, Coleraine, Co. Londonderry BT52 2JB

A quality, well run family park convenient for the Causeway coast, Tullans Farm is one of the most popular in the area. It has a quiet, heart of the country feel, yet the University town of Coleraine is within a mile, the seaside resort Portrush and Portstewart five miles and a shopping centre a five minute drive. Tullans Farm has earned a reputation for its spotlessly clean toilet block and well cared for appearance. In a central position, fronted by a parking space, stands a long white building housing the sanitary facilities and reception. Around the park roads are gravel and 20 of the 32 pitches are on hardstanding; all have electric hook-ups (10A). In season the owners organise barbecues, barn dances and line dancing (funds in aid of charity).

Facilities: The toilet and shower rooms, including a family shower unit, are spacious, modern and include facilities for people with disabilities. Laundry and washing up room with sinks, washing machine, dryers and a large fridge. Play area. TV lounge and barn used for indoor recreation.

Charges 2002

Per unit incl. all persons	
and electricity	£10.00 - £11.00
awning	£1.00
family tent	£10.00
2 man tent	£7.00

Special Queen's Jubilee offers. No credit cards. Tel/Fax: 028 7034 2309. E-mail: tullansfarm@ hotmail.com. Reservations: Advised for peak times. **Open** March - 31 October.

Directions: From the Lodge Road roundabout (south end of Coleraine) turn east onto A29 Portrush ring road and proceed for ½ mile. Turn right at sign for park and Windy Hall. Park is clearly signed on left.

Bellemont Caravan Park

860 10 Islandtasserty Road, Coleraine, Co. Londonderry BT52 2PN

Close to Coleraine and Portstewart, this new, well kept park makes an immediately favourable impression with its white concrete roads, its perfect grass areas and well laid out appearance. The gently sloping ground rises at the far right of the park to give views over Portstewart and towards the sea. To the left of the entrance and security gate are five privately owned caravan holiday homes. There are 30 touring pitches, all with hardstanding, electric hook-up and water. These are spacious and well distributed around this open, parkland style setting. In a central position stands a gleaming white building, with flower tubs decorating the forecourt, which houses reception and heated sanitary facilities. Bellemont makes a good base for visiting the university town of Coleraine, the resorts and beaches of Portstewart and Portrush, or famous sights such as Dunluce Castle, Carrick-a-Rede rope bridge, the Giant's Causeway, plus the ports and harbours which follow the North Antrim coastline. There are no tent pitches.

Facilities: Toilet facilities with good sized showers (token operated). En-suite unit for disabled visitors. Laundry room with two washing machines, two dryers and iron (token operated), plus dishwashing sink and drainer to the outside. Play area for children with swings and slide on a bark surface. Dogs are not accepted.

Charges 2001

Per unit incl. all persons	£10.50
with electricity	£12.00
awning	£1.50

No credit cards. Tel: 028 7082 3872. Reservations: Contact site. **Open** Easter - 30 September.

Directions: From Lodge Road roundabout on eastern outskirts of Coleraine follow A29 north to fourth roundabout. Continue towards Portrush and site is clearly signed on left after ¼ mile.

Banbridge Touring Caravan and Camping Park

200 Newry Road, Banbridge, Co. Down BT32 3NB

This conveniently situated touring park on the main A1 Belfast - Newry road is an ideal place for a stopover if travelling between Southern and Northern Ireland. It is within easy towing distance of the main ports or would make an ideal base for discovering many tourist attractions such as the Bronte Homeland or Scarna Visitor Centre. A tiny site, with 8 hardstanding pitches and electrical connections (6A), it is part of the Banbridge Gateway Tourist Information Centre complex. The centre is an attractive building of modern design surrounded by a well maintained garden area and car park. Housed inside, apart from the offices of the centre and a bureau de change, is a display areas for Irish crafts. The restaurant and coffee shop within the complex (10.00-17.00 hrs daily) serves lunchtime specials, scones, cakes, etc. The touring park, located in the far left hand corner of the complex, is enclosed with ranch fencing, plus a security gate and barrier. The town of Banbridge is 1 mile.

Facilities: Excellent, ultra-modern toilet facilities, spotlessly clean and key operated, include two showers, good facilities for disabled people and an outside, covered dishwashing area. Extensive children's play area with safety base. **Off site:** Shops, restaurants, pubs and all services within 1 mile. Fishing, bicycle hire or golf within 3 miles.

Charges 2002

Per unit incl. electricity	£8.00
tent	£4.00

Max. stay 5 consecutive nights. Refundable key deposit (gate, WCs and showers) £20. Tel: 028 4062 3322. Fax: 028 4062 3114. E-mail: banbridge @nitic.net. Reservations: Contact centre during office hours (summer: Mon-Sat 09.00-19.00, Sun. 14.00-18.00; winter: Mon-Sat 10.00-17.00, Sun. closed). It is essential to arrive during opening hours to obtain keys. **Open** all year (except Christmas and New Year), but closed Sundays Oct - May incl.

Directions: Follow signs to Tourist Information Centre off the A1 Belfast - Newry dual carriageway, 1 mile south of Banbridge.

Tollymore Forest Caravan Park

Tollymore Forest Park, Newcastle, Co. Down BT33 6PW

This popular park, for tourers only, is located within the parkland of Tollymore Forest. It is discreetly situated away from the public footpaths and is noted for its scenic surroundings. The forest park, which is approached by way of an ornate gateway and majestic avenue of Himalayan cedars, covers an area of almost 500 hectares. It is backed by the Mourne mountains and situated two miles from the beaches and resort of Newcastle. The site is attractively laid out with hardstanding pitches, 72 of which have electricity (6A). The Head Ranger at Tollymore is helpful and ensures that the caravan site is efficiently run and quiet, even when full. Exploring the forest park is part of the pleasure of staying here, and of note are the stone follies, bridges and entrance gates. The Shimna and Spinkwee rivers flow through the park adding a refreshing touch and tree lovers appreciate the arboretum with its many rare species.

Facilities: Toilet blocks, timbered in keeping with the setting, are clean and modern with wash cubicles, facilities for disabled people, dishwashing and laundry area. **Off site**: Confectionery shop and tea room nearby. Small grocery shop a few yards from the exit gate of the park with gas available.

Charges 2001

Per unit incl. car and occupants	£7.00 - £11.00
electricity	£1.50

Low season mid-week special rates. Tel: 028 4372 2428. Reservations: Advisable in high season and for B.Hs. and made with £10 deposit. Contact: Tollymore Forest Park (Administration), 176 Tullybrannigan Road, Newcastle, Co. Down BT33 0PW. **Open** all year.

Directions: Approach Newcastle on the A24. Before entering the town, at roundabout, turn right on to A50 signed Castlewellan and follow signs for Tollymore Forest Park.

Gortin Glen Caravan and Camping Park

1 Lisnaharney Road, Lislap, Omagh, Co. Tyrone BT79 7UG

Pronounced 'Gorchin', this excellent, truly peaceful site is deep in Gortin Glen with splendid views of the surrounding hills and forest. The very large Gortin Glen Forest embraces the 405 ha. forest park which has a 5 mile scenic road offering breathtaking views, picnic areas, nature trails, wildlife enclosures and an indoor exhibit, all open to the public. Within the park is a camping area with 24 individually numbered pitches, all with hardstanding and electricity (13A). All pitches are spacious with room for an awning. In addition there are separate areas for tents and attractive self catering cottages. A barbecue area is located behind the main block. Reception is well stocked with tourist information on local attractions which include the Ulster History Park, Ulster American Folk Park and Sperrin Heritage Centre.

Facilities: The toilet block has four controllable hot showers (10p for 8 minutes) and good facilities for people with disabilities, which mothers may also use for children. Laundry room with two washing machines and two dryers. Dishwashing area with free hot water. TV/games room with table tennis and full sized snooker table. Children's play area with safety base and provision for ball games. **Off site**: Shops are in Gortin village (3 miles).

Charges guide

Per caravans	£8.50 (£51 per week)
tent acc. to size	£4.00 - £8.50 (£24 - £51 per week)
electricity	£1.50
awning	50p

Youth groups of 10 or more £1.50 per person, per night. Tel: 028 8164 8108. FAX: as phone. E-mail: gortinholidaypark@omagh.gov.uk. Reservations: Made with £15 fee for B.H. weekends. **Open** all year.

Directions: From Omagh take B48 road signed Gortin. Proceed north for approx. seven miles and turn left immediately after Ulster History Park into site.

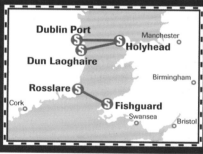

 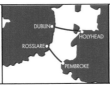

REPUBLIC OF IRELAND

For information on all parts of Southern Ireland contact:

Irish Tourist Board
Tel: 020 7493 3201 Fax: 020 7493 9065
E-mail: info@irishtouristboard.co.uk

Internet: http://www.ireland.travel.ie

'You're welcome' is not said lightly to the visitor who sets foot in Ireland, it is said with sincerity. On this `Emerald Isle' you will find friendly and hospitable people, spectacular scenery and a selection of good campsites to suit your particular needs. Whether you choose to be sited by a lough shore, at the foothills of a mountain range or close by golden sands, the scenery is stunning and the pace of life slow. With the help of information and maps available from the Tourist Office you discover for yourself, not only the beauty spots, but also many historic and interesting routes to follow. In such areas we have endeavoured to locate well run sites that range from family parks where children can find day long amusement, to the more simple site offering total relaxation, all of good quality.

A British visitor to the Republic of Ireland does not require a passport (and one may take the dog!). British currency is accepted in most outlets although we quote charges in Euros (€).

Travel insurance is advisable when travelling in the south.

To telephone the Irish Republic from the UK, replace the first `0' given in the number with the country code: 00 353. For example: (094) 88100 becomes 00 353 94 88100.

The population of the Republic (26 counties) is just over 3.5 million. Dublin is the largest city with 1,058,264 inhabitants, Cork is the second with 420,510 inhabitants.

Signposts are mostly bilingual. Whilst Ireland has gradually converted to metric measurements, it should be noted that most of the black on white finger-post signs are in miles and the newer green and white ones are in kilometres.

Gas cylinders in the UK and Ireland are not compatible. In Ireland the Euro-system that has a click-on regulator is used. The cylinders used in Ireland have a different shape, weight and size to those used in Britain.

Irish Caravan Council

Ireland, one of Europe's best kept secrets, is the Caravan and Camping destination for the discerning traveller. You take control of your holiday from start to finish, go as you please, and do as little or as much as you like. It's all on offer in Ireland: rugged coastlines, inland waterways, lakes and rivers, Celtic monuments, churches and castles, rolling hills and lush green valleys. Plus, of course, Ireland's legendary hostelries and the friendliest people you're ever likely to meet. Pick up a copy of the 2002 Caravan and Camping Guide at your local tourist office today - it's a breath of fresh air.

Alternatively contact ICC direct at:
Fax: 00 353 98 28237.
E-mail: info@camping-ireland.ie
Website: http//www.camping-ireland.ie
Boite Postale: ICC, Box 4443, Dublin 2, Ireland

Knockalla Caravan and Camping Park

Portsalon, Co. Donegal

864

What adds to the popularity of this site is its location, nestling between the slopes of the Knockalla Mountains and Ballymastocker Bay amidst the breathtaking scenery of County Donegal. The fact that the beach here has been named 'the second most beautiful beach in the world' is not surprising. Approached by an unclassified but short road, Knockalla's elevated situation commands a panoramic view of the famed Bay, Lough Swilly, Inishowen Peninsula and Dunree Head. The family run park is partly terraced giving an attractive, orderly layout with reception, shop and restaurant in a central position and the touring area sited to the left of reception. All 50 pitches have electrical hook-ups and hardstanding, offering a choice of tarmac only or with an adjoining grass to allow for awnings. Tents are pitched on a lower level facing reception and to the far left of the tourers, with caravan holiday homes placed around the right hand perimeter and to the rear of the park. Specialities at the shop and café are home made scones, apple cakes, jams, etc. with a takeaway or table service. Full Irish breakfasts are served.

Facilities: The main toilet block, tastefully refurbished and kept clean and fresh, can be heated. Showers (token). Dishwashing area and campers' kitchen with hot water. Laundry service operated by staff. Motorcaravan service points. Gas available. Children's play area and TV/games room. Shop and cafe (both July/Aug, plus B.H. w/ends). **Off site**: Golf 5 km, fishing, riding and bicycle hire within 16 km.

Charges 2001

Per motorhome, caravan or family tent	€ 13,97
awning	€ 1,90
tent for 1 or 2 persons	€ 10,16
extra person	€ 3,80
electricity (5A)	€ 1,90

No credit cards. Tel: 074 59108 or 074 53213. Reservations: Advisable for July/Aug and B.H. w/ends. **Open** 17 March - 17 September.

Directions: From Letterkenny take R245 to Rathmelton. Continue on R245 to Milford. Turn right on R246 to Kerrykeel. In village turn left towards Portsalon and at second crossroads turn right onto Portsalon/Knockalla coast road. Turn right to park at sign.

Greenlands Caravan and Camping Park

Rosses Point, Co. Sligo

869

Just off the N15 road and 8 km. from Sligo town, this is a well run park at Rosses Point, in the sand hills adjoining a championship golf course. It is thoughtfully laid out with small tents placed to the front of reception and the hardstanding touring pitches separated from the trailer tent pitches which occupy the rear. The ground is undulating and adds interest to the overall appearance. Your view depends on where you are pitched - look towards Coney Island and the Blackrock lighthouse which guards the bay, take in the sight of Benbulben Mountain or appreciate the seascape and the water lapping the resort's two bathing beaches. Electric hook-ups (10A) are available for touring units. This is an excellent base from which to explore the 'Yeats Country' and discover the beauty spots immortalised in his poems, such places as Lissadell, Dooney Rock, the Isle of Innisfree and the poet's burial place at Drumcliffe.

Facilities: Modern toilet facilities, recently extended and refitted, are kept exceptionally clean, with hot showers (token) dishwashing and laundry sinks, washing machine, dryer and iron. Motorcaravan service point. New campers' kitchen. Information point and TV room beside reception. Sand pit for children and outdoor chess and draughts sets. Night security. **Off site**: Mini-market, restaurant and evening entertainment in the village. Fishing and boat launching 100 m, golf 50 m, bicycle hire 8 km, riding 14 km.

Charges 2002

Per unit	€ 12,70
person	€ 0,65
hiker/cyclist incl. tent	€ 8,25
awning or pup tent	€ 1,25
electricity (10A)	€ 2,50

Weekly rates available. Tel: 071 77113. Reservations: Contact park. **Open** Easter - mid-September.

Directions: From Sligo city travel approx. 800 m. north on N15 road, turn left onto R291 signed Rosses Point. Continue for 6.5 km. and park is on right after village.

Gateway Caravan and Camping Park

870 Ballinode, Sligo, Co. Sligo

Convenient for the beauty spots immortalised by the poet W. B. Yeats, this is one of the northwest's most popular parks and it warrants the highest accolade for its excellent design and standards. Its situation 1.2 km. from Sligo centre means this cultural city is easily accessible, yet Gateway's off-the-road location, screened by mature trees and fencing, offers a quiet relaxing environment. After the entrance, past the family bungalow and to the left is the reception and services block which is fronted by columns. Incorporated in this building are three separate rooms – one for TV, snooker and board games, the second for satellite TV and the third for selected video viewing. A passage divides the elongated building which also houses the sanitary facilities. There are 30 fully serviced touring pitches with hardstanding and satellite TV connection, 10 grass pitches with electrical hook-up for tents and 10 caravan holiday homes for hire. Touring pitches stand to the right and centre of the park, holiday homes to the left and rear, with tents pitched at the top left. Evening relaxation could mean a 3 km. drive to romantic Half Moon Bay, or a drink in the fascinating surroundings of Farrells Brewery, which faces the caravan park.

Facilities: Fully equipped toilet facilities include baby units in both male and female areas. Showers and a room for disabled visitors (with WC and shower) are entered from the outside of this block which can be heated. In an adjacent building is a dishwashing area, laundry room, fully equipped campers' kitchen plus a large indoor games room and a toddlers room with play houses and fixed toys. An outdoor children's play area faces reception. **Off site**: Fishing or bicycle hire within 2 km, golf 8 km, riding 12 km.

Charges 2001

Per unit incl. 2 persons	€ 12,70
adult or child in July/Aug	€ 0,63
m/cyclist incl. tent	€ 10,79
hiker or cyclist incl. tent	€ 6,35
electricity (10A)	€ 2,54

7 nights for price of 6 if pre-paid. Tel/Fax: 071 45618. E-mail: gateway@oceanfree.net. Reservations: Contact site. **Open** all year, excl. 18 Dec. - 6 Jan.

Directions: Site is 1.2 km. northeast of Sligo city, off the N16 Enniskillen - Belfast road. Approaching from the north on the N15, turn left at second traffic lights into Ash Lane, continue for 1.1 km. and turn left at traffic lights on N16 Sligo - Enniskillen road. Site entrance is on left in 50 m.

Cong Caravan and Camping Park

874 Lisloughrey, Quay Road, Cong, Connemara, Co. Mayo

THE ALAN ROGERS'
travel service

To Book	
Ferry	✓
Pitch	✓
Accommodation	✗

01892 55 98 98

It would be difficult to find a more idyllic and famous spot for a caravan park than Cong. Situated close to the shores of Lough Corrib, Cong's scenic beauty was immortalised in the film 'The Quiet Man'. This immaculately kept park is 1.6 km. from the village of Cong, near the grounds of the magnificent and renowned Ashford Castle. The owner's house that incorporates reception, shop and the hostel, stands to the fore of the site. Toilet facilities and the holiday hostel accommodation are entered from the courtyard area. These are tastefully decorated, kept very clean and heated when necessary. The 40 grass pitches, 36 with electricity, are placed at a higher level to the rear, with the tent area below and to the side – the policy is for campers to choose a pitch rather than have one allocated. When not spending time around the village of Cong with its picturesque river setting and Monastic relics, there is much to keep the active camper happy. Not least of the on site attractions at this park is a mini cinema showing 'The Quiet Man' film nightly all season.

Facilities: Toilet facilities for the campsite include hot showers with curtains (on payment). Dishwashing area. Launderette service. Central bin depot. Barbecue, games room and extensive children's play area. Shop. Catering is a feature – full Irish or continental breakfast, dinner or packed lunch may be ordered, or home baked bread and scones purchased in the shop. Bicycle hire. **Off site**: Riding or golf within 2 km, fishing and boat slipway 500 m.

Charges 2001

Per pitch	€ 7,62 - € 8,89
adult	€ 1,90
child	€ 1,59
awning	€ 2,54
electricity (16A)	€ 2,54
hiker/cyclist incl. tent and 1 person	€ 8,25

Tel: 092 46089. Fax: 092 46448. E-mail: quiet.man. cong@iol.ie. Reservations: Contact park. **Open** all year.

Directions: Leave N84 road at Ballinrobe to join R334/345 signed Cong. Turn left at end of the R345 (opposite entrance to Ashford Castle), take next road on right (approx. 300 m) and the park is on right (200 m).

Belleek Caravan and Camping Park

875 Ballina, Co. Mayo

Belleek has a quiet woodland setting, only minutes from Ballina, a famed salmon fishing centre. With excellent pitches and toilet block, the family owners are committed to ensuring that it is immaculate at all times. From the entrance gate, the park is approached by a drive that passes reception and leads to 58 well spaced pitches. With a very neat overall appearance, 32 pitches have hardstanding, 35 have electricity hook-ups, and you may choose your pitch. Sports facilities within a short distance of the park include pitch and putt, a swimming pool, tennis and bicycle hire. Other local attractions are the Blue Flag beach at Ross, Ceide Fields (Neolithic farm), Down Patrick Head, Mayo North Heritage Centre or a seaweed bath at Kilcullen's Bath House, Enniscrone.

Facilities: Spotlessly clean, tastefully decorated toilet block providing showers (token), baby sink and facilities for disabled people. Laundry sink, two washing machines and two dryers. TV room and games room with table tennis and football game. Campers' kitchen and emergency accommodation with beds provided. Children's play area, ball game area, basketball and tennis courts. New barbecue area. Reception includes a shop (June-Sept) and a tea room that also serves breakfasts. **Off site:** fishing 1 km, bicycle hire 3 km.

Charges guide

Per unit	€ 7,62 - € 8,89
adult or child	€ 1,27
m/cyclist and tent	€ 4,44 - € 5,71
hiker or cyclist and tent	€ 3,81 - € 5,08
awning	free - € 1,27
electricity (10A)	€ 1,90

No credit cards. Tel: 096 71533. E-mail: lenahan@ indigo.ie. Reservations: Contact park. **Open** 15 March - 8 October; by arrangement all year.

Directions: Take R314 Ballina - Killala road. Park is signed on right after approx. 2.5 km. from Ballina.

Parkland Caravan and Camping Park

877 Westport, Co. Mayo

Located in the grounds of an elegant country estate, this popular park offers the choice of a 'pitch only' booking, or a 'special deal' (min. stay 3 nights). This includes free admission to Westport House and children's animal and bird park, plus other activities, such as boating and fishing on the lake and river, pitch and putt, 'slippery dip', ball pond and 'supabounce', hillside train rides and new flume ride. Stay one week or more and all the above are free, plus tennis, a par-3 golf course and 20% discount on bar food in the Horse and Wagon bar on the site. From Westport Quay, you enter the grounds of the estate by way of a tree lined road that crosses the river and leads to the site. In an attractive, sheltered area of the parkland, set in the trees, are 155 pitches. There are 65 with hardstanding and 76 electric hook-ups. The gate is closed 11.30 pm.- 9 am. with good site lighting around the site If late, vehicles must be parked in the car park. Early in the season the site may not be fully prepared, and only minimal facilities may be available. Westport is an attractive town with splendid Georgian houses and traditional shop fronts. There are many good restaurants and pubs.

Facilities: Toilet facilities are provided at various points on the site, plus a 'super-loo' located in the farmyard buildings. Facilities for disabled people. Dishwashing and laundry sinks, washing machines and dryers plus free ironing facilities. Well stocked shop in the farmyard reception area. Bar offers food and musical entertainment (all 1/6-31/8). No dogs are accepted. **Off site:** Within 5 km. of the estate are an 18 hole golf course and deep sea angling on Clew Bay.

Charges guide

Per unit excl. free facilities (see above)	
pitch only	€ 20,32 - € 31,11
hiker or cyclist	€ 15,24 - € 16,51
electricity	incl.

No credit cards. Tel: 098 27766. Fax: 098 25206. E-mail: camping@westporthouse.ie. Reservations: Contact park. **Open** 19 May - 9 September.

Directions: Take R335 Westport - Louisburgh road and follow signs for Westport Quay, then turn right into Westport House Country Estate.

Knock Caravan and Camping Park

878

Claremorris Road, Knock, Co. Mayo

This park is immediately south of the world famous shrine that receives many visitors. Comfortable and clean, the square shaped campsite is kept very neat with tarmac roads and surrounded by clipped trees. The pitches are of a decent size accommodating 38 caravans or motor-caravans, 20 tents and 15 caravan holiday homes. All pitches have hardstanding (5 doubles) and there are 52 electrical connections (13A), with an adequate number of water points. There is also an overflow field. Because of the religious connections of the area, the site is very busy in August and indeed there are unlikely to be any vacancies at all for 14-16 August. Besides visiting the shrine and Knock Folk Museum, it is also a good centre for exploring scenic Co. Mayo.

Facilities: Two heated toilet blocks have good facilities for disabled visitors and a nice sized rest room attached, hot showers (on payment) and adequate washing and toilet facilities. Laundry and dishwashing room. Motorcaravan service points. Gas supplies. Children's playground. **Off site:** Fishing 5 km, golf or riding 11 km.

Charges 2001

Per unit	€ 12,06 - € 12,70
hiker or cyclist and tent	€ 7,62 - € 8,89
electricity (13A)	€ 1,90

No credit cards. Tel: 094 88100 or 88223. FAX: 094 88295. E-mail: info@knock-shrine.ie. Reservations: Taken for any length, no deposit, but see editorial for August. **Open** 1 March - 31 October.

Directions: Take N17 to the Knock site which is just south of the village. Camp site is well signed.

 Alan Rogers' discount
Two for one admission (adults) to Knock Folk Museum

Carra Caravan and Camping Park

879

Belcarra, Castlebar, Co. Mayo

This is an ideal location for those seeking a real Irish village experience on a 'value for money' park. Small, unpretentious and family run, it is located in Belcarra, a regular winner of the 'Tidiest Mayo Village' award. Nestling at the foot of a wooded drumlin, it is surrounded by rolling hills and quiet roads which offer an away from it all feeling, yet Castlebar the county's largest town is only an 8 km. drive. On the pleasant 1.5 acre park, the 20 unmarked touring pitches, 14 with electric hook-up (13A), are on flat ground enclosed by ranch fencing and shaded in parts by trees. A novel idea at Carra is eight horse-drawn caravans for hire. Also of interest are the talks that the owner Sean and daughter Deirdre give on the area.

Facilities: The basic toilet block has adequate, well equipped showers (on payment), Combined kitchen, dishwashing, laundry area with fridge/freezer, sink, table, chairs, washing machine and dryer. Comfortable lounge with TV, books and magazines located at reception. **Off site:** Village shops, a post office and 'Flukies' cosy bar which serves Irish breakfast and where Irish stew is a speciality. Leisure centre and tennis courts. Recommended walks with maps provided. Free fishing area and special walkway to the river. Golf 8 km.

Charges 2002

Per unit incl. all persons	€ 8,00
electricity	€ 1,50

No credit cards. Tel: 094 32054. Fax: 094 32351. E-mail: post@mayoholidays.com. Reservations: Contact park. **Open** 8 June - 21 September (bookings may be accepted outside this period).

Directions: From Castlebar take N60 Claremorris road for 8.5 km. southeast and turn right at sign for Belcarra. Continue for 4.5 km. to village and site on left at end of village.

Lough Ree East Caravan and Camping Park

896

Ballykeeran, Athlone, Co. Westmeath

This touring park is alongside the river, screened by trees but reaching the water's edge. Drive into the small village of Ballykeeran and the park is discreetly located behind the main street. The top half of the site is in woodland and after the reception and sanitary block, Lough Ree comes into view; the remaining pitches run down to the shoreline. There are 60 pitches, 20 with hardstanding and 52 with electricity. With fishing right on the doorstep there are boats for hire and the site has its own private mooring buoys, plus a dinghy slip and harbour.

Facilities: The toilet block, is clean without being luxurious. Hot showers (token). Dishwashing sinks outside. New laundry room. A wooden chalet houses a pool room and campers' kitchen. **Off site:** Golf or riding 4 km. Restaurant and 'singing' pub close.

Charges guide

Per adult	€ 3,17
child (under 14 yrs)	€ 1,27
pitch	€ 2,54 - € 6,08
awning	€ 2,54
electricity	€ 1,27

No credit cards. Tel: 0902 78561 or 74414. Fax: 0902 77017. E-mail: athlonecamping@eircom.net. Reservations: Contact park. **Open** 1 April - 2 Oct.

Directions: From Athlone take N55 towards Longford for 4.8 km. Park is in the village of Ballykeeran, clearly signed.

Hodson Bay Caravan and Camping Park

882

Kiltoom, Athlone, Co. Roscommon

This picturesque park is in a tranquil, wooded setting on the shores of Lough Ree on the River Shannon in central Ireland. Part of a 100-acre working farm, the site offers 19 pitches with electricity for caravans and motorcaravans and 15 for tents, on flat grass. The reception block provides a lounge area no shop but there is a mini-market at the top of the road. An hotel serving bar snacks and a carvery is close. You may fish, swim, go boating or just walk along the park's own path by the lough shore. Barbecues are permitted on site and by the lough.

Facilities: The central toilet block is well kept with hot showers on payment (08.00 - 12.00 and 16.00 - 21.00 hrs), plus sufficient washing and toilet facilities and good facilities for disabled people. Dishwashing room at the rear of the block with two sinks (hot water on payment). Spin and tumble dryers are available for use after you take your laundry to reception where it is put through an industrial machine for you. Campers' kitchen. TV room. Dogs are not accepted. **Off site**: Riding 3 km. Bicycle hire 6 km.

Charges 2001

Per adult or child	€ 1,27
caravan or family tent	€ 8,89
car	€ 1,27
motorcaravan	€ 10,16
hiker/cyclist and tent	€ 8,25
awning	€ 2,54
electricity	€ 2,54
hardstanding	€ 1,27

Tel: 0902 92448. Reservations: Made for high season with € 6,35 deposit. **Open** 1 June - 1 September.

Directions: Leave N6 at Roscommon/Sligo junction to join N61. Travel 4 km. and turn right onto minor road. Site is clearly signed. Continue to park at the end of this road (2.4 km).

Táin Holiday Village

889

Carlingford Lough, Omeath, Co. Louth

THE ALAN ROGERS'
travel service

ook
✓
✓
ommodation ✗
92 55 98 98

This holiday complex is one of the most extensive in Ireland and is exactly what a family seeking non-stop entertainment might want. The touring park is within the 10-acre fun packed holiday village, overlooking Carlingford Lough with views towards the Mourne mountains, whilst nestling at the foot of the Cooley mountains. The area for tourers is situated to the far right of the main buildings with entry through a security gate (deposit required for key). There are 87 pitches with hardstanding and electrical hook-ups, plus 10 pitches for tents. Young trees are planted and will eventually add more detail to this well laid out, but open site. Included in the site fees is the use of the 40,000 sq.ft. of indoor leisure facilities. These include a heated pool with slides, flumes and rafts, an indoor water play pool, an indoor play area with free fall, ball pool, climbing room and nets, also a sports hall, gym and games room, a jacuzzi, steam room and sun beds. Not least at Táin is a hands-on Science Interactive Centre.

Facilities: The fully equipped sanitary block is kept clean and can be heated. Facilities for disabled visitors. Dishwashing and laundry sinks. Washing machines and iron. Motorcaravan services. Licensed restaurant with varied menus. Good bar and lounge (all limited opening outside July/Aug). Indoor swimming pool complex (4-9 pm daily), indoor play area and sports hall. Outdoor activities include two adventure playgrounds, tennis courts and watersports. **Off site**: Fishing, bicycle hire or riding 2 km, golf 5 km

Charges 2001

Per unit incl. 2 persons	
on fully serviced gravel pitch	€ 24,13 - € 26,66
tent on grass area	€ 21,59 - € 24,13
extra person	€ 5,08 - € 6,35

Min. 2 nights in high season; for 1 night only prices are higher. Tel: 042 9375385. Fax: 042 9375417. Reservations: Made with deposit. **Open** 17 March - 31 October.

Directions: From Newry take B79/R173 road signed Omeath. Site is 1.6 km. south of Omeath village, on the left.

Green Gables Caravan and Camping Park

906 Geashill, Tullamore, Co. Offaly

A peaceful, relaxing environment in the heart of Ireland's Bogland, Green Gables enjoys a natural meadow-like setting in keeping with the wide open countryside that enhances this county. This park is maturing and offers top class facilities but most importantly, a friendly reception - in fact, here you experience Irish hospitality at its best. From the park entrance the drive leads to a parking area, clearly defined by a roundabout and a huge Ice Age stone from Boora Bog, known as 'Mona'. Reception, the Gables tea rooms and a patio area lie to the right, approached by a gateway and gravel path. Apart from 8 hardstanding pitches towards the rear of the park, the remainder are on grass. Electric hook-ups (10A) are provided on 14 pitches and tents are catered for. The ground is gently sloping and the perimeter is surrounded by hedging. Getting out of the village can mean taking a train from Portarlington station to Dublin city. If preferring the countryside there are cycle tours, the Grand Canal walking routes or a Bog Train tour through the historic bogland, one of Offaly's many attractions.

Facilities: The spotlessly clean heated toilet block is well cared for and includes baby changing space. There are excellent facilities for disabled people, a laundry area and a washing up sink. Motorcaravan service point. Gas supplies. **Off site:** The village of Geashill is 50 m. with old houses, stone walls, shops and three pubs. The proprietor at Hamilton's welcomes Green Gables campers in his pub where Irish culture abounds. Riding 5 km, fishing, bicycle hire or golf 10 km.

Charges 2002

Per unit	€ 11,00
small tent	€ 8,00
adult	€ 1,50
child	€ 0,75
hiker or cyclist and tent	€ 6,50
electricity (10A)	€ 2,00

No credit cards. Tel/Fax: 0506 43760. E-mail: ggcp@iol.ie. Reservations: Contact park. Open Easter - 31 September

Directions: From Tullamore take R420 east for 12 km. to village of Geashill. Site is on right at end of village.

Shankill Caravan and Camping Park

911 Shankill, Co. Dublin

Shankill is a long-established park that makes an excellent overnight halt within easy reach of Dublin Port and Dun Laoghaire ferries. It also makes an ideal base for visiting Dublin with a bus departing from the site entrance every 15 minutes. The Dart fast train also leaves from Shankill village at 15 minute intervals. With lovely views of the Dublin mountains, the site is set in pleasant grounds with an abundance of mature trees, shrubs and well kept flower beds which gives it a park-like appearance. Additionally there are broad tarmac roads and night lighting. There are 82 unmarked pitches, 66 of which are for tourers. Some have hardstanding and 40 have electric hook-ups (10A). Reception staff are pleasant, helpful and willing to give advice on visiting the city or local tourist spots.

Facilities: The two sanitary blocks, although showing signs of age and certainly not ultra modern, offer basic but adequate facilities which are kept clean, with piping hot water to sinks and showers (on payment). Laundry sinks, ironing facilities and dishwashing area. Basic foodstuffs can be purchased at reception. No double-axle vans are permitted. **Off site:** The site is located within a three minute walk of the village with shops, restaurants, supermarkets. The seaside resort of Bray is a 5 minute drive.

Charges guide

Per unit	€ 8,25 - € 8,89
adult	€ 1,27
child	€ 0,63
hiker or cyclist	€ 6,98 - € 7,62
electricity	€ 1,27

Tel: 01 282 0011. Fax: 01 282 0108. E-mail: shankillcaravan@eircom.net. Reservations: Not possible in advance. **Open** all year.

Directions: Site is 15 km. south of Dublin off the N11. From Dublin take N11 Wexford road for 15 km. and turn left at Bray, Shankill sign. Then follow signs to site on right.

Co. Dublin

Camac Valley Tourist Caravan and Camping Park

Naas Road, Clondalkin, Dublin 22

Opened in '96, this campsite is not only well placed for Dublin, but also offers a welcome stopover if travelling to the more southern counties from the north of the country, or vice versa. Despite its close proximity to the city, being located in the 300 acre Corkagh Park gives it a 'heart of the country' atmosphere. The site entrance and sign are distinctive and can be spotted in adequate time when approaching on the busy N7. Beyond the entrance gate and forecourt stands an attractive timber fronted building. Its design includes various roof levels and spacious interior layout, with large windows offering a view of the site. Housed here is reception, information, reading, TV and locker rooms plus shop and sanitary facilities. There are 163 pitches, 48 for tents placed to the fore and the hardstandings for caravans laid out in bays and avenues with electrical connections, drainage and water points. Young trees separate pitches and roads are of tarmac. After a day of sightseeing in Dublin, which can be reached by bus from the site, Camac Valley offers an evening of relaxation with woodland and river walks in the park or a number of first class restaurants and pubs nearby.

Facilities: Heated sanitary facilities include good sized showers (token), facilities for disabled people, baby changing room, laundry and washing up. Children's playground with wooden play frames and safety base. Shop and coffee bar (open June, July and August). Automatic gate and 24 hour security. Dogs are not accepted in July/Aug. **Off site**: Fishing 8 km, bicycle hire 1.5 km, riding 9 km, golf 6 km.

Charges 2001

Per unit incl. 2 adults	€ 11,43 - 15,24
incl. up to 4 children	€ 12,70 - 17,78
extra person	€ 1,27
child (under 7 yrs)	€ 0,63
motorcyclist, cyclist or hiker with tent	€ 5,08 - 5,71
electricity (10A)	€ 2,54

Tel: 01 464 0644. FAX: 01 464 0643. E-mail: camacmorriscastle@tinet.ie. Reservations: Advance bookings necessary. (max. stay operates at certain times). **Open** all year.

Directions: From north follow signs for West Link and M50 motorway. Exit M50 at junction 9 onto N7 Cork road. Site is on right of dual carriageway (beside Green Isle Hotel) after 2 km. and is clearly signed. At City West business park, cross over bridge and return on dual-carriageway following camp signs - site is on left after 800 m.

Co. Wicklow

Roundwood Caravan and Camping Park

Roundwood, Co. Wicklow

In the heart of the Wicklow mountains, this park is under new management, but still maintains high standards. It is neatly laid out with rows of trees dividing the different areas and giving an attractive appearance. There are 31 pitches for caravans and motorcaravans, all with electricity (5A) and 27 with hardstanding, plus 40 pitches for tents, arranged off tarmac access roads. There are excellent walks around the Varty Lakes and a daily bus service to Dublin city. Close by are the Wicklow and Sally Gap, Glendalough, Powerscourt Gardens, plus many other places of natural beauty. Apart from its scenic location, this site is well placed for the ferry ports.

Facilities: The sanitary block is kept clean, with adequate washing and toilet facilities, plus spacious showers on payment. The block also houses two dishwashing sinks and good laundry facilities, but ask at reception as machines are not self-service. Motorcaravan service point. Campers' kitchen and dining room. TV room. Children's adventure playground. Bicycle hire. **Off site**: Roundwood village has shops, pubs, restaurants, takeaway food, and a Sunday market. Fishing or golf 1 km.

Charges 2002

Per unit	€ 8,90 - € 10.20
adult	€ 2,55
child (under 14 yrs)	€ 1,99
electricity	€ 1,90

No credit cards. Tel/Fax: 01 2818163. E-mail: dicksonn@indigo.ie. Reservations: Accepted without deposit and advisable for July/Aug. Open 31 March - 1 October.

Directions: Turn off N11 Dublin - Wexford road at Kilmacanogue towards Glendalough and then 15 km. to Roundwood.

Valley Stopover and Caravan Park

Valleyview, Killough, Kilmacanogue, Co. Wicklow

914

In a quiet, idyllic setting in the picturesque Rocky Valley, this small, neat, family run park is convenient for the Dublin ferries. Situated in the grounds of the family home, covering three-quarters of an acre, it can be used either as a transit site or for a longer stay. It will appeal to those who prefer the more basic 'CL' type site. There are 15 grassy pitches, 11 with electric hook-ups, 3 hardstandings, 2 water points, night lighting and a security gate. Staying put here you are only minutes from Enniskerry which lies in the glen of the Glencullen river. Here you can enjoy a delight of forest walks, or visit Powerscourt, one of the loveliest gardens in Ireland. To be at the sea, travel 6 km. to Bray and you are in one of the oldest seaside resorts in the country.

Facilities: Toilet facilities, spotlessly clean when we visited, are housed in one unit and consist of two WCs with washbasins, mirrors, etc. and a shower (on payment). Dishwashing and laundry sink, a spin dryer and a campers' kitchen. Full cooked Irish breakfast is available in the family guest house. **Off site:** Fishing 16 km, bicycle hire 7 km (can be delivered), riding 3 km, golf 7 km.

Charges 2001

Per caravan or tent with car	€ 10,16
motorcaravan	€ 8,89
tent with bicycle	€ 4,44
electricity	€ 1,27
awning	€ 1,27

No credit cards. Tel: 01 282 9565. E-mail: mabelrowan@hotmail.com. Reservations: Advised for July/Aug. **Open** Easter - 31 October.

Directions: Turn off N11 Dublin - Wexford road at Kilmacanogue, following signs for Glendalough. Continue for 1.6 km and take right fork signed 'Waterfall'. Park is first opening on the left in approx. 200 m.

Alan Rogers' discount
Less 10%

River Valley Caravan and Camping Park

Redcross Village, Co. Wicklow

915

THE ALAN ROGERS'
travel service

To Book
Ferry ✓
Pitch ✓
Accommodation ✗

01892 55 98 98

In the small country village of Redcross, in the heart of County Wicklow, you will find this popular, family run park. Based here you are within easy reach of beauty spots such as the Vale of Avoca (Ballykissangel), Glendalough and Powerscourt, plus the safe beach of Brittas Bay. The 100 touring pitches at River Valley are mostly together in a dedicated area, all have electricity connections (6A) and offer a choice of hardstanding or grass – you select your pitch. Within this 12-acre site children can find day long amusement, whether it be Fort Apache, the adventure playground, the tiny tots playground, or at the natural mountain stream where it is safe to paddle. There is also a pets corner with a 'fat belly pig'. An attractive wine and coffee bar with a conservatory is inviting, or an alternative may be the restaurant where home made, traditional dishes are on the menu (1/6-31/8). The late arrivals area has electricity hook-ups, water and night lighting.

Facilities: A luxurious new sanitary block has a modern, well designed appearance making it a special feature. Facilities for disabled visitors are excellent and there is hot water for dishwashing. Laundry area. Campers' kitchen. Motorcaravan service points. Gas available. Wine/coffee bar and restaurant. TV and games room. Three tennis courts. Par 3 golf course. Bowling green. Sports complex with badminton courts and indoor football and basketball. Adventure and tiny tots playgrounds. Rally area. Caravan storage. No dogs are accepted in July/Aug.

Charges 2001

Per unit incl. 2 adults	€ 12,70 - € 13,97
small tent	€ 10,16 - € 11,43
extra adult	€ 3,81
child (under 15 yrs)	€ 1,27
m/cyclist, cyclist or hiker and tent	€ 6,35 - € 7,62
electricity	€ 1,90

Tel: 0404 41647. Fax: 0404 41677. E-mail: info@rivervalleypark.ie. Reservations: Made with deposit. **Open** 12 March - 13 September.

Directions: From Dublin follow N11 Wexford road. Turn right in Rathnew and left under railway bridge onto the Wexford-Arklow road. Continue for 11 km. and turn right at Doyle's Pub. Park is in Redcross village, under 5 km.

Moat Farm Caravan and Camping Park

Donard, Co. Wicklow

Here is a true feel of the countryside – this site is part of a working sheep farm – that also offers incredible vistas across a scenic landscape, yet is within driving distance of Dublin and Rosslare. Driving into the village of Donard you little suspect that alongside the main street lies a pleasant, well cared for and tranquil five-acre campsite. The entrance is approached by way of a short road where the ruins of a Medieval church sit high overlooking the forecourt and reception. There are 40 pitches for caravans and tents. Spacious pitches with hardstanding line both sides of a broad avenue, incorporating awning space, and all with electricity and drainage points. A separate area is for tents. This site makes a good base for touring or going on foot, for this area is a walker's paradise with a 30 minute circular walk around the perimeter of the site.

Facilities: The toilet block is kept clean and includes spacious showers, facilities for visitors with disabilities, and a well equipped laundry room. A recent extension has added a new campers' kitchen and a large recreation/entertainment room with an open fire. Three large barbecues and a patio area are provided. Caravan storage. **Off site:** Mountain climbing or sites of archaeological interest nearby. Fishing 3 km, bicycle hire 15 km, golf 13 km.

Charges 2001

Per caravan, motorcaravan or family tent	€ 10,16
adult	€ 1,27
child	€ 0,64
tent (1 or 2 persons)	€ 7,62
m/cyclist, hiker or cyclist incl. tent	€ 6,35
electricity (10A)	€ 1,90

No credit cards. Tel/Fax: 045 404727. E-mail: nuala@wicklowhills.com. Reservations: Contact site. **Open** all year.

Directions: Park is 18 km. south of Blessington, 1 hour from Dublin via N4, N7 and N81 or 1½ hours from Rosslare via N80 and N81. Site is clearly signed.

Forest Farm Caravan and Camping Park

Dublin Road, Athy, Co. Kildare

This new site makes an excellent stopover if travelling from Dublin to the southeast counties. It is signed on the N78 and approached by a 500 m. avenue of tall pines. Part of a working farm, the campsite spreads to the right of the modern farmhouse, which also provides B&B. The owners have cleverly utilised their land to create a site which offers 64 unmarked touring pitches on level ground. Of these, 32 are for caravans, all with electricity connections and 10 with hardstanding, and 32 places are available for tents. Full Irish breakfasts are served at the farmhouse and farm tours are arranged on request.

Facilities: The centrally located, red brick toilet block is heated and double glazed, providing quality amenities including a spacious shower unit for disabled visitors, a family room with shower and WC. It also houses a laundry room, a campers' kitchen with dishwashing sinks, a fridge/freezer, cooker, table and chairs and a comfortable lounge/games room (a TV can be provided). Basketball net, sand pit and picnic tables.

Charges 2001

Per unit incl. 2 adults	€ 8,89 - € 11.34
child	€ 1,27
1 or 2 person tent	€ 3,81 - € 5,08
m/cyclist, hiker or cyclist incl. tent	€ 3,81 - € 5,08
electricity (13A)	€ 1,90

Stay 7 nights, pay for 6. No credit cards. Tel: 0507 31231 or 33070. Fax: 0507 31231. E-mail: forestfarm@eircom.net. Reservations: Contact site. **Open** all year.

Directions: Site is 4.8 km. northeast of Athy town off the main N78 Athy - Kilcullen road.

The Alan Rogers' Travel Service

We have recently extended The Alan Rogers Travel Service. This unique service enables our readers to reserve their holidays as well as ferry crossings and comprehensive insurance cover at extremely competitive rates. Whilst the majority of participating sites are in France, we are now also able to offer a selection of some of the very best sites in Ireland and The Channel Islands.

One simple telephone call to our Travel Service on 01892 559898 is all that is needed to make all the arrangements. Why not take advantage of our years' of experience of camping and caravanning. We would be delighted to discuss your holiday plans with you, and offer advice and recommendations.

Share our experience and let us help to ensure that your holiday will be a complete success. The new Alan Rogers Travel Service Tel. 01892 55 98 98

Nore Valley Park

923 Annamult, Bennettsbridge, Co. Kilkenny

This lovely site is set on a grassy hillock overlooking the valley and the river Nore, with a woodland setting behind. Situated on a working farm, it offers 60 pitches, 30 for caravans and motorcaravans, all with electrical hook-up and hardstanding. The owners pride themselves on their home baking and farm produce and during high season cooked breakfasts are available in the small café. The reception area at the entrance is in an attractive courtyard and unusual facilities within the courtyard include a sand pit, pedal go-karts, tractor rides and a straw loft play area for wet weather. This is an ideal park for families, offering children and adults alike the opportunity to feed the animals (goats, lambs, ducks, chickens, and donkey). It is 11 km. from Kilkenny, renowned for its castle, history and crafts, and 3 km. from the village of Bennettsbridge, where there are shops and eating places. Note: the tractor rides, go-karts and the café are closed on Sundays.

Facilities: The modern toilet block is kept spotlessly clean and can be heated. Two units suitable for disabled visitors. Dishwashing sinks. Laundry room with washing machine and dryer. Motorcaravan services. The original block in the courtyard is used mainly in the low season. Basic items such as milk, bread and camping gaz available from reception. Café (June-Aug). Comfortable lounge next to reception area. Games room with pool table. Fenced children's play area. Crazy golf. Bicycle hire. **Off site**: Outdoor pursuits nearby such as canoeing, walking or fishing (4 km). Riding 6 km. Golf 10 km.

Charges 2001

Per person	€ 1,27
caravan	€ 10,79
trailer or chalet tent	€ 10,16
motorcaravan	€ 9,52
family tent	€ 10,16
2 person tent	€ 6,98
awning or extra small tent	€ 2,54
electricity (6A)	€ 1,90

Tel: 056 27229. Fax: 056 27748. E-mail: norevalleypark@eircom.net. Reservations: Contact park. **Open** 1 March - 31 October.

Directions: From Kilkenny take R700 to Bennettsbridge. Just before the bridge turn right at sign for Stoneyford and after approx. 3 km. site is signed Nore Valley Park.

Tree Grove Caravan and Camping Park

924 Danville House, Kilkenny, Co. Kilkenny

The entrance gate to this small family run site is easily spotted off the R700 road. Tree Grove is within walking distance of medieval Kilkenny, known for its elegance and famed for its beer and cats. An orderly, neat park, it has instant appeal because its young owners are friendly and have insisted on a logical layout to suit both the terrain and campers needs. It is terraced with the lower terrace to the right of the wide sweeping driveway laid out with 11 hardstanding pitches for caravans. All 30 pitches have electrical hook-ups (10A) and plenty of water points are to be found. On a higher level, is a grass area for hikers and cyclists with further caravan and tent pitches sited near the elevated sanitary block. If needed more grass pitches face reception which is temporarily housed in a mobile unit. Whilst there are mature trees at the entrance and around the site perimeter, many shrubs have been effectively placed together with flower troughs. On the patio there are bench seats with tables and umbrellas. Tents to rent on site. There is much to see and do around the ancient city of Kilkenny (1.5 km) with its cobbled streets and castle. County Touring Routes are worth following.

Facilities: House plants add decoration inside the toilet block giving a cared for look to this modern building which includes a family room with shower, WC and washbasin which can be used by disabled people. Laundry room. Open, covered kitchen for campers with fridge, work-top, sink and electric kettle adjoins a comfortable games/TV room with pool table, and easy chairs. Bicycle hire. **Off site**: Fishing 500 m, riding 1 km. Golf 2 or 15 km.

Charges 2001

Per unit incl. 2 persons	€ 10,79
extra person	€ 1,27
1 man tent	€ 6,35
2 man tent	€ 8,25
car	€ 1,27
awning	€ 1,27
electricity (10A)	€ 1,90

No credit cards. Tel: 056 70302. Fax: 056 21512. mail: treecc@iol.ie. Reservations: Contact site. **Open** 1 March - 15 November.

Directions: Travelling north on the N10 Waterford/Kilkenny Road turn right at roundabout on ring road. Continue to 2nd roundabout and turn right onto R700. Site is 150 m. on right.

Co. Wexford

Morriscastle Strand Caravan and Camping Park

Kilmuckridge, Co. Wexford

930

Whether you use this park as a stopover, to or from Rosslare Port, or choose it for a longer stay, you will find it to be a quiet relaxing location. Situated minutes from the pretty village of Kilmuckridge it offers well maintained and clean facilities. There are 145 privately owned caravan holiday homes on site but these are unobtrusive and kept separate by high hedging. The entrance to the touring park is to the right of reception by way of a tarmac drive. This leads to the secluded, gently sloping, grass pitches which enjoy an open aspect. They overlook marshland which attracts wild geese and ducks, whilst the sea brings in crabs, eels and fish. To the right of the site lie the sand-hills and pathways to the beach which is supervised by lifeguards in high season. The 100 pitches are numbered and marked by concrete slabs, each with an electrical hook-up (5A) and drainage point. Spacing can be a little tight in high season when the park gets very busy. Kilmuckridge is approximately 3 km. with an assortment of shops, pubs offering nightly entertainment and top class restaurants, such as The Rafters, a picturesque spot which helps characterise this charming village.

Facilities: Two toilet blocks house all the toilet facilities, including unisex showers (on payment). There is provision for disabled people, a baby bath, campers' kitchen, dishwashing area, launderette, and outside cold showers. Good night lighting. Shop, snacks and takeaway in high season. Games room. Two tennis courts. Football field and children's play area. Dogs are only accepted in certain areas (not with tents). **Off site:** Golf 5 km.

Charges 2001

Per unit incl. 2 persons	€ 12,70 - € 15,24
incl. up to 4 children	€ 13,97 - € 17,78
extra person	€ 5,08
child (under 7 yrs)	€ 2,54
m/cyclist, cyclist or hiker with tent	€ 5,71 - € 6,35
awning	€ 2,54
electricity (5A)	€ 1,27

Tel: 053 30124 or 053 30212 (off season 01 453 5355). Fax: 053 30365 (off season 01 454 5916). E-mail: camacmorriscastle@eircom.net. Reservations: Made with deposit; contact site by phone or letter (use off season numbers Oct - April). **Open** 1 May - 30 September.

Directions: Site is 25 km. east of Enniscorthy. Travelling south on N11 Dublin/Wexford road branch onto R741 at Gorey. Continue for 19 km. to Ballyedmund. Turn left at petrol station and follow signs for Kilmuckridge and site.

Co. Waterford

Newtown Cove Camping and Caravan Park

Tramore, Co. Waterford

934

Well run and friendly, this small park is only five minutes walk from the beautiful Newton Cove. It offers views of the famous and historic Metal Man and is 2.5 km. from Tramore beach and 11 km. from Waterford. Neatly set out on gently sloping grass with an abundance of shrubs and bushes, there are 40 pitches. All have electrical connections (10A), some hardstanding also, with access by well lit tarmac roads. There are around 50 privately owned caravan holiday homes. A modern building at the entrance houses reception, the amenities and further sanitary facilities. The village of Tramore, with a wide range of shops and eating houses, is close and there is a choice of many delightful cliff walks in the immediate vicinity.

Facilities: The main sanitary block at the bottom end of the site is not very modern but has been retiled and provides good facilities including a bathroom. Showers on payment (50p token from reception). Also here are a campers' kitchen with cooking facilities (20p), lounge, dishwashing room and small laundry. Small shop (1/7- 30/8). TV room. Games room. Small children's play area in centre of park. **Off site:** Golf 800 m. Fishing 400 m, riding 3 km.

Charges 2002

Per unit incl. 2 persons	€ 12,50 - € 14,00
extra adult	€ 1,50 - € 2,00
child	free - € 1,50
hiker, cyclist or motorcyclist	€ 5,00 - € 6,50
awning	€ 1,50 - € 2,50
electricity (10A)	€ 2,00

No credit cards. No single sex groups. Tel: 051 381979. E-mail: newtown_cove@iol.ie. Reservations: Not necessary or accepted but for information contact park. **Open** Easter, then 1 May - 30 September.

Directions: From Tramore on R675 coast road to Dungarvan. Turn left 2 km. from town centre, following signs.

Casey's Caravan Park, Clonea, Dungarvan

933 Clonea, Dungarvan, Co. Waterford

Set on 20 acres of flat grass, edged by mature trees, this family run park offers 284 pitches which include 154 touring pitches, 118 with electrical hook-ups and 30 with hardstanding. The remainder are occupied by caravan holiday homes. There is direct access from the park to a sandy, Blue Flag beach with a resident lifeguard during July/Aug. A highly recommended leisure centre is adjacent should the weather be inclement. The park is 5½ km. from Dungarvan, a popular town for deep sea angling, from which charter boats can be hired and three 18 hole golf courses are within easy distance. Recommended drives include the scenic Vee, the Comeragh Drive and the coast road to Tramore.

Facilities: The central toilet block (key system), has good facilities kept spotlessly clean, with showers on payment, washing up sinks and small laundry with machine and dryer. A further luxurious and modern block provides an excellent campers' kitchen, laundry room and toilet for disabled visitors. Large children's adventure play area with bark surface in its own field (not supervised by staff). Games room with pool table, table tennis and amusements. TV lounge. Crazy golf. Gas supplies. Full time security staff in high season. **Off site:** Two village stores near the beach. Golf.

Charges 2001

Per unit	€ 14,60 - € 15,24
hiker or cyclist	€ 5,71
electricity (5A)	€ 1,27

No credit cards. Tel: 058 41919. Reservations: Are made in low season, but not between 9 July - 15 Aug; contact park. **Open** 27 April - 9 September.

Directions: From Dungarvan centre follow R675 east for 3.5 km. Look for signs on the right to Clonea Bay and site. Site is approx. 1.5 km.

 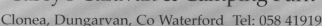

Casey's Caravan & Camping Park

Clonea, Dungarvan, Co Waterford Tel: 058 41919

Top class facilities
Playground
Electric sites for tents & tourers (5A)
Dungarvan town 3.5 miles
Choice of scenic views to visit
Adjacent hotel with 19 metre pool
and leisure centre with bowling alley

Two ablution blocks
with laundry & kitchen
Games room and TV room
EU Blue Flag beach
Two nearby shops with takeaway
Deep sea and river angling
18 hole golf course in easy reach

Streamstown Caravan and Camping Park

942 Streamstown, Roscrea, Co. Tipperary

This family run site, set on a dairy farm in the centre of Ireland, is conveniently situated off the N7 Dublin - Limerick road. It makes a good overnight halt or for a longer stay if you are seeking a quiet, restful location with little to disturb the peace. This is a working farm and the owners, who are friendly and welcoming, are in the process of improving and developing their site. What impresses most here is the tidy overall appearance with neatly trimmed hedging, tables placed around the grass areas and with flower baskets a special feature. There are 27 pitches, 10 with hardstanding and separated by low hedges. The remainder are on grass and more suitable for unit with awnings. Nearby pubs offer traditional music evenings and mountain walking and fishing can be enjoyed in the area.

Facilities: The sanitary facilities, which were of an acceptable level of cleanliness when we visited, are housed in a modern block, although showers, toilets and washbasins are of the older type and slightly out of keeping with the outside appearance. Good camper's kitchen with fridge/freezer and electric cooker. Good quality children's play area with safety surface. TV and pool room.

Charges 2001

Per unit	€ 9,98
adult	€ 2,54
child	€ 1,27
m/cyclist, cyclist or hiker incl tent	€ 7,62
electricity (10A)	€ 1,90

Tel/Fax: 0505 21519. E-mail: streamstown caravanpark@eircom.net. Reservations: Contact site. **Open** 1 April – 1 Nov.

Directions: From Roscrea centre follow signs for R491 Shirone. Continue towards Shirone following camp signs for approx. 2.5 km and site entrance is on left.

Co. Tipperary
Carrick-on-Suir Caravan and Camping Park

Kilkenny Road, Carrick-on-Suir, Co. Tipperary

This memorable little site is not only conveniently situated off the main N24 between Waterford and Clonmel, but its owner, Frank O'Dwyer, is an excellent ambassador for his county. On his quiet, family run site campers are guaranteed the finest example of 'Cead Mile Failte' it is possible to encounter - personal attention and advice on where to go and what to see in the area is all part of the service. The entrance to the park is immediately past the O'Dwyers' shop, through a gate which is closed at 11 pm. The tarmac drive leads past tall hedges and well kept shrubs to the right and several caravan holiday homes (for hire) to the left. The touring park lies to the rear with scenic views to the wooded hills. At present there are 40 level pitches, 33 with electricity (6/10A) and several with hardstanding, but this number is to be extended. What makes this little site distinctive is its excellent, well designed sanitary block which has a sparkling clean freshness. Within a short drive is the 'magic road', the Mahon Falls, a slate quarry or a romantic river walk. Carrick is well placed en-route to the west, only 1½ hours from Rosslare.

Facilities: Toilet facilities include plenty of hot water each morning. Laundry room with washing machine. Dishwashing area. Camper's kitchen with TV. Motorcaravan service point. Good grocery shop with a selection of fine wines. Gas supplies. Good night lighting. **Off site**: Fishing 1 km, riding 6 km, golf 3 km. Carrick town centre is five minutes walk for shops, pubs, restaurants, etc. plus a castle which is open to the public.

Charges 2001

Per unit incl. 2 adults	€ 13,97
extra adult	€ 3,37
child	€ 2,54
electricity	6A €1,17, 10A €1,86
hiker/cyclist incl. tent	€ 2,54

Tel: 051 640461. E-mail: coscamping@eircom.net. Reservations: Contact site. **Open** 1 March - 1 November.

Directions: Approaching town on N24 road, follow signs for R690 in the direction of Kilkenny. Site is north of town, clearly signed at junction with R697.

Co. Tipperary
The Apple Camping and Caravan Park

Moorstown, Cahir, Co. Tipperary

This fruit farm and campsite combination offers an idyllic country holiday venue in one of the most delightful situations imaginable. For tourers only, it is located off the N24, midway between Clonmel and Cahir. Entrance is by way of a 300 m. drive which follows straight through the heart of the farm. Apple trees guard the route, as do various non-fruit tree species, which are named and of interest to guests who are free to spend time walking the paths around the farm. When we visited, strawberries were being gathered – the best we had tasted all season. Reception is housed with the other site facilities in a large farmyard barn. Although a rather unusual arrangement, it is very effective. The 32 pitches are in a secluded situation behind the barns and are mostly grass with a few hardstandings, with electricity connections to 24. The towns of Cahir and Clonmel are of historic interest and the countryside around boasts rivers, mountains, Celtic culture and scenic drives.

Facilities: Toilet facilities, kept very clean, quite modern in design and with heating, comprise showers, washbasins with mirrors, electric points, etc. in functional units occupying two corners of the large floor space with an attractive, well maintained appearance. Facilities for disabled visitors. Also in the barn are dishwashing sinks and a fridge/freezer for campers to use. Motorcaravan service point. Tennis court, basketball/football pitch and children's play area. Dogs are not accepted. **Off site**: Fishing, golf, bicycle hire and riding within 6 km.

Charges 2002

Per person	€ 4,50 - € 5,00
child (0-12 yrs)	€ 2,50 - € 3,00
electricity (13A)	€ 2,00
(no charge per unit)	

Less 20% for groups of 4 or more. No credit cards. Tel: 052 41459. Fax: 052 42774. E-mail: con.traas@theapplefarm.com. Reservations: Contact site. **Open** 1 May - 30 September.

Directions: Park is 300 m. off main N24, 9.6 km. northwest of Clonmel, 6.4 km. southeast of Cahir.

 Alan Rogers' discount
Free bottle of apple juice or fruit in season

Parsons Green Caravan and Camping Park

938 Clogheen, Co. Tipperary

In a tranquil and scenic location, this small, family run park commands panoramic views toward the Vee Gap and Knockmealdown Mountains. In open style, surrounded by low ranch fencing, it offers 34 pitches with hardstanding for caravans and motorcaravans and 10 on grass, all with electrical connections (6A), plus 20 pitches for tents. There is a range of things to do and see including a garden area, river walks, picnic area, an extensive farm museum, a pet field with selection of domestic and rare animals and birds, pony and trap rides, boating on the small lake and trout fishing river. If not sitting back enjoying the scenic surroundings or participating in the many activities, there is much to see and do in this area. The manager at Parson's Green, would be more than pleased to pinpoint places of interest.

Facilities: Toilet facilities to the top right of the site close to reception, are kept clean and include good facilities for disabled people (shower and toilet). Laundry area with washing machines, dryer and sinks, plus dishwashing sinks. Coffee shop and takeaway. Children's playground. Minigolf. Fishing. TV/games room. Campers' kitchen and function room. **Off site:** Village within 500 m. (footpath and lighting) with shops, pubs, bank, post office, etc. Riding and golf 8 miles.

Charges 2001

Per caravan, family tent or motorcaravan	€ 6,35
small tent	€ 5,08
adult	€ 2,54
child	€ 1,27
awning	€ 1,27
electricity (6A)	€ 1,27

No credit cards. Tel: 052 65290. Fax: 052 65504. Reservations: Contact site. **Open** all year.

Directions: Site is in the village of Clogheen, 200 m. off the R665, 24 km. west of Clonmel, 19 km. east of Mitchelstown.

Curraghchase Caravan and Camping Park

945 Coillte Forest Park, Kilcornan, Co. Limerick

Approached by a long, tree-lined avenue that sets it well back from the main road, this tranquil 39 acre park is set in 600 acres of beech forest (known as the Coillte Forest Park), 21 km. from Limerick City. Touring pitches have hardstanding with drainage and electric hook-ups, with a separate grassy area allocated for 40 tents. Behind the main block is a small 'sun trap' picnic area. There are many lovely forest walks, a nature trail and a number of rare orchids can be found. Within the forest are the ruins of Curragh (or Currah) Chase House, which was once the home of the poet Aubrey de Vere. Fishing, riding, golf and Adare village, with its interesting historical buildings and shopping facilities, are within 10 km.

Facilities: One large amenities building houses a well stocked shop, TV lounge, a games room with table tennis and seating for an excellent campers' kitchen and the sanitary facilities which are basic. Hot water is free and showers are separated by a partition, sharing a large base with single drain and a communal dressing area with hooks and benches. Dishwashing sinks are in the campers' kitchen. Small laundry with washing machines, dryers and iron. Children's play area with a bark safety base.

Charges guide

Per caravan or family tent	€ 12,70
tent incl. 1 or 2 persons	€ 6.25
electricity	€ 1.27

No credit cards. Tel: 061 396349 (or 061 337322 off season). Fax: 061 338271. E-mail: okeeffe_e@ ecoillte.ie. Reservations: Advisable in high season - contact site. **Open** 1 May - 10 September.

Directions: From Limerick city take N69 Foynes road; park entrance is at Kilcornan. Park also signed from Adare on the N20.

Blarney Caravan and Camping Park

Stone View, Blarney, Co. Cork

948

There is a heart of the country feel about this 'on the farm' site, yet the city of Cork is only an 8 km. drive. What makes this friendly, family run park so appealing is its secluded location and neatly laid out, open appearance. The terrain on the three acre park is elevated and gently sloping, commanding views towards Blarney Castle and the surrounding mountainous countryside. The 40 pitches, 30 of which have hardstanding and 10A electrical connections, are with caravans sited to the centre and left and tents pitched to the right. There are gravel roads, well tended young shrubs and a screen of mature trees and hedging marks the park's perimeter. In the Blarney area, apart from the castle, house and gardens, there are shops, restaurants, pubs with traditional music and an abundance of outdoor pursuits such as walking, riding and fishing.

Facilities: Well kept toilet areas, one new, are housed in converted farm buildings with reception and small shop. Facilities for disabled visitors. Laundry room with sinks, washing machine, dryer and ironing. Dishwashing area in the large campers' kitchen. Motorcaravan service point. Shop (1/6-31/8). TV lounge. 18 hole golf and pitch and putt course. Night lighting. **Off site:** Public bar and restaurant 100 m. serving food all day. Within easy reach of the ports of Cork and Rosslare.

Charges 2001

Per caravan, family tent or motorhome	€ 6,35 - 7,62
car and small tent	€ 5,08 - 6,35
adult	€ 3,17
child	€ 1,27
hiker/cyclist and tent	€ 4,44 - 5,08
m/cyclist per person	€ 5,08 - 5,71
electricity (10A)	€ 2,54
awning	€ 1,27 - 1,90

7 nights for price of 6, if pre-paid. Tel/Fax: 021 4385167. E-mail: con.quill@camping-ireland.ie. Reservations: Contact park. **Open** all year.

Directions: Site is 8 km. northwest of Cork, just off the N20. Take N20 from Cork for approx. 6 km. and then left on R617 to Blarney. Site clearly signed at Esso station in village, in approx. 2 km.

The Meadow Camping Park

Glandore, Co. Cork

950

The stretch of coast from Cork to Skibbereen reminds British visitors of Devon before the era of mass tourism. This is rich dairy country, the green of the meadows matching the emerald colours of the travel posters. Thanks to the warm and wet Gulf Stream climate, it is also a county of gardens – and keen gardeners. The Meadows is best described not as a site, but as a one acre garden surrounded, appropriately, by lush meadows. It lies 1.5 km. east of the fishing village of Glandore. A further 5 km. west is the regional centre, Skibbereen, beyond which the landscape moves from unspoilt Devon to unspoilt Cornwall. The owners, who live on the park, have cunningly arranged accommodation for 19 pitches among the flower beds and shrubberies of their extended garden. Space is rather tight and towed caravans are therefore not encouraged. There are 6 hardstandings for motorcaravans with 5A electric hook-ups. Among the homely features are a sitting room and a well equipped kitchen, and breakfast is available on request. Note: tents and motorcaravans only.

Facilities: Facilities are limited but well designed and immaculately maintained. Showers on payment. Washing machine and dryer. American motorhomes accepted with additional charge according to length. Dogs are not accepted. **Off site:** Fishing or riding 2 km, fishing, swimming, boat launching and sailing at Glandore (2 km).

Charges 2001

Per unit incl. 2 persons	€ 11,43 - 12,70
extra person	€ 3,81
child (under 12)	€ 1,27
hiker or cyclist incl. tent per person	€ 5,08 - 5,71
electricity (5A)	€ 1,27

No credit cards. Tel: 028 33280. E-mail: themeadow @oceanfree.net. Reservations: Please phone site for details. **Open** 15 March - 30 September.

Directions: Park is 1.5 km. east of Glandore, off N71 road, on R597 mid-way between Leap and Rosscarbery (coast road).

Barleycove Holiday Park

952 Crookhaven, Co. Cork

This long established, family owned park enjoys an idyllic situation tucked between the golden sands of Barleycove and Crookhaven Harbour on the scenic Mizen Peninsula. It is within an 8 km. drive of Mizen Head, Ireland's most south-westerly point, and approached along a route of unspoilt rugged countryside, offering the ideal 'away from it all' environment. It is a well cared for park with a neat and tidy appearance. Mobile homes are sited around the perimeter and within a field to the right. The 85 touring pitches all have electricity hook-ups (5A). Some are on grass in bays of 12, divided by timber fencing, others are unfenced on hardstanding with drainage and rubbish disposal. Tents have a dedicated grass area. Apart from discovering the natural beauty of this peninsula, of interest is Mizen Head Signal Station visitor centre, reached by a suspension bridge. Alternatively, the local friendly pubs and quality seafood restaurant at Heron's Cove offer a memorable evening out.

Facilities: Three toilet blocks, kept clean and well maintained, provide free hot showers, open style wash areas, plus a vanity unit. Laundry, with washing machines, dryer and spin dryer, washing-up sinks. Motorcaravan service point. Cafe/takeaway (July/Aug) with outside seating. Well stocked mini-market. Ice packs at reception. Games room with table tennis, pool tables and games machines. Tennis court (free). Pitch and putt. Activities for children are organised in high season. Security gate and night watchman. Dogs are not accepted.

Charges 2001

Per family unit	€ 13,00 - 16,50
2 person unit	€ 11,50 - 13,50
awning (high season only)	€ 3,00
hiker, cyclist or m/cyclist with tent	€ 4,00 - 5,00
hardstanding	free - € 1,25
electricity	free - € 1,25

Tel: 028 35302 (low season 021 4346466). Fax: 021 4307230. Reservations: Contact park. **Open** Easter - 16 September.

Directions: Site is 35 km. southwest of Bantry. From N71 Bantry/Cork road join R591 (3.2 km. south of Bantry) and follow signs for Crookhaven via Durrus, Toormore and Goleen. Site on right before Crookhaven village.

Eagle Point Caravan and Camping Park

951 Ballylickey, Bantry, West Cork

Midway between the towns of Bantry and Glengarriff, the spectacular peninsula of Eagle Point juts into Bantry Bay. The first impression is of a spacious country park rather than a campsite. As far as the eye can see this 20 acre, landscaped, part-terraced park, with its vast manicured grass areas separated by mature trees, shrubs and hedges, runs parallel with the shoreline. Suitable for all ages, this is a well run park devoted to tourers, with campers pitched mostly towards the shore. It provides 125 pitches (60 caravans, 65 tents), and electric hook-ups, thus avoiding overcrowding during peak periods. A wet weather timbered building towards the water's edge houses a TV room - the brightly decorated interior is guaranteed to brighten the dullest of days. Eagle Point makes an excellent base for watersports enthusiasts - swimming is safe and there is a slipway for small craft.

Facilities: Three well maintained, well designed toilet blocks are above expected standards. Laundry and dishwashing. Motorcaravan services. Children's play area. Tennis courts. Football field to the far right, well away from the pitches. Fishing. Supermarket at park entrance. Dogs are not accepted. **Off site**: Bicycle hire 6 km, riding 10 km, golf 2 km.

Charges 2001

Per unit	€ 16,51 - 17,78
extra adult	€ 5,08
m/cyclist, hiker or cyclist, per person	€ 6,35
extra car	€ 2,54
electricity (6A)	€ 1,27

Tel: 027 50630. E-mail: eaglepointcamping@ eircom.net. Reservations: Bookings not essential. **Open** 27 April - 30 September.

Directions: Take N71 to Bandon, then R586 Bandon to Bantry, N71 Bantry to Glengarriff. 6.4 km. (4 miles) from Bantry; park entrance is opposite Burmah petrol station.

Creveen Lodge Caravan and Camping Park

957 Healy Pass, Lauragh, Co. Kerry

The address of this park is rather confusing, but Healy Pass is the well known scenic summit of the road (R574) crossing the Beara Peninsula, which lies between Kenmare Bay to the north and Bantry Bay to the south. Several kilometres inland from the north coast road (R571), the R574 starts to climb steeply southward towards the Healy Pass. Here, on the mountain foothills, is Creveen Lodge, a working hill farm with a quiet, homely atmosphere. Although not so famed as the Iveragh Peninsula, around which runs the Ring of Kerry, the northern Beara is a scenically striking area of County Kerry. Creveen Lodge, commanding views across Kenmare Bay, is divided among three gently sloping fields separated by trees. To allow easy access, the steep farm track is divided into a simple one-way system. There are 20 pitches, 16 for tents, 4 for caravans, with an area of hardstanding for motorcaravans, and electrical connections are available. The park is carefully tended with neat rubbish bins and rustic picnic tables informally placed. This is walking and climbing countryside or, of interest close by, is Derreen Gardens.

Facilities: Well appointed and immaculately maintained, the small toilet block provides showers on payment (€ 0,65), plus a communal room with a fridge, freezer, TV, ironing board, fireplace, tables and chairs. Reception is in the farmhouse which also offers guests a comfortable sitting room. Full Irish breakfast is served on request. Children's play area. **Off site**: Water sports, riding, 'Seafari' cruises, shops and a restaurant nearby. Fishing 2 km, bicycle hire 9 km, boat launching 9 km.

Charges 2002

Per unit	€ 9,00
person	€ 1,30
hiker or cyclist incl. tent, per person	€ 4,75
electricity	€ 1,30

No credit cards. Tel: 064 83131. E-mail: info@ creveenlodge.com. Reservations: Write to site with an S.A.E. **Open** Easter - 31 October.

Directions: Park is on the Healy Pass road (R574) 1.5 km. southeast of Lauragh.

Wave Crest Caravan and Camping Park

956 Caherdaniel, Ring of Kerry, Co. Kerry

It would be difficult to imagine a more dramatic location than Wave Crest's on the Ring of Kerry coast. Huge boulders and rocky outcrops tumble from the park entrance on the N70 down to the seashore which forms the most southern promontory on the Ring of Kerry. There are spectacular southward views from the park across Kenmare Bay to the Beara peninsula. Sheltering on grass patches in small coves that nestle between the rocks and shrubbery, are 65 hardstanding pitches and 20 on grass offering seclusion. Electricity connections are available (13A). A unique feature is the TV room, an old stone farm building with a thatched roof. Its comfortable interior includes a stone fireplace heated by a converted cast iron marker buoy. Caherdaniel is known for its cheerful little pubs and distinguished restaurant. The Derrynane National Park Nature Reserve is only a few kilometres away, as is Derrynane Cove and Bay. This park would suit older people looking for a quiet, relaxed atmosphere.

Facilities: Two blocks house the sanitary facilities and include hot showers (on payment), toilet for disabled people and dishwashing sinks. Laundry service. Small shop and takeaway service (May - Sept). Children's play area. Fishing and boat launching. **Off site**: Riding 1 km, bicycle hire or golf 10 km. Small beach near and Derrynane Hotel with bar and restaurant.

Charges 2001

Per unit	€ 11,43
small tent	€ 10,16
adult	€ 1,27
child	€ 0,63
hiker or cyclist incl. tent, per person	€ 4,44
m/cyclist incl. tent	€ 5,08
electricity (13A)	€ 1,27

Tel: 066 9475188 or 9475483. Fax: 066 9475188. E-mail: wavecrest@eircom.net. Reservations: Write for details. **Open** 15 March - 15 October.

Directions: On the N70 (Ring of Kerry), 1½ km. east of Caherdaniel.

Fossa Caravan and Camping Park

Fossa, Killarney, Co. Kerry

959

THE ALAN ROGERS'
travel service

To Book
Ferry ✓
Pitch ✓
Accommodation ✗

01892 55 98 98

This mature, well equipped park is in a scenic location, ten minutes drive from the town centre. Fossa Caravan Park is recognisable by its forecourt on which stands a distinctive building housing a roof top restaurant, reception area, shop and petrol pumps. The well laid out park is divided in two - the touring area lies to the right, tucked behind the main building, and to the left is an open grass area mainly for campers. Touring pitches, with electricity and drainage, have hardstanding and are angled between shrubs and trees in a tranquil, well cared for garden setting. To the rear at a higher level are 50 caravan holiday homes. These are unobtrusive and sheltered by the thick foliage of the wooded slopes which climb high behind the park. Not only is Fossa convenient for Killarney (5.5 km), it is also en-route for the famed 'Ring of Kerry', and makes an ideal base for walkers and golfers.

Facilities: Modern toilet facilities kept spotlessly clean include showers on payment. Laundry room, washing up area. Campers' kitchen. Shop (April - Sept). Restaurant (mid-May - end Aug) and takeaway (July/Aug). TV lounge. Children's play area, picnic area. Games room. Bicycle hire. Night lighting and security patrol. **Off site**: Fishing or golf 2 km, riding 3 km.

Charges 2001

Per unit	€ 3,81 - 4,44
adult	€ 3,81
child (under 14 yrs)	€ 1,27
1 or 2 man tent	€ 3,17 - 3,81
m/cycle and tent per person	€ 5,08 - 5,71
electricity (10/15A)	€ 2,54
awning	€ 2,54

Tel: 064 31497. Fax: 064 34459. E-mail: campingholidays@ireland.com. Reservations: Advisable in high season and made for min. 3 nights with deposit. **Open** 1 April - 30 September.

Directions: Approaching Killarney from all directions, follow signs for N72 Ring of Kerry/Killorglin. At last roundabout join R562/N72. Continue for 5.5 km. and Fossa is the second park to the right.

FOSSA CARAVAN & CAMPING PARK

✱ Ample hardstanding & electric hook-up ✱ Separate tent area
✱ Modern toilets ✱ Shaving points ✱ Hairdryers ✱ Hot showers
✱ Facilities for the disabled ✱ Full laundry facilities ✱ Campers kitchen
✱ Free wash-up facilities ✱ On site shop open 7 days Easter to Sept.
✱ Restaurant (June-Aug) ✱ Take away (July/Aug)
✱ Children's playground ✱ Tennis court ✱ Games room ✱ TV room ✱ Bicycles for hire
✱ Mobile homes for hire ✱ Hostel accommodation

FOR FREE COLOUR BROCHURE WRITE TO:
Brosnan Family, Fossa Caravan & Camping Park, Fossa, Killarney, Co. Kerry, Ireland
Telephone: (064) 31497   Fax: (064) 34459

Anchor Caravan Park

Castlegregory, Co. Kerry

955

Of County Kerry's three long, finger like peninsulas which jut into the sea, Dingle is the most northerly. Tralee is the main town and Anchor Caravan Park is 20 km. west of this famed town and under 4 km. south of Castlegregory on Tralee Bay. A secluded and mature, five acre park, it is enclosed by shrubs and trees, with a gateway leading to a beautiful, sandy beach which is safe for bathing, boating and shore fishing. There are 30 pitches, all with electric hook-ups and some also with drainage and water points. Although there are holiday homes for hire, these are well apart from the touring pitches. In this area of great beauty, miles of sand abounds and taking in the panorama of mountain scenery from the top of the Conor Pass is a wonderful experience.

Facilities: Toilet facilities (entry by key) are kept clean (three or four times daily in busy periods) providing showers on payment (€ 0,50), two private cabins, toilet with handrail, dishwashing and laundry facilities (incl. clothes lines). Motorcaravan services. Two children's play areas. Games/TV room. Night lighting. **Off site**: Beautiful sandy beach 2 minutes. Fishing 2 km. Riding or bicycle hire 3 km. Golf 4 km.

Charges 2002

Per unit incl. all persons	€ 13,00 - 14,00
small tent incl. 1 or 2 persons	€ 11,00 - 12,00
m/cyclist, hiker or cyclist incl. tent	€ 10,00
electricity	€ 2,00
awning	€ 2,50

No credit cards. Tel/Fax: 066 7139157. E-mail: anchorcaravanpark@eircom.net. Reservations: Contact site. **Open** Easter - 30 September.

Directions: From Tralee follow the Dingle coast road for 19 km. Park is signposted from Camp junction.

Glenross Caravan and Camping Park

960 Glenbeigh, Ring of Kerry

Its situation on the spectacular Ring of Kerry and the Kerry Way gives Glenross an immediate advantage, and scenic grandeur around every bend of the road is guaranteed as Glenbeigh is approached. Quietly located before entering the village, the park commands a fine view of Rossbeigh Strand, which is within walking distance. On arrival, a good impression is created with the park well screened from the road, with a new stone entrance and gates. There are 34 touring pitches, including some hardstanding pitches with electricity, and 6 caravan holiday homes, all attractively laid out. There is no catering on site but the Glenbeigh Hotel is popular and village shops are near. Not least is the Kerry Bog Village where you can go back in time in this reconstructed pre-famine village.

Facilities: Well maintained modern toilet block includes facilities for laundry and dishwashing. Motorcaravan service point. Games room. Bicycle hire. Shelter for campers. Sun lounge and barbecue patio. **Off site**: Watersports and tennis near, riding and fishing 200 m. and golf 500 m.

Charges 2001

Per unit	€ 4,44 - 5,08
adult	€ 5,08
child (under 14 yrs)	€ 1,27
awning	€ 1,27 - 1,90
electricity (10A)	€ 2,16 - 2,54
m/cyclist and tent	€ 6,35 - 6,66
hiker or cyclist and tent	€ 5,72 - 6,35

No credit cards. Tel: 066 9768451 (May-Aug) or 064 31590 at other times. Fax: 064 37474. E-mail: fwbcamping@tinet.ie. Reservations: Write to site for details. **Open** 4 May - 10 September.

Directions: Park is on the N70 Killorglin - Glenbeigh road, on the right just before entering the village.

Mannix Point Camping and Caravan Park

961 Cahirciveen, Co. Kerry

A quiet and peaceful, beautifully located seashore park, it is no exaggeration to describe Mannix Point as a nature lovers' paradise. Situated in one of the most spectacular parts of the Ring of Kerry, overlooking the Portmagee Channel towards Valentia Island, the park commands splendid views in all directions. It is flat and open being right on marshland which teems with wildlife (a two acre nature reserve) with direct access to the beach and seashore. The owner has planted around 500 plants with plans for around 1,000 more trees and shrubs. There are 42 pitches, 15 for tourers and 27 for tents, with electrical connections (6A) available. A charming old fisherman's cottage has been converted to provide reception. A cosy sitting room with turf fire, and 'emergency' dormitory for campers, is a feature of this site. There is no television, but compensation comes in the form of a knowledgeable, hospitable owner who is a Bord Fáilte registered local tour guide. This park retains a wonderful air of Irish charm aided by occasional impromptu musical evenings. Watersports, bird watching, walking and photography can all be pursued. Local cruises to Skelligs Rock with free transport to and from the port for walkers and cyclists. This is also an ideal resting place for people walking the Kerry Way.

Facilities: Toilet facilities, now upgraded and immaculate, have well designed showers. Modern campers' kitchen. Laundry facilities with washing machines and dryer. Motorcaravan service facilities. Dogs are not accepted in July and August. **Off site**: Bicycle hire 800 m. riding 3 km, golf 14 km.

Charges 2001

Per adult	€ 5,08
child	€ 3,05
caravan or motorcaravan	€ 3,05
tent	no charge
electricity (6A)	€ 1,52
m/cycle	€ 0,95

Book 7 nights, pay 6. Reductions for groups if pre-paid. No credit cards. Tel/Fax: 066 9472806. E-mail: mannixpoint@mail.com. Reservations: Made with deposit of one night's fee. **Open** 15 March - 15 October, the rest of the year also, if you write first.

Directions: Park is 250 m. off the N70 Ring of Kerry road, 800 m. southwest of Cahirciveen (or Cahersiveen) on the road towards Waterville.

Co. Kerry
White Villa Farm Caravan and Camping Park
Cork Road (N22), Killarney, Co. Kerry

963

This is a very pleasing small touring park in scenic surroundings on the N22 Killarney-Cork road. It is set on a 100 acre family operated dairy farm which stretches as far as the River Flesk, yet is only minutes away from Killarney town. Trees and shrubs surround the park but dominant is a magnificent view of the MacGillicuddy's Reeks. There are 25 pitches for caravans and tents, 15 with hardstanding and a grass area for awnings, electricity (10A), water points and night lighting. An unusual novelty is old school desks placed around the site, plus an antique green telephone box. One can also enjoy walking through the oak wood, fishing on the Flesk or visiting the site's own National Farm Museum.

Facilities: The toilet block, a sandstone coloured building to the rear of the park, is kept spotlessly clean and houses showers (on payment), a good toilet/shower room for disabled visitors, laundry room, clothes lines and dishwashing sinks. Motorcaravan service area. Campers' kitchen with TV. Children's play area and basketball. Bicycle hire. Max. 2 dogs per pitch are accepted (not certain breeds). **Off site:** Riding, golf and boat launching 5 km. Killarney town and the National Park 10 minutes away.

Charges 2002

Per unit	€ 3,00 - 3,50
adult	€ 4,00
child under 14 yrs	€ 1,30
14-18 yrs	€ 2,00
m/cyclist, hiker or cyclist incl. tent	€ 5,00 - 5,50
electricity	€ 2,00

No credit cards. Tel: 064 32456 or 31414. E-mail: killarneycamping@eircom.net. Reservations: Made with deposit (€ 15 or UK£10). **Open** 25 March - 16 October.

Directions: Park is 3 km. east from Killarney town on N22 Cork road. Park entrance is 500 m. east of N22/N72 junction. From Killarney follow N22 Cork road signs and 'White Villa Farm' finger signs from Park Road roundabout. From Kenmare take R569 via Kilgarvan to the N22, then as above.

Co. Kerry
Fleming's White Bridge Caravan Park
White Bridge, Ballycasheen Road, Killarney, Co. Kerry

962

THE ALAN ROGERS' travel service

To Book
Ferry ✓
Pitch ✓
Accommodation ✗

01892 55 98 98

Once past the county border, the main road from Cork to Killarney (N22) runs down the valley of the Flesk river. On the final approach to Killarney off the N22 Cork road, the river veers away from the road to enter the Lower Lake. On this prime rural position, between the road and the river, and within comfortable walking distance of the town, is Fleming's White Bridge, a nine acre woodland park. The ground is flat, landscaped and generously adorned with flowers, shrubs and trees. There are now 92 pitches (46 caravans and 46 tents) that extend beyond a wooden bridge to an area surrounded by mature trees and where a new toilet block, one of three, is sited. This is obviously a park of which the owners are very proud, and the family personally supervise the reception and grounds, maintaining high standards of hygiene, cleanliness and tidiness. The park's location so close to Ireland's premier tourism centre makes this park an ideal base to explore Killarney and the southwest.

Facilities: Three toilet blocks are maintained to high standards. Dishwashing sinks. Motorcaravan service point. Campers' drying room and two laundries. Shop (1/6-1/9). Two TV rooms and a games room. Fishing (advice and permits provided). Canoeing (own canoes). Bicycle hire. Woodland walks. **Off site:** Riding 3 km, golf 2 km.

Charges 2001

Per unit	€ 4,44 - 5,08
small tent/car or motorcaravan	€ 3,81 - 4,44
adult	€ 5,08
child (under 14 yrs)	€ 1,27
awning	€ 1,27 - 1,90
electricity (10A)	€ 2,54 - 3,81
m/cyclist and tent	€ 6,35 - 6,67
hiker or cyclist and tent	€ 5,71 - 6,35

Tel: 064 31590. Fax: 064 37474. E-mail: fwbcamping@eircom.net. Reservations: Advised for high season; contact park. **Open** 17 March - 31 October.

Directions: From Cork and Mallow: at N72/N22 junction continue towards Killarney and take first turn left (signed Ballycasheen Road). Proceed for 300 m. to archway entrance on left. From Limerick: follow N22 Cork road. After passing Super Valu and Killarney Heights Hotel take first right (signed Ballycasheen Road) and continue as above. From Kenmare: On N71, pass Gleneagles Hotel and Flesk Bridge. Turn right before Shell filling station into Woodlawn Road and Ballycasheen Road for continue 2 km. to archway.

The Flesk Muckross Caravan and Camping Park

Muckross Road, Killarney, Co. Kerry

At the gateway to the National Park and Lakes, near Killarney town, this family run, seven acre park has undergone extensive development and offers high quality standards. Pitches are well spaced and have electricity (10A), water, and drainage connections; 21 also have hardstanding with a grass area for awnings. The grounds have been well cultivated with further shrubs, plants and an attractive barbecue and patio area. This is to the left of the sanitary block and is paved and sunk beneath the level roadway. Surrounded by a garden border, it has tables and chairs, making a pleasant communal meeting place commanding excellent views of Killarney's mountains.

Facilities: Modern, clean toilet blocks are well designed and equipped. Baby bath/changing room. Laundry room. Campers' kitchen with dishwashing sinks. Bar. Comfortable games room. Other on site facilities include petrol pumps, supermarket (all year), delicatessen and café (March - Oct) with extra seating on the sun terrace. Night lighting and night time security checks. Winter caravan storage. **Off site:** Fishing 300 m, boat launching 2 km.

Charges 2002

Per unit	€ 4,50 - 5,00
adult	€ 5,75
child (under 14 yrs)	€ 1,50
small tent incl. 1 or 2 persons	€ 4,00 - 4,50
m/cylist incl. tent	€ 6,50 - 7,00
hiker or cyclist incl. tent	€ 6,00 - 6,50
awning	€ 2,00
electricity	€ 3,00

Tel: 064 31704. FAX: 064 34681. E-mail: killarneylakes@eircom.net. Reservations: Advisable in peak periods, write to park. **Open** 29 March - 30 September.

Directions: From Killarney town centre follow the N71 and signs for Killarney National Park. Site is 1.5 km. on the left beside the Gleneagle Hotel.

FLESK MUCKROSS
CARAVAN PARK

Family run, 7 acre park, situated at the gateway to 25,000 acres of National Park and lakes.

AA award winning sanitation facilities 1994/5

Just 1 mile (1.5 km) from Killarney town on the N71 south of Kenmare,

adjacent to Gleneagle Hotel and leisure centre

MUCKROSS, KILLARNEY
CO. KERRY, IRELAND   Prop: Johnny & Sinead Courtney

Phone: 064-31704
Fax: 064-34681

The Alan Rogers' Travel Service

THE ALAN ROGERS'
travel service

Book   ✓
rry   ✓
ch
commodation ✗

892 55 98 98

We have recently extended The Alan Rogers Travel Service. This unique service enables our readers to reserve their holidays as well as ferry crossings and comprehensive insurance cover at extremely competitive rates. Whilst the majority of participating sites are in France, we are now also able to offer a selection of some of the very best sites in Ireland and The Channel Islands.

One simple telephone call to our Travel Service on 01892 559898 is all that is needed to make all the arrangements. Why not take advantage of our years' of experience of camping and caravanning. We would be delighted to discuss your holiday plans with you, and offer advice and recommendations.

Share our experience and let us help to ensure that your holiday will be a complete success. The new Alan Rogers Travel Service Tel. 01892 55 98 98

Woodlands Park Touring Caravan and Camping Park

965 Dan Spring Road, Tralee, Co. Kerry

Tralee is not only the Capital of County Kerry and gateway to the Dingle Peninsula, it is also Ireland's fastest growing visitor destination, with Woodlands its newest touring caravan park. Although only a 10 minute walk from the town centre, this park is located on a 16 acre elevated site approached by a short roadway and bridge that straddles the River Lee. Once on site the town seems far removed, with a countryside environment taking over. Hedging, trees, grazing fields and the distant Slieve Mish Mountain create the setting. The owners of Woodlands have designed and equipped their park to a high standard. A distinctive feature is its impressive yellow coloured building which houses an 'on top' family dwelling and ground floor services. There are 92 pitches with hardstanding, electricity, water and drainage plus night light, to the left and centre behind the main building, and a grass area for 40 tents is to the right. Young shrubs, cordyline trees and flower beds have been planted around the park and a security barrier is in operation. Interesting is the award winning 'Kerry the Kingdom' museum with its incredible time car trip through the Middle Ages. Evening entertainment in Tralee means a selection of singing pubs, restaurants and the National Folk Theatre.

Facilities: Heated sanitary facilities include sizeable showers (token) and provision for disabled guests. Campers' kitchen and dishwashing sinks. Laundry room with washing machines and dryer. Café/snack bar. Shop. Games room. TV and adult room. Fenced adventure play area. **Off site:** The nearby Aqua Dome offers half price admission after 6 pm. Golf 6 km, riding 2 km. Blue flag beaches on the Dingle Peninsula.

Charges 2001

Per unit incl. 2 adults	€ 13,33 - 13,97
plus 2 children	€ 15,87 - 16,51
small tent incl.2 adults	€ 12,70 - 13,33
m/cyclist incl. tent	€ 5,71 - 6,35
hiker or cyclist incl. tent	€ 5,08 - 6,03
extra adult	€ 4,44
child (under14)	€ 1,27
electricity (10A)	€ 2,22

Tel: (066) 7121235. Fax: (066) 7181199. E-mail: wdlands@eircom.net. Reservations: Advisable for high season. **Open** 15 March - 30 September.

Directions: Site is 1 km. southwest of Tralee town centre. From N21/N69/N86 junction south of Tralee follow camp signs for 2.4 km. to park, 200 m. off the N86 Tralee - Dingle road.

CHANNEL ISLANDS

Weymouth   Poole

Jersey

Jersey Tourism
Liberation Square, St Helier, Jersey JE1 1BB
Tel: (01534) 500700 Fax: (01534) 500899
www.jersey.com

Guernsey and Herm

States of Guernsey Tourist Board
PO Box 13, White Rock, Guernsey
Tel: (01481) 723552

Sark

Sark Tourism Office
Sark (via Guernsey), Channel Islands.
Tel: (01481) 832345

A visit to the Channel Islands offers a holiday in part of the British Isles, but in an area which has a definitely continental flavour. Of course, you don't need a passport or to change your money, although the proximity of the islands to the French coast might tempt one to take a day trip. All the islands have beautiful beaches and coves, pretty scenery and fascinating histories. Jersey is probably more commercially orientated, with more entertainment provided, while Guernsey will suit those who prefer a quieter, more peaceful holiday. For total relaxation, one of the smaller islands, such as Sark or Herm, where no cars are allowed, might appeal. Shopping in all the islands has the advantage of no mainland VAT – particularly useful for buying cameras, watches, jewellery and clothes.

Camping holidays on the islands are limited to TENTS only - caravans and motorcaravans are not permitted due to the narrow and sometimes crowded nature of the roads. Trailer tents (with canvas roof and walls) are permitted but on Jersey advance reservations must be made. Contact the Island Tourism authorities for more detailed information. Some of the parks we feature offer tents and camping equipment for hire, which may prove a popular option for some, and cars are also easily rented on the main islands.

Since all the parks cater solely for tents, rather than caravans or motorcaravans, this means that there tend to be very limited waste water emptying points and almost no chemical disposal facilities. We are advised that on both Jersey and Guernsey, that political pressure is being placed for a change of policy in order to develop tourism. Guernsey is trying for caravans on the basis that, once they are on site, then only the car will run around the island, while Jersey is pushing for motorcaravans under a certain length. Both developments are under consideration – contact the relevant tourist board for the latest information.

Travel between mainland Britain and the Channel Islands is not cheap, particularly if you take your car. However the Condor wave-piercing catamaran service has made travelling to the Channel Islands a very easy and much quicker proposition than ever before. We used this service, which now carries cars, and were most impressed, in respect of the speed (From Poole, Guernsey is only some 2½ hours travelling time, Jersey 1 hour longer), the comfort and the onboard service. These craft are surprisingly spacious with room to walk around (and even to go outside), a bar and snack bar and duty-free shopping facilities. Condor offer a range of fares, including a Family Saver deal. Condor may be contacted at on tel: (01305) 761551.

Photo: Jersey Tourism

Jersey, Guernsey and St. Malo

The fast car ferry service

If you're travelling to the Channel Islands or Western France for your holiday next year, the first thing you need is your copy of a Condor 2002 Car Ferries Brochure.

With services up to 3 times daily from Weymouth or Poole you can be in Jersey in 3 hours, Guernsey in 2 hours or St. Malo in as little as $4^1/_2$ hours.

Information & Booking 0845 345 2000

ONLY WE DUTY FREE

CONDOR
Ferries

Jersey

Rozel Camping Park

971 Rozel, St Martin, Jersey, Channel Islands JE3 6AX

This family owned park is within walking distance of the famous Jersey Zoo and the pretty harbour and fishing village of Rozel where the north coast cliff path commences. The surrounding countryside is quieter than many areas of the island. A car is probably necessary to reach the main island beaches, although a bus service does run to St Helier from close by. The park itself is quietly situated at the top of a valley (the French coast can be seen on a clear day) and is surrounded by trees providing shelter. There are two main camping areas providing 100 pitches of which some 15 are used for fully equipped tents to hire. Some pitches, mainly for smaller tents are arranged on terraced areas. The remainder are on a higher, flat field where pitches are arranged in bays with hedges growing to separate them into groups. Parking is permitted by the tents and some electrical connections are available. In addition to package deals for tent hire and travel, the site offers a good range of camping equipment for hire on a daily basis. Boats are accepted by prior arrangement.

Facilities: Two heated sanitary buildings offer first rate facilities including a bathroom for disabled people with a shower, toilet and washbasin in the lower block with an access ramp. Family shower room in the upper block with a small heater for cooler weather. Dishwashing facilities under cover. Laundry and make up room. Shop. Attractive, sheltered swimming pool (June-Sept) with children's pool and sunbathing areas. Play equipment. Crazy golf. Games room, reading and TV room. Bicycle hire. Torches useful. Dogs are not accepted. **Off site**: Fishing 1 mile, riding 3 miles, golf 4 miles.

Charges 2001

Per person	£5.00 - £7.20
child (3-11 yrs)	half price
electricity	£1.50

Tent hire and travel packages. Tel: (01534) 856797. Fax: (01534) 856127. E-mail: rozelcamping@jerseyhols.com. Reservations: Made for any length with £40 deposit; balance due 14 days before arrival. **Open** 1 May - 8 September.

Directions: On leaving the harbour by Route du Port Elizabeth, take A1 east through the tunnel and the A17. At the fourth set of traffic lights turn left on A6. Keep in the middle lane. Continue to Five Oaks and on to St Martin's church. Turn right, then immediately left at the 'Royal' onto the B38 to Rozel and the park is on the right.

Jersey

Beuvelande Camp Site

972 St Martin, Jersey, Channel Islands JE3 6EZ

What a pleasant surprise we had when we called here - the outstanding sanitary building gives campers facilities normally associated with top class hotels. A licensed restaurant with covered terrace area is also situated in this building, open morning and evening all season, but perhaps a few less hours at quiet times. There are 150 pitches, 60 with fully equipped tents for hire, but with plenty of space for those with their own tents. Some electric hook ups are available and cars may be parked next to your tent. Torches would be useful. Car hire can be arranged and bicycle hire is possible from the site. This family run park prides itself on quality, cleanliness and hospitality.

Facilities: The toilet block is tiled top to bottom and spotlessly clean, with controllable showers, two fully equipped bathrooms for disabled people, and a baby room. Plenty of dishwashing facilities and a laundry can now be found in the original sanitary building. Games room and TV room. Well stocked shop open 8 am. - 7 pm. during peak times and stocks gas. Ice pack and battery charging services for a small charge. Outdoor heated swimming pool (41 x 17 ft) with a sun terrace. Simple play equipment for children. **Off site**: Fishing, golf or riding within 3 km.

Charges guide

Per adult	£5.00 - £7.00
child 8-14 yrs	£3.50
2-8 yrs	£2.50
dog	£2.00

Single sex groups not accepted. No credit cards. Tel: (01534) 853575, 852223 or 851156. Fax: (01534) 857788. Reservations: Made with £30 deposit; contact park for details. **Open** 1 May - 15 September.

Directions: On leaving the harbour by Route du Port Elizabeth, take A1 east through the tunnel and the A17. At the fourth set of traffic lights turn left on A6. Continue to Five Oaks and on to St Martin's RC church, then right into La Longue Rue, right again Rue de L'Orme then left to site.

Fauxquets Valley Farm Campsite

978 Castel, Guernsey, Channel Islands GY5 7QA

THE ALAN ROGERS'
travel service

To Book
Ferry ✓
Pitch ✓
Accommodation ✗

01892 55 98 98

Situated in the rural centre of the island, Fauxquets is in a pretty sheltered valley, hidden down narrow lanes away from busy roads and is run by the Guille family. A car would be useful here to reach the beaches, St Peter Port and other attractions, although there is a bus service each day (20 minutes walk). It was once a dairy farm, but the valley side has now been developed into an attractive camp site, with the old farm buildings as its centre. Plenty of trees, bushes and flowers have been planted to separate pitches and to provide shelter around the various fields which are well terraced. The 86 touring pitches are of a good size, most marked, numbered and with electricity, and there is lots of open space. There are also 15 smaller places for backpackers. The site has 23 fully equipped tents for hire, but there are no tour operators. The Haybarn licensed restaurant and bar provides (15/6-31/8) breakfast, morning coffee and cake and evening meals. There is plenty of room to sit around the heated swimming pool, including a large grassy terrace with sun-beds provided. A torch would be useful.

Facilities: The toilet facilities are good with free, controllable hot showers, some washbasins set in flat surfaces, with others in private cabins and with a shower, baby bath and changing unit for children. Hairdryers and irons are free. Dishwashing facilities under cover (free hot water) and a tap to take away hot water. Laundry room with free iron. Heated swimming pool (20 x 45 ft.) with paddling pool. Restaurant. Bar. Small shop (Easter-15/9) with ice-pack hire and gas. TV room and table tennis rooms. Small children's play area and play field. Nature walk. Bicycle hire. **Off site:** Fishing and boat launching 3 miles, riding and golf 2 miles

Charges 2001

Per adult	£4.50 - £5.20
child (at school)	half price
electricity	£2.50

Fully equipped tents with fridge for hire. Tel: (01481) 255460. Fax: (01481) 251797. E-mail: fauxquets@ campingguernsey.freeserve.co.uk. Reservations: Made for independent campers for any length, with £50 deposit. Tent hire details from site. **Open** Easter - 15 September.

Directions: From St Peter Port harbour take second exit from roundabout. At top of hill, turn left at 'filter in turn' into Queens Road, then right at next filter. Follow straight through traffic lights and down hill past Hospital, through pedestrian lights and straight on at another set of lights at top of hill. Continue for ¾ mile, then turn right opposite at sign for German Underground Hospital. Fourth left is pedestrian entrance, cars carry on for 400 yds to gravel entrance on left.

Vaugrat Camping

977 St Sampson's, Guernsey, Channel Islands GY2 4TA

Vaugrat Camping is a neat, well tended site, close to the beach in the northwest of the island. Owned and run by the Laine family, it is centred around attractive and interesting old granite farm buildings dating back to the 15th century, with a gravel courtyard and colourful flower beds. It provides 150 pitches on flat grassy meadows, that are mostly surrounded by trees, banks and hedges to provide shelter. Tents are arranged around the edges of the fields, giving open space in the centre, and while pitches are not marked, there is sufficient room and cars may be parked next to tents. Only couples and families are accepted and the site is well run and welcoming. It also offers 25 fully equipped tents for hire. Housed in the old farmhouse, now a listed building, are the reception area, and shop and upstairs the Coffee Barn, with views to the sea, where breakfast is served; one can also sit here in the evenings. A cider room complete with the ancient presses is now the games/TV room.

Facilities: Well kept sanitary facilities are in two buildings, one of which is in the courtyard, with hot showers on payment. Unit for disabled visitors with shower, basin and toilet (although there is a 6" step into the building). Laundry room with washing machine, dryer and iron. Second block near the camping fields provides one private cabin for ladies and dishwashing facilities. Shop with ice pack hire (main season only). Café. Dogs are not accepted. Torches may be useful. **Off site:** Bus service within easy reach. Car or bicycle hire can be arranged. Fishing, riding and golf within 1½ miles. Hotel and bar nearby.

Charges 2001

Per adult £5.50; child (under 14 yrs)	£4.40
car or boat	£1.05

Families and couples only. Fully equipped tents to hire (details from site). Tel: (01481) 57468. Fax: (01481) 51841. E-mail: adgould@globalnet.co.uk. Reservations: Made for independent campers for any length, with £10 deposit and balance on arrival. **Open** 1 May - 30 September.

Directions: On leaving St Peter Port, turn right onto coast road for 1½ miles. At filter turn left into Vale Road. Straight over at two sets of lights then first left turn by church. Follow to crossroads (garage opposite) turn right. Carry on past Peninsula Hotel, then second left, signed for site. Site on left after high stone wall (400 yds) with concealed entrance.

Herm

Seagull Campsite

983 Herm Island, Channel Islands GY1 3HR

This tiny site, and indeed the island of Herm, will appeal to those who are looking for complete tranquillity and calm. Reached by boat (20 minutes and approx. £6 return fare for adults, £3 for children) from Guernsey, the 500 acre island allows no cars only tractors on its narrow roads and paths (no bicycles either). One is free to stroll around the many paths, through farmland, heath and around the coast, where there are beautiful beaches. The campsite is a 20 minute uphill walk from the harbour, but your luggage will be transported for you by tractor. It consists of several terraced areas offering a total of 80 pitches, and 30 fully equipped tents for hire on flat grass areas. There are no electricity hook-ups. One may bring one's own tent and equipment or hire a tent and equipment (but not bedding, crockery and lighting) from the site. Herm is definitely not for those who like entertainment and plenty of facilities, but for total relaxation, with the absence of any bustle and noise it takes some beating!

Facilities: Small, modern, but open, toilet block on site. Hot showers (£1 payment - there is a shortage of water on Herm). Freezer for ice-packs. The harbour village is about ten minutes walk down the hill where there is a small shop for provisions, gas, a post office, pub, restaurants and café. Fishing on the island. No dogs or pets are allowed. Torches useful.

Charges 2001

Fixed site charge (irrespective of length of stay)	
incl. transportation of luggage	£6.00
Per adult	£4.60
child (under 14 yrs)	£2.30

Equipped tents for hire. Groups of single people not accepted. Tel: (01481) 722377. Fax: (01481) 700334. E-mail: camping@herm-island.com. Reservations: Made for any length with £20 deposit. Details of hire tents from above address. **Open** 14 May - first w/end in September.

Directions: Reached by boat from St Peter Port - report to Administration Office on arrival. Do not take your car as it is unlikely you will be able to park long term in St Peter Port.

Sark

Pomme de Chien Campsite

987 Sark, Channel Islands

'The island where time stands still' is an apt description of Sark, one of the smallest inhabited Channel Islands, some 45 minutes from Guernsey by boat. There is no airport, no cars or motorcycles and (apart from a tractor-drawn 'train' up Harbour Hill) the only transport is by bicycle or horse-drawn carriage. However everything you are likely to need for a tranquil holiday is provided with several small shops, pubs, hotels, restaurants, a Tourist Office and even two banks! Situated five minutes from the shops and ten from the beach, the Pomme de Chien campsite on Sark is tiny in terms of the number of pitches, totalling only 20, of which 8 are occupied by large, fully equipped frame tents (of excellent quality) for rent. The remainder are for campers with their own tents (no caravans, motorcaravans or trailer tents of course). The pitches themselves are large, on fairly level ground, but none have electricity hook-ups. There is a warm welcome from the owners Chris and Jill Rang with the famous charm of Sark. Baggage can be transferred from the harbour right to the site by tractor trailer, at a cost of 60p per item.

Facilities: A new sanitary block was added in 1999 with free hot showers (large, with bench and hook), toilets and washbasins. Dishwashing sinks are outside. Dogs are not accepted and torches are necessary. **Off site**: Fishing 10 mins. walk, bicycle hire 5 mins.

Charges 2001

Per adult	£4.50 - £5.00
child	£2.50 - £3.00

Fully equipped hire tents from £160 per week. No credit cards. Tel: (01481) 832316. Reservations: Write to site. **Open** all year - independent campers May - Sept. for hire tents.

Directions: Take the tractor drawn 'train' up Harbour Hill (60p; you can walk but it is a ten minute hike). Once at the top take road leading off left, then second right, and follow the lane to the site entrance. Reception is at house with white gates.

Open All Year

The following parks are understood to accept caravanners and campers all year round, although the list also includes some parks open for at least 10 months. These parks are marked with a star (✸) – please refer to the park's individual entry for details. It is always wise to phone the park to check as, for example, facilities available may be reduced.

ENGLAND

002 Cardinney ✸
006 River Valley ✸
018 Carnon Downs
037 Budemeadows
044 Dolbeare
071 Hidden Valley
080 Higher Longford
081 Riverside
091 Ross Park ✸
092 Finlake
135 Quantock Orchard
140 Isle of Avalon
142 Southfork
144 Baltic Wharf
145 Bath
148 Home Farm
150 Long Hazel ✸
151 Bath Chew Valley
152 Waterrow
167 Alderbury
170 C&C Club Devizes
177 Binghams Farm
181 Newlands
202 Ulwell Cottage ✸
203 Wareham Forest
208 Merley Court ✸
227 Oakdene ✸
228 Lytton Lawn ✸
229 Sandy Balls
236 Hill Cottage Farm ✸
245 The Orchards ✸
249 Kite Hill Farm
260 Barnstones
262 Wysdom
275 Highclere Farm ✸
281 C&C Club Chertsey
289 White Rose ✸
293 Sheepcote Valley
294 Honeybridge
295 Washington
303 Tanner Farm
304 Broadhembury
305 Pine Lodge
307 C&C Club Canterbury
309 Black Horse Farm
326 Abbey Wood
327 Crystal Palace
330 The Grange ✸
331 Low House
340 Old Brick Kilns ✸
342 Two Mills ✸

347 Breckland Meadows ✸
355 Old Manor
358 Ferry Meadows
369 Bainland
373 Skegness Sands
376 Tallington Lakes ✸
385 Rivendale ✸
390 Bosworth Water Trust
392 Riverside
394 Smeaton's Lakes
407 Somers Wood
413 Moreton-in-Marsh
414 C&C Club Winchcombe ✸
421 Lickhill Manor
430 Poston Mill
439 Westbrook Park
440 Stanmore Hall
441 Beaconsfield Farm
442 Severn Gorge
443 Oxon Hall
454 St Helens in the Park ✸
474 Jasmine Park ✸
528 Abbey Farm
529 Royal Umpire
535 Holgates ✸
536 Willowbank ✸
556 Sykeside
557 Wild Rose
574 White Water
576 Percy Wood ✸
580 Ord House

WALES

593 Cwmcarn Forest
595 Afon Lodge ✸
604 Pencelli Castle
606 Tredegar House
633 Daisy Bank
637 Hendre Mynach ✸
659 Beddgelert ✸
660 Bryn Gloch
668 James'

SCOTLAND

692 Cressfield
693 Park of Brandedleys
695 Brighouse Bay
697 The Monks' Muir
702 Aird Donald
703 Gibson Park
705 Edinburgh
724 Lomond Woods
727 Auchterarder
768 Glenmore ✸
785 Linnhe Lochside ✸

NORTHERN IRELAND

842 Tollymore Forest
843 Banbridge
850 LoanEden
856 Gortin Glen

IRISH REPUBLIC

870 Gateway ✸
874 Cong
908 Forest Farm
910 Camac Valley
911 Shankhill ✸
916 Moat Farm
938 Parsons Green
948 Blarney
961 Mannix Point

CHANNEL ISLANDS

987 Pomme de Chien

No Dogs!

For the benefit of those who want to take their dogs with them and for those who do not like dogs on the parks they visit, we list here the parks which have indicated to us that they do not accept dogs. If you are planning to take your dog we do, however, advise that you phone the park first to check - there may be limits on numbers, breeds, etc. or times of the year when they are excluded.

NEVER - these parks do not accept dogs at any time:

020	Newquay	410	Cotswold Hoburne	889	Tain
025	Pentewan Sands	453	Northcliffe	906	Green Gables
087	Beverley Park	555	Limefitt Park	941	The Apple
138	Blue Anchor	598	Moreton Farm	950	The Meadow
149	Greenacres	604	Pencelli Castle	951	Eagle Point
213	Grove Farm	635	Barcdy	952	Barleycove
230	Ashurst	704	Slatebarns	971	Rozel
305	Pine Lodge	782	Oban Divers	977	Vaugrat
306	Yew Tree	860	Bellemont	983	Seagull Campsite
312	Gate House Wood	877	Parkland	987	Pomme de Chien
327	Crystal Palace	882	Hodson Bay		

SOMETIMES - these parks do not accept dogs at certain times of the year:

072	Easewell	not high season	452	Flower of May	not July/Aug.
085	Galmpton	not July/Aug.	629	Glan-y-Mor	not 14/7-31/8
208	Merley Court	not 14/7-31/8	910	Camac Valley	not July/Aug.
210	Sandford Park	only after 2/9	915	River Valley	not July/Aug.
211	Pear Tree	not July/Aug.	961	Mannix Point	not July/Aug.

MAYBE - accepted at any time but with certain restrictions:

001	Chacewater	not all breeds	397	Glencote	max. 2
003	Ayr	max.1	420	The Boyce	max. 2; not all breeds
015	Sea View	not all breeds	440	Stanmore Hall	max. 2
048	Boscrege	max. 3	441	Beaconsfield	max. 2
049	Mullion	max. 1	442	Severn Gorge	max. 2
069	Stowford	max. 2	452	Flower of May	by arrangement
071	Hidden Valley	max. 2	463	Ripley	max. 2
072	Easewell	max. 1	464	Goose Wood	max. 2
085	Galmpton	max. 2	470	Nostell Priory	max. 2
090	Widdecombe	not all breeds	476	Riverside	by arrangement
093	Ashburton	not all breeds	530	Kneps Farm	max. 2
095	River Dart	max. 2	535	Holgates	not all breeds
102	Oakdown	not all breeds	554	Falbarrow	max. 1
141	Broadway	not all breeds	557	Wild Rose	not all breeds
154	Batcombe	max. 1, not all breeds	571	Doe Park	by arrangement
181	Newlands	max. 2	575	Waren	by arrangement
204	Manor Farm	owner's discretion	576	Percy Wood	not all breeds
210	Sandford Park	max. 1	580	Ord House	by arrangement
225	Bashley Park	max. 1	593	Cwmcarn	by arrangement
228	Lytton Lawn	max. 1	597	Noble Court	max. 1
247	Southland	by arrangement	628	Aeron Coast	max. 1 per unit
257	Lincoln Farm	max. 2	636	Pen-y-Garth	by arrangement
290	Horam Manor	max. 2	664	Home Fram	max. 2
304	Broadhembury	max. 2	665	Hunters Hamlet	max. 2
311	Quex	over 2 by arrangement	693	Brandedleys	max. 2
330	The Grange	max. 2; not all breeds	699	Moretonhall	by arrangement
342	Two Mills	max. 2; not all breeds	730	Blair Castle	max. 2
343	Kelling Heath	max. 2	731	Twenty Shilling	max. 2
351	Liffens	max. 1	764	Dunroamin	max. 2
355	Old Manor	max. 2	769	Torvean	max. 1
367	Lakeside	max. 2	770	Pitgrudy	max. 2
370	Pilgrims Way	by arrangement	785	Linnhe	max 2
376	Tallington	max. 2	963	White Villa	max. 2; not all breeds
396	Silvertrees	not all breeds			

Fishing

We are pleased to include details of parks which provide facilities for fishing on the site. Many other parks, particularly in Scotland and Ireland, are in popular fishing areas and have facilities within easy reach. Where we have been given details, we have included this information in the individual site reports. It is always best to contact individual parks to check that they provide for your individual requirements.

ENGLAND

006	River Valley
017	Trevella
022	Trevornick
025	Pentewan Sands
038	Wooda Farm
075	Minnows
077	Clifford Bridge
079	Harford Bridge
081	Riverside
092	Finlake
095	River Dart
097	Cofton
106	Yeatheridge Farm
109	Peppermint Park
137	Burrowhayes Farm
138	Blue Anchor
139	Old Oaks
142	Southfork
145	Bath
148	Home Farm
174	Golden Cap
176	Wood Farm
178	Freshwater
201	Sandyholme
213	Grove Farm
229	Sandy Balls
236	Hill Cottage Farm
245	The Orchards
261	Bo Peep
269	Wellington
281	Chertsey
282	Horsley
290	Horam Mano
292	Bay View
303	Tanner Farm
321	Lee Valley
340	Old Brick Kilns
343	Kelling Heath
344	Gatton Waters
348	Little Lakeland
367	Lakeside
375	Foreman's Bridge
390	Bosworth Water Trust
392	Riverside
394	Smeaton's Lakes
397	Glencote
410	Cotswold Hoburne
419	Kingsgreen
420	The Boyce
421	Lickhill Manor
430	Poston Mill
431	Luck's All
432	Broadmeadow
433	The Millpond
438	Fernwood
439	Westbrook
441	Beaconsfield Farm
451	Thorpe Hall
461	Moorside
464	Goose Wood
466	Woodhouse Farm
470	Nostell Priory
472	Knight Stainforth Hall
473	Far Grange
528	Abbey Farm
529	Royal Umpire
554	Fallbarrow
555	Limefitt
560	Pennine View
571	Doe Park

WALES

592	The Bridge
593	Cwmcarn
597	Noble Court
659	Beddgelert
660	Bryn Gloch
667	The Plassey

SCOTLAND

691	Hoddom Castle
695	Brighouse Bay
700	Strathclyde
726	Ardgartan
727	Auchterarder
766	Spindrift
771	Ardmair Point
772	Woodend
780	Resipole Farm
784	North Ledaig
785	Linnhe
786	Glendaruel

NORTHERN IRELAND

831	Carnfunnock
834	Drumaheglis
850	LoanEden
852	Share

IRISH REPUBLIC

877	Parkland
896	Lough Ree
930	Morriscastle Strand
938	Parsons Green
951	Eagle Point
956	Wave Crest
962	White Bridge
963	White Villa Farm

Bicycle Hire

We understand that the following parks have bicycles to hire on site or can arrange for bicycles to be delivered. However, we would recommend that you contact the park to check as the situation can change.

ENGLAND

011	Calloose
014	Penrose Farm
015	Sea View
022	Trevornick
025	Pentewan Sands
026	Penhaven
033	Killigarth Manor
036	Lakefield
049	Mullion
069	Stowford Farm
104	Old Cotmore Farm
135	Quantock Orchard
139	Old Oaks
140	Isle of Avalon
141	Broadway House
149	Greenacres
178	Freshwater Beach
205	Rowlands Wait
210	Sandford Park
213	Grove Farm Meadow
225	Bashley Park
227	Oakdene
229	Sandy Balls
235	Red Shoot
258	Cotswold View
340	Old Brick Kilns
351	Liffens
356	Highfield Farm
375	Foreman's Bridge
380	Highfields
430	Poston Mill
456	Golden Square
466	Woodhouse Farm
471	Rudding
472	Knight Stainforth Hall
555	Limefitt
557	Wild Rose
580	Ord House
581	Fallowfield Dene

WALES

604	Pencelli Castle

SCOTLAND

695	Brighouse Bay
696	Crossburn
697	Monks Muir
691	Hoddom Castle
700	Strathclyde
723	Trossachs
724	Lomond Woods
774	Loch Grehornish
786	Glendaruel

NORTHERN IRELAND

852	Share

IRISH REPUBLIC

874	Cong
875	Belleek
913	Roundwood
923	Nore Valley
924	Tree Grove
959	Fossa
960	Glenross
962	Flemings White Bridge
963	White Villa Farm

CHANNEL ISLANDS

971	Rozel
972	Beuvelande
977	Vaugrat
978	Fauxquets Valley

Photo: Jersey Tourism

Golf

We understand that the following parks have facilities for playing golf on site. Where facilities are within easy reach and we have been given details, we have included this information in the individual site reports. However, we recommend that you contact the park to check that the facility meets your requirements.

022	Trevornick		452	Flower of May
038	Wooda Farm		471	Rudding
069	Stowford Farm		667	The Plassey
072	Easewell Farm		691	Hoddom Castle
101	Lady's Mile		695	Brighouse Bay
107	Woolacombe Bay		769	Torvean
175	Highlands End		780	Resipole Farm
225	Bashley Park		831	Carnfunnock
367	Lakeside Park		877	Parkland
369	Bainland		915	River Valley
407	Somers Wood		948	Blarney
430	Poston Mill			

Horse Riding

We understand that the following parks have horse riding stables on site. Where facilities are within easy reach and we have been given details, we have included this information in the individual site reports. However, we would recommend that you contact the park to check that the facility meets your requirements.

036	Lakefield		262	Wysdom
038	Wooda Farm		290	Horam Manor
069	Stowford Farm		295	Washington
092	Finlake		695	Brighouse Bay
106	Yeatheridge Farm		730	Blair Castle
137	Burrowhayes Farm		850	LoanEden
178	Freshwater Beach		916	Moat Farm
229	Sandy Balls			

Boat Launching

We understand that the following parks have boat slipways on site. Where facilities are within easy reach and we have been given details, we have included this information in the individual site reports. However, we would recommend that you contact the park to check that the facility meets your requirements.

025	Pentewan Sands		784	North Ledaig
175	Highlands End		785	Linnhe
269	Wellington		831	Carnfunnock
390	Bosworth		834	Drumaheglis
421	Lickhill Manor		850	LoanEden
554	Fallbarrow		852	Share
695	Brighouse Bay		877	Parkland
700	Strathclyde		896	Lough Ree
726	Ardgartan		951	Eagle Point
771	Ardmair Point		956	Wave Crest
780	Resipole Farm		961	Mannix Point

Adults Only

The following parks have made the decision not to accept children.

001	Chacewater (30 yrs+)	345	Little Haven (14 yrs+)
139	The Old Oaks (18 yrs+)	407	Somers Wood
151	Bath Chew Valley	441	Beaconsfield Farm (25 yrs+)
152	Waterrow (18 yrs+)	461	Moorside (16 yrs+)
168	Plough Lane	551	The Larches
177	Binghams Farm	565	The Ashes
342	Two Mills	633	Daisy Bank
344	Gatton Waters (18 yrs+)		

The following parks also do not accept children at certain times or in certain areas of their site:

380 Highfields Camping and Caravan Park - in one area only
438 Fernwood Caravan Park - in one area only
440 Stanmore Hall Touring Park (21 yrs) - 31 grass pitches only
479 Bronte Caravan Park - in certain areas
443 Oxon Hall Touring Park   - in one area only

Naturist Parks

We feature just one naturist site in this guide: 024 Southleigh Manor Naturist Club. 029 Carlyon Bay provides a separate area for naturist campers.

This is a Life Saver

According to police sources about three quarters of all fatal motorway accidents involve a tyre failure. Of course some of them are clearly identifiable incidents where a blown tyre causes an accident. Some are slightly more complex like when a motorist stops to change a tyre and is hit by a passing vehicle.

The problem isn't actually tyres going bang. That only happened in the days when we all used inner tubes. With modern radial ply tyres they are more likely to lose a little pressure over a period of time. If you hear a bang it's more likely that the tyre has been running soft for some time, and what you just heard was the tyre parting company with the wheel.

Over the generations lots of solutions to punctured tyres have appeared - and just as soon disappeared. Of course there are puncture sealants, but they aren't the answer either. The problem isn't punctures, its not knowing that you've got a puncture until it is too late.

Recently our caravan journalist friends have been trying to persuade us to look at a product called Tyron Wheel Safety Bands, so in 2001 at the NEC caravan show, we spent some time on the Tyron stand finding out what it was all about - and we're convinced to the extent that I'm now fitting them to my historic rally car's wheels for the Rallye Monte Carlo next January! Tyron is a simple device which fits inside the wheel. You still use your ordinary wheels and tyres and if you swap your caravan or motor caravan you can probably swap the Tyron bands to your new purchase.

All Tyron does is prevent the tyre coming off the wheel. That means you won't loose control of your vehicle and you can keep driving until you can find somewhere safe to change the wheel. The German TUV organisation approve Tyron as a high-speed run-flat device. Tyron is already used on police cars, ambulances, fire engines, military vehicles, trucks carrying dangerous loads and ... well the list is endless.

This is an editorial piece, not an advert. So we aren't begging you to go out and fit Tyron. What we are asking you to do is do your own research. When you have we think you'll be as convinced as we are to fit Tyron as well.

www.insure4europe.com

Taking your own tent, caravan or motorhome abroad?

Looking for the best cover at the best rates?

Our prices considerably undercut most high street prices and the 'in-house insurance' of many tour operators whilst offering equivalent (or higher) levels of cover.

Our annual multi-trip policies offer superb value, covering you not only for your european camping holiday but also subsequent trips abroad for the next 12 months.

Total Peace of Mind

To give you total peace of mind during your holiday our insurance policies have been specifically tailored to cover most potential eventualities on a self-drive camping holiday. Each is organised through Voyager Insurance Services Ltd who specialize in travel insurance for Europe and for camping in particular. All policies are underwritten by UK Insurance, part of the Green Flag Group.

24 Hour Assistance

Our personal insurance provides access to the services of International Medical Rescue (IMR), one of the UK's largest assistance companies. Experienced multi-lingual personnel provide a caring and efficient service 24 hours a day.

European vehicle assistance cover is provided by Green Flag who provide assistance to over 3 million people each year. With a Europe-wide network of over 7,500 garages and agents you know you're in very safe hands.

Both IMR and green flag are very used to looking after the needs of campsite-based holidaymakers and are very familiar with the location of most European campsites, with contacts at garages, doctors and hospitals nearby.

Save with an Annual policy

If you are likely to make more than one trip to Europe over the next 12 months then our annual multi-trip policies could save you a fortune. Personal cover for a couple starts at just £85 and the whole family can be covered for just £105.
Cover for up to 17 days wintersports participation is included.

Low Cost Annual multi-trip insurance

Premier Annual Europe self-drive
including 17 days wintersports

£85 per couple

Premier Annual Europe self-drive
including 17 days wintersports

£105 per family

Low Cost Combined Personal and Vehicle Assistance Insurance

Premier Family Package
10 days cover for vehicle, 2 adults plus dependent children under 16.

£68*

Premier Couples Package
10 days cover for vehicle and 2 adults

£55*

* Motorhomes, cars towing trailers and caravans, all vehicles over 4 years old and holidays longer than 10 days attract supplements – ask us for details. See leaflet for full terms and conditions.

Gerry and Chris Bullock's Page

Who are they and why give them a page?

Gerry and Chris are both disabled. Chris has been a wheelchair user for many years and Gerry has, as he puts it, a bionic leg and wrist! (He says "I use Chris's wheelchair as my zimmer frame".)

For many years they have been involved with all aspects of camping and motor caravanning for the disabled with various publications, and were the original authors of the MMM Mobility Guide. They also assist people such as the National Trust regarding access difficulties and problems that arise and have been known to visit cities around the country and assist the local tourist boards regarding access reports. They have over the years become 'experts' in finding parks/sites that also offer good facilities for the wheelchair users that are truly useable. This has been very helpful for disabled campers and also for site owners with whom they share their findings. They have also looked very carefully at the Disabled Discrimination Act, which comes into force in 2004 and have tried (as with most acts, quite a minefield) to note any points that may be of relevance to site owners and of which they should be aware.

Here are some of the things they look for when inspecting sites:

Access to the facilities block.
Are there special facilities either for wheelchair users or walking disabled?
What facilities are on offer?
En-suite or separate or just a W.C.?
What does the room offer and is it suitable?
The shower and its access for the user?
Handrails - are they adequate?
Sink - its height and the type of taps?
Height of mirrors and other accessories?
Is there an emergency cord?

They also look at the site from the wheelchair user's (non powered) point of view.

Kerbs and paths
Roads and their surfaces
Grass and the general condition of the pitches
Access to other areas

Of course they look at all parks with the attitude that you cannot expect a small (say 20 to 30 pitch, private park) to offer the same quality or range of equipment as a large commercial or club owned site. They recommend that disabled campers join one of the larger clubs, as their disabled rooms are usually of a very high standard. They try to make disabled campers aware of one point - that they must remember that "camping is still sleeping in a field", whether you are in a tent, a caravan or a motorhome; that you will not find the same facilities as you may find in your converted home, it will not be all concrete and tarmac, with all rooms and areas accessible. These are things that may only be found in a specialist hotel and if essential, that should be the type of holiday you should look at.

What they try to do is offer a list of sites that have been inspected and that readers can rely on. Please note: To ensure suitable pitching when you visit a campsite chosen as most suitable for its facilities for disabled visitors, we would advise booking. Giving information of your requirements to the site means that they can place you as best as possible (but please be patient as it is hard to please everyone no matter how hard they try).

If readers require any further information, or have any suggestions, or any site owners need any assistance, Gerry and Chris would like to hear from you. Their address is:

97 Stalham Road, Hoveton, Norwich, Norfolk NR12 8EF Telephone: 01603 784152

NOTE. They advise that they are not looking at facilities for persons with special needs. They leave this to the such people as the Sue Ryder Foundation, etc. which cater very well in this field.

Following visits this year, Chris and Gerry have made the following comments:

ENGLAND

206 Wilksworth Farm Caravan Park

Excellent en-suite disabled room, roadways tarmac, speed humps, advance booking for disabled pitch, slightly hilly site, level pitches, access to coffeeshop, very helpful staff.

229 Sandy Balls Holiday Park

Excellent en-suite disabled room; radar key; access to most areas; level site; hard standings; disabled friendly site; speed humps.

303 Tanner Farm Touring Park

Two disabled units- one with shower, one with bath; roadways tarmac; level site; level pitches; hardstandings; key from reception; pre-booking.

305 Pine Lodge Touring Park

Excellent en-suite disabled room - sliding door; roadways tarmac; pitches level; hardstandings; pre-booking; some parts of site hilly.

384 Lime Tree Park

Large en-suite disabled room; tarmac roadways; steep hill onto and off touring site; level pitches.

385 Rivendale

Superb en-suite disabled room; slight ramp; roadways hardcore (advised assistance); level pitches; hard standings; access to other areas; assistance offered to café users (upstairs); hill up to site from reception.

577 Dunstan Hill C&C Club Site

Excellent en-suite disabled room (emergency cords); roadways hardcore; level site; hardstandings; level pitches; pre-booking.

SCOTLAND

691 Hoddom Castle Caravan Park

One of the most spacious en-suite disabled rooms seen; roadways tarmac; some level pitches; hardstandings; some hilly parts on site; access shop, reception, games room; speed humps; key from reception; pre-booking.

699 Mortonhall Caravan Park

Spacious en-suite disabled room; roadways tarmac; level pitches; slight ramp; disabled w.c. at reception; access to shop/reception; booking essential.

704 Slatebarns Caravan Park

Excellent en-suite disabled room; slight ramp; roadways hardcore; hardstandings; some hilly parts on site; access to reception; key from reception; pre booking.

724 Lomond Woods Holiday Park

Good en-suite disabled room; hard standings; roadways tarmac; speed humps; slight ramp; key from reception; pre booking.

726 Ardgartan Caravan and Camping Site

Good en-suite disabled room; roadways tarmac and hardcore; slight ramp; hardstandings; some parts of site hill; access to reception; pre-booking.

732 Witches Craig Caravan Park

Good en-suite disabled room; tarmac roadways; level site; level pitches; hardstandings; speed humps; key from reception.

781 C&C Club Site Oban

Excellent en-suite disabled room; emergency cord; roadways hardcore; slight ramp; level site ; hardstandings; level pitches; key from reception; pre-booking.

IRELAND

905 Green Gables Caravan Park

Good en-suite disabled room; concrete paths; roadways hardcore; hard standings; level pitches; access all areas including café and reception.

915 River Valley Caravan Park

Excellent en-suite disabled room; all roadways and paths tarmac; all pitches level; hardstandings; disabled friendly site.

930 Morriscastle Strand

Good disabled room; site sloping; roadways tarmac; advise assistance on site with wheelchair.

Chris and Gerry have visited the following parks in preious years. Please contact them if you are interested in their coments:

011 Calloose Caravan Park
016 Newperran Tourist Park
018 Carnon Downs Caravan Park
021 Hendra Holiday Park
075 Minnows Camping and Caravan Park
088 Dornafield
091 Ross Park
144 Baltic Wharf Caravan Club Site
145 Bath Marina and Caravan Park
203 Wareham Forest Tourist Park
258 Cotswold View Caravan Site
293 Sheepcote Valley Caravan Club Site
327 Crystal Palace Caravan Club Site
325 Lee Valley Campsite

330 The Grange Country Park
339 Dower House Touring Park
340 The Old Brick Kilns
343 Kelling Heath Holiday Park
347 Breckland Meadows
348 Little Lakeland Caravan Park
350 Woodhill Park
355 Old Manor Touring Park
358 Ferry Meadows Caravan Club Site
365 Cherry Tree Site
373 Skegness Sands Touring Site
404 C&C Club Site Clent Hills
411 Tewksbury Caravan Club Site
442 Seven Gorge Caravan Park

The MOTOR Caravanners' CLUB

™

From the moment you join the club
YOU ENJOY ALL THESE PRIVILEGES AND SERVICES

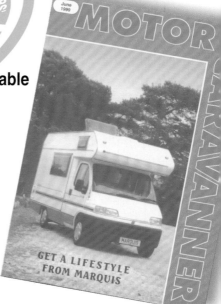

- Monthly Magazine
- UK. & European Touring Service
- UK. Sites Guide
- Discounted Insurance Rates available
- Breakdown Recovery Service
- Camping Card (CCI) International
- "Snail" Know-How Booklets
- Discounted rates for Cross Channel Ferries and Overseas Travel Insurance
- Year round Social Events, Weekend Meets and Holiday Rallies

GET A LIFESTYLE FROM MARQUIS

It's a great club for enjoyment, interest, making friends, help and advice, weekend meets for you and all the family.

For membership details write:
THE MOTOR CARAVANNERS' CLUB LTD. FREEPOST (1292) TWICKENHAM, TW2 5BR TEL: 0181 893 3883 (OFFICE HOURS)
E-mail: motorcaravanners@msn.com

Club
THE ROAD TO ENJOYMENT

F.I.C.

If you're interested in the

ALAN ROGERS' GOOD CAMPS GUIDE

you'll probably be interested in

THE GOOD MAGAZINE GUIDE

ON SALE
the first
Thursday of
the month

ON SALE
the second
Thursday of
the month

For tests and touring features 12 months of the year choose Britain's premier caravan and motorhome magazines.

On sale at most good newsagents or by subscription - telephone

01778 391134

ON SALE
the fourth
Thursday of
the month

Reports by Readers

We always welcome reports from readers concerning parks which they have visited. Generally reports provide us with invaluable feedback on parks already featured in the Guide or, in the case of those not featured in our Guide, they provide information which we can follow up with a view to adding them in future editions.

However, if you have a complaint about a site, this should be addressed to the campsite owner, preferably in person before you leave.

Please make your comments either on this form or on plain paper. It would be appreciated if you would indicate the approximate dates when you visited the park and, in the case of potential new parks, provide the correct name and address and, if possible, include a park brochure. Send your reports to:

Alan Rogers' Guides, Manor Garden, Burton Bradstock, Bridport DT6 4QA

Name of Park and Ref. No. (or address for new recommendations):

. . . .

. . . .

Dates of Visit: . . . .

Comments:

Reader's Name and Address: . . . .

. . . .

. . . .

. . . .

APPLE MOTORHOME HIRE LTD

97 St Ronans Road, Southsea, Portsmouth, Hants, PO4 0PR United Kingdom
Tel: 023 9235 3071 Fax: 023 9235 3071
e-mail: hire@apple-motorhome.co.uk website: www.apple-motorhome.co.uk

APPLE MOTORHOME HIRE

THE SOUTH'S ONLY SUPPLIER OF BENIMAR MOTORHOMES

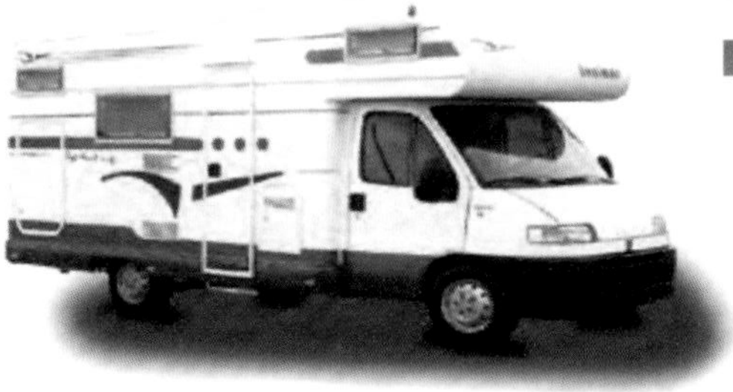

Choice of right / left hand drive

European breakdown cover

Comprehensive insurance

Unlimited mileage

All models supplied by Apple Motorhome Hire include as standard – 2.8 Turbo Diesel engine, PAS, central heating, double-glazing, blinds, screens and curtains, shower compartment, 90 litre 3-way fridge, water heater, 125 litre fresh water capacity, Thetford cassette with electric flush, electric step, rear corner steadies, roof rack and ladder.

TRY BEFORE YOU BUY

One week money-back test hire if you subsequently decide to buy a brand new Benimar motorhome from us within three months, (ask for details)

COLLECTION and DELIVERY

Collect your motorhome from our offices in Portsmouth or, alternatively, let us deliver to a destination of your choice, (a small charge may be applied for delivery outside of a 50 mile radius of Portsmouth).

P&O PORTSMOUTH

A FULL COLOUR BROCHURE AND PRICE LIST AVAILABLE ON REQUEST

Also available from RDH Motorhome Hire, Nottingham Tel: (0870) 752727 (Sales) 7585050 (Hire) 7583030 (Fax)
e-mail: motorhomes@rdh.co.uk website: www.rdh.co.uk

Thinking about a towbar?

Think Witter and you'll be in good company. With over 5 million sold, Witter are undoubtedly Britain's most popular towbar. Why? Because Witter towbars come with the additional security of the Shield of Safety that guarantees the bar for the life of the vehicle and not simply its warranty period.

The Witter Shield of Safety also symbolises a tradition of excellence started over 50 years ago. It continues today through investment in design, manufacture and quality standards. It brings you towbars made in the UK with an unrivalled reputation for strength, quality and reliability.

Look for the Witter sign at over 250 specialists throughout the UK where your towbar will be fitted with expertise and care.

The right direction

WITTER
TOWBAR SYSTEMS

See Yellow Pages for your nearest dealer or contact us at: Witter Towbars, Chester CH1 3LL. Tel: (01244) 284500 Fax: (01244) 284577 www.witter-towbars.co.uk

South West England and the New Forest

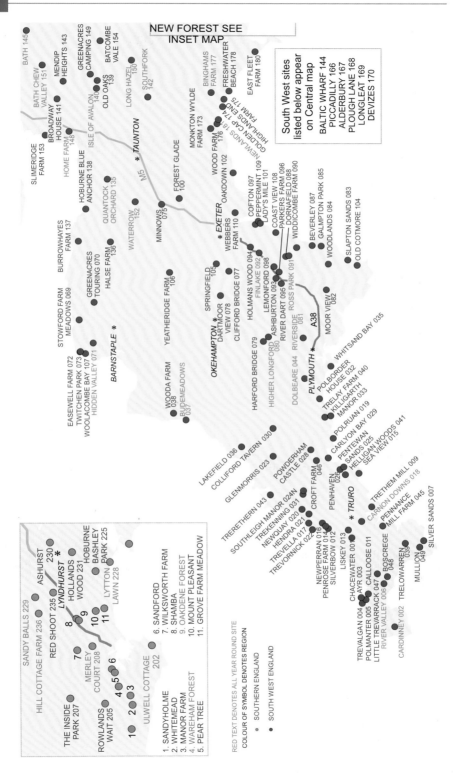

NEW FOREST SEE INSET MAP

South West sites listed below appear on Central map
BALTIC WHARF 144
PICCADILLY 166
ALDERBURY 167
PLOUGH LANE 168
LONGLEAT 169
DEVIZES 170

BATH 145
BATH CHEW VALLEY 151
MENDIP HEIGHTS 143
GREENACRES CAMPING 149
BATCOMBE VALE 154
SOUTHFORK 142
BROADWAY HOUSE 141
HOME FARM 148
OLD OAKS 139
LONG HAZEL 150
BINGHAMS FARM 177
FRESHWATER 178
EAST FLEET BEACH 178
SLIMERIDGE FARM 153
ISLE OF AVALON 140
* TAUNTON
MONKTON WYLDE FARM 173
NEWLANDS GOLDEN CAP 174
HIGHLANDS FARM 175
HOBURNE BLUE ANCHOR 138
QUANTOCK ORCHARD 135
WATERROW 152
M5
FOREST GLADE 100
WOOD FARM 176
MINNOWS 075
COFTON 097
PEPPERMINT 109
LADY'S MILE 101
* EXETER OAKDOWN 102
WEBBERS FARM 110
BEVERLEY 087
GALMPTON PARK 085
WOODLANDS 084
SLAPTON SANDS 083
OLD COTMORE 104
BURROWHAYES FARM 137
STOWFORD FARM MEADOWS 069
GREENACRES TOURING 070
HALSE FARM 136
YEATHERIDGE FARM 106
SPRINGFIELD 105
COAST VIEW 108
PARKERS FARM 096
DORNAFIELD 088
WIDDICOMBE FARM 090
BARNSTAPLE *
EASEWELL FARM 072
TWITCHEN PARK 073
WOOLACOMBE BAY 107
HIDDEN VALLEY 071
WOODA FARM 038
BUDEMEADOWS 037
OKEHAMPTON *
DARTMOOR VIEW 078
CLIFFORD BRIDGE 077
FINLAKE 092
HOLMANS WOOD 094
LEMONFORD 098
RIVER DART 095
ASHBURTON 093
RIVERSIDE 081
ROSS PARK 091
A38
MOOR VIEW 082
HARFORD BRIDGE 079
HIGHER LONGFORD 080
DOLBEARE 044
PLYMOUTH *
WHITSAND BAY 035
LAKEFIELD 036
COLLIFORD TAVERN 030
GLENMORRIS 023
POWDERHAM CASTLE 028
CROFT FARM 046
POLBORDER HOUSE 032
TRELAY FARM 040
KILLIGARTH MANOR 033
POLRUAN 019
CARLYON BAY 029
PENTEWAN SANDS 025
HELLIGAN WOODS 041
SEA VIEW 015
TRERETHEN 043
SOUTHLEIGH MANOR 024N
TREKENNING 031
NEWQUAY 020
HENDRA 021
TREVELLA 017
TREVORNICK 022
NEWPERRAN 016
PENROSE FARM 014
SILVERBOW 012
LISKEY 013
CHACEWATER 00
AYR 003
CALLOOSE 011
PENHAVEN 02
* TRURO
TRETHEM MILL 009
CARNON DOWNS 018
PENNANCE MILL FARM 045
TREVALGAN 004
POLMANTER 005
LITTLE TREVARRACK 047
RIVER VALLEY 006
CARDINNEY 002
BOSCREGE 048
TRELOWARREN 039
MULLION 049
SILVER SANDS 007

RED TEXT DENOTES ALL YEAR ROUND SITE
COLOUR OF SYMBOL DENOTES REGION
● SOUTHERN ENGLAND
● SOUTH WEST ENGLAND

SANDY BALLS 229
HILL COTTAGE FARM 236
RED SHOOT 235
ASHURST 230
LYNDHURST *
HOLLANDS WOOD 231
HOBURNE BASHLEY 225
LYTTON 7 LAWN 228
MERLEY COURT 208
ROWLANDS WAIT 205
THE INSIDE PARK 207
ULWELL COTTAGE 202

1. SANDYHOLME
2. WHITEMEAD
3. MANOR FARM
4. WAREHAM FOREST
5. PEAR TREE
6. SANDFORD
7. WILKSWORTH FARM
8. SHAMBA
9. OAKDENE FOREST
10. MOUNT PLEASANT
11. GROVE FARM MEADOW

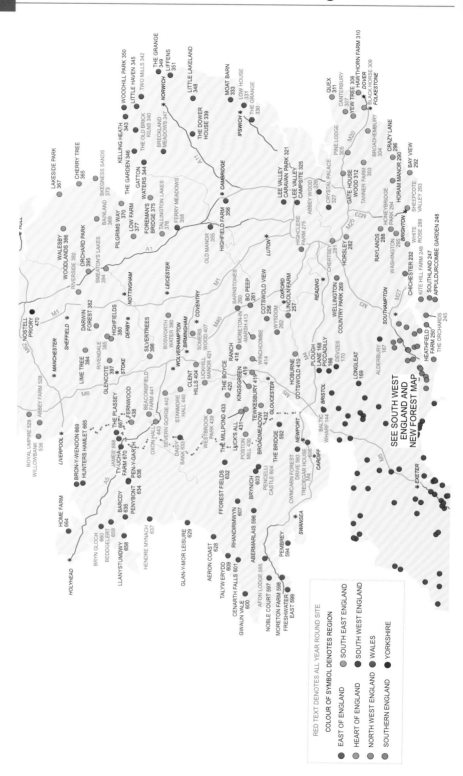

THE GRANGE 349
LIFFENS 351
WOODHILL PARK 350
LITTLE HAVEN 345
TWO MILLS 342
KELLING HEATH 343
THE OLD BRICK KILNS 340
THE GARDEN 346
GATTON WATERS 344
NORWICH
LITTLE LAKELAND 348
THE DOWER HOUSE 339
BRECKLAND MEADOWS 347
LOW HOUSE 330
MOAT BARN 333
THE GRANGE 330
IPSWICH
LAKESIDE PARK 367
CHERRY TREE 365
SKEGNESS SANDS 373
BAINLAND 369
WALESBY WOODLANDS 366
RIVERSIDE 392
ORCHARD PARK 395
SMEATON'S LAKES
PILGRIMS WAY 370
LOW FARM 377
FOREMANS WATERS 344
FERRY MEADOWS 358
TALLINGTON LAKES
CAMBRIDGE
HIGHFIELD FARM 356
LEE VALLEY CARAVAN PARK 321
LEE VALLEY CAMPSITE 325
ABBEY WOOD
HIGHCLERE FARM 275
QUEX 311
CANTERBURY 307
YEW TREE 306
HAWTHORN FARM 310
DOVER
BLACK HORSE 309
FOLKESTONE
PINE LODGE 305
BROADHEMBURY 304
HONEYBRIDGE 288
BAY VIEW 292
CRAZY LANE 296
HORAM MANOR 290
SHEEPCOTE VALLEY 293
CRYSTAL PALACE 327
CHERTSEY 281
GATE HOUSE WOOD 312
TANNER FARM 303
HORSLEY 282
M23
M20
M25
M26
M2
RAYLANDS 288
WASHINGTON 295
BRIGHTON 295
WHITE ROSE 289
CHICHESTER 232
SOUTHLAND 247
APPULDURCOMBE GARDEN 248
A11
A14
A1
A1
OLD MANOR 355
LUTON*
READING
WELLINGTON COUNTRY PARK 269
M1
M40
BARNSTONES 260
HIGH ASH 413
BO PEEP 261
OXFORD 259
LINCOLN FARM 257
COTSWOLD VIEW 258
WYSDOM 262
COVENTRY
SOMERS 421
LICKHILL WOOD 407
MORETON-IN-MARSH 413
WINCHCOMBE 414
HOBURNE COTSWOLD 410
PLOUGH LANE 168
PICCADILLY 166
DEVIZES 170
LONGLEAT 169
WELLINGTON 247
ALDERBURY 167
HEATHFIELD FARM 250
KITE HILL FARM 249
THE ORCHARDS 245
M4
M27
SOUTHAMPTON
SEE SOUTH WEST ENGLAND AND NEW FOREST MAP
ROYAL UMPIRE 528
WILLOWBANK 536
ABBEY FARM 528
NOSTELL PRIORY 470
LIVERPOOL*
MANCHESTER
SHEFFIELD
DARWIN FOREST 382
HIGHFIELDS 380
DERBY
RIVENDALE 385
LIME TREE 384
GLENCOTE 397
STOKE
SILVERTREES 398
NOTTINGHAM
LEICESTER
M1
M6
BOSWORTH WATER 390
BIRMINGHAM
BEACONSFIELD FARM 441
FERNWOOD 438
THE PLASSEY 667
SEVERN GORGE 442
STANMORE HALL 440
CLENT HILLS 404
THE BOYCE 420
KINGSGREEN 419
RANCH 418
TEWKESBURY 419
BROADMEADOW 432
GLOUCESTER
WESTBROOK PARK 439
THE MILLPOND 433
LUCKS ALL 431
POSTON MILL 430
OXON HALL 443
DAISY BANK 633
BRON-Y-WENDON 669
HUNTERS HAMLET 665
JAMES' 668
TY-UCHA FARM 670
PEN-Y-GARTH 636
PENYBONT 634
BARCDY 635
FERNWOOD
HOME FARM 664
BRYN GLOCH 660
BEDDGELERT 659
LLANYSTUMDWY 658
HENDRE MYNACH 637
HOLYHEAD*
AERON COAST 628
GLAN-Y-MOR LEISURE 629
THE ERYDD 609
CENARTH FALLS 601
RHANDIRMWYN 607
ABERMARLAIS 596
TALYWERYDD 600
GWAUN VALE
BRYNICH 603
PENCELLI CASTLE 604
THE BRIDGE 592
TREDEGAR HOUSE 606
NEWPORT
CWMCARN FOREST DRIVE 744
BALTIC WHARF 144
CARDIFF
BRISTOL
M5
FFOREST FIELDS 632
FREEST 599
MORETON FARM 598
NOBLE COURT 597
AFON LODGE 595
PEMBREY 594
SWANSEA
EXETER

Scotland and Northern England

RED TEXT DENOTES
ALL YEAR ROUND SITE

COLOUR OF SYMBOL
DENOTES REGION

- CUMBRIA
- NORTHUMBRIA
- NORTH WEST ENGLAND
- SCOTLAND
- YORKSHIRE

SCOURIE 773

WOODEND 772
DUNROAMIN 764
ARDMAIR POINT 771
PITGRUDY 770

STAFFIN 775
LOCH GRESHORNISH 774
SPINDRIFT 766
TORVEAN 769 INVERNESS
ADEN COUNTRY PARK 753
ABERLOUR GARDENS 754
RERAIG 776
GRANTOWN-ON-SPEY 767
HUNTLY CASTLE 755
FAICHEM PARK 778
GLENMORE 768
ABERDEEN

LINNHE LOCHSIDE 785
A93

GLEN NEVIS 783
BLAIR CASTLE 730
RESIPOLE FARM 780 INVERCOE 779
NETHER CRAIG 728
A90

OBAN 781
NORTH LEDAIG 784
DUNDEE

OBAN DIVERS 782
TWENTY SHILLING 731
CRAIGTOUN MEADOWS 729
ARDGARTAN 726
AUCHTERARDER 727
TROSSACHS 723
WITCHES CRAIG 732
GLENDARUEL 786
LOMOND WOOD 724
TANTALLON 706
EDINBURGH 705 EDINBURGH
MONKS' MUIR 697
GLASGOW
MORTONHALL 699
DRUM MOHR 698
STRATHCLYDE 700
SLATEBARNS 704
ORD HOUSE 580
CROSSBURN 696
WAREN 575
GIBSON PARK 703
DUNSTAN HILL 577
CULZEAN CASTLE 701
PERCY WOOD 576

BROWN RIGG 578
CRESSFIELD 692
HODDOM CASTLE 691
PARK OF BRANDEDLEYS 693
FALLOWFIELD DENE 581
NEWCASTLE UPON TYNE
AIRD DONALD 702
A1(M)
BRIGHOUSE BAY 695
SEAWARD 690
THE LARCHES 551
M6
DOE PARK 571
WATERFOOT 561
WHITE WATER 574
COVE 562
WILD ROSE 557
BARNARD CASTLE 572

NORTHCLIFFE 453
SYKESIDE 556
PENNINE VIEW 560
ROSEDALE 477
ST HELENS IN THE PARK 454
LIMEFITT PARK 555
BROMPTON ON SWALE 480
VALE OF PICKERING 460
CAYTON VILLAGE 455
SKELWITH FOLD 552
WESTMORLAND 559
CONSTABLE BURTON HALL 469
FOXHOLME 458
SCARBOROUGH
WALLS 553
STREET HEAD 468
SEE INSET MAP
GOLDEN SQUARE 456
FLOWER OF MAY 452
FALLBARROW PARK 554
THE ASHES 565
RIVERSIDE MEADOWS 476
LEBBERSTON 478
HOLGATES 535
WOODHOUSE FARM 466
JASMINE PARK 474
BRIDLINGTON
KNIGHT STAINFORTH HALL 472
GOOSE WOOD 464
MOORSIDE 461
THORPE HALL 451
WOOD NOOK 467
RIPLEY 463
FANGFOSS OLD STATION 465
FAR GRANGE 473
HOWGILL LODGE 475
RUDDING 471
YORK
YORK

PART OF YORKSHIRE
KNEPS FARM 530
BRONTE 479
BLACKPOOL
BRADFORD
M62
PIPERS HEIGHT 531
PRESTON
NOSTELL PRIORY 470
HULL
ROYAL UMPIRE 529
M62

Ireland and the Channel Islands

RED TEXT DENOTES
ALL YEAR ROUND SITE

● SITE NAME ABBREVIATED
REFERENCE NUMBER

■ ALAN ROGERS'
TRAVEL SERVICE SITE

COLOUR OF SYMBOL
DENOTES REGION

● CHANNEL ISLANDS
● NORTHERN IRELAND
● REPUBLIC OF IRELAND

KNOCKALLA 864
BELLEMONT 860   BUSH 835
COLERAINE   TULLANS FARM 859
LONDONDERRY   DRUMAHEGLIS 834
STRABANE   CARNFUNNOCK 831
BALLYMENA   LARNE
GORTIN GLEN 856   CURRAN COURT 832
DONEGAL   OMAGH   COOKSTOWN   BANGOR
LOANEDEN 850   BELFAST
GREENLANDS 869   SLIGO   ENNISKILLEN   ARMAGH
GATEWAY 870   SHARE 852   BANBRIDGE 843
BELLEEK 875   NEWRY   TOLLYMORE FOREST 842
PARKLAND 877   CAVAN   DUNDALK   TAIN 889
CARRA 879   KNOCK 878
CONG 874
HODSON BAY 882   LOUGH REE (EAST) 896
GALWAY   ATHLONE
GREEN GABLES 906   CAMAC VALLEY 910   DUBLIN
SHANKHILL 911
NAAS   VALLEY 914
STREAMSTOWN   PORTLAOISE   ROUNDWOOD 913
942   FOREST FARM 908   MOAT FARM 916   WICKLOW
RIVER VALLEY 915
CURRAGHCHASE 945   LIMERICK   KILKENNY   TREE GROVE 924
NORE VALLEY 923
ANCHOR 955   TRALEE   TIPPERARY   APPLE 941   MORRISCASTLE STRAND 930
WOODLANDS PARK 965   CARRICK-ON-SUIR 939
GLENROSS 960   FOSSA 959   CLONMEL   WEXFORD
MANNIX POINT 961   KILLARNEY   PARSONS GREEN 938   WATERFORD   ROSSLARE
WHITE VILLA FARM 963
THE FLESK 964   FLEMING'S WHITEBRIDGE 962   CASEY'S 933   NEWTOWN COVE 934
WAVE CREST 956   BLARNEY 948
CREVEEN LODGE 957   EAGLE POINT 951   CORK
THE MEADOW 950
BARLEYCOVE 952

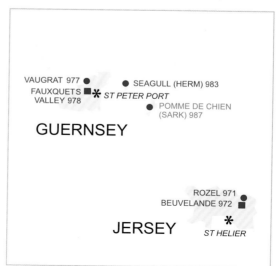

VAUGRAT 977   SEAGULL (HERM) 983
FAUXQUETS   ST PETER PORT
VALLEY 978   POMME DE CHIEN
(SARK) 987

GUERNSEY

ROZEL 971
BEUVELANDE 972

JERSEY   *
ST HELIER

Town and Village Index

Town and Village Index

Town and Village Index

Campsite Index

ENGLAND

South West England

New Parks: *Parks that are new to the guide this year are highlighted in bold type in this index.*